RAGAN

MICROECONOMICS

CHRISTOPHER T.S. RAGAN

McGILL UNIVERSITY

PEARSON

Toronto

Editorial Director: Claudine O'Donnell
Acquisitions Editor: Megan Farrell
Marketing Manager: Loula March
Program Manager: Patricia Ciardullo
Project Manager: Andrea Falkenberg
Manager of Content Development: Suzanne Schaan
Developmental Editor: Keriann McGoogan
Media Editor: Simon Bailey
Media Developer: Olga Avdyeyeva
Production Services: Cenveo® Publisher Services
Permissions Project Manager: Joanne Tang
Photo and Text Permissions Research:
Integra Publishing Services
Interior and Cover Designer: Anthony Leung
Cover Image: © cowardlion / Shutterstock (container box); © donvictorio / Shutterstock

Vice-President, Cross Media and Publishing Services: Gary Bennett

7   18

Library and Archives Canada Cataloguing in Publication
Ragan, Christopher, author   Microeconomics / Christopher T.S.
Ragan. — 15th Canadian edition.

Includes index.
ISBN **978-0-13-391043-8** (hardback)

1. Microeconomics—Textbooks. 2. Microeconomics—Canada—Textbooks. I. Title.

HB172.R35 2016   338.5   C2015-908617-5

ISBN 978-0-13-391043-8

Brief Contents

Contents

List of Boxes

Applying Economic Concepts

Lessons from History

Extensions in Theory

To the Instructor

Economics is a living discipline, changing and evolving in response to developments in the world economy and in response to the research of many thousands of economists throughout the world. Through fifteen editions, *Microeconomics* has evolved with the discipline. Our purpose in this edition, as in the previous fourteen, is to provide students with an introduction to the major issues facing the world's economies, to the methods that economists use to study those issues, and to the policy problems that those issues create. Our treatment is everywhere guided by three important principles:

1. Economics is *scientific*, in the sense that it progresses through the systematic confrontation of theory by evidence. Neither theory nor data alone can tell us much about the world, but combined they tell us a great deal.

2. Economics is *useful*, and it should be seen by students to be so. An understanding of economic theory combined with knowledge about the economy produces many important insights about economic policy. Although we stress these insights, we are also careful to point out cases in which too little is known to support strong statements about public policy. Appreciating what is not known is as important as learning what is known.

3. We strive always to be *honest* with our readers. Although we know that economics is not always easy, we do not approve of glossing over difficult bits of analysis without letting readers see what is happening and what has been assumed. We take whatever space is needed to explain why economists draw their conclusions, rather than just asserting the conclusions. We also take pains to avoid simplifying matters so much that students would have to unlearn what they have been taught if they continue their study beyond the introductory course. In short, we have tried to follow Albert Einstein's advice:

Everything should be made as simple as possible, but not simpler.

CURRENT ECONOMIC ISSUES

In writing the fifteenth edition of *Microeconomics,* we have tried to reflect the major economic issues that we face in the early twenty-first century.

Living Standards and Economic Growth

One of the most fundamental economic issues is the determination of overall living standards. Adam Smith wondered why some countries become wealthy while others remain poor. Though we have learned much about this topic in the past 240 years since Adam Smith's landmark work, economists recognize that there is still much we do not know.

The importance of technological change in determining increases in overall living standards is a theme that permeates both the microeconomics and macroeconomics halves of this book. Chapter 8 explores how firms deal with technological change at the micro level, and how changes in their economic environment lead them to create new products and new production processes. Chapters 11 and 12 discuss how imperfectly competitive firms often compete through their innovative practices, and the importance for policymakers of designing competition policy to keep these practices as energetic as possible.

We are convinced that no other introductory economics textbook places as much emphasis on technological change and economic growth as we do in this book. Given the importance of continuing growth in living standards and understanding where that growth comes from, we believe this emphasis is appropriate. We hope you agree.

Financial Crisis, Recession, and Recovery

The collapse of U.S. housing prices in 2007 led to a global financial crisis the likes of which had not been witnessed in a century, and perhaps longer. A deep recession, experienced in many countries, followed quickly on its heels. These dramatic events reawakened many people to two essential facts about economics. First, modern economies *can and do* go into recession. This essential fact had perhaps been forgotten by many who had become complacent after more than two decades of economic prosperity. Second, financial markets are crucial to the operation of modern economies. Like an electricity system, the details of financial markets are a mystery to most people, and the system itself is often ignored when it is functioning properly. But when financial markets cease to work smoothly and interest rates rise while credit flows decline, we are all reminded of their importance. In this sense, the financial crisis of 2007–2008 was like a global power failure for the world economy.

The financial crisis had micro causes and macro consequences. The challenges of appropriate regulation for financial and nonfinancial firms are explored in Chapters 12 and 16. The market for financial capital and the determination of interest rates are examined in Chapter 15. And debates regarding the appropriate role of the government in a market economy occur throughout the book, including in Chapters 1, 5, 16, 17, and 18.

Globalization

Enormous changes have occurred throughout the world over the last few decades. Flows of trade and investment between countries have risen so dramatically that it is now common to speak of the "globalization" of the world economy. Today it is no longer possible to study any economy without taking into account developments in the rest of the world.

Throughout its history, Canada has been a trading nation, and our policies relating to international trade have often been at the centre of political debates. International trade shows up in many parts of this textbook, but it is the exclusive focus of two chapters. Chapter 33 discusses the theory of the gains from trade; Chapter 34 explores trade policy, with an emphasis on NAFTA and the WTO.

The forces of globalization are with us to stay. In this fifteenth edition of *Microeconomics*, we have done our best to ensure that students are made aware of the world outside Canada and how events elsewhere in the world affect the Canadian economy.

The Role of Government

Between 1980 and 2008, the political winds shifted in Canada, the United States, and many other countries. Political parties that previously advocated a greater role for government in the economy argued the benefits of limited government. But the political winds shifted again with the arrival of the financial crisis and global recession in 2008, which led governments the world over to take some unprecedented actions. Many soon argued that we were observing the "end of laissez-faire" and witnessing the return of "big government." But was that really true?

Has the *fundamental* role of government changed significantly over the past 35 years? In order to understand the role of government in the economy, students must understand the benefits of free markets as well as the situations that cause markets to fail. They must also understand that governments often intervene in the economy for reasons related more to equity than to efficiency.

In this fifteenth edition of *Microeconomics*, we continue to incorporate the discussion of government policy as often as possible. Here are but a few of the many examples that we explore:

- tax incidence (in Chapter 4)
- the effects of minimum wages and rent controls (in Chapter 5)
- economic regulation and competition policy (in Chapter 12)
- pay equity policy (in Chapter 13)
- environmental policies (in Chapter 17)
- the disincentive effects of income taxes (in Chapter 18)

THE BOOK

Economic growth, financial crisis and recession, globalization, and the role of government are pressing issues of the day. Much of our study of economic principles and the Canadian economy has been shaped by these issues. In addition to specific coverage of growth and internationally oriented topics, growth and globalization appear naturally throughout the book in the treatment of many topics once thought to be entirely "domestic."

Most chapters of *Microeconomics* contain some discussion of economic policy. We have two main goals in mind when we present these discussions:

1. We aim to give students practice in using economic theory, because applying theory is both a wonderfully effective teaching method and a reliable test of students' grasp of theory.

2. We want to introduce students to the major policy issues of the day and to let them discover that few policy debates are as "black and white" as they often appear in the press.

Both goals reflect our view that students should see economics as useful in helping us to understand and deal with the world around us.

Structure and Coverage

To open Part 1, Chapter 1 begins with an informal presentation of seven major issues of the day. We then introduce scarcity and choice, and this leads to a discussion of the market as a coordinating device. Finally, we turn to alternative economic systems. Comparisons with command economies help to establish what a market economy is *by showing what it is not*. Chapter 2 makes the important distinction between positive and normative inquiries and goes on to an introductory discussion of the construction and testing of economic theories.

Part 2 deals with demand and supply. After introducing price determination and elasticity in Chapters 3 and 4, we apply these tools in Chapter 5. The case studies are designed to provide practice in applying the tools rather than to give full coverage of each case presented. Chapter 5 also has an intuitive and thorough treatment of economic value and market efficiency.

Part 3 presents the foundations of demand and supply. The theory of consumer behaviour is developed via marginal utility theory in Chapter 6, which also provides an introduction to consumer surplus and an intuitive discussion of income and substitution effects. The Appendix to Chapter 6 covers indifference curves, budget lines, and the derivation of demand curves using indifference theory. Chapter 7 introduces the firm as an institution and develops short-run costs. Chapter 8 covers long-run costs and the principle of substitution and goes on to consider shifts in cost curves due to technological change. The latter topic is seldom if ever covered in the micro part of elementary textbooks, yet applied work on firms' responses to changing economic signals shows it to be extremely important.

The first two chapters of Part 4, Chapters 9 and 10, present the standard theories of perfect competition and monopoly with a thorough discussion of price discrimination and some treatment of international cartels. Chapter 11 deals with monopolistic competition and oligopoly, which are the market structures most commonly found in Canadian industries. Strategic behaviour plays a central part in the analysis of this chapter. The first half of Chapter 12 deals with the efficiency of competition and the inefficiency of monopoly. The last half of the chapter deals with regulation and competition policy.

Part 5 begins with Chapter 13, which discusses the general principles of factor pricing and how factor prices are influenced by factor mobility. Chapter 14 then examines the operation of labour markets, addressing issues such as wage differentials, discrimination, labour unions, and the current trend of rising income inequality. Chapter 15 discusses investment in physical capital, the role of the interest rate, and the overall functioning of capital markets.

The first chapter of Part 6 (Chapter 16) provides a general discussion of market success and market failure and outlines the arguments for and against government intervention in a market economy. Chapter 17 deals with environmental regulation, with a detailed discussion of market-based policies and an introduction to the issue of global climate change. Chapter 18 analyzes taxes, public expenditure, and the main elements of Canadian

social policy. These three chapters expand on the basics of microeconomic analysis by providing current illustrations of the relevance of economic theory to contemporary policy situations.

We hope you find this menu both attractive and challenging; we hope students find the material stimulating and enlightening. Many of the messages of economics are complex—if economic understanding were only a matter of common sense and simple observation, there would be no need for professional economists and no need for textbooks like this one. To understand economics, one must work hard. Working at this book should help readers gain a better understanding of the world around them and of the policy problems faced by all levels of government. Furthermore, in today's globalized world, the return to education is large. We like to think that we have contributed in some small part to the understanding that increased investment in human capital by the next generation is necessary to restore incomes to the rapid growth paths that so benefited our parents and our peers. Perhaps we may even contribute to some income-enhancing accumulation of human capital by some of our readers.

SUBSTANTIVE CHANGES TO THIS EDITION

We have revised and updated the entire text with guidance from feedback from both users and nonusers of the previous editions of this book. For this edition, we have aimed to reduce the book's length by about 10 percent, and this required streamlining many discussions and deleting some boxes. As always, we have striven very hard to improve the teachability and readability of the book. We have focused the discussions so that each major point is emphasized as clearly as possible, without distracting the reader with nonessential points. As in recent editions, we have kept all core material in the main part of the text. Three types of boxes (Applying Economic Concepts, Lessons from History, and Extensions in Theory) are used to show examples or extensions that can be skipped without fear of missing an essential concept. But we think it would be a shame to skip too many of them, as there are many interesting examples and policy discussions in these boxes.

What follows is a brief listing of the main changes that we have made to the textbook.

Part 1: What is Economics?

In Chapter 1 we have added income inequality to the initial list of motivating topics, deleted the box on the failure of central planning, and have deleted the appendix on graphing (given that this topic is well-covered in Chapter 2).

Part 2: An Introduction to Demand and Supply

In Chapter 3 on demand and supply, we have provided a fuller discussion of weather shocks, and have added a numerical example of a demand-and-supply model. We have deleted the box on weather events as well as the box on the algebra of market equilibrium. In Chapter 4 on elasticity, we have clarified the discussion by adding summary tables for each type of elasticity and have deleted the box on the algebra of tax incidence. We have also clarified the distinction between normal and inferior goods and provided numerical examples to demonstrate this distinction. Lastly, we have added a new small box on economic development and income elasticities. In Chapter 5 we have deleted the former opening section on the interaction of markets.

Part 3: Consumers and Producers

In Chapter 7 on the theory of the firm, we have streamlined the discussion of diminishing marginal returns, deleted the box on idle capital equipment and flat cost curves, and have added a new box on the flat marginal cost curves (and high fixed costs) characteristic of many digital products. In Chapter 8 on firms in the long run, we have added the example of Ford's River Rouge factory to illustrate diseconomies of scale. Also in Chapter 8, we have streamlined the discussion of the three aspects of technological change, and deleted the box on the evolution of personal banking.

Part 4: Market Structure and Efficiency

We have streamlined several small parts of Chapter 9, and have deleted the discussion of sunk costs and a firm's exit from the industry. In Chapter 10 we added a new discussion of why monopolies are rare, which now feeds into the discussion on entry barriers. We removed the box on Irish pubs, added modern examples to the existing box on creative destruction, and streamlined the discussion of cartels. In Chapter 11 on imperfect competition, we have rewritten the entire first section, streamlined the section on oligopoly in practice, and deleted the box about OPEC. In Chapter 12 we have shortened the discussion of market structure and efficiency, deleted the box on allocative efficiency and income distribution, and also deleted the box on innovation and imperfect competition.

Part 5: Factor Markets

In Chapter 13, the short section on income distribution, together with the box on income inequality, have been moved to Chapter 14 where we now have an expanded discussion of the ongoing trend in Canada and elsewhere toward greater income inequality. In Chapter 14 on labour markets, we have re-worked the introduction, which now motivates the chapter's topics with the figure on the changing shares of Canadian employment over the past century. We have streamlined the discussions of wage differentials and bilateral monopoly. In Chapter 14 we have also deleted the box on the development of labour unions as well as the old final section on the "good jobs/bad jobs" debate. The chapter now ends with a new section on rising income inequality, with current data, various possible explanations, and some policy discussion.

Part 6: Government in the Market Economy

In Chapter 16 we have clarified our discussions of common-property resources, moral hazard, and the preferences for public provision. We have removed the brief discussion of economic growth from the "broader social goals" discussion, and have streamlined the discussion of government intervention and failure. In Chapter 17 on environmental policy we have removed the discussion of uncertainty and the choice between emissions taxes and "cap and trade" systems and have added a new box providing examples of pollution pricing. The old section on past (and mostly ineffective) Canadian climate policy has been deleted, as has the box on the open letter from economists. We have added a new section on current Canadian climate policy, which focuses on provincial policies currently in place.

Part 12: Canada in the Global Economy

In Chapter 32 on the gains from trade, we have clarified our discussion of scale economies and intra-industry trade. In Chapter 33 we have vastly streamlined the discussion of the WTO (and GATT) and we have deleted the box on the transformation of Canadian trade.

* * *

If you are moved to write to us (and we hope that you will be!), please do. You can send any comments or questions regarding the text (or any of the supplementary material, such as the *Instructor's Manual*, the *TestGen*, or the web-based MyEconLab to:

Christopher Ragan
Department of Economics
McGill University
855 Sherbrooke St. West
Montreal, Quebec H3A 2T7
e-mail: christopher.ragan@mcgill.ca

To the Student

Welcome to what is most likely your first book about economics! You are about to encounter what is for most people a new way of thinking, which often causes people to see things differently than they did before. But learning a new way of thinking is not always easy, and you should expect some hard work ahead. We do our best to be as clear and logical as possible and to illustrate our arguments whenever possible with current and interesting examples.

You must develop your own technique for studying, but the following suggestions may prove helpful. Begin by carefully considering the Learning Objectives at the beginning of a chapter. Read the chapter itself relatively quickly in order to get the general idea of the argument. At this first reading, you may want to skip the boxes and any footnotes. Then, after reading the Summary and the Key Concepts (at the end of each chapter), reread the chapter more slowly, making sure that you understand each step of the argument.

With respect to the figures and tables, be sure you understand how the conclusions that are stated in boldface at the beginning of each caption have been reached. You should be prepared to spend time on difficult sections; occasionally, you may spend an hour on only a few pages. Paper and pencil are indispensable equipment in your reading. It is best to follow a difficult argument by building your own diagram while the argument unfolds rather than by relying on the finished diagram as it appears in the book.

The end-of-chapter Study Exercises require you to practise using some of the concepts that you learned in the chapter. These will be excellent preparation for your exams. To provide you with immediate feedback, we have posted Solutions to Selected Study Exercises on MyEconLab (www.myeconlab.com). We strongly advise that you should seek to understand economics, not to memorize it.

The red numbers in square brackets in the text refer to a series of mathematical notes that are found starting on page M-1 at the end of the book. For those of you who like mathematics or prefer mathematical argument to verbal or geometric exposition, these may prove useful. Others may disregard them.

In this edition of the book, we have incorporated many elements to help you review material and prepare for examinations. A brief description of all the features in this book is given in the separate section that follows.

We encourage you to make use of MyEconLab that accompanies this book (www.myeconlab.com) at the outset of your studies. MyEconLab contains a wealth of valuable resources to help you. MyEconLab provides Solutions to Selected Study Exercises. It also includes many additional practice questions, some of which are modelled on Study Exercises in the book. You can also find an electronic version of the textbook. For more details about MyEconLab, please see the description on the inside front cover of your text.

Over the years, the book has benefited greatly from comments and suggestions we have received from students. Please feel free to send your comments to christopher.ragan@mcgill.ca. Good luck, and we hope you enjoy your course in economics!

Features of This Edition

We have made a careful effort with this edition to incorporate features that will facilitate the teaching and learning of economics.

- A set of **Learning Objectives** at the beginning of each chapter, correlated to the **Chapter Outline,** clarifies the skills and knowledge to be learned in each chapter. These same learning objectives are used in the chapter summaries, as well as in the *Study Guide*.

- **Major ideas** are highlighted with a yellow background in the text.
- **Key terms** are boldfaced where they are defined in the body of the text, and they are restated with their definitions in the margins. In the index at the back of the book, each key term and the page reference to its definition are boldfaced.

- The **colour scheme for figures** consistently uses the same colour for each type of curve. For example, all demand curves are blue and all supply curves are red.
- **A caption for each figure and table** summarizes the underlying economic reasoning. Each caption begins with a boldfaced statement of the relevant economic conclusion.

- **Applying Economic Concepts** boxes demonstrate economics in action, providing examples of how theoretical material relates to issues of current interest.
- **Extensions in Theory** boxes provide a deeper treatment of a theoretical topic that is discussed in the text.
- **Lessons from History** boxes contain discussions of a particular policy debate or empirical finding that takes place in a historical context.
- **Photographs with short captions** are interspersed throughout the chapters to illustrate some of the arguments.

- **Chapter Summaries** are organized using the same numbered heading as found in the body of the chapter. The relevant Learning Objective (LO) numbers are given in red next to each heading in the summary.

- **Key Concepts** are listed near the end of each chapter.
- A set of **Study Exercises** is provided for each chapter. These often quantitative exercises require the student to analyze problems by means of computations, graphs, or explanations.

- A set of **Mathematical Notes** is presented in a separate section near the end of the book. Because mathematical notation and derivations are not necessary to understand the principles of economics but are more helpful in advanced work, this seems to be a sensible arrangement. References in the text to these mathematical notes are given by means of red numbers in square brackets.

- A **Timeline of Great Economists,** extending from the mid-seventeenth century to the late twentieth century, is presented near the end of the book. Along this timeline we have placed brief descriptions of the life and works of some great economists, most of whom the reader will encounter in the textbook. The timeline also includes some major world events in order to give readers an appreciation of when these economists did their work.
- **Economists on Record,** on the inside of the back cover, provides some classic quotations that are relevant to the study and practice of economics.
- For convenience, a list of the **Common Abbreviations Used in the Text** is given inside the front cover.

Supplements

MYECONLAB

The Ragan MyEconLab has been designed and refined with a single purpose in mind: to create those moments of understanding that transform the difficult into the clear and obvious. With homework, quiz, test, activity, and tutorial options, instructors can manage all their assessment needs in one program.

- All of the end-of-chapter study exercises are assignable and automatically graded in MyEconLab.
- The Gradebook records each student's performance and time spent on the Tests and Study Plan and generates reports by student or by chapter.
- The Gradebook records each student's performance and time spent on the Tests and Study Plan and generates reports by student or by chapter.
- Test Bank questions are also assignable for test, quiz, or homework and auto-graded in the MyEconLab.

MyEconLab also includes the following features.

Adaptive Learning

MyEconLab's Study Plan is now powered by a sophisticated adaptive learning engine that tailors learning material to meet the unique needs of each student. MyEconLab's new Adaptive Learning Study Plan monitors students' performance on homework, quizzes, and tests and continuously makes recommendations based on that performance.

If a student is struggling with a concept such as supply and demand, or having trouble calculating a price elasticity of demand, the Study Plan provides customized remediation activities—a pathway based on personal proficiencies, the number of attempts, back on track. Students will also receive recommendations for additional practice in the form of rich multimedia learning aids such as videos, an interactive eText, Help Me Solve This tutorials, and graphing tools.

The Study Plan can extrapolate a student's future trouble spots and provide learning material and practice to avoid pitfalls. In addition, students who are showing a high degree of success with the assessment material are offered a chance to work on future topics based on the professor's course coverage preferences. This personalized and adaptive feedback and support ensure that your students are optimizing their current and future course work and mastering the concepts, rather than just memorizing and at guessing answers.

You can learn more about adaptive learning at http://www.myeconlab.com/product-info/adaptive.

Economics in the News

Economics in the News is a turnkey solution to bringing current news into the classroom. Updated weekly during the academic year, two relevant articles (one micro, one macro) are uploaded with questions that may be assigned for homework or for classroom discussion.

Digital Interactives

Digital Interactives immerse students in a fundamental economic principle, helping them to learn actively. They can be presented in class as a visually stimulating, highly engaging lecture tool, and can also be assigned with assessment questions for grading. Digital Interactives are designed for use in traditional, online, and hybrid courses, and many incorporate real-time, as well as data display and analysis tools. To learn more, and for a complete list of digital interactives, visit www.myeconlab.com.

Learning Catalytics

Learning Catalytics is a bring-your-own-device classroom engagement tool instructors can use to ask students questions utilizing 18 different question types, allowing students to participate in real time during lectures. With Learning Catalytics you can:

- Engage students in real time, using open-ended tasks to probe student understanding.
- Promote student participation using any modern Web-enabled device they already have—laptop, smartphone, or tablet.
- Address misconceptions before students leave the classroom.
- Understand immediately where students are and adjust your lecture accordingly.
- Improve your students' critical thinking skills.
- Engage with and record the participation of every student in your classroom.

Learning catalytics gives you the flexibility to create your own questions to fit your course exactly or choose from a searchable question library Pearson has created.

For more information, visit learningcatalytics.com.

Dynamic Study Modules

Dynamic Study Modules, which focus on key topic areas and are available from within MyEconLab, are an additional way for students to obtain tailored help. These modules work by continuously assessing student performance and activity on discrete topics and provide personalized content in real time to reinforce concepts that target each student's particular strengths and weaknesses.

Each Dynamic Study Module, accessed by computer, smartphone, or tablet, promotes fast learning and long-term retention. Because MyEconLab and Dynamic Study Modules help students stay on track and achieve a higher level of subject-matter mastery, more class time is available for interaction, discussion, collaboration, and exploring applications to current news and events.

Instructors can register, create, and access all of their MyEconLab courses at www.myeconlab.com.

Pearson eText

Pearson eText gives students access to the text whenever and wherever they have online access to the Internet. eText pages look exactly like the printed text, offering powerful new functionality for students and instructors. Users can create notes, highlight text in different colours, create bookmarks, zoom, click hyperlinked words and phrases to view definitions, and view in single-page or two-page view.

INSTRUCTOR'S RESOURCES

These instructor supplements are available for download from a password-protected section of Pearson Canada's online catalogue (www.pearsoncanada.ca/highered). Navigate to your book's catalogue page to view a list of those supplements that are available. Speak to your local Pearson sales representative for details and access.

Instructor's Manual

- An **Instructor's Manual** (in both Word and PDF format) written by Christopher Ragan. It includes full solutions to all the Study Exercises.

Computerized Test Bank

- **Computerized Test Bank.** Pearson's computerized test banks allow instructors to filter and select questions to create quizzes, tests or homework. Instructors can revise questions or add their own, and may be able to choose print or online options. These questions are also available in Microsoft Word format.

PowerPoint Slides

- **PowerPoint® Slides,** covering the key concepts of each chapter, that can be adapted for lecture presentations.

Image Library

- An **Image Library,** consisting of all the figures and tables from the textbook in gif format. These files can easily be imported into PowerPoint slides for class presentation.

Additional Topics

- **Additional Topics,** written by Christopher Ragan, offering optional topics on a wide variety of economic subjects. A list of these topics is included in the text; students can access them on MyEconLab (www.myeconlab.com).

TECHNOLOGY SPECIALISTS

Learning Solutions Managers. Pearson's Learning Solutions Managers work with faculty and campus course designers to ensure that Pearson technology products, assessment tools, and online course materials are tailored to meet your specific needs. This highly qualified team is dedicated to helping schools take full advantage of a wide range of educational resources, by assisting in the integration of a variety of instructional materials and media formats. Your local Pearson Canada sales representative can provide you with more details on this service program.

Acknowledgements

It would be impossible to acknowledge here by name all the teachers, colleagues, and students who contributed to the development and improvement of this book over its previous fourteen editions. Hundreds of users have written to us with specific suggestions, and much of the credit for the improvement of the book over the years belongs to them. We can no longer list them individually but we thank them all sincerely.

For the development of this fifteenth edition, we are grateful to the many people who offered informal suggestions. We would also like to thank the following instructors who provided us with formal reviews of the textbook. Their observations and recommendations were extremely helpful.

- Medoune Seck, CEGEP John Abbott College
- Paul T. Dickinson, McGill University
- Mark Raymond, Saint Mary's University
- Cheryl Jenkins, John Abbott College
- Kevin Richter, Douglas College
- Fulton Tom, Langara College
- Mayssun El-Attar Vilalta, McGill University

We would like to express our thanks to the many people at Pearson Canada involved in the development and production of this textbook. We would especially like to thank three individuals with whom we worked closely. Megan Farrell (Acquisitions Editor); Keriann McGoogan (Senior Developmental Ediotor); Loula March (Marketing Manager) all showed their professionalism, dedication, and enthusiasm in guiding this book through the publication and marketing processes. We would also like to thank the many sales representatives who work to bring this book to professors across the country. These individuals have been a pleasure to work with each step along the way, and we are deeply grateful for their presence and their participation and delighted to consider them friends as well as professional colleagues.

Our thanks also to the many people at Pearson with whom we work less closely but who nonetheless toil behind the scenes to produce this book, including Andrea Falkenberg, Vastavikta Sharma and Anthony Leung.

Thanks also to Cat Haggert for copyediting, Jeannie Gilmore for the technical review, and to Joel Gladstone for proofreading, all of whom provided an invaluable service with their attention to detail.

In short, we realize that there is a great deal more involved in producing a book than *just* the writing. Without the efforts of all of these dedicated professionals, this textbook simply would not exist. Our sincere thanks to all of you.

Thanks also to Simon Altman for his detailed and diligent work in assembling the necessary data for updating this fifteenth edition.

Finally, Ingrid Kristjanson is deeply involved in each revision of this textbook. Without her participation, the quality and efficiency of this project would suffer greatly. In addition, for the past four editions she has played a leading role in the improvement, rewriting, and expansion of the electronic Testbank. With her involvement, the lengthy revision of the textbook and its supplements continues to be an enriching and pleasant experience.

Christopher Ragan

About the Author

Chris Ragan received his B.A. in economics from the University of Victoria, his M.A. from Queen's University, and his Ph.D. from the Massachusetts Institute of Technology in Cambridge, Massachusetts in 1990. He then joined the Department of Economics at McGill University in Montreal, where he has taught graduate courses in macroeconomics and international finance and undergraduate courses in macroeconomic theory and policy, current economic issues, and financial crises. Over the years he has taught principles of economics (micro and macro) to thousands of students at McGill and maintains a reputation on campus as being "super-excited" about economics. In 2007, Chris Ragan was awarded the Noel Fieldhouse Teaching Award from McGill for teaching excellence.

Professor Ragan's research focuses mainly on the design and implementation of macroeconomic policy in Canada. He has been privileged to serve the federal government in Ottawa as Special Advisor to the Governor of the Bank of Canada and as the Clifford Clark Visiting Economist at the Department of Finance. He currently serves as the chair of Canada's Ecofiscal Commission, a five-year project of independent economists and advisors to promote the greater use of pollution pricing in the Canadian economy.

Chris Ragan used the third edition of this textbook as an undergraduate student in 1981 and joined Richard Lipsey as a co-author in 1997 for the book's ninth edition. For several editions, Lipsey and Ragan worked diligently to maintain the book's reputation as the clearest and most comprehensive introductory economics textbook in Canada. Although Professor Ragan is now the sole listed author, this fifteenth edition of *Economics* still owes much to the dedication of previous authors, including Richard Lipsey, Douglas Purvis, and Gordon Sparks.

1 Economic Issues and Concepts

CHAPTER OUTLINE	LEARNING OBJECTIVES (LO)
	After studying this chapter you will be able to
1.1 WHAT IS ECONOMICS?	1 explain the importance of scarcity, choice, and opportunity cost, and how each is illustrated by the production possibilities boundary.
1.2 THE COMPLEXITY OF MODERN ECONOMIES	2 view the market economy as self-organizing in the sense that order emerges from a large number of decentralized decisions.
	3 explain how specialization gives rise to the need for trade, and how trade is facilitated by money.
	4 identify the economy's decision makers and see how their actions create a circular flow of income and expenditure.
1.3 IS THERE AN ALTERNATIVE TO THE MARKET ECONOMY?	5 describe how all actual economies are mixed economies, having elements of free markets, tradition, and government intervention.

MANY of the challenges we face in Canada and around the world are primarily economic. Others that appear to be mainly environmental, social, or political usually have a significant economic dimension. Wars and civil unrest throughout history have often had economic roots, with antagonists competing for control over vital resources; global climate change is a phenomenon that engages the attention of the scientific and environmental communities, but the economic implications of both the problem and its solutions will be tremendous; population aging in Canada and other developed countries will have consequences for the structure of our societies, but it will also have significant economic effects; and the existence of poverty, whether in Canada or in the much poorer nations of the world, most certainly has economic causes and consequences. We begin by discussing several issues that are currently of pressing concern, both inside and outside of Canada. Then, we'll move on to acquiring the knowledge and tools we need to better understand these and many other issues.

Productivity Growth Productivity growth lies at the heart of the long-term increase in average living standards. Productivity is a measure of how much output (or income) is produced by one hour of work effort, and it has been rising gradually over the past century. In recent years, however, productivity growth has been slowing in Canada, and economists have been examining the cause of the slowdown and also examining what policies, if any, might reverse this trend. If your living standards are to improve over your lifetime as much as your grandparents' did over theirs, Canada's rate of productivity growth will need to increase significantly.

Population Aging The average age of the Canadian population is steadily rising, due both to a long-term decline in fertility and to an increase in average life-expectancy. This population aging has several effects. First, since people eventually retire as they approach their "golden years," there will be a decline in the growth rate of Canada's labour force. As a result, some firms and industries will find it more difficult to find workers, and wages are likely to rise. Second, since our publicly funded health-care system tends to spend much more on seniors than it does on younger Canadians, there will be a significant increase in public health-care spending that will put difficult demands on governments' fiscal positions. This same demographic problem is being encountered in most developed countries.

Climate Change Climate change is a global phenomenon that has important implications for most nations on Earth. The long-term increase in the emission of greenhouse gases—caused largely from the burning of fossil fuels such as oil, coal, and natural gas—has led to an accumulation of these gases in the atmosphere and is contributing to a long-term increase in Earth's average temperature. The rise in temperature is leading to the melting of polar ice caps, a slow increase in sea level, a creeping expansion of the world's great deserts, and reductions in agricultural productivity. Global climate change presents a challenge for the design of better economic policy, aimed at reducing greenhouse-gas emissions without unduly slowing the growth of material living standards.

Global Financial Stability The collapse of the U.S. housing market in 2007–2008 led to the failure of several major financial institutions and caused a global financial crisis. The largest and most synchronized worldwide recession in over 70 years followed in its wake. The crisis led most of the world's major governments to intervene considerably in their economies—by providing assistance to their financial institutions and by directly expanding expenditures on goods and services. By 2014 most of these economies had emerged from recession but were nonetheless still experiencing slow economic recoveries. Most governments were also actively redesigning their financial regulations to reduce the likelihood that similar events would occur in the future. The quest for "financial stability" has become a policy imperative in many countries.

Rising Government Debt The aggressive government response to the global financial crisis led to massive new public spending in an effort to dampen the effects of the recession. Governments' budget deficits increased for several years, and thus government debt in most countries increased significantly between 2008 and 2015. Early in this period it became clear that government debt in some European countries (especially Greece, Portugal, Ireland, Italy, and Spain) was so high that bondholders were no longer prepared to purchase new government bonds or renew their existing holdings of bonds. The resulting upward spike in interest rates made it almost impossible for these countries to carry out their regular business without special financial assistance from other governments or from the International Monetary Fund. The political tensions created among European governments threatened to spell the end of Europe's common currency, the euro. These issues are still largely unresolved.

Globalization   Canada is a small nation that relies significantly on trade with the rest of the world for its prosperity. We sell our lumber and oil and beef to the world, as we do our engineering and legal and financial services. As consumers we buy a wide variety of products from the rest of the world, including coffee, leather shoes, and fine wine; our firms also buy many inputs from abroad, including machine tools, software, and some specialized raw materials. In short, international trade and the ongoing process of globalization are crucial to Canada's economic prosperity. Yet globalization also presents some challenges. A decision to reduce tariffs on imported goods generates temporary costs for those Canadians who are displaced from their previously protected occupations. And greater competition for Canadian firms from those in developing countries may lead to a decline in some middle-level Canadian jobs.

Growing Income Inequality   In Canada and most other developed countries, the past three decades have seen a rise in income inequality. Particularly dramatic has been the increase in the share of national income going to the richest one percent of individuals, all while the incomes of those in the "middle classes" have grown very slowly. The causes of this rising inequality are hotly debated among economists, but most agree that the nature and pace of technological change and the growing ability of firms to locate their production facilities in lower-wage developing countries are contributing factors. There is also considerable debate regarding what government actions could be taken to slow or reverse the increase in income inequality, and whether the benefits of those actions in terms of reduced inequality would be justified by the associated costs.

These seven issues are only a small sample of the many economic issues that confront Canada and other countries. To understand any of them it is necessary to have a basic understanding of economics—how markets work, how prices are determined, in what sense markets sometimes fail to work well, and how government policy can be used to improve outcomes. These are the main topics of this book. There is a lot to learn, and not many weeks in your college or university course. So, let's get started at the very beginning.

1.1 WHAT IS ECONOMICS?

The issues described in the introduction would not matter much if we lived in an economy of such plenty that there was always enough to fully satisfy everyone's wants. If we could always get all the things we wanted, it wouldn't be so important to be more productive in our work. Rapid growth in health-care spending would not be such a problem if governments had no limits on what they could spend, or if there were not problems associated with high levels of government debt. And there would be no need to trade with other countries if Canada could easily and cheaply produce coffee, clothing, electronic components, and all those other things that we currently import from foreign lands. But such an economy with unlimited products is impossible. Why?

The short answer is because we live in a world of *scarcity*. Compared with the desires of individuals for things such as better food, clothing, housing, education, clean water and health care, the existing supplies of resources are clearly inadequate. They are sufficient to produce only a small fraction of the goods and services that we desire. This scarcity gives rise to the basic economic problem of choice. If we cannot have everything we want, we must choose what we will and will not have.

One definition of *economics* comes from the great economist Alfred Marshall (1842–1924), who we will encounter at several points in this book: "Economics is a study of mankind in the ordinary business of life." A more informative definition is:

> **Economics is the study of the use of scarce resources to satisfy unlimited human wants.**

Scarcity is inevitable and is central to economic problems. What are society's resources? Why is scarcity inevitable? What are the consequences of scarcity?

Resources

A society's resources are often divided into the three broad categories of land, labour, and capital. *Land* includes all natural endowments, such as arable land, forests, lakes, crude oil, and minerals. *Labour* includes all mental and physical human resources, including entrepreneurial capacity and management skills. *Capital* includes all manufactured aids to production, such as tools, machinery, and buildings. Economists call such resources **factors of production** because they are used to produce the things that people desire. We divide what is produced into goods and services. **Goods** are tangible (e.g., cars and shoes), and **services** are intangible (e.g., legal advice and education). People use goods and services to satisfy their wants. The act of making them is called **production**, and the act of using them is called **consumption**.

factors of production Resources used to produce goods and services; frequently divided into the basic categories of land, labour, and capital.

goods Tangible products, such as cars or shoes.

services Intangible products, such as legal services and education.

production The act of making goods or services.

consumption The act of using goods or services to satisfy wants.

Scarcity and Choice

For almost all of the world's 7.3 billion people, scarcity is real and ever-present. As we said earlier, relative to our desires, existing resources are inadequate; there are enough to produce only a fraction of the goods and services that we want.

But aren't the developed nations rich enough that scarcity is no longer a problem? After all, they are "affluent" societies. Whatever affluence may mean, however, it does not mean the end of the problem of scarcity. Canadian families that earn $80 000 per year, approximately the average after-tax income for a Canadian family in 2016 but a princely amount by *world* standards, have no trouble spending it on things that seem useful to them, and they would certainly have no trouble convincing you that their resources are scarce relative to their desires.

Because resources are scarce, all societies face the problem of deciding what to produce and how much each person will consume. Societies differ in who makes the choices and how they are made, but the need to choose is common to all. Just as scarcity implies the need for choice, so choice implies the existence of cost. A decision to have more of one thing requires a decision to have less of something else. The less of "something else" can be thought of as the cost of having more of that "one thing."

Scarcity implies that choices must be made, and making choices implies the existence of costs.

Opportunity Cost To see how choice implies cost, we look first at a trivial example and then at one that affects all of us; both examples involve precisely the same fundamental principles.

Consider the choice David faces when he goes out for pizza and beer with his friends. Suppose that he has only $16 for the night and that each beer costs $4 and each slice of pizza costs $2. David would like to have 4 slices of pizza and 3 beers, but this would cost $20 and is therefore unattainable given David's scarce resources of $16. There are several combinations, however, that are attainable: 8 slices of pizza and 0 beers; 6 slices of pizza and 1 beer; 4 slices of pizza and 2 beers; 2 slices of pizza and 3 beers; and 0 slices of pizza and 4 beers.

David's possible choices are illustrated in Figure 1-1. The numbers of slices of pizza are shown on the horizontal axis; the numbers of beers are shown on the vertical axis. The downward-sloping line connects the five possible combinations of beer and pizza that use up all of David's resources—$16. This is David's *budget line*. Notice that point A shows a combination that lies outside the line because its total cost is more than $16; Point A is *unattainable* to David. If David could buy fractions of a beer and of a slice of pizza, *all* points that lie on or inside the line would be *attainable* combinations.

In this setting David can ask himself, "What is the cost of one beer?" One answer is that the cost is $4. An equivalent answer, assuming that he wanted to spend all of this $16 on these two items, is that the cost of one beer is the two slices of pizza he must give up to get it. In fact, we say in this case that two slices of pizza is the *opportunity cost* of one beer, since they are the opportunity David must give up to get one extra beer.

Every time a choice is made, opportunity costs are incurred.

As simple as it may seem, the idea of opportunity cost is one of the central insights of economics. Here is a precise definition: The **opportunity cost** of choosing any one alternative is the value of the next best alternative that is given up. That is, it is the cost measured in terms of other goods and services that could have been obtained instead. If, for example, resources that could have produced 20 km of road are best used instead to produce one hospital, the opportunity cost of a hospital is 20 km of road; looked at the other way round, the opportunity cost of 20 km of road is one hospital.

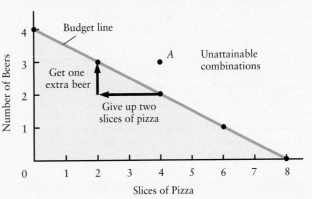

FIGURE 1-1 Choosing Between Pizza and Beer

Scarce resources force a choice among competing alternatives. Given a total of $16 to spend on $2 slices of pizza and $4 beers, some choices are unattainable, such as point A. The five points on the green line show *all* combinations that are attainable by spending the $16. If it were possible to buy parts of a beer and parts of a slice of *pizza*, then all combinations on the line and in the green area would be attainable. If the entire $16 is to be spent, the choice between more pizza and more beer involves an opportunity cost. The *slope* of the green line reflects opportunity costs. The opportunity cost of one extra slice of pizza is half of a beer; the opportunity cost of one extra beer is two slices of pizza.

opportunity cost The value of the next best alternative that is forgone when one alternative is chosen.

APPLYING ECONOMIC CONCEPTS 1-1

The Opportunity Cost of Your University Degree

The opportunity cost of choosing one thing is what must be given up as the best alternative. Computing the opportunity cost of a college or university education is a good example to illustrate which factors are included in the computation of opportunity cost. You may also be surprised to learn how expensive your university degree really is!*

Suppose that a bachelor's degree requires four years of study and that each year you spend $6500 for tuition fees—approximately the average at Canadian universities in 2016—and a further $1500 per year for books and materials. Does this mean that the cost of a university education is only $32 000? Unfortunately not; the true cost of a university degree to a student is much higher.

The key point is that the opportunity cost of a university education does not include just the out-of-pocket expenses on tuition and books. You must also take into consideration *what you are forced to give up* by choosing to attend university. Of course, if you were not studying you could have done any one of a number of things, but the relevant one is *the one you would have chosen instead*—your best alternative to attending university.

Suppose your best alternative to attending university was to get a job. In this case, the opportunity cost of your university degree must include the earnings that you would have received had you taken that job. Suppose your (after-tax) annual earnings would have been $25 000 per year, for a total of $100 000 if you had stayed at that job for four years. To the direct expenses of $32 000, we must therefore add $100 000 for the earnings that

you gave up by not taking a job. This brings the true cost of your university degree—the opportunity cost—up to $132 000!

Notice that the cost of food, lodging, clothing, and other living expenses did not enter the calculation of the opportunity cost in this example. The living expenses must be incurred in either case—whether you attend university or get a job.

If the opportunity cost of a degree is so high, why do students choose to go to university? Maybe students simply enjoy learning and are prepared to incur the high cost to be in the university environment. Or maybe they believe that a university degree will significantly increase their future earning potential. In Chapter 14 we will see that this is true. In this case, they are giving up four years of earnings at one salary so that they can invest in building their skills in the hope of enjoying many more years in the future at a considerably higher salary.

Whatever the reason for attending college or university, the recognition that a post-secondary degree is very expensive should convince students to make the best use of their time while they are there. Read on!

---

* This box considers only the cost *to the student* of a university degree. For reasons that will be discussed in detail in Part Six of this book, provincial governments heavily subsidize post–secondary education in Canada. Because of this subsidy, the cost *to society* of a university degree is generally much higher than the cost to an individual student.

See *Applying Economic Concepts 1-1* for an example of opportunity cost that should seem quite familiar to you: the opportunity cost of getting a university degree.

Production Possibilities Boundary   Although David's choice between pizza and beer may seem to be a trivial consumption decision, the nature of the decision is the same whatever the choice being made. Consider, for example, the choice that any country must face between producing goods for final consumption (such as food and clothing) and goods for investment purposes used to increase future production (such as machines and factories).

If resources are fully and efficiently employed it is not possible to have more of *both* consumption and investment goods. As the country devotes more resources to producing consumption goods it must take resources away from producing investment goods. The opportunity cost of the extra consumption goods is the value of the investment goods forgone.

The choice is illustrated in Figure 1-2. Because resources are scarce, some combinations—those that would require more than the total available supply of resources for their production—cannot be attained. The negatively sloped curve on the graph divides the combinations that can be attained from those that cannot. Points above and to the right of this curve cannot be attained because there are not enough resources, points below and to the left of the curve can be attained without using all of the available resources, and points on the curve can just be attained if all the available resources are used efficiently. The curve is called the **production possibilities boundary**. (Sometimes "boundary" is replaced with "curve" or "frontier.") It has a negative slope because when all resources are being used efficiently, producing more of one good requires producing less of others.

production possibilities boundary A curve showing which alternative combinations of output can be attained if all available resources are used efficiently; it is the boundary between attainable and unattainable output combinations.

> **A production possibilities boundary illustrates three concepts: scarcity, choice, and opportunity cost. Scarcity is indicated by the unattainable combinations outside the boundary; choice, by the need to choose among the alternative attainable points along the boundary; and opportunity cost, by the negative slope of the boundary.**

The shape of the production possibilities boundary in Figure 1-2 implies that an increasing amount of consumption goods must be given up to achieve equal successive increases in the production of investment goods. This shape, referred to as *concave* to the origin, indicates that the opportunity cost of either good increases as we increase the amount of it that is produced. A straight-line boundary, as in Figure 1-1, indicates that the opportunity cost of one good stays constant, no matter how much of it is produced.

The concave shape in Figure 1-2 is the way economists usually draw a country's production possibilities boundary. The shape occurs because each factor of production is not equally useful in producing all goods. To see why differences among factors of production are so important, suppose we begin at point *c* in Figure 1-2, where most resources are devoted to the production of consumption goods, and then consider gradually shifting more and more resources toward the production of investment goods. We might begin by shifting the use of iron ore and other raw materials. These resources may not be very well suited to producing consumption goods (like food) but may be essential for producing tools, machinery, and factories. This shift of resources will therefore lead to a small reduction in the output of consumption goods but a substantial increase in the output of investment goods. Thus, the opportunity cost of producing more units of investment goods, which is equal to the forgone consumption goods, is

FIGURE 1-2 A Production Possibilities Boundary

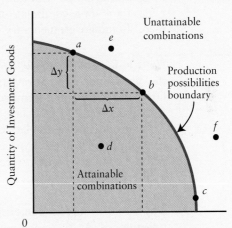

The negatively sloped boundary shows the combinations that are attainable when all resources are used efficiently. The production possibilities boundary separates the attainable combinations of goods, such as *a*, *b*, *c*, and *d*, from unattainable combinations, such as *e* and *f*. Points *a*, *b*, and *c* represent full and efficient use of society's resources. Point *d* represents either inefficient use of resources or failure to use all the available resources. If production changes from point *a* to point *b*, an opportunity cost is involved. The opportunity cost of producing Δx more consumption goods is the necessary reduction in the production of investment goods equal to Δy.

small. But as we shift more and more resources toward the production of investment goods, and therefore move along the production possibilities boundary toward point *a*, we must shift more and more resources that are actually quite well suited to the production of consumption goods, like arable agricultural land. As we produce more and more investment goods (by devoting more and more resources to producing them), the amount of consumption goods that must be forgone to produce one *extra* unit of investment goods rises. That is, the opportunity cost of producing one good rises as more of that good is produced.

Four Key Economic Problems

Modern economies involve millions of complex production and consumption activities. Despite this complexity, the basic decisions that must be made are not very different from those that were made in ancient and primitive economies in which people worked with few tools and bartered with their neighbours. In all cases, scarcity, opportunity cost, and the need for choice play crucial roles. Whatever the economic system, whether modern or ancient or complex or primitive, there are four key economic problems.

resource allocation The allocation of an economy's scarce resources among alternative uses.

What Is Produced and How?
This question concerns the *allocation* of scarce resources among alternative uses. This **resource allocation** determines the quantities of various goods that are produced. Choosing to produce a particular combination of goods means choosing a particular allocation of resources among the industries or regions producing the goods. What determines which goods are produced and which ones are not?

Is there some combination of the production of goods that is "better" than others? If so, should governments try to alter the pattern of production in this direction?

What Is Consumed and by Whom?
Economists seek to understand what determines the distribution of a nation's total output among its people. Who gets a lot, who gets a little, and why? Should governments care about this *distribution* of consumption and, if so, what tools do they have to alter it?

If production takes place on the production possibilities boundary, then how about consumption? Will the economy consume exactly the same goods that it produces? Or will the country's ability to trade with other countries permit the economy to consume a different combination of goods?

Why Are Resources Sometimes Idle?
Sometimes large numbers of workers are unemployed. At the same time, the managers and owners of offices and factories could choose to produce more goods and services. For some reason, however, these resources—land, labour, and factories—lie idle. Thus, in terms of Figure 1-2, the economy sometimes operates inside its production possibilities boundary.

Why are resources sometimes idle? Should governments worry about such idle resources, or is there some reason to believe that such occasional idleness is necessary for a well-functioning economy?

Is Productive Capacity Growing?
The capacity to produce goods and services grows rapidly in some countries, grows slowly in others, and actually declines in others. Growth in productive capacity can be represented by an outward shift of the production possibilities boundary, as shown in Figure 1-3. If an economy's capacity to

produce goods and services is growing, some combinations that are unattainable today will become attainable in the future. What are the determinants of such growth and can governments do anything to influence them?

Economics and Government Policy

Questions relating to what is produced and how, and what is consumed and by whom, fall within the realm of microeconomics. **Microeconomics** is the study of the causes and consequences of the allocation of resources as it is affected by the workings of the price system and government policies that seek to influence it. Questions relating to the idleness of resources and the growth of the economy's productive capacity fall within the realm of macroeconomics. **Macroeconomics** is the study of the determination of economic aggregates, such as total output, total employment, and the rate of economic growth.

The design and effectiveness of government policy matters for each of our four key economic problems. When asking what combination of goods and services is produced in the economy, and whether some combinations might be better than others, government policy enters the discussion. In later chapters we will examine situations called *market failures*, which arise when free markets lead to too much of some goods being produced (like pollution) and too little of others (like national parks). Government policy could be used to alter the allocation of the economy's resources to correct these market failures.

When asking who gets to consume the economy's output, it is natural to discuss the *fairness* regarding the distribution of consumption across individuals. Do free markets lead to fair outcomes? Can we even decide objectively what is fair and what is unfair? We will see throughout this book that many government policies are designed with fairness in mind. We will also encounter an ongoing debate about how much the government should try to improve the fairness of market outcomes. Some argue that it is reasonable to do so; others argue that attempts to improve fairness often lead to reductions in market efficiency that impose large costs on society.

Government policy is also part of the discussion of why a nation's resources are sometimes idle and what can be done to reduce such idleness. For example, when the Canadian economy entered a major global recession in 2009, the federal and provincial governments increased their spending significantly in an attempt to dampen the decline in aggregate output that was then occurring. Some critics argue that such "fiscal stimulus" packages cannot increase overall output, since the increase

microeconomics The study of the causes and consequences of the allocation of resources as it is affected by the workings of the price system.

macroeconomics The study of the determination of economic aggregates such as total output, employment, and growth.

FIGURE 1-3 The Effect of Economic Growth on the Production Possibilities Boundary

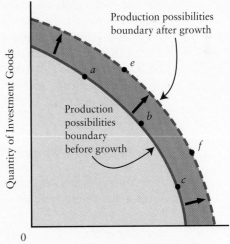

Economic growth shifts the boundary outward and makes it possible to produce more of all products. Before growth in productive capacity, points *a*, *b*, and *c* were on the production possibilities boundary and points *e* and *f* were unattainable. After growth, points *e* and *f* and many other previously unattainable combinations are attainable.

in government spending will simply displace private spending. Others argue that recessions are caused largely by a reduction in private spending, and that an increase in government spending can be an effective replacement to sustain the level of economic activity. Such debates lie at the heart of macroeconomic policy, and we have much to say about them in this book.

1.2 THE COMPLEXITY OF MODERN ECONOMIES

If you want a litre of milk, you go to your local grocery store and buy it. When the grocer needs more milk, he orders it from the wholesaler, who in turn gets it from the dairy, which in turn gets it from the dairy farmer. The dairy farmer buys cattle feed and electric milking machines, and he gets power to run all his equipment by putting a plug into a wall outlet where the electricity is supplied as he needs it. The milking machines are made from parts manufactured in several different places in Canada, the United States, and overseas. The parts themselves are made from materials produced in a dozen or more countries.

As it is with the milk you drink, so it is with everything else that you buy. When you go to a store, or shop online, what you want is normally available. Those who make these products find that all the required components and materials are available when they need them—even though these things typically come from many different parts of the world and are made by many people who have no direct dealings with one another.

Your own transactions are only a small part of the remarkably complex set of transactions that takes place every day in a modern economy. Shipments arrive daily at our ports, railway terminals, and airports. These shipments include raw materials, such as iron ore, logs, and oil; parts, such as automobile engines, transistors, and circuit boards; tools, such as screwdrivers, lathes, and digging equipment; perishables, such as fresh flowers, coffee beans, and fruit; and all kinds of manufactured goods, such as washing machines, computers, and cell phones. Trains and trucks move these goods among thousands of different destinations within Canada. Some go directly to consumers. Others are used by local firms to manufacture their products—some of which will be sold domestically and others exported to other countries. Remarkably, no one is actually *organizing* all of this economic activity.

The Nature of Market Economies

An *economy* is a system in which scarce resources—labour, land, and capital—are allocated among competing uses. Let's consider how this all happens in a market economy.

Self-Organizing   Early in the development of modern economics, thoughtful observers wondered how such a complex set of decisions and transactions gets organized. Who coordinates the whole set of efforts? Who makes sure that all the activities fit together, providing jobs to produce the things that people want and delivering those things to where they are wanted? The answer, as we said above, is nobody!

A great insight of early economists was that an economy based on free-market transactions is *self-organizing*.

A market economy is self-organizing in the sense that when individual consumers and producers act independently to pursue their own self-interests, the collective outcome is coordinated—there is a "spontaneous economic order." In that order, millions of transactions and activities fit together to produce the things that people want within the constraints set by the resources that are available to the nation.

The great Scottish economist and political philosopher Adam Smith (1723–1790),[1] who was the first to develop this insight fully, put it this way:

It is not from the benevolence of the butcher, the brewer, or the baker, that we expect our dinner, but from their regard to their own interest. We address ourselves, not to their humanity but to their self-love, and never talk to them of our own necessities but of their advantages.

Smith is not saying that benevolence is unimportant. Indeed, he praises it in many other passages of his book. He is saying, however, that the massive number of economic interactions that characterize a modern economy are not all motivated by benevolence. Although benevolence does motivate some of our actions, often the very dramatic ones, the vast majority of our everyday actions are motivated by self-interest. Self-interest is therefore the foundation of economic order.

Adam Smith wrote An Inquiry into the Nature and Causes of the Wealth of Nations in 1776. *Now referred to by most people simply as* The Wealth of Nations, *it is considered to be the beginning of modern economics.*

Efficiency   Another great insight, which was hinted at by Smith and fully developed over the next century and a half, was that this spontaneously generated economic order is relatively *efficient*. Loosely speaking, efficiency means that the resources available to the nation are organized so as to produce the various goods and services that people want to purchase and to produce them with the least possible amount of resources.

An economy organized by free markets behaves almost as if it were guided by "an invisible hand," in Smith's now-famous words. This does not literally mean that a supernatural presence runs a market economy. Instead it refers to the relatively efficient order that emerges spontaneously out of the many independent decisions made by those who produce, sell, and buy goods and services. The key to explaining this market behaviour is that these decision makers all respond to the same set of prices, which are determined in markets that respond to overall conditions of national scarcity or plenty. Much of this book is devoted to a detailed elaboration of how this market order is generated and how efficiently that job is done.

That free markets usually generate relatively efficient outcomes does not mean that they are *always* efficient or that everyone views the outcomes as desirable or even *fair*. Free markets sometimes fail to produce efficient outcomes, and these failures often provide a motivation for government intervention. In addition, many market outcomes may be efficient but perceived by many to be quite unfair. For example, we will see that an efficient labour market may nonetheless lead to large differentials in wages, with some individuals receiving low incomes while others receive enormous incomes. So, while a central aspect of economics is the study of how markets allocate resources efficiently, much emphasis is also placed on what happens when markets fail in various ways.

---

[1] Throughout this book, we encounter many great economists from the past whose ideas shaped the discipline of economics. At the back of the book you will find a timeline that begins in the 1600s. It contains brief discussions of many of these thinkers and places them in their historical context.

Incentives and Self-Interest   Lying at the heart of modern economies are *incentives* and *self-interest*. Individuals generally pursue their own self-interest, buying and selling what seems best for them and their families. They purchase products that they want rather than those they dislike, and they buy them when it makes sense given their time and financial constraints. Similarly, they sell products, including their own labour services, in an attempt to improve their own economic situation. When making such decisions about what to buy or sell and at what prices, people respond to *incentives*. Sellers usually want to sell more when prices are high because by doing so they will be able to afford more of the things they want. Similarly, buyers usually want to buy more when prices are low because by doing so they are better able to use their scarce resources to acquire the many things they desire.

With self-interested buyers and sellers responding to incentives when determining what they want to buy and sell, the overall market prices and quantities are determined by their collective interactions. Changes in their preferences or productive abilities lead to changes in their desired transactions and thus to fluctuations in market prices and quantities.

Of course, individuals are not motivated *only* by self-interest. For most people, love, faith, compassion, and generosity play important roles in their lives, especially at certain times. Behavioural economists devote their research to better understanding how these motivations influence individuals' economic behaviour. But none of this detracts from the importance of understanding the crucial role played in a modern economy by incentives and self-interest.

The Decision Makers and Their Choices

Three types of decision makers operate in any economy. The first is *consumers*. Sometimes we think of consumers as being individuals and sometimes we think in terms of families or households. Consumers purchase various kinds of goods and services with their income; they usually earn their income by selling their labour services to their employers.

The second type of decision maker is *producers*. Producers may be firms that are interested in earning profits or they may be non-profit or charitable organizations. In any case, producers hire workers, purchase or rent various kinds of material inputs and supplies, and then produce and sell their products. In the cases of charitable organizations, their products are often distributed for free.

The third type of decision maker is *government*. Like producers, governments hire workers, purchase or rent material and supplies, and produce goods and services. Unlike most producers, however, governments usually provide their goods and services at no direct cost to the final user; their operations are financed not by revenue from the sale of their products but instead by the taxes they collect from individual consumers and producers. In addition to producing and providing many goods and services, governments create and enforce laws, and design and implement regulations that must be followed by consumers and producers.

How Are Decisions Made?   How do consumers, producers, and governments make decisions? We will be examining how and why governments make decisions in detail throughout this book, so we will leave that until later. For now, let's focus on how consumers and producers make their decisions. Economists usually assume that consumers' and producers' decisions are both "maximizing" and "marginal." What does this mean?

Maximizing Decisions. Economists usually assume that consumers and producers make their decisions in an attempt to do as well as possible for themselves. In the jargon of economics, people are assumed to be *maximizers*. When individuals decide how much of their labour services to sell to producers and how many products to buy from them, they are assumed to make choices designed to maximize their well-being, or *utility*. When producers decide how much labour to hire and how many goods to produce, they are assumed to make choices designed to maximize their *profits*. We explore the details of utility and profit maximization in later chapters.

Marginal Decisions. Firms and consumers who are trying to maximize usually need to weigh the costs and benefits of their decisions *at the margin*. For example, when you consider buying a new shirt, you know the *marginal cost* of the shirt—that is, how much you must pay to get it—and you need to compare that cost to the *marginal benefit* that you will receive—the *extra* satisfaction you get from having that shirt. If you are trying to maximize your utility, you will buy the new shirt only if you think the benefit to you in terms of extra utility exceeds the marginal cost.

Similarly, a producer attempting to maximize its profits and considering whether to hire an extra worker must determine the *marginal cost* of the worker—the extra wages that must be paid—and compare it to the *marginal benefit* of the worker—the increase in sales revenues the extra worker will generate. A producer interested in maximizing its profit will hire the extra worker only if the benefit in terms of extra revenue exceeds the cost in terms of extra wages.

> In order to achieve their objectives, maximizing consumers and producers make marginal decisions; they decide whether they will be made better off by buying or selling a little more or a little less of any given product.

The Flow of Income and Expenditure Figure 1-4 shows the basic decision makers and the flows of income and expenditure that they set up. Individuals own factors of production. They sell the services of these factors to producers and receive payments in return. These are their incomes. Producers use the factor services that they buy to make goods and services. They sell these to individuals, receiving payments in return. These are the incomes of producers. These basic flows of income and expenditure pass through markets. Individuals sell the services of the factor that they own in what are collectively called *factor markets*. When you get a part-time job during university, you are participating in the factor market—in this case, a market for labour. Producers sell their outputs of goods and services in what are collectively called *goods markets*. When you purchase a haircut, an airplane ticket, or a new pair of shoes, for example, you are participating in the goods market.

The prices that are determined in these markets determine the incomes that are earned. People who get high prices for their factor services earn high incomes; those who get low prices earn low incomes. The *distribution of income* refers to how the nation's total income is distributed among its citizens. This is largely determined by the price that each type of factor service receives in factor markets.

Production and Trade

Individual producers decide which goods to produce and how to produce them. Production is a very complex process in any modern economy. For example, a typical

FIGURE 1-4 **The Circular Flow of Income and Expenditure**

The red line shows the flow of goods and services; the blue line shows the payments made to purchase these. Factor services flow from individuals who own the factors (including their own labour) through factor markets to firms that use them to make goods and services. These goods and services then flow through goods markets to those who consume them. Money payments flow from firms to individuals through factor markets. These payments become the income of individuals. When they spend this income buying goods and services, money flows through goods markets back to producers.

specialization of labour The specialization of individual workers in the production of particular goods or services.

division of labour The breaking up of a production process into a series of specialized tasks, each done by a different worker.

car manufacturer assembles a product out of thousands of individual parts. It makes some of these parts itself. Most are subcontracted to parts manufacturers, and many of the major parts manufacturers subcontract some of their work to smaller firms. The same is true for most other products you can imagine purchasing. Such complex production displays two characteristics noted long ago by Adam Smith—*specialization* and the *division of labour*.

Specialization   In ancient hunter–gatherer societies and in modern subsistence economies, most people make most of the things they need for themselves. However, from the time that people first engaged in settled agriculture and then began to live in towns, people have specialized in doing particular jobs. Artisan, soldier, priest, and government official were some of the earliest specialized occupations. Economists call this allocation of different jobs to different people the **specialization of labour**. There are two fundamental reasons why specialization is extraordinarily efficient compared with universal self-sufficiency.

First, individual abilities differ, and specialization allows individuals to do what they can do relatively well while leaving everything else to be done by others. The economy's total production is greater when people specialize than when they all try to be self-sufficient. This is true for individuals, but it is also true for entire countries, and it is one of the most fundamental principles in economics: the principle of *comparative advantage*. A much fuller discussion of comparative advantage is found in Chapter 32, where we discuss the gains from international trade.

The second reason why specialization is more efficient than self-sufficiency concerns changes in people's abilities that occur *because* they specialize. A person who concentrates on one activity becomes better at it than someone who produces many different things. This is called *learning by doing*.

The Division of Labour   Throughout most of history each artisan who specialized in making some product made the whole of that product. But over the last several hundred years, many technical advances have made it efficient to organize production methods into large-scale firms organized around what is called the **division of labour**. This term refers to specialization *within* the production process of a particular product. For example, in most mass-production factories, work is divided into highly specialized tasks by using specialized machinery. Each worker repeatedly does one or a few small tasks that represents only a small fraction of those necessary to produce any one product.

Money and Trade   People who specialize in doing only one thing must satisfy most of their wants by consuming things made by other people. In early societies the exchange of goods and services took place by simple mutual agreement among neighbours. In the course of time, however, trading became centred on particular gathering places called markets. For example, the French markets or trade fairs of Champagne were known throughout Europe as early as the eleventh century. Even now, many small towns in Canada have regular market days. Today, however, the term "market" has a much broader meaning, referring to any institutions that allow buyers and sellers to transact with each other, which could be by meeting physically or by trading over the Internet. Also, we use the term "market economy" to refer to a society in which people specialize in productive activities and meet most of their material wants through voluntary market transactions with other people.

Specialization must be accompanied by trade. People who produce only one thing must trade most of it with other people to obtain all the other things they want.

Early trading was by means of **barter**, the trading of goods directly for other goods. But barter is costly in terms of time spent searching out satisfactory exchanges. If a farmer has wheat but wants a hammer, he must find someone who has a hammer and wants wheat. A successful barter transaction thus requires what is called a *double coincidence of wants*.

barter An economic system in which goods and services are traded directly for other goods and services.

Money eliminates the cumbersome system of barter by separating the transactions involved in the exchange of products. If a farmer has wheat and wants a hammer, she merely has to find someone who wants wheat. The farmer takes money in exchange. Then she finds a person who wants to sell a hammer and gives up the money for the hammer.

Money greatly facilitates trade, which itself facilitates specialization.

Globalization   Market economies constantly change, largely as a result of the development of new technologies and the new patterns of production and trade that result. Many of the recent changes are referred to as *globalization*, a term often used loosely to mean the increased importance of international trade.

Though international trade dates back thousands of years, what is new in the last few decades is the globalization of manufacturing. Assembly of a product may take place in the most industrialized countries, but the hundreds of component parts are manufactured in dozens of different countries and delivered to the assembly plant "just in time" for assembly.

Two major causes of globalization are the rapid reduction in transportation costs and the revolution in information technology that have occurred in the past 50 years. The cost of moving products around the world fell greatly over the last half of the twentieth century because of containerization and the increasing size of ships. Our ability to transmit and analyze data increased even more dramatically, while the costs of doing so fell sharply. For example, today $1000 buys an ultra-slim tablet or laptop computer that has the same computing power as a "mainframe" computer that in 1970 cost $10 million and filled a large room. This revolution in information and communication technology has made it possible to coordinate economic transactions around the world in ways that were difficult and costly 50 years ago and quite impossible 100 years ago.

The revolution in shipping and in computer technology has drastically reduced communication and transportation costs. This reduction in costs lies at the heart of globalization.

Through the ongoing process of globalization, national economies are ever more linked to the global economy.

Globalization comes with challenges, however. As Canadian firms relocate production facilities to countries where costs are lower, domestic workers are laid off and must search for new jobs, perhaps needing retraining in the process. The location of production facilities in countries with lower environmental or human-rights records raises difficult questions about the standards that should be followed by Canadian-owned firms in foreign lands. And firms often use the threat of relocation in an attempt to extract financial assistance from governments, placing those governments in difficult positions. These concerns have led in recent years to "anti-globalization protests" that have raised awareness of some of the costs associated with the process of globalization. We have more to say about these issues in Chapters 33 and 34.

1.3 IS THERE AN ALTERNATIVE TO THE MARKET ECONOMY?

In this chapter we have discussed the elements of an economy based on free-market transactions—what we call a *market economy*. Are there any alternatives to this type of economy? To answer this question we first need to identify various types of economic systems.

Types of Economic Systems

It is helpful to distinguish three pure types of economies, called *traditional, command,* and *free-market economies*. These economies differ in the way in which economic decisions are coordinated. But no actual economy fits neatly into one of these three categories—all real economies contain some elements of each type.

traditional economy An economy in which behaviour is based mostly on tradition.

Traditional Economies   A **traditional economy** is one in which behaviour is based primarily on tradition, custom, and habit. Young men follow their fathers' occupations. Women do what their mothers did. There is little change in the pattern of goods produced from year to year, other than those imposed by the vagaries of nature. The techniques of production also follow traditional patterns, except when the effects of an occasional new invention are felt. Finally, production is allocated among the members according to long-established traditions.

Such a system works best in an unchanging environment. Under such static conditions, a system that does not continually require people to make choices can prove effective in meeting economic and social needs.

Traditional systems were common in earlier times. The feudal system, under which most people in medieval Europe lived, was a largely traditional society. Peasants, artisans, and most others living in villages inherited their positions in that society. They also usually inherited their specific jobs, which they handled in traditional ways.

command economy An economy in which most economic decisions are made by a central planning authority.

Command Economies   In command economies, economic behaviour is determined by some central authority, usually the government, or perhaps a dictator, which makes most of the necessary decisions on what to produce, how to produce it, and who gets to consume which products and in what quantities. Such economies are characterized by the *centralization* of decision making. Because centralized decision makers usually create elaborate and complex plans for the behaviour that they want to impose, the terms **command economy** and *centrally planned economy* are usually used synonymously.

The sheer quantity of data required for the central planning of an entire modern economy is enormous, and the task of analyzing it to produce a fully integrated plan can hardly be exaggerated. Moreover, the plan must be continually modified to take account not only of current data but also of future trends in labour and resource supplies and technological developments. This is a notoriously difficult exercise, not least because of the unavailability of all essential, accurate, and up-to-date information.

Until about 40 years ago, more than one-third of the world's population lived in countries that relied heavily on central planning. Today, after the collapse of the Soviet Union and the rapid expansion of markets in China, the number of such countries is small. Even in countries in which central planning is the proclaimed system, as in Cuba and North Korea, increasing amounts of market determination are gradually being permitted.

Free-Market Economies   In the third type of economic system, the decisions about resource allocation are made without any central direction. Instead, they result from innumerable independent decisions made by individual producers and consumers. Such a system is known as a **free-market economy** or, more simply, a *market economy*. In such an economy, decisions relating to the basic economic issues are *decentralized*. Despite the absence of a central plan, these many decentralized decisions are nonetheless coordinated. The main coordinating device is the set of market-determined prices—which is why free-market systems are often called *price systems*.

In a pure market economy, all these decisions are made by buyers and sellers acting through unhindered markets. The government provides the background of defining property rights and protecting citizens against foreign and domestic enemies but, beyond that, markets determine all resource allocation and income distribution.

free-market economy An economy in which most economic decisions are made by private households and firms.

Mixed Economies   Economies that are fully traditional or fully centrally planned or wholly free-market are pure types that are useful for studying basic principles. When we look in detail at any actual economy, however, we discover that its economic behaviour is the result of some mixture of central control and market determination, with a certain amount of traditional behaviour as well.

In practice, every economy is a mixed economy in the sense that it combines significant elements of all three systems in determining economic behaviour.

mixed economy An economy in which some economic decisions are made by firms and households and some by the government.

Furthermore, within any economy, the degree of the mix varies from sector to sector. For example, in some planned economies, the command principle was used more often to determine behaviour in heavy-goods industries, such as steel, than in agriculture. Farmers were often given substantial freedom to produce and sell what they wanted in response to varying market prices.

When economists speak of a particular economy as being centrally planned, we mean only that the degree of the mix is weighted heavily toward the command principle. When we speak of one as being a market economy, we mean only that the degree of the mix is weighted heavily toward decentralized decision making.

Although no country offers an example of either system working alone, some economies, such as those of Canada, the United States, France, and Hong Kong, rely much more heavily on market decisions than others, such as the economies of China, North Korea, and Cuba. Yet even in Canada, the command principle has some sway.

Karl Marx argued that free-market economies could not be relied on to ensure an equitable distribution of income. He advocated a system of central planning in which government owns most of the means of production.

Crown corporations, legislated minimum wages, rules and regulations for environmental protection, quotas on some agricultural outputs, and restrictions on the import of some items are just a few examples.

The Great Debate   ~read later~

As we saw earlier, in 1776 Adam Smith was one of the first people to analyze the operation of markets, and he stressed the relative efficiency of free-market economies. A century later, another great economist and political philosopher, Karl Marx (1818–1883), argued that although free-market economies would indeed be successful in producing high levels of output, they could not be relied on to ensure that this output would be fairly distributed among citizens. He argued the benefits of a centrally planned system in which the government could ensure a more equitable distribution of output.

Beginning with the Soviet Union in the early 1920s, many nations adopted systems in which conscious government central planning replaced the operation of the free market. For almost a century, a great debate then raged on the relative merits of command economies versus market economies. Along with the Soviet Union, the countries of Eastern Europe and China were command economies for much of the twentieth century. Canada, the United States, and most of the countries of Western Europe were, and still are, primarily market economies. The apparent successes of the Soviet Union and China in the 1950s and 1960s, including the ability to mobilize considerable resources into heavy industries, suggested to many observers that the command principle was at least as good for organizing economic behaviour as the market principle. Over the long run, however, planned economies proved to be a failure of such disastrous proportions that they seriously depressed the living standards of their citizens.

During the last decade of the twentieth century, most of the world's centrally planned economies began the difficult transition back toward freer markets. These transitions occurred at different paces in different countries, but in most cases the initial few years were characterized by significant declines in output and employment. Twenty-five years later, however, most of the "transition" economies are experiencing growth rates above the ones they had in their final years as centrally planned economies. Living standards are on the rise.

The large-scale failure of central planning suggests the superiority of decentralized markets over centrally planned ones as mechanisms for allocating an economy's scarce resources. Put another way, it demonstrates the superiority of mixed economies with substantial elements of market determination over fully planned command economies. However, it does *not* demonstrate, as some observers have asserted, the superiority of completely free-market economies over mixed economies.

There is no guarantee that completely free markets will, on their own, handle such urgent matters as controlling pollution, providing public goods (like national defence), or preventing financial crises, such as occurred in 2008 in most of the developed countries. Indeed, as we will see in later chapters, much economic theory is devoted to explaining why free markets often *fail* to do these things. Mixed economies, with significant elements of government intervention, are needed to do these jobs.

Furthermore, acceptance of the free market over central planning does not provide an excuse to ignore a country's pressing social issues. Acceptance of the benefits of the free market still leaves plenty of scope to debate the most appropriate levels and types of government policies directed at achieving specific social goals. It follows that there is still considerable room for disagreement about the degree of the mix of market and government determination in any modern mixed economy—room enough to accommodate such divergent views as could be expressed by conservative, liberal, and modern social democratic parties.

So, the first answer to the question about the existence of an alternative to the market economy is no: There is no *practical* alternative to a mixed system with major reliance on markets but some government presence in most aspects of the economy. The second answer is yes: Within the framework of a mixed economy there are substantial alternatives among many different and complex mixes of free-market and government determination of economic life.

Government in the Modern Mixed Economy

Market economies in today's advanced industrial countries are based primarily on voluntary transactions between individual buyers and sellers. Private individuals have the right to buy and sell what they want, to accept or refuse work that is offered to them, and to move where they want when they want. However, some of the most important institutions in our societies govern the transactions between buyers and sellers.

> **Key institutions are private property and freedom of contract, both of which must be maintained by active government policies. The government creates laws of ownership and contract and then provides the institutions, such as police and courts, to enforce these laws.**

In modern mixed economies, governments go well beyond these important basic functions. They intervene in market transactions to correct what economists call *market failures*. These are well-defined situations in which free markets do not work well. Some products, called *public goods*, are usually not provided at all by markets because their use cannot usually be restricted to those who pay for them. Defence and police protection are examples of public goods. In other cases, private producers or consumers impose costs called *externalities* on those who have no say in the transaction. This is the case when factories pollute the air and rivers. The public is harmed but plays no part in the transaction. In yet other cases, financial institutions, such as banks, mortgage companies, and investment houses, may indulge in risky activities that threaten the health of the entire economic system. These market failures explain why governments sometimes intervene to alter the allocation of resources.

Also, important issues of *equity* arise from letting free markets determine people's incomes. Some people lose their jobs because firms are reorganizing to become more efficient in the face of new technologies. Others keep their jobs, but the market places so little value on their services that they face economic deprivation. The old and the chronically ill may suffer if their past circumstances did not allow them to save enough to support themselves. For many reasons of this sort, almost everyone accepts some government intervention to redistribute income.

These are some of the reasons all modern economies are mixed economies. Throughout most of the twentieth century in advanced industrial societies, the mix had been shifting toward more and more government participation in decisions about the allocation of resources and the distribution of income. Starting in the early 1980s, a worldwide movement began to reduce the degree of government participation in economies. With the onset of the global financial crisis in 2008, however, there has been some movement back toward a greater involvement of government in the economy. These shifts in the market/government mix, and the reasons for them, are some of the major issues that will be studied in this book.

SUMMARY

1.1 WHAT IS ECONOMICS?   LO 1

- Scarcity is a fundamental problem faced by all economies. Not enough resources are available to produce all the goods and services that people would like to consume.
- Scarcity makes it necessary to choose. All societies must have a mechanism for choosing what goods and services will be produced and in what quantities.
- The concept of opportunity cost emphasizes the problem of scarcity and choice by measuring the cost of obtaining a unit of one product in terms of the number of units of other products that could have been obtained instead.

- A production possibilities boundary shows all the combinations of goods that can be produced by an economy whose resources are fully and efficiently employed. Movement from one point to another along the boundary requires a reallocation of resources.
- Four basic questions must be answered in all economies: What is produced and how? What is consumed and by whom? Why are resources sometimes idle? Is productive capacity growing?
- Issues of government policy enter into discussions of all four questions.

1.2 THE COMPLEXITY OF MODERN ECONOMIES   LO 2, 3, 4

- A market economy is self-organizing in the sense that when individual consumers and producers act independently to pursue their own self-interest, the collective outcome is coordinated.
- Incentives and self-interest play a central role for all groups of decision makers: consumers, producers, and governments.
- Individual consumers are assumed to make their decisions in an effort to maximize their well-being or utility. Producers' decisions are assumed to be designed to maximize their profits.

- The interaction of consumers and producers through goods and factor markets is illustrated by the circular flow of income and expenditure.
- Modern economies are based on the specialization and division of labour, which necessitate the exchange (trading) of goods and services. Exchange takes place in markets and is facilitated by the use of money.
- Driven by the ongoing revolution in transportation and communications technology, the world economy is rapidly globalizing.

1.3 IS THERE AN ALTERNATIVE TO THE MARKET ECONOMY?   LO 5

- We can distinguish three pure types of economies: traditional, command, and free-market. In practice, all economies are mixed economies.
- By the late 1980s, most countries with centrally planned economies had failed to produce minimally acceptable living standards for their citizens. These countries are now moving toward greater market determination and less state command in their economies.

- Governments play an important role in modern mixed economies. They create and enforce important background institutions such as private property and freedom of contract. They intervene to correct market failures. They also redistribute income in the interests of equity.

KEY CONCEPTS

Resources
Scarcity and the need for choice
Choice and opportunity cost
Production possibilities boundary
The self-organizing economy

Incentives and self-interest
Specialization
The division of labour
Trade and money
Globalization

Traditional economies
Command economies
Free-market economies
Mixed economies

STUDY EXERCISES

MyEconLab

Make the grade with MyEconLab: Study Exercises marked in ⊕ can be found on MyEconLab. You can practise them as often as you want, and most feature step-by-step guided instructions to help you find the right answer.

❶ Fill in the blanks to make the following statements correct.

 a. The three general categories of any economy's resources are _____, _____, and _____. Economists refer to these resources as the _____ of production.
 b. When we use any resource, the benefit given up by not using it in its best alternative way is known as the _____ of that resource.
 c. The concepts of scarcity, choice, and opportunity cost can be illustrated by a curve known as the _____.
 d. When looking at a production possibilities boundary, any point that is outside the boundary demonstrates _____. The _____ slope of the production possibilities boundary demonstrates _____.
 e. A straight-line production possibilities boundary (PPB) indicates that the opportunity cost of each good is _____, no matter how much of that good is produced. A PPB that is concave to the origin indicates that a(n) _____ amount of one good must be given up to produce more of the other good.
 f. Consider an economy producing two goods, A and B, with a PPB that is concave to the origin. As the economy produces more of good A and less of good B, its opportunity cost of producing A _____.

❷ Consider your decision whether to go skiing for the weekend. Suppose transportation, lift tickets, and accommodation for the weekend cost $300. Suppose also that restaurant food for the weekend will cost $75. Finally, suppose you have a weekend job that you will have to miss if you go skiing, which pays you $120 (after tax) for the one weekend day that you work. What is the opportunity cost of going skiing? Do you need any other information before computing the opportunity cost?

❸ Suppose you own an outdoor recreation company and you want to purchase all-terrain vehicles (ATVs) for your summer business and snowmobiles for your winter business. Your budget for new vehicles this year is $240 000. ATVs cost $8000 each and snowmobiles cost $12 000 each.

 a. Draw the budget line for your purchase of new vehicles.
 b. What is the opportunity cost of one ATV?
 c. What is the opportunity cost of one snowmobile?
 d. Does the opportunity cost of one ATV depend on how many you purchase? Why or why not?

❹ Suppose one factory produces residential windows and doors. The following scenarios describe various straight-line production possibilities boundaries for this factory. Each scenario describes the numbers of doors that could be produced in one day if all the factory's resources were devoted to producing doors and the number of windows that could be produced in one day if all the factory's resources were devoted to producing windows. For each scenario, calculate the opportunity cost to the factory owner of producing one extra door.

 a. 1000 windows; 250 doors
 b. 500 windows; 500 doors
 c. 1200 windows; 400 doors
 d. 942 windows; 697 doors
 e. 450 doors; 600 windows

❺ Explain the three economic concepts illustrated by the production possibilities boundary.

❻ Consider an economy that produces only food and clothing. Its production possibilities boundary is shown below.

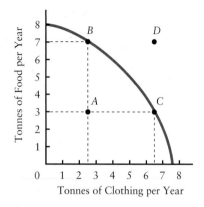

a. If the economy is at point *A*, how many tonnes of clothing and how many tonnes of food are being produced? At point *B*? At point *C*?

b. What do we know about the use of resources when the economy is at point *A*? At point *B*? At point *C*?

c. If the economy is at point *B*, what is the opportunity cost of producing one more tonne of food? What is the opportunity cost of producing one more tonne of clothing?

d. What do we know about the use of resources at point *D*? How would it be possible for the economy to produce at point *D*?

7 Choiceland has 250 workers and produces only two goods, *X* and *Y*. Labour is the only factor of production, but some workers are better suited to producing *X* than *Y* (and vice versa). The table below shows the maximum levels of output of each good possible from various levels of labour input.

Number of Workers Producing *X*	Annual Production of *X*	Number of Workers Producing *Y*	Annual Production of *Y*
0	0	250	1300
50	20	200	1200
100	45	150	900
150	60	100	600
200	70	50	350
250	75	0	0

a. Draw the production possibilities boundary for Choiceland on a scale diagram, with the production of *X* on the horizontal axis and the production of *Y* on the vertical axis.

b. Compute the opportunity cost of producing an extra 15 units of *X* if the economy is initially producing 45 units of *X* and 900 units of *Y*. How does this compare to the opportunity cost if the economy were initially producing 60 units of *X* and 600 units of *Y*?

c. If the economy is producing 40 units of *X* and 600 units of *Y*, what is the opportunity cost of producing an extra 20 units of *X*?

d. Suppose now that the technology associated with producing good *Y* improves, so that the maximum level of *Y* that can be produced from any given level of labour input increases by 10 percent. Explain (or show in a diagram) what happens to the production possibilities curve.

8 For each of the following events, describe the likely effect on the country's production possibilities boundary (PPB). Start with a PPB like the one below and draw the likely change. "In each case, specify the appropriate labels for both axes in the diagram."

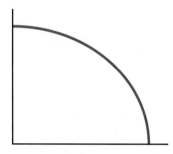

a. Suppose the country has a 10-year civil war that destroys much of its infrastructure.

b. Suppose a small country produces only food and clothing. A new agricultural technology is then introduced that doubles the amount of food that can be produced per year.

c. Suppose a small country produces only food and clothing. An earthquake destroys many of the clothing factories, but the ability to produce food is unaffected.

d. The country admits approximately 250 000 immigrants *each year*, many of whom join the labour force.

9 Explain why a technological improvement in the production of one good means that a country can now produce more of *other* goods than it did previously. Hint: Draw a country's production possibilities boundary to help answer this question.

10 Suppose you and a friend are stranded on an island and must gather firewood and catch fish to survive. Through experience, you know that if each of you spends an entire day on either activity, the result is given in the following table:

	Fish	Firewood (bundles)
You	6	3
Your friend	8	2

a. What is the opportunity cost for you to gather an additional bundle of firewood? What is your friend's opportunity cost of gathering an extra bundle of firewood?

b. Assuming that you and your friend specialize, what allocation of tasks maximizes total output for your one day of joint effort?

c. Suppose you both decide to work for two days according to the allocation in part (b). What is the total amount of output? What would it have been had you chosen the reverse allocation of tasks?

11 In this chapter we used a simple idea of a production possibilities boundary to illustrate the concepts of scarcity, choice, and opportunity cost. We assumed there were only two goods—call them X and Y. But we all know that any economy produces many more than just two goods. Explain why the insights illustrated in Figure 1-2 are more general, and why the assumption of only two goods is a useful one.

12 What is the difference between microeconomics and macroeconomics?

13 For each of the following situations, explain how a change in the stated "price" is likely to affect your incentives regarding the stated decision.

a. the price of ski-lift tickets; your decision to purchase a ski-lift ticket

b. the hourly wage for your weekend job; the decision to not work and go skiing on the weekend instead

c. the fine for speeding; your decision to speed on the highway

d. the weight of your course grade attached to an assignment; your decision to work hard on that assignment

e. the level of tuition fees at your college or university; your decision to attend that college or university

14 State and explain two reasons why the specialization of labour is more efficient than universal self-sufficiency.

15 Consider the market for doctors' services. In what way has this market taken advantage of the specialization of labour?

16 List the four main types of economic systems and their main attributes.

17 As we said in the text, the average family income in Canada is about $80 000 per year. Imagine a hypothetical world in which *all* Canadian families had this income.

a. In such a world, would poverty exist in Canada?

b. In such a world, would scarcity exist in Canada?

c. Explain the difference between poverty and scarcity.

18 Comment on the following statement: "One of the mysteries of semantics is why the government–managed economies ever came to be called planned and the market economies unplanned. It is the former that are in chronic chaos, in which buyers stand in line hoping to buy some toilet paper or soap. It is the latter that are in reasonable equilibrium—where if you want a bar of soap or a steak or a shirt or a car, you can go to the store and find that the item is magically there for you to buy. It is the liberal economies that reflect a highly sophisticated planning system, and the government-managed economies that are primitive and unplanned."

2 Economic Theories, Data, and Graphs

CHAPTER OUTLINE	LEARNING OBJECTIVES (LO) After studying this chapter, you will be able to
2.1 POSITIVE AND NORMATIVE STATEMENTS	1 distinguish between positive and normative statements.
2.2 BUILDING AND TESTING ECONOMIC THEORIES	2 explain why and how economists use theories to help them understand the economy. 3 understand the interaction between economic theories and empirical observation.
2.3 ECONOMIC DATA	4 identify several types of economic data, including index numbers, time-series and cross-sectional data, and scatter diagrams.
2.4 GRAPHING ECONOMIC THEORIES	5 see that the slope of a line on a graph relating two variables shows the "marginal response" of one variable to a change in the other.

IF you follow the news, whether online, TV, newspaper, or radio, you are likely to hear the views of economists being discussed—about debt crises, unemployment, income inequality, attempts to reform the health-care system, environmental policy, changes to corporate income-tax rates, or a myriad of other issues. Where do economists' opinions come from? Are they supported by hard evidence, and if so, why do economists sometimes disagree with each other over important issues?

Economics is a social science, and in this chapter we explore what it means to be "scientific" in the study of economics. Along the way we will learn much about theories, predictions, data, testing, and graphing—economists use all of these tools and techniques in their attempt to understand the economic world. We begin with the important distinction between positive and normative statements.

2.1 POSITIVE AND NORMATIVE STATEMENTS

Economists give two broad types of advice, called *normative* and *positive*. For example, they sometimes advise that the government ought to try harder to reduce unemployment. When they say such things, they are giving normative advice; in this case, they are making judgements about the value of the various things that the government could do with its limited resources and about the costs and benefits of reducing unemployment. Advice that depends on a value judgement is normative—it tells others what they *ought* to do.

Another type of advice is illustrated by the statement "If the government wants to reduce unemployment, reducing employment-insurance benefits is an effective way of doing so." This is positive advice. It does not rely on a judgement about the value of reducing unemployment. Instead, the expert is saying, "If this is what you want to do, here is a way to do it."

Normative statements depend on value judgements and cannot be evaluated solely by a recourse to facts. In contrast, **positive statements** do not involve value judgements. They are statements about matters of fact, and so disagreements about them are appropriately dealt with by an appeal to evidence. The distinction between positive and normative is fundamental to scientific progress. Much of the success of modern science depends on the ability of scientists to separate their views on *what does happen* in the world from their views on *what they would like to happen*. For example, until the eighteenth century almost everyone believed that Earth was only a few thousand years old. Evidence then began to accumulate that Earth was billions of years old. This evidence was hard for most people to accept, since it ran counter to a literal reading of many religious texts. Many did not want to believe the evidence. Nevertheless, scientists, many of whom were religious, continued their research because they refused to allow their feelings about what they wanted to believe to affect their scientific search for the truth. Eventually, all scientists and most members of the public came to accept that Earth is about 4.5 billion years old.

> **normative statement** A statement about what ought to be; it is based on a value judgement.

> **positive statement** A statement about what actually is, was, or will be; it is not based on a value judgement.

> Distinguishing what is actually true from what we would like to be true requires distinguishing between positive and normative statements.

Examples of both types of statements are given in Table 2-1. All five positive statements in the table are assertions about the nature of the world in which we live. In contrast, the five normative statements involve value judgements. Notice two things about the positive/normative distinction. First, positive statements need not be true. Statement C is almost certainly false, and yet it is positive, not normative. Second, the inclusion of a value judgement in a statement does not necessarily make the statement itself normative. Statement D is a positive statement about the value judgements that people hold. We could conduct a survey to check if people really do prefer low unemployment to low inflation. We could ask them and we could observe how they voted. There is no need for the economist to rely on a value judgement to check the validity of the statement itself.

We leave you to analyze the remaining eight statements to decide precisely why each is either positive or normative. Remember to apply the two tests. First, is the statement only about actual or alleged facts? If so, it is a positive one. Second, are value judgements necessary to assess the truth of the statement? If so, it is normative.

TABLE 2-1 Positive and Normative Statements

Positive	Normative
A Raising interest rates encourages people to save.	F People should be encouraged to save.
B High rates of income tax encourage people to evade paying taxes.	G Governments should arrange taxes so that people cannot avoid paying them.
C Lowering the price of cigarettes leads people to smoke less.	H The government should raise the tax on cigarettes to discourage people from smoking.
D The majority of the population would prefer a policy that reduced unemployment to one that reduced inflation.	I Unemployment is a more important social problem than inflation.
E Government financial assistance to commercial banks is ineffective at preventing job losses.	J Government should not spend taxpayers' money on supporting commercial banks.

Disagreements Among Economists

Economists often disagree with one another in public discussions, frequently because of poor communication. They often fail to define their terms or their points of reference clearly, and so they end up "arguing past" each other, with the only certain result being that the audience is left confused.

Economists often disagree with one another in the media or at conferences, but their debates are more often about normative issues than positive ones.

Another source of disagreement stems from some economists' failure to acknowledge the full state of their ignorance. There are many points on which the evidence is far from conclusive. In such cases, a responsible economist makes clear the extent to which his or her view is based on judgements about the relevant (and uncertain) facts.

Many other public disagreements are based on the positive/normative distinction. Different economists have different values, and these normative views play a large part in most discussions of public policy. Many economists stress the importance of individual responsibility and argue, for example, that lower employment insurance benefits would be desirable because people would have a greater incentive to search for a job. Other economists stress the need for a generous "social safety net" and argue that higher employment insurance benefits are desirable because human hardship would be reduced. In such debates, and there are many in economics, it is the responsibility of the economist to state clearly what part of the proffered advice is normative and what part is positive.

Because the world is complex and because no issue can be settled beyond any doubt, economists rarely agree unanimously on an issue. Nevertheless, there is an impressive amount of agreement on many aspects of how the economy works and what happens when governments intervene to alter its workings. A survey published in the *American Economic Review,* perhaps the most influential economics journal, showed strong

APPLYING ECONOMIC CONCEPTS 2-1

Where Economists Work

This chapter discusses the theoretical and empirical tools that economists use. After reading this material, you might wonder where economists find jobs and what kind of work they actually do. The skills of economists are demanded in many parts of the economy by governments, private businesses and crown corporations, non-profit organizations, and universities.

In Ottawa and the provincial and territorial capitals, economists are hired in most government departments to analyze the effects of government policies and to design ways to improve those policies. At Finance Canada, economists design and analyze the income-tax system and the effects of current spending programs. At Environment Canada, they help design and evaluate policies aimed at reducing water and air pollution. At Industry Canada, they study the sources of productivity growth and design policies to encourage innovation in the private sector. At the Bank of Canada, economists research the link between interest rates, the aggregate demand for goods and services, and the rate of increase in prices. They also monitor developments in the global economy and their effects on the Canadian economy. Statistics Canada employs many economists to design methods of collecting and analyzing data covering all aspects of Canadian society.

The analysis of economic policies also takes place in independent research organizations, often called "think tanks." The C.D. Howe Institute in Toronto is one of Canada's best-known think tanks, and it regularly publishes papers on topics ranging from monetary policy and the state of public pensions to the effects of immigration and the challenges in reforming Canada's policies for foreign development assistance. Other think tanks include the Institute for Research on Public Policy, the Canadian Centre for Policy Alternatives, the Fraser Institute, the Centre for the Study of Living Standards, and

the Conference Board of Canada. All of these independent and non-profit organizations hire economists to study economic issues and then write and edit the economic publications that address them.

Private and public (crown) corporations in many sectors of the economy also hire economists in a variety of positions. Economists at Canadian Pacific Railway monitor how changes in world commodity prices will lead to changes in Canadian resource production and thus to changes in the demand for their rail transport services. Economists at Manitoba Hydro study the link between economic growth and electricity demand to help the firm with its long-run investment decisions. Those at Export Development Canada examine how economic and political risks in various countries influence the demand for the products of Canadian exporters. Economists at Bombardier are hired to determine how ongoing negotiations within the World Trade Organization will affect tariff levels in various countries and how these changes will affect the demand for Bombardier jets.

Finally, many economists are hired by universities all over the world to teach students like you and to conduct research on a wide variety of economic topics. Some of this research is theoretical and some is empirical, using data to test economic theories. Other academic economists focus their research on the design and implementation of better economic policy, and often spend considerable time interacting with the economists employed by government departments.

Training in economics provides useful analytical skills that are valuable for learning about the workings of a complex economic world. There is no shortage of demand for people who can think clearly and analytically about economic issues. This course could well be the start of a great career for you. Study hard!

agreement among economists on many propositions, including "Rent control leads to a housing shortage" (85 percent yes), "Tariffs usually reduce economic welfare" (93 percent yes), and "A minimum wage increases unemployment among young workers" (79 percent yes). Notice that all these are positive rather than normative statements. Other examples of these areas of agreement will be found in many places throughout this book.

Interesting stats

Whether they agree or disagree with one another, economists are in demand in many sectors of the economy. See *Applying Economic Concepts 2-1* for a discussion of the many organizations that employ economists.

2.2 BUILDING AND TESTING ECONOMIC THEORIES

The economic world is complex. Many things are changing at the same time, and it is difficult to distinguish cause from effect. By examining data carefully, however, regularities and trends can be detected. To better understand these patterns in the data, economists develop *theories*, which they sometimes call *models*. Theories are used to both explain events that have already happened and to help predict events that might happen in the future.

What Are Theories?

Theories are constructed to explain things. For example, economists may seek to explain what determines the quantity of eggs bought and sold in a particular month in Manitoba and the price at which they are sold. Or they may seek to explain what determines the quantity of oil bought and sold around the world on a particular day and the price at which it is traded. As part of the answer to such questions, economists have developed theories of demand and supply—theories that we will study in detail in the next three chapters. These and all other theories are distinguished by their *variables*, *assumptions*, and *predictions*.

variable Any well-defined item, such as the price or quantity of a commodity, that can take on various specific values.

Variables   The basic elements of any theory are its variables. A **variable** is a well-defined item, such as a price or a quantity, that can take on different possible values.

In a theory of the egg market, the variable *quantity of eggs* might be defined as the number of cartons of 12 Grade A large eggs. The variable *price of eggs* is the amount of money that must be given up to purchase each carton of eggs. The particular values taken by those two variables might be 20 000 cartons per week at a price of $2.60 in July 2014, 18 000 cartons per week at a price of $2.75 in July 2015, and 19 500 cartons per week at a price of $2.95 in July 2016.

endogenous variable A variable that is explained within a theory. Sometimes called an *induced variable* or a *dependent variable.*

exogenous variable A variable that is determined outside the theory. Sometimes called an *autonomous variable* or an *independent variable.*

There are two broad categories of variables that are important in any theory. An **endogenous variable** is one whose value is determined within the theory. An **exogenous variable** influences the endogenous variables but is itself determined outside the theory. To illustrate the difference, the price of eggs and the quantity of eggs are endogenous variables in our theory of the egg market—our theory is designed to explain them. The state of the weather, however, is an exogenous variable. It may well affect the number of eggs consumers demand or producers supply, but we can safely assume that the state of the weather is not influenced by the market for eggs.

Assumptions   A theory's assumptions concern motives, directions of causation, and the conditions under which the theory is meant to apply.

Motives.   The theories we study in this book make the fundamental assumption that everyone pursues his or her own self-interest when making economic decisions. Individuals are assumed to strive to maximize their *utility*, while firms are assumed to try to maximize their *profits*. Not only are they assumed to know what they want, but we also assume that they know how to go about getting it within the constraints they face.

Direction of Causation.   When economists assume that one variable is related to another, they are usually assuming some causal link between the two. For example, when the amount of wheat that producers want to supply is assumed to increase when the weather improves, the causation runs from the weather to the supply of wheat. Producers supply more wheat because the growing conditions improve; they are not assumed to experience better weather as a result of their increased supply of wheat.

Conditions of Application.   Assumptions are often used to specify the conditions under which a theory is meant to hold. For example, a theory that assumes there is "no government" usually does not mean literally the absence of government but only that the theory is meant to apply when governments are not significantly affecting the situation being studied.

Although assumptions are an essential part of all theories, students are often concerned about those that seem unrealistic. An example will illustrate some of the issues involved. Much of the theory that we are going to study in this book uses the assumption that owners of firms attempt to make as much money as they can—that is, to maximize their profits. The assumption of profit maximization allows economists to make predictions about the behaviour of firms, such as "firms will supply more output if the market price increases."

Profit maximization may seem like a rather crude assumption. Surely, for example, the managers of firms sometimes choose to protect the environment rather than pursue certain highly polluting but profitable opportunities. Does this not discredit the assumption of profit maximization by showing it to be unrealistic?

The answer is no; to make successful predictions, the theory does not require that managers be solely and unwaveringly motivated by the desire to maximize profits at all times. All that is required is that profits be a sufficiently important consideration that a theory based on the assumption of profit maximization will lead to explanations and predictions that are substantially correct. It is not always appropriate to criticize a theory because its assumptions seem unrealistic. A good theory abstracts in a useful way; a poor theory does not. If a theory has ignored some genuinely important factors, its predictions will usually be contradicted by the evidence.

> **All theory is an abstraction from reality. If it were not, it would merely duplicate the world in all its complexity and would add little to our understanding of it.**

Predictions   A theory's predictions are the propositions that can be deduced from it. They are often called *hypotheses*. For example, a prediction from a theory of the oil market is that a rise in the world price for oil will lead Canadian oil producers to produce and supply more oil. Another prediction in the same market is that a decision by the members of the OPEC cartel to reduce their annual output of oil will lead to an increase in the world price. The economic logic behind such predictions will be explained in several chapters of this book; for now we can proceed to see how economists *test* such predictions or hypotheses.

Testing Theories

A theory is tested by confronting its predictions with empirical evidence. For example, is an increase in the world price of oil *actually* followed by an increase in oil production by Canadian producers? A theory ceases to be useful when it cannot predict better than an alternative theory. When a theory consistently fails to predict better than an available alternative, it is either modified or replaced. Figure 2-1 illustrates the interaction between theory and empirical observation that occurs in economics.

> **The scientific approach is central to the study of economics: Empirical observation leads to the construction of theories, theories generate specific predictions, and the predictions are tested by more detailed empirical observation.**

Statistical Analysis   Most theories generate a prediction of the form "If *X* increases, then *Y* will also increase." A specific example is "If national income rises, the level

FIGURE 2-1   The Interaction Between Theory and Empirical Observation

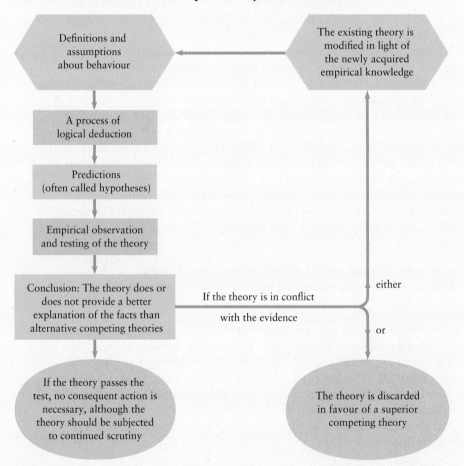

Theory and observation are in continuous interaction. Starting (at the top left) with the assumptions of a theory and the definitions of relevant terms, the theorist deduces by logical analysis everything that is implied by the assumptions. These implications are the predictions or the hypotheses of the theory. The theory is then tested by confronting its predictions with evidence. If the theory is in conflict with facts, it will usually be amended to make it consistent with those facts (thereby making it a better theory), or it will be discarded, to be replaced by a superior theory. The process then begins again: The new or amended theory is subjected first to logical analysis and then to empirical testing.

of employment will rise." Statistical analysis can be used to test such predictions. In practice, the same data can be used simultaneously to test whether a relationship exists between X and Y, and, if it does exist, to provide an estimate of the magnitude of that relationship.

Because economics is primarily a non-laboratory science, it lacks the controlled experiments central to such sciences as physics and chemistry. Economics must therefore use millions of uncontrolled "experiments" that are going on every day in the marketplace. Households are deciding what to purchase given changing prices and incomes, firms are deciding what to produce and how, and governments are involved in the economy through their various taxes, subsidies, and regulations. Because all these activities can be observed and recorded, a mass of data is continually being produced by the economy.

The variables that interest economists—such as the level of employment, the price of a laptop, and the output of automobiles—are generally influenced by many forces that vary simultaneously. If economists are to test their theories about relations among specific variables, they must use statistical techniques designed for situations in which other things *cannot* be held constant. Fortunately, such techniques exist, although their application is usually neither simple nor straightforward.

Later in this chapter we provide a discussion of some graphical techniques for describing data and displaying some of the more obvious relationships. Further examination of data involves techniques studied in elementary statistics courses. More advanced courses in econometrics deal with the array of techniques designed to test economic hypotheses and to measure economic relations in the complex circumstances in which economic evidence is often generated.

Correlation Versus Causation   Suppose you want to test your theory's prediction that "If X increases, Y will also increase." You are looking for a *causal* relationship from X to Y, because a change in X is predicted to *cause* a change in Y. When you look at the data, suppose you find that X and Y are positively correlated—that is, when X rises, Y also tends to rise. Is your theory supported? It might appear that way, but there is a potential problem.

A finding that X and Y are positively correlated means only that X and Y tend to move together. This correlation is *consistent* with the theory that X causes Y, but it is *not* direct evidence of this causal relationship. The causality may be in the opposite direction—from Y to X. Or X and Y may have no direct causal connection; they may instead be jointly caused by some third variable, Z.

Here is an example. Suppose your theory predicts that individuals who get more education will earn higher incomes as a result—the causality in this theory runs from education to income. In the data, suppose we find that education and income are positively correlated (as they are). This should not, however, be taken as direct evidence for the causal prediction. The data are certainly consistent with that theory, but they are also consistent with others. For example, individuals who grow up in higher-income households may "buy" more education, just as they buy more clothes or entertainment. In this case, income causes education, rather than the other way around. Another possibility is that education and income are positively correlated because the personal characteristics that lead people to become more educated— ability and motivation—are the same characteristics that lead to high incomes. In this case, the *causal* relationship runs from personal characteristics to both income and education.

Most economic predictions involve causality. Economists must take care when testing predictions to distinguish between correlation and causation. Correlation can establish that the data are consistent with the theory; establishing causation usually requires advanced statistical techniques.

2.3 ECONOMIC DATA

Economists use real-world observations to test their theories. For example, did the amount that people saved last year rise—as the theory predicts it should have—when a large tax cut increased their after-tax incomes? To test this prediction we need reliable data for people's incomes and their savings.

Political scientists, sociologists, anthropologists, and psychologists often collect for themselves the data they use to formulate and test their theories. Economists are unusual among social scientists in mainly using data collected by others, often government statistical agencies. In economics there is a division of labour between collecting data and using them to test theories. The advantage is that economists do not need to spend much of their scarce research time collecting the data they use. The disadvantage is that they are often not as well informed about the limitations of the data collected by others as they would be if they had collected the data themselves.

After data are collected, they can be displayed in various ways, many of which we will see later in this chapter. They can be laid out in tables. They can be displayed in various types of graphs. And when we are interested in relative movements rather than absolute ones, the data can be expressed in *index numbers*. We begin with a discussion of index numbers.

index number A measure of some variable, conventionally expressed relative to a base period, which is assigned the value 100.

TABLE 2-2 Volume of Steel and Newsprint Output

Year	Volume of Steel (thousands of tonnes)	Volume of Newsprint (thousands of rolls)
2007	200	3200
2008	210	3100
2009	225	3000
2010	215	3200
2011	250	3100
2012	220	3300
2013	265	3100
2014	225	3300
2015	255	3100
2016	230	3200
2017	245	3000

Comparing the time paths of two data series is difficult when absolute numbers are used. Since steel output and newsprint output have quite different absolute numbers, it is difficult to detect which time series is more volatile.

Index Numbers

Economists frequently look at data on prices or quantities and explore how specific variables change over time. For example, they may be interested in comparing the time paths of output in two industries: steel and newsprint. The problem is that it may be difficult to compare the time paths of the two different variables if we just look at the "raw" data.

Table 2-2 shows some hypothetical data for the volume of output in the steel and newsprint industries. Because the two variables are measured in different units, it is not immediately clear which of the two variables is more volatile or which, if either, has an upward or a downward trend.

It is easier to compare the two paths if we focus on *relative* rather than *absolute* changes. One way to do this is to construct some **index numbers**.

TABLE 2-3 **Constructing Index Numbers**

Year	Steel Procedure		Index	Newsprint Procedure		Index
2007	(200/200) × 100	=	100.0	(3200/3200) × 100	=	100.0
2008	(210/200) × 100	=	105.0	(3100/3200) × 100	=	96.9
2009	(225/200) × 100	=	112.5	(3000/3200) × 100	=	93.8
2010	(215/200) × 100	=	107.5	(3200/3200) × 100	=	100.0
2011	(250/200) × 100	=	125.0	(3100/3200) × 100	=	96.9
2012	(220/200) × 100	=	110.0	(3300/3200) × 100	=	103.1
2013	(265/200) × 100	=	132.5	(3100/3200) × 100	=	96.9
2014	(225/200) × 100	=	112.5	(3300/3200) × 100	=	103.1
2015	(255/200) × 100	=	127.5	(3100/3200) × 100	=	96.9
2016	(230/200) × 100	=	115.0	(3200/3200) × 100	=	100.0
2017	(245/200) × 100	=	122.5	(3000/3200) × 100	=	93.8

Index numbers are calculated by dividing the value in the given year by the value in the base year and multiplying the result by 100. The 2017 index number for steel tells us that steel output in 2017 was 22.5 percent greater than in the base year, 2007. The 2017 index number for newsprint tells us that newsprint output in 2017 was 93.8 percent of the output in the base year, 2007.

How to Build an Index Number We start by taking the value of the variable at some point in time as the "base" with which the values in other periods will be compared. We call this the *base period*. In the present example, we choose 2007 as the base year for both series. We then take the output in each subsequent year, called the "given year," divide it by the output in the base year, and then multiply the result by 100. This gives us an index number for the output of steel and a separate index number for the output of newsprint. For each index number, the value of output in the base year is equal to 100. The details of the calculations are shown in Table 2-3.

An index number simply expresses the value of some variable in any given year as a percentage of its value in the base year. For example, the 2017 index of steel output of 122.5 tells us that steel output in 2017 was 22.5 percent greater than in 2007. In contrast, the 2017 index for newsprint output of 93.8 tells us that newsprint output in 2017 was only 93.8 percent of the output in 2007—that is, output was 6.2 percent lower in 2017 than in 2007. The results in Table 2-3 allow us to compare the relative fluctuations in the two series. It is apparent from the values in the table that the output of steel has shown significantly more percentage variability than has the output of newsprint. This is also clear in Figure 2-2.

The formula of any index number is

$$\text{Value of index in any given period} = \frac{\text{Absolute value in given period}}{\text{Absolute value in base period}} \times 100$$

Care must be taken, however, when using index numbers. The index number always tells you the percentage change compared with the base year, but when comparing an

FIGURE 2-2   Index Values for Steel and Newsprint Output

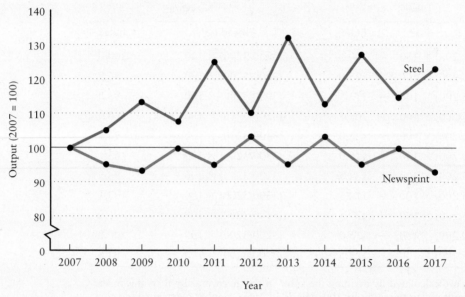

Comparing the time paths of two variables is much easier when index numbers are used. Since both index numbers are equal to 100 in the base year, relative volatility and trends become clear. Steel output is clearly more volatile in percentage terms than newsprint output. Steel output also has an upward trend, whereas newsprint output appears to have little or no trend.

index number across non-base years, the percentage change in the index number is *not* given by the absolute difference in the values of the index number. For example, if you want to know how much steel output changed from 2011 to 2013, we know from Table 2-3 that the index number for steel output increased from 125.0 to 132.5. But this is not an increase of 7.5 percent. The *percentage* increase in steel output is computed as $(132.5 - 125.0)/125.0 = 7.5/125.0 = 0.06$, or 6 percent.

More Complex Index Numbers   Perhaps the most famous index number used by economists is the index of average prices—the Consumer Price Index (CPI). This is a price index of the *average* price paid by consumers for the typical basket of goods that they buy. The inclusion of the word "average," however, makes the CPI a more complex index number than the ones we have constructed here.

With what you have just learned, you could construct separate index numbers for the price of beef, the price of coffee, and the price of orange juice. But to get the Consumer Price Index, we need to take the *average* of these separate price indexes (plus thousands of others for the goods and services we have ignored here). But it cannot be a simple average. Instead, it must be a *weighted* average, in which the weight assigned to each price index reflects the relative importance of that good in the typical consumer's basket of goods and services. For example, since the typical consumer spends a tiny fraction of income on sardines but a much larger fraction of income on housing, the weight on the "sardines" price index in the CPI is very small and the weight on the "housing" price index is very large. The result is that even huge swings in the price of sardines have negligible effects on the CPI, whereas much more modest changes in the price of housing have noticeable effects on the CPI.

We will spend much more time discussing the Consumer Price Index when we study macroeconomics beginning in Chapter 19. For now, keep in mind the usefulness of the simple index numbers we have constructed here. They allow us to compare the time paths of different variables.

Graphing Economic Data

A single economic variable, such as unemployment, national income, or the average price of a house, can come in two basic forms.

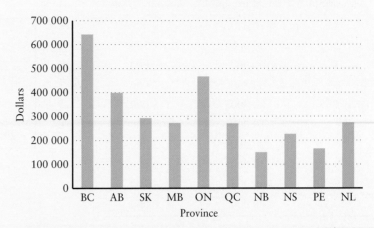

FIGURE 2-3 **A Cross-Sectional Graph of Average House Prices for 10 Canadian Provinces, 2015**

(*Source:* Adapted from MLS® Statistics ©2015 The Canadian Real Estate Association; www.crea.ca/content/national-average-price-map)

Cross-Sectional and Time-Series Data   The first is called **cross-sectional data,** which means a number of different observations on one variable all taken in different places at the same point in time. Figure 2-3 shows an example. The variable in the figure is the average selling price of a house in each of the 10 Canadian provinces in March 2015. The second type of data is called **time-series data.** It refers to observations of one variable at successive points in time. The data in Figure 2-4 show the unemployment rate for Canada from 1978 to 2015. Note in Figures 2-3 and 2-4 that in each case the figure is showing the behaviour of a *single* economic variable.

cross-sectional data A set of observations of a variable made at the same time across several different units (such as households, firms, or countries).

time-series data A set of observations of a variable made at successive periods of time.

FIGURE 2-4   **A Time-Series Graph of the Canadian Unemployment Rate, 1978–2015**

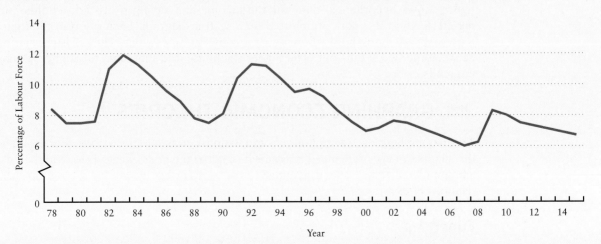

(*Source:* Annual average of monthly, seasonally adjusted data from Statistics Canada, CANSIM Table 282-0087; both sexes, 15 years and over)

FIGURE 2-5 A Scatter Diagram of Household Income and Saving in 2016

Household	Annual Income	Annual Saving
1	$ 70 000	$10 000
2	30 000	2 500
3	100 000	12 000
4	60 000	7 000
5	80 000	8 000
6	10 000	500
7	20 000	2 000
8	50 000	5 000
9	40 000	4 200
10	90 000	8 000

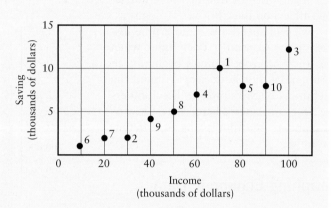

Saving tends to rise as income rises. The table shows the amount of income earned by ten (hypothetical) households together with the amount they saved during the same year. The scatter diagram plots the income and saving for the ten households listed in the table. The number on each dot refers to the household in the corresponding row of the table.

scatter diagram A graph showing two variables, one measured on the horizontal and the other on the vertical axis. Each point represents the values of the variables for a particular unit of observation.

Scatter Diagrams Another way data can be presented is in a **scatter diagram**. It is designed to show the relation between two different variables. To plot a scatter diagram, values of one variable are measured on the horizontal axis and values of the second variable are measured on the vertical axis. Any point on the diagram relates a specific value of one variable to a corresponding specific value of the other.

The data plotted on a scatter diagram may be either cross-sectional data or time-series data. An example of the former is shown in Figure 2-5. The table in the figure shows hypothetical data for the income and saving of 10 households during 2016, and these data are plotted on a scatter diagram. Each point in the figure represents one household, showing its income and its saving. The positive relation between the two stands out. The higher the household's income, the higher its saving tends to be.

2.4 GRAPHING ECONOMIC THEORIES

Theories are built on assumptions about relationships between variables. For example, the quantity of eggs demanded is assumed to fall as the price of eggs rises, and the total amount an individual saves is assumed to rise as his or her income rises. How can such relations be expressed?

Functions

When one variable, X, is related to another variable, Y, in such a way that to every value of X there is only one possible value of Y, we say that Y is a *function* of X. When we write this relation down, we are expressing a *functional relation* between the two variables.

Here is a specific but hypothetical example. Consider the relation between an individual's annual income, which we denote by the symbol Y, and the amount that person spends on goods and services during the year, which we denote by the symbol C (for consumption). Any particular example of the relation between C and Y can be expressed several ways: in words, in a table, in a mathematical equation, or in a graph.

Words.   When income is zero, the person will spend $800 a year (either by borrowing the money or by spending past savings), and for every extra $1 of income the person will increase spending by 80 cents.

Table.   This table shows selected values of the person's income and consumption.

Annual Income	Consumption	Reference Letter
$ 0	$ 800	p
2 500	2 800	q
5 000	4 800	r
7 500	6 800	s
10 000	8 800	t

Mathematical Equation. $C = \$800 + 0.8Y$ is the equation of the relation just described in words and displayed in the table. As a check, you can first see that when Y is zero, C is $800. Further, you can see that every time Y increases by $1, the level of C increases by 0.8($1), which is 80 cents.

Graph.   Figure 2-6 shows the points from the preceding table and the line representing the equation given in the previous paragraph. Comparison of the values on the graph with the values in the table, and with the values derived from the equation just stated, shows that these are alternative expressions of the same relation between C and Y.

Graphing Functions

Different functions have different graphs, and we will see many of these in subsequent chapters. Figure 2-6 is an example of a relation in which the two variables move together. When income goes up, consumption goes up. In such a relation the two variables are *positively related* to each other.

Figure 2-7 is an example of variables that move in opposite directions. As the amount spent on pollution reduction goes up, the amount of remaining pollution goes down. In such a relation the two variables are *negatively related* to each other.

Both of these graphs are straight lines. In such cases the variables are *linearly related* to each other (either positively or negatively).

FIGURE 2-6   Income and Consumption

FIGURE 2-7 Linear Pollution Reduction

Pollution as a linear function of clean-up expenditure. Between points *A* and *B* it costs $2000 to reduce pollution by 1000 tonnes. The cost of pollution reduction is the same elsewhere on the line. The slope of the line, –0.5, indicates that any $1 expenditure on pollution clean-up reduces the amount of pollution by 0.5 tonnes.

The Slope of a Straight Line Slopes are important in economics. They show you how much one variable changes as the other changes. The slope is defined as the amount of change in the variable measured on the vertical axis per unit change in the variable measured on the horizontal axis. In the case of Figure 2-7 it tells us how many tonnes of pollution, symbolized by *P*, are removed per dollar spent on reducing pollution, symbolized by *E*. Consider moving from point *A* to point *B* in the figure. If we spend $2000 more on clean-up, we reduce pollution by 1000 tonnes. This is 0.5 tonnes per dollar spent. On the graph the extra $2000 is indicated by ΔE, the arrow indicating that *E* rises by 2000. The 1000 tonnes of pollution reduction is indicated by ΔP, the arrow showing that pollution falls by 1000. (The Greek uppercase letter delta, Δ, stands for "the change in.") To get the amount of pollution reduction per dollar of expenditure, we merely divide one by the other. In symbols this is $\Delta P / \Delta E$.

If we let *X* stand for whatever variable is measured on the horizontal axis and *Y* for whatever variable is measured on the vertical axis, the slope of a straight line is $\Delta Y / \Delta X$. [1][1]

The equation of the line in Figure 2-7 can be computed in two steps. First, note that when *E* = 0, the amount of remaining pollution, *P*, is equal to 6 (thousand tonnes). Thus, the line meets the vertical axis (*E* = 0) when *P* = 6. Second, we have already seen that the slope of the line, $\Delta P / \Delta E$, is equal to −0.5, which means that for every one-unit increase in *E*, *P* falls by 0.5 unit. We can thus state the equation of the line as

$$P = 6 - (0.5)E$$

where both *P* and *E* are expressed as thousands of units (tonnes and dollars, respectively).

Non-linear Functions Although it is sometimes convenient to simplify the situation by assuming two variables to be linearly related, this is seldom the case over their whole range. Non-linear relations are much more common than linear ones. In the case of reducing pollution, it is usually quite cheap to eliminate the first units of pollution. Then, as the environment gets cleaner and cleaner, the cost of further clean-up tends to increase because more and more sophisticated and expensive methods need to be used. As a result, Figure 2-8 is more realistic than Figure 2-7. Inspection of Figure 2-8 shows that as more and more is spent, the amount of pollution reduction for an additional $1 of clean-up expenditure gets smaller and smaller. This is shown by the diminishing slope of the curve as we move rightward along it. For example, as we move from point

---

[1] Red numbers in square brackets indicate mathematical notes that are found in a separate section at the back of the book.

FIGURE 2-8 Non-linear Pollution Reduction

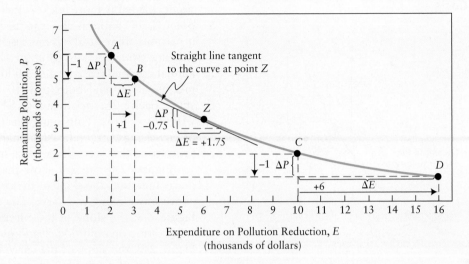

Pollution as a non-linear function of clean-up expenditure. The slope of the curve changes as we move along it. Between points *A* and *B*, it costs $1000 to reduce pollution by 1000 tonnes. Between points *C* and *D*, it costs $6000 to reduce pollution by 1000 tonnes. At point *Z*, the slope of the curve is equal to the slope of the straight line tangent to the curve at point *Z*. The slope of the tangent line is $-0.75/1.75 = -0.43$.

A to point *B*, an increase in expenditure of $1000 is required to reduce pollution by 1000 tonnes. Thus, each tonne of pollution reduction costs $1. But as we move from point *C* (where we have already reduced pollution considerably) to point *D*, an extra $6000 must be spent in order to reduce pollution by 1000 tonnes. At that point, each tonne of pollution reduction therefore costs $6.

Economists call the change in pollution when a bit more or a bit less is spent on clean-up the *marginal* change. The figure shows that the slope of the curve at each point measures this marginal change. It also shows that in the type of curve illustrated, the marginal change per dollar spent is diminishing as we spend more on pollution reduction. There is always a payoff to more expenditure over the range shown in the figure, but the payoff diminishes as more is spent. This relation can be described as *diminishing marginal response*. We will see such relations many times in what follows, so we emphasize now that diminishing marginal response does not mean that the *total* response is diminishing. In Figure 2-8, the total amount of pollution continues to fall as more and more is spent on clean-up. But diminishing marginal response does mean that the amount of pollution reduced per dollar of expenditure gets less and less as the total expenditure rises.

Figure 2-9 shows a graph in which the marginal response is increasing. The graph shows the relationship between annual production costs and annual output for a firm that makes hockey sticks. Notice that the more sticks produced annually, the higher the firm's total costs. This is shown by the positive slope of the line. Notice also that as more and more hockey sticks are produced, the extra amount that the firm must pay to produce each extra stick rises. For example, as the firm moves from point *A* to point *B*, annual costs rise by $30 000 in order to increase its annual output by 10 000 hockey

FIGURE 2-9 **Increasing Marginal Production Costs**

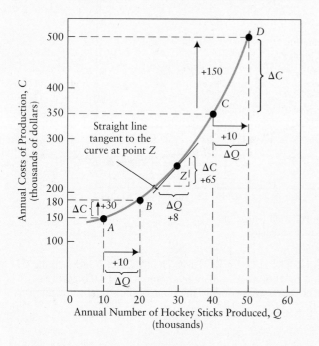

Marginal costs increase as annual output rises. From point A to point B, an extra annual output of 10 000 hockey sticks increases annual costs by $30 000. Each extra stick costs $3. From point C to point D, an extra output of 10 000 hockey sticks increases annual costs by $150 000. Each extra hockey stick then costs $15. This is a case of increasing marginal cost. At point Z, the slope of the curve is equal to the slope of the straight line tangent to the curve at point Z. The slope of the tangent line is 65/8 = 8.13.

sticks. Each extra stick costs $3 ($30 000/ 10 000 = $3). But when the firm is already producing many more hockey sticks, such as at point C, its factory is closer to its capacity and it becomes more costly to increase production. Moving from point C to point D, the firm's annual costs increase by $150 000 in order to increase its annual output by 10 000 hockey sticks. Each extra stick then costs $15 ($150 000 /10 000 = $15). This figure illustrates a case of *increasing marginal cost*, a characteristic of production that we will see often in this book.

Figures 2-8 and 2-9 show that with non-linear functions the slope of the curve changes as we move along the curve. For example, in Figure 2-8, the slope of the curve falls as the expenditure on pollution clean-up increases. In Figure 2-9, the slope of the curve increases as the volume of production increases.

How, exactly, do we measure the slope of a curved line? The answer is that we use the slope of a straight line *tangent to that curve* at the point that interests us. For example, in Figure 2-8, if we want to know the slope of the curve at point Z, we draw a straight line that touches the curve *only* at point Z; this is a tangent line. The slope of this line is −0.75/1.75 = −0.43. Similarly, in Figure 2-9, the slope of the curve at point Z is given by the slope of the straight line tangent to the curve at point Z. The slope of this line is 65/8 = 8.13.

For non-linear functions, the slope of the curve changes as X changes. Therefore, the marginal response of Y to a change in X depends on the value of X.

Functions with a Minimum or a Maximum   So far, all the graphs we have shown have had either a positive or a negative slope over their entire range. But many relations change directions as the independent variable increases. For example, consider a firm that is attempting to maximize its profits and is trying to determine how much output to produce. The firm may find that its unit production costs are lower than the market price of the good, and so it can increase its profit by producing more. But as it increases its level of production, the firm's unit costs may be driven up because the capacity of the factory is being approached. Eventually, the firm may find that extra output will actually cost so much that its profits are *reduced*. This is a relationship that we will study in detail in later chapters, and it is illustrated in Figure 2-10. Notice that when profits are maximized at point A, the slope of the curve is zero (because a tangent to the curve at point A is horizontal), and so the *marginal response* of profits to output is zero.

Now consider an example of a function with a minimum. You probably know that when you drive a car, the fuel consumption per kilometre depends on your speed. Driving very slowly uses a lot of fuel per kilometre travelled. Driving very fast also uses a lot of fuel per kilometre travelled. The best fuel efficiency—the lowest fuel consumption per kilometre travelled—occurs at a speed of approximately 95 kilometres per hour. The relationship between speed and fuel consumption is shown in Figure 2-11 and illustrates a function with a minimum. Note that at point *A* the slope of the curve is zero (because a tangent to the curve at point *A* is horizontal), and so the *marginal response* of fuel consumption to speed is zero.

At either a minimum or a maximum of a function, the slope of the curve is zero. Therefore, at the minimum or maximum the marginal response of *Y* to a change in *X* is zero.

FIGURE 2-10   Profits as a Function of Output

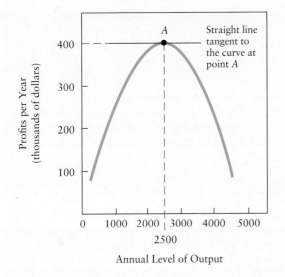

Profits rise and then eventually fall as output rises. When the firm is producing fewer than 2500 units annually, the marginal response of profit to output is positive—that is, an increase in output leads to an increase in profit. Beyond 2500 units annually, the marginal response is negative—an increase in output leads to a reduction in profit. At point *A*, profits are maximized and the marginal response of profit to output is zero. Because the tangent at point *A* is horizontal, the slope of the curve is zero at that point.

FIGURE 2-11   Average Fuel Consumption as a Function of Speed

Average fuel consumption falls and then rises as speed increases. Average fuel consumption in litres per kilometre travelled is minimized at point *A* at a speed of approximately 95 kilometres per hour (km/h). At speeds less than 95 km/h, the marginal response is negative—that is, an increase in speed reduces fuel consumption per kilometre. At speeds above 95 km/h, the marginal response is positive—an increase in speed increases fuel consumption per kilometre. At 95 km/h, the marginal response is zero and fuel consumption per kilometre is minimized.

A Final Word

We have done much in this chapter. We have discussed why economists develop theories (or models) to help them understand economic events in the real world. We have also discussed how they test their theories and how there is a continual back-and-forth process between empirical testing of predictions and refining the theory. Finally, we have devoted considerable time and space to exploring the many ways that data can be displayed in graphs and how economists use graphs to illustrate their theories.

Many students find themselves intimidated when they are first confronted with all the details about graphing. But try not to worry. You may not yet be a master of all the graphing techniques that we have discussed in this chapter, but you will be surprised at how quickly it all falls into place. And, as is true for most skills, there is no substitute for practice. In the next three chapters we will encounter many graphs. But we will start simply and then slowly attempt more complicated cases. We are confident that in the process of learning some basic economic theories you will get enough practice in graphing that you will very soon look back at this chapter and realize how straightforward it all is.

SUMMARY

2.1 POSITIVE AND NORMATIVE STATEMENTS   LO 1

- A key to the success of scientific inquiry lies in separating positive statements about the way the world works from normative statements about how one would like the world to work.

- Normative statements involve value judgements and cannot be disproven. Positive statements, at least in principle, can be disproven with an appeal to evidence.

2.2 BUILDING AND TESTING ECONOMIC THEORIES   LO 2, 3

- Theories (sometimes called models) are designed to explain and predict what we see. A theory consists of a set of definitions of the variables to be discussed, a set of assumptions about how things behave, and the conditions under which the theory is meant to apply.
- A theory provides predictions of the type "If one event occurs, then another event will also occur."
- Theories are tested by checking their predictions against evidence. In economics, testing is almost always done using the data produced by the world of ordinary events.

- Economists make use of statistical analysis when testing their theories. They must take care to make the distinction between correlation and causation.
- The progress of any science lies in finding better explanations of events than are now available. Thus, in any developing science, one must expect to discard some existing theories and replace them with demonstrably superior alternatives.

2.3 ECONOMIC DATA   LO 4

- Index numbers express economic series in relative form. Values in each period are expressed in relation to the value in the base period, which is given a value of 100.
- Economic data can be graphed in three different ways. Cross-sectional graphs show observations taken at the same time. Time-series graphs show observations on one variable taken over time. Scatter diagrams show many points, each of which refers to specific observations on two different variables.

2.4 GRAPHING ECONOMIC THEORIES   LO 5

- A functional relation can be expressed in words, in a table giving specific values, in a mathematical equation, or in a graph.
- A graph of two variables has a positive slope when they both increase or decrease together and a negative slope when they move in opposite directions.
- The marginal response of a variable gives the amount it changes in response to a change in a second variable.

When the variable is measured on the vertical axis of a diagram, its marginal response at a specific point on the curve is measured by the slope of the line at that point.
- Some functions have a maximum or minimum point. At such points, the marginal response is zero.

KEY CONCEPTS

Positive and normative statements
Endogenous and exogenous variables
Theories and models
Variables, assumptions, and predictions

Correlation versus causation
Functional relations
Positive and negative relations
  between variables

Positively and negatively sloped curves
Marginal responses
Maximum and minimum values

STUDY EXERCISES

MyEconLab   Make the grade with MyEconLab: Study Exercises marked in ⊕ can be found on MyEconLab. You can practise them as often as you want, and most feature step-by-step guided instructions to help you find the right answer.

❶ Determine whether each of the following statements is positive or normative.

   a. The government should impose stricter regulations on the banking sector to avoid future financial crises.

   b. Financial aid to developing countries has no impact on per capita GDP in those countries.

   c. Tuition fee increases at Canadian universities lead to reduced access for low-income students.

   d. It is unfair that Canadians have universal access to health care but not to dental care.

   e. Canadians currently have too much personal debt.

❷ In the following examples, identify the exogenous (or independent) variable and the endogenous (or dependent) variable.

   a. The amount of rainfall on the Canadian prairies determines the amount of wheat produced in Canada.

   b. When the world price of coffee increases, there is a change in the price of a cup of coffee at Tim Hortons.

   c. If student loans were no longer available, there would be fewer students attending university.

   d. An increase in the tax on gasoline leads people to drive more fuel-efficient vehicles.

❸ Fill in the blanks to make the following statements correct.

   a. Economists have designed _____ to better explain and predict the behaviour we observe in the world around us.

   b. A variable, such as price or quantity, that is determined within a theory is known as a(n) _____ variable. A variable that is determined outside the theory is known as a(n) _____ variable.

   c. When, based on a theory, we claim that "If A occurs, then B will follow," we are making a _____ that can then be tested by _____ observation.

   d. If we observe that when variable A decreases, variable B also decreases, we can say that the two variables are _____. We cannot necessarily say that there is a _____ relationship between A and B.

   e. An important assumption that is made in economics is that individuals and firms pursue their own _____. We assume that individuals seek to maximize their _____ and firms seek to maximize their _____.

4 An examination of data reveals a positive correlation between the demand for new homes and the price of lumber. Which of the following conclusions can be correctly inferred from the existence of this correlation? Why?

a. An increase in the demand for homes causes an increase in the price of lumber.
b. The observed correlation is consistent with a theory that an increase in demand for new homes causes an increase in the price of lumber.

5 Use the appropriate graph—time-series, cross-sectional, or scatter diagram—to illustrate the economic data provided in each part below.

a. The Canadian-dollar price of one U.S. dollar (the "exchange rate") in 2011:

January	0.994
February	0.988
March	0.977
April	0.958
May	0.968
June	0.977
July	0.956
August	0.982
September	1.003
October	1.019
November	1.026
December	1.024

b. A comparison of average household expenditures across provinces in 2010:

British Columbia	$72 486
Alberta	84 087
Saskatchewan	69 237
Manitoba	66 330
Ontario	74 521
Quebec	61 536
New Brunswick	59 943
Nova Scotia	61 907
Prince Edward Island	58 194
Newfoundland and Labrador	60 139

c. Per capita growth rates of real GDP and investment rates for various countries, averaged over the period 1950–2009:

Country	Average Growth Rate (% per year)	Average Investment Rate (% of GDP)
Canada	2.0	18.2
Austria	3.1	22.0
Japan	4.0	26.6
United States	1.9	18.1
United Kingdom	2.0	14.5
Spain	3.4	23.0
Norway	2.8	27.4
South Korea	5.1	27.2
Iceland	2.7	28.0

6 Suppose you want to create a price index for the price of a particular physics textbook over ten years in your university bookstore. The price of the book on September 1 of each year is as follows:

Year	Price ($)	Year	Price ($)
2000	85	2006	120
2001	87	2007	125
2002	94	2008	127
2003	104	2009	127
2004	110	2010	130
2005	112		

a. The base year is 2000. Construct a physics textbook price index.
b. What is the percentage increase in the price of the book between the base year and 2005?
c. What is the percentage increase in the price of the book from 2007 to 2010?
d. Are the data listed above time-series or cross-sectional data? Explain why.

7 Suppose you want to create a price index for the price of a personal pizza across several Canadian university campuses, as of March 1, 2016. The data are as follows:

University	Price per Pizza
Dalhousie	$6.50
Laval	5.95
McGill	6.00
Queen's	8.00
Waterloo	7.50
Manitoba	5.50
Saskatchewan	5.75
Calgary	6.25
UBC	7.25
Victoria	7.00

a. Using Calgary as the "base university," construct the Canadian university pizza price index.

b. At which university is pizza the most expensive, and by what percentage is the price higher than in Calgary?

c. At which university is pizza the least expensive, and by what percentage is the price lower than in Calgary?

d. Are the data listed above time-series or cross-sectional data? Explain why.

8 According to Statistics Canada, Canada's exports and imports of energy (combined totals of fossil fuels, hydro, and nuclear, all measured in petajoules) over a five-year period were as follows:

	Exports	Imports
2005	8662	3139
2006	8899	2977
2007	9331	3124
2008	9302	3010
2009	7902	2945

a. Using 2005 as the base year, construct index numbers for each of exports and imports.

b. Were exports or imports more volatile over this time period? Explain how you know.

c. Using your constructed index numbers, what was the percentage change in exports and imports from 2007 to 2009?

d. Can you provide a possible explanation for why Canada's exports of energy fell so dramatically from 2007 to 2009?

9 Use the following figure to answer the questions below.

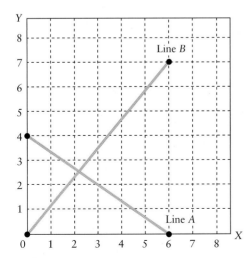

a. Is the slope of Line *A* positive or negative? Line *B*?

b. Calculate the slope of Line *A*. Write the equation describing the line in the form $Y = mX + b$, where *m* is the slope of the line and *b* is a constant term.

c. Calculate the slope of Line *B*. Write the equation describing the line in the form $Y = mX + b$, where *m* is the slope of the line and *b* is a constant term.

10 Suppose the relationship between the government's tax revenue (*T*) and national income (*Y*) is represented by the following equation: $T = 10 + 0.25Y$. Plot this relationship on a scale diagram, with *Y* on the horizontal axis and *T* on the vertical axis. Interpret the equation.

11 Consider the following three specific functions for a functional relation between *X* and *Y*:

i) $Y = 50 + 2X$
ii) $Y = 50 + 2X + 0.05X^2$
iii) $Y = 50 + 2X - 0.05X^2$

a. For the values of *X* of 0, 10, 20, 30, 40, and 50, plot *X* and *Y* on a scale diagram for each specific function. Connect these points with a smooth line.

b. For each function, state whether the slope of the line is constant, increasing, or decreasing as the value of *X* increases.

c. Describe for each function how the marginal change in *Y* depends on the value of *X*.

12 For each of the functional relations listed below, plot the relations on a scale diagram (with *X* on the horizontal axis and *Y* on the vertical axis) and compute the slope of the line.

a. $Y = 10 + 3X$
b. $Y = 20 + 4X$
c. $Y = 30 + 5X$
d. $Y = 10 + 5X$

13 Suppose we divide Canada into three regions: the West, the Centre, and the East. Each region has an unemployment rate, defined as the number of people unemployed, expressed as a fraction of that region's labour force. The table that follows shows each region's unemployment rate and the size of its labour force.

Region	Unemployment Rate	Labour Force
West	5.5%	5.3 million
Centre	7.2%	8.4 million
East	12.5%	3.5 million

a. Compute an unemployment rate for Canada using a simple average of the rates in the three regions. Is this the "right" unemployment rate for Canada as a whole? Explain why or why not.

b. Now compute an unemployment rate for Canada using weights that reflect the size of that region's labour force as a proportion of the overall Canadian labour force. Explain the difference in this unemployment rate from the one in part (a). Is this a "better" measure of Canadian unemployment? Explain why.

14 Draw three graphs in which the dependent variable increases at an increasing rate, at a constant rate, and at a diminishing rate. Then draw three graphs in which it decreases at an increasing, constant, and diminishing rate. State a real relation that each of these graphs might describe, other than the ones given in the text of this chapter.

15 The following questions will provide practice working with simple linear functions. All questions refer to a coordinate graph with the variable X on the horizontal axis and the variable Y on the vertical axis.

a. If two points on a straight line are $(X = 3, Y = 2)$ and $(X = 12, Y = 5)$, what is the slope of the line?
b. If point A is at $(X = 20, Y = 20)$ and point B is at $(X = 10, Y = 40)$, what is the slope of the straight line joining points A and B?
c. What is the slope of the function described by $Y = 12\,000 - 0.5X$?
d. What is the slope of a line described by $Y = 6.5X$?
e. What is the slope of a line described by $Y = 27 + 3.2X$?
f. What is the Y-intercept of the function $Y = 1000 + mX$?
g. What is the Y-intercept of the function $Y = -100 + 10X$?
h. What is the X-intercept of the function $Y = 10 - 0.1X$?
i. Suppose ABC Corp. spends $100 000 per year on some basic level of advertising, regardless of its revenues. In addition, the company spends 15 percent of each dollar of revenue on extra advertising. Write a mathematical equation that describes the functional relation between advertising (A) and revenue (R).

16 The figure below shows a monthly cost curve for the production of Good X.

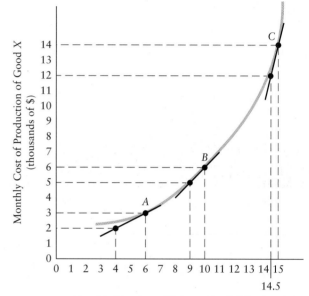

a. Calculate the slope of this non-linear function at points A, B, and C.
b. Is the marginal response of the cost of production of Good X to the change in the quantity produced of Good X increasing or decreasing?
c. Is the slope of this function increasing or decreasing as the volume of production increases?

3 Demand, Supply, and Price

CHAPTER OUTLINE	LEARNING OBJECTIVES (LO)
	After studying this chapter, you will be able to
3.1 **DEMAND**	1 list the factors that determine the quantity demanded of a good.
	2 distinguish between a shift of the demand curve and a movement along the demand curve.
3.2 **SUPPLY**	3 list the factors that determine the quantity supplied of a good.
	4 distinguish between a shift of the supply curve and a movement along the supply curve.
3.3 **THE DETERMINATION OF PRICE**	5 explain the forces that drive market price to equilibrium, and how equilibrium price is affected by changes in demand and supply.

WE are now ready to study the important question of how markets work. The answer leads us to develop a simple model of supply and demand. And though there is much more to economics than just demand and supply (as many following chapters will illustrate), this is an essential starting point for understanding how a market economy functions.

As a first step, we need to understand what determines the demand for and the supply of particular products. Then we can see how demand and supply together determine the prices of products and the quantities that are bought and sold. Finally, we examine how the price system allows the economy to respond to changes in demand and supply. The concepts of demand and supply help us to understand the price system's successes and failures, and the consequences of many government policies.

This chapter deals with the basic elements of demand, supply, and price. In the next two chapters we use the theory of demand and supply to discuss such issues as the effects of gasoline taxes, legislated minimum wages, rent controls, and the burden of payroll taxes.

3.1 DEMAND

What determines the demand for any given product? How have Canadian consumers responded to the recent declines in the prices of smartphones and tablet computers? How will they respond to the next sudden change in the price of gasoline or coffee? We start by developing a theory designed to explain the demand for some typical product.

Quantity Demanded

quantity demanded The amount of a good or service that consumers want to purchase during some time period.

The total amount of any particular good or service that consumers want to purchase during some time period is called the **quantity demanded** of that product. It is important to notice two things about this concept.

First, quantity demanded is a *desired* quantity. It is the amount that consumers want to purchase when faced with a particular price of the product, other products' prices, their incomes, their tastes, and everything else that might matter. It may be different from the amount that consumers actually succeed in purchasing. If sufficient quantities are not available, the amount that consumers want to purchase may exceed the amount that they actually purchase. (For example, think of standing in line to purchase tickets to a show, only to find out that the show is sold out before you get to the head of the line.) To distinguish these two concepts, the term *quantity demanded* is used to refer to desired purchases, and such phrases as *quantity bought* or *quantity exchanged* are used to refer to actual purchases.

Second, quantity demanded refers to a *flow* of purchases, expressed as so much per period of time: 1 million units per day, 7 million per week, or 365 million per year. For example, being told that the quantity of new cars demanded (at current prices) in Canada is 50 000 means nothing unless you are also told the period of time involved. For a country as large as Canada, 50 000 cars demanded per day would be an enormous rate of demand, whereas 50 000 per year would be a very small rate of demand. The important distinction between *stocks* and *flows* is discussed in *Extensions in Theory 3-1*.

The total amount of some product that consumers in the relevant market want to buy during a given time period is influenced by the following important variables: [2]

- Product's own price
- Consumers' income
- Prices of other products
- Tastes
- Population
- Significant changes in weather

We will discuss the separate effects of each of these variables later in the chapter. For now, we focus on the effects of changes in the product's own price. But how do we analyze the distinct effect of changes in this one variable when all variables are likely to be changing at once? Since this is difficult to do, we consider the influence of the variables one at a time. To do this, we hold all variables constant except the product's own price. Then we let the product's price vary and study how its change affects quantity demanded. We can do the same for each of the other variables in turn, and in this way we can come to understand the importance of each variable.

Holding all other variables constant is often described by the expressions "other things being equal," "other things given," or the equivalent Latin phrase, *ceteris*

EXTENSIONS IN THEORY 3-1

The Distinction Between Stocks and Flows

An important conceptual issue that arises frequently in economics is the distinction between *stock* and *flow* variables. Economic theories use both, and it takes a little practice to keep them straight.

As noted in the text, a flow variable has a time dimension—it is so much *per unit of time*. For example, the quantity of Grade A large eggs purchased in Edmonton is a flow variable. No useful information is conveyed if we are told that the number purchased was 2000 dozen eggs unless we are also told the period of time over which these purchases occurred. Two thousand dozen eggs per hour would indicate a much more active market in eggs than would 2000 dozen eggs per month.

In contrast, a stock variable is a variable whose value has meaning *at a point in time*. Thus, the number of eggs in the egg producer's warehouse on a particular day—for example, 10 000 dozen eggs on September 3, 2016—is a stock variable. All those eggs are there at one time, and they remain there until something happens to change the stock held in the warehouse.

The terminology of stocks and flows can be understood using an analogy to a bathtub. At any moment, the tub holds so much water. This is the *stock*, and it can be measured in terms of the volume of water, say, 100 litres. There might also be water flowing into the tub from the tap; this *flow* is measured as so much water per unit time, say, 10 litres per minute.

The distinction between stocks and flows is important. Failure to keep them straight is a common source of error. Note, for example, that a stock variable and a flow variable cannot be added together without specifying some time period for which the flow persists. We cannot add the stock of 100 litres of water in the tub to the flow of 10 litres per minute to get 110 litres. The new stock of water will depend on how long the flow persists; if it lasts for 20 minutes, the new stock will be 300 litres; if the flow persists for 60 minutes, the new stock will be 700 litres (or the tub will overflow!).

The amount of income earned is a flow; it is so much per year or per month or per hour. The amount of a consumer's expenditure is also a flow—so much spent per week or per month or per year. The amount of money in a bank account (earned, perhaps, in the past but unspent) is a stock—just so many thousands of dollars. The key test is always whether a time dimension is required to give the variable meaning.

---

paribus. When economists speak of the influence of the price of gasoline on the quantity of gasoline demanded, *ceteris paribus*, they refer to what a change in the price of gasoline would do to the quantity of gasoline demanded *if all other variables that influence the demand for gasoline did not change.*

Quantity Demanded and Price[1]

We are interested in studying the relationship between the quantity demanded of a product and that product's price. We therefore hold all other influences constant and ask, "How will the quantity demanded of a product change as its price changes?"

A basic economic hypothesis is that the price of a product and the quantity demanded are related *negatively*, other things being equal. That is, the lower the price, the higher the quantity demanded; the higher the price, the lower the quantity demanded.

---

[1] In this chapter we explore a product's demand curve for the market as a whole—what we often call the *market demand curve*. In Chapter 6 we discuss how this market demand curve is derived by adding up, or *aggregating*, the demands of different individuals.

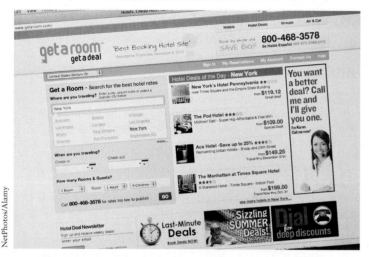

Changes in prices lead most consumers to alter their choices. For example, as prices for hotel rooms fall, vacationers may be more likely to take weekend trips.

The great British economist Alfred Marshall (1842–1924) called this fundamental relation the "law of demand." In Chapter 6, we will derive the law of demand as a prediction that follows from more basic assumptions about the behaviour of individual consumers. For now, let's simply explore why this relationship seems reasonable. Products are used to satisfy desires and needs, and there is almost always more than one product that will satisfy any desire or need. Hunger may be alleviated by eating meat or vegetables; a desire for green vegetables can be satisfied by broccoli or spinach. The desire for a vacation may be satisfied by a trip to the ocean or to the mountains; the need to get there may be satisfied by different airlines, a bus, a car, or a train. For any general desire or need, there are almost always many different products that will satisfy it.

Now consider what happens if income, tastes, population, and the prices of all other products remain constant and the price of only one product changes. As the price goes up, that product becomes an increasingly expensive means of satisfying a desire. Many consumers will decide to switch wholly or partly to other products. Some consumers will stop buying it altogether, others will buy smaller amounts, and still others may continue to buy the same quantity. But the overall effect is that less will be demanded of the product whose price has risen. For example, as meat becomes more expensive, some consumers will switch to meat substitutes; others may forgo meat at some meals and eat less meat at others. Taken together as a group, consumers will want to buy less meat when its price rises.

Conversely, as the price goes down, the product becomes a cheaper way of satisfying a desire. Households will demand more of it as they substitute away from other products whose prices have not fallen. For example, if the price of tomatoes falls, many shoppers will buy more tomatoes and less of other vegetables.

Demand Schedules and Demand Curves

demand schedule A table showing the relationship between quantity demanded and the price of a commodity, other things being equal.

A **demand schedule** is one way of showing the relationship between quantity demanded and the price of a product, other things being equal. It is a table showing the quantity demanded at various prices.

The table in Figure 3-1 shows a hypothetical demand schedule for apples.[2] It lists the quantity of apples that would be demanded at various prices, given the assumption that all other variables are held constant. The table gives the quantities demanded for five selected prices, but in fact a separate quantity would be demanded at every possible price.

---

[2] We realize that apples are not a very exciting product to discuss, and many students wonder why we do not instead use cell phones, restaurant meals, or cars as our hypothetical example. The model of demand and supply, however, best applies to products that are demanded by many consumers and supplied by many producers, each of which offers for sale a virtually identical ("homogeneous") version of the product. For this reason, we have chosen a simple agricultural product, but we could have illustrated the same principles with beef, wheat, copper, newsprint, oil, and a whole host of what economists call "commodities."

FIGURE 3-1   The Demand for Apples

A Demand Schedule for Apples

Reference Point	Price ($ per bushel)	Quantity Demanded (thousands of bushels per year)
U	20	110
V	40	85
W	60	65
X	80	50
Y	100	40

A Demand Curve for Apples

Both the table and the graph show the total quantity of apples that would be demanded at various prices, *ceteris-paribus*. For example, row W indicates that if the price of apples were $60 per bushel, consumers would desire to purchase 65 000 bushels of apples per year, holding constant the values of the other variables that affect quantity demanded. The demand curve, labelled D, relates quantity of apples demanded to the price of apples; its negative slope indicates that quantity demanded increases as price falls.

A second method of showing the relationship between quantity demanded and price is to draw a graph. The five price–quantity combinations shown in the table are plotted in Figure 3-1. Price is plotted on the vertical axis, and the quantity demanded is plotted on the horizontal axis.

The curve drawn through these points is called a **demand curve**. It shows the quantity that consumers would like to buy at each price. The negative slope of the curve indicates that the quantity demanded increases as the price falls. Each point on the demand curve indicates a single price–quantity combination. The demand curve as a whole shows something more.

demand curve The graphical representation of the relationship between quantity demanded and the price of a commodity, other things being equal.

The demand curve represents the relationship between quantity demanded and price, other things being equal; its negative slope indicates that quantity demanded increases when price decreases.

When economists speak of *demand* in a particular market, they are referring not just to the particular quantity being demanded at the moment (i.e., not just to one point on the demand curve) but to the entire demand curve—to the relationship between desired purchases and all the possible prices of the product.

The term **demand** therefore refers to the entire relationship between the quantity demanded of a product and the price of that product. In contrast, a single point on a demand schedule or curve is the quantity demanded at that point. This distinction between "demand" and "quantity demanded" is an extremely important one and we will examine it more closely later in this chapter.

demand The entire relationship between the quantity of a commodity that buyers want to purchase and the price of that commodity, other things being equal.

FIGURE 3-2   An Increase in the Demand for Apples

| | Demand Schedules | | Demand Curves |
| | | | |

Price ($ per bushel)	Quantity Demanded (thousands of bushels per year when average annual income is $50 000)	Quantity Demanded (thousands of bushels per year when average annual income is $60 000)
p	D_0	D_1
20	110 U	140 U'
40	85 V	115 V'
60	65 W	95 W'
80	50 X	80 X'
100	40 Y	70 Y'

An increase in annual household income increases the quantity demanded at each price (for all normal goods). This is shown by the rightward shift in the demand curve, from D_0 to D_1. When average income rises from $50 000 to $60 000 per year, quantity demanded at a price of $60 per bushel rises from 65 000 bushels per year to 95 000 bushels per year. A similar rise occurs at every other price.

Shifts in the Demand Curve   A demand curve is drawn with the assumption that everything except the product's own price is being held constant. But what if other things change, as they often do? For example, consider an increase in average household income while the price of apples remains constant. If consumers spend some of their extra income on apples, the new quantity demanded cannot be represented by a point on the original demand curve. It must be represented on a new demand curve that is to the right of the old curve. Thus, a rise in income that causes more apples to be demanded *at each price* shifts the demand curve for apples to the right, as shown in Figure 3-2. This shift illustrates the operation of an important general rule.

A change in any of the variables (other than the product's own price) that affect the quantity demanded will shift the demand curve to a new position.

A demand curve can shift in two important ways. In the first case, more is desired at each price—the demand curve shifts rightward so that each price corresponds to a higher quantity than it did before. In the second case, less is desired at each price—the demand curve shifts leftward so that each price corresponds to a lower quantity than it did before. Figure 3-3 shows increases and decreases in demand, and the associated shifts in the demand curve.

Let's now consider five important causes of shifts in the demand curve.

1. Consumers' Income.   If *average* income rises, consumers as a group can be expected to desire more of most products, other things being equal. Goods for which the quantity demanded increases when income rises are called *normal goods*; goods for which the quantity demanded falls when income rises are called *inferior goods*. The term *normal* *goods* reflects economists' empirical finding that the demand for most goods rises when income rises. We therefore expect that a rise in average consumer income shifts the demand curve for most products to the right, indicating that more will be demanded at any given price. Such a shift is illustrated in Figure 3-2. (We discuss normal and inferior goods in the next chapter.)

2. Prices of Other Goods.   We saw that the negative slope of a product's demand curve occurs because the lower its price, the cheaper the product becomes relative to other products that can satisfy the same needs or desires. These other products are called **substitutes in consumption**. Another way for the same change to come about is that the price of the substitute product rises. For example, apples can become cheap relative to oranges either because the price of apples falls or because the price of oranges rises. Either change will increase the amount of apples that consumers want to buy as some consumers substitute away from oranges and toward apples. Thus, a rise in the price of a substitute for a product shifts the demand curve for the product to the right. More will be demanded at each price.

> **substitutes in consumption** Goods that can be used in place of another good to satisfy similar needs or desires.

  Complements in consumption are products that tend to be used jointly. Cars and gasoline are complements; so are golf clubs and golf balls, and airplane flights to Calgary and ski-lift tickets in Banff. Because complements tend to be consumed together, a fall in the price of one will increase the quantity demanded of *both* products. Thus, a fall in the price of a complement for a product will shift that product's demand curve to the right. More will be demanded at each price. For example, a fall in the price of airplane trips to Calgary will lead to a rise in the demand for ski-lift tickets in Banff, even though the price of those lift tickets is unchanged. (The demand curve for ski-lift tickets will shift to the right.)

> **Complements in consumption** Goods that tend to be consumed together.

3. Tastes.   Tastes have a powerful effect on people's desired purchases. A change in tastes may be long-lasting, such as the shift from typewriters to computers, or it may be a short-lived fad as is common with many electronic games. In either case, a change in tastes in favour of a product shifts the demand curve to the right. More will be demanded at each price. Of course, a change in tastes against some product has the opposite effect and shifts the demand curve to the left.

4. Population.   If there is an increase in population with purchasing power, the demands for all the products purchased by the new people will rise. Thus, we expect that an increase in population will shift the demand curves for most products to the right, indicating that more will be demanded at each price.

5. Significant Changes in Weather.   The demands for some products are affected by dramatic changes in the weather. During winter, for example, a cold snap will lead to increases in demand for electricity, natural gas, and other energy sources used to heat homes and buildings. More snowfall will increase the demand by some people for ski vacations and for others their demand for beach vacations in southern destinations will increase. During summer, a hot spell increases the demand for air conditioners and the electricity to power them, and a dry spell will increase farmers' demand for water to irrigate their crops.

FIGURE 3-3   Shifts in the Demand Curve

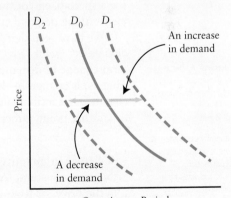

A rightward shift in the demand curve from D_0 to D_1 indicates an increase in demand; a leftward shift from D_0 to D_2 indicates a decrease in demand. An increase in demand means that more is demanded at each price. A decrease in demand means that less is demanded at each price.

Movements Along the Curve Versus Shifts of the Whole Curve Suppose you read in today's newspaper that a sharp increase in the world price of coffee beans has been caused by an increased worldwide demand for coffee. Then tomorrow you read that the rising price of coffee is reducing the typical consumer's purchases of coffee, as shoppers switch to other beverages. The two stories appear to contradict each other. The first associates a rising price with rising demand; the second associates a rising price with declining demand. Can both statements be true? The answer is yes—because the two statements actually refer to different things. The first describes a shift in the demand curve; the second describes a movement along the demand curve in response to a change in price.

Consider first the statement that the increase in the price of coffee has been caused by an increased demand for coffee. This statement refers to a shift in the demand curve for coffee—in this case, a shift to the right, indicating more coffee demanded at each price. This shift, as we will see later in this chapter, will increase the price of coffee.

Now consider the second statement—that less coffee is being bought because of its rise in price. This refers to a movement along the *new* demand curve and reflects a change between two specific quantities demanded, one before the price increased and one afterward.

Possible explanations for the two stories are as follows:

1. A rise in population and income in coffee-drinking countries shifts the demand curve for coffee to the right. This, in turn, raises the price of coffee (for reasons we will soon study in detail). This was the first newspaper story.

2. The rising price of coffee is causing each individual household to cut back on its coffee purchases. The cutback is represented by an upward movement to the left along the *new* demand curve for coffee. This was the second newspaper story.

To prevent the type of confusion caused by our two newspaper stories, economists use a specialized vocabulary to distinguish between shifts of demand curves and movements along demand curves.

We have seen that "demand" refers to the *entire* demand curve, whereas "quantity demanded" refers to a particular *point* on the demand curve. Economists reserve the term **change in demand** to describe a change in the quantity demanded at *every* price. That is, a change in demand refers to a shift of the entire demand curve. The term **change in quantity demanded** refers to a movement from one point on a demand curve to another point, either on the same demand curve or on a new one.

> **change in demand** A change in the quantity demanded at each possible price of the commodity, represented by a shift in the whole demand curve.

> **change in quantity demanded** A change in the specific quantity of the good demanded, represented by a change from one point on a demand curve to another point, either on the original demand curve or on a new one.

> **A change in quantity demanded can result from a shift in the demand curve with the price constant, from a movement along a given demand curve due to a change in the price, or from a combination of the two. [3]**

We consider these three possibilities in turn.

An increase in demand means that the whole demand curve shifts to the right; at any given price, an increase in demand causes an increase in quantity demanded. For example, in Figure 3-2 the shift in the demand curve for apples from D_0 to D_1 represents an increase in demand, and at a price of $40 per bushel, quantity demanded increases from 85 000 bushels to 115 000 bushels, as indicated by the move from V to V'.

A movement down and to the right along a demand curve represents an increase in quantity demanded. For example, in Figure 3-2, with the demand for apples given by the curve D_1, an increase in price from $40 to $60 per bushel causes a movement along D_1 from V' to W', and quantity demanded decreases from 115 000 bushels to 95 000 bushels.

When there is a change in demand *and* a change in the price, the overall change in quantity demanded is the net effect of the shift in the demand curve and the movement along the new demand curve. Figure 3-4 shows the combined effect of an increase in demand, shown by a rightward shift in the whole demand curve, and an upward movement to the left along the new demand curve caused by an increase in price. The increase in demand causes an increase in quantity demanded at the initial price, whereas the movement along the new demand curve causes a decrease in the quantity demanded. Whether quantity demanded rises or falls overall depends on the relative magnitudes of these two changes.

3.2 SUPPLY

What determines the supply of any given product? Why do Canadian oil producers extract and sell more oil when the price of oil is high? Why do Canadian cattle ranchers raise and sell more beef when the price of cattle-feed falls? We start by developing a theory designed to explain the supply of some typical product.

FIGURE 3-4 Shifts of and Movements Along the Demand Curve

An increase in demand means that the demand curve shifts to the right, and hence quantity demanded is higher at each price. A rise in price causes a movement upward and to the left along the demand curve, and hence quantity demanded falls. The demand curve is originally D_0 and price is p_0, which means that quantity demanded is Q_0. Suppose demand increases to D_1, which means that at any particular price, there is a larger quantity demanded; for example, at p_0, quantity demanded is now Q_1. Now suppose the price rises above p_0. This causes a movement up and to the left along D_1, and quantity demanded falls below Q_1. As the figure is drawn, the quantity demanded at the new price p_2 is less than Q_1 but greater than Q_0. So in this case the combined effect of the increase in demand and the rise in price is an increase in quantity demanded from Q_0 to Q_2.

Quantity Supplied

The amount of some good or service that producers want to sell in some time period is called the **quantity supplied** of that product. Quantity supplied is a flow; it is so much per unit of time. Note also that quantity supplied is the amount that producers are willing to offer for sale; it is not necessarily the amount that they succeed in selling, which is expressed by *quantity sold* or *quantity exchanged*.

quantity supplied The amount of a commodity that producers want to sell during some time period.

As a general rule, any event that makes production of a specific product more profitable will lead firms to supply more of it. The quantity supplied of a product is influenced by the following key variables: [4]

- Product's own price
- Prices of inputs
- Technology

- Some government taxes or subsidies
- Prices of other products
- Number of suppliers

The situation with supply is the same as that with demand: There are several influencing variables, and we will not get far if we try to discover what happens when they all change at the same time. Again, we use the convenient *ceteris paribus* assumption to study the influence of the variables one at a time.

Quantity Supplied and Price

We begin by holding all other influences constant and ask, "How do we expect the total quantity of a product supplied to vary with its own price?"

> A basic economic hypothesis is that the price of the product and the quantity supplied are related *positively,* other things being equal. That is, the higher the product's own price, the more its producers will supply; the lower the price, the less its producers will supply.

In later chapters we will derive this hypothesis as a prediction from more basic assumptions about the behaviour of individual profit-maximizing firms. For now we simply note that as the product's price rises, producing and selling this product becomes a more profitable activity. Firms interested in increasing their profit will therefore choose to increase their supply of the product.

Supply Schedules and Supply Curves

supply schedule A table showing the relationship between quantity supplied and the price of a commodity, other things being equal.

supply curve The graphical representation of the relationship between quantity supplied and the price of a commodity, other things being equal.

The general relationship just discussed can be illustrated by a **supply schedule,** which shows the relationship between quantity supplied of a product and the price of the product, other things being equal. The table in Figure 3-5 presents a hypothetical supply schedule for apples. A **supply curve,** the graphical representation of the supply schedule, is also illustrated in Figure 3-5. Each point on the supply curve represents a specific price–quantity combination; however, the whole curve shows something more.

> The supply curve represents the relationship between quantity supplied and price, other things being equal; its positive slope indicates that quantity supplied increases when price increases.

When economists make statements about the conditions of *supply,* they are not referring just to the particular quantity being supplied at the moment—that is, not to just one point on the supply curve. Instead, they are referring to the entire supply curve, to the complete relationship between desired sales and all possible prices of the

FIGURE 3-5 **The Supply of Apples**

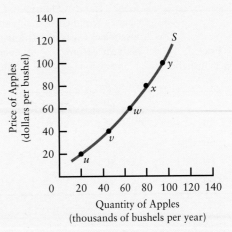

A Supply Schedule for Apples

Reference Point	Price ($ per bushel)	Quantity Supplied (thousands of bushels per year)
u	20	20
v	40	45
w	60	65
x	80	80
y	100	95

A Supply Curve for Apples

Both the table and the graph show the quantities that producers want to sell at various prices, *ceteris paribus*. For example, row *w* indicates that if the price of apples were $60 per bushel, producers would want to sell 65 000 bushels per year. The supply curve, labelled *S*, relates quantity of apples supplied to the price of apples; its positive slope indicates that quantity supplied increases as price increases.

product. **Supply** refers to the entire relationship between the quantity supplied of a product and the price of that product, other things being equal. A single point on the supply curve refers to the *quantity supplied* at that price.

Shifts in the Supply Curve   A shift in the supply curve means that at each price there is a change in the quantity supplied. An increase in the quantity supplied at each price is shown in Figure 3-6. This change appears as a rightward shift in the supply curve. In contrast, a decrease in the quantity supplied at each price would appear as a leftward shift. For supply, as for demand, there is an important general rule:

> **A change in any of the variables (other than the product's own price) that affects the quantity supplied will shift the supply curve to a new position.**

Let's now consider five possible causes of shifts in supply curves.

1. Prices of Inputs.   All things that a firm uses to produce its outputs, such as materials, labour, and machines, are called the firm's *inputs*. Other things being equal, the higher the price of any input used to make a product, the less profit there will be from making that product. We expect, therefore, that the higher the price of any input used by a firm, the less the firm will produce and offer for sale at any given price of the product. A rise in the price of inputs therefore shifts the supply curve for the product to the left, a fall in the price of inputs makes production more profitable and therefore shifts the supply curve to the right.

2. Technology.   At any given time, what is produced and how it is produced depend on the state of knowledge. Over time, however, knowledge changes. The enormous

supply The entire relationship between the quantity of some commodity that producers wish to sell and the price of that commodity, other things being equal.

FIGURE 3-6   An Increase in the Supply of Apples

Supply Schedules

Price ($ per bushel)	Quantity Supplied (thousands of bushels per year before innovation)	Quantity Supplied (thousands of bushels per year after innovation)
p	S_0	S_1
20	20 u	50 u'
40	45 v	75 v'
60	65 w	95 w'
80	80 x	110 x'
100	95 y	125 y'

Supply Curves

A cost-saving innovation increases the quantity supplied at each price. This is shown by the rightward shift in the supply curve, from S_0 to S_1. As a result of a cost-saving innovation, the quantity that is supplied at a price of $100 per bushel rises from 95 000 to 125 000 bushels per year. A similar rise occurs at every price.

increase in production per worker that has been going on in industrial societies for over 200 years is due largely to improved methods of production. The Industrial Revolution is more than a historical event; it is a present reality. Discoveries in chemistry have led to lower costs of production for well-established products, such as paints, as well as to a large variety of new products made of plastics and synthetic fibres. Silicon chips and fibre optics have radically changed products, such as cell phones, computers, and surgical devices, and the consequent development of smaller computers has revolutionized the production and lowered the costs of countless other non-electronic products.

Any technological innovation that decreases the amount of inputs needed per unit of output reduces production costs and hence increases the profits that can be earned at any given price of the product. Because increased profitability leads to increased willingness to produce, this change shifts the supply curve to the right.

A reduction or deterioration in technology is very rare, although in the agricultural sector significant changes in weather can have a similar effect. Drought, excessive rain, or flooding can all massively reduce the supply of wheat and other crops growing in temperate climates. In tropical climates, hurricanes can wipe out a coffee or banana crop, and a cold snap or frost can decimate the supply of fruit.

3. Government Taxes or Subsidies.   We have seen that anything increasing firms' costs will shift the supply curve to the left, and anything decreasing firms' costs will shift the supply curve to the right. As we will see in later chapters, governments often levy special taxes on the production of specific goods, such as gasoline, cigarettes, and alcohol. These taxes make the production and sale of these goods less profitable. The result is that the supply curve shifts to the left.

For other goods, governments often subsidize producers—that is, they pay producers a specific amount for each unit of the good produced. This often occurs for agricultural products, especially in the United States and the European Union. In such situations, the subsidy increases the profitability of production and shifts the supply curve to the right. For example, environmental concerns have led the U.S. and Canadian governments in recent years to provide subsidies for the production of biofuels. These subsidies have caused the supply curve for biofuels to shift to the right.

4. Prices of Other Products.   Changes in the price of one product may lead to changes in the supply of some other product because the two products are either *substitutes* or *complements* in the production process.

A prairie farmer, for example, can plant his field in wheat or oats. If the market price of oats falls, thus making oat production less profitable, the farmer will be more inclined to plant wheat. In this case, wheat and oats are said to be *substitutes* in production—for every extra hectare planted in one crop, one fewer hectare can be planted in the other. In this example, a reduction in the price of oats leads to an increase in the supply of wheat.

An excellent example in which two products are *complements* in production is oil and natural gas, which are often found together below Earth's surface. If the market price of oil rises, producers will do more drilling and increase their production of oil. But as more oil wells are drilled, the usual outcome is that more of *both* natural gas and oil are discovered and then produced. Thus, the rise in the price of oil leads to an increase in the supply of the complementary product—natural gas.

5. Number of Suppliers.   For given prices and technology, the total amount of any product supplied depends on the number of firms producing that product and offering it for sale. If profits are being earned by current firms, then more firms will choose to enter this industry and begin producing. The effect of this increase in the number of suppliers is to shift the supply curve to the right. Similarly, if the existing firms are losing money, they will eventually leave the industry; such a reduction in the number of suppliers shifts the supply curve to the left.

Movements Along the Curve Versus Shifts of the Whole Curve   As with demand, it is important to distinguish movements along supply curves from shifts of the whole curve. Economists reserve the term **change in supply** to describe a shift of the whole supply curve—that is, a change in the quantity that will be supplied at every price. The term **change in quantity supplied** refers to a movement from one point on a supply curve to another point, either on the same supply curve or on a new one. In other words, an increase in supply means that the whole supply curve has shifted to the right, so that the quantity supplied at any given price has increased; a movement up and to the right along a supply curve indicates an increase in the quantity supplied in response to an increase in the price of the product.

change in supply A change in the quantity supplied at each possible price of the commodity, represented by a shift in the whole supply curve.

change in quantity supplied A change in the specific quantity supplied, represented by a change from one point on a supply curve to another point, either on the original supply curve or on a new one.

A change in quantity supplied can result from a change in supply with the price constant, a movement along a given supply curve because of a change in the price, or a combination of the two.

An exercise you might find useful is to construct a diagram similar to Figure 3-4, emphasizing the difference between a shift of the supply curve and a movement along the supply curve.

3.3 THE DETERMINATION OF PRICE

So far we have considered demand and supply separately. We now come to a key question: How do the two forces of demand and supply interact to determine price? Before considering this question, you should know that the demand-and-supply model does *not* apply to all markets. See *Applying Economic Concepts 3-1* for a discussion of why the model in this chapter applies well to apples (and many other "commodities") but not to many more interesting products, such as iPhones (and a whole range of "differentiated" products).

The Concept of a Market

Originally, the term *market* designated a physical place where products were bought and sold. We still use the term this way to describe such places as Granville Island Market in Vancouver, Kensington Market in Toronto, or Jean Talon Market in Montreal. Once developed, however, theories of market behaviour were easily extended to cover products, such as wheat or oil, that can be purchased anywhere in the world at a price that tends to be uniform the world over. Today we can also buy and sell most consumer products in markets that exist online. The idea that a *market* must be a single geographic location where consumers can go to buy something became obsolete long ago.

market Any situation in which buyers and sellers can negotiate the exchange of goods or services.

For present purposes, a **market** may be defined as existing in any situation (such as a physical place or an electronic medium) in which buyers and sellers negotiate the exchange of goods or services.

Individual markets differ in the degree of *competition* among the various buyers and sellers. In the next few chapters we will examine markets in which the number of buyers and sellers is sufficiently large that no one of them has any appreciable influence on the market price. This is a rough definition of what economists call *perfectly competitive markets*. Starting in Chapter 10, we will consider the behaviour of markets in which there are small numbers of either sellers or buyers. But our initial theory of markets, based on the interaction of demand and supply, will be a very good description of the markets for such things as wheat, pork, newsprint, coffee, copper, oil, and many other commodities.

Market Equilibrium

The table in Figure 3-7 brings together the demand and supply schedules from Figures 3-1 and 3-5. The quantities of apples demanded and supplied at each price can now be compared.

There is only one price, $60 per bushel, at which the quantity of apples demanded equals the quantity supplied. At prices less than $60 per bushel, there is a shortage of apples because the quantity demanded exceeds the quantity supplied. This is a situation of **excess demand**. At prices greater than $60 per bushel, there is a surplus of apples because the quantity supplied exceeds the quantity demanded. This is a situation of **excess supply**. This same story can also be told in graphical terms. The quantities demanded and supplied at any price can be read off the two curves; the excess supply or excess demand is shown by the horizontal distance between the curves at each price.

excess demand A situation in which, at the given price, quantity demanded exceeds quantity supplied.

excess supply A situation in which, at the given price, quantity supplied exceeds quantity demanded.

To examine the determination of market price, let's suppose first that the price is $100 per bushel. At this price, 95 000 bushels are offered for sale, but only 40 000 bushels are demanded. There is an excess supply of 55 000 bushels per year. Apple sellers are then likely to cut their prices to get rid of this surplus. And purchasers, observing

APPLYING ECONOMIC CONCEPTS 3-1

Why Apples but Not iPhones?

The demand-and-supply model that we have developed in this chapter does *not* apply to the markets for all goods and services, and there is a good reason why our example throughout the chapter has been apples and not, for example, iPhones, cars, brand-name clothing, or even textbooks. Three conditions must be satisfied in order for price determination in a market to be well described by the demand-and-supply model.

1. There must be a large number of consumers of the product, each one small relative to the size of the market.

2. There must be a large number of producers of the product, each one small relative to the size of the market.

3. Producers must be selling identical or "homogeneous" versions of the product.

The first assumption ensures that no single consumer is large enough to influence the market price through their buying actions. This is satisfied in most markets, although there are important exceptions. For example, Canadian provincial governments are dominant purchasers of prescription drugs in Canada, and their *market power* tends to keep prices below what they would otherwise be.

The second assumption ensures that no single producer is large enough to influence the market price through their selling actions. There are many markets in which this is not true. For example, DeBeers controls the sale of a large fraction of the world's rough diamonds, and thus it can alter the market price through its sales restrictions. Hydro Quebec is the sole producer of electricity in the province of Quebec and sets the price that consumers pay. In contrast, most producers of fruits and vegetables are very small relative to the size of the market and have no ability to influence the market price.

The third assumption ensures that there will be a single price in the market because producers have no ability to *differentiate* their product from those of other producers. This condition is satisfied in many markets for commodities—steel, aluminum, copper, wheat, oil, natural gas, lumber, newsprint, beef, pork, etc. But it is *not* satisfied in the markets for many consumer products such as smartphones and other electronic devices, cars and motorcycles, clothing, and fast food and other restaurant meals. In these cases, each producer sells a different version of the product and spends considerable advertising resources trying to convince consumers to purchase their version. In these markets, differentiated products sell at different prices.

When *all three* conditions are satisfied, economists use the demand-and-supply model to explain the determination of market price and quantity. This model has proven to be very successful in explaining outcomes in markets such as oil, steel, copper, wheat, soybeans, beef, pork, newsprint, lumber, foreign currencies, financial assets like stocks and bonds—and apples!

So be careful when you try to apply the demand-and-supply model. It works very well in describing the events in many markets, but not so well for others. Later chapters in this book will examine the more complex markets for which we need a more advanced model.

---

the stock of unsold apples, will begin to offer less money for the product. In other words, *excess supply causes downward pressure on price.*

Now consider the price of $20 per bushel. At this price, there is excess demand. The 20 000 bushels produced each year are snapped up quickly, and 90 000 bushels of desired purchases cannot be made. Rivalry between would-be purchasers may lead them to offer more than the prevailing price to outbid other purchasers. Also, sellers may begin to ask a higher price for the quantities that they do have to sell. In other words, *excess demand causes upward pressure on price.*

Finally, consider the price of $60. At this price, producers want to sell 65 000 bushels per year, and purchasers want to buy that same quantity. There is neither a shortage nor a surplus of apples. There are no unsatisfied buyers to bid the price up, nor are there unsatisfied sellers to force the price down. Once the price of $60 has been reached, therefore, there will be no tendency for it to change.

FIGURE 3-7 The Equilibrium Price of Apples

Demand and Supply Schedules

Price ($ per bushel)	Quantity Demanded	Quantity Supplied	Excess Demand (+) or Excess Supply (−)
	(thousands of bushels per year)		
p	D	S	D–S
20	110	20	+90
40	85	45	+40
60	65	65	0
80	50	80	−30
100	40	95	−55

Demand and Supply Curves

The equilibrium price corresponds to the intersection of the demand and supply curves. At any price above $60, there is excess supply and thus downward pressure on price. At any price below $60, there is excess demand and thus upward pressure on price. Only at a price of $60 is there no pressure for price to change. Equilibrium occurs at point *E*, at a price of $60 and quantity exchanged equal to 65 000 bushels.

equilibrium price The price at which quantity demanded equals quantity supplied. Also called the *market-clearing price*.

Equilibrium implies a state of rest, or balance, between opposing forces. The **equilibrium price** is the one toward which the actual market price will tend. Once established, it will persist until it is disturbed by some change in market conditions that shifts the demand curve, the supply curve, or both.

> **The price at which the quantity demanded equals the quantity supplied is called the equilibrium price, or the market-clearing price. [5]**

disequilibrium price A price at which quantity demanded does not equal quantity supplied.

disequilibrium A situation in a market in which there is excess demand or excess supply.

Any price at which the market does not "clear"—that is, quantity demanded does not equal quantity supplied—is called a **disequilibrium price**. Whenever there is either excess demand or excess supply in a market, that market is said to be in a state of **disequilibrium**, and the market price will be changing.

Figure 3-7 makes it clear that the equilibrium price occurs where the demand and supply curves intersect. Below that price, there is excess demand and hence upward pressure on the existing price. Above that price, there is excess supply and hence downward pressure on the existing price.[3]

---

[3] When economists graph a demand (or supply) curve, they put the variable to be explained (the dependent variable) on the horizontal axis and the explanatory variable (the independent variable) on the vertical axis. This is "backward" to what is usually done in mathematics. The rational explanation of what is now economists' odd practice is buried in the history of economics and dates back to Alfred Marshall's *Principles of Economics* (1890) [6]. For better or worse, Marshall's scheme is now used by all economists, although mathematicians never fail to wonder at this example of the odd ways of economists.

Changes in Market Equilibrium

Changes in any of the variables, other than price, that influence quantity demanded or supplied will cause a shift in the demand curve, the supply curve, or both. There are four possible shifts: an increase in demand (a rightward shift in the demand curve), a decrease in demand (a leftward shift in the demand curve), an increase in supply (a rightward shift in the supply curve), and a decrease in supply (a leftward shift in the supply curve).

To discover the effects of each of the possible curve shifts, we use the method known as **comparative statics**.[4] With this method, we derive predictions about how the *endogenous* variables (equilibrium price and quantity) will change following a change in a single *exogenous* variable (the variables whose changes cause shifts in the demand and supply curves). We start from a position of equilibrium and then introduce the change to be studied. We then determine the new equilibrium position and compare it with the original one. The difference between the two positions of equilibrium must result from the change that was introduced, because everything else has been held constant.

The changes caused by each of the four possible curve shifts are shown in Figure 3-8. Study the figure carefully. Previously, we had given the axes specific labels, but because it is now intended to apply to any product, the horizontal axis is simply labelled "Quantity." This means quantity per period in whatever units output is measured. "Price," the vertical axis, means the price measured as dollars per unit of quantity for the same product.

The effects of the four possible curve shifts are as follows:

1. An increase in demand causes an increase in both the equilibrium price and the equilibrium quantity exchanged.

2. A decrease in demand causes a decrease in both the equilibrium price and the equilibrium quantity exchanged.

3. An increase in supply causes a decrease in the equilibrium price and an increase in the equilibrium quantity exchanged.

4. A decrease in supply causes an increase in the equilibrium price and a decrease in the equilibrium quantity exchanged.

Demonstrations of these effects are given in the caption to Figure 3-8. The intuitive reasoning behind each is as follows:

1. **An increase in demand (the demand curve shifts to the right).** An increase in demand creates a shortage at the initial equilibrium price, and the unsatisfied buyers bid up the price. This rise in price causes a larger quantity to be supplied, with the result that at the new equilibrium more is exchanged at a higher price.

Commodities & Futures					
	Price (US$)	Chg		Price (US$)	Chg
Crude Oil	96.57	−0.27	Lumber	292.50	−4.40
Natural Gas	2.816	0.041	Cocoa	2400.00	−33.00
Heating Oil	3.1244	−0.0073	Corn	829.25	−2.00
Gold	1642.70	−0.20	Soybeans	1727.50	−5.00
Silver	29.48	−0.034	Oat	393.25	−3.75
Copper	3.4565	−0.0045	Live Cattle	124.775	0.15
Platinum	1524.10	16.30	Wood Pulp	865.00	3.50
Palladium	629.75	5.55	Lean Hogs	75.175	−0.625

Many commodities like those listed here are actively traded in international markets and their equilibrium prices fluctuate daily.

Source: Based on the data from "Commodities & Futures," TMX Money, tmx.quotemedia.com/futures.php. Accessed August 22, 2012.

comparative statics The derivation of predictions by analyzing the effect of a change in a single exogenous variable on the equilibrium.

---

[4] The term *static* is used because we are not concerned with the actual path by which the market goes from the first equilibrium position to the second, or with the time taken to reach the second equilibrium. Analysis of these movements would be described as *dynamic analysis*.

FIGURE 3-8   Shifts in Demand and Supply Curves

(i) The effect of shifts in the demand curve

(ii) The effect of shifts in the supply curve

Shifts in either demand or supply curves will generally lead to changes in equilibrium price and quantity. In part (i), suppose the original demand and supply curves are D_0 and S, which intersect to produce equilibrium at E_0, with a price of p_0 and a quantity of Q_0. An increase in demand shifts the demand curve to D_1, taking the new equilibrium to E_1. Price rises to p_1 and quantity rises to Q_1. Starting at E_0, a decrease in demand shifts the demand curve to D_2, taking the new equilibrium to E_2. Price falls to p_2 and quantity falls to Q_2.

In part (ii), the original demand and supply curves are D and S_0, which intersect to produce equilibrium at E_0, with a price of p_0 and a quantity of Q_0. An increase in supply shifts the supply curve to S_1, taking the new equilibrium to E_1. Price falls to p_1 and quantity rises to Q_1. Starting at E_0, a decrease in supply shifts the supply curve from S_0 to S_2, taking the new equilibrium to E_2. Price rises to p_2 and quantity falls to Q_2.

2. **A decrease in demand (the demand curve shifts to the left).** A decrease in demand creates a surplus at the initial equilibrium price, and the unsuccessful sellers bid the price down. As a result, less of the product is supplied and offered for sale. At the new equilibrium, both price and quantity exchanged are lower than they were originally.

3. **An increase in supply (the supply curve shifts to the right).** An increase in supply creates a surplus at the initial equilibrium price, and the unsuccessful suppliers force the price down. This drop in price increases the quantity demanded, and the new equilibrium is at a lower price and a higher quantity exchanged.

4. **A decrease in supply (the supply curve shifts to the left).** A decrease in supply creates a shortage at the initial equilibrium price that causes the price to be bid up. This rise in price reduces the quantity demanded, and the new equilibrium is at a higher price and a lower quantity exchanged.

By using the tools we have learned in this chapter, we can link many real-world events that cause demand or supply curves to shift and thus lead to changes in market prices and quantities. For example, economic growth in rapidly developing countries like China and India leads to increases in global demand for a wide range of products such as steel, cement, copper, and glass. *Ceteris paribus*, this economic growth will increase the equilibrium prices of these products. For another example, consider the rapid development of hydraulic fracturing ("fracking") in the United States. In recent years, use of this technology has led to an enormous increase in the supply of natural gas in the North American market, which, *ceteris paribus*, has caused a decrease in the equilibrium price.

It is worth noting that real-world demand and supply shifts are often not isolated events. More realistic is that one event causes a shift in the demand curve while some other event occurring at the same time causes a shift in the supply curve. For example, an increase in Calgary's population may lead to an increase in demand for residential accommodation while, at the same time, increased construction of condos and houses increases the supply. If these demand and supply shifts occur at the same time and are of the same magnitude, there may be no noticeable effect on the equilibrium price (although equilibrium quantity would increase).

Readers are referred to several Study Exercises at the end of this chapter to work through examples of demand and supply shifts, and the predicted effects on equilibrium price and quantity.

A Numerical Example

Changes in market equilibrium can also be examined by using a simple algebraic model. For example, consider the (hypothetical) wholesale market for potatoes in Atlantic Canada in 2016. The price is the dollar price per 100 kg and the quantity is the number of 100 kg units (in thousands). The demand and supply curves are:

$$Q^D = 100 - 3p$$
$$Q^S = 20 + 2p$$

Notice that the many things shifting the demand curve (such as income, tastes, etc.) are not explicitly shown in the demand equation. Instead, their effect is already represented in the constant term of 100. The demand equation shows that for every $1 increase in the price, quantity demanded falls by 3000 units per year. Similarly, the many things shifting the supply curve are not shown explicitly, but their effect is shown inside the constant term of 20. From the supply equation it is clear that each $1 increase in the price leads to an increase in quantity supplied of 2000 units per year.

In order to determine the market equilibrium, we need to find the single price at which $Q^D = Q^S$. By setting $Q^D = Q^S$, we get:

$$100 - 3p = 20 + 2p$$

which can be rewritten to get:

$$80 = 5p$$
$$\Rightarrow p = 16$$

The equilibrium price for potatoes is therefore $16 per 100 kg unit. To find the equilibrium quantity, we substitute this price into *either* the demand or supply equation. Using the demand equation, we get

$$Q^D = 100 - 3(16) = 52$$

So the equilibrium quantity of potatoes in Atlantic Canada in 2016 is 52 000 units (of 100 kg each). Readers are directed to the Study Exercises at the end of this chapter to work through other algebraic and numerical examples of market equilibrium.

Relative Prices

The theory we have developed explains how individual prices are determined by the forces of demand and supply. To facilitate matters, we have made *ceteris paribus* assumptions. Specifically, we have assumed the constancy of all prices except the one we are studying. This assumption forces us to make the distinction between *absolute* prices and *relative* prices.

The price of a product is the amount of money that must be spent to acquire one unit of that product. This is called the **absolute price** or *money price*. A **relative price** is the ratio of two absolute prices; it expresses the price of one good in terms of (relative to) another.

We have been reminded several times that what matters for demand and supply is the price of the product in question *relative to the prices of other products*; that is, what matters is the relative price. For example, if the price of carrots rises while the prices of other vegetables are constant, we expect consumers to reduce their quantity demanded of carrots as they substitute toward the consumption of other vegetables. In this case, the *relative* price of carrots has increased. But if the prices of carrots and all other vegetables are rising at the same rate, the relative price of carrots is constant. In this case we expect no substitution to take place between carrots and other vegetables.

> In microeconomics, whenever we refer to a change in the price of one product, we mean a change in that product's relative price, that is, a change in the price of that product relative to the prices of all other goods.

absolute price The amount of money that must be spent to acquire one unit of a commodity. Also called money price.

relative price The ratio of the money price of one commodity to the money price of another commodity; that is, a ratio of two absolute prices.

SUMMARY

3.1 DEMAND

LO 1, 2

- The amount of a product that consumers want to purchase is called *quantity demanded*. It is a flow expressed as so much per period of time. It is determined by tastes, income, the product's own price, the prices of other products, and population.
- The relationship between quantity demanded and price is represented graphically by a demand curve that shows how much will be demanded at each market price. Quantity demanded is assumed to increase as the price of the product falls, other things held constant. Thus, demand curves are negatively sloped.

- A shift in a demand curve represents a change in the quantity demanded at each price and is referred to as a *change in demand*.
- An increase in demand means the demand curve shifts to the right; a decrease in demand means the demand curve shifts to the left.
- It is important to make the distinction between a movement along a demand curve (caused by a change in the product's price) and a shift of a demand curve (caused by a change in any of the other determinants of demand).

3.2 SUPPLY

LO 3, 4

- The amount of a good that producers wish to sell is called *quantity supplied*. It is a flow expressed as so much per period of time. It depends on the product's own price, the costs of inputs, the number of suppliers, government taxes or subsidies, the state of technology, and prices of other products.

- The relationship between quantity supplied and price is represented graphically by a supply curve that shows how much will be supplied at each market price. Quantity supplied is assumed to increase as the price of the product increases, other things held constant. Thus, supply curves are positively sloped.

- A shift in the supply curve indicates a change in the quantity supplied at each price and is referred to as a *change in supply*.
- An increase in supply means the supply curve shifts to the right; a decrease in supply means the supply curve shifts to the left.

- It is important to make the distinction between a movement along a supply curve (caused by a change in the product's price) and a shift of a supply curve (caused by a change in any of the other determinants of supply).

3.3 THE DETERMINATION OF PRICE

LO 5

- The *equilibrium price* is the price at which the quantity demanded equals the quantity supplied. At any price below equilibrium, there will be excess demand; at any price above equilibrium, there will be excess supply. Graphically, equilibrium occurs where the demand and supply curves intersect.
- Price rises when there is excess demand and falls when there is excess supply. Thus, the actual market price will be pushed toward the equilibrium price. When it is reached, there will be neither excess demand nor excess supply, and the price will not change until either the supply curve or the demand curve shifts.

- By using the method of *comparative statics*, we can determine the effects of a shift in either demand or supply. An increase in demand raises both equilibrium price and equilibrium quantity; a decrease in demand lowers both. An increase in supply raises equilibrium quantity but lowers equilibrium price; a decrease in supply lowers equilibrium quantity but raises equilibrium price.
- The absolute price of a product is its price in terms of money; its relative price is its price in relation to other products.

KEY CONCEPTS

Stock and flow variables
Ceteris paribus or "other things being equal"
Quantity demanded
Demand schedule and demand curve

Change in quantity demanded versus change in demand
Quantity supplied
Supply schedule and supply curve
Change in quantity supplied versus change in supply

Equilibrium, equilibrium price, and disequilibrium
Comparative statics
Relative and absolute prices

STUDY EXERCISES

MyEconLab Make the grade with MyEconLab: Study Exercises marked in ● can be found on MyEconLab. You can practise them as often as you want, and most feature step-by-step guided instructions to help you find the right answer.

● Fill in the blanks to complete the statements about a supply-and-demand model, as applied in the following situations.

a. Consider the market for cement in Toronto. If, *ceteris paribus*, half the producers in this market shut down, the _____ curve for cement will shift to the _____, indicating a(n) _____ in _____.

b. Consider the market for Canadian softwood lumber (a normal good). If, *ceteris paribus*, average incomes in both Canada and the United States rise over several years, the _____ curve for

lumber will shift to the _____, indicating a(n) _____ in _____.

c. Consider the market for Quebec artisanal cheeses. If, *ceteris paribus*, the price of imported cheeses from France rises significantly, the _____ curve for Quebec cheeses will shift to the _____, indicating a(n) _____ in _____.

d. Consider the market for milk in the United States. If, *ceteris paribus*, the U.S. government decreases subsidies to dairy farmers, the _____ curve for milk will shift to the _____, indicating a(n) _____ in _____.

e. Consider the world market for shipping containers. If, *ceteris paribus*, the price of steel (a major input) rises, the _____ curve for shipping containers will shift to the _____, indicating a(n) _____ in _____.

f. Consider the market for hot dog buns. If, *ceteris paribus,* the price of wieners doubles, the _____ curve for hot dog buns will shift to the _____, indicating a(n) _____ in _____.

② Fill in the blanks to make the following statements correct.

a. *Ceteris paribus*, the price of a product and the quantity demanded are related _____.

b. *Ceteris paribus*, the price of a product and the quantity supplied are related _____.

c. At any price above the equilibrium price there will be excess _____. At any price below the equilibrium price there will be excess _____.

d. The equilibrium price is the price at which quantity demanded _____ quantity supplied.

e. An increase in demand for some product will usually cause its equilibrium price to _____ and also cause an increase in _____.

f. A decrease in the supply of some product will usually cause its equilibrium price to _____ and also cause a decrease in _____.

③ The following table shows hypothetical demand schedules for sugar for three separate months. To help make the distinction between changes in demand and changes in quantity demanded, choose the wording to make each of the following statements correct.

Price/kg	Quantity Demanded for Sugar (in kilograms)		
	October	November	December
$1.50	11 000	10 500	13 000
1.75	10 000	9 500	12 000
2.00	9 000	8 500	11 000
2.25	8 000	7 500	10 000
2.50	7 000	6 500	9 000
2.75	6 000	5 500	8 000
3.00	5 000	4 500	7 000
3.25	4 000	3 500	6 000
3.50	3 000	2 500	5 000

a. When the price of sugar rises from $2.50 to $3.00 in the month of October there is a(n) (*increase/ decrease*) in (*demand for/quantity demanded of*) sugar of 2000 kg.

b. We can say that the demand curve for sugar in December shifted (*to the right/to the left*) of November's demand curve. This represents a(n) (*increase/decrease*) in demand for sugar.

c. An increase in the demand for sugar means that quantity demanded at each price has (*increased/ decreased*), while a decrease in demand for sugar means that quantity demanded at each price has (*increased/decreased*).

d. In the month of December, a price change for sugar from $3.50 to $2.75 per kilogram would mean a change in (*demand for/quantity demanded of*) sugar of 3000 kg.

e. Plot the three demand schedules on a graph and label each demand curve to indicate whether it is the demand for October, November, or December.

④ Classify the effect of each of the following as (i) a change in the demand for fish or (ii) a change in the quantity of fish demanded. Illustrate each diagrammatically.

a. The government of Canada closes the Atlantic cod fishery.

b. People buy less fish because of a rise in fish prices.

c. The Catholic Church relaxes its ban on eating meat on Fridays.

d. The price of beef falls and, as a result, consumers buy more beef and less fish.

e. Fears of mercury poisoning lead locals to shun fish caught in nearby lakes.

f. It is generally alleged that eating fish is better for one's health than eating meat.

⑤ Are the following two observations inconsistent?

a. Rising demand for housing causes prices of new homes to soar.

b. Many families refuse to buy homes as prices become prohibitive for them.

⑥ Consider households' demand for chicken meat. For each of the events listed below, state and explain the likely effect on the demand for chicken. How would each event be illustrated in a diagram?

a. A medical study reports that eating chicken reduces the likelihood of suffering from particular types of heart problems.

b. A widespread bovine disease leads to an increase in the price of beef.

c. Average household income increases.

⑦ For each of the following statements, determine whether there has been a change in supply or a change in quantity supplied. Draw a demand-and-supply diagram for each situation to show either a movement along the supply curve or a shift of the supply curve.

a. The price of Canadian-grown peaches skyrockets during an unusually cold summer that reduces the size of the peach harvest.

b. An increase in income leads to an increase in the price of family-restaurant meals, and to an increase in their sales.

c. Technological improvements in electronic publishing lead to price reductions for e-books and an increase in e-book sales.

d. A low-carb diet becomes popular and leads to a reduction in the price of bread and less bread being sold.

8 The following supply and demand schedules describe a hypothetical Canadian market for potash.

Price ($ per tonne)	Quantity Supplied (million tonnes)	Quantity Demanded (million tonnes)
280	8.5	12.5
300	9.0	11.0
320	9.5	9.5
340	10.0	8.0
360	10.5	6.5
380	11.0	5.0

a. What is the equilibrium price of potash?

b. How much potash would actually be purchased if the price was $280 per tonne?

c. How much potash would actually be sold if the price was $360 per tonne?

d. At a price of $280 per tonne, is there excess supply or demand? How much?

e. At a price of $360 per tonne, is there excess supply or demand? How much?

f. If the price is $280 per tonne, describe the forces that will cause the price to change.

g. If the price is $360 per tonne, describe the forces that will cause the price to change.

9 The following diagram describes the hypothetical demand and supply for canned tuna in Canada in 2016.

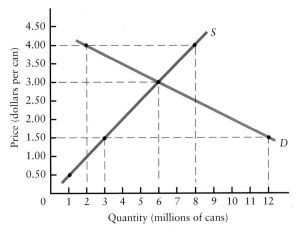

a. Suppose the price of a can of tuna is $4.00. What is the quantity demanded? What is the quantity supplied? At this price, is there a shortage or a surplus? By what amount?

b. Suppose the price of a can of tuna is $1.50. What is the quantity demanded? What is the quantity supplied? At this price, is there a shortage or a surplus? By what amount?

c. What is the equilibrium price and quantity in this market?

10 Consider the world market for a particular quality of coffee beans. The following table shows the demand and supply schedules for this market.

Price (per kilogram)	Quantity Demanded	Quantity Supplied
	(millions of kilograms per year)	
$2.00	28	10
$2.40	26	12
$3.10	22	13.5
$3.50	19.5	19.5
$3.90	17	22
$4.30	14.5	23.5

a. Plot the demand and supply schedules on a diagram.

b. Identify the amount of excess demand or supply associated with each price.

c. Identify the equilibrium price in this market.

d. Suppose that a collection of national governments were somehow able to set a minimum price for coffee equal to $3.90 per kilogram. Explain the outcome in the world coffee market.

11 Early in 2011, the world price of copper reached a record high of over $10 000 per tonne. Two events appeared to lie behind this high price. First, China's rapid economic growth and the massive building of infrastructure. Second, an explosion closed a major Chilean port used for shipping a substantial fraction of the world's copper output. Use a demand-and-supply diagram to illustrate these events in the copper market, and explain how each event shifts either the demand curve or the supply curve.

12 There has been explosive growth in the demand for the green leafy vegetable kale in recent years, as consumers learned of its health benefits. The demand curve has shifted significantly rightward. However, the price of a bunch of kale in the grocery store has been fairly stable. Draw a demand-and-supply diagram showing the market for kale, and explain how the price of kale could remain stable in the face of such an enormous growth in demand. (Hint: there are two possible scenarios in which the equilibrium price does not change.)

13 Consider the world market for wheat. Suppose there is a major failure in Russia's wheat crop because of a severe drought. Explain the likely effect on the equilibrium price and quantity in the world wheat market. Also explain why Canadian wheat farmers certainly benefit from Russia's drought. The following diagrams provide a starting point for your analysis.

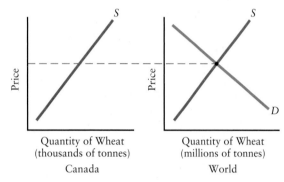

14 Assume you have the following information for the global market for agricultural commodity X. For each scenario, use demand and supply analysis to provide a likely explanation for the change in market equilibrium. The prices are per bushel and the quantities are millions of bushels.

Scenario	August 2015	August 2016
a.	$p^* = \$142\ Q^* = 315$	$p^* = \$180\ Q^* = 315$
b.	$p^* = \$142\ Q^* = 315$	$p^* = \$128\ Q^* = 360$
c.	$p^* = \$142\ Q^* = 315$	$p^* = \$135\ Q^* = 275$
d.	$p^* = \$142\ Q^* = 315$	$p^* = \$142\ Q^* = 400$

15 This question requires you to solve a supply-and-demand model algebraically. Letting p be the price of

the product, suppose the demand and supply functions for some product are given by

$$Q^D = 100 - 3p$$
$$Q^S = 10 + 2p$$

a. Plot both the demand curve and the supply curve.
b. What is the condition for equilibrium in this market?
c. By imposing the condition for equilibrium, solve for the equilibrium price.
d. Substitute the equilibrium price into either the demand or the supply function to solve for the equilibrium quantity. Check to make sure you get the same answer whether you use the demand function or the supply function.
e. Now suppose there is an increase in demand so that the new demand function is given by

$$Q^D = 180 - 3p$$

Compute the new equilibrium price and quantity. Is your result consistent with the "law" of demand?
f. Now suppose that with the new demand curve in place, there is an increase in supply so that the new supply function is given by $Q^S = 90 + 2p$. Compute the new equilibrium price and quantity.

16 Find the equilibrium price and quantity for each of the following pairs of demand and supply functions.

a. $Q^D = 10 - 2P$ $Q^S = 5 + 3P$
b. $Q^D = 1270 - 10P$ $Q^S = 1000 + 20P$
c. $Q^D = 100 - 0.25P$ $Q^S = 40 + 0.25P$
d. $Q^D = 6000 - 0.2P$ $Q^S = 4000 + 0.8P$
e. $Q^D = 10\ 000 - 100P$ $Q^S = 100P$

4 Elasticity

CHAPTER OUTLINE	LEARNING OBJECTIVES (LO)
	After studying this chapter you will be able to
4.1 PRICE ELASTICITY OF DEMAND	**1** explain what price elasticity of demand is and how it is measured.
	2 explain the relationship between total expenditure and price elasticity of demand.
4.2 PRICE ELASTICITY OF SUPPLY	**3** explain what price elasticity of supply is and how it is measured.
4.3 ELASTICITY MATTERS FOR EXCISE TAXES	**4** see how elasticity of demand and supply determine the effects of an excise tax.
4.4 OTHER DEMAND ELASTICITIES	**5** measure the income elasticity of demand and be able to distinguish between normal and inferior goods.
	6 measure cross elasticity of demand and be able to distinguish between substitute and complement goods.

THE model of demand and supply predicts the direction of changes in equilibrium price and quantity in response to various shifts in demand and supply curves. For many purposes, however, it is not enough to know merely whether price and quantity rise or fall; it is also important to know by how much each changes.

For example, during the 2011 civil war in Libya, that country's oil production was sharply reduced for over six months. As a result, global oil production fell by over 1.5 million barrels per day, a decline of just under 2 percent. This drop in the world supply of oil led to an immediate 20-percent increase in the world price, which persisted until Libya's production returned to more normal levels after the end of the civil war. How can we explain why the increase in the price of oil in this situation was 20 percent rather than 50 percent or only 5 percent? As we will see in this chapter, the shapes of the demand and supply curves determine the sensitivity of prices and quantities to various economic shocks. Precise measures of these sensitivities are provided by what are called the *elasticity* of demand and supply.

4.1 PRICE ELASTICITY OF DEMAND

Suppose there is a decrease in the supply of some farm crop—that is, a leftward shift in the supply curve. We saw in Chapter 3 that such a decrease in supply will cause the equilibrium price to rise and the equilibrium quantity to fall. But by how much will each change? The answer depends on what is called the *price elasticity of demand*.

Loosely speaking, demand is said to be *elastic* when quantity demanded is quite responsive to changes in price. When quantity demanded is relatively unresponsive to changes in price, demand is said to be *inelastic*.

The importance of elasticity is illustrated in Figure 4-1. The two parts of the figure have the same initial equilibrium, which is then disturbed by the same leftward shift in the supply curve. But the demand curves are different in the two parts of the figure, and so the sizes of the changes in equilibrium price and quantity are also different.

Part (i) of Figure 4-1 illustrates a case in which the quantity that consumers demand is quite responsive to price changes—that is, demand is relatively *elastic*. The reduction in supply pushes up the price, but because the quantity demanded is quite responsive to changes in price (demand is elastic), only a small change in price is necessary to restore equilibrium.

Part (ii) of Figure 4-1 shows a case in which quantity demanded is quite unresponsive to price changes—that is, demand is relatively *inelastic*. As in part (i), the decrease in supply at the original price causes a shortage that increases the price. However, in

FIGURE 4-1   The Effects of a Supply Shift with Two Different Demand Curves

(i) Relatively elastic demand   (ii) Relatively inelastic demand

The more responsive the quantity demanded is to changes in price, the less the change in equilibrium price and the greater the change in equilibrium quantity resulting from any given shift in the supply curve. Both parts of the figure are drawn to the same scale. They show the same initial equilibrium, E_0, and the same shift in the supply curve, from S_0 to S_1. In each part, initial equilibrium is at price p_0 and output Q_0 and the new equilibrium, E_1, is at p_1 and Q_1. In part (i), the effect of the reduction in supply is a slight rise in the price and a large decrease in quantity. In part (ii), the effect of the identical reduction in supply is a large increase in the price and a relatively small decrease in quantity.

this case quantity demanded does not fall much in response to the rise in price (demand is inelastic). The result is that equilibrium price rises more, and equilibrium quantity falls less, than in the first case.

In both cases shown in Figure 4-1, the supply curves and their shifts are identical. The sizes of the effects on the equilibrium price and quantity are different only because of the different elasticities of demand.

The Measurement of Price Elasticity

In Figure 4-1, we were able to say that the demand curve in part (i) showed more responsiveness to price changes than the demand curve in part (ii) because two conditions were fulfilled. First, both curves were drawn on the same scale. Second, the initial equilibrium prices and quantities were the same in both parts of the figure. Let's see why these conditions matter.

First, by drawing both figures on the same scale, we saw that the demand curve that *looked* steeper actually did have the larger absolute slope. (The slope of a demand curve tells us the amount by which price must change to cause a unit change in quantity demanded.) If we had drawn the two curves on different scales, we could have concluded nothing about which demand curve actually had the greater slope.

Second, because we started from the same price–quantity equilibrium in both parts of the figure, we did not need to distinguish between *percentage* changes and *absolute* changes. If the initial prices and quantities are the same in both cases, the larger absolute change is also the larger percentage change. However, when we want to deal with different initial price–quantity equilibria, we need to decide whether we are interested in absolute or percentage changes.

To see why the difference between absolute and percentage change matters, consider the changes in price and quantity demanded for three different products: cheese, T-shirts, and coffee machines. The information is shown in Table 4-1. Should we conclude that the demand for coffee machines is not as responsive to price changes as the demand for cheese? After all, price cuts of $2 cause quite a large increase in the quantity of cheese demanded, but only a small increase in the quantity demanded of coffee machines. It should be obvious that a $2 price reduction is a large price cut for a low-priced product and an insignificant price cut for a high-priced product. In Table 4-1, each price reduction is $2, but they are clearly different proportions of the respective prices. It is usually more revealing to know the *percentage* change in the prices of the various products.

For similar reasons, knowing the change in the quantity demanded is not very revealing unless the initial quantity demanded is also known. An increase of 7500 kilograms is quite a significant change if the quantity formerly bought was 15 000 kilograms, but it is insignificant if the quantity formerly bought was 10 million kilograms.

TABLE 4-1 Price Reductions and Corresponding Increases in Quantity Demanded for Three Products

Product	Reduction in Price	Increase in Quantity Demanded (per month)
Cheese	$2 per kilogram	7500 kilograms
T-shirts	$2 per shirt	25 000 shirts
Coffee machines	$2 per machine	500 machines

For each of the three products, the data show the change in quantity demanded resulting from the same absolute fall in price. The data are fairly uninformative about the responsiveness of quantity demanded to price because they do not tell us either the original price or the original quantity demanded.

TABLE 4-2 Price and Quantity Information Underlying Data of Table 4-1

Product	Unit	Original Price ($)	New Price ($)	Average Price ($)	Original Quantity	New Quantity	Average Quantity
Cheese	kilogram	5.00	3.00	4.00	116 250	123 750	120 000
T-shirts	shirt	17.00	15.00	16.00	187 500	212 500	200 000
Coffee machines	machine	81.00	79.00	80.00	9 750	10 250	10 000

These data provide the appropriate context for the data given in Table 4-1. The table relates the $2 per-unit price reduction of each product to the actual prices and quantities demanded.

Table 4-2 shows the original and new levels of price and quantity. Note that it also shows the *average* price and *average* quantity. These averages will be necessary for our computation of elasticity.

The **price elasticity of demand,** the measure of responsiveness of the quantity of a product demanded to a change in that product's price, is symbolized by the Greek letter eta, η. It is defined as follows:

$$\eta = \frac{\text{Percentage change in quantity demanded}}{\text{Percentage change in price}}$$

This measure is called the price elasticity of demand, or simply demand elasticity. Because the variable causing the change in quantity demanded is the product's own price, the term *own-price elasticity of demand* is also used.

The Use of Average Price and Quantity in Computing Elasticity   Table 4-3 shows the percentage changes for price and quantity using the data from Table 4-2. The caption in Table 4-3 stresses that the demand elasticities are computed by using changes in price and quantity measured in terms of the *average* values of each. Averages are used to avoid the ambiguity caused by the fact that when a price or quantity changes, the change is a different percentage of the original value than it is of the new value. For example, the $2.00 change in the price of cheese shown in Table 4-2 represents a 40 percent change in the original price of $5.00 but a 66.7 percent change in the new price of $3.00.

TABLE 4-3 Calculation of Demand Elasticities

Product	(1) Percentage Decrease in Price	(2) Percentage Increase in Quantity	(3) Elasticity of Demand (2) ÷ (1)
Cheese	50.0	6.25	0.125
T-shirts	12.5	12.5	1.0
Coffee machines	2.5	5.0	2.0

Elasticity of demand is the percentage change in quantity demanded divided by the percentage change in price. The percentage changes are based on average prices and quantities shown in Table 4-2. For example, the $2.00-per-kilogram decrease in the price of cheese is 50 percent of the average price $4.00. A $2.00 change in the price of coffee machines is only 2.5 percent of the average price per machine of $80.00.

Using average values for price and quantity means that the measured elasticity of demand between any two points on the demand curve, call them *A* and *B*, is independent of whether the movement is from *A* to *B* or from *B* to *A*. In the example of cheese in Table 4-2 and

4-3, the $2.00 change in the price of cheese is unambiguously 50 percent of the average price of $4.00, and that percentage applies to a price increase from $3.00 to $5.00 or to a price decrease from $5.00 to $3.00.

Once we have computed the average prices and quantities as in Table 4-2, the algebraic formula for price elasticity is straightforward. Suppose we have an initial price of p_0 and an initial quantity of Q_0. We then consider a new price of p_1 and a new quantity of Q_1 (both price–quantity combinations lie on the demand curve for the product). The formula for price elasticity is then

$$\eta = \frac{\dfrac{\Delta Q}{\overline{Q}}}{\dfrac{\Delta p}{\overline{p}}} = \frac{\dfrac{Q_1 - Q_0}{\overline{Q}}}{\dfrac{p_1 - p_0}{\overline{p}}}$$

where $\overline{p}$ is the average price and $\overline{Q}$ is the average quantity. In the case of cheese from Table 4-2, we have

$$\eta = \frac{\dfrac{(123\ 750 - 116\ 250)}{120\ 000}}{\dfrac{(5.00 - 3.00)}{4.00}} = \frac{7500/120\ 000}{2.0/4.0} = \frac{0.0625}{0.5} = 0.125$$

as shown in Table 4-3. Notice that elasticity is *unit free*—even though prices are measured in dollars and quantity of cheese is measured in kilograms, the elasticity of demand has no units.

We leave it to you to use this formula to confirm the price elasticities for T-shirts and coffee machines shown in Table 4-3. [7]

Interpreting Numerical Elasticities   Because demand curves have negative slopes, an increase in price is associated with a decrease in quantity demanded, and vice versa. Because the percentage changes in price and quantity have opposite signs, demand elasticity is a negative number. However, here we will ignore the negative sign and speak of the measure as a positive number, as we have done in the illustrative calculations in Table 4-3. Thus, the more responsive the quantity demanded to a change in price, the greater the elasticity and the larger is η.

The numerical value of demand elasticity can vary from zero to infinity. First consider the extreme cases. Elasticity is zero when a change in price leads to *no change* in quantity demanded. This is the case of a vertical demand curve, and it is quite rare because it indicates that consumers do not alter their consumption at all when price changes. At the other extreme, elasticity is very large when even a very small change in price leads to an enormous change in quantity demanded. In these situations, the demand curve is very flat, almost horizontal. (In the rare limiting case, the demand curve is perfectly horizontal and elasticity is infinite.) Most of reality lies between the extremes of vertical and horizontal demand curves. We divide this "realistic" range of elasticities into two regions.

When the percentage change in quantity demanded is less than the percentage change in price (elasticity less than 1), there is said to be **inelastic demand**. When the percentage change in quantity demanded is greater than the percentage change in price (elasticity greater than 1), there is said to be **elastic demand**. The dividing line between these two cases occurs when the percentage change in quantity demanded is exactly

inelastic demand Following a given percentage change in price, there is a smaller percentage change in quantity demanded; elasticity is less than 1.

elastic demand Following a given percentage change in price, there is a greater percentage change in quantity demanded; elasticity is greater than 1.

FIGURE 4-2 Elasticity Along a Linear Demand Curve

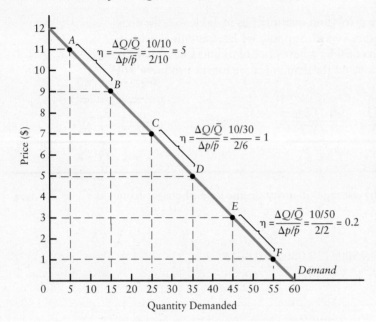

Moving down a linear demand curve, price elasticity falls continuously, even though the slope is constant. For each of the three intervals shown, the absolute change in the price is $2 and the absolute change in quantity demanded is 10 units. But for low quantities (and high prices) along an interval such as *AB*, these percentage changes are quite different than with high quantities (and low prices), such as for interval *EF*. The result is that price elasticity falls as we move down and to the right along a linear demand curve. Elasticity approaches infinity as we get closer to where the demand curve intersects the vertical axis; elasticity approaches zero as we get closer to where the demand curve intersects the horizontal axis.

equal to the percentage change in price, and so elasticity is equal to 1. Here we say that demand is *unit elastic*.

A demand curve need not, and usually does not, have the same elasticity over its whole length. Figure 4-2 shows that a negatively sloped linear demand curve does not have a constant elasticity, even though it does have a constant slope. A linear demand curve has constant elasticity only when it is vertical or horizontal. Figure 4-3 illustrates these two cases, in addition to a third case of a particular *non-linear* demand curve that also has a constant elasticity.

What Determines Elasticity of Demand?

Elasticity of demand is mostly determined by the *availability of substitutes* and the *time period* under consideration.

Availability of Substitutes   Some products, such as margarine, broccoli, Dell PCs, and Toyota cars, have quite close substitutes—butter, other green vegetables, Toshiba PCs, and Mazda cars. A change in the price of these products, *with the prices of the substitutes remaining constant,* can be expected to cause much substitution. A fall in the price of broccoli leads consumers to buy more broccoli and less of other green vegetables, and a rise in price leads consumers to buy less broccoli as they substitute toward other green vegetables.

A related point concerns *product definition.* Products defined more broadly, such as *all* foods or *all* clothing or *all* methods of transportation, have many fewer satisfactory substitutes than do products defined much more narrowly. A rise in their prices can be expected to cause a smaller fall in quantities demanded than would be the case if close substitutes were available. For example, there are far more substitutes for Diet Pepsi than there are for the broader categories of diet colas, soft drinks, or all beverages. As a result, the demand elasticity for Diet Pepsi is significantly higher than for beverages overall.

> **Products with close substitutes tend to have elastic demands; products with no close substitutes tend to have inelastic demands. Narrowly defined products have more elastic demands than do more broadly defined products.**

Short Run and Long Run Demand elasticity also depends to a great extent on the time period being considered. Because it takes time to develop satisfactory substitutes, a demand that is inelastic in the short run may prove to be elastic when enough time has passed. A dramatic example of this principle occurred in 1973–1974 when output restrictions by the Organization of Petroleum Exporting Countries

FIGURE 4-3 **Three Demand Curves with Constant Elasticity**

Each of these demand curves has a constant elasticity. D_1 has zero elasticity: The quantity demanded is equal to Q_0, independent of the price. D_2 has infinite elasticity at the price p_0: A small price increase from p_0 decreases quantity demanded from an indefinitely large amount to zero. D_3 has unit elasticity: A given percentage increase in price brings an equal percentage decrease in quantity demanded at all points on the curve; it is a rectangular hyperbola for which price times quantity demanded is a constant.

(OPEC) increased the world price of oil by 400 percent. In the short run, which lasted several years, the demand for oil was very inelastic. In the long run, however, the high price of oil led to significant adjustments such as the use of smaller and more fuel-efficient cars, more efficient home heating, and alternative fuel sources. The same general principle applies whenever consumers or firms adjust their buying habits in response to a price change.

> **The response to a price change, and thus the measured price elasticity of demand, will tend to be greater the longer the time span.**

For products for which substitutes only develop over time, it is helpful to identify two kinds of demand curves. A *short-run demand curve* shows the immediate response of quantity demanded to a change in price. The *long-run demand curve* shows the response of quantity demanded to a change in price after enough time has passed to develop or switch to substitute products.

Figure 4-4 shows the short-run and long-run effects of an increase in supply. In the short run, the supply increase leads to a movement down the relatively inelastic short-run demand curve; it thus causes a large fall in price but only a small increase in quantity. In the long run, demand is more elastic; thus long-run equilibrium has price and quantity above those that prevailed in short-run equilibrium.

FIGURE 4-4 Short-Run and Long-Run Equilibrium Following an Increase in Supply

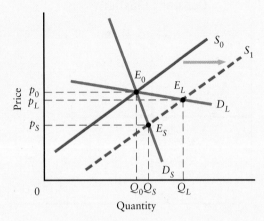

The magnitude of the changes in the equilibrium price and quantity following a shift in supply depends on the time allowed for demand to adjust. The initial equilibrium is at E_0, with price p_0 and quantity Q_0. Supply then increases and the supply curve shifts from S_0 to S_1.

Immediately following the increase in supply, the relevant demand curve is the short-run curve D_S, and the new equilibrium immediately following the supply shock is E_S. Price falls sharply to p_S, and quantity rises only to Q_S. In the long run, the demand curve is the more elastic one given by D_L, and equilibrium is at E_L. The long-run equilibrium price is p_L (greater than p_S), and quantity is Q_L (greater than Q_S).

The terminology for elasticity and the interpretation of various elasticity values is difficult at the beginning, but the more you work with the concept the easier it gets. Readers are referred to the Study Exercises at the end of this chapter for practice. Table 4-4 offers a summary of the terminology for price elasticity of demand.

Elasticity and Total Expenditure

We know that quantity demanded increases as price falls, but what happens to the total expenditure on that product? It turns out that the response of total expenditure depends on the price elasticity of demand.

TABLE 4-4 Summary of Price Elasticity of Demand (η)

Numerical Measure (absolute value)	What We Call It	What It Means
$\eta = 0$	perfectly inelastic	Quantity demanded does not change as the price changes. Demand curve is vertical.
$0 < \eta < 1$	inelastic	The percentage change in quantity demanded is smaller than the percentage change in price.
$\eta = 1$	unit elastic	The percentage change in quantity demanded is equal to the percentage change in price.
$\eta > 1$	elastic	The percentage change in quantity demanded is larger than the percentage change in price.
$\eta = $ infinity	perfectly elastic	Buyers are prepared to buy all they can at the given price. Demand curve is horizontal.

To see the relationship between the elasticity of demand and total expenditure, we begin by noting that total expenditure at any point on the demand curve is equal to price times quantity:

$$\text{Total expenditure} = \text{Price} \times \text{Quantity}$$

Because price and quantity move in opposite directions along a demand curve, the change in total expenditure is ambiguous if all we know about the demand curve is that it has a negative slope. The change in total expenditure depends on the *relative* changes in the price and quantity. As an example, consider a price decline of 10 percent. If quantity demanded rises by more than 10 percent (elastic demand), then the quantity change will dominate and total expenditure will rise. In contrast, if quantity demanded increases by less than 10 percent (inelastic demand), then the price change will dominate and total expenditure will fall. If quantity demanded increases by exactly 10 percent (unit elastic demand), then the two percentage changes exactly offset each other and total expenditure will remain unchanged.

Figure 4-5 illustrates the relationship between elasticity and total expenditure; it is based on the linear demand curve in Figure 4-2. Total expenditure at each of a number of points on the demand curve is calculated in the table, and the general relationship

FIGURE 4-5   Total Expenditure and Quantity Demanded

Price ($)	Quantity Demanded	Expenditure ($)
12	0	0
10	10	100
8	20	160
6	30	180
4	40	160
2	50	100
0	60	0

The change in total expenditure on a product in response to a change in price depends on the elasticity of demand. The table and graph are based on the demand curve shown in Figure 4-2. For quantities demanded that are less than 30, elasticity of demand is greater than 1, and hence any increase in quantity demanded will be proportionately larger than the fall in price that caused it. In that range, total expenditure increases as price falls. For quantities greater than 30, elasticity of demand is less than 1, and hence any increase in quantity demanded will be proportionately smaller than the fall in price that caused it. In that range, total expenditure decreases as price falls. The maximum of total expenditure occurs where the elasticity of demand equals 1.

between total expenditure and quantity demanded is shown by the plotted curve. In the figure we see that expenditure reaches its maximum when elasticity is equal to 1. [8]

The world wheat market provides a good example of the relationship between elasticity and total expenditure. This market is strongly influenced by weather conditions in the major wheat-producing countries. If one major wheat-producing country, like Russia, suffers a significant failure in its wheat crop, the world supply curve for wheat shifts to the left and the equilibrium world price rises. Because the world demand for wheat is inelastic, the world's total expenditure on wheat will rise. In this case, even though many individual Russian wheat producers will be worse off because their crop failed, the total income of the *world's* wheat producers will increase. One other observation is relevant: Wheat producers in other countries, like Canada, benefit by selling their (unchanged) crop at a higher world price. And the less elastic the world demand for wheat, the more the price will rise as a result of the Russian crop failure, and thus the *more* Canadian wheat farmers will benefit.

4.2 PRICE ELASTICITY OF SUPPLY

price elasticity of supply (η_s)
A measure of the responsiveness of quantity supplied to a change in the product's own price.

The concept of elasticity can be applied to supply as well as to demand. **Price elasticity of supply** measures the responsiveness of the quantity supplied to a change in the product's price. It is denoted η_S and defined as follows:

$$\eta_S = \frac{\text{Percentage change in quantity supplied}}{\text{Percentage change in price}}$$

This is often called *supply elasticity*. The supply curves considered in this chapter all have positive slopes: An increase in price causes an increase in quantity supplied. Such supply curves all have positive elasticities because price and quantity change in the same direction.

Figure 4-6 shows a simple linear supply curve to illustrate the measurement of supply elasticity. Between points A and B, the change in price is $1.50 and the average price is $4.25. Between the same two points, the change in quantity supplied is 20 units and the average quantity is 40 units. The value of supply elasticity between points A and B is therefore

$$\eta_S = \frac{\Delta Q/\overline{Q}}{\Delta p/\overline{p}} = \frac{20/40}{1.50/4.25} = \frac{0.5}{0.353} = 1.42$$

As was the case with demand, care must be taken when computing supply elasticity. Keep in mind that even though the supply curve may have a constant slope, the measure of supply elasticity may be different at different places on the curve. When $\eta_S > 1$, supply is said to be elastic; when $\eta_S < 1$, supply is said to be inelastic.

Some important special cases need to be noted. If the supply curve is vertical—the quantity supplied does not change as price changes—then elasticity of supply is zero. A horizontal supply curve has

FIGURE 4-6 Computing Price Elasticity of Supply

Supply elasticity is computed using average price and average quantity supplied. Between points A and B, the elasticity of supply is 1.42. The same approach shown here can be used to compute elasticity between any two points on the supply curve.

an infinite elasticity of supply: There is one critical price at which output is supplied but where a small drop in price will reduce the quantity that producers are willing to supply from an indefinitely large amount to zero. Between these two extremes, elasticity of supply varies with the shape of the supply curve.[1]

Determinants of Supply Elasticity

Because much of the treatment of demand elasticity carries over to supply elasticity, we can cover the main points quickly.

Ease of Substitution   The ease of substitution can vary in production as well as in consumption. If the price of a product rises, how much more can be produced profitably? This depends in part on how easy it is for producers to shift from the production of other products to the one whose price has risen. If agricultural land and labour can be readily shifted from wheat to canola, for example, the supply of each crop will be more elastic than if they cannot. Or if a factory that produces snowmobiles can easily be refitted to produce Jet Skis, then the supply of each product will be more elastic than if the factory and equipment could not be easily modified. We will see in Chapter 7 that the ease of substitution in production is closely related to the firm's technology and influences its cost structure.

Short Run and Long Run   As with demand, length of time for response is important. It may be difficult to change quantity supplied in response to a price increase in a matter of weeks or months but easy to do so over years. An obvious example relates to oil production. New oil fields can be discovered, wells drilled, and pipelines built over years but not in a few months. Thus, the elasticity of oil supply is much greater over five years than over one year.

As with demand, it is useful to make the distinction between the short-run and the long-run supply curves. The *short-run supply curve* shows the immediate response of quantity supplied to a change in price given producers' current capacity to produce the good. The *long-run supply curve* shows the response of quantity supplied to a change in price after enough time has passed to allow producers to adjust their productive capacity.

> The long-run supply for a product is more elastic than the short-run supply.

Figure 4-7 illustrates the short-run and long-run effects of an increase in demand. The immediate effect of

---

[1] Here is another special case that is often puzzling at first glance. Consider a linear supply curve that begins at the origin. It is easy to show that the elasticity of supply along such a curve is always 1—no matter how steep the supply curve is! See Study Exercise #10 at the end of this chapter to explore this further.

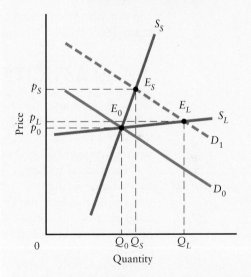

FIGURE 4-7   Short-Run and Long-Run Equilibrium Following an Increase in Demand

The size of the changes in the equilibrium price and quantity following a shift in demand depends on the time frame of the analysis. The initial equilibrium is at E_0, with price p_0 and quantity Q_0. Demand then increases from D_0 to D_1.

Immediately following the demand shift, the relevant supply curve is the short-run curve S_S, so that the new equilibrium immediately following the demand shock is at E_S. Price rises sharply to p_S, and quantity rises only to Q_S. In the long run, the supply curve is the more elastic one given by S_L. The long-run equilibrium is at E_L; price is p_L (less than p_S) and quantity is Q_L (greater than Q_S).

TABLE 4-5   Summary of Price Elasticity of Supply (η_S)

Numerical Measure	What We Call It	What It Means
$\eta_S = 0$	perfectly inelastic	Quantity supplied does not change as the price changes. Supply curve is vertical.
$0 < \eta_S < 1$	inelastic	The percentage change in quantity supplied is smaller than the percentage change in price.
$\eta_S > 1$	elastic	The percentage change in quantity supplied is larger than the percentage change in price.
$\eta_S = $ infinity	perfectly elastic	Sellers are prepared to sell all they can at the given price. Supply curve is horizontal.

the shift in demand is a sharp increase in price and only a modest increase in quantity. The inability of firms to change their output in the short run in response to the increase in demand means that the market-clearing response is mostly an increase in price. Over time, however, as firms are more able to increase production, the consequences of the demand shift fall more on quantity and less on price.

As with demand, the terminology for supply elasticity becomes clearer with time and practice. See the Study Exercises at the end of this chapter to work through several examples. Table 4-5 summarizes the terminology for price elasticity of supply.

4.3 ELASTICITY MATTERS FOR EXCISE TAXES

We have spent much time examining price elasticity (of both demand and supply) and how to measure it. But why should we care about this? In this section, we explore the important concept of *tax incidence* and show that elasticity is crucial to determining whether consumers or producers (or both) end up bearing the burden of excise taxes.

The federal and provincial governments in Canada levy special sales taxes called **excise taxes** on many goods, such as cigarettes, alcohol, and gasoline. At the point of sale of the product, the sellers collect the tax on behalf of the government and then remit the tax collections. When the sellers write their cheques to the government, these firms feel that they are the ones paying the whole tax. Consumers, however, argue that *they* are the ones shouldering the burden of the tax because the tax causes the price of the product to rise. Who actually bears the burden of the tax?

The question of who *bears the burden* of a tax is called the question of **tax incidence**. A straightforward application of demand-and-supply analysis will show that tax incidence has nothing to do with whether the government collects the tax directly from consumers or from firms.

excise tax A tax on the sale of a particular product.

tax incidence The location of the burden of a tax—that is, the identity of the ultimate bearer of the tax.

> **The burden of an excise tax is distributed between consumers and sellers in a manner that depends on the relative elasticities of supply and demand.**

Let's consider a case where the government imposes an excise tax on gasoline. The analysis begins in Figure 4-8. To simplify the problem, we analyze the case where there is initially no tax. The equilibrium without taxes is illustrated by the solid supply and demand curves. What happens when a tax of *t* cents per litre of gasoline is introduced?

With an excise tax, the price paid by the consumer, called the *consumer price,* and the price ultimately received by the seller, called the *seller price,* must differ by the amount of the tax, *t*.

In terms of the figure, we can analyze the effect of the tax by considering a new supply curve S' that is above the original supply curve S by the amount of the tax, *t*. This reduction in supply, caused by the imposition of the excise tax, will cause a movement *along* the demand curve, reducing the equilibrium quantity. At this new equilibrium, E_1, the consumer price rises to p_c (greater than p_0), the seller price falls to p_s (less than p_0), and the equilibrium quantity falls to Q_1. Notice that the difference between the consumer price and the seller price is exactly the amount of the excise tax, *t*.

Note also that the quantity demanded *at the consumer price* is equal to the quantity supplied *at the seller price,* a condition that is required for equilibrium. As shown in the figure, compared with the original equilibrium, the consumer price is higher and the seller price is lower, although in each case the change in price is less than the full extent of the excise tax. The difference between p_0 and p_c is the amount of the tax that the consumer ends up paying; the difference between p_0 and p_s is the amount of the tax the seller ends up paying. The burden of the excise tax is shared between consumers and sellers in proportion to the rise in price to consumers relative to the fall in price received by sellers.

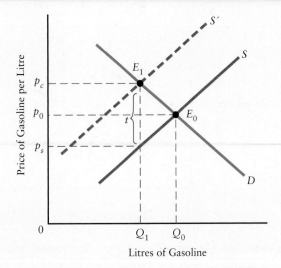

FIGURE 4-8   The Effect of a Gasoline Excise Tax

The burden of an excise tax is shared by consumers and producers. The original supply and demand curves for gasoline are given by the solid lines S and D; equilibrium is at E_0 with price p_0 and quantity Q_0. When an excise tax of *t* per litre is imposed, the supply curve shifts up to the dashed line S', which lies above the original supply curve by the amount of the tax, *t*. The new equilibrium is at E_1. The tax increases the consumer price but by less than the full amount of the tax, and reduces the seller price, also by less than the full amount of the tax. The tax also reduces the equilibrium quantity exchanged.

> After the imposition of an excise tax, the difference between the consumer and seller prices is equal to the tax. In the new equilibrium, the quantity exchanged is less than what occured without the tax.

The role of the relative elasticities of supply and demand in determining the incidence of the excise tax is illustrated in Figure 4-9. In part (i), demand is inelastic relative to supply; as a result, the fall in quantity is quite small, whereas the price paid by consumers rises by almost the full extent of the tax. Because neither the price received by sellers nor the quantity sold changes very much, sellers bear little of the burden of the tax. In part (ii), supply is inelastic relative to demand; in this case, consumers can more easily substitute away from gasoline. There is little change in the price, and hence they bear little of the burden of the tax, which falls mostly on suppliers. Notice in Figure 4-9 that the size of the upward shift in supply is the same in the two cases, indicating the same tax in both cases.

> When demand is inelastic relative to supply, consumers bear most of the burden of excise taxes. When supply is inelastic relative to demand, producers bear most of the burden.

FIGURE 4-9   Elasticity and the Incidence of an Excise Tax

(i) Inelastic demand, elastic supply

(ii) Inelastic supply, elastic demand

The distribution of the burden of an excise tax between consumers and producers depends on the relative elasticities of supply and demand. In both parts of the figure, the initial supply and demand curves are given by S and D; the initial equilibrium is at E_0 with equilibrium price p_0 and quantity Q_0. A tax of t cents per litre of gasoline is imposed, causing the supply curve to shift up by the amount of the tax to S'. The new equilibrium is at E_1. The consumer price rises to p_c, the seller price falls to p_s, and the quantity falls to Q_1. Sellers bear little of the burden of the tax in the first case (and consumers bear a lot), whereas consumers bear little of the burden in the second case (and sellers bear a lot).

So, who *really* pays for increases in a gasoline tax? The demand for gasoline is inelastic in the short run, both overall and relative to supply. The result is that consumers bear most of the burden of gasoline taxes. Over time, however, as consumers adapt their behaviour and use more substitutes, the demand for gasoline is more elastic. Over time, therefore, more of the burden of a gasoline tax falls on producers.

4.4 OTHER DEMAND ELASTICITIES

The price of the product is not the only important variable determining the quantity demanded for that product. Changes in income and changes in the prices of other products also lead to changes in quantity demanded, and elasticity is a useful concept in measuring their effects.

Income Elasticity of Demand

Income elasticity of demand (η_Y) A measure of the responsiveness of quantity demanded to a change in income.

An important determinant of demand is the income of the customers. The responsiveness of demand to changes in income is termed the **income elasticity of demand** and is symbolized η_Y.

$$\eta_Y = \frac{\text{Percentage change in quantity demanded}}{\text{Percentage change in income}}$$

normal good A good for which quantity demanded rises as income rises—its income elasticity is positive.

For most goods, increases in income lead to increases in demand—their income elasticity is positive. These are called **normal goods**. Goods for which demand decreases in response to a rise in income have negative income elasticities and are called **inferior goods.**

Inferior good A good for which quantity demanded falls as income rises—its income elasticity is negative.

Normal Goods   The income elasticity of normal goods can be greater than 1 (elastic) or less than 1 (inelastic), depending on whether the percentage change in quantity demanded is greater or less than the percentage change in income that brought it about.

Income Inelastic.   If income elasticity is positive but less than one, we say the demand for this good is *income inelastic*. Suppose average annual income in Canada rises from $47 500 to $52 500, an increase (calculated at the average value of $50,000) of 10 percent. Suppose also that this increase in income leads to an increase in quantity demanded of snow shovels, from 784 000 to 816 000, an increase (calculated at the average value of 800 000) of 4 percent. The income elasticity of demand for snow shovels is therefore

$$\eta_Y = \frac{4\%}{10\%} = 0.4$$

Income Elastic.   If income elasticity is positive and greater than one, we say the demand for this good is *income elastic*. Suppose the same 10 percent increase in average income leads to an increase in the quantity demanded of snowboards from 510 000 to 690 000, an increase (calculated at the average value of 600 000) of 30 percent. The income elasticity of demand for snowboards is therefore

$$\eta_Y = \frac{30\%}{10\%} = 3$$

Luxuries Versus Necessities.   Empirical studies find that basic food items—such as vegetables, bread, and cereals—usually have positive income elasticities less than 1 (so an increase in income of 10 percent leads to an increase in quantity demanded of less than 10 percent). Such goods are often called **necessities.** In contrast, more expensive foods—such as prime cuts of meat, prepared meals, and wine—usually have positive income elasticities greater than 1 (so an increase in income of 10 percent leads to an increase in quantity demanded of more than 10 percent). These products are often called **luxuries.**

necessities Products for which the income elasticity of demand is positive but less than 1.

luxuries Products for which the income elasticity of demand is positive and greater than 1.

> **The more necessary an item is in the consumption pattern of consumers, the lower is its income elasticity.**

Income elasticities for any one product also vary with the level of a consumer's income. When incomes are low, consumers may eat almost no green vegetables and consume lots of starchy foods, such as bread and pasta; when incomes are higher, they may eat cheap cuts of meat and more green vegetables along with their bread and pasta; when incomes are higher still, they are likely to eat higher-quality and prepared foods of a wide variety.

Inferior Goods   Notice that both necessities and luxuries have positive income elasticities and thus are *normal* goods. In contrast, *inferior* goods have a negative income elasticity because an increase in income actually leads to a *reduction* in quantity demanded. An example of an inferior good for some consumers might be ground beef or packages of instant noodles; as consumers' incomes rise, they reduce their demand for these products and consume more of higher-quality items.

LESSONS FROM HISTORY 4-1

Economic Development and Income Elasticities

How the demand for goods and services reacts to changes in income has important economic effects. In most Western countries during the twentieth century, economic growth caused the level of income to double every 20 to 30 years. This rise in income was shared to some extent by almost all citizens. As they found their incomes increasing, they increased their demands for most products. In the first part of that century, however, the demands for some products (such as food and basic clothing) were income-inelastic, whereas the demands for durable goods (such as cars and TVs) were income-elastic. As a result, the demand for food and clothing grew less rapidly than did the demand for cars and TVs. Later in the century, as incomes rose still further, the income elasticity of demand for manufactured durables fell while that for services (such as restaurant meals and entertainment) increased. During this period the ongoing income growth led the demand for services to grow more rapidly than the demand for durable goods.

In some developing countries, where per capita incomes today are close to those of the Western nations at the beginning of the twentieth century, it is the demands for durable manufactured goods that are increasing most rapidly as income rises. In future years (assuming that the current growth of income continues), these same countries will likely experience the same shift in demand toward services that was experienced by the Western countries in the last part of the twentieth century.

The uneven impact of the growth of income on the demands for different products has important effects on the pattern of employment. For example, in Western countries, employment in agriculture fell during the first part of the twentieth century, while employment in manufacturing rose. In the last half of the century, employment in manufacturing fell gradually whereas employment in services increased rapidly (and employment in agriculture continued its gradual decline). We will see many other consequences of these demand shifts later in this book.

Note, however, that it is generally easier to find examples of inferior goods for an individual than it is for the market as a whole. With any given individual, it is relatively easy to determine which products they consume less of as their income rises. Once we aggregate all consumers into a market, however, and the unusual behaviour of some consumers offsets those of others, we tend to find that the demand for most products is normal. Increases in average income lead to increases in the market demand for most products.

Historically, as a nation's income grows, demand for various goods and services changes depending on the associated income elasticities. See *Lessons from History* 4-1 for a brief discussion of this point.

Cross Elasticity of Demand

The responsiveness of quantity demanded to changes in the price of *another* product is called the **cross elasticity of demand**. It is denoted η_{XY} and defined as follows:

cross elasticity of demand (η_{XY}) A measure of the responsiveness of the quantity of one product demanded to changes in the price of another product.

$$\eta_{XY} = \frac{\text{Percentage change in quantity demanded of good } X}{\text{Percentage change in price of good } Y}$$

The change in the price of good Y causes the *demand curve* for good X to shift. If X and Y are substitutes, an increase in the price of Y leads to an increase in the demand for X. If X and Y are complements, an increase in the price of Y leads to a reduction in demand for X. In either case, we are holding the price of X constant. We therefore measure the change in the quantity demanded of X (at its unchanged price) by measuring the shift of the demand curve for X.

Cross elasticity can vary from minus infinity to plus infinity. Complementary products, such as cars and gasoline, have negative cross elasticities. A rise in the price of gasoline will lead to a decline in the demand for cars, as some people decide to do without a car and others decide not to buy an additional car. Substitute products, such as cars and public transport, have positive cross elasticities. A rise in the price of cars will lead to a rise in the demand for public transport as some people shift from cars to public transport.

The positive or negative signs of cross elasticities tell us whether goods are substitutes or complements.

Measures of cross elasticity sometimes prove helpful in defining whether producers of similar products are in competition with each other. For example, glass bottles and aluminum cans have a high cross elasticity of demand. The producer of bottles is thus in competition with the producer of cans. If the bottle company raises its price, it will lose substantial sales to the can producer. In contrast, men's shoes and women's shoes have a low cross elasticity, and thus a producer of men's shoes is not in close competition with a producer of women's shoes. If the former raises its price, it will not lose many sales to the latter. Knowledge of cross elasticity can be important in matters of *competition policy,* in which the issue is whether a firm in one industry is or is not competing with firms in another industry. We discuss competition policy in more detail in Chapter 12.

Income elasticity and cross elasticity are also concepts that become clearer with practice. See the Study Exercises at the end of this chapter to work through some examples. Table 4-6 offers a brief summary of the concepts.

TABLE 4-6   Summary of Income Elasticity of Demand (η_Y)

Numerical Measure	What We Call It	What It Means
$\eta_Y < 0$	inferior good	An increase in income leads to a reduction in quantity demanded.
$0 < \eta_Y < 1$	normal good (income in elastic) —necessity	The percentage change in quantity demanded is smaller than the percentage change in income.
$\eta_Y > 1$	normal good (income elastic) —luxury	The percentage change in quantity demanded is larger than the percentage change in income.

Summary of Cross Elasticity of Demand (η_{XY})

Numerical Measure	What We Call It	What It Means
$\eta_{XY} < 0$	complements	When the price of one good rises, the quantity demanded of the other good falls.
$\eta_{XY} > 0$	substitutes	When the price of one good rises, the quantity demanded of the other good increases.

SUMMARY

4.1 PRICE ELASTICITY OF DEMAND

- Price elasticity of demand is a measure of the extent to which the quantity demanded of a product responds to a change in its price. Represented by the symbol η, it is defined as

$$\eta = \frac{\text{Percentage change in quantity demanded}}{\text{Percentage change in price}}$$

- The percentage changes are usually calculated as the change divided by the average value. Elasticity is defined to be a positive number, and it can vary from zero to infinity.
- When elasticity is less than 1, demand is inelastic—the percentage change in quantity demanded is less than the percentage change in price. When elasticity exceeds 1, demand is elastic—the percentage change in quantity demanded is greater than the percentage change in price.
- The main determinant of demand elasticity is the availability of substitutes for the product. Any one of a group of close substitutes will have a more elastic demand than will the group as a whole.
- Items that have few substitutes in the short run tend to develop many substitutes when consumers and producers have time to adapt. Therefore, demand is more elastic in the long run than in the short run.
- Elasticity and total expenditure are related. If elasticity is less than 1, total expenditure is positively related with price. If elasticity is greater than 1, total expenditure is negatively related with price. If elasticity is 1, total expenditure does not change as price changes.

4.2 PRICE ELASTICITY OF SUPPLY

- Elasticity of supply measures the extent to which the quantity supplied of some product changes when the price of that product changes. Represented by the symbol η_S, it is defined as

$$\eta_S = \frac{\text{Percentage change in quantity supplied}}{\text{Percentage change in price}}$$

- Supply tends to be more elastic in the long run than in the short run because it usually takes time for producers to alter their output in response to price changes.

4.3 ELASTICITY MATTERS FOR EXCISE TAXES

- The distribution of the burden of an excise tax between consumers and producers depends on the relative elasticities of supply and demand for the product.
- The less elastic demand is relative to supply, the more of the burden of an excise tax falls on the consumers.

The more elastic demand is relative to supply, the more of the burden of an excise tax falls on producers.

4.4 OTHER DEMAND ELASTICITIES

- Income elasticity of demand is a measure of the extent to which the quantity demanded of some product changes as income changes. Represented by the symbol η_Y, it is defined as

$$\eta_Y = \frac{\text{Percentage change in quantity demanded}}{\text{Percentage change in income}}$$

- Normal goods have a positive income elasticity; inferior goods have a negative income elasticity.

- Cross elasticity of demand is a measure of the extent to which the quantity demanded of one product changes when the price of a different product changes. Represented by the symbol η_{XY}, it is defined as

$$\eta_{XY} = \frac{\text{Percentage change in quantity demanded of good } X}{\text{Percentage change in price of good } Y}$$

- It is used to define products that are substitutes for one another (positive cross elasticity) and products that are complements for one another (negative cross elasticity).

KEY CONCEPTS

Price elasticity of demand
Inelastic and perfectly inelastic
  demand
Elastic and perfectly elastic demand
Relationship between demand elasti-
  city and total expenditure

Elasticity of supply
Short-run and long-run responses to
  shifts in demand and supply
The burden of an excise tax
Consumer price and seller price
Income elasticity of demand

Normal goods and inferior goods
Luxuries and necessities
Cross elasticity of demand
Substitutes and complements

STUDY EXERCISES

MyEconLab Make the grade with MyEconLab: Study Exercises marked in ⊕ can be found on MyEconLab. You can practise them as often as you want, and most feature step-by-step guided instructions to help you find the right answer.

① Fill in the blanks to make the following statements correct.

  a. When a 10 percent change in the price of a good brings about a 20 percent change in its quantity demanded, we calculate the price elasticity of demand to be _____. We can say that demand for this good is _____.

  b. When a 10 percent change in the price of a good brings about a 4 percent change in its quantity demanded, we calculate the price elasticity of demand to be _____. We can say that demand for this good is _____.

  c. When a 10 percent change in the price of a good brings about a 10 percent change in its quantity demanded, we calculate the price elasticity of demand to be _____. We can say that demand for this good is _____.

② A hypothetical demand schedule for comic books in a small town is provided below.

Price	Quantity Demanded	Total Expen-diture	Percent Change in Price	Percent Change in Quantity Demanded	Elastic-ity of Demand
$11	1	_____			
9	3	_____	_____	_____	_____
7	5	_____	_____	_____	_____
5	7	_____	_____	_____	_____
3	9	_____	_____	_____	_____
1	11	_____	_____	_____	_____

  a. Fill in the table and calculate the price elasticity of demand over each price range. Be sure to use average prices and quantities when computing the percentage changes.

  b. Plot the demand curve and show the elasticities over the different ranges of the curve.

  c. Explain why demand is more elastic at the higher prices.

③ Suppose the market for frozen orange juice is in equilibrium at a price of $2.00 per can and a quantity of 4200 cans per month. Now suppose that at a price of $3.00 per can, quantity demanded falls to 3000 cans per month and quantity supplied increases to 4500 cans per month.

  a. Draw the appropriate diagram for this market.

  b. Calculate the price elasticity of demand for frozen orange juice between the prices of $2.00 and $3.00. Is the demand elastic or inelastic?

  c. Calculate the elasticity of supply for frozen orange juice between the prices of $2.00 and $3.00. Is the supply elastic or inelastic?

  d. Explain in general what factors would affect the elasticity of demand for frozen orange juice.

  e. Explain in general what factors would affect the elasticity of supply of frozen orange juice.

④ From the following quotations, what, if anything, can you conclude about elasticity of demand?

  a. "Good weather resulted in record wheat harvests and sent wheat prices tumbling. The result has been disastrous for many wheat farmers."

  b. "Ridership always went up when bus fares came down, but the increased patronage never was enough to prevent a decrease in overall revenue."

c. "As the price of cell phones fell, producers found their revenues soaring."

d. "Coffee to me is an essential good—I've just gotta have it no matter what the price."

e. "The soaring price of condominiums does little to curb the strong demand in Vancouver."

5 Suppose you are advising an industry association on the predicted effects of a price change on quantity demanded and total expenditure on their product. The current price is $1.00 per unit, and quantity demanded is 2500 units per day. Based on extensive empirical studies, you know that price elasticity of demand for the product is 0.5. If the price increases to $2.00 per unit, what is the predicted percentage change in quantity demanded? Will total expenditure increase or decrease?

6 What would you predict about the relative price elasticity of demand for each of the following items? Explain your reasoning.

a. food
b. vegetables
c. leafy vegetables
d. leafy vegetables sold at your local supermarket
e. leafy vegetables sold at your local supermarket on Wednesdays

7 Suppose a stamp dealer buys the only two existing copies of a stamp at an auction. After the purchase, the dealer goes to the front of the room and burns one of the stamps in front of the shocked audience. What must the dealer believe in order for this to be a wealth-maximizing action? Explain with a demand-and-supply diagram.

8 For each of the following events, state the relevant elasticity concept. Then compute the measure of elasticity, using average prices and quantities in your calculations. In all cases, assume that these are *ceteris paribus* changes.

a. When the price of movie tickets is reduced from $14.00 to $11.00, ticket sales increase from 1200 to 1350.

b. As average household income in Canada increases by 10 percent, annual sales of BMWs increase from 56 000 to 67 000.

c. After a major failure of Brazil's coffee crop sent coffee prices up from $3.00 per kilogram to $4.80 per kilogram, sales of tea in Canada increased from 7500 kg per month to 8000 kg per month.

d. An increase in the world demand for pulp (used in producing newsprint) increases the price by 14 percent. Annual Canadian production increases from 8 million tonnes to 11 million tonnes.

e. Marta increases her purchases of organic fruits and vegetables from 40 kilos per year to 80 kilos per year as her income rises from $60 000 to $69 000 per year.

f. When private school tuition fees increased from an average of $17 500 per year to $22 500 per year, schools recorded a drop in annual enrolment from 12 000 students to 8000 students.

9 The following table shows the demand schedule for PlayStation video games.

	Price (per unit)	Quantity Demanded (per year)	Total Expenditure
A	$30	400 000	_____
B	35	380 000	_____
C	40	350 000	_____
D	45	320 000	_____
E	50	300 000	_____
F	55	260 000	_____
G	60	230 000	_____
H	65	190 000	_____

a. Compute total expenditure for each row in the table.

b. Plot the demand curve and the total expenditure curve.

c. Compute the price elasticities of demand between points A and B, B and C, C and D, and so on.

d. Over what range of prices is the demand for video games elastic? Explain.

e. Over what range of prices is the demand for video games inelastic? Explain.

10 Consider the following straight-line supply curves. In each case, p is the price (measured in dollars per unit) and Q^S is the quantity supplied of the product (measured in thousands of units per month).

i) $p = 2Q^S$
ii) $p = 4Q^S$
iii) $p = 5Q^S$
iv) $p = 10Q^S$

a. Plot each supply curve on a scale diagram. In each case, plot point A (which corresponds to price equal to $20) and point B (which corresponds to price equal to $40).

b. For each supply curve, compute the price elasticity of supply between points A and B.

c. Explain why the slope of a supply curve is not the same as the elasticity of supply.

⑪ This is a challenging question intended for those students who like mathematics. It will help you work through the issue of tax incidence. Consider the market for gasoline. Suppose the market demand and supply curves are as given below. In each case, quantity refers to millions of litres of gasoline per month; price is the price per litre (in cents).

$$\text{Demand: } p = 80 - 5Q^D$$

$$\text{Supply: } p = 24 + 2Q^S$$

a. Plot the demand and supply curves on a scale diagram.
b. Compute the equilibrium price and quantity.
c. Now suppose the government imposes a tax of 14 cents per litre. Show how this affects the market equilibrium. What is the new "consumer price" and what is the new "producer price"?
d. Compute the total revenue raised by the gasoline tax. What share of this tax revenue is "paid" by consumers, and what share is "paid" by producers?

(Hint: If the consumer price were unchanged from the pre-tax equilibrium, we would say that consumers pay none of the tax.)

⑫ Suppose a local government votes to impose an excise tax of $1.00 per bottle on the sales of bottled water. (Assume that all bottles are identical and residents cannot shop elsewhere.) Before the tax, the equilibrium price and quantity are $1.00 and 2000 bottles per day. After the tax is imposed, market equilibrium adjusts to a price of $1.80 and a quantity of 1400 bottles per day.

a. Draw the supply and demand diagram before and after the excise tax is imposed.
b. How much revenue from the tax does the local government collect each day?
c. After imposition of the tax, what is the after-tax price received by the sellers? What is the total after-tax revenue received per day by the sellers?
d. Who bears most of the burden of this excise tax, and why?

5 Price Controls and Market Efficiency

CHAPTER OUTLINE	LEARNING OBJECTIVES (LO)
	After studying this chapter, you will be able to
5.1 GOVERNMENT-CONTROLLED PRICES	1 describe how the presence of legislated price ceilings and price floors affect equilibrium price and quantity.
5.2 RENT CONTROLS: A CASE STUDY OF PRICE CEILINGS	2 compare the short-run and long-run effects of legislated rent controls.
5.3 AN INTRODUCTION TO MARKET EFFICIENCY	3 describe the relationship between economic surplus and the efficiency of a market.
	4 explain why government interventions that cause prices to deviate from their market-clearing levels tend to be inefficient for society as a whole.

OVER the past two chapters, we have developed the model of demand and supply that you can now use to analyze individual markets. A full understanding of the basic theory, however, comes only with practice. This chapter will provide some practice by analyzing several examples, including minimum wages, rent controls, and output quotas. These are all examples of government policies that control either the price or quantity traded in a given market. We will see how these types of controls affect both consumers and producers.

An important economic concept that we will study in more detail in later chapters is the "efficiency" of markets. We will introduce this concept in this chapter and see what it means to maximize "economic surplus" for society as a whole. Finally, we will look at how government policies that intervene in markets can influence the efficiency of those markets.

5.1 GOVERNMENT-CONTROLLED PRICES

In a number of important cases, governments control the price at which a product must be bought and sold in the domestic market. Here we examine the general consequences of such policies. Later, we look at some specific examples.

In a free market the equilibrium price equates the quantity demanded with the quantity supplied. Government *price controls* are policies that attempt to hold the price at some *disequilibrium* value. Some controls hold the market price below its equilibrium value, thus creating a shortage at the controlled price. Other controls hold price above its equilibrium value, thus creating a surplus at the controlled price.

Disequilibrium Prices

When controls hold the price at some disequilibrium value, what determines the quantity *actually traded* on the market? This is not a question we have to ask when examining a free market because the price adjusts to equate quantity demanded with quantity supplied. But this adjustment cannot take place if the government is controlling the price. So, in this case, what determines the quantity actually exchanged?

The key to the answer is the fact that any *voluntary* market transaction requires both a willing buyer and a willing seller. So, if quantity demanded is less than quantity supplied, demand will determine the amount actually exchanged, while the rest of the quantity supplied will remain in the hands of the unsuccessful sellers. Conversely, if quantity demanded exceeds quantity supplied, supply will determine the amount actually exchanged, while the rest of the quantity demanded will represent unsatisfied demand of would-be buyers. Figure 5-1 illustrates the general conclusion:

> At any disequilibrium price, quantity exchanged is determined by the *lesser* of quantity demanded or quantity supplied.

Price Floors

Governments sometimes establish a *price floor*, which is the minimum permissible price that can be charged for a particular good or service. A price floor that is set at or below the equilibrium price has no effect because the free-market equilibrium remains attainable. If, however, the price floor is set above the equilibrium, it will raise the price, in which case it is said to be *binding*.

Price floors may be established by rules that make it illegal to sell the product below the prescribed price, as in the case of a legislated minimum wage. Or the government may establish a price floor by announcing that it will guarantee a certain price by buying any excess supply. Such guarantees are a feature of many agricultural income-support policies.

FIGURE 5-1 The Determination of Quantity Exchanged in Disequilibrium

In disequilibrium, quantity exchanged is determined by the lesser of quantity demanded and quantity supplied. At E, the market is in equilibrium, with quantity demanded equal to quantity supplied. For any price below p_0, the quantity exchanged will be determined by the supply curve. For any price above p_0, the quantity exchanged will be determined by the demand curve. Thus, the solid portions of the S and D curves show the actual quantities exchanged at different disequilibrium prices.

FIGURE 5-2   A Binding Price Floor

A binding price floor leads to excess supply. The free-market equilibrium is at E, with price p_0 and quantity Q_0. The government now establishes a binding price floor at p_1. Actual quantity exchanged is then Q_1, and there is excess supply equal to Q_1Q_2.

The effects of a binding price floor are illustrated in Figure 5-2, which establishes the following key result:

> **Binding price floors lead to excess supply.** Either an unsold surplus will exist, or someone (usually the government) must enter the market and buy the excess supply.

The consequences of excess supply differ from product to product. If the product is labour, subject to a minimum wage, excess supply translates into people without jobs (unemployment). If the product is wheat, and more is produced than can be sold to consumers, the surplus wheat will accumulate in grain elevators or government warehouses. These consequences may or may not be worthwhile in terms of the other goals achieved. But worthwhile or not, these consequences are inevitable in a competitive market whenever a price floor is set above the market-clearing equilibrium price.

Why might the government want to incur these consequences? One reason is that the people who succeed in selling their products at the price floor are better off than if they had to accept the lower equilibrium price. Workers and farmers are among the politically active, organized groups who have gained much by persuading governments to establish price floors enabling them to sell their goods or services at prices above free-market levels. If the demand is inelastic, as it often is for agricultural products, producers earn more income in total (even though they sell fewer units of the product). The losses are spread across the large and diverse set of consumers, each of whom suffers only a small loss.

Applying Economic Concepts 5-1 examines the case of a legislated minimum wage in more detail, and explains the basis of the often-heard claim that minimum wages increase unemployment. We discuss the effects of minimum wages in greater detail in Chapter 14, when we examine various labour-market issues.

Price Ceilings

A *price ceiling* is the maximum price at which certain goods and services may be legally exchanged. Price ceilings on oil, natural gas, and rental housing have been frequently imposed by federal and provincial governments. If the price ceiling is set above the equilibrium price, it has no effect because the free-market equilibrium remains attainable. If, however, the price ceiling is set below the free-market equilibrium price, the price ceiling lowers the price and is said to be *binding*. The effects of binding price ceilings are shown in Figure 5-3, which establishes the following conclusion:

> **Binding price ceilings lead to excess demand, with the quantity exchanged being less than in the free-market equilibrium.**

Allocating a Product in Excess Demand   Free markets with flexible prices eliminate excess demand by allowing prices to rise, thereby allocating the available supply among would-be purchasers. Because this adjustment cannot happen in the presence of a binding price ceiling, some other method of allocation must be adopted. Experience suggests what we can expect.

If stores sell their available supplies on a *first-come, first-served* basis, people will rush to stores that are said to have stocks of the product. Buyers may wait hours to get into the store, only to find that supplies are exhausted before they can be served. This is why standing in lines became a way of life in the centrally planned economies of the Soviet Union and Eastern Europe, in which price controls and product shortages were pervasive.

In market economies, "first-come, first-served" is often the basis for allocating tickets to concerts and sporting events when promoters set a price at which demand exceeds the supply of available seats. In these cases, ticket "scalpers" often buy blocks of tickets and then resell them at market-clearing prices. Storekeepers (and some ticket sellers) often respond to excess demand by keeping goods "under the counter" and selling only to customers of their own choosing. When sellers decide to whom they will and will not sell their scarce supplies, allocation is said to be by **sellers' preferences.**

FIGURE 5-3   A Price Ceiling and Black-Market Pricing

A binding price ceiling causes excess demand and invites a black market. The equilibrium point, E, is at a price of p_0 and a quantity of Q_0. If a price ceiling is set at p_1, the quantity demanded will rise to Q_1 and the quantity supplied will fall to Q_2. Quantity actually exchanged will be Q_2. But if all the available supply of Q_2 were sold on a black market, the price to consumers would rise to p_2. If black marketeers buy at the ceiling price of p_1 and sell at the black-market price of p_2, their profits are represented by the shaded area.

sellers' preferences Allocation of products in excess demand by decisions of the sellers.

If the government dislikes the allocation of products by long line-ups or by sellers' preferences, it can choose to *ration* the product. To do so, it prints only enough ration coupons to match the quantity supplied at the price ceiling and then distributes the coupons to would-be purchasers, who then need both money and coupons to buy the product. The coupons may be distributed equally among the population or on the basis of some criterion, such as age, family status, or occupation. Rationing of this sort was used by Canada and many other countries during both the First and Second World Wars, when the supply of many products were reserved for military purposes.

Black Markets   Binding price ceilings usually give rise to black markets. A **black market** is any market in which transactions (which are themselves legal) take place at prices that violate a legal price control.

black market A situation in which products are sold at prices that violate a legal price control.

> **Binding price ceilings always create the potential for a black market because a profit can be made by buying at the controlled price and selling at the (illegal) black-market price.**

Figure 5-3 illustrates the extreme case, in which all the available supply is sold on a black market. We say this case is extreme because there are law-abiding people in every society and because governments ordinarily have at least *some* power to enforce their price ceilings. Although some units of a product subject to a binding price ceiling will be sold on the black market, it is unlikely that all of that product will be.

APPLYING ECONOMIC CONCEPTS 5-1

Minimum Wages and Unemployment

All Canadian governments, provincial, territorial, and federal, have legislated minimum wages. For those industries covered by provincial or territorial legislation (which includes most industries except banking, airlines, trucking, and railways), the minimum wage in 2015 ranged from a low of $10.30 per hour in the Northwest Territories to a high of $11.25 per hour in Nunavut and Ontario. This box examines the effects of implementing a minimum wage in a competitive labour market and provides a basis for understanding the often-heard claim that minimum wages lead to an increase in unemployment.

The accompanying figure shows the demand and supply curves for labour services in a fully competitive market with Employment on the horizontal axis and Hourly Wage Rate on the vertical axis. In the absence of any legislated minimum wage, the equilibrium in the labour market would be a wage equal to w_0 and a level of employment equal to E_0.

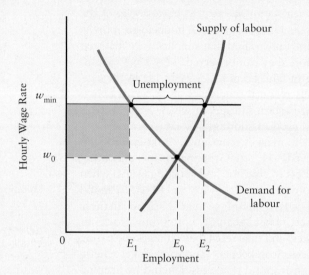

Does the existence of a black market mean that the goals sought by imposing price ceilings have been thwarted? The answer depends on what the goals are. Three common goals that governments have when imposing price ceilings are:

1. To restrict production (perhaps to release resources for other uses, such as wartime military production)

2. To keep specific prices down

3. To satisfy notions of equity in the consumption of a product that is temporarily in short supply (such as building supplies immediately following a natural disaster)

When price ceilings are accompanied by a significant black market, it is not clear that any of these objectives are achieved. First, if producers are willing to sell (illegally) at prices above the price ceiling, nothing restricts them to the level of output of Q_2 in Figure 5-3. As long as they can receive more than a price of p_1, they have an incentive to increase their production. Second, black markets clearly frustrate the second objective since the *actual* prices are not kept down; if quantity supplied remains below Q_0, then the black-market price will be *higher* than the free-market equilibrium price, p_0. The third objective may also be thwarted, since with an active black market it is likely that much of the product will be purchased only by those who can afford the high black-market price.

To the extent that binding price ceilings give rise to a black market, it is likely that the government's objectives motivating the imposition of the price ceiling will be thwarted.

Now suppose the government introduces a minimum wage equal to w_{min} that is greater than w_0. The increased wage has two effects. First, by increasing the cost of labour services to firms, the minimum wage reduces the level of employment to E_1. The second effect is to increase the quantity supplied of labour services to E_2. Thus, the clear effect of the binding minimum wage, as seen in the figure, is to generate unemployment—workers that want a job in this market but are unable to get one—equal to the amount E_1E_2.

Whom does this policy benefit? And whom does it harm? The owners of firms are clearly made worse off since they are now required to pay a higher wage than before the minimum wage was imposed. They respond to this increase in costs by reducing their use of labour. Some (but not all) workers are made better off. The workers who are lucky enough to keep their jobs—E_1 workers in the figure—get a higher wage than before. The shaded area shows the redistribution of income away from firms and toward these fortunate workers. Some workers are harmed by the policy—the ones who lose their jobs as a result of the wage increase, shown in the figure as the quantity E_1E_0.

These are the effects of minimum wages in a competitive labour market—one in which there are many firms and many workers, none of whom have the power to influence the market wage. In Chapter 14 we will examine non-competitive labour markets, and we will then see that minimum wages may have a different effect on the market. This different behaviour of competitive and non-competitive markets in the presence of minimum wages probably accounts for the disagreements among economists and policymakers regarding the effects of minimum wage legislation. Until we proceed to that more advanced discussion, however, the analysis of a competitive labour market in this box provides an excellent example of the economic effects of a binding price floor in specific circumstances.

The market for health care in Canada is an important example in which market-clearing prices are not charged; instead, the price is controlled at zero and the services are rationed by customers having to wait their turn to be served. No black market has arisen, although when some Canadians travel to the United States and pay cash for health-care services that they cannot get quickly enough in Canada, or when they pay cash for the limited services provided by Canadian private clinics, the effects are similar to those that occur in a black market. Even though there is not enough of the product available in the public system to satisfy all demand at the controlled price of zero, many people's sense of social justice is satisfied because health care, at least in principle, is freely and equally available to everyone. In recent years, there has been a great deal of debate regarding potential reforms to Canada's health-care system; we discuss this debate in more detail in Chapter 18.

5.2 RENT CONTROLS: A CASE STUDY OF PRICE CEILINGS

For long periods over the past hundred years, rent controls existed in London, Paris, New York, and many other large cities. In Sweden and Britain, where rent controls on apartments existed for decades, shortages of rental accommodations were chronic. When rent controls were initiated in Toronto and Rome, severe housing shortages developed, especially in those areas where demand was rising.

Rent controls provide a vivid illustration of the short- and long-term effects of this type of market intervention. Note, however, that the specifics of rent-control laws vary greatly and have changed significantly since they were first imposed many decades ago.

In particular, current laws often permit exemptions for new buildings and allowances for maintenance costs and inflation. Moreover, in many countries rent controls have evolved into a "second generation" of legislation that focuses on *regulating* the rental housing market rather than simply controlling the price of rental accommodation.

In this section, we confine ourselves to an analysis of rent controls that are aimed primarily at holding the price of rental housing below the free-market equilibrium value. It is this "first generation" of rent controls that produced dramatic results in such cities as London, Paris, New York, and Toronto.

The Predicted Effects of Rent Controls

Binding rent controls are a specific case of price ceilings, and therefore Figure 5-3 can be used to predict some of their effects:

1. There will be a shortage of rental housing because quantity demanded will exceed quantity supplied. Since rents are held below their free-market levels, the available quantity of rental housing will be less than if free-market rents had been charged.

2. The shortage will lead to alternative allocation schemes. Landlords may allocate by sellers' preferences, or the government may intervene, often through security-of-tenure laws, which protect tenants from eviction and thereby give them priority over prospective new tenants.

3. Black markets will appear. For example, landlords may (illegally) require tenants to pay "key money" reflecting the difference in value between the free-market and the controlled rents. In the absence of security-of-tenure laws, landlords may force tenants out when their leases expire in order to extract a large entrance fee from new tenants.

The unique feature of rent controls, however, as compared with price controls in general, is that they are applied to a highly *durable product* that provides services to consumers for long periods. Once built, an apartment can be used for decades. As a result, the immediate effects of rent control are typically quite different from the long-term effects.

The short-run supply response to the imposition of rent controls is usually quite limited. Some conversions of apartment units to condominiums (that are not covered by the rent-control legislation) may occur, but the quantity of apartments does not change much. The short-run supply curve for rental housing is quite *inelastic*.

In the long run, however, the supply response to rent controls can be quite dramatic. If the expected rate of return from building new rental housing falls significantly below what can be earned on other investments, funds will go elsewhere. New construction will be halted, and old buildings will be converted to other uses or will simply be left to deteriorate. The long-run supply curve of rental accommodations is highly *elastic*.

Figure 5-4 illustrates the housing shortage that worsens as time passes under rent control. Because the short-run supply of housing is inelastic, the controlled rent causes only a moderate housing shortage in the short run. Indeed, most of the shortage comes from an increase in the quantity demanded rather than from a reduction in quantity supplied. As time passes, however, fewer new apartments are built, more conversions take place, and older buildings are not replaced (and not repaired) as they wear out. As a result, the quantity supplied shrinks steadily and the extent of the housing shortage worsens.

Along with the growing housing shortage comes an increasingly inefficient use of rental accommodation space. Existing tenants will have an incentive to stay where they are even though their family size, location of employment, or economic circumstances may change. Since they cannot move without giving up their low-rent accommodation, some may accept lower-paying jobs nearby simply to avoid the necessity of moving. Thus, a situation will arise in which existing tenants will hang on to accommodation even if it is poorly suited to their needs, while individuals and families who are newly entering the housing market will be unable to find any rental accommodation except at black-market prices.

The province of Ontario instituted rent controls in 1975 and tightened them on several subsequent occasions. The controls permitted significant increases in rents only where these were needed to pass on cost increases. As a result, the restrictive effects of rent controls were felt mainly in areas where demand was increasing rapidly (as opposed to areas where only costs were increasing rapidly).

During the mid- and late-1990s, the population of Ontario grew substantially but the stock of rental housing did not keep pace. A shortage developed in the rental-housing market, and was especially acute in Metro Toronto. This growing housing shortage led the Conservative Ontario government in 1997 to loosen rent controls, in particular by allowing landlords to increase the rent as much as they saw fit *but only as tenants vacated the apartment.* Not surprisingly, this policy had both critics and supporters. Supporters argued that a loosening of controls would encourage the construction of apartments and thus help to reduce the housing shortage. Critics argued that landlords would harass existing tenants, forcing them to move out so that rents could be increased for incoming tenants. (Indeed, this behaviour happened in rent-controlled New York City, where a landlord pleaded guilty to hiring a "hit man" to kill some tenants and set fires to the apartments of others to scare them out so that rents could be increased!)

Rent control still exists in many Canadian provinces, and the governments place limits on the annual rate of increase of rents. In Ontario in 2015, for example, the maximum allowable increase was 1.6 percent, although landlords could apply to the regulatory body for permission to have a larger increase.

FIGURE 5-4   The Short-Run and Long-Run Effects of Rent Controls

Rent control causes housing shortages that worsen as time passes. The free-market equilibrium is at point E. The controlled rent of r_c forces rents below their free-market equilibrium value of r_1. The short-run supply of housing is shown by the perfectly inelastic curve S_S. Thus, quantity supplied remains at Q_1 in the short run, and the housing shortage is Q_1Q_2. Over time, the quantity supplied shrinks, as shown by the long-run supply curve S_L. In the long run, there are only Q_3 units of rental accommodations supplied, fewer than when controls were instituted. The long-run housing shortage of Q_3Q_2 is larger than the initial shortage of Q_1Q_2.

Who Gains and Who Loses?

Existing tenants in rent-controlled accommodations are the principal gainers from a policy of rent control. As the gap between the controlled and the free-market rents grows, and as the stock of available housing falls, those who are still lucky enough to live in rent-controlled housing gain more and more.

Landlords suffer because they do not get the rate of return they expected on their investments. Some landlords are large companies, and others are wealthy individuals. Neither of these groups attracts great public sympathy, even though the rental companies' shareholders are not all rich. But some landlords are people of modest means who may have put their retirement savings into a small apartment block or a house or two.

Perhaps the most striking effect of rent control is the long-term decline in the amount and quality of rental housing.

They find that the value of their savings is diminished, and sometimes they find themselves in the ironic position of subsidizing tenants who are far better off than they are.

The other important group of people who suffer from rent controls are *potential future* tenants. The housing shortage will hurt some of them because the rental housing they will require will not exist in the future. These people, who wind up living farther from their places of employment or in apartments otherwise inappropriate to their situations, are invisible in debates over rent control because they cannot obtain housing in the rent-controlled jurisdiction. Thus, rent control is often stable politically even when it causes a long-run housing shortage. The current tenants benefit, and they outnumber the current landlords, while the potential tenants, who are harmed, are nowhere to be seen or heard.

Policy Alternatives

Most rent controls today are meant to protect lower-income tenants, not only against "profiteering" by landlords in the face of severe local shortages but also against the steadily rising cost of housing. The market solution is to let rents rise sufficiently to cover the rising costs. The higher rents, however, will force some people to make agonizing choices, both to economize on housing and to spend a higher proportion of total income on it, which mean consuming less housing and less of other things as well.

If governments do not want to accept this market solution, there are many things they can do, but they cannot avoid the fundamental fact that good housing requires *someone* to spend considerable resources. Binding rent controls create housing shortages. The shortages can be removed only if the government, at taxpayer expense, either subsidizes housing production or produces public housing directly.

Alternatively, the government can make housing more affordable to lower-income households by providing income assistance directly to these households, thereby giving them access to higher-quality housing than they could otherwise afford. Whatever policy is adopted, it is important to recognize that providing greater access to rental accommodations has a resource cost. The costs of providing additional housing cannot be voted out of existence; all that can be done is to transfer the costs from one set of persons to another.

5.3 AN INTRODUCTION TO MARKET EFFICIENCY

In this chapter we have seen the effects of governments intervening in competitive markets by setting price floors and price ceilings. In both cases, we noted that the imposition of a controlled price generates benefits for some individuals and costs for others. For example, in the case of the legislated minimum wage (a price floor), firms are made worse off by the minimum wage, but workers who retain their jobs are made better off. Other workers, those unable to retain their jobs at the higher wage, may be made worse off. In the example of legislated rent controls (a price ceiling), landlords are made worse off by the rent controls, but some tenants are made better off. Those tenants who are no longer able to find an apartment when rents fall are made worse off.

Is it possible to determine the *overall* effects of such policies, rather than just the effects on specific groups? For example, can we say that a policy of legislated minimum wages, while harming firms, nonetheless makes *society as a whole* better off because it helps workers more than it harms firms? Or can we conclude that the imposition of rent controls makes society as a whole better off because it helps tenants more than it harms landlords?

To address such questions, economists use the concept of *market efficiency*. We will explore this concept in more detail in later chapters, but for now we simply introduce the idea and see how it helps us understand the overall effects of price controls. We begin by taking a slightly different look at market demand and supply curves.

Demand as "Value" and Supply as "Cost"

In Chapter 3 we saw that the market demand curve for any product shows, for each possible price, how much of that product consumers want to purchase. Similarly, we saw that the market supply curve shows how much producers want to sell at each possible price. But we can turn things around and view these curves in a slightly different way—by starting with any given quantity and asking about the price. Specifically, we can consider the highest price that consumers are *willing to pay* and the lowest price that producers are *willing to accept* for any given unit of the product. As we will see, viewing demand and supply curves in this manner helps us think about how society as a whole benefits by producing and consuming any given amount of some product.

Let's begin by considering the market demand curve for pizza, as shown in part (i) of Figure 5-5. Each point on the demand curve shows the highest price consumers are willing to pay for a given pizza. (We assume for simplicity that all pizzas are identical.) At point *A* we see that consumers are willing to pay up to $20 for the 100th pizza, and at point *B* consumers are willing to pay up to $15 for the 200th pizza. In both cases, these maximum prices reflect the subjective *value* consumers place on that particular pizza. In general, for each pizza, the price on the demand curve shows the value to consumers from consuming that pizza.

The reason the demand curve is downward sloping is that not all consumers are the same. Some consumers value pizza so highly that they are willing to pay $20 for a pizza; others are prepared to pay only $10, while some value pizza so little that they are prepared to pay only $5. There is nothing special about pizza, however. What is true for the demand for pizza is true for the demand for any other product.

> For each unit of a product, the price on the market demand curve shows the value to consumers from consuming that unit.

Now let's consider the market supply curve for pizza, shown in part (ii) of Figure 5-5. Each point on the market supply curve shows the lowest price firms are willing to accept to produce and sell a given pizza. (We maintain our simplifying assumption that all pizzas are identical.) At point *E* firms are willing to accept a price no lower than $5 for the 100th pizza, and at point *F* firms are willing to accept a price no lower than $10 for the 200th pizza. The lowest acceptable price as shown on the supply curve reflects the *additional cost* firms incur to produce each given pizza. To see this, consider the production of the 200th pizza at point *F*. If the firm's total costs increase by $10 when this pizza is produced, the firm will be able to increase its profits as long as it can sell that pizza at a price greater than $10. If it sells the pizza at any price below $10, its profits will decline. If it sells the pizza at a price of exactly $10, its profits will neither rise nor fall. Thus, for a profit-maximizing firm, the *lowest acceptable price* for the 200th pizza is $10.

FIGURE 5-5   Reinterpreting the Demand and Supply Curves for Pizza

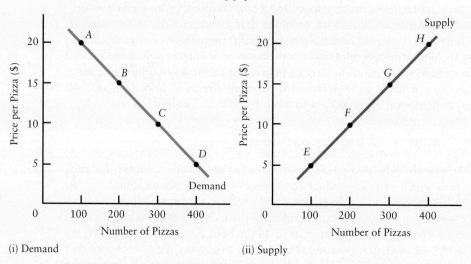

(i) Demand   (ii) Supply

For each pizza, the price on the demand curve shows the value consumers receive from consuming that pizza; the price on the supply curve shows the additional cost to firms of producing that pizza. Each point on the demand curve shows the maximum price consumers are willing to pay to consume that unit. This maximum price reflects the value that consumers get from that unit of the product. Each point on the supply curve shows the minimum price firms are willing to accept for producing and selling that unit. This minimum price reflects the additional costs firms incur by producing that unit.

The reason the supply curve is upward sloping is that not all producers are the same. Some are so good at producing pizzas (low-cost producers) that they would be willing to accept $5 per pizza; others are less easily able to produce pizzas (high-cost producers) and hence would need to receive $15 in order to produce and sell the identical pizza. What is true for the supply of pizza is true for the supply of other products:

> **For each unit of a product, the price on the market supply curve shows the lowest acceptable price to firms for selling that unit. This lowest acceptable price reflects the additional cost to firms from producing that unit.**

Economic Surplus and Market Efficiency

Once the demand and supply curves are put together, the equilibrium price and quantity can be determined, just as in Chapter 3. This brings us to the important concept of *economic surplus*. We continue with our pizza example in Figure 5-6, which shows the demand and supply curves together. Consider a quantity of 100 pizzas. For each one of those 100 pizzas, the value to consumers is given by the height of the demand curve. The additional cost to firms from producing each of these 100 pizzas is shown by the height of the supply curve. For the entire 100 pizzas, the difference between the value to consumers and the additional costs to firms is called *economic surplus* and is shown by the shaded area ① in the figure.

> **For any given quantity of a product, the area below the demand curve and above the supply curve shows the economic surplus associated with the production and consumption of that product.**

What does this economic surplus represent? The economic surplus is the net value that *society as a whole* receives by producing and consuming these 100 pizzas. It arises because firms and consumers have taken resources that have a lower value (as shown by the height of the supply curve) and transformed them into something valued more highly (as shown by the height of the demand curve). To put it differently, the value from consuming the 100 pizzas is greater than the cost of the resources necessary to produce those 100 pizzas—flour, yeast, tomato sauce, cheese, and labour. Thus, the act of producing and consuming those 100 pizzas "adds value" and generates benefits for society as a whole.

We are now ready to introduce the concept of market efficiency. In later chapters, after we have explored consumer and firm behaviour in greater detail, we will have a more detailed discussion of efficiency.

Economists say that a market for any specific product is efficient if the quantity of the product produced and consumed is such that the economic surplus in that market is maximized. Note that this refers to the *total* surplus but not its distribution between consumers and producers. For example, as we will see in the next section, the removal of a binding set of rent controls will increase total surplus and thus improve the efficiency of the market. At the same time, however, some tenants will be made worse off while some landlords will be made better off. The fact that total surplus has increased means that, at least in principle, it would be possible for those who gain to compensate those who lose so that everyone ends up being better off. When economists say that "society gains" when market efficiency is enhanced, even though these compensations rarely occur, there is an implicit value judgement being made that the benefits to those who gain outweigh the costs to those who lose.

Let's apply this concept of efficiency to the pizza market shown in Figure 5-6 and ask, What level of pizza production and consumption is efficient? Consider the quantity of 100 pizzas. At this quantity, the shaded area ① shows the total economic surplus that society receives from producing and consuming 100 pizzas. But if output were to increase beyond 100 pizzas, more economic surplus would be generated because the value placed by consumers on additional pizzas is greater than the additional costs associated with their production. Specifically, if production and consumption were to increase to 200 pizzas, additional economic surplus would be generated, as shown by shaded area ②. Continuing this logic, we see that the amount of economic surplus is *maximized* when the quantity is 250 units, and at that quantity the total economic surplus is equal to the sum of areas ①, ②, and ③.

What would happen if the quantity of pizzas were to rise further, say to 300 units? For any pizzas beyond 250, the value placed on these pizzas by consumers is *less than* the additional costs associated with their production. In this case, producing the last 50 pizzas would actually *decrease* the amount of economic

FIGURE 5-6 Economic Surplus in the Pizza Market

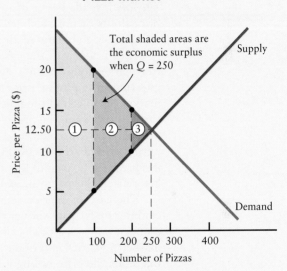

For any quantity of pizzas, the area below the demand curve and above the supply curve shows the economic surplus generated by the production and consumption of those pizzas. The demand curve shows the value consumers place on each additional pizza; the supply curve shows the additional cost associated with producing each pizza. For example, consumers value the 100th pizza at $20, whereas the additional cost to firms of producing that 100th pizza is $5. The economic surplus generated by producing and consuming this 100th pizza is therefore $15 ($20 − $5). For any range of quantity, the shaded area between the curves over that range shows the economic surplus generated by producing and consuming those pizzas.

Economic surplus in the pizza market is maximized—and thus market efficiency is achieved—at the free-market equilibrium quantity of 250 pizzas and price of $12.50. At this point, total economic surplus is the sum of the three shaded areas.

surplus in this market because society would be taking highly valued resources (flour, cheese, etc.) and transforming them into pizzas which are valued less.

In our example of the pizza market, as long as the price is free to adjust to excess demands or supplies, the equilibrium price and quantity will be determined where the demand and supply curves for pizza intersect. In Figure 5-6, the equilibrium quantity is 250 pizzas, the quantity that maximizes the amount of economic surplus in the pizza market. In other words, the free interaction of demand and supply will result in market efficiency. This result in the pizza market suggests a more general rule:

A competitive market will maximize economic surplus and therefore be efficient when price is free to achieve its market-clearing equilibrium level.[1]

Market Efficiency and Price Controls

At the beginning of this section we asked whether we could determine if *society as a whole* is made better off or worse off as a result of the government's imposition of price floors or price ceilings. With an understanding of economic surplus and market efficiency, we are now ready to consider these questions.

Let's begin with the case of a price floor, as shown in part (i) of Figure 5-7. The free-market equilibrium is shown by point E, with price p_0 and quantity Q_0. When the government imposes a price floor at p_1, the quantity exchanged falls to Q_1. In the free-market case, each of the units of output between Q_0 and Q_1 generates some economic surplus. But when the price floor is put in place, these units of the good are no longer produced or consumed, and thus they no longer generate any economic surplus. The purple shaded area is called the *deadweight loss* caused by the binding price floor, and it represents the overall loss of economic surplus to society. The size of the deadweight loss reflects the extent of *market inefficiency*.

The case of a price ceiling is shown in part (ii) of Figure 5-7. The free-market equilibrium is again shown by point E, with price p_0 and quantity Q_0. When the government imposes a price ceiling at p_2, the quantity exchanged falls to Q_2. In the free-market case, each unit of output between Q_0 and Q_2 generates some economic surplus. But when the price ceiling is imposed, these units of the good are no longer produced or consumed, and so they no longer generate any economic surplus. The purple shaded area is the *deadweight loss* and represents the overall loss of surplus to society caused by the policy. The size of the deadweight loss reflects the extent of market inefficiency.

The imposition of a binding price ceiling or price floor in an otherwise free and competitive market leads to market inefficiency.

It is worth repeating a central point: binding price floors and price ceilings do more than merely redistribute a given amount of economic surplus between buyers and sellers. They also lead to a reduction in the quantity of the product transacted and a reduction in total economic surplus. Society as a whole receives less economic surplus as compared with the free-market case.

---

[1] In Part 6 of this book, we will see some important exceptions to this rule when we discuss "market failures."

FIGURE 5-7   Market Inefficiency with Price Controls

(i) Binding price floor   (ii) Binding price ceiling

Binding price floors and price ceilings in competitive markets lead to a reduction in overall economic surplus and thus to market inefficiency. In both parts of the figure, the free-market equilibrium is at point E with price p_0 and quantity Q_0. In part (i), the introduction of a price floor at p_1 reduces quantity to Q_1. In part (ii), the introduction of a price ceiling at p_2 reduces quantity to Q_2. In both parts, the shaded area shows the reduction in overall economic surplus—the deadweight loss—created by the price floor or ceiling. Both outcomes display market inefficiency.

One Final Application: Output Quotas

Before ending this chapter, it is useful to consider one final application of government intervention in a competitive market, and to examine the effects on overall economic surplus and market efficiency. Figure 5-8 illustrates the effects of introducing a system of *output quotas* in a competitive market. Output quotas are commonly used in Canadian agriculture, especially in the markets for milk, butter, and cheese. Output quotas are sometimes used in other industries as well; for example, they are often used in large cities to regulate the number of taxi drivers.

The equilibrium in the free-market case is at point E, with price p_0 and quantity Q_0. When the government introduces an output quota, it restricts total output of this product to Q_1 units and then distributes quotas—"licences to produce"—among the producers. With output restricted to Q_1 units, the market price rises to p_1, the price that consumers are willing to pay for this quantity of the product. The purple shaded area—the deadweight loss of the output quota—shows the overall loss of economic surplus as a result of the quota-induced output restriction.

As you can see from Figure 5-8, the output restriction created by the quota leads to an increase in the product's price. If demand for the product is inelastic, as is the case in the dairy markets where quotas are commonly used, total income to producers rises as a result of the reduction

FIGURE 5-8   The Inefficiency of Output Quotas

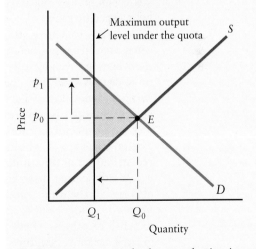

Binding output quotas lead to a reduction in output and a reduction in overall economic surplus. The free-market equilibrium is at point E with price p_0 and quantity Q_0. Suppose the government then restricts total quantity to Q_1 by issuing output quotas to firms. The market price rises to p_1. The shaded area shows the reduction in overall economic surplus—the deadweight loss—created by the quota system.

in output. (Refer back to Figure 4-5 in Chapter 4.) But since their output falls, firms' production costs are also reduced. The introduction of a quota system therefore leads to a rise in revenues and a fall in production costs—a clear benefit for producers! Not surprisingly, individual producers are often trying to increase their holdings of quotas so as to increase their production and profits.

There is a catch, however: producers must incur a very high cost in order to purchase the quotas. (The high price for quotas reflects the profits they can generate.) For example, an average dairy farm in Ontario or Quebec has about 90 cows and produces about 2300 litres of milk per day. The market value of the quota required to produce this amount of milk is approximately $2.2 million. The ownership of a quota therefore represents a considerable asset for those producers who were lucky enough to receive it (for free) when it was initially issued by the government. But for new producers wanting to get into the industry, the need to purchase an expensive quota represents a considerable obstacle. These large costs from purchasing the quota offset the benefits from selling the product at the (quota-induced) high price.

A Cautionary Word

In this chapter we have examined the effects of government policies to control prices in otherwise free and competitive markets, and we have shown that such policies usually have two results. First, there is a redistribution between buyers and sellers; one group is made better off while the other group is made worse off. Second, there is a reduction in the overall amount of economic surplus generated in the market; the result is that the outcome is inefficient and society as a whole is made worse off.

The finding that government intervention in otherwise free markets leads to inefficiency should lead one to ask why government would ever intervene in such ways. The answer in many situations is that the government policy is motivated by the desire to help a specific group of people and that the overall costs are deemed to be a worthwhile price to pay to achieve the desired effect. For example, legislated minimum wages are often viewed by politicians as an effective means of reducing poverty—by increasing the wages received by low-wage workers. The costs such a policy imposes on firms, and on society overall, may be viewed as costs worth incurring to redistribute economic surplus toward low-wage workers. Similarly, the use of output quotas in certain agricultural markets is sometimes viewed by politicians as an effective means of increasing income to specific farmers. The costs that such quota systems impose on consumers, and on society as a whole, may be viewed by some as acceptable costs in achieving a redistribution of economic surplus toward these farmers.

In advocating these kinds of policies, ones that redistribute economic surplus but also reduce the total amount of economic surplus available, policymakers are making *normative* judgements regarding which groups in society deserve to be helped at the expense of others. These judgements may be informed by a careful study of which groups are most genuinely in need, and they may also be driven by political considerations that the current government deems important to its prospects for re-election. In either case, there is nothing necessarily "wrong" about the government's decision to intervene in these markets, even if these interventions lead to inefficiency. Not surprisingly, however, decisions like this are often controversial and hotly debated.

The job of the economist is to carefully analyze the effects of such policies, taking care to identify both the distributional effects and the implications for the overall amount of economic surplus generated in the market. This is *positive* analysis, emphasizing the *actual* effects of the policy rather than what might be *desirable*. These analytical results can then be used as inputs to the decision-making process, where they will be combined with normative and political considerations before a final policy decision is reached. In many parts of this textbook, we will encounter policies that governments implement (or consider implementing) to alter market outcomes, and we will examine the effects of those policies. A full understanding of why specific policies are implemented requires paying attention to the effects of such policies on both the overall amount of economic surplus and the distribution of that surplus.

SUMMARY

5.1 GOVERNMENT-CONTROLLED PRICES

LO 1

- Government price controls are policies that attempt to hold the price of some product at a disequilibrium value—a value that could not be maintained in the absence of the government's intervention.
- A binding price floor is set above the equilibrium price; a binding price ceiling is set below the equilibrium price.
- Binding price floors lead to excess supply. Either the potential sellers are left with quantities that cannot

be sold, or the government must step in and buy the surplus.
- Binding price ceilings lead to excess demand and provide a strong incentive for black marketeers to buy at the controlled price and sell at the higher free-market (illegal) price.

5.2 RENT CONTROLS: A CASE STUDY OF PRICE CEILINGS

LO 2

- Rent controls are a form of price ceiling. The major consequence of binding rent controls is a shortage of rental accommodations and the allocation of rental housing by sellers' preferences.

- Because the supply of rental housing is much more elastic in the long run than in the short run, the extent of the housing shortage caused by rent controls worsens over time.

5.3 AN INTRODUCTION TO MARKET EFFICIENCY

LO 3, 4

- Demand curves show consumers' willingness to pay for each unit of the product. For any given quantity, the area below the demand curve shows the overall value consumers place on that quantity of the product.
- Supply curves show the lowest price producers are prepared to accept in order to produce and sell each unit of the product. This lowest acceptable price for each additional unit reflects the firm's costs required to produce each additional unit.
- For any given quantity exchanged of a product, the area below the demand curve and above the supply curve (up

to that quantity) shows the economic surplus generated by the production and consumption of those units.
- A market's surplus is maximized when the quantity exchanged is determined by the intersection of the demand and supply curves. This outcome is said to be efficient.
- Policies that intervene in otherwise free and competitive markets—such as price floors, price ceilings, and output quotas—generally lead to a reduction in the total amount of economic surplus generated in the market.

KEY CONCEPTS

Price controls: floors and ceilings
Allocation by sellers' preferences

Black markets
Rent controls
Short-run and long-run supply curves
   of rental accommodations

Economic surplus
Market efficiency
Inefficiency of price controls and
   output quotas

STUDY EXERCISES

MyEconLab   Make the grade with MyEconLab: Study Exercises marked in ● can be found on MyEconLab. You can practise them as often as you want, and most feature step-by-step guided instructions to help you find the right answer.

● Consider the market for straw hats on a tropical island. The demand and supply schedules are given below.

Price ($)	Quantity Demanded	Quantity Supplied
1	1000	200
2	900	300
3	800	400
4	700	500
5	600	600
6	500	700
7	400	800
8	300	900

Fill in the blanks to make the following statements correct.

a. The equilibrium price for straw hats is _____. The equilibrium quantity demanded and quantity supplied is _____.
b. Suppose the government believes that no islander should have to pay more than $3 for a hat. The government can achieve this by imposing a (n) _____.
c. At the government-controlled price of $3 there will be a(n) _____ of _____ hats.
d. Suppose now that the government believes the island's hat makers are not paid enough for their hats and that islanders should pay no less than $6 for a hat. They can achieve this by imposing a (n) _____.
e. At the new government-controlled price of $6 there will be a(n) _____ of _____ hats.

● The following questions are about resource allocation in the presence of price ceilings and price floors.

a. A binding price ceiling leads to excess demand. What are some methods, other than price, of allocating the available supply?
b. A binding price floor leads to excess supply. How might the government deal with this excess supply?
c. Why might the government choose to implement a price ceiling?
d. Why might the government choose to implement a price floor?

● Consider the market for rental housing in Yourtown. The demand and supply schedules for rental housing are given in the table.

Price ($ per month)	Quantity Demanded (thousands of units)	Quantity Supplied (thousands of units)
1100	40	80
1000	50	77
900	60	73
800	70	70
700	80	67
600	90	65
500	100	60

a. In a free market for rental housing, what is the equilibrium price and quantity?
b. Now suppose the government in Yourtown decides to impose a ceiling on the monthly rental price. What is the highest level at which such a ceiling could be set in order to have any effect on the market? Explain your answer.
c. Suppose the maximum rental price is set equal to $500 per month. Describe the effect on quantity demanded, supplied, and exchanged in the rental-housing market.
d. Suppose a black market develops in the presence of the rent controls in part (c). What is the black-market price that would exist if all of the quantity supplied were sold on the black market?

● Explain and show in a diagram why the short-run effects of rent control are likely to be less significant than the long-run effects.

● In cities experiencing rapid growth, like Calgary and Saskatoon, it is often claimed that the "overheated" real estate market puts housing out of reach of ordinary Canadians. Not surprisingly, governments often debate how best to deal with this issue. Who bears the heaviest cost when rents are kept artificially low by each of the following means?

a. legislated rent controls
b. a subsidy to tenants equal to some fraction of their rent
c. the provision of public housing which is made available at below-market rents

6 Consider the market for burritos in a hypothetical Canadian city, blessed with thousands of hungry students and dozens of small burrito stands. The demand and supply schedules are shown in the table.

Price ($)	Quantity Demanded (thousands of burritos per month)	Quantity Supplied (thousands of burritos per month)
0	500	125
1.00	400	175
1.50	350	200
2.00	300	225
2.50	250	250
3.00	200	275
3.50	150	300
4.00	100	325
5.00	0	375

a. Graph the demand and supply curves. What is the free-market equilibrium in this market?
b. What is the dollar value of the total economic surplus in this market in the free-market equilibrium? What area in your diagram represents this economic surplus?
c. Suppose the local government, out of concern for the students' welfare, enforces a price ceiling on burritos at a price of $1.50. Show in your diagram the effect on price and quantity exchanged.
d. Are students better off as a result of this policy? Explain.
e. What happens to overall economic surplus in this market as a result of the price ceiling? Show this in the diagram.

7 Consider the market for some product X that is represented in the demand-and-supply diagram.

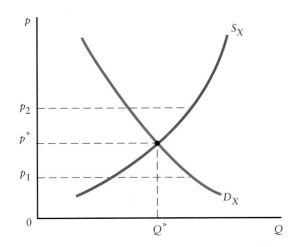

a. Suppose the government decides to impose a price floor at p_1. Describe how this affects price, quantity, and market efficiency.
b. Suppose the government decides to impose a price floor at p_2. Describe how this affects price, quantity, and market efficiency.
c. Suppose the government decides to impose a price ceiling at p_1. Describe how this affects price, quantity, and market efficiency.
d. Suppose the government decides to impose a price ceiling at p_2. Describe how this affects price, quantity, and market efficiency.

8 The diagrams below show the supply and demand curves in the market for widgets. In each diagram the free market equilibrium price and quantity are p^* and Q^*.

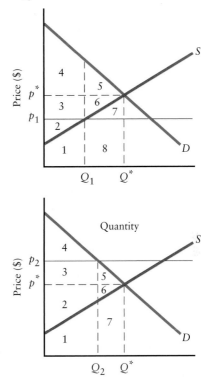

a. In part (i), if the price of widgets is at its market-clearing equilibrium level, p^*, identify the areas on the graph that sum to this market's total economic surplus.
b. In part (i), suppose the government imposes a price ceiling at price p_1. Identify the areas on the graph that represent the reduction in economic surplus as a result of this price control.
c. In part (ii), if the price of widgets is at its market-clearing equilibrium level, p^*, identify the areas on the graph that sum to this market's total economic surplus.

d. In part (ii), suppose the government imposes a price floor at price p_2. Identify the areas on the graph that represent the reduction in economic surplus as a result of this price control.

e. For parts (i) and (ii), describe the effect on market efficiency of the price controls. Is society as a whole better off?

9 The diagram below shows supply and demand curves in the Canadian market for soybeans. The free market equilibrium price and quantity are p^* and Q^*.

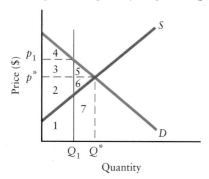

a. If the price of soybeans is at its market-clearing equilibrium level, p^*, identify the areas on the graph that sum to this market's total economic surplus.

b. Suppose the government imposes an output quota at Q_1. Identify the areas on the graph that represent the reduction in economic surplus as a result of this government's imposition of the quota.

c. Describe the effect of this quota on market efficiency. Is society as a whole better off?

10 Consider the market for milk in Saskatchewan. If p is the price of milk (cents per litre) and Q is the quantity of litres (in millions per month), suppose that the demand and supply curves for milk are given by

$$\text{Demand: } p = 225 - 15Q^D$$

$$\text{Supply: } p = 25 + 35Q^S$$

a. Assuming there is no government intervention in this market, what is the equilibrium price and quantity?

b. Now suppose the government guarantees milk producers a price of $2 per litre and promises to buy any amount of milk that the producers cannot sell. What are the quantity demanded and quantity supplied at this guaranteed price?

c. How much milk would the government be buying (per month) with this system of price supports and how much is the government paying for this milk?

d. Who pays for the milk that the government buys? Who is helped by this policy and who is harmed?

11 This question is related to the use of output quotas in the milk market in the previous question. Suppose the government used a quota system instead of direct price supports to assist milk producers. In particular, it issued quotas to existing milk producers for 1.67 million litres of milk per month.

a. If milk production is exactly equal to the amount of quotas issued, what price do consumers pay for milk?

b. Compared with the direct price controls in the previous question, whose income is higher under the quota system? Whose is lower?

12 Consider a simple demand-and-supply model of a competitive labour market in a small town. The demand and supply curves for labour are given by

$$\text{Demand: } w = 18 - 3L^D$$

$$\text{Supply: } w = 3 + 2L^S$$

where w is the wage ($ per hour) and L is the number of hours of employment (measured in thousands of hours per month).

a. Plot the demand and supply curves to scale.

b. Solve for the equilibrium level of w and L in the case of no government intervention.

c. Now suppose that the town council imposes a minimum wage equal to $10 per hour. What is the new level of employment?

d. Identify in your diagram the area that is the deadweight loss. Compute its size, measured in thousands of dollars per month.

6 Consumer Behaviour

CHAPTER OUTLINE	LEARNING OBJECTIVES (LO)
	After studying this chapter you will be able to
6.1 MARGINAL UTILITY AND CONSUMER CHOICE	**1** describe the difference between marginal and total utility.
	2 explain how utility-maximizing consumers adjust their expenditure until the marginal utility per dollar spent is equalized across products.
6.2 INCOME AND SUBSTITUTION EFFECTS OF PRICE CHANGES	**3** understand how the slope of any demand curve is determined by the income and substitution effects of price changes.
6.3 CONSUMER SURPLUS	**4** see that consumer surplus is the "bargain" the consumer gets by paying less for the product than the maximum price he or she is willing to pay.
	5 explain the "paradox of value."

NOW we need to go "behind the scenes" of demand curves to understand why they are downward sloping. So far, we have studied the demand and supply model and used it to analyze market outcomes, but we have not explained the consumer behaviour that underlies the demand curve itself. The first and second parts of this chapter provide alternative approaches to understanding how consumers make the decisions that underlie their demand curves. The third and final section examines an important implication of having negatively sloped demand curves and introduces the concept of consumer surplus (part of the economic surplus that we discussed in Chapter 5) which shows how much consumers really benefit from their market transactions.

6.1 MARGINAL UTILITY AND CONSUMER CHOICE

Consumers make all kinds of decisions—they choose to drink coffee or tea, to go to a movie, to go out for dinner, to buy mobile devices, and to purchase houses and condos. As we discussed in Chapter 1, economists assume that in making their choices, consumers are motivated to maximize their **utility**, the total satisfaction they derive from the goods and services they consume.

Although utility cannot be measured directly, it is still a useful concept. You know that you derive satisfaction—or utility—from eating a good meal, listening to music, buying new shoes, or taking a walk through a park. And we need some way to think about how you as a consumer make your decisions. As we will see in this chapter, it is possible to construct a useful theory of consumer behaviour based on the assumption of *utility maximization*.

In developing our theory of consumer behaviour, we begin by considering the consumption of a single product. It is useful to distinguish between the consumer's **total utility**, which is the full satisfaction resulting from the consumption of that product by a consumer, and the consumer's **marginal utility**, which is the *additional* satisfaction resulting from consuming *one more unit* of that product. For example, the total utility of consuming five bottles of fruit juice per day is the total satisfaction that those five juices provide. The marginal utility of the fifth juice consumed is the additional satisfaction provided by the consumption of that fifth juice each day.[1]

> **utility** The satisfaction that a consumer receives from consuming some good or service.

> **total utility** The consumer's total satisfaction resulting from the consumption of a given product.

> **marginal utility** The additional satisfaction obtained from consuming one additional unit of a product.

Diminishing Marginal Utility

The central hypothesis of utility theory, often called the *law of diminishing marginal utility*, is as follows:

> **The utility that any consumer derives from *successive* units of a particular product consumed over some period of time diminishes as total consumption of the product increases (holding constant the consumption of all other products).**

Consider your utility from using clean water, for drinking, bathing, washing your dishes and clothes, and all its other purposes. Some minimum quantity is very important and you would, if necessary, give up a considerable sum of money to obtain that quantity of water. The total utility you receive from that basic quantity of water is very high. You will, of course, consume more than this bare minimum, but your *marginal* utility of *successive* litres of water used over a period of time will decline steadily.

We will consider evidence for this hypothesis later, but you can convince yourself that it is at least reasonable by asking a few questions. How much money would be needed to induce you to reduce your consumption of water by one litre per week? The answer is *very little*. How much would induce you to reduce it by a second litre? By a third litre? To only one litre consumed per week? The answer to the last question is *quite a lot*. The fewer litres you are already using, the higher the marginal utility of one additional litre of water.

---

[1] Technically, incremental utility is measured over a discrete interval, such as from four juices to five juices, whereas marginal utility is a rate of change measured over an infinitesimal interval. However, common usage applies the word *marginal* when the last unit is involved, even if a one-unit change is not infinitesimal.[9]

Utility Schedules and Graphs

In Figure 6-1 we make the assumption that utility can be measured (in units we call "utils"), and thus the different amount of utility received from consuming different units can be compared. This is a helpful assumption in allowing us to see the important difference between total and marginal utility. The figure illustrates the assumptions that have been made about utility, using Alison's daily consumption of fruit juice as an example. The table shows that Alison's total utility rises as she drinks more bottles of juice per day. However, the utility that she gets from each *additional* juice per day is less than that of the previous one—that is, her marginal utility declines as the quantity she consumes rises. [10]

The data are graphed in the two parts of Figure 6-1.

Maximizing Utility

As already noted, economists assume that consumers try to make themselves as well off as they possibly can, given their circumstances. In other words, consumers seek

FIGURE 6-1   Alison's Total and Marginal Utility from Drinking Juice

Number of Bottles of Juice Alison Drinks per Day	Alison's Total Utility (number of "utils")	Alison's Marginal Utility (number of "utils")
0	0	
		30
1	30	
		20
2	50	
		15
3	65	
		10
4	75	
		8
5	83	
		6
6	89	
		4
7	93	
		3
8	96	
		2
9	98	
		1
10	99	

Total utility rises, but marginal utility declines, as consumption increases. The marginal utility of 20, shown as the second entry in the third column, arises because Alison's total utility increases from 30 to 50—a difference of 20—with consumption of the second juice. To indicate that the marginal utility is associated with the change from one level of consumption to another, the values in the third column are recorded between the rows of the values in the second column.

to maximize their total utility subject to the constraints they face—in particular, their income and the market prices of various products.

The Consumer's Decision   Now that we have examined the concepts of total utility and marginal utility, we are ready to examine how someone like Alison could consume juice and burritos in a way that maximizes her utility. Of course, we could ask the same question about any two goods, or any number of goods, but we will focus on juice and burritos to keep the example simple.

We begin with the answer: a utility-maximizing consumer should consume juice and burritos to the point at which the marginal utility *per dollar spent* on the last juice is just equal to the marginal utility *per dollar spent* on the last burrito.

> **A utility-maximizing consumer allocates expenditures so that the marginal utility obtained from the last dollar spent on each product is equal.**

To understand this result, let's consider an example. Imagine that Alison's utility from the last dollar spent on juice is three times her utility from the last dollar spent on burritos. In this case, Alison can increase her total utility by spending less on burritos and spending more on juice.

If Alison wants to *maximize* her utility, she will continue to switch her expenditure from burritos to juice as long as her last dollar spent on juice yields more utility than her last dollar spent on burritos. This switching, however, reduces the quantity of burritos consumed and, given the law of diminishing marginal utility, raises the marginal utility of burritos. At the same time, switching increases the quantity of juice consumed and thereby lowers the marginal utility of juice.

Eventually, the marginal utilities will have changed enough so that the utility received from the last dollar spent on juice is just equal to the utility received from the last dollar spent on burritos. At this point, Alison gains nothing from further switches. (In fact, switching further would *reduce* her total utility.)

So much for the specific example. What can we say more generally about utility maximization? Suppose we denote the marginal utility of the last unit of product X by MU_X and its price by p_X. Let MU_Y and p_Y refer, respectively, to the marginal utility of a second product Y and its price. The marginal utility per dollar spent on X will be MU_X/p_X. For example, if the last unit of X increases utility by 30 and costs \$3, its marginal utility per dollar is $30/3 = 10$. If the last unit of Y increases utility by 10 and costs \$1, its marginal utility per dollar is $10/1 = 10$. With these numbers, the marginal utilities from the last dollar spent on X and Y are equal.

The condition required for a consumer to be maximizing utility, for any pair of products, is

$$\frac{MU_X}{p_X} = \frac{MU_Y}{p_Y} \tag{6-1}$$

This equation says that a utility-maximizing consumer will allocate expenditure so that the utility gained from the last dollar spent on one product is equal to the marginal utility gained from the last dollar spent on any other product.

This is the fundamental equation of marginal utility theory. With only a given amount of income to spend, a consumer demands each product up to the point at which the marginal utility per dollar spent on it is the same as the marginal utility per dollar spent on every other product. When this condition is met for all products, the consumer cannot increase utility further by reallocating expenditure. That is, utility will be maximized. (Of course, if she gets more income to spend, she can raise her total utility by buying more of each product.)

An Alternative Interpretation   If we rearrange the terms in Equation 6-1, we can gain additional insight into consumer behaviour.

$$\frac{MU_X}{MU_Y} = \frac{p_X}{p_Y} \tag{6-2}$$

The right side of this equation is the *relative* price of the two products. It is determined by the market and is beyond Alison's control. She reacts to these market prices but is powerless to change them. The left side is the *relative* ability of the two products to add to Alison's utility. This is within her control because in determining the quantities of different products to buy, she also determines their marginal utilities.

If the two sides of Equation 6-2 are not equal, Alison can increase her total utility by rearranging her purchases of X and Y. Suppose that the price of X is \$4 and the price of Y is \$2. The right-hand side of Equation 6-2 is then $p_X/p_Y = 4/2 = 2$. Remember that Alison can do nothing to change the right-hand side of this equation—the prices are determined in the market and are beyond her control. Suppose also that Alison is currently purchasing X and Y such that the marginal utility for X is 12 and the marginal utility for Y is 4. The left-hand side of Equation 6-2 is then $MU_X/MU_Y = 12/4 = 3$. In this case $MU_X/MU_Y > p_X/p_Y$. Alison can increase her total utility by increasing her purchases of X (which have a high MU) and reducing her purchases of Y (which have a low MU) until the ratio MU_X/MU_Y is equal to 2, the same as the ratio of the prices. At this point Alison cannot increase her total utility any further by rearranging her purchases between the two products.

Consider what Alison is doing. She is faced with a set of prices that she cannot change. She responds to these prices and maximizes her utility by adjusting the things that she *can* change—the quantities of the various products she purchases—until Equation 6-2 is satisfied for all pairs of products.

Is This Realistic?   It may seem unrealistic to argue that consumers maximize utility in the precise way we have described. After all, not many of us stand in the aisles of a store and compute ratios of marginal utilities and prices and then adjust our consumption exactly as suggested by Equation 6-2. Keep in mind, though, that utility theory is used by economists to predict how consumers will behave when faced with such events as changing prices and incomes. As long as consumers seek to do the best they can for themselves with their limited resources, the consumer's actual thought process does not concern us. The theory is not meant to be a description of *how* they reach their decisions but is rather a convenient way of discovering the *implications* of their maximizing behaviour. Like many theories, utility-maximization theory leads to predictions that can be tested empirically. Economists continue to use the theory of utility maximization because its predictions are rarely rejected by the data. One of the most important of these predictions is that consumers who act as if they are following a rule like Equation 6-2 have negatively sloped demand curves for goods and services. In the next section we derive this result.

The Consumer's Demand Curve

To derive the consumer's demand curve for a product, we need to ask what happens when there is a change in the price of that product. As an example, let us derive Alison's demand curve for fruit juice. Consider Equation 6-2 and let X represent juice and Y represent *all other products taken together*. In this case, the price of Y is interpreted as the average price of all other products. What will Alison do if, with all other prices remaining constant, there is an increase in the price of juice? Alison cannot avoid suffering some loss in utility—whereas her income is unchanged, it costs more to buy each juice and the same to buy each unit of everything else. She might decide to spend less on everything else and increase her spending on juice in order to hold her juice consumption constant. But she can do better than that. To see why, notice that when the price of juice rises, the right side of Equation 6-2 increases. But, until Alison adjusts consumption, the left side is unchanged. Thus, after the price changes but before Alison reacts, the following situation exists:

$$\frac{MU \text{ of juice}}{MU \text{ of } Y} < \frac{\text{Price of juice}}{\text{Price of } Y}$$

What does Alison do to restore the equality? The hypothesis of diminishing marginal utility tells us that as she buys fewer bottles of juice, the *marginal* utility of juice will rise and thereby increase the ratio on the left side. Thus, in response to an increase in the price of juice, with all other prices constant, Alison reduces her consumption of juice until the marginal utility of juice rises sufficiently that Equation 6-2 is restored. This would be Alison's utility-maximizing response to the increase in the price of juice.

This analysis leads to the basic prediction of demand theory:

A rise in the price of a product (with all other determinants of demand held constant) leads each utility-maximizing consumer to reduce the quantity demanded of the product.

Market Demand Curves

If this is what each consumer does, it is also what all consumers taken together do. Thus, the theory of consumer behaviour that we have considered here predicts a negatively sloped market demand curve as well as a negatively sloped demand curve for each individual consumer.

As we first saw in Chapter 3, market demand curves show the relationship between the product's price and the amount demanded by all consumers together. The market demand curve is the horizontal sum of the demand curves of all individual consumers. It is the horizontal sum because we want to add quantities demanded at any given price, and quantities are measured in the horizontal direction on a conventional demand curve.

Figure 6-2 illustrates a market made up of only two consumers: Arun and Bashira. At a price of $3, Arun purchases 2 units and Bashira purchases 4 units; thus, together they purchase 6 units, yielding one point on the market demand curve. No matter how many consumers are involved, the process is the same: Add the quantities demanded by all consumers at each price, and the result is the market demand curve.

FIGURE 6-2   Market and Individual Demand Curves

(i) Arun   (ii) Bashirah   (iii) Arun and Bashirah

The market demand curve is the horizontal sum of all the individual demand curves. At any given price, the quantity demanded by Arun is added to the quantity demanded by Bashira to yield the total quantity demanded by the market. However large the number of consumers in the market, the derivation of the market demand curve follows the same summation process.

6.2 INCOME AND SUBSTITUTION EFFECTS OF PRICE CHANGES

We have just seen the relationship between the *law of diminishing marginal utility* and the slope of the consumer's demand curve for some product. Here we consider an alternative method for understanding the slope of an individual's demand curve.

Let's consider Tristan, a student who loves to eat—and especially loves to eat ice cream. A fall in the price of ice cream affects Tristan in two ways. First, it provides an incentive to buy more ice cream (and less of other things) because eating ice cream is now a cheaper way to satisfy his desire to eat. Thus, a reduction in the price of ice cream—which, with all other prices constant means a fall in the *relative* price of ice cream—leads Tristan to *substitute* away from other products toward ice cream.

Second, because the price of ice cream has fallen, Tristan has more *purchasing power* or **real income** available to spend on all products. Suppose the price of premium ice cream fell from $5 to $4 per litre and Tristan was in the habit of eating half a litre of ice cream a day. In the course of a 30-day month, Tristan could keep his ice cream habit unchanged but save $15, money that would be available for any purpose—more ice cream, blueberry muffins, rounds of mini golf, or photocopies of your economics notes.

Let's now explore these two separate effects in a little more detail.

real income Income expressed in terms of the purchasing power of money income—that is, the quantity of goods and services that can be purchased with the money income.

The Substitution Effect

To isolate the effect of the change in relative price when the price of ice cream falls, we can consider what would happen if we also reduce Tristan's money income to restore the original purchasing power. Suppose Tristan's uncle sends him a monthly allowance for ice cream, and when the price of ice cream falls, the allowance is reduced by $15 so that Tristan can buy just as much ice cream—and everything else—as he could before. Tristan's purchasing power will be unchanged. If his behaviour remains unchanged, however, he will no longer be maximizing his utility. Recall that utility maximization requires that the ratio of marginal utility to price be the same for all goods. In our example, with no change in behaviour, the quantities (and hence marginal utilities) and the prices of all goods other than ice cream are unchanged. The quantity of ice cream is also unchanged, but the price has fallen. To maximize his utility after the price of ice cream falls, Tristan must therefore increase his consumption (reduce his marginal utility) of ice cream and reduce his consumption of other goods. In other words, he must *substitute* away from other goods and toward ice cream.

When purchasing power is held constant, the change in the quantity demanded of a product whose relative price has changed is called the **substitution effect** of the price change.[2]

> The substitution effect increases the quantity demanded of a product whose price has fallen and reduces the quantity demanded of a product whose price has risen.

substitution effect The change in the quantity of a product demanded resulting from a change in its relative price (holding real income constant).

The Income Effect

To examine the substitution effect, we reduced Tristan's *money* income following the price reduction so that we could see the effect of the relative price change, holding purchasing power constant. Now we want to see the effect of the change in purchasing power, *holding relative prices constant at their new value*. To do this, suppose that after Tristan has adjusted his purchases to the new price and his reduced money income, he convinces his uncle to increase his allowance by $15 to restore it to its original amount. If we assume that ice cream is a normal good, Tristan will increase his consumption of ice cream (even beyond the increase we have already seen as a result of the substitution effect). The change in the quantity of ice cream demanded as a result of Tristan's reaction to increased real income is called the **income effect**.

income effect The change in the quantity of a product demanded resulting from a change in real income (holding relative prices constant).

> The income effect leads consumers to buy more of a product whose price has fallen, provided that the product is a normal good.

Notice that the size of the income effect depends on the amount of income spent on the product whose price changes and on the amount by which the price changes. In our example, if Tristan were initially spending half of his income on ice cream, a reduction in the price of ice cream from $5 to $4 would be equivalent to a 10 percent increase in real income (20 percent of 50 percent). Now consider a different case: The price of gasoline falls by 20 percent. For a consumer who was spending 5 percent of income on gas, this is equivalent to a 1 percent increase in real income (20 percent of 5 percent).

---

[2] This measure, which isolates the substitution effect by holding the consumer's purchasing power constant, is known as the Slutsky effect. A related but slightly different measure that holds the consumer's level of utility constant is discussed in the appendix to this chapter.

The Slope of the Demand Curve

We have now divided Tristan's response to a change in the price of ice cream into a substitution effect and an income effect. Of course, when the price changes, Tristan moves directly from the initial consumption pattern to the final one; we do not observe any "halfway" consumption pattern. However, by breaking this movement into two parts for analytical purposes, we are able to study Tristan's total change in quantity demanded as a response to a change in relative prices plus a response to a change in real income.

What is true for Tristan is also true, in general terms, for all consumers. The substitution effect leads consumers to increase their quantity demanded of goods whose prices fall. The income effect leads consumers to buy more of all normal goods whose prices fall.

Putting the income and substitution effects together gives the following general statement:

> **Because of the combined operation of the income and substitution effects, the demand curve for any normal good will be negatively sloped. A fall in price will increase the quantity demanded.**

Figure 6-3 illustrates how the combination of the substitution effect and the income effect determines the slope of any demand curve. In each part of the figure, we begin at point A with the price p_0. We then consider a reduction in the price to p_1. In each case, the substitution effect (shown by the green arrow) increases the quantity demanded. In each case there is also an income effect (the red arrow), but the size and sign of the income effect differs in each case. The sum of the income and substitution effects determines the total effect of the price change and thus how overall quantity demanded responds to the price reduction. Note that all normal goods have negatively sloped demand curves. The same is true for *most* inferior goods. The figure illustrates why in the case of an inferior good the income effect must be very strong in order to generate a positively sloped demand curve. This is a very rare case in economics, but there is some interesting history behind it.

Giffen Goods   Great interest was generated by the English economist Sir Robert Giffen (1837–1910) when he claimed to observe a situation with an *upward*-sloping demand curve. He observed that when the price of bread increased (due to an increase in the price of imported wheat), members of the British working class *increased* their consumption of bread.

As described in Figure 6-3, products with positively sloped demand curves are known as **Giffen goods**, and they have two key characteristics. First, the good must be an inferior good, meaning that a reduction in real income leads households to purchase *more* of that good. Second, the good must take a large proportion of total household expenditure and therefore have a large income effect. Bread was indeed a dietary staple of the British working classes during the nineteenth century. A rise in the price of bread would therefore cause a large reduction in people's real income. This could lead people to eat more bread (and less meat) in order to consume enough calories to stay alive. Though possible, such cases are all but unknown today for in all but the poorest societies, typical households do not spend large proportions of their incomes on any single inferior good.

Giffen good An inferior good for which the income effect outweighs the substitution effect so that the demand curve is positively sloped.

FIGURE 6-3 **Income and Substitution Effects of a Price Change**

(i) Normal good
(ii) Inferior good
(iii) (Inferior) Giffen good

Demand curves for normal goods are negatively sloped. Demand curves for inferior goods are negatively sloped unless the income effect outweighs the substitution effect. In each of the diagrams, the initial price is p_0 and the initial quantity demanded is Q_0. Thus, A is a point on all three demand curves. For all three goods, a price reduction to p_1 creates a substitution effect that increases quantity demanded to Q_0^S.

For normal goods in part (i), the reduction in price increases real income and leads to a further increase in quantity demanded. The income effect is shown as the increase from Q_0^S to Q_1. The total effect of the price change is therefore the change from Q_0 to Q_1, and point B is on the negatively sloped demand curve.

For inferior goods, the price reduction causes an increase in real income that leads to a reduction in quantity demanded. If the good makes up a small fraction of the consumer's total expenditure, which is the case for most goods, then this income effect will be small. In part (ii), the income effect reduces quantity demanded from Q_0^S to Q_1, and so the total effect of the price change is the change from Q_0 to Q_1. In this case, the income effect does not fully offset the substitution effect and so the demand curve is still negatively sloped through point B. In part (iii), the income effect is very large, reducing quantity demanded from Q_0^S to Q_1, and the overall change is therefore a reduction in quantity demanded from Q_0 to Q_1. In this case the demand curve is positively sloped through point B. This is the case of a Giffen good.

Conspicuous Consumption Goods   A second case of positively sloped demand curves relates to what are called *conspicuous consumption goods*. Thorstein Veblen (1857–1929), in *The Theory of the Leisure Class,* noted that some products were consumed not for their intrinsic qualities but because they had "snob appeal." He suggested that the more expensive such a commodity became, the greater might be its ability to confer status on its purchaser.

Consumers might value diamonds, for example, precisely because everyone knows they are expensive. Thus, a fall in price might lead them to stop buying diamonds and to switch to a more satisfactory object of conspicuous consumption. They may behave in the same way with respect to luxury cars, buying them *because* they are expensive. Does this sort of behaviour violate our basic theory of utility maximization?

Two comments are in order. First, in a case where individuals appear to buy more goods at a higher price *because of the high price*, there is actually something else going on in addition to a price change. What really appeals to such individuals is that *other people think* they paid a high price—this is the basis for the "snob appeal." But such snobs would still buy more at a lower price (and hence still have negatively sloped demand curves) as long as they were absolutely sure that other people *thought* they had paid the high price. As one advertising slogan for a discount department store puts it, "Only you know how little you paid."

Second, even if such conspicuous consumers do exist, it is still unlikely that the *market* demand curve is positively sloped. Countless lower-income consumers would be glad to buy diamonds or BMWs if these commodities were sufficiently inexpensive, and their behaviour would likely offset the behaviour of the relatively few higher-income "snobs".

6.3 CONSUMER SURPLUS

We have now studied two alternative methods to explain why demand curves have a negative slope, the first using marginal utility theory and the second using substitution and income effects. In this section we use marginal utility theory to introduce the important concept of *consumer surplus*. We will revisit the distinction between *marginal* and *total* utility and see how confusion between these two concepts led to a famous paradox in the history of economic theory.

The Concept

Imagine yourself facing an either/or choice concerning some particular product, say, ice cream: You can have the amount you are now consuming, or you can have none of it. Suppose you would be *willing* to pay as much as $100 per month for the eight litres of gourmet ice cream that you now consume, rather than do without it. Further, suppose you *actually* buy those eight litres for only $40. What a bargain! You have paid $60 less than the most you were willing to pay. Actually, this sort of bargain occurs every day in the economy. Indeed, it is so common that the $60 "saved" in this example has been given a name: *consumer surplus*. **Consumer surplus** is the difference between the total value that consumers place on all the units consumed of some product and the payment they actually make to purchase that amount of the product.

Consumer surplus is a direct consequence of negatively sloped demand curves.[3] This is easiest to understand if you think of an individual's demand curve as showing his or her willingness to pay for successive units of the product. (You may recall our discussion of this point in Chapter 5.) To illustrate the concept, suppose we have interviewed Moira and displayed the information from the interview in the table in Figure 6-4. Our first question to Moira is, "If you were drinking no milk at all, how much would you be willing to pay for one litre per week?" With no hesitation she replies, "$6.00." We then ask, "If you had already consumed that one litre, how much would you be willing to pay for a second litre per week?" After a bit of thought, she answers, "$3.00." Adding one litre per week with each question, we discover that she would be willing to pay $2.00 to get a third litre per week and $1.60, $1.20, $1.00, $0.80, $0.60, $0.50, and $0.40 for successive litres from the fourth to the tenth litre per week.

consumer surplus The difference between the total value that consumers place on all units consumed of a product and the payment that they actually make to purchase that amount of the product.

---

[3] Consumer surplus is part of what, in Chapter 5, we called economic surplus when we discussed market efficiency. We will return to a detailed discussion of market efficiency in Chapter 12.

FIGURE 6-4 **Moira's Consumer Surplus on Milk Consumption**

Litres of Milk Moira Consumes per Week	Amount Moira Is Willing to Pay to Obtain This Litre	Moira's Consumer Surplus If She Actually Pays $1.00 per Litre
First	$6.00	$5.00
Second	3.00	2.00
Third	2.00	1.00
Fourth	1.60	0.60
Fifth	1.20	0.20
Sixth	1.00	0.00
Seventh	0.80	—
Eighth	0.60	—
Ninth	0.50	—
Tenth	0.40	—

Consumer surplus on each unit consumed is the difference between the market price and the maximum price that the consumer is willing to pay to obtain that unit. The table shows the value that Moira puts on successive litres of milk consumed each week. Her negatively sloped demand curve shows that she would be willing to pay progressively smaller amounts for each additional litre consumed. If the market price is $1.00 per litre, Moira will buy six litres of milk per week and pay the amount in the dark shaded area. The total value she places on these six litres is the entire shaded area. Her consumer surplus is the light shaded area.

The sum of the values that she places on each litre of milk gives us the *total value* that she places on all ten litres. In this case, Moira values the 10 litres of milk per week at $17.10. This is the amount that she would be willing to pay if she faced the either/or choice of 10 litres or none. This is also the amount she would be willing to pay if she were offered the milk one litre at a time and charged the maximum she was willing to pay for each litre.

However, Moira does not have to pay a different price for each litre of milk she consumes each week; she can buy all she wants at the prevailing market price. Suppose the price is $1.00 per litre. She will buy six litres per week because she values the sixth litre just at the market price but all earlier litres at higher amounts. She does not buy a seventh litre because she values it at less than the market price.

Because Moira values the first litre at $6.00 but gets it for $1.00, she makes a "profit" of $5.00 on that litre. Between her $3.00 valuation of the second litre and what she has to pay for it, she makes a "profit" of $2.00, a $1.00 profit on the third litre, and so on. This "profit," which is shown in the third column of the table, is Moira's consumer surplus on each litre of milk.

We can calculate Moira's total consumer surplus of $8.80 per week by summing her surplus on each litre that she actually purchases; we can calculate the same total by first summing what she would be willing to pay for all six litres, which is $14.80, and then subtracting the $6.00 that she actually does pay.

For any unit consumed, consumer surplus is the difference between the maximum amount the consumer is willing to pay for that unit and the price the consumer actually pays.

The data in the first two columns of the table give Moira's demand curve for milk. It is her demand curve because she will go on buying litres of milk as long as she values each litre at least as much as the market price she must pay for it. When the market price is $6.00 per litre, she will buy only one litre; when it is $3.00, she will buy two litres; and so on. The total valuation is the area below her demand curve, and consumer surplus is the part of the area that lies above the price line.

Figure 6-5 shows that the same relationship holds for the smooth market demand curve that indicates the total amount that all consumers would buy at each price. Figure 6-4 is a bar chart because we allowed Moira to vary her consumption only in discrete units of one litre at a time. Had we allowed her to vary her consumption of milk one drop at a time, we could have traced out a continuous curve similar to the one shown in Figure 6-5.

The market demand curve shows the valuation that consumers place on each unit of the product. For any given quantity, the area under the demand curve and above the price line shows the consumer surplus received from consuming those units.

The Paradox of Value

Early economists and philosophers, struggling with the problem of what determines the relative prices of products, encountered what they called the *paradox of value*. Why is it that water, which is essential to life, has a low price, while diamonds, which are mainly used for jewellery (and a few industrial uses), have a high price? Surely we value water more highly than diamonds? This paradox could not adequately be explained until the theory of marginal utility was developed.

The early economists thought the price, or "value" of a good, depended only on the demand by consumers. This view left out two important aspects of the determination of price that we now understand. First, supply plays just as important a role as demand in determining price. Second, consumers purchase units of a good until the marginal value of the last unit purchased is equal to its market price. Figure 6-6 shows a demand and supply diagram for water and for diamonds. Water has a plentiful supply, and hence a low price; diamonds have a relatively scarce supply and hence a high price.

FIGURE 6-5 Consumer Surplus for the Market

Consumer surplus if market price = p_0

Market price

p_0

D

0   Q_0

Quantity Consumed per Period

Total consumer surplus is the area under the demand curve and above the price line. The area under the demand curve shows the total valuation that consumers place on all units consumed. For example, the total value that consumers place on Q_0 units is the entire shaded area under the demand curve up to Q_0. At a market price of p_0, the amount paid for Q_0 units is the dark shaded area. Hence, consumer surplus is the light shaded area.

FIGURE 6-6   Resolving the Paradox of Value

(i) Water

(ii) Diamonds

The market price of a product does not just reflect the total value that consumers place on that product; supply also matters. The graph presents hypothetical demand curves for water and diamonds. The total value that consumers place on Q_w units of water, as shown by the total shaded area under the demand curve, is great. The total value that consumers place on Q_d units of diamonds is shown by the total shaded area under the demand curve for diamonds. This is clearly less than the total value placed on water.

The large supply of water makes water plentiful and makes water low in price, as shown by p_w in part (i) of the figure. The relatively low supply of diamonds makes diamonds scarce and keeps diamonds high in price, as shown by p_d in part (ii) of the figure. The high total value for water, combined with its low price, leads to a large consumer surplus for water. For diamonds, the low total value and high price lead to a small consumer surplus.

The next part of resolving this paradox is to distinguish between the marginal value and the total value of water and diamonds. Since water has a low price, consumers will use water to the point where the *marginal* value placed on the last unit consumed is very low. However, remember that the *total* value placed on all units consumed is shown by the area under the demand curve—which for water is very high. Diamonds, on the other hand, have a very high market price and so consumption will stop at a level where the marginal value placed on the last unit purchased is equally high. For diamonds, though, the *total* value on all units consumed is very low.

This paradox of value, easily illustrated with the example of water and diamonds, also provides a good illustration of consumer surplus. Water has a high total value and a low price, which leads to a large consumer surplus; diamonds have a low total value and a high price, and therefore relatively little consumer surplus.

The paradox of value can be resolved by understanding (1) the market price of a good depends on both demand and supply, and (2) the difference between the *total* and *marginal* value that consumers place on a good. Water has a low price and low marginal value, but a high total value. Diamonds have a high price and high marginal value, but a low total value.

The same paradox exists in many markets, including labour markets. As we all know, professional hockey players earn many times more than nurses and doctors, even though most consumers probably place more total value on health care than they do on sports entertainment. But top-quality hockey players have a set of skills that are in much shorter supply than even highly skilled medical professionals, and this difference in supply helps to explain their different incomes. We have much more to say about the operation of labour markets in Chapters 13 and 14.

SUMMARY

6.1 MARGINAL UTILITY AND CONSUMER CHOICE   LO 1, 2

- Marginal utility theory distinguishes between the total utility from the consumption of all units of some product and the incremental (or marginal) utility derived from consuming one more unit of the product.
- The basic assumption in marginal utility theory is that the utility consumers derive (over some given time period) from the consumption of successive units of a product diminishes as the number of units consumed increases.
- Utility-maximizing consumers make their choices such that the utilities derived from the last dollar spent on each product are equal. For two goods X and Y, utility will be maximized when

$$\frac{MU_X}{p_X} = \frac{MU_Y}{p_Y}$$

- Demand curves have negative slopes because when the price of one product falls, each consumer responds by increasing purchases of that product sufficiently to restore the ratio of that product's marginal utility to its now lower price (MU/p) to the same level achieved for all other products.
- Market demand curves for any product are derived by horizontally summing all of the individual demand curves for that product.

6.2 INCOME AND SUBSTITUTION EFFECTS OF PRICE CHANGES   LO 3

- A change in the price of a product generates both an income effect and a substitution effect. The substitution effect is the reaction of the consumer to the change in relative prices, with purchasing power (real income) held constant. The substitution effect leads the consumer to increase purchases of the product whose relative price has fallen.
- The income effect is the reaction of the consumer to the change in purchasing power (real income) that is caused by the price change, holding relative prices constant at their new level. A fall in one price will lead to an

increase in the consumer's real income and thus to an increase in purchases of all normal goods.
- The combined income and substitution effects ensure that the quantity demanded of any normal good will increase when its price falls, other things being equal. Normal goods, therefore, have negatively sloped demand curves.
- An inferior good will have a negatively sloped demand curve unless the income effect is strong enough to outweigh the substitution effect. This situation is very rare and is called a Giffen good.

6.3 CONSUMER SURPLUS   LO 4, 5

- For each unit of a product, consumer surplus is the difference between what consumers are willing to pay for that unit and what consumers actually pay for that unit.
- Consumer surplus arises because demand curves are negatively sloped and consumers purchase units of a product up to the point where the marginal value equals the market price. On all units before the marginal unit,

consumers value the product more than the price and hence they earn consumer surplus.
- Price is related to the marginal value that consumers place on having a bit more or a bit less of some product; it bears no necessary relationship to the total value that consumers place on all of the units consumed of that product. The paradox of value involves confusion between total value and marginal value.

KEY CONCEPTS

Total utility and marginal utility
Utility maximization
Equality of *MU/p* across different products

Slope of the demand curve
Market and individual demand curves
Income effect and substitution effect

Giffen goods and conspicuous consumption goods
Consumer surplus
The paradox of value

STUDY EXERCISES

MyEconLab Make the grade with MyEconLab: Study Exercises marked in ⊕ can be found on MyEconLab. You can practise them as often as you want, and most feature step-by-step guided instructions to help you find the right answer.

1 Fill in the blanks to make the following statements correct.

a. Utility theory is based on the hypothesis that the _____ received from each additional unit of the good _____ as total consumption of the good increases.

b. A utility-maximizing consumer will allocate expenditure such that the _____ per dollar spent on each product is _____ for all products.

c. An equation that represents a utility-maximizing pattern of consumption of two goods, *A* and *B*, is _____.

d. Marginal utility analysis tells us that a rise in the price of a good, *ceteris paribus*, leads each consumer to reduce the _____ of the good. This, in turn, predicts a _____ demand curve.

2 The table below shows how Brett's utility increases as the number of avocados he consumes (per month) increases. Brett's utility is measured in utils, a name that economists invented to describe units of utility.

Avocados	Total Utility (in utils)	Marginal Utility (in utils)
Zero	0	_____
First	100	_____
Second	185	_____
Third	245	_____
Fourth	285	_____
Fifth	315	_____
Sixth	335	_____
Seventh	345	_____
Eighth	350	_____

a. Plot Brett's total utility on a scale diagram, with utils on the vertical axis and the number of avocados (per month) on the horizontal axis.

b. Compute the marginal utility for each avocado and fill in the table.

c. Plot the marginal utility on a scale diagram, with utils on the vertical axis and the number of avocados (per month) on the horizontal axis. (Make sure to plot marginal utility at the midpoints between units.)

d. Explain why it is reasonable that Brett's utility increases by smaller and smaller amounts for each successive avocado consumed.

3 In each of the cases listed below, identify whether Claudia's expenditure on each product should rise or fall in order to maximize her utility.

Case	Price of X ($)	Marginal Utility of X (units of utility)	Price of Y ($)	Marginal Utility of Y (units of utility)
A	10	2	5	3
B	12	4	4	2
C	3	1	6	2
D	4	2	4	2
E	3	4	4	3

4 Luc allocates his total monthly household expenditures between only two goods, restaurant meals and "all other goods." Suppose the price of each restaurant meal is $20 and the price of each unit of "all other goods" is $10. In each case below, assuming that Luc is maximizing his utility, determine the marginal utility (*MU*) received from the unmentioned good.

a. The *MU* he is currently receiving from his consumption of restaurant meals is 100.
b. The *MU* he is currently receiving from his consumption of "all other goods" is 40.
c. The *MU* he is currently receiving from his consumption of restaurant meals is 56.
d. The *MU* he is currently receiving from his consumption of "all other goods" is 122.

5 Use the following diagram to answer the questions below about marginal and total utility for the consumption of Good X.

a. What is the total utility of consuming 500 units of the good? 600 units? 700 units?
b. How does the marginal utility of the 100th unit compare to that for the 200th or 500th? How do you know?
c. How is the law of diminishing marginal utility demonstrated in this diagram?
d. What is the marginal utility of consuming Good X when total utility is at its maximum?

6 Sally consumes only two goods, shoes and "everything else." For five different shopping trips (each with different prices), the prices and Sally's marginal utilities are shown below.

	Shoes		Everything Else	
	MU	Price ($)	*MU*	Price ($)
Trip 1	125	250	50	100
Trip 2	100	200	50	100
Trip 3	75	150	50	100
Trip 4	50	100	50	100
Trip 5	25	50	50	100

a. Is Sally maximizing her total utility on each shopping trip? Explain why or why not.
b. Using what you have learned in this chapter about marginal utility, explain how the number of shoes consumed is changing as their price changes.
c. Can you detect the shape of Sally's demand curve for shoes from the data shown in the table?

7 Both diagrams below show the income and substitution effects of a rise in price from p_0 to p_1. In each case the substitution effect is illustrated by the change in quantity demanded from Q_0 to Q^*; the income effect is illustrated by the change in quantity demanded from Q^* to Q_1.

a. Is Good X a normal or an inferior good? Explain.
b. Is Good Y a normal or an inferior good? Explain.
c. For each of Goods X and Y, explain whether the income effect is working in the same direction or the opposite direction as the substitution effect.

d. For Good Y, how large would the income effect need to be for this to be a Giffen good? What would the demand curve look like in this case?

8 Suppose there is a 10 percent increase in the prices of the following products. Keeping in mind how large a fraction of a typical consumer's budget these items are, explain whether you think the income effect in each case would be small or large, and why.

a. salt
b. jeans
c. all fruits and vegetables
d. gasoline
e. mini-vans
f. rental apartments
g. luxury cars
h. all electronic equipment
i. vacations to Cuba
j. fee for one-day car rentals

9 In what situations do the substitution effect and the income effect work in the same direction to produce a downward-sloping demand curve? In what situations do they have opposing effects?

10 Rupert really loves pizza, but he eventually tires of it. The table below shows the highest price that Rupert is willing to pay for each successive pizza per week.

Pizza	Rupert's Willingness to Pay
First	$18
Second	$16
Third	$13
Fourth	$9
Fifth	$4
Sixth	$0

a. Suppose Rupert were to eat five pizzas per week. What is the total value Rupert would place on his five weekly pizzas?
b. If the market price is $10 per pizza, how many pizzas will Rupert buy and eat per week?
c. If the market price is $10 per pizza, what is the weekly consumer surplus that Rupert gets from eating pizza?

11 Use the following diagram of a market for potted plants to answer the questions below about consumer surplus.

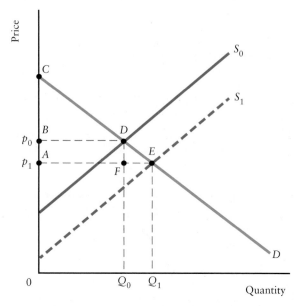

a. With demand curve D and supply curve S_0, the equilibrium price and quantity in this market are p_0 and Q_0. At the price p_0, what is the area that represents total consumer surplus in this market? (Use the letter point labels to describe the area.)
b. Now suppose supply increases to S_1. Determine the new equilibrium price and quantity. What is the area that now represents total consumer surplus?
c. At the new lower price, what is the area that represents the increased consumer surplus earned on the original units purchased?
d. At the new lower price, what is the area that represents consumer surplus earned on the new units purchased?

12 See the diagrams at the bottom of the next page. Consider the supply-and-demand diagrams depicting the markets for X and Y, respectively. In the market for good X, supply is perfectly elastic, indicating that producers are prepared to supply any amount of X at price p_0.

a. In the market for X, demand increases from D_0 to D_1. Explain what happens to the total value that consumers place on X.
b. Explain how the increase in demand for X alters the marginal value that consumers place on X.
c. In the market for Y, a technological improvement causes supply to increase from S_0 to S_1, causing price to fall from p_0 to p_1. Explain what happens

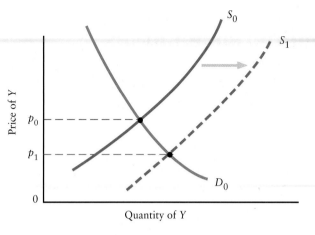

to the total value that consumers place on a given quantity of Y.

d. Explain why the increase in supply leads consumers to reduce their marginal value of Y even though there has been no change in their preferences regarding Y (and thus no shift in the demand curve).

⑬ Consider the market for some product. The demand and supply curves are given by:

$$\text{Demand: } p = 30 - 4Q^D$$

$$\text{Supply: } p = 6 + 2Q^S$$

a. Plot the demand and supply curves on a scale diagram. Compute the equilibrium price (p^*) and quantity (Q^*).

b. Show in the diagram the total value that consumers place on Q^* units of the good.

c. What is the value that consumers place on an additional unit of the good?

d. Now suppose that production costs fall, and thus the market supply curve shifts to a new position given by $p = 2 + 2Q^S$. How do consumers now value an additional unit of the good?

e. Explain why consumers' marginal value has fallen even though there has been no change in their preferences (and thus no change in the demand curve).

⑭ Using marginal utility theory, discuss why newspaper publishers are prepared to use vending machines that allow customers to pay for one newspaper and remove several, whereas candy and soft-drink producers use vending machines that allow customers to remove only the single product that is purchased.

⑮ Many medical and hospital services in Canada are provided at zero direct cost to all Canadians and are financed out of general government revenues.

a. What would be the marginal value of such services consumed by each Canadian if the government provided the necessary resources to satisfy all demand?

b. How does your answer to part (a) relate to the total value that Canadians probably place on medical services?

⑯ The diamond-water paradox is the classic example of the paradox of value, but the concept can be applied to many other market situations. Show in a diagram and explain why a cardiac surgeon earns far less than an NHL hockey star. Does society "value" the hockey player more than the surgeon?

Appendix to Chapter 6
Indifference Curves

In Chapter 6, we studied the theory of demand; here we extend the theory by considering in more detail the assumptions about consumer behaviour that underlie the theory of demand.

The history of demand theory has seen two major breakthroughs. The first was marginal utility theory, which we used in Chapter 6. By distinguishing total and marginal values, this theory helped to explain the so-called paradox of value. The second breakthrough came with indifference theory, which showed that the stringent assumption of measurable utility (required for marginal utility theory) could be dispensed with. Indifference theory is based on the much weaker assumption that consumers can always say which of two consumption bundles they prefer without having to say by *how much* they prefer it. In other words, even if we are unable to measure a consumer's utility, indifference theory gives us a fully coherent way to think about individual and market demand curves.

6A.1 INDIFFERENCE CURVES

Suppose Hugh currently has available some specific bundle of goods, say, 18 units of clothing and 10 units of food. Now offer him an alternative bundle of, say, 13 units of clothing and 15 units of food. This alternative combination of goods has 5 fewer units of clothing and 5 more units of food than the first one. Whether Hugh prefers this new bundle depends on the relative valuation that he places on 5 more units of food and 5 fewer units of clothing. If he values the extra food more than the forgone clothing, he will prefer the new bundle to the original one. If he values the extra food less than the forgone clothing, he will prefer the original bundle. If Hugh values the extra food the same as the forgone clothing, he is said to be indifferent between the two bundles.

Suppose that after much trial and error, we have identified several bundles between which Hugh is indifferent. In other words, all bundles give him equal satisfaction or utility. They are shown in the table in Figure 6A-1.

Of course, there are combinations of the two products other than those enumerated in the table that will give Hugh the same level of utility. All of these combinations are shown in Figure 6A-1 by the smooth curve that passes through the points plotted from the table. This curve, called an indifference curve, shows all combinations of products that yield Hugh the same utility.

> The consumer is indifferent between the combinations indicated by any two points on one indifference curve.

Any points above the curve show combinations of food and clothing that Hugh prefers to points on the curve. Consider, for example, the combination of 20 units of food and 18 units of clothing, represented by point *g* in Figure 6A-1. Although it may not be obvious that this bundle must be preferred to bundle *a* (which has more clothing but less food), it is obvious that it will be preferred to bundle *c* because both less clothing and less food are represented at *c* than at *g*. Inspection of the graph shows that any point above the curve will be superior to some points on the curve in the sense that it will contain both more food and more clothing than those points on the curve. However, because all points on the curve are equal in Hugh's eyes, any point above the curve must be superior to all points on the curve. By a similar argument, all points below and to the left of the curve represent bundles that are inferior to bundles represented by points on the curve.

> Any point above an indifference curve is preferred to any point along that same indifference curve; any point on the curve is preferred to any point below it.

FIGURE 6A-1 **Hugh's Indifference Curve**

Alternative Bundles Giving Hugh Equal Utility

Bundle	Clothing (units)	Food (units)
a	30	5
b	18	10
c	13	15
d	10	20
e	8	25
f	7	30

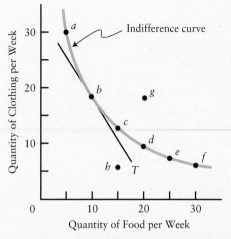

This indifference curve shows combinations of food and clothing that yield equal utility and between which Hugh is indifferent. The smooth curve through the points is an indifference curve; all combinations on it give Hugh equal utility. Point *g* above the line is a preferred combination to any point on the line; point *h* below the line is an inferior combination to any point on the line. The slope of the line *T* gives the marginal rate of substitution at point *b*. Moving down the indifference curve from *b* to *f*, the slope flattens, showing that the more food and the less clothing Hugh has, the less willing he is to sacrifice further clothing to get more food.

Diminishing Marginal Rate of Substitution

How much clothing would Hugh be willing to give up to get one more unit of food but to keep his utility unchanged? The answer to this question measures what is called Hugh's marginal rate of substitution of clothing for food. The marginal rate of substitution (MRS) is the amount of one product that a consumer is willing to give up to get one more unit of another product and remain indifferent.

The first basic assumption of indifference theory is that the algebraic value of the MRS between two goods is always negative.

A negative MRS means that to increase consumption of one product, Hugh is prepared to decrease consumption of a second product. The negative value of the marginal rate of substitution is indicated graphically by the negative slope of indifference curves.

Consider a case in which Hugh has a lot of clothing and only a little food. Common sense suggests that he might be willing to give up quite a bit of plentiful clothing to get one more unit of scarce food. It suggests as well that if Hugh had little clothing and a lot of food he would be willing to give up only a little scarce clothing to get one more unit of already plentiful food.

This example illustrates the hypothesis of diminishing marginal rate of substitution. The less of one product, *A,* and the more of a second product, *B,* that the consumer has already, the smaller the amount of *A* that the consumer will be willing to give up to get one additional unit of *B*. The hypothesis says that the marginal rate of substitution changes when the amounts of two products consumed change. The graphical expression of this hypothesis is that any indifference curve becomes flatter as the consumer moves downward and to the right along the curve. In Figure 6A-1, a movement downward and to the right means that Hugh is consuming less clothing and more food. The decreasing steepness of the curve means that Hugh is willing to sacrifice less and less clothing to get each additional unit of food. [11]

Diminishing MRS is the second basic assumption of indifference theory.

The hypothesis of diminishing marginal rate of substitution is illustrated in Table 6A-1, which is based on the example in Figure 6A-1. The last column of the table shows the rate at which Hugh is prepared to sacrifice units of clothing per unit of food obtained. At first, Hugh will sacrifice 2.4 units of clothing to get 1 unit more of food, but as his consumption of clothing diminishes and his consumption of food increases, Hugh becomes less and less willing to sacrifice further clothing for more food.

The Indifference Map

So far, we have constructed only a single indifference curve for Hugh. However, starting at any other point in Figure 6A-1, such as *g*, there will be other combinations that will give Hugh equal utility. If the points indicating all of these combinations are connected, they will form another indifference curve. This exercise can be repeated many times, and we can thereby generate many indifference curves for Hugh. The farther any indifference curve is from the origin, the higher will be the level of Hugh's utility given by any of the points on the curve.

A set of indifference curves is called an indifference map, an example of which is shown in Figure 6A-2. It specifies the consumer's tastes by showing his rate of substitution between the two products for every possible level of current consumption of these products.

When economists say that a consumer's tastes are given, they do not mean that the consumer's current consumption pattern is given; rather, they mean that the consumer's entire indifference map is given.

TABLE 6A-1 Hugh's Marginal Rate of Substitution Between Clothing and Food

Movement	(1) Change in Clothing	(2) Change in Food	(3) Marginal Rate of Substitution (1) ÷ (2)
From *a* to *b*	12	5	2.4
From *b* to *c*	5	5	1.0
From *c* to *d*	3	5	0.6
From *d* to *e*	2	5	0.4
From *e* to *f*	1	5	0.2

The marginal rate of substitution of clothing for food declines (in absolute value) as the quantity of food increases. This table is based on Figure 6A-1. When Hugh moves from *a* to *b*, he gives up 12 units of clothing and gains 5 units of food; he remains at the same level of overall utility. At point *a*, Hugh is prepared to sacrifice 12 units of clothing for 5 units of food (i.e., 12/5 = 2.4 units of clothing per unit of food obtained). When he moves from *b* to *c*, he sacrifices 5 units of clothing for 5 units of food (a rate of substitution of 1 unit of clothing for each unit of food).

FIGURE 6A-2 Hugh's Indifference Map

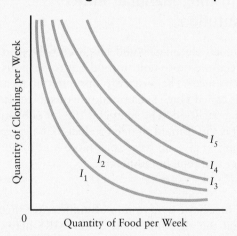

An indifference map consists of a set of indifference curves. All points on a particular curve indicate alternative combinations of food and clothing that give Hugh equal utility. The farther the curve is from the origin, the higher is the level of utility it represents. For example, I_5 is a higher indifference curve than I_4, which means that all the points on I_5 give Hugh a higher level of utility than do the points on I_4.

6A.2 THE BUDGET LINE

Indifference curves illustrate consumers' tastes. To develop a complete theory of their choices, we must also illustrate the available alternatives. These are shown as the solid line *ab* in Figure 6A-3. That line, called a budget line, shows all the combinations of food and clothing that Hugh can buy if he spends a fixed amount of money, in this case his entire money income of $720 per week, at fixed prices of the products (in this case, $12 per unit for clothing and $24 per unit for food).

Properties of the Budget Line

The budget line has several important properties:

1. Points on the budget line indicate bundles of products that use up the consumer's entire income. (Try, for example, the point 20C, 20F.)

2. Points between the budget line and the origin indicate bundles of products that cost less than the consumer's income. (Try, for example, the point 20C, 10F.)

3. Points above the budget line indicate combinations of products that cost more than the consumer's income. (Try, for example, the point 30C, 40F.)

The budget line shows all combinations of products that are available to the consumer given his money income and the prices of the goods that he purchases.

We can also show Hugh's alternatives with an equation that uses symbols to express the information contained in the budget line. Let E stand for Hugh's money income, which must be equal to his total expenditure on food and clothing. If p_F and p_C represent the money prices of food and clothing, respectively, and F and C represent the quantities of food and clothing that Hugh chooses, then his spending on food is equal to p_F times F, and his spending on clothing is equal to p_C times C. Thus the equation for the budget line is

$$E = p_F \times F + p_C \times C$$

The Slope of the Budget Line

Look again at Hugh's budget line in Figure 6A-3. The vertical intercept is 60 units of clothing, and the horizontal intercept is 30 units of food. Thus the slope is equal to –2. The minus sign means that increases in Hugh's purchases of one of the goods must be accompanied by decreases in his purchases of the other. The numerical value of the slope indicates how much of one good must be given up to obtain an additional unit of the other; in our example, the slope of –2 means that Hugh must forgo the purchase of 2 units of clothing to acquire 1 extra unit of food.

Recall that in Chapter 3 we contrasted the absolute, or money, price of a product with its relative

FIGURE 6A-3 **Hugh's Budget Line**

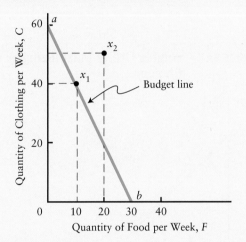

The budget line shows the quantities of goods available to a consumer given money income and the prices of goods. Any point in this diagram indicates a combination (or bundle) of so much food and so much clothing. Point x_1, for example, indicates 40 units of clothing and 10 units of food per week.

With an income of $720 a week and prices of $24 per unit for food and $12 per unit for clothing, Hugh's budget line is *ab*. This line shows all the combinations of F and C available to him if he spends the entire $720 per week. He could spend all this money income on clothing and obtain 60 units of clothing and zero food each week. Or he could go to the other extreme and purchase only food, buying 30 units of F and zero units of C. Hugh could also choose an intermediate position and consume some of both goods—for example, spending $240 to buy 10 units of F and $480 to buy 40 units of C (point x_1). Points above the budget line, such as x_2, are not attainable.

price, which is the ratio of its absolute price to that of some other product or group of products. One important point is that the relative price determines the slope of the budget line. In terms of our example of food and clothing, the slope of the budget line is determined by the relative price of food in terms of clothing, p_F/p_C; with the price of food (p_F) at $24 per unit and the price of clothing (p_C) at $12 per unit, the slope of the budget line (in absolute value) is 2. [12]

The significance of the slope of Hugh's budget line for food and clothing is that it reflects his opportunity cost of food in terms of clothing. To increase food consumption while maintaining expenditure constant, Hugh must move along the budget line and therefore consume less clothing; the slope of the budget line determines how much clothing he must give up to obtain an additional unit of food.

> The opportunity cost of food in terms of clothing is measured by the (absolute value of the) slope of the budget line, which is equal to the relative price ratio, p_F/p_C.

In the example, with fixed income and with the relative price of food in terms of clothing (p_F/p_C) equal to 2, Hugh must forgo the purchase of 2 units of clothing to acquire 1 extra unit of food. The opportunity cost of a unit of food is thus 2 units of clothing. Notice that the relative price (in our example, p_F/p_C = 2) is consistent with an infinite number of absolute prices. If p_F = $40 and p_C = $20, it is still necessary to sacrifice 2 units of clothing to acquire 1 unit of food.[4] Thus relative, not absolute, prices determine opportunity cost.

6A.3 THE CONSUMER'S UTILITY-MAXIMIZING CHOICES

An indifference map describes the preferences of a consumer, and a budget line describes the possibilities available to a consumer. To predict what a con-

sumer will actually do, both sets of information must be combined, as is done in Figure 6A-4. Hugh's budget line is shown by the straight line, and the curves from the indifference map are also shown. Any point on the budget line is attainable, but which point will Hugh actually choose?

Because Hugh wants to maximize utility, he wants to reach the highest attainable indifference curve. Inspection of Figure 6A-4 shows that if Hugh purchases any bundle on the budget line at a point cut by an indifference curve, he can reach a higher indifference curve. Only when the bundle purchased is such that the indifference curve is tangent to the budget line is it impossible for Hugh to reach a higher curve by altering his purchases.

FIGURE 6A-4 Hugh's Utility-Maximizing Choice

The consumer's utility is maximized at A, where an indifference curve is tangent to the budget line. Hugh has a money income of $720 per week and faces money prices of $12 per unit for clothing and $24 per unit for food. A combination of units of clothing and food indicated by point *a* on I_1 is attainable but, by moving along the budget line, Hugh can reach higher indifference curves. The same is true at *b* on I_2 and at *c* on I_3. At A, however, where an indifference curve (I_4) is tangent to the budget line, Hugh cannot reach a higher curve by moving along the budget line.

---

[4] Of course, with a given income, Hugh can afford much less of each at these higher money prices, but the opportunity cost of food in terms of clothing remains unchanged.

The consumer's utility is maximized at the point where an indifference curve is tangent to the budget line. At that point, the consumer's marginal rate of substitution for the two goods is equal to the relative prices of the two goods.

The intuitive explanation for this result is that if Hugh values goods differently from the way the market does, there is room for profitable exchange. Hugh can give up some of the good that he values relatively less than the market does and take in return some of the good that he values relatively more than the market does. When he is prepared to exchange goods at the same rate as they can be traded on the market, there is no further opportunity for him to raise utility by substituting one product for the other.

The theory thus proceeds by supposing that Hugh is presented with market prices that he cannot change and then by analyzing how he adjusts to these prices by choosing a bundle of goods such that, at the margin, his own subjective valuation of the goods coincides with the valuations given by market prices.

We will now use this theory to predict the typical consumer's response to a change in income and in prices.

The Consumer's Response to a Change in Income

A change in Hugh's money income will, *ceteris paribus*, shift his budget line. For example, if Hugh's income doubles, he will be able to buy twice as much of both food and clothing compared with any combination on his previous budget line. His budget line will therefore shift out parallel to itself to indicate this expansion in his consumption possibilities. (The fact that it will be a parallel shift is established by the previous demonstration that the slope of the budget line depends only on the relative prices of the two products.)

For each level of Hugh's income, there will be a utility-maximizing point at which an indifference curve is tangent to the relevant budget line. Each such utility-maximizing position means that Hugh is doing as well as possible at that level of income. If we move the budget line through all possible levels of income

FIGURE 6A-5 **Income-Consumption Line**

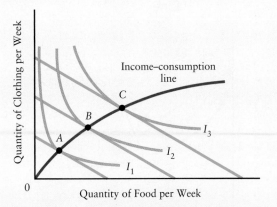

The income-consumption line shows how the consumer's purchases react to a change in money income with relative prices being held constant. Increases in Hugh's money income cause a parallel outward shift of his budget line, moving his utility-maximizing point from A to B to C. By joining all the utility-maximizing points, Hugh's income-consumption line is traced out.

and if we join up all the utility-maximizing points, we will trace out what is called an income-consumption line, an example of which is shown in Figure 6A-5. This line shows how Hugh's consumption bundle changes as his income changes, with relative prices being held constant.

The Consumer's Response to a Change in Price

We already know that a change in the relative prices of the two goods changes the slope of the budget line. Given the price of clothing, for each possible price of food there is a different utility-maximizing consumption bundle for Hugh. If we connect these bundles, at a given money income, we will trace out a price-consumption line, as shown in Figure 6A-6. Notice that in this example, as the relative prices of food and clothing change, the quantities of food and clothing that Hugh purchases also change. In particular, as the price of food falls, Hugh buys more food and less clothing.

FIGURE 6A-6 Hugh's Price-Consumption Line

The price-consumption line shows how the consumer's purchases react to a change in one price with money income and other prices being held constant. Decreases in the price of food (with money income and the price of clothing held constant) pivot Hugh's budget line from *ab* to *ac* to *ad*. Hugh's utility-maximizing bundle moves from *A* to *B* to *C*. By joining all the utility-maximizing points, a price-consumption line is traced out, showing that Hugh purchases more food and less clothing as the price of food falls.

6A.4 DERIVING THE CONSUMER'S DEMAND CURVE

What happens to the consumer's demand for some product, say, gasoline, as the price of that product changes, holding constant the prices of all other goods?

If there were only two products purchased by consumers, we could derive a demand curve for one of the products from the price-consumption line like the one we showed for Hugh in Figure 6A-6. When there are many products, however, a change in the price of one product generally causes substitution toward (or away from) all other goods. Thus, we would like to have a simple way of representing the individual's tastes in a world of many products.

In part (i) of Figure 6A-7, a new type of indifference map is plotted in which litres of gasoline per month are measured on the horizontal axis and the value of all other goods consumed per month is plotted on the vertical axis. We have in effect used "everything but gasoline" as the second product. The indifference curves in this figure then show the rate at which the consumer is prepared to substitute gasoline for money (which allows him to buy all other goods) at each level of consumption of gasoline and of all other goods.

To illustrate the derivation of demand curves, we use the numerical example shown in Figure 6A-7. The consumer is assumed to have an after-tax money income of $4000 per month. This level of money income is plotted on the vertical axis, showing that if the consumer consumes no gasoline, he can consume $4000 worth of other goods each month. When gasoline costs $1.50 per litre, the consumer could buy a maximum of 2667 litres per month. This set of choices gives rise to the innermost budget line. Given the consumer's tastes, utility is maximized at point *A*, consuming 600 litres of gasoline and $3100 worth of other products.

Next, let the price of gasoline fall to $1.00 per litre. Now the maximum possible consumption of gasoline is 4000 litres per month, giving rise to the middle budget line in the figure. The consumer's utility is maximized, as always, at the point where the new budget line is tangent to an indifference curve. At this point, *B*, the consumer is consuming 1200 litres of gasoline per month and spending $2800 on all other goods. Finally, let the price fall to 50 cents per litre. The consumer can now buy a maximum of 8000 litres per month, giving rise to the outermost of the three budget lines. The consumer maximizes utility by consuming 2200 litres of gasoline per month and spending $2900 on other products.

If we let the price vary over all possible amounts, we will trace out a complete price-consumption line, as shown in Figure 6A-7. The points derived in the preceding paragraph are merely three points on this line.

We have now derived all that we need to plot the consumer's demand curve for gasoline, now that we know how much the consumer will purchase at each price. To draw the curve, we merely replot the data from part (i) of Figure 6A-7 onto a demand graph, as shown in part (ii) of Figure 6A-7.

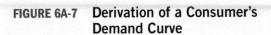

FIGURE 6A-7 Derivation of a Consumer's Demand Curve

(i) Price–consumption line

(ii) Demand curve

Every point on the price-consumption line corresponds to both a price of the product and a quantity demanded; this is the information required for a demand curve. In part (i), the consumer has a money income of $4000 and alternatively faces prices of $1.50, $1.00, and $0.50 per litre of gasoline, choosing positions A, B, and C at each price. The information for litres of gasoline demanded at each price is then plotted in part (ii) to yield the consumer's demand curve. The three points a, b, and c in part (ii) correspond to the points A, B, and C in part (i).

Like part (i), part (ii) has quantity of gasoline on the horizontal axis. By placing one graph under the other, we can directly transcribe the quantity determined on the upper graph to the lower one. We first do this for the 600 litres consumed on the innermost budget line. We now note that the price of gasoline that gives rise to that budget line is $1.50 per litre. Plotting 600 litres against $1.50 in part (ii) produces the point a, derived from point A in part (i). This is one point on the consumer's demand curve. Next we consider the middle budget line, which occurs when the price of gasoline is $1.00 per litre. We take the figure of 1200 litres from point B in part (i) and transfer it to part (ii). We then plot this quantity against the price of $1.00 to get the point b on the demand curve. Doing the same thing for point C yields the point c in part (ii): price 50 cents, quantity 2200 litres.

Repeating the operation for all prices yields the demand curve in part (ii). Note that the two parts of Figure 6A-7 describe the same behaviour. Both parts measure the quantity of gasoline on the horizontal axes; the only difference is that in part (i) the price of gasoline determines the slope of the budget line, whereas in part (ii) the price of gasoline is plotted explicitly on the vertical axis.

Income and Substitution Effects

The price-consumption line in part (i) of Figure 6A-7 indicates that as price decreases, the quantity of gasoline demanded increases, thus giving rise to the negatively sloped demand curve in part (ii). As we saw in Chapter 6, the key to understanding the negative slope of the demand curve is to distinguish between the income effect and the substitution effect of a change in price. We can make this distinction more precisely, and somewhat differently, by using indifference curves.

In Chapter 6, we examined the substitution effect of a reduction in price by eliminating the income effect. We did this by reducing money income until the consumer could just purchase the original bundle of goods. We then examined how the change in relative prices affected the consumer's choices. In indifference theory, however, the income effect is removed by changing money income until the original level of utility—the original indifference curve—can just be achieved. This method results in a slightly different measure of the

FIGURE 6A-8 **The Income and Substitution Effects of a Price Change**

The substitution effect is defined by sliding the budget line around a fixed indifference curve; the income effect is defined by a parallel shift of the budget line. The original budget line is at *ab*, and a fall in the price of gasoline takes it to *aj*. The original utility-maximizing point is at A_0 with Q_0 of gasoline being consumed, and the new utility-maximizing point is at A_2 with Q_2 of gasoline being consumed. To remove the income effect, imagine reducing the consumer's money income until the original indifference curve is just attainable. We do this by shifting the line *aj* to a parallel line nearer the origin $a_1 j_1$ that just touches the indifference curve that passes through A_0. The intermediate point A_1 divides the quantity change into a substitution effect $Q_0 Q_1$ and an income effect $Q_1 Q_2$.

income effect, but the principle involved in separating the total change into an income effect and a substitution effect is exactly the same as in Chapter 6.

The separation of the two effects according to indifference theory is shown in Figure 6A-8. The figure shows in greater detail part of the price-consumption line first drawn in Figure 6A-7. Points A_0 and A_2 are on the price-consumption line for gasoline; A_0 is the consumer's utility-maximizing point at the initial price, whereas A_2 is the consumer's utility-maximizing point at the new price.

We can think of the separation of the income and substitution effects as occurring in the following way. After the price of the good has fallen, we reduce money income until the original indifference curve can just be obtained. The consumer moves from point A_0 to an intermediate point A_1, and this response is defined as the substitution effect. Then, to measure the income effect, we restore money income. The consumer moves from the point A_1 to the final point A_2, and this response is defined as the income effect.

STUDY EXERCISES

1 Consider Katie's preferences for magazines and ice cream cones. Several "consumption bundles" are shown in the table below.

Bundle	Ice Cream Cones	Magazines
a	9	0
b	7	2
c	6	2
d	5	3
e	4	4
f	4	3
g	3	4
h	2	6
i	0	6

a. On a scale diagram with the quantity of ice cream cones on the vertical axis and the quantity of magazines on the horizontal axis, plot the various bundles.

b. Suppose that Katie is indifferent between bundles c and i. She is also indifferent between bundles d, g, and h, but all three of these are preferred to c or i. Finally, suppose that, of the bundles shown in the table, bundle e is Katie's favourite. Draw three indifference curves showing this information.

c. Consider bundles e, f, and g. What can you conclude about how Katie would rank these bundles?

2 Continue with Katie from the previous question. Katie has a monthly allowance of $36 that she chooses to divide between magazines and ice cream cones. Magazines cost $6 each and ice cream cones cost $4 each.

a. For each of the consumption bundles shown in the table, compute the total expenditure. Which ones can Katie afford, and which ones can't she afford?

b. Draw Katie's budget line. What is the slope of the line?

c. Given Katie's monthly budget constraint, which bundle does she choose to maximize her utility?

3 Debra travels to Mexico and enjoys both burritos and Coronas. The diagram shows her utility-maximizing choices.

a. If the budget line is line 1, describe why point A is Debra's utility-maximizing choice.

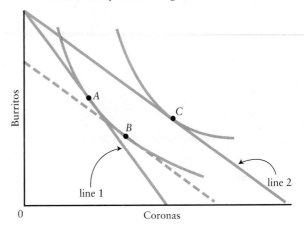

b. What event can explain why the budget line moves to line 2?

c. What is the meaning of point B in the figure?

d. Suppose Coronas are a normal good for Debra. What does this restriction imply about the location of point C? Is this restriction satisfied in the diagram?

e. Suppose Coronas were an inferior good for Debra. How would this information be reflected in her choice following the move of the budget line to line 2?

4 Consider your sets of indifference curves for

i. Coke and chips
ii. Coke and Pepsi

Explain why these sets of indifference curves are likely to look different. Illustrate with a diagram. What does this difference imply about the magnitude of the substitution effects in response to changes in the price of Coke?

7 Producers in the Short Run

CHAPTER OUTLINE	LEARNING OBJECTIVES (LO)
	After studying this chapter, you will be able to
7.1 WHAT ARE FIRMS?	1 identify the various forms of business organization and discuss the different ways that firms can be financed.
7.2 PRODUCTION, COSTS, AND PROFITS	2 distinguish between accounting profits and economic profits.
7.3 PRODUCTION IN THE SHORT RUN	3 understand the relationships among total product, average product, and marginal product; and the law of diminishing marginal returns.
7.4 COSTS IN THE SHORT RUN	4 explain the difference between fixed and variable costs, and the relationships among total costs, average costs, and marginal costs.

IN Chapter 6, we went behind the scenes of the demand curve to understand how it is determined by the behaviour of consumers. In this chapter and the next, we go behind the scenes of the supply curve to understand how it is determined by the behaviour of firms.

We begin by comparing the firms that we see in the real world with those that appear in economic theory. Next we introduce the concepts of costs, revenues, and profits, and we outline the key role that profits play in determining the allocation of a nation's resources. To determine the most profitable quantity for a firm to produce and supply to the market, we need to see how its costs vary with its output.

When examining the relationship between output and cost, *time* plays an important role. In this chapter, we focus on the short run, where a firm can change only some of its inputs, and output is governed by the famous "law of diminishing returns." In the next chapter we examine the firm's behaviour in the long run—when all the firm's inputs are variable—and in the very long run—when the state of technology changes. There we encounter "scale economies" and firms' incentives for research and development.

7.1 WHAT ARE FIRMS?

We start by taking a brief look at the concept of a firm. How are firms organized? How are they financed? What are their goals?

Organization of Firms

A firm can be organized in any one of six different ways.

1. A **single proprietorship** has one owner–manager who is personally responsible for all aspects of the business, including its debts.

2. An **ordinary partnership** has two or more joint owners, each of whom is personally responsible for all the partnership's debts.

3. The **limited partnership**, which is less common than an ordinary partnership, provides for two types of partners. *General partners* take part in the running of the business and are liable for all the firm's debts. *Limited partners* take no part in the running of the business, and their liability is limited to the amount they actually invest in the enterprise.

4. A **corporation** is a firm regarded in law as having an identity of its own; its owners are not personally responsible for anything that is done in the name of the firm, though its directors may be. The shares of a *private* corporation are not traded on any stock exchange (such as the Toronto or New York Stock Exchanges), whereas the shares of a *public* corporation are.

5. A **state-owned enterprise** is owned by the government but is usually under the direction of a more or less independent, state-appointed board. Although its ownership differs, the organization and legal status of a state-owned enterprise are similar to those of a corporation. In Canada, such state-owned enterprises are called *Crown corporations*.

6. **Non-profit organizations** are established with the explicit objective of providing goods or services to customers but having any profits that are generated remain with the organization and not claimed by individuals. In many cases, some goods or services are sold to consumers while others are provided free of charge. Non-profit firms therefore earn their revenues from a combination of sales and donations. An example is your local YMCA—it sells memberships to consumers for use of the health facilities, but it also raises funds to provide free services to needy individuals in the community.

Firms that have locations in more than one country are often called **multinational enterprises (MNEs)**. Having locations in several countries is very unusual for single proprietorships and ordinary partnerships, but is common for limited partnerships (such as large law and accounting firms) and very common for large corporations. The number and importance of MNEs have increased greatly over the last few decades. A large amount of international trade represents business transactions of MNEs—between different corporations, as well as between different regional operations of the same corporation. MNEs play an increasing role in the ongoing process of globalization.

single proprietorship A firm that has one owner who is personally responsible for the firm's actions and debts.

ordinary partnership A firm that has two or more joint owners, each of whom is personally responsible for the firm's actions and debts.

limited partnership A firm that has two classes of owners: general partners, who take part in managing the firm and are personally liable for the firm's actions and debts, and limited partners, who take no part in the management of the firm and risk only the money that they have invested.

corporation A firm that has a legal existence separate from that of the owners.

state-owned enterprise A firm that is owned by the government. In Canada, these are called *Crown corporations*.

non-profit organizations Firms that provide goods and services with the objective of just covering their costs. These are often called NGOs, for non-governmental organizations.

multinational enterprises (MNEs) Firms that have operations in more than one country.

Finally, note that not all production in the economy takes place within firms. Many government agencies provide goods and services, such as defence, roads, primary and secondary education, and health-care services. In most of these cases, goods and services are provided to citizens without charging directly for their use; costs are financed through the government's general tax revenues.

Financing of Firms

The money a firm raises for carrying on its business is sometimes called its financial capital, as distinct from its real capital, which is the firm's physical assets, such as factories, machinery, offices, and fleets of vehicles. Although the use of the term *capital* to refer to both an amount of money and a quantity of goods can be confusing, it will usually be clear from the context which sense is being used.

The basic types of financial capital used by firms are *equity* and *debt*. Equity is the funds provided by the owners of the firm. Debt is the funds borrowed from creditors (individuals or institutions) outside the firm.

Equity In individual proprietorships and partnerships, one or more owners provide much of the required funds. A corporation acquires funds from its owners in return for stocks, shares, or equities (as they are variously called). These are basically ownership certificates. The money goes to the company and the shareholders become owners of the firm, risking the loss of their money and gaining the right to share in the firm's profits. Profits that are paid out to shareholders are called **dividends**.

dividends Profits paid out to shareholders of a corporation.

One easy way for an established firm to raise money is to retain current profits rather than paying them out to shareholders. Financing investment from such *retained earnings* adds to the value of the firm and hence raises the market value of existing shares.

Debt The firm's creditors are not owners; they have lent money in return for some form of loan agreement, or IOU. Firms often borrow from commercial banks or other financial institutions, who channel money from their depositors to borrowers. Firms can also choose to borrow money directly from non-bank lenders, with whom there are many possible types of loan agreements, which are collectively called *debt instruments* or **bonds**. Two characteristics are common to all loan agreements. First, they carry an obligation to repay the amount borrowed, called the *principal* of the loan. Second, they carry an obligation to make some form of payment to the lender called *interest*. The time at which the principal is to be repaid is called the *redemption date* of the debt. The amount of time between the issue of the debt and its redemption date is called its *term*.

bond A debt instrument carrying a specified amount, a schedule of interest payments, and (usually) a date for redemption of its face value.

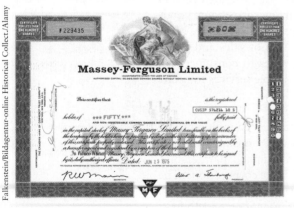

Falkenstein/Bildagentur-online Historical Collect./Alamy

Many firms raise money by issuing shares and selling them to investors. For example, in 1928 the Canadian Pacific Railway Company (which still exists today) issued this share certificate and sold it to Westminster Bank, Ltd.

Goals of Firms

Economists generally make two key assumptions about firm behaviour. First, firms are assumed to be profit-maximizers, seeking to make as much profit for their owners as possible. Second, each firm is assumed to be a single, consistent decision-making unit.

Recall from Chapter 2 that assumptions are used to simplify a theory so that economists can focus on the essential aspects of the issue. These two key assumptions about firms allow economists to ignore details related to how firms are organized and focus on deriving straightforward predictions about their market behaviour—predictions that can be subjected to empirical study.

Is maximizing profit the only thing firms care about? In recent years there has been much public discussion of the need for firms to be "socially responsible" in addition to being motivated by the pursuit of profits. Some people argue that every firm has a responsibility to society that goes well beyond the responsibility to its shareholders. Others disagree and argue that by maximizing profits, firms are providing a valuable service to society. For a discussion of both sides of this interesting debate, see *Applying Economic Concepts 7-1*.

7.2 PRODUCTION, COSTS, AND PROFITS

We must now specify a little more precisely the concepts of production, costs, and profits that are used by economists.

Production

In order to produce the goods or services that it sells, each firm needs inputs. Hundreds of inputs enter into the production of any specific output. Among the many inputs entering into car production, for example, are steel, rubber, spark plugs, electricity, the site of the factory, machinists, accountants, spray-painting machines, forklift trucks, lawyers, and managers. These inputs can be grouped into four broad categories:

- inputs that are outputs from some other firm, such as spark plugs, electricity, and steel
- inputs that are provided directly by nature, such as the land owned or rented by the firm
- inputs that are the services of labour, provided by workers and managers employed by the firm
- inputs that are the services of physical capital, such as the facilities and machines used by the firm

The items that make up the first group of inputs are called **intermediate products** because they are the output of one firm but the input for another. If these intermediate products are traced back to their sources, all production can be accounted for by the services of the other three kinds of input, which we first discussed in Chapter 1 and which are called *factors of production*. These are the gifts of nature, such as soil and raw materials, called *land*; physical and mental efforts provided by people, called *labour*; and factories, machines, and other human-made aids to production, called *capital*.

The **production function** describes the technological relationship between the inputs that a firm uses and the output that it produces. In terms of functional notation, a simplified production function (in which we ignore the role of land) is written as

$$Q = f(K, L)$$

intermediate products All outputs that are used as inputs by other producers in a further stage of production.

production function A functional relation showing the maximum output that can be produced by any given combination of inputs.

APPLYING ECONOMIC CONCEPTS 7-1

Is It Socially Responsible to Maximize Profits?

In recent years there has been growing public discussion of the need for firms, especially large ones, to behave in a socially responsible manner. Advocates of this view start from the position that unadorned capitalism, and the associated goal of profit maximization, does not serve the broader public interest: corporate profits clearly help firms' shareholders, but the public interest is not being served. In this view, corporate social responsibility must involve more than simply maximizing profits.

Others argue that firms should indeed focus on the goal of maximizing profits and that, by doing so, they are providing significant benefits to their customers and their employees, not just their shareholders. In addition, it is the pursuit of profits that leads firms to develop new products and production methods, innovations that lie at the heart of ongoing improvements in overall living standards. This opposing view is grounded in the same insight of Adam Smith's that we saw in Chapter 1—that the pursuit of private gain creates benefits for society as a whole.

What about corporate profits generated through a production process that damages the environment? Surely there are costs imposed on society when firms, through their profit-maximizing decisions, are led to emit poisonous effluents into the air or into local waterways. Or how about firms—such as investment banks or mortgage brokers—making unethical business decisions and thereby earning profits at the expense of other parties? Isn't simple profit maximization in these cases socially irresponsible?

One response is that it is the duty of governments to set rules in the public interest and then leave firms free to maximize their profits within the constraints set by those rules. For example, the government can design and enforce environmental, labour, banking, accounting, and tax regulations deemed to be in the public interest. Faced with these laws and regulations, private firms are then free to take whatever action is expected to maximize their profits; violations of the established laws or regulations will be met with appropriate penalties. Such a division of responsibilities—the government setting the rules and the firms maximizing profits within the implied constraints—recognizes that although private firms are usually not good judges of the public interest, they are quite good at making decisions about how best to use scarce resources in order to satisfy consumers' desires. Government policymakers, through a process that involves consultation with various groups in society, and the trading off of competing demands, are usually better placed to judge what is and is not in the overall public interest.

This position still recognizes two methods for modifying corporate behaviour. Those who believe that certain corporate actions are not in the public interest can try to convince policymakers to design new rules that will make it costly for firms to continue such actions. Various non-governmental organizations (NGOs), ranging from environmental organizations to consumer-advocacy groups, can play an important role in identifying and publicizing poor corporate behaviour, and also in lobbying the government for change. If the case is persuasive, and sufficient public pressure can be brought to bear on the policymakers, policies will eventually be changed. An example is the relatively recent design of environmental protection policies. Many years ago, Canadian firms could pollute the environment with impunity, whereas today many types of pollution are illegal and some emissions are closely monitored by government agencies. Another more recent example is the push by governments for improved financial-market regulation following the global financial crisis of 2008 that caused a major world-wide recession.

A second way that firms can be encouraged to change their behaviour is through the expression of consumers' preferences in the marketplace. If enough consumers dislike a certain activity by a specific firm, and these views can be expressed clearly enough in terms of consumers' demand for the firm's products, the firm may be convinced to change its behaviour. In this case, new laws or regulations may not be required; the firm decides, on the basis of the possible decline in sales it will suffer if it continues its unpopular activities, that a change in its behaviour is required for profit maximization. One example occurred when Nike was heavily criticized for contracting its production to Asian "sweatshops," where workers were treated very poorly. A widespread boycott of Nike products began and Nike eventually responded by improving working conditions and allowing independent monitors into its factories. The threat of a loss of sales was so powerful that competing companies Reebok and Adidas, who had not yet attracted any negative publicity, began making improvements in their factories just to prevent being tarred by the Nike brush.

What is the bottom line? Corporations *do* change their behaviour over time—in response to changes in laws and regulations, and also in response to changes in consumer attitudes. If governments can be relied upon to establish and enforce rules and regulations in the public interest, and consumers continue to actively express their preferences through their decisions in the marketplace, then firms may be able to be socially responsible and profit seeking at the same time.

where Q is the flow of output, K is the flow of capital services, and L is the flow of labour services.[1] f is the production function itself. Changes in the firm's technology, which alter the relationship between inputs and output, are reflected by changes in the function f. The production function specifies the *maximum* amount of output that can be obtained from any given amounts of inputs.

Costs and Profits

Firms arrive at what they call *profits* by taking the revenues they obtain from selling their output and subtracting all the costs associated with their inputs. When all costs have been correctly deducted, the resulting profits are the return to the owners' financial investment in the firm.

The robotic equipment used inside an auto assembly plant is an example of capital. These machines deliver a flow of capital services to the firm that uses them.

Economic Versus Accounting Profits   Compared with accountants, economists use somewhat different concepts of costs and profits. When accountants measure profits, they begin with the firm's revenues and then subtract all of the *explicit* costs incurred by the firm. By explicit costs, we mean the costs that actually involve a purchase of goods or services by the firm. The obvious explicit costs include the hiring of workers, the rental of equipment, interest payments on debt, and the purchase of intermediate inputs.[2]

$$\text{Accounting profits} = \text{Revenues} - \text{Explicit costs}$$

Like accountants, economists subtract from revenues all explicit costs, but they also subtract some *implicit* costs that accountants ignore. These are items for which there is no market transaction but for which there is still an opportunity cost for the firm that should be included in the complete measure of costs. The two most important implicit costs are the opportunity cost of the owner's time and the opportunity cost of the owner's capital. When this more complete set of costs is subtracted from the firm's revenues, the result is called **economic profit** and is sometimes called *pure profit.*

$$\begin{aligned}\text{Economic profits} &= \text{Revenues} - (\text{Explicit costs} + \text{Implicit costs})\\ &= \text{Accounting profits} - \text{Implicit costs}\end{aligned}$$

economic profit The difference between the revenues received from the sale of output and the opportunity cost of the inputs used to make the output. Negative economic profits are called economic losses.

Opportunity Cost of Time.   Especially in small and relatively new firms, owners spend a tremendous amount of their time developing the business. Often they pay themselves far less than they could earn if they were instead to offer their labour services to other firms. For example, an entrepreneur who opens a restaurant may pay herself only $1000 per month while she is building her business, even though she could earn $4000 per month in her next best alternative job. In this case, there is an *implicit* cost

---

[1] Remember that production is a flow: it is so many units per period of time. For example, when we say that production rises from 100 to 101 units, we mean that the rate of production has risen from 100 units each period to 101 units each period.

[2] *Depreciation* is also among the firm's explicit costs, even though it does not involve a market transaction. Depreciation is a cost to the firm that arises because of the wearing out of its physical capital.

to her firm of $3000 per month that would be missed by the accountant who measures only the explicit cost of her wage at $1000 per month.[3]

Opportunity Cost of Financial Capital. What is the opportunity cost of the financial capital that owners have invested in a firm? This question applies equally to small, owner-operated businesses and to large corporations. The answer is best broken into two parts. First, ask what could be earned by lending this amount to someone else in a riskless loan. The owners could have purchased a government bond, which has no significant risk of default. Suppose the return on this is 3 percent per year. This amount is the risk-free rate of return on capital. It is clearly an opportunity cost, since the firm could close down operations, lend out its money, and earn a 3 percent return. Next, ask what the firm could earn in addition to this amount by lending its money to another firm where risk of default was equal to the firm's own risk of loss. Suppose this is an additional 4 percent. This is the risk premium, and it is clearly also a cost. If the firm does not expect to earn this much in its own operations, it could close down and lend its money out to some equally risky firm and earn 7 percent (3 percent pure return plus 4 percent risk premium).

> Economists include both implicit and explicit costs in their measurement of profits, whereas accountants include only explicit costs. Economic profits are therefore less than accounting profits.

Table 7-1 compares economic and accounting profits for a hypothetical owner-operated firm that produces gourmet soups. In that example, both accounting profits and economic profits are positive (though accounting profits are larger). Another possibility, however, is that a firm has positive *accounting* profits even though it has zero *economic* profits. If a firm's *accounting* profits represent a return just equal to what is available if the owner's capital and time were used elsewhere, then opportunity costs are just being covered. In this case, there are zero *economic* profits, even though the firm's accountant will record positive profits.

Is one of these concepts better than the other? No. Firms are interested in the financial return to their owners, which is what they call *profits*. They must also conform with tax laws, which define

TABLE 7-1 **Accounting Versus Economic Profit for Ruth's Gourmet Soup Company**

Total Revenues ($)		2000
Explicit Costs ($)		
Wages and Salaries	500	
Intermediate Inputs	400	
Rent	80	
Interest on Loan	100	
Depreciation	80	
Total Explicit Costs	1160	
Accounting Profit		840
Implicit Costs ($)		
Opportunity Cost of Owner's Time	160	
Opportunity Cost of Owner's		
$1500 Capital		
(a) risk-free return of 3%	45	
(b) risk premium of 4%	60	
Total Implicit Costs	265	
Economic Profit		575

Economic profits are less than accounting profits because of implicit costs. The table shows a simplified version of a real profit-and-loss statement. Accounting profits are computed as revenues minus explicit costs (including depreciation), and in the table are equal to $840 for the period being examined. When the correct opportunity cost of the owner's time (in excess of what is recorded in wages and salaries) and capital are recognized as implicit costs, the firm appears less profitable. Economic profits are still positive but equal only $575.

---

[3] For larger firms that are not operated by their owners, this element of implicit costs is not relevant because the owners usually do not work at the firm. In these cases, the salaries to the firm's managers appear in the firm's accounts as explicit costs.

profits in the same way. In contrast, economists are interested in how profits affect resource allocation; their definition is best for that purpose and is the definition used throughout this book. Let's see why economic profit is a useful concept when thinking about resource allocation.

Profits and Resource Allocation   If all firms in some industry are earning economic profits, the owners of factors of production will want to move resources into the industry, because the earnings available to them are greater there than in alternative uses. If, in some other industry, firms are incurring economic losses, some or all of this industry's resources are more highly valued in other uses, and owners of the resources will want to move them to those other uses.

> Economic profits and losses play a crucial signalling role in the workings of a free-market system.

Economic profits in an industry are the signal that resources can profitably be moved into that industry. Losses are the signal that the resources can profitably be moved elsewhere. Only if there are zero economic profits (which means that revenues exactly cover opportunity costs) is there no incentive for resources to move into or out of an industry. We will examine the role of profits and losses in determining industry entry and exit in Chapters 9 and 10.

Profit-Maximizing Output

From this point on, when we talk about a firm's profit, we will *always* mean economic profit, where all explicit and implicit costs are considered. Our next step in developing a theory of supply is to determine the level of output that maximizes a firm's economic profit, to which we give the symbol π (the lowercase Greek letter pi). This is the difference between the total revenue (TR) each firm derives from the sale of its output and the total cost (TC) of producing that output:

$$\pi = TR - TC$$

By determining the profit-maximizing level of output for any given firm, we will be closer to understanding that firm's supply curve, which naturally helps us to better understand the origin of market supply curves. Firms make output decisions over quite different time horizons, however, and we must briefly examine this point before exploring the relationship between a firm's costs, profits, and output.

Time Horizons for Decision Making

Economists classify the decisions that firms make into three types: (1) how best to use existing plant and equipment—the *short run*; (2) what new plant and equipment and production processes to select, given known technical possibilities—the *long run*; and (3) how to encourage, or adapt to, the development of new techniques—the *very long run*.

short run A period of time in which the quantity of some inputs cannot be changed.

fixed factor An input whose quantity cannot be changed in the short run.

variable factor An input whose quantity can be changed over the time period under consideration.

The Short Run   The **short run** is a time period in which the quantity of some inputs, called **fixed factors**, cannot be changed. A fixed factor is usually an element of capital (such as plant and equipment), but it might be land, the services of management, or even the supply of skilled labour. Inputs that are not fixed but instead can be varied in the short run are called **variable factors**.

The short run does not correspond to a specific number of months or years. In some industries, it may extend over many years; in others, it may be a matter of months or even weeks. In the electric power industry, for example, it takes three or more years to acquire and install a steam turbine generator. An unforeseen increase in demand will involve a long period during which the extra demand must be met with the existing capital equipment. In contrast, a car mechanic's shop may be able to acquire new equipment in a few weeks. An increase in demand will have to be met with the existing stock of capital for only a brief time, after which it can be adjusted to the level made desirable by the higher demand.

The short run is the length of time over which some of the firm's factors of production are fixed.

long run A period of time in which all inputs may be varied, but the existing technology of production cannot be changed.

The Long Run   The **long run** is a time period in which all inputs may be varied but in which the basic technology of production cannot be changed. Like the short run, the long run does not correspond to a specific length of time.

The long run corresponds to the situation the firm faces when it is planning to go into business, to expand the scale of its operations, to branch out into new products or new areas, or to change its method of production. The firm's *planning decisions* are long-run decisions because they are made from given technological possibilities but with freedom to choose from a variety of production processes that will use factor inputs in different proportions.

The long run is the length of time over which all of the firm's factors of production can be varied, but its technology is fixed.

very long run A period of time that is long enough for the technological possibilities available to a firm to change.

The Very Long Run   Unlike the short run and the long run, the **very long run** is a period of time in which the technological possibilities available to a firm will change. Modern industrial societies are characterized by continually changing technologies that lead to new and improved products and production methods.

The very long run is the length of time over which all the firm's factors of production and its technology can be varied.

For the remainder of this chapter, we consider costs and production in the short run. We continue with our simplified situation in which there are only two factors of production—labour and capital. We will assume that capital is the fixed factor whereas labour is the variable factor. In the next chapter, we explore the firm's decisions in the long run and the very long run.

7.3 PRODUCTION IN THE SHORT RUN

Consider a company in Regina that produces specialty wooden skateboards. The firm owns a small factory with the necessary machinery and equipment—this is the firm's stock of capital, and we will assume that it is fixed in quantity. We call these the *fixed* factors of production. The firm also purchases intermediate inputs, such as wood, glue, and electricity, and, of course, hires workers. The intermediate inputs and the labour services are the firm's *variable* inputs.

In the following discussion, we will focus on the relationship between the firm's use of labour and the firm's production of skateboards. In particular, we want to know—with a fixed amount of capital—how output changes as the firm increases or decreases its amount of labour. The table in Figure 7-1 shows three different ways of looking at how output varies with the quantity of labour services.

FIGURE 7-1 **Total, Average, and Marginal Products in the Short Run**

Quantity of Labour (L)	Total Product (TP)	Average Product $\left(AP = \dfrac{TP}{L}\right)$	Marginal Product $\left(MP = \dfrac{\Delta TP}{\Delta L}\right)$
(1)	(2)	(3)	(4)
0	0		
			3
1	3	3	
			4
2	7	3.5	
			6
3	13	4.3	
			9
4	22	5.5	
			13
5	35	7.0	
			20
6	55	9.2	
			25
7	80	11.4	
			18
8	98	12.3	
			9
9	107	11.9	
			6
10	113	11.3	
			4
11	117	10.6	
			2
12	119	9.9	

(i) Total product

(ii) Average and marginal product

The relation of output to changes in the quantity of the variable factor (labour) can be looked at in three different ways. As the quantity of labour increases, total output increases, as shown in column 2. The average product in column 3 is found by dividing the total product in column 2 by the quantity of labour shown in the corresponding row of column 1. The marginal product is shown between the rows because it refers to the change in output from one level of labour input to another. The curves are plotted from the data in the table. In part (i), the *TP* curve shows the total product steadily rising, first at an increasing rate, then at a decreasing rate. This causes both the average and the marginal product curves in part (ii) to rise at first and then decline. Where *AP* reaches its maximum, $MP = AP$.

Total, Average, and Marginal Products

total product (*TP*) Total amount produced by a firm during some time period.

Total product (*TP*) is the total amount that is produced during a given period of time. For any given amount of the fixed factor, total product will change as more or less of the variable factor is used. This variation is shown in columns 1 and 2 of the table in Figure 7-1. Part (i) of Figure 7-1 plots the schedule from the table. (The shape of the curve will be discussed shortly.)

average product (*AP*) Total product divided by the number of units of the variable factor used in its production.

Average product (*AP*) is the total product divided by the number of units of the variable factor used to produce it. If we let the number of units of labour be denoted by *L*, the average product is given by

$$AP = \frac{TP}{L}$$

Notice in column 3 of the table that as more labour is used, average product first rises and then falls. The level of labour input at which average product reaches a maximum (8 units of labour in the example) is called the *point of diminishing average productivity*. Up to that point, average product is increasing; beyond that point, average product is decreasing.

marginal product (*MP*) The change in total output that results from using one more unit of a variable factor.

Marginal product (*MP*) is the *change* in total product resulting from the use of one additional unit of the variable factor. [13] Recalling that the Greek letter Δ (delta) means "the change in," marginal product is given by

$$MP = \frac{\Delta TP}{\Delta L}$$

Computed values of marginal product are shown in column 4 of the table in Figure 7-1. The values in this column are placed between the other rows of the table to stress that the concept refers to the *change* in output caused by the *change* in quantity of the variable factor. For example, the increase in labour from 3 to 4 units ($\Delta L = 1$) increases output from 13 to 22 ($\Delta TP = 9$). Thus, the *MP* equals 9, and it is recorded between 3 and 4 units of labour. Note that *MP* in the table first rises and then falls as the amount of labour increases. The level of labour input at which marginal product reaches a maximum (between 6 and 7 units of labour in this example) is called the *point of diminishing marginal productivity*.

Part (ii) of Figure 7-1 plots the *AP* and *MP* curves from the table. Although three different curves are shown in Figure 7-1, they are all aspects of the same single relationship described by the production function. As we vary the quantity of labour, with capital being fixed, output changes. Sometimes it is interesting to look at total product, sometimes at average product, and sometimes at the marginal product.

We will see later in this chapter that understanding firms' costs requires understanding how total, average, and marginal products are related to one another. We now turn to examining two aspects of this relationship.

law of diminishing returns The hypothesis that if increasing quantities of a variable factor are applied to a given quantity of fixed factors, the marginal product of the variable factor will eventually decrease.

Diminishing Marginal Product

The variations in output that result from applying more or less of a variable factor to a given quantity of a fixed factor are the subject of a famous economic hypothesis, referred to as the **law of diminishing returns**.

The law of diminishing returns states that if increasing amounts of a variable factor are applied to a given quantity of a fixed factor (holding the level of technology constant), eventually a situation will be reached in which the marginal product of the variable factor declines.

Notice in Figure 7-1 that the marginal product curve rises at first and then begins to fall with each successive increase in the quantity of labour.

The common sense explanation of the law of diminishing returns is that in order to increase output in the short run, more and more of the variable factor is combined with a given amount of the fixed factor. As a result, each successive unit of the variable factor has less and less of the fixed factor to work with. When the fixed factor is capital and the variable factor is labour, each worker (or worker hour) gets a declining amount of capital to assist it in producing more output. It is not surprising, therefore, that sooner or later, equal increases in work effort eventually begin to add less and less to total output.

To illustrate the concept, consider the number of workers in our skateboard manufacturing firm, which has only a given amount of factory space and machinery. If there is only one worker, that worker must do all the tasks, shifting from one to another and becoming competent at each. As a second, third, and subsequent workers are added, each can specialize in one task, becoming expert at it. One can cut the wood into the required pieces, the second can glue the pieces together, a third worker can do the necessary planing and sanding, while a fourth worker attaches the wheels. This process, as we noted in Chapter 1, is called the *division of labour*. If additional workers allow more efficient divisions of labour, marginal product will rise: each newly hired worker will add more to total output than each previous worker did. However, according to the law of diminishing returns, when there is only an unchanging amount of physical capital the scope for such increases must eventually disappear, and sooner or later the marginal products of additional workers must decline. When the decline takes place, each additional worker will increase the total output of skateboards by less than did the previous worker.

Eventually, as more and more workers are employed, marginal product may reach zero and even become negative. It is not hard to see why if you consider the extreme case, in which there would be so many workers in a limited space that additional workers would simply get in the way, thus reducing the total output of skateboards (a negative marginal product).

Empirical confirmation of diminishing marginal returns occurs frequently. Some examples are illustrated in *Applying Economic Concepts 7-2*.

The Average–Marginal Relationship

We have so far examined the concept of diminishing *marginal* returns; but *average* returns are also usually expected to diminish. If increasing quantities of a variable factor are applied to a given quantity of fixed factors, the average product of the variable factor will eventually decrease. [14]

Notice that in part (ii) of Figure 7-1, the *MP* curve cuts the *AP* curve at the *AP*'s maximum point. This is not a matter of luck or the way the artist just happened to draw the figure. Rather, it illustrates a fundamental property of the relationship between average and marginal product curves, one that is important to understand.

APPLYING ECONOMIC CONCEPTS 7-2

Three Examples of Diminishing Returns

Sport Fishing

British Columbia's Campbell River, a noted sport-fishing area, has long been the centre of a thriving, well-promoted tourist trade. As sport fishing has increased over the years, the total number of fish caught has steadily increased, but the number of fish *per person fishing* has decreased and the average hours fished for each fish caught has increased.*

Pollution Control

When Southern California Edison was required to modify its Mojave power plant to reduce the amount of pollutants emitted into the atmosphere, it discovered that a series of filters applied to the smokestacks could do the job. A single filter eliminated one-half of the discharge. A second filter could not reduce the same absolute amount and hence reduce the total discharge to zero. Instead, five additional filters were required, and even then the remaining discharge would still be 3 percent of the original amount. In other words, increasing the number of filters leads to diminishing marginal returns in pollution reduction.

Portfolio Diversification

Investors in the stock market typically like to reduce the risk of their portfolios. This risk—typically measured with a statistical concept called the *standard deviation*—can be reduced by purchasing the stocks of several different companies rather than just one or two. However, the mathematics of finance shows that the greatest reduction in risk is achieved when you increase the number of individual stocks from one to two. After this point, adding more stocks still reduces risk but at a decreasing rate. These diminishing marginal returns to reducing risk have led many investment advisers to suggest that a sensible portfolio should contain stocks from no more than 15 to 20 well-chosen companies.

---

*For a *given stock of fish* and increasing numbers of boats, this example is a good illustration of the law of diminishing returns. But in recent years the story has become more complicated as overfishing has depleted the stock of fish. We examine the reasons for overfishing in Chapter 16.

The average product curve slopes upward as long as the marginal product curve is *above* it; whether the marginal product curve is itself sloping upward or downward is irrelevant. For example, if an additional worker is to raise the average product of all workers, that additional worker's output must be greater than the average output of the other workers. In other words, in order for the average product to rise when a new worker is added, the marginal product (the output of the new worker) must exceed the average product. [15]

The relationship between marginal and average measures is very general. If the marginal is greater than the average, the average must be rising; if the marginal is less than the average, the average must be falling. For example, if you had a 3.6 cumulative grade point average (GPA) last semester and in this (marginal) semester you get only a 3.0 GPA, your cumulative GPA will fall. To increase your cumulative GPA, you must score better in this (marginal) semester than you have on average in the past—that is, to increase the average, the marginal must be greater than the average.

7.4 COSTS IN THE SHORT RUN

We now shift our attention from production to costs. The majority of firms cannot influence the prices of the inputs that they use; instead, they must pay the going market price for their inputs. For example, an electronic game maker in Montreal, a petrochemicals producer in Sarnia, a rancher in Red Deer, and a boat builder in Prince Rupert are each too small a part of the total demand for the factors that they use to be able to influence their prices significantly. The firms must pay the going rent for the land they need, the going wage rate for the labour they employ, and the going interest rate that banks charge for loans; so it is with most other firms. Given these prices and the physical returns summarized by the product curves, the costs of producing different levels of output can be calculated.

Defining Short Run Costs

Several different types of costs are relevant in the short run, and we must be careful to get them straight. They are all related to the product concepts we have just discussed.

Total Cost (TC). **Total cost** is the sum of all costs that the firm incurs to produce a given level of output. Total cost is divided into two parts: *total fixed cost* and *total variable cost*.

$$TC = TFC + TVC$$

total cost (TC) The total cost of producing any given level of output; it can be divided into total fixed cost and total variable cost.

Total Fixed Cost (TFC). **Total fixed cost** is the cost of the fixed factor(s). This does not vary with the level of output; it is the same whether output is 1 unit or 1000 units. Total fixed cost is also referred to as *overhead cost*. An example of a fixed cost is the annual cost associated with renting a factory (or servicing the debt incurred to build a factory). Whether the level of output increases or decreases, this annual fixed cost does not change.

total fixed cost (TFC) All costs of production that do not vary with the level of output.

Total Variable Cost (TVC). **Total variable cost** is the cost of the variable factors. It varies directly with the level of output—that is, it rises when output rises and it falls when output falls. Examples of variable costs are the cost of labour and intermediate inputs that are used to produce output. As the level of output increases or decreases, the amount of labour and intermediate inputs required for production changes in the same direction.

total variable cost (TVC) Total costs of production that vary directly with the level of output.

Average Total Cost (ATC). The total cost of producing any given number of units of output divided by that number of units tells us the **average total cost** per unit of output. We let Q be the total units of output (what we earlier referred to as total product, TP). Since total cost is split into fixed and variable costs, we can also divide average total cost into its fixed and variable components:

$$ATC = TC/Q$$

$$ATC = AFC + AVC$$

average total cost (ATC) Total cost of producing a given output divided by the number of units of output; it can also be calculated as the sum of average fixed costs and average variable costs. Also called *unit cost* or *average cost*.

Average Fixed Cost (AFC). Total fixed cost divided by the number of units of output tells us the average fixed cost per unit of output. **Average fixed cost** declines continually as output increases because the amount of the fixed cost attributed to each unit of output falls. This is known as *spreading overhead*.

$$AFC = TFC/Q$$

average fixed cost (AFC) Total fixed cost divided by the number of units of output.

Average Variable Cost (AVC). Total variable cost divided by the number of units of output tells us the average variable cost per unit of output. For reasons that we will soon see, **average variable cost** first declines as output rises, reaches a minimum, and then increases as output continues to rise.

$$AVC = TVC/Q$$

average variable cost (AVC) Total variable cost divided by the number of units of output.

Marginal Cost (MC). The increase in total cost resulting from a one-unit increase in the level of output is called **marginal cost**. (Marginal costs are always marginal *variable*

marginal cost (MC) The increase in total cost resulting from increasing output by one unit.

costs because fixed costs do not change as output varies.) Marginal cost is calculated as the change in total cost divided by the change in output that brought it about: [16]

$$MC = \Delta TC / \Delta Q$$

Short-Run Cost Curves

Using the firm's production relationships from Figure 7-1, suppose the price of labour is $20 per unit and the price of capital is $10 per unit. Also suppose the firm has 10 units of capital (the fixed factor). The firm's resulting costs are shown in Table 7-2.

Columns 4 through 6 in Table 7-2 show the firm's total costs. TFC is simply $10 per unit of capital times 10 units of capital. TVC is $20 per unit of labour times the increasing amount of labour shown in column 2. TC is the sum of TFC and TVC. Columns 7 through 9 show the average costs. For each average cost concept, the number is computed as the total cost from columns 4, 5, or 6 divided by the number of units of output shown in column 3.

Column 10 shows the marginal cost. For each change in the level of output, MC is equal to the change in TC divided by the change in output. For example, as output increases from 22 to 35 units (which occurs when L rises from 4 to 5), total costs rise from $180 to $200. Thus, marginal cost over this range of output is equal to $20/13 = $1.54.

The graphs in Figure 7-2 plot the cost curves from the data in Table 7-2. Part (i) plots the various total cost curves and shows that TVC rises at a decreasing rate until output is approximately 60 units. For output levels above 60, TVC rises at an

TABLE 7-2   Short-Run Costs: Fixed Capital and Variable Labour

Inputs		Output	Total Costs			Average Costs			Marginal Cost
Capital (K) (1)	Labour (L) (2)	(Q) (3)	Fixed (TFC) (4)	Variable (TVC) (5)	Total (TC) (6)	Fixed (AFC) (7)	Variable (AVC) (8)	Total (ATC) (9)	(MC) (10)
10	0	0	$100	$0	$100	—	—	—	
10	1	3	100	20	120	$33.33	$6.67	$40.00	$6.67
10	2	7	100	40	140	14.29	5.71	20.00	5.00
10	3	13	100	60	160	7.69	4.62	12.31	3.33
10	4	22	100	80	180	4.55	3.64	8.18	2.22
10	5	35	100	100	200	2.86	2.86	5.71	1.54
10	6	55	100	120	220	1.82	2.18	4.00	1.00
10	7	80	100	140	240	1.25	1.75	3.00	0.80
10	8	98	100	160	260	1.02	1.63	2.65	1.11
10	9	107	100	180	280	0.93	1.68	2.62	2.22
10	10	113	100	200	300	0.88	1.77	2.65	3.33
10	11	117	100	220	320	0.85	1.88	2.74	5.00
10	12	119	100	240	340	0.84	2.02	2.86	10.00
10	13	120	100	260	360	0.83	2.17	3.00	20.00

These cost schedules are computed from the product curves of Figure 7-1, given the price of capital of $10 per unit and the price of labour of $20 per unit.

FIGURE 7-2   Total, Average, and Marginal Cost Curves

(i) Total cost curves

(ii) Marginal and average cost curves

These curves are plotted from the data in Table 7-2. In part (i), total fixed cost does not vary with output. Total variable cost and total cost ($TC = TVC + TFC$) rise with output, first at a decreasing rate, then at an increasing rate. The total cost curves in (i) give rise to the average and marginal curves in (ii). Average fixed cost (*AFC*) declines as output increases. Average variable cost (*AVC*) and average total cost (*ATC*) fall and then rise as output increases. Marginal cost (*MC*) does the same, intersecting the *ATC* and *AVC* curves at their minimum points. Capacity output is at the minimum point of the *ATC* curve, which is an output of about 107 in this example.

increasing rate. Total fixed costs (*TFC*), of course, do not vary as the level of output changes. Since *TFC* is horizontal, the shape of *TC* comes from the shape of *TVC*.

Part (ii) of Figure 7-2 plots the average cost curves and the marginal cost curve. Notice that the *MC* curve cuts the *ATC* curve and the *AVC* curve at their lowest points. This is another example of the relationship between a marginal and an average curve. The *ATC* and *AVC* curves slope downward whenever the *MC* curve is below them; they slope upward whenever the *MC* curve is above them. Now let's consider the various curves in a little more detail.

The AFC, AVC, and ATC Curves   In part (ii) of Figure 7-2, the average fixed cost (*AFC*) curve is steadily declining as output rises. Since there is a given amount of capital with a total fixed cost of $100, increases in the level of output lead to a steadily declining fixed cost per unit of output. This is the phenomenon of *spreading overhead*.

The average variable cost (*AVC*) curve shows the variable cost per unit of output. It declines as output rises, reaching a minimum at approximately 100 units of output. As output increases above this level, *AVC* rises.

Since average total cost (*ATC*) is simply the sum of *AFC* and *AVC*, it follows that the *ATC* curve is derived geometrically by vertically adding the *AFC* and *AVC* curves. That is, for each level of output, the point on the *ATC* curve is derived by adding together the values of *AFC* and *AVC*. The result is an *ATC* curve that declines initially as output increases, reaches a minimum, and then rises as output increases further. Economists usually refer to this as a "U-shaped" *ATC* curve.

The MC Curve   Figure 7-2 also shows the marginal cost (*MC*) curve. Notice that the points on the curve are plotted at the *midpoint* of the output interval shown in the table (because marginal cost refers to the *change* in cost as output rises from one level to another). For example, when we plot the marginal cost of $1.54 as output increases from 22 to 35 units, the point is plotted at an output level of 28.5 units (the midpoint between 22 and 35). The *MC* curve declines steadily as output initially increases, reaches a minimum somewhere near 70 units of output, and then rises as output increases further.

Why U-Shaped Cost Curves?   It is clear from Figure 7-2 that the *AVC*, *ATC*, and *MC* curves are all U-shaped. What explains this shape?

Recall that the *MP* and *AP* curves in Figure 7-1 are both "hill-shaped" (an inverted "U") whereas the *AVC* and *MC* curves are both U-shaped. Is this just a coincidence, or is there some relationship between the two sets of curves? The answer is that this is no coincidence. Since labour input adds directly to cost, it should not surprise you that the relationship between labour input and output—the *AP* and *MP* curves—is closely linked to the relationship between output and cost—the *AVC* and *MC* curves.

Consider first the relationship between the *AP* and *AVC* curves. The *AP* curve shows that as the amount of labour input increases, the average product of labour rises, reaches a maximum, and then eventually falls. But each unit of labour adds the same amount to total variable cost ($20 in this example). Thus, each additional worker adds the same amount to cost but a different amount to output. When output per worker (*AP*) is rising, the variable cost per unit of output (*AVC*) is falling, and when output per worker (*AP*) is falling, average variable cost (*AVC*) is rising. *AVC* is at its minimum when *AP* reaches its maximum. [17]

Eventually diminishing average product of the variable factor implies eventually increasing average variable cost.

Exactly the same logic applies to the relationship between the *MP* and *MC* curves. Since each unit of labour adds the same amount to cost but has a different marginal product, it follows that when *MP* is rising *MC* is falling, and when *MP* is falling *MC* is rising. The *MC* curve reaches its minimum when the *MP* curve reaches its maximum. [18]

Eventually diminishing marginal product of the variable factor implies eventually increasing marginal costs.

Finally, we can return to the *ATC* curve to consider its shape. Since *ATC* = *AFC* + *AVC*, the *ATC* curve gets its shape from both the *AFC* and the *AVC* curves. The *AFC* curve is steadily declining as a given amount of overhead (fixed factor) is spread over an increasing number of units of output. And the *AVC* curve is U-shaped for the reasons we have just seen regarding the relationship between *AP* and *AVC*. It follows that the *ATC* curve begins to rise (after reaching its minimum) only when the effect of the increasing *AVC* dominates the effect of the declining *AFC*. We therefore see the *ATC* curve reaching its minimum at a level of output above where *AVC* reaches its minimum.

Capacity

The level of output that corresponds to the minimum short-run average total cost is often called the *capacity* of the firm. When used in this sense, capacity is the largest output that can be produced without encountering rising average costs per unit. In part (ii) of Figure 7-2, capacity output is about 107 units, but higher outputs can be achieved, provided that the firm is willing to accept the higher per-unit costs that accompany any level of output that is "above capacity." A firm that is producing at an output less than the point of minimum average total cost is said to have *excess capacity*.

This technical definition gives the word *capacity* a meaning that is different from the one used in everyday speech, in which it often means an upper limit that cannot be exceeded. The technical definition is, however, a useful concept in economic and business discussions.

The cost curves we have been discussing are typical in an industrial setting, such as for firms producing steel or newsprint or machinery or even computers and smartphones. In these cases, the existence of a fixed factor, such as a factory with a given amount of machinery and equipment, usually leads to clear cases of diminishing marginal returns and thus to the U-shaped cost curves as shown in Figure 7-2.

Many students wonder, however, if the same logic applies when firms are producing movies or computer software or smartphone apps or digital versions of books, magazines, or newspapers. *Applying Economic Concepts 7-3* examines the cost curves for products that have high one-time development costs but extremely low marginal costs.

Shifts in Short-Run Cost Curves

Remember that a firm's short-run cost curves are drawn holding two things constant. First, the amount of the fixed factor used by the firm is held constant (indeed, it is the

APPLYING ECONOMIC CONCEPTS 7-3

The Digital World: When Diminishing Returns Disappear Altogether

Many digital products have large initial costs associated with their creation and development, but near-zero costs associated with their unit-by-unit sales to customers. For example, a blockbuster movie may cost hundreds of millions of dollars to produce, but the cost of streaming that movie over Netflix is close to zero. The cost of developing an electronic game may also be very high, but once it is available for download on the firm's website, the cost of selling an additional unit is approximately zero. The same is true for all computer software, apps, and a whole range of digital products where the sale of an additional copy involves extremely low marginal costs.

In these situations, the firm's cost curves can still be drawn, but the key difference is that the law of diminishing marginal returns does not apply: the MC curve is at the same very low value for all units of output. But if every additional unit (beyond the first) costs the same

low amount, then average variable costs are also constant and equal to marginal costs. In this case, however, average *total* costs decline sharply because of the spreading of the large fixed costs. The accompanying figure shows the cost curves for such a firm.

The MC (and AVC) curve is flat at a very low level, showing that marginal cost is near zero for all units of output. The ATC curve begins very high and drops sharply as output rises, and continues falling indefinitely, asymptotically approaching the MC curve.

One implication of this cost structure is that large sales volumes may be necessary in order to reduce average costs significantly. For example, suppose the fixed development cost of a computer game is $5 million and the marginal cost on all units is $1 per unit (the costs of processing the online transaction). If only 200 000 units are sold, a selling price of $26 per unit would be required to cover all costs; in contrast, if 2.5 million units could be sold, any price above $3 per unit would fully cover costs and generate economic profits as well.

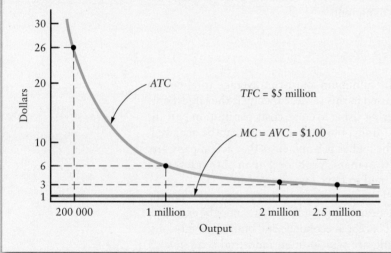

TFC = $5 million

MC = AVC = $1.00

Most firms with cost structures of this kind are producing and selling products that are considerably *differentiated* from those of their corporate rivals. We will see in Chapters 10 and 11 how this differentiation gives firms the ability to influence their own prices. Until then, the central message is simple: many digital products have constant and near-zero marginal costs and so are a good example of settings where diminishing marginal returns are not present.

existence of such a fixed factor that ensures we are in the short run). Second, factor prices—the price per unit of labour and the price per unit of capital—are held constant. How would changes in factor prices and in the amount of the fixed factor affect the firm's short-run cost curves?

Changes in Factor Prices   Factor prices change frequently, sometimes dramatically, and such changes naturally affect firms' costs. Consider a change in the wage, the price of a unit of labour services. An increase in the wage increases variable costs, leaves fixed costs unaffected, and therefore increases the firm's total costs. Since marginal costs are always marginal *variable* costs, such a change will also increase the firm's marginal costs. An increase in the price of the variable factor will therefore cause an upward shift in the firm's ATC and MC curves, as shown in Figure 7-3.

Now consider an increase in the price of a unit of the fixed factor. The firm's total *fixed* costs will rise, but its variable costs will be unaffected. Thus, in a diagram like Figure 7-3, the *ATC* curve will shift up but the *MC* curve will not move.

Changes in the Amount of the Fixed Factor   In the short run, the firm has a fixed amount of some factor of production. Economists usually think of physical capital as the fixed factor in the short run, especially the physical capital embodied in a plant or factory. What happens to the firm's production costs if it increases the size of its factory?

There are two effects from such a change. First, once the larger factory is in place, the firm's total fixed costs have increased. Second, the increase in the size of the factory means that labour and other variable factors now have more (or better) physical capital with which to work, and this generally increases their average and marginal product, and thus reduces marginal and average costs (at any given level of output). What is the combined effect of these two forces?

The overall effect on the *ATC* curve is difficult to predict without having more information about the firm's technology. It depends on how much the firm's output rises when it increases its use of *all* factors. In other words, we need to have more detailed information about the firm's production function before we know how a change in the firm's plant size will affect its *ATC* curve.

Changing from one plant size to another is considered by economists to be a long-run decision by the firm. This brings us to the next chapter, in which we explore how firms make decisions in a setting in which all factors of production are variable.

FIGURE 7-3   An Increase in Variable Factor Prices

A change in the price of a variable factor shifts the average total cost curve and the marginal cost curve. The original average total cost and marginal cost curves are shown by ATC_0 and MC_0. A rise in the price of a variable input—for example, the wage rate—raises the cost of producing each level of output. As a result, the average total cost curve and the marginal cost curve shift upward to ATC_1 and MC_1.

SUMMARY

7.1 WHAT ARE FIRMS?   LO 1

- Production is organized either by private-sector firms, which take four main forms—single proprietorships, ordinary partnerships, limited partnerships, and corporations—or by state-owned enterprises and non-profit organizations.
- Modern firms finance themselves by selling shares, using their retained earnings, or borrowing from lenders, such as banks.

- A firm's profit is the difference between its total revenue and its total costs.
- Economists usually assume that firms attempt to maximize profits.

7.2 PRODUCTION, COSTS, AND PROFITS   LO 2

- The production function relates inputs of factor services to output.
- Accounting profit is the difference between the firm's revenues and its explicit costs, including labour costs, capital costs, the costs of intermediate inputs, and depreciation.

- Economic profit is the difference between the firm's revenues and total costs, including both explicit and implicit costs. Implicit costs include the opportunity cost of the owner's time and capital.

- Economic profits play a key role in resource allocation. Positive economic profits attract resources into an industry; negative economic profits induce resources to move elsewhere.
- Economists divide the firm's production decisions into three time frames. The short run involves decisions in which one or more factors of production are fixed. The long run involves decisions in which all factors are variable but technology is unchanging. The very long run involves decisions in which technology can change.

7.3 PRODUCTION IN THE SHORT RUN   LO 3

- The theory of short-run costs is concerned with how output varies as different amounts of the variable factors are combined with given amounts of the fixed factors. Total, average, and marginal product curves describe relationships between output and the quantity of the variable factors of production.
- The law of diminishing returns asserts that if increasing quantities of a variable factor are combined with given quantities of fixed factors, the marginal and the average products of the variable factor will eventually decrease. For given factor prices, this hypothesis implies that marginal and average costs will eventually rise as output rises.

7.4 COSTS IN THE SHORT RUN   LO 4

- Short-run average total cost curves are often U-shaped because average product increases at low levels of output but eventually declines sufficiently to offset advantages of spreading overheads.
- The *MC* curve is downward sloping when *MP* is rising; it is upward sloping when *MP* is falling.
- The output corresponding to the minimum point of a short-run average total cost curve is called the plant's capacity.
- Changes in factor prices shift the short-run cost curves—upward when prices rise and downward when prices fall.

KEY CONCEPTS

Forms of business organization
Methods of financing firms
Profit maximization
Inputs and factors of production
Accounting versus economic profits

Economic profits and resource allocation
Short run, long run, and very long run
Total product, average product, and marginal product

The law of diminishing returns
Total cost, marginal cost, and average cost
Short-run cost curves
Capacity

STUDY EXERCISES

MyEconLab   Make the grade with MyEconLab: Study Exercises marked in ● can be found on MyEconLab. You can practise them as often as you want, and most feature step-by-step guided instructions to help you find the right answer.

❶ Fill in the blanks to make the following statements correct.

 a. The relationship between the inputs of factor services and output is called the ____
 b. A firm earning positive accounting profits could have zero _____ if the owner's capital is earning exactly its opportunity cost.
 c. A firm's planning decisions made when some inputs are variable but others are fixed are made in the time period known as the ____. The time period over which all factors are variable but technology is fixed is known as the ____.

❷ Fill in the blanks to make the following statements correct.

 a. The ____ tells us that as more of a variable factor is used in combination with given quantities of fixed factors, the marginal product of the variable factor will eventually decrease.

b. The ____ is the change in total output resulting from the use of one additional unit of the variable factor.

c. If average product and marginal product curves are plotted on a graph, the *AP* curve is rising as long as the *MP* curve lies ____ the *AP* curve. The *AP* curve is falling when the *MP* curve lies ____ the *AP* curve.

❸ Fill in the blanks to make the following statements correct.

a. For given factor prices, when average product per worker is at a maximum, average variable cost is at a ____.

b. If marginal costs are above average costs, then producing one more unit of output will ____ the average cost.

c. The level of output that corresponds to a firm's minimum short-run average total cost is called the ____ of the firm.

❹ For each of the costs listed below, identify whether it is an explicit or implicit cost to a firm. Which costs would be subtracted from a firm's total revenue to calculate economic profit, and which to calculate accounting profit?

a. hourly wages to the firm's employees
b. depreciation of the firm's physical assets
c. the risk-free 2% return the firm's owners could receive on their financial capital instead of investing it in the firm
d. annual rental payments for a production facility
e. the additional wages the owner/manager could have received in alternative employment
f. the risk premium of 3% that the owners of the firm could earn on their financial capital if they invested it in an equally risky venture

❺ Consider the revenues and costs in 2013 for Spruce Decor Inc., an Alberta-based furniture company entirely owned by Mr. Harold Buford.

Furniture Sales	$ 645 000
Catalogue Sales	$ 12 000
Labour Costs	$ 325 000
Materials Costs	$ 157 000
Advertising Costs	$ 28 000
Debt-Service Costs	$ 32 000

a. What would accountants determine Spruce Decor's profits to be in 2013?

b. Suppose Mr. Buford has $400 000 of capital invested in Spruce Decor. Also suppose that equally risky enterprises earn a 16 percent annual rate of return on capital. What is the opportunity cost for Mr. Buford's capital?

c. What are the *economic* profits for Spruce Decor in 2013?

d. If Spruce Decor's economic profits were typical of furniture makers in 2013, what would you expect to happen in this industry? Explain.

❻ A carpenter quits his job at a furniture factory to open his own cabinetmaking business. In his first two years of operation, his sales average $100 000 per year and his operating costs for wood, workshop and tool rental, utilities, and miscellaneous expenses average $70 000 per year. Now his old job at the furniture factory is again available. What is the lowest wage at which he should decide to return to his old job? Why?

❼ Wacky Wintersports Inc. can produce snowboards according to the following schedule.

Units of Labour (per week)	Number of Snowboards (per week)	Average Product	Marginal Product
0	0	—	—
1	2	—	—
2	5	—	—
3	9	—	—
4	14	—	—
5	18	—	—
6	21	—	—
7	23	—	—
8	24	—	—

a. Complete the table by calculating the marginal and average products.

b. Plot the *AP* and *MP* curves on a single graph, and identify the point of diminishing marginal productivity.

❽ Consider an example of a production function that relates the monthly production of widgets to the monthly use of capital and labour services. Suppose the production function takes the following specific algebraic form:

$$Q = KL - (0.1) L^2$$

where Q is the output of widgets, K is the input of capital services, and L is the input of labour services.

a. Suppose that, in the short run, K is constant and equal to 10. Fill in the following table.

K	L	Q
10	5	—
10	10	—
10	15	—
10	20	—
10	25	—
10	30	—
10	40	—
10	50	—

b. Using the values from the table, plot the values of Q and L on a scale diagram, with Q on the vertical axis and L on the horizontal axis. (This is analogous to the TP curve in Figure 7-1.)

c. Now suppose that K increases to 20 because the firm increases the size of its widget factory. Recompute the value of Q for each of the alternative values of L. Plot the values of Q and L on the same diagram as in part (b).

d. Explain why an increase in K increases the level of Q (for any given level of L).

9 The following table shows how the total output of skates (per month) changes when the quantity of the variable input (labour) changes. The firm's amount of capital is fixed.

Hours of Labour (per month)	Pairs of Skates (per month)	Average Product	Marginal Product
100	200	—	—
120	260	—	—
140	350	—	—
160	580	—	—
180	720	—	—
200	780	—	—
220	800	—	—
240	810	—	—

a. Compute the average product of labour for each level of output and fill in the table. Plot the AP curve on a scale diagram.

b. Compute the marginal product of labour for each interval (that is, between 100 and 120 hours, between 120 and 140 hours, and so on). Fill in the table and plot the MP curve on the same diagram. Remember to plot the value for MP at the midpoint of the output intervals.

c. Is the "law of diminishing marginal returns" satisfied?

d. Explain the relationship between the marginal product of labour and the average product of labour.

10 This question requires you to understand the relationship between total product, average product, and marginal product. Each of the diagrams below shows how total product (TP) changes as the quantity of the variable input (which we call L) changes. These reflect four *different* production functions.

a. In each case, describe in words how total output depends on the amount of variable input.

b. For each production function, draw a diagram showing the average product (AP) curve. (Recall that AP is given by total output divided by total variable input. The value of AP is also equal to the slope of a straight line from the origin to the TP curve.)

c. On the same diagram, draw the marginal product (MP) curve. (Recall that MP is given by the *change* in total output divided by the *change* in the variable input. The value of MP is also equal to the slope of a tangent line to the TP curve.)

d. Is the relationship between AP and MP discussed in the text satisfied by each of the production functions?

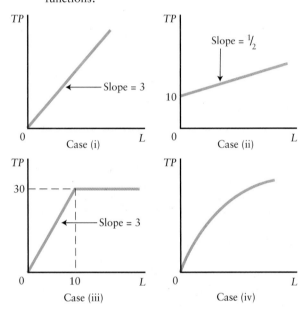

11 In 1921, a classic set of experiments with chemical fertilizers was performed at the Rothampsted Experimental Station, an agricultural research institute in Hertfordshire, England. Researchers applied different amounts of a particular fertilizer to ten apparently identical plots of land. The results for one test, using identical seed grain, are listed in the following table. Create a graph with the fertilizer dose on the horizontal axis and output on the vertical axis. (With no fertilizer, output = 100.) Compute the average and marginal product of fertilizer, and identify the (approximate) points of diminishing average and marginal productivity.

Plot	Fertilizer Dose	Output Index*
1	15	104.2
2	30	110.4
3	45	118.0
4	60	125.3
5	75	130.2
6	90	131.4
7	105	131.9
8	120	132.3
9	135	132.5
10	150	132.8

*Output without fertilizer = 100.

⑫ Consider the table below, which shows the total fixed costs (*TFC*) and total variable costs (*TVC*) for producing specialty bicycles in a small factory with a fixed amount of capital.

Output Per Year (thousands of bicycles)	TFC	TVC	AFC	AVC	ATC
		(thousands of dollars)			
1	200	40	—	—	—
2	200	70	—	—	—
3	200	105	—	—	—
4	200	120	—	—	—
5	200	135	—	—	—
6	200	155	—	—	—
7	200	185	—	—	—
8	200	230	—	—	—
9	200	290	—	—	—
10	200	350	—	—	—
11	200	425	—	—	—

a. Compute average fixed costs (*AFC*) for each level of output.
b. Compute average variable costs (*AVC*) for each level of output.
c. Compute average total cost (*ATC*) for each level of output. What level of output (per year) is the firm's capacity?
d. Plot the *AFC*, *AVC*, and *ATC* curves on a scale diagram with dollars on the vertical axis and the level of output on the horizontal axis.

⑬ Each of the following situations describes a firm's production and costs during a given year.

a. Firm A is producing 20 000 units of output, incurring a total cost of $1 000 000 and total variable cost of $600 000. What is Firm A's average fixed cost?
b. Firm B is producing 20 000 units of output, incurring a total cost of $100 000 and total fixed cost of $20 000. What is Firm B's average variable cost?
c. Firm C is producing 750 units of output. Average variable cost is $10 per unit and average fixed cost is $5 per unit. What is Firm C's total cost?
d. Firm D is producing 400 units of output. Average total cost is $12 and average fixed cost is $4. What is Firm D's total variable cost?
e. Firm E is producing 1 250 000 units of output, incurring a total cost of $20 million and total variable cost of $18 million. What is Firm E's average fixed cost?

⑭ An electronic-parts manufacturer with U-shaped short-run cost curves is producing 10 000 units per month and has short-run costs as follows:

ATC = $6.50
AVC = $4.50
AFC = $2.00
MC = $6.90

a. At this level of output, has the firm started experiencing diminishing marginal and average returns? How do you know?
b. At this level of output, is the firm operating below, at, or above its capacity? How do you know?

⑮ The table below shows the total daily output for a firm producing specialty cakes, and operating with a fixed amount of capital. The cost of labour is $100 per unit per day and the fixed cost of the capital is $1000 per day.

Units of Labour (per day)	Total Output (per day)	TFC	TVC	TC	MC	AFC	AVC	ATC
10	100							
20	300							
30	900							
40	1320							
50	1500							
60	1620							
70	1680							

a. Using the information provided, compute all of the short-run costs for this firm and complete the table. Remember to record the marginal costs *between* the rows indicating total cost.
b. Assuming that labour is only hired in increments of 10 units, what is this firm's capacity level of output?
c. At what level of labour employed per day does the firm encounter diminishing marginal productivity of labour?

⑯ Hilda's Handbags Inc. is incurring total costs of production in the short run of $30 000 per day. The firm's average variable cost equals $100 per unit and its average fixed cost equals $50 per unit.

a. How many units is the firm producing per day?
a. What are the firm's total variable costs at this output level?
c. What are the firm's total fixed costs at this output level?

8 Producers in the Long Run

CHAPTER OUTLINE	LEARNING OBJECTIVES (LO)
	After studying this chapter you will be able to
8.1 THE LONG RUN: NO FIXED FACTORS	**1** explain why profit maximization requires firms to equate marginal product per dollar spent for all factors.
	2 explain why profit-maximizing firms substitute away from factors whose prices have risen and toward factors whose prices have fallen.
	3 understand the relationship between short-run and long-run cost curves.
8.2 THE VERY LONG RUN: CHANGES IN TECHNOLOGY	**4** discuss the importance of technological change and why firms are motivated to innovate.

IN the first part of this chapter we look at the long run, in which firms are free to vary all factors of production. Recall from the end of the previous chapter that different amounts of the fixed factor lead to different short-run cost curves. The choice faced by a firm in the long run is to determine how much of the fixed factor to install—that is, to decide *which* of the several short-run cost curves to use. Some firms use a great deal of capital and only a small amount of labour. Others use less capital and more labour. Here we examine the effects these choices have on firms' costs, and we look at the conditions that influence these choices.

In the second part of the chapter, we examine the *very* long run, a period of analysis over which technology changes. The discussion concerns the improvements in technology and productivity that have dramatically increased output and incomes in all industrial countries over centuries. Firms are among the most important economic actors that cause technological advances to take place. As in the short and long run, firms respond to events, such as changes in factor prices. But in the very long run, firms often respond by innovating—that is, by developing *new* technologies.

Throughout this chapter, we should remember that the lengths of the various "runs" under consideration are defined by the kinds of changes that can take place, not by calendar time. Thus, we would expect actual firms in any given time period to be on their short-run cost curves, as described in Chapter 7; to choose among alternative short-run cost curves in the long run, as described in the first part of this chapter; and to change technologies in the very long run as described in the latter part of this chapter.

8.1 THE LONG RUN: NO FIXED FACTORS

In the short run, when at least one factor is fixed, the only way to adjust output is to adjust the input of the variable factors. In the long run, when all factors can be varied, there are numerous ways to produce any given output. For example, the firm could use complex automated machines and few workers, or simple machines and many workers. Thus, firms in the long run must choose the type and amount of plant and equipment and the size of their labour force.

In making these choices, the profit-maximizing firm will try to be **technically efficient**, which means using no more of all inputs than necessary—that is, the firm does not want to waste any of its valuable inputs. For example, consider the situation faced by a crate-manufacturing firm. If the firm is *able* to produce 100 crates per day by using two machines and eight workers, the firm would be technically *inefficient* if it decided instead to produce only 90 crates per day while still employing the same amount of (expensive) labour and capital. If the firm decides that it wants to produce only 90 crates per day, technical efficiency requires that it use fewer workers, fewer machines, or both.

Technical efficiency is not enough for profits to be maximized, however. In order to maximize its profit, the firm must choose from among the many technically efficient options the one that produces a given level of output at the lowest cost. For example, if the firm decides to produce 100 crates per day, it still must decide whether to use two simple machines and eight workers, or perhaps four automated machines and six workers. If it wants to maximize its profits, it should choose the lowest-cost combination of labour and capital.

Such choices about how much capital and labour to use are *long-run* choices because both labour and capital are assumed to be variable. These long-run planning decisions are important. A firm that decides to build a new steel mill and invest in the required machinery can choose among many alternatives. Once installed, that equipment is fixed for a long time. If the firm makes a poor choice, its survival may be threatened; if it chooses well, it may be rewarded with large profits.

> **technical efficiency** When a given number of inputs are combined in such a way as to maximize the level of output.

Profit Maximization and Cost Minimization

Any firm that seeks to maximize its profits in the long run should select the production method that produces its output at the lowest possible cost. This implication of the hypothesis of profit maximization is called **cost minimization**: From among the many technically efficient methods of production available to it, the profit-maximizing firm will choose the least costly means of producing whatever level of output it chooses.

Long-Run Cost Minimization If it is possible to substitute one factor for another to keep output constant while reducing total cost, the firm is currently not minimizing its

> **cost minimization** An implication of profit maximization that firms choose the production method that produces any given level of output at the lowest possible cost.

costs. In such a situation, the firm should substitute one factor for another factor as long as the marginal product of the one factor *per dollar spent on it* is greater than the marginal product of the other factor *per dollar spent on it*. The firm is not minimizing its costs whenever these two magnitudes are unequal. For example, if an extra dollar spent on labour produces more output than an extra dollar spent on capital, the firm can reduce costs by spending less on capital and more on labour.

Suppose we use K to represent capital, L to represent labour, and p_L and p_K to represent the prices per unit of the two factors. The necessary condition for cost minimization is then

$$\frac{MP_K}{p_K} = \frac{MP_L}{p_L} \tag{8-1}$$

Whenever the ratio of the marginal product of each factor to its price is not equal for all factors, there are possibilities for factor substitutions that will reduce costs (for a given level of output).

To see why Equation 8-1 must be satisfied when costs are being minimized, consider an example in which the equation is *not* satisfied. Suppose the marginal product of capital is 40 units of output and the price of one unit of capital is $10. Also suppose the marginal product of labour is 20 units of output and the price of one unit of labour is $2. Then we have

$$\frac{MP_K}{p_K} = \frac{40}{10} = 4 < \frac{MP_L}{p_L} = \frac{20}{2} = 10$$

Thus, the last dollar spent on capital adds only 4 units to output, whereas the last dollar spent on labour adds 10 units to output. In this case, the firm can reduce the cost of producing its current level of output by using more labour and less capital. Specifically, suppose the firm used 2 more units of labour and 1 fewer unit of capital. The 2 more units of labour would cause output to rise by 40 units and costs to increase by $4; the 1 fewer unit of capital would cause output to fall back by 40 units and costs to decline by $10. After this substitution of labour for capital, output would be unchanged but costs would be lower by $6. Thus, the original combination of factors was not a cost-minimizing one.

Of course, as the firm substitutes between labour and capital, the marginal products of both factors, MP_L and MP_K, will change. Specifically, the law of diminishing marginal returns says that with other inputs held constant, an increase in the amount of one factor used will decrease that factor's marginal product. As the firm in the previous example reduces its use of K and increases its use of L, MP_K will rise and MP_L will fall. These changes help to restore the equality in Equation 8-1.

By rearranging the terms in Equation 8-1, we can look at the cost-minimizing condition a bit differently.

$$\frac{MP_K}{MP_L} = \frac{p_K}{p_L} \tag{8-2}$$

Oil is a very important input in many industries. Increases in the price of oil will lead profit-maximizing firms to substitute away from oil toward other factors of production, whenever that is technically possible.

Skip Nall/Photodisc/Getty Images

The ratio of the marginal products on the left side compares the contribution to output of the last unit of capital and the last unit of labour. The right side shows how the cost of an additional unit of capital compares to the cost of an additional unit of labour. If the two sides of Equation 8-2 are the same, then the firm cannot make any substitutions between labour and capital to reduce costs (if output is held constant). However, with the marginal products and factor prices used in the example above, the left side of the equation equals 2 but the right side equals 5; the last unit of capital is twice as productive as the last unit of labour but it is five times more expensive. It will thus pay the firm to switch to a method of production that uses less capital and more labour. Only when the ratio of marginal products is exactly equal to the ratio of factor prices is the firm using the cost-minimizing production method.[1]

> **Profit-maximizing firms adjust the quantities of factors they use to the prices of the factors given by the market.**

The Principle of Substitution   The preceding discussion suggests that profit-maximizing (and therefore cost-minimizing) firms will react to changes in factor prices by changing their methods of production. This is referred to as the **principle of substitution**.

Suppose the firm's use of capital and labour currently satisfies Equation 8-1. Then consider a decrease in the price of capital while the price of labour remains unchanged. The least-cost method of producing any output will now use less labour and more capital than was required to produce the same output before the factor prices changed.

principle of substitution The principle that methods of production will change if relative prices of inputs change, with relatively more of the cheaper input and relatively less of the more expensive input being used.

> **Methods of production will change if the relative prices of factors change. Relatively more of the cheaper factor and relatively less of the more expensive factor will be used.**

The principle of substitution plays a central role in resource allocation because it relates to the way in which individual firms respond to changes in relative factor prices that are caused by the changing relative scarcities of factors in the economy as a whole. Individual firms are motivated to use less of factors that become scarcer to the economy and more of factors that become more plentiful. Here are four examples of the principle of substitution in action.

In recent decades, advances in information and communications technology (ICT), and massive declines in the price of ICT capital, have changed many everyday activities, including banking. Banks used to employ thousands of tellers to handle deposits and withdrawals at hundreds of branches across Canada. But now most retail bank transactions are done at automated teller machines (ATMs) or over the Internet by computer or smartphone. Banks have followed the principle of substitution by substituting away from labour and toward ICT capital as the price of the latter has declined.

The principle of substitution can also explain why methods of producing the same product often differ across countries. In Canada, where labour is generally highly skilled and expensive, farmers use advanced machinery to economize on labour. In many developing countries, however, where labour is abundant and capital is scarce,

---

[1] The appendix to this chapter provides a graphical analysis of this condition, which is similar to the analysis of consumer behaviour that we developed in the appendix to Chapter 6.

In many developing countries, labour is used much more intensively in agriculture than is the case in richer, developed countries. This does not mean methods are somehow "backward" in the developing countries; the intensive use of labour reflects a cost-minimizing response to low wages.

a much less mechanized method of production is appropriate. The Western engineer who believes that these countries are inefficient because they are using methods long ago discarded in the West is missing the truth about efficiency in the use of resources: Where factor scarcities differ across nations, so will the cost-minimizing methods of production.

The principle of substitution also shows that firms can be induced to substitute between capital and material inputs, such as fuel. With increases in the world price of oil, airlines have reduced their reliance on expensive jet fuel (derived from oil) by substituting toward planes that are constructed with lighter materials and have more fuel-efficient jet engines. In these situations, the increase in the price of fuel leads the airlines to change their *type* of capital equipment—to substitute away from jets that use a lot of fuel toward ones that are more fuel efficient.

Our final example involves a cross-country comparison of how firms substitute between capital and electricity. In North America, the price of electricity is quite low, and hotels usually do not worry about the extra expense when customers leave lights and air conditioning on when they leave their rooms during the day. In Europe and Central America, however, where electricity is far more expensive, many hotels are built so that all lights and air conditioning inside the room automatically turn off when you leave the room. The high price of electricity leads these firms to substitute toward a different kind of capital—one that uses less electricity.

Long-Run Cost Curves

We have been discussing a typical firm's cost-minimizing choices between various factors of production. Remember that these are *long-run* decisions because we are assuming that the firm is free to alter the amounts of all factors of production. As we have seen, when all factors can be varied, there exists a least-cost method of producing any given level of output. Thus, with given factor prices, there is a minimum achievable cost for each level of output; if this cost is expressed in terms of dollars per unit of output, we obtain the long-run average cost of producing each level of output. When this minimum cost of producing each level of output is plotted on a graph, the result is called a **long-run average cost (*LRAC*) curve**. Figure 8-1 shows one such curve.

The *LRAC* curve is determined by the firm's current technology and by the prices of the factors of production. It is a "boundary" in the sense that points below it are unattainable; points on the curve, however, are attainable if sufficient time elapses for all inputs to be adjusted. To move from one point on the *LRAC* curve to another requires an adjustment in *all* factor inputs, which may, for example, require building a larger factory with more machinery.

long-run average cost (*LRAC*) curve The curve showing the lowest possible cost of producing each level of output when all inputs can be varied.

The *LRAC* curve is the boundary between cost levels that are attainable, with known technology and given factor prices, and those that are unattainable.

FIGURE 8-1   A "Saucer-Shaped" Long-Run Average Cost Curve

The long-run average cost (*LRAC*) curve is the boundary between attainable and unattainable levels of costs. If the firm wants to produce output Q_0, the lowest attainable cost is c_0 per unit. Thus, point C_0 is on the *LRAC* curve. At point C_1, the firm has achieved the lowest possible average cost of producing Q_1. Suppose a firm is producing at Q_0 and desires to increase output to Q_1. In the long run, a larger plant can be built and the average cost of c_1 can be attained. However, in the short run, it will not be able to vary all factors, and thus costs per unit will be above c_1—say, c_2. For a range of output beginning at Q_m, the firm attains its lowest possible average cost of production for the given technology and factor prices.

Just as the short-run cost curves discussed in Chapter 7 relate to the production function describing the physical relationship between factor inputs and output, so does the *LRAC* curve. The difference is that in deriving the *LRAC* curve, there are no fixed factors of production. Since all costs are variable in the long run, we do not need to distinguish among *AVC*, *AFC*, and *ATC*, as we did in the short run; in the long run, there is only one *LRAC* for any given set of input prices.

The Shape of the Long-Run Average Cost Curve   The *LRAC* curve shown in Figure 8-1 first falls and then rises. Like the short-run cost curves we saw in Chapter 7, this curve is often described as U-shaped, although empirical studies suggest it is often "saucer-shaped." Consider the three portions of any saucer-shaped *LRAC* curve.

1. Decreasing Costs.   Over the range of output from zero to Q_m, the firm has falling long-run average costs: An expansion of output permits a reduction of average costs. When long-run average costs fall as output rises, the firm is said to have **economies of scale**. Because the *LRAC* curve is drawn under the assumption of constant factor prices, the decline in long-run average cost occurs because output is increasing *more than* in proportion to inputs as the scale of the firm's production expands. Over this range of output, the decreasing-cost firm is often said to enjoy long-run **increasing returns.**[2]

economies of scale Reduction of long-run average costs resulting from an expansion in the scale of a firm's operations so that more of all inputs is being used.

increasing returns (to scale) A situation in which output increases more than in proportion to inputs as the scale of a firm's production increases. A firm in this situation is a decreasing-cost firm.

---

[2] Economists shift back and forth between speaking in physical terms ("increasing returns") and cost terms ("decreasing costs"). As the text explains, the same relationship can be expressed either way.

Increasing returns may occur as a result of increased opportunities for specialization of tasks made possible by the division of labour. Even the most casual observation of the differences in production techniques used in large and small plants shows that larger plants use greater specialization. These differences arise because large, specialized equipment is useful only when the volume of output that the firm can sell justifies using that equipment. For example, assembly lines which intensively use expensive robotics are cost-minimizing techniques for producing cars and trucks only when individual operations are repeated thousands of times.

2. Constant Costs. In Figure 8-1, the firm's long-run average costs fall until output reaches Q_m, which is known as the firm's **minimum efficient scale**. It is the smallest level of output at which $LRAC$ reaches its minimum. The $LRAC$ curve is then flat over some range of output. With such a flat portion, the firm encounters constant costs over the relevant range of output, meaning that the firm's long-run average costs do not change as its output rises. Because factor prices are assumed to be fixed, the firm's output must be increasing *exactly in proportion to* the increase in inputs. When this happens, the constant-cost firm is said to have **constant returns**.

3. Increasing Costs. When the $LRAC$ curve is rising, a long-run expansion in production is accompanied by a rise in average costs. If factor prices are constant, the firm's output must be increasing *less than* in proportion to the increase in inputs. When this happens, the increasing-cost firm is said to encounter long-run **decreasing returns**. Decreasing returns imply that the firm suffers some *diseconomies of scale.*

Such diseconomies may be associated with the difficulties of managing and controlling an enterprise as its size increases. At first, there may be scale economies as the firm grows and benefits from greater specialization. But sooner or later, planning and coordination problems may multiply more than in proportion to the growth in size. If so, costs per unit of output will rise.

Other diseconomies are the possible alienation of the labour force as size increases; it becomes more difficult to provide appropriate supervision as more layers of supervisors and middle managers come between the person at the top and the workers on the shop floor. Control of middle-range managers may also become more difficult. As the firm becomes larger, managers may begin to pursue their own goals rather than devote all of their efforts to making profits for the firm.

In the early 1900s, Henry Ford pioneered the use of assembly lines in his automobile production facilities, and was successful at significantly reducing per unit production costs. In an attempt to reduce costs further, Ford built the massive River Rouge plant in Dearborn, Michigan, which began production in 1928 as the largest integrated facility in the world. But organizational complexities and alienation of the labour force plagued the plant, and costs were actually higher there than at other, smaller Ford facilities. Over time, the Ford Motor Company reduced the size of the River Rouge plant and focussed on building smaller factories across the country, and around the world.

Note that long-run decreasing returns differ from short-run diminishing returns. In the short run, at least one factor is fixed, and the law of diminishing returns ensures that returns to the variable factor will eventually diminish. In the long run, all factors are variable, and it is possible that physically diminishing returns will never be encountered—at least as long as it is genuinely possible to increase inputs of all factors.

The Relationship Between Long-Run and Short-Run Costs The short-run cost curves from the previous chapter and the long-run cost curve studied in this chapter are all derived from the same production function. Each curve assumes given prices for all

minimum efficient scale (MES) The smallest output at which $LRAC$ reaches its minimum. All available economies of scale have been realized at this point.

constant returns (to scale) A situation in which output increases in proportion to inputs as the scale of production is increased. A firm in this situation is a constant-cost firm.

decreasing returns (to scale) A situation in which output increases less than in proportion to inputs as the scale of a firm's production increases. A firm in this situation is an increasing-cost firm.

factor inputs. The *LRAC* curve shows the lowest cost of producing any output when all factors are variable. Each short-run average total cost (*SRATC*) curve shows the lowest cost of producing any output when one or more factors are fixed.

No short-run cost curve can fall below the long-run cost curve because the *LRAC* curve represents the lowest attainable cost for each possible output.

As the level of output is changed, a different-size plant is normally required to achieve the lowest attainable cost. Figure 8-2 shows that the *SRATC* curve lies above the *LRAC* curve at all levels of output except Q_0.

Note that any individual *SRATC* curve is just one of many such curves, each one corresponding to a different plant size. The single *SRATC* curve in Figure 8-2 shows how costs vary as output is varied, holding the plant size constant. Figure 8-3 shows a family of *SRATC* curves, along with a single *LRAC* curve. The *LRAC* curve is sometimes called an *envelope curve* because it encloses (or envelops) a series of *SRATC* cost curves by being tangent to them.

Each *SRATC* curve is tangent to the *LRAC* curve at the level of output for which the quantity of the fixed factor is optimal, and lies above it for all other levels of output.

FIGURE 8-2 **_LRAC_ and _SRATC_ Curves**

Each *SRATC* curve is tangent at some point to the *LRAC* curve. With given technology, each plant size gives rise to a different *SRATC* curve. The *SRATC* curve shown corresponds to the optimal plant size for producing Q_0 units of output because the average cost, c_0, is the lowest attainable. For output levels less than or greater than Q_0, such as Q_1 or Q_2, the plant size embodied in $SRATC_0$ is not optimal because the cost given by the $SRATC_0$ curve is greater than the minimum possible cost, given by the *LRAC* curve.

For example, if the firm wants to increase production from Q_0 to Q_2 in the short run, its average total costs will rise above the *LRAC* curve to point x. To achieve the minimum possible cost of producing output Q_2 in the long run, the firm must increase its plant size. By doing so the firm moves to a different *SRATC* curve, one that is tangent to the *LRAC* curve at output Q_2.

FIGURE 8-3 **The Relationship Between the LRAC Curve and the SRATC Curves**

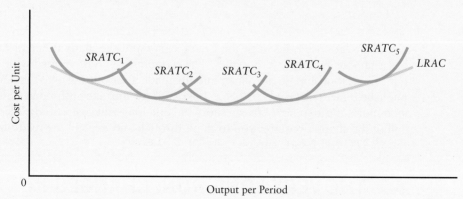

To every point on the LRAC curve, there is an associated SRATC curve tangent at that point. Each short-run curve is drawn for a given plant size, and shows how costs vary if output varies (holding constant the size of the plant). The level of output at the tangency between each *SRATC* curve and the *LRAC* curve shows the level of output for which the plant size is optimal.

LESSONS FROM HISTORY 8-1

Jacob Viner and the Clever Draftsman

Jacob Viner (1892–1970) was born in Montreal and studied economics at McGill University under Stephen Leacock (1869–1944). Viner was clearly an outstanding student and, according to some of his McGill classmates, knew much more about economics than did Leacock, who was actually better known as a humorist than an economist. Viner was such a good economist that he was the first person to work out the relationship between a firm's long-run average costs and its short-run average costs. He went on to teach economics at the University of Chicago and at Princeton University and became one of the world's leading economic theorists.

If you find the relationship between *SRATC* and *LRAC* hard to understand you may take some comfort from the fact that when Jacob Viner first worked out this relationship, and published it in 1931, he made a crucial mistake. In preparing a diagram like Figure 8-3, he instructed his draftsman to draw the *LRAC* curve through the *minimum points* of all the *SRATC* curves, "but so as to never lie above" the *SRATC* curves. Viner later said of the draftsman: "He is a mathematician, however, not an economist, and he saw some mathematical objection to this procedure which I could not succeed in understanding. I could not persuade him to disregard his scruples as a craftsman and to follow my instructions, absurd though they might be."

Viner's mistake was to require that the draftsman connect all the *minimum* points of the *SRATC* curves

rather than to construct the curve that would be the *lower envelope* of all the *SRATC* curves. The former curve can, of course, be drawn, but it is not the *LRAC* curve. The latter curve is the *LRAC* curve and is tangent to each *SRATC* curve.

Since Viner's article was published in 1931, generations of economics students have experienced great satisfaction when they finally figured out his crucial mistake. Viner's famous article was often reprinted, for its fame was justly deserved, despite the importance of the mistake. But Viner always rejected suggestions that he correct the error because he did not want to deprive other students of the pleasure of feeling one up on him.

The economic sense of the fact that tangency is not at the minimum points of *SRATC* rests on the subtle distinction between the least-cost method of utilizing a *given plant* and the least-cost method of producing a *given level of output*. The first concept defines the minimum of any given *SRATC* curve, whereas the second defines a point on the *LRAC* curve for any given level of output. It is the second concept that interests us in the long run. If bigger plants can achieve lower average costs, there will be a gain in building a bigger plant *and underutilizing it* whenever the gains from using the bigger plant are enough to offset the costs of underutilizing the plant. If there are gains from building bigger plants (i.e., if *LRAC* is declining), some underutilization is always justified.

The relationship between the *LRAC* curve and the many different *SRATC* curves has a famous history in economics. The economist who is credited with first working out this relationship, Jacob Viner, initially made a serious mistake that ended up being published; *Lessons From History 8-1* explains his mistake and shows how it illustrates an important difference between short-run and long-run costs. Study Exercise #7 at the end of the chapter requires you to think through and explain the relationship between the *SRATC* and *LRAC* curves.

8.2 THE VERY LONG RUN: CHANGES IN TECHNOLOGY

In the long run, profit-maximizing firms faced with given technologies choose the cost-minimizing mix of factors to produce their desired level of output. Firms are therefore on, rather than above, their *LRAC* curves. In the very long run, however, there are changes in the available techniques and resources. Such changes cause *shifts* in *LRAC* curves.

The decrease in costs that can be achieved by choosing from among available factors of production, known techniques, and alternative levels of output is necessarily limited by the existing state of knowledge. In contrast, improvements by invention and innovation are potentially limitless.

Technological change refers to all changes in the available techniques of production. There are countless examples, including the invention of the assembly line, the development of robotics, the invention of fuel-efficient jet engines, the creation of new medical and drug treatments, the creation of the Internet, and the development of wireless communication devices. To measure the extent of technological change, economists usually use the notion of **productivity**, defined as a measure of output produced per unit of input used. Two widely used measures of productivity are output per worker and output per hour of work. The rate of increase in productivity provides one measure of technological change.

Most economists believe that productivity growth driven by technological change is the primary cause of rising material living standards over decades and centuries. If you want to know why your real income (purchasing power) is likely to be several times that enjoyed by your great-grandparents 75 or 100 years ago, the reason is that you are likely to be much more productive than they were. Your greater productivity is due to better health, better skills, and the fact that you work with much better equipment than did workers back then.

In recent years, however, the rate of productivity growth in Canada has been slowing, and it has also become clear that it is below the rate of growth in other developed countries like the United States and the United Kingdom. The importance of productivity growth in sustaining our rising path of living standards has led economists in universities and government to spend a great deal of effort researching the causes of the slowdown as well as policies that might encourage faster productivity growth. See *Applying Economic Concepts 8-1* for more on this important issue.

technological change Any change in the available techniques of production.

productivity Output produced per unit of some input; frequently used to refer to labour productivity, measured by total output divided by the amount of labour used.

Technological Change

Technological change was once thought to be mainly a random process, brought about by inventions made by crackpots and eccentric scientists working in garages and scientific laboratories. As a result of recent research by historians and economists, we now know better.

Many changes in technology are based on scientific discoveries made in such non-profit organizations as universities and government research laboratories; others come out of laboratories run by private firms. Whatever their origin, most technological advances are put into practice by firms in search of profits. A firm that first develops a new product, a new wrinkle on an old product, or a new process that lowers production costs gets a temporary advantage over its competitors. This advantage creates profits that persist until others can copy what the original firm has done. So in the very long run, the search for profit takes the form not just of choosing the most efficient technique among known alternatives but also of inventing and innovating new products and processes. Since firms do this in search of profits, we say that the technological change is *endogenous* to the economic system rather than something that just occurs for unknown reasons.

Sometimes innovations come from new ideas that are the next extension of existing knowledge, where the motivation is to raise profits by developing these opportunities. Examples include new features in Facebook or the developments of new apps for smartphones. At other times innovations are a response to some obvious challenge. For example, rising fuel prices and the growing recognition of problems associated with the

APPLYING ECONOMIC CONCEPTS 8-1

The Significance of Productivity Growth

Long ago, economics was known as the "dismal science" because some of its predictions were grim. Thomas Malthus (1766–1834) and other Classical economists predicted that the pressure of more and more people on the world's limited resources would cause a decline in output per person because of the law of diminishing returns. Human history would see more and more people living less and less well and the surplus population, which could not be supported, dying off from hunger and disease.

This prediction has proven wrong for industrialized countries for two main reasons. First, their populations have not expanded as rapidly as predicted by early economists, who were writing before birth-control techniques were widely used. Second, technological advances have been so important during the past 150 years that output has increased much faster than the population. We have experienced sustained growth in productivity that has permitted significant increases in output per person—often referred to as material living standards. As the accompanying figure shows, real output per

employed worker in Canada increased by 335 percent between 1926 and 2014, an average annually compounded growth rate of 1.68 percent.

Even such small annual productivity increases are a powerful force for increasing material living standards over many years. Our great-grandparents would have regarded today's standard of living in most industrialized countries as unattainable. An apparently modest rate of increase in productivity of 2 percent per year leads to a doubling of per capita output every 36 years.[*]

Because of the importance of productivity growth in raising long-run material living standards, it is not surprising that explaining the sources of technological progress has become a very active area of research among both academic and government economists.

---

[*] The mathematical "rule of 72" says that for any variable growing at X percent per year, 72/X gives the approximate number of years required for the variable to double.

The Path of Canadian Labour Productivity, 1926–2014

(*Source:* Based on the data from Statistics Canada, CANSIM database. Output as measured by Real GDP: Series V3862685, Table 380-0017. Employment: Series V2091072.)

burning of fossil fuels have led to a rapid development of all-electric vehicles and the battery technology necessary to make them effective substitutes to gasoline-powered cars.

Consider three aspects of technological change: *new techniques, improved inputs,* and *new products*.

New Techniques Throughout the nineteenth and twentieth centuries, changes in the techniques available for producing existing products have been dramatic; this is called *process innovation*. Two examples where the product is largely the same but the techniques for producing them have changed dramatically are road building and electricity production. A century ago, roads and railways were built by gangs of workers who used buckets, shovels, and draft horses. Today, bulldozers, giant trucks, and other specialized equipment have banished the workhorse completely from construction sites and to a great extent have displaced the pick-and-shovel worker. Before the Second World War, electricity was generated either by burning fossil fuels or by harnessing the power of flowing water. After the Second World War, many countries developed large-scale nuclear generating capacity that displayed enormous economies of scale. In recent years, however, the development of small-scale, gas-combustion turbines has permitted inexpensive construction of small generating stations that can produce electricity at a lower average cost than the much larger nuclear, hydro, or fossil fuel–burning generating stations. The product—electricity—is absolutely unchanged, but the techniques of production have changed markedly over the past several decades.

Improved Inputs Improvements in material inputs are constantly occurring. For example, the type and quality of metals have changed. Steel has replaced iron, and aluminum substitutes for steel in a process of change that makes a statistical category such as "primary metals" seem unsatisfactory. Even for a given category such as steel, today's product is lighter, stronger, and more flexible than the "same" product manufactured only 20 years ago. Furthermore, the modern "materials revolution" allows new materials to be tailor-made for the specific purposes for which they are required.

> The invention of new production techniques and the development of new and better inputs are important aspects of technological improvement. They lead to reductions in firms' costs and a downward shift in *LRAC* curves.

New technologies and improved inputs are key aspects of technological change, and they are both reasons that firms' *LRAC* curves shift downward over time. A third aspect is not directly related to costs but rather to the new products that are invented as a result of technological change.

New Products New goods and services are constantly being invented and marketed; this is called *product innovation*. DVDs, smartphones, MRIs, CAT scans, DNA tests, personal GPS devices, 3D printers, driverless cars, drones, and many other products did not exist 30 years ago. Other products have changed so dramatically that the only connection they have with the "same" product

Environmental concerns combined with increases in the world price of oil have led to the development of hybrid and fully electric cars.

Kevin Dietsch/UPI Photo/Landov

from the past is the name. Today's Ford car is very different from a 1920 Ford, and it is even different from a 1990 Ford in size, safety, and gasoline consumption. Modern jet aircraft are revolutionary compared with the first passenger jet aircraft, which were in turn many times larger and faster than the DC-3, the workhorse of the airlines during the 1930s and 1940s. Beyond having wings and engines, the DC-3 itself bore little resemblance to the Wright brothers' original flying machine.

The development of new products is a crucial part of the steady increase in living standards.

Firms' Choices in the Very Long Run

Firms respond to market signals that indicate changes in the economic environment. For example, consider the situation faced by Dofasco—a major steel producer located in Hamilton, Ontario—when the price of coal (a major input) increases and is expected to remain at the higher level for some time. How can Dofasco respond to this change in the economic environment?

One option for Dofasco is to make a long-run response by substituting away from the use of coal by changing its production techniques within the confines of existing technology. This might involve switching to other fuels (whose prices have not increased) to operate Dofasco's enormous blast furnaces. Another option is to invest in research in order to develop new production techniques that innovate away from coal (and other fuels as well), such as the design of blast furnaces that require less fuel to process each unit of iron ore.

Faced with increases in the price of an input, firms may either *substitute away* or *innovate away* from the input—or do both over different time horizons.

It is important to recognize that these two options can involve quite different actions and can ultimately have quite different implications for productivity. For example, consider three different responses to an increase in Canadian labour costs. One firm relocates its production activities to Mexico or India, where labour costs are relatively low and hence labour-intensive production techniques remain quite profitable. A second firm chooses to reduce its use of labour but increase its use of capital equipment. These two firms have, in different ways, chosen to *substitute away* from the higher-priced Canadian labour. A third firm devotes resources to developing new production techniques, perhaps by using robotics or other new equipment. This firm has *innovated away* from higher-priced Canadian labour.

All three are possible reactions to the changed circumstances. The first two are largely well understood in advance and will lead to reduced costs relative to continued reliance on the original production methods. The third response, depending on the often unpredictable results of the innovation, may fail completely or it may succeed and so reduce costs sufficiently to warrant the investment in research and development and may even lead to substantially more effective production techniques that allow the firm to maintain an advantage over its competitors for a number of years. Invention and innovation are subject to great uncertainties that are hard to estimate in advance. For this reason, they must produce large profits when they do succeed in order to induce inventing firms to incur the costs of pushing into the unknown.

SUMMARY

8.1 THE LONG RUN: NO FIXED FACTORS

- There are no fixed factors in the long run. Profit maximizing firms choose from the available alternatives the least-cost method of producing any specific output.
- Profit-maximizing firms must minimize the cost of producing any given level of output. The condition for cost minimization is

$$\frac{MP_K}{MP_L} = \frac{p_K}{p_L}$$

- The principle of substitution states that, in response to changes in factor prices, profit-maximizing firms will substitute toward the cheaper factors and substitute away from the more expensive factors.

- A long-run average cost curve represents the boundary between attainable and unattainable costs for the given technology and given factor prices.
- The shape of the *LRAC* curve depends on the relationship of inputs to outputs as the whole scale of a firm's operations changes. Increasing, constant, and decreasing returns lead, respectively, to decreasing, constant, and increasing long-run average costs.
- The *LRAC* and *SRATC* curves are related. Each *SRATC* curve represents a specific plant size and is tangent to the *LRAC* curve at the level of output for which that plant size is optimal.

8.2 THE VERY LONG RUN: CHANGES IN TECHNOLOGY

- Over the very long run, the most important influence on costs of production and on material standards of living has been increases in output made possible by technological improvements.
- Technological improvements usually lead to downward shifts in firms' *LRAC* curves.
- Changes in technology are often *endogenous responses* to changing economic signals; that is, they result from the firms' responses to changes in the economic environment.

- There are three important kinds of technological change: developments of new production techniques, improved inputs, and new products. All three play an important role in increasing material living standards.
- To understand any industry's response to changes in its operating environment, it is important to consider the effects of endogenous innovations in technology as well as substitution based on changes in the use of existing technologies.

KEY CONCEPTS

The implication of cost minimization
The interpretation of $MP_K/MP_L = p_K/p_L$
The principle of substitution

Increasing, constant, and decreasing returns
Economies and diseconomies of scale
LRAC curve as an envelope of *SRATC* curves

Technological change and productivity growth
Changes in technology as endogenous responses

STUDY EXERCISES

MyEconLab Make the grade with MyEconLab: Study Exercises marked in ⊕ can be found on MyEconLab. You can practise them as often as you want, and most feature step-by-step guided instructions to help you find the right answer.

❶ Fill in the blanks to make the following statements correct.

    a. In the long run, if a firm is maximizing its profits while producing a given level of output, then this firm is also _____ its costs.

    b. In the long run, all factors of production are _____. There are no _____ factors.

    c. Profit-maximizing firms employ factors of production such that the marginal products per dollar spent on each factor are _____.

d. Firms adjust their methods of production in response to changes in relative prices. This is known as the _____.

2 The long-run average cost curve is often saucer-shaped. Fill in the blanks to make the following statements about the $LRAC$ curve correct.

a. Over the range of output where the $LRAC$ curve is falling, the firm is experiencing _____ or _____. As output increases, average costs are _____.

b. When the $LRAC$ curve reaches its minimum, the firm has reached its _____. If the curve is flat over some range of output, we say the firm is exhibiting _____.

c. Over the range of output in which the $LRAC$ curve is rising, the firm is experiencing _____ or _____. As output increases, average costs are _____.

d. The $LRAC$ curve represents the _____ for each level of output.

e. Each short-run average total cost curve is _____ at some point to the $LRAC$ curve. The $LRAC$ curve shows the lowest possible cost of producing any output when all factors are _____. The $SRATC$ curve shows the lowest possible cost of producing any output when one or more factors are _____.

3 Explain why a profit-maximizing firm must also minimize costs.

4 Industrial Footwear Inc. uses capital and labour to produce workboots. Suppose this firm is using capital and labour such that the MP_K is equal to 80 and the MP_L is equal to 20. For each set of per-unit prices of capital and labour given below, determine whether Industrial Footwear Inc. is minimizing its costs. If it is not, determine the direction of factor substitution the firm should make in order to do so.

a. $P_K = \$2$ $P_L = \$10$
b. $P_K = \$20$ $P_L = \$5$
c. $P_K = \$40$ $P_L = \$5$

5 Use the principle of substitution to predict the effect in each of the following situations.

a. During the past 30 years, technological advances in the computer industry have led to dramatic reductions in the price of equipment. At the same time, real wages have increased slowly.

b. The ratio of land costs to building costs is much higher in big cities than in small cities.

c. Wages of textile workers and shoe machinery operators are higher in Canada than in the Southern United States, but the price of capital equipment is approximately the same.

d. In China's cities, wage rates for labour are rising faster than the price of capital equipment.

6 The following table shows the marginal product of capital and labour for each of several methods of producing 1000 kilograms of flour per day.

Production Method	MP_K	MP_L
A	14	3
B	12	6
C	10	9
D	8	12
E	6	15
F	4	18
G	2	21

a. As we move from A to G, are the production methods becoming more or less _capital intensive_? Explain.

b. If capital costs $8 per unit and labour costs $4 per unit, which production method minimizes the cost of producing 1000 kg of flour?

c. For each of the methods that are not cost minimizing (with the factor prices from part (b)), describe how the firm would have to adjust its use of capital and labour to minimize costs.

d. Now suppose the price of capital falls to $4 per unit and the price of labour rises to $6 per unit. Which method now minimizes costs?

7 Consider the following diagram of $SRATC$ and $LRAC$ curves.

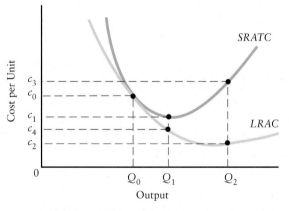

a. The $SRATC$ curve is drawn for a given plant size. Given this plant size, what is the level of output that minimizes short-run average costs? What are unit costs in the short run at this level of output?

b. What is the level of output for which this plant size is optimal in the long run? What are unit costs in the short run at this level of output?

c. Explain the economics of why c_1 is greater than c_4.

d. Suppose the firm wants to increase output to Q_2 in the short run. How is this accomplished, and what would unit costs be?

e. Suppose the firm wants to increase output to Q_2 in the long run. How is this accomplished, and what would unit costs be?

8 The following diagram shows three possible *SRATC* curves and an *LRAC* curve for a single firm producing light bulbs, where each *SRATC* curve is associated with a different-sized plant.

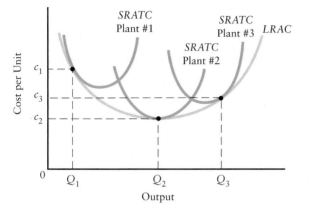

a. If the firm is producing Q_1 light bulbs with Plant #1, what are the firm's average costs?
b. At Q_1, does the firm display decreasing, constant, or increasing costs?
c. How does your answer in part (b) relate to the concept of *economies of scale*?
d. Repeat parts (a), (b), and (c) for output level Q_2 with Plant #2 and output level Q_3 with Plant #3.

9 In the text, we stated that the *LRAC* curve eventually slopes upward because of *diseconomies of scale*. In the previous chapter we saw that the *SRATC* curve eventually slopes upward because of *diminishing marginal product of the variable factor*.

a. Explain the difference between *diseconomies of scale* and *diminishing marginal product of the variable factor*. Why is one a short-run concept and the other a long-run concept?
b. Draw a diagram with short-run and long-run average cost curves that illustrates *for the same level of output* both diseconomies of scale and diminishing marginal product of the variable factor.

10 In the text, we stated that the *LRAC* curve initially slopes downward because of *economies of scale*. In the previous chapter we saw that the *SRATC* curve can initially slope downward because of *spreading overhead*.

a. Explain the difference between *economies of scale* and *spreading overhead*. Why is one a short-run concept and the other a long-run concept?
b. Draw a diagram with short-run and long-run average cost curves that illustrates *for the same level of output* both economies of scale and spreading overhead.

11 This question combines the various concepts from Questions 9 and 10.

a. Draw a diagram with short-run and long-run average cost curves that illustrates *for the same level of output* economies of scale in the long run but diminishing marginal product for the variable factor in the short run.
b. Draw a diagram with short-run and long-run average cost curves that illustrates *for the same level of output* diseconomies of scale in the long run but falling average total costs in the short run.

12 This question relates to the material in the Appendix. The following table shows several methods of producing 500 rubber tires per day. There are two factors, labour and capital, with prices per unit of $3 and $6, respectively.

Production Method	Units of Labour	Units of Capital	Total Cost
A	110	20	—
B	90	25	—
C	70	33	—
D	50	43	—
E	30	55	—
F	10	70	—

a. Compute the total cost for each production method and fill in the table.
b. Which production method minimizes costs for producing 500 tires?
c. Plot the isoquant for 500 tires, with units of capital on the vertical axis and units of labour on the horizontal axis.
d. Given the factor prices, draw the isocost line that corresponds to the cost-minimizing production method.
e. Now suppose the price of labour rises to $5 per unit but the firm still wants to produce 500 tires per day. Explain how a cost-minimizing firm adjusts to this change (with no change in technology).

The production function gives the relationship between the factor inputs that the firm uses and the output that it obtains. In the long run, the firm can choose among many different combinations of inputs that yield the same output. The production function and the long-run choices open to the firm can be represented graphically by using *isoquants*.

8A.1 ISOQUANTS

The table in Figure 8A-1 illustrates a hypothetical example in which several combinations of two inputs, labour and capital, can produce a given quantity of output. The data from the table are plotted graphically in Figure 8A-1. A smooth curve is drawn through the points to indicate that there are additional ways, which are not listed in the table, of producing the same output.

This curve is called an *isoquant*. It shows the whole set of technically efficient factor combinations for producing a given level of output. This is an example of graphing a relationship among three variables in two dimensions. It is analogous to the contour line on a map, which shows all points of equal altitude, and to an indifference curve (discussed in the Appendix to Chapter 6), which shows all combinations of products that yield the consumer equal utility.

As we move from one point on an isoquant to another, we are *substituting one factor for another* while holding output constant. If we move from point *b* to point *c*, we are substituting 1 unit of labour for 3 units of capital.

The marginal rate of substitution measures the rate at which one factor is substituted for another with output being held constant.

Sometimes the term *marginal rate of technical substitution* is used to distinguish this concept from the analogous one for consumer theory (the marginal rate of substitution) that we examined in Chapter 6.

Graphically, the marginal rate of substitution is measured by the slope of the isoquant at a particular point. We adopt the standard practice of defining the marginal rate of substitution as the negative of the slope of the isoquant so that it is a positive number. The table in Figure 8A-1 shows the calculation of some marginal rates of substitution between various points on an isoquant. [19]

The marginal rate of substitution is related to the marginal products of the factors of production. To see how, consider an example. Suppose at the present level of inputs of labour and capital, the marginal product of labour is 2 units of output and the marginal product of capital is 1 unit of output. If the firm reduces its use of capital and increases its use of labour to keep output constant, it needs to add only one-half unit of labour for 1 unit of capital given up. If, at another point on the isoquant with more labour and less capital, the marginal products are 2 for capital and 1 for labour, the firm will have to add 2 units of labour for every unit of capital it gives up. The general proposition is this:

The marginal rate of (technical) substitution between two factors of production is equal to the ratio of their marginal products.

Economists assume that isoquants satisfy two important conditions: they are downward sloping, and they are convex when viewed from the origin. What is the economic meaning of these conditions?

The downward slope indicates that each factor input has a positive marginal product. If the input of one factor is reduced and that of the other is held constant, output will be reduced. Thus, if one input is decreased, production can be held constant only if the other factor input is increased.

To understand the convexity of the isoquant, consider what happens as the firm moves along the isoquant of Figure 8A-1 downward and to the right. Labour is being added and capital reduced to keep

FIGURE 8A-1 An Isoquant

Alternative Methods of Producing a Given Level of Output

Method	K	L	ΔK	ΔL	Marginal Rate of Substitution (absolute value of $\Delta K/\Delta L$)
a	18	2			
b	12	3	−6	1	6.00
c	9	4	−3	1	3.00
d	6	6	−3	2	1.50
e	4	9	−2	3	0.67
f	3	12	−1	3	0.33
g	2	18	−1	6	0.17

An isoquant describes the firm's alternative methods for producing a given level of output. Method *a* uses a great deal of capital (*K*) and very little labour (*L*). As we move down the table, labour is substituted for capital in such a way as to keep output constant. Finally, at the bottom, most of the capital has been replaced by labour. The marginal rate of substitution between the two factors is calculated in the last three columns of the table. Note that as we move down the table, the marginal rate of substitution declines.

When the isoquant is plotted, it is downward sloping and convex. The downward slope reflects the requirement of technical efficiency: Keeping the level of output constant, a reduction in the use of one factor requires an increase in the use of the other factor. The convex shape of the isoquant reflects a diminishing marginal rate of (technical) substitution.

output constant. If labour is added in increments of exactly 1 unit, how much capital can be dispensed with each time? The key to the answer is that both factors are assumed to be subject to the law of diminishing returns. Thus, the gain in output associated with each additional unit of labour added is *diminishing*, whereas the loss of output associated with each additional unit of capital forgone is *increasing*. Therefore, it takes ever-smaller reductions in capital to compensate for equal increases in labour. Viewed from the origin, therefore, the isoquant is convex.

An Isoquant Map

The isoquant of Figure 8A-1 is for a given level of output. Suppose it is for 6 units. In this case, there is another isoquant for 7 units, another for 7000 units, and a different one for every other level of output. Each isoquant refers to a specific level of output and connects combinations of factors that are technically efficient methods of producing that output. If we plot a representative set of these isoquants from the same production function on a single graph, we get an *isoquant map* like that in

FIGURE 8A-2 An Isoquant Map

An isoquant map shows a set of isoquants, one for each level of output. Each isoquant corresponds to a specific level of output and shows factor combinations that are technically efficient methods of producing that output.

Figure 8A-2. The higher the level of output along a particular isoquant, the farther the isoquant is from the origin.

8A.2 COST MINIMIZATION

Finding the cost-minimizing method of producing any output requires knowledge of the factor prices. Suppose capital is priced at $4 per unit and labour at $1 per unit. An *isocost line* shows alternative combinations of factors that a firm can buy for a given total cost. Four different isocost lines appear in Figure 8A-3. The slope of each isocost line reflects *relative* factor prices. For given factor prices, a series of parallel isocost lines will reflect the alternative levels of expenditure on factor purchases that are available to the firm. The higher the level of expenditure, the farther the isocost line is from the origin.

In Figure 8A-4, the isoquant and isocost maps are brought together. The cost-minimizing method of production must be a point on an isoquant that just touches (is tangent to) an isocost line. If the isoquant cuts the isocost line, it is possible to move along the isoquant and reach a lower level of cost. Only at a point of tangency is a movement in either direction along the isoquant a movement to a higher cost level.

As shown in Figure 8A-4, the lowest attainable cost of producing 6 units is $24, and this requires using 12 units of labour and 3 units of capital.

> **The least-cost position is given graphically by the tangency point between the isoquant and the isocost lines.**

The slope of the isocost line is given by the ratio of the prices of the two factors of production. The slope of the isoquant at any point is given by the ratio of their marginal products. When the firm reaches its cost-minimizing position, it has equated the price ratio (which is given to it by the market) with the ratio of the marginal products (which it can adjust by changing its usage of the factors). In symbols,

$$\frac{MP_L}{MP_K} = \frac{p_L}{p_K}$$

This is the same condition that we derived in the text (see Equation 8-2), but here we have derived it by using the isoquant analysis of the firm's decisions. [20]

Note the similarity of this condition for a cost-minimizing firm to Equation 6-2, where we saw how

FIGURE 8A-3   Isocost Lines

Each isocost line shows alternative factor combinations that require the same expenditure. The graph shows the four isocost lines that result when labour costs $1 per unit and capital $4 per unit and when expenditure (total cost, *TC*) is held constant at $12, $24, $36, and $48, respectively.

utility maximization for a consumer requires that the ratio of marginal utilities of consuming two products must equal the ratio of the two product prices. Both conditions reveal the basic principle that the decision makers (consumers or producers) face market prices beyond their control and so adjust quantities (consumption or factor inputs) until they are achieving their objective (utility maximization or cost minimization).

The Principle of Substitution

Suppose with technology unchanged (that is, for a given isoquant map), the price of one factor changes. In particular, suppose with the price of capital unchanged at $4 per unit, the price of labour rises from $1 to $4 per unit. Originally, the cost-minimizing factor combination for producing 6 units of output was 12 units of labour and 3 units of capital. Total cost was $24. To produce that same output in the same way would now cost $60 at the new factor prices. Figure 8A-5 shows why this production method is no longer the cost-minimizing one. The slope of the isocost line has changed, which makes it efficient to substitute the now relatively cheaper

FIGURE 8A-4   Cost Minimization

Cost minimization occurs at points of tangency between isoquant and isocost lines. The isoquant map of Figure 8A-2 and the isocost lines of Figure 8A-3 are brought together. Consider point A. It is on the 6-unit isoquant and the $24 isocost line. Thus, it is possible to achieve the output $Q = 6$ for a total cost of $24. There are other ways to achieve this output, for example, at point B, where $TC = \$48$. Moving along the isoquant from point A in either direction increases cost. Similarly, moving along the isocost line from point A in either direction lowers output. Thus, either move would raise cost per unit.

FIGURE 8A-5   The Effects of a Change in Factor Prices on Costs and Factor Proportions

(i) The effect on the isocost line of an increase in the price of labour

(ii) Substitution of capital for labour resulting from an increase in the price of labour

An increase in the price of labour pivots the isocost line inward, increasing its slope. This changes the cost-minimizing method of producing any level of output. In part (i), the rise in the price of L from $1 to $4 per unit (with the price of K being held constant at $4) pivots the $24 isocost line inward to the dashed line. Any output previously produced for $24 will cost more at the new prices if it uses any labour. The new cost of using the factor combination at A rises from $24 to $60. In part (ii), the steeper isocost line is tangent to the $Q = 6$ isoquant at C, not A, so that more capital and less labour is used. Costs at C are $48, higher than they were before the price increase but not as high as they would be if the factor substitution had not occurred.

capital for the relatively more expensive labour. The change in slope of the isocost line illustrates the principle of substitution.

Changes in relative factor prices will cause a partial replacement of factors that have become relatively more expensive by factors that have become relatively cheaper.

Of course, substitution of capital for labour cannot fully offset the effects of a rise in the cost of labour, as Figure 8A-5(i) shows. Consider the output attainable for $24. In the figure, there are two isocost lines representing $24 of outlay—at the old and new prices of labour. The new isocost line for $24 lies inside the old one (except where no labour is used). The $24 isocost line must therefore be tangent to a lower isoquant. Thus, if production is to be held constant, higher costs must be accepted. However, because of substitution, it is not necessary to accept costs as high as those that would accompany an unchanged factor proportion. In the example, 6 units can be produced for $48 rather than the $60 that would be required if no change in factor proportions were made.

This analysis leads to the following predictions:

A rise in the price of one factor with all other factor prices held constant will (1) shift the cost curves of products that use that factor upward and (2) lead to a substitution of factors that are now relatively cheaper for the factor whose price has risen.

Both of these predictions were stated in Chapter 8; now they have been derived formally by the use of isoquants and isocost lines.

9 Competitive Markets

CHAPTER OUTLINE	LEARNING OBJECTIVES (LO)
	After studying this chapter you will be able to
9.1 **MARKET STRUCTURE AND FIRM BEHAVIOUR**	**1** explain the difference between competitive behaviour and a competitive market.
9.2 **THE THEORY OF PERFECT COMPETITION**	**2** list the four key assumptions of the theory of perfect competition.
9.3 **SHORT-RUN DECISIONS**	**3** derive a competitive firm's supply curve.
	4 determine whether competitive firms are making profits or losses in the short run.
9.4 **LONG-RUN DECISIONS**	**5** explain the role played by profits, entry, and exit in determining a competitive industry's long-run equilibrium.

DOES MasterCard compete with Visa? Does a wheat farmer from Biggar, Saskatchewan, compete with a wheat farmer from Brandon, Manitoba? If we use the ordinary meaning of the word *compete*, the answer to the first question is plainly yes, and the answer to the second question is no.

MasterCard and Visa both advertise extensively to persuade consumers to use their credit cards, so these two firms actively compete against each other, with additional profits for one firm sometimes coming at the expense of the other.

The farmer in Saskatchewan, however, can do nothing to affect either the sales or the profits of the Manitoba farmer. Even if the Saskatchewan farmer could

do something to influence the profits of the Manitoba farmer, there would be no point in doing so, since changes in the profits of the Manitoba farmer would not affect the Saskatchewan farmer.

In this chapter we examine what economists call *competitive markets*, in which firms—like the farmers in the example above—do *not* actively compete with one another. To sort out the questions of who is competing with whom and in what sense, it is useful to distinguish between the behaviour of individual firms and the type of market in which they operate. Economists are interested in two different concepts—*competitive market structure* and *competitive behaviour*.

9.1 MARKET STRUCTURE AND FIRM BEHAVIOUR

market structure All features of a market that affect the behaviour and performance of firms in that market, such as the number and size of sellers, the extent of knowledge about one another's actions, the degree of freedom of entry, and the degree of product differentiation.

market power The ability of a firm to influence the price of its product.

The term **market structure** refers to all the features that may affect the behaviour and performance of the firms in a market, such as the number of firms or the type of product they sell. In this chapter, we focus on a *competitive* market structure.

Competitive Markets

Economists say that firms have **market power** when they can influence the price of their product. The *competitiveness* of the market is the degree to which individual firms *lack* such market power.

> A market is said to be competitive when its firms have little or no market power. The more market power the firms have, the less competitive is the market.

Visa "competes" very actively in the credit-card market against Mastercard and American Express, but economists nonetheless refer to the structure of this market as non-competitive.

The extreme form of competitive market structure occurs when each firm has zero market power. In such a case, there are so many firms in the market that each must accept the price set by the forces of demand and supply. The firms perceive themselves as being able to sell as much as they choose at the prevailing market price and as having no power to influence that price. If the firm charged a higher price, it would make no sales; so many other firms would be selling at the market price that buyers would take their business elsewhere.

This extreme is called a *perfectly competitive market*. In such a market there is no need for individual firms to compete actively with one another because none has any power over the market. One firm's ability to sell its product does not depend on the behaviour of any other firm. For example, the Saskatchewan and Manitoba wheat farmers operate in a perfectly competitive market over which they have no power. Neither can change the market price for wheat by altering their own behaviour.

Competitive Behaviour

In everyday language, the term *competitive behaviour* refers to the degree to which individual firms actively vie with one another for business. For example, MasterCard and Visa clearly engage in competitive behaviour. It is also true, however, that both companies have some real power over their market. Each has the power to decide the fees that people will pay for the use of their credit cards, within limits set by buyers' tastes, the fees of competing cards, and some government regulations. Either firm could raise its fees and still continue to attract some customers. Even though they actively compete with each other, they do so in a market that does not have a perfectly competitive structure.

In contrast, the Saskatchewan and Manitoba wheat farmers do not engage in competitive behaviour because the only way they can affect their profits is by changing their own outputs of wheat or their own production costs.

The distinction that we have just made between behaviour and structure explains why firms in perfectly competitive markets (e.g., the Saskatchewan and Manitoba wheat producers) do not compete actively with each other, whereas firms that do compete actively with each other (e.g., MasterCard and Visa) do not operate in perfectly competitive markets.

9.2 THE THEORY OF PERFECT COMPETITION

The perfectly competitive market structure—usually referred to simply as **perfect competition**—applies directly to a number of markets, especially many agricultural and raw-materials markets. It also provides an important benchmark for comparison with other market structures.

perfect competition A market structure in which all firms in an industry are price takers, and in which there is freedom of entry into and exit from the industry.

The Assumptions of Perfect Competition

In addition to the fundamental assumption that firms seek to maximize their profits, the theory of perfect competition is built on a number of assumptions relating to each firm and to the industry as a whole.

1. All the firms in the industry sell an identical product. Economists say that the firms sell a **homogeneous product**.

2. Consumers know the nature of the product being sold and the prices charged by each firm.

3. The level of each firm's output at which its long-run average cost reaches a minimum is small relative to the *industry's* total output. (This is a precise way of saying that each firm is small relative to the size of the industry.)

4. The industry is characterized by *freedom of entry and exit*; that is, any new firm is free to enter the industry and start producing if it so wishes, and any existing firm is free to cease production and leave the industry. Existing firms cannot block the entry of new firms, and there are no legal prohibitions or other barriers to entering or exiting the industry.

homogeneous product In the eyes of purchasers, every unit of the product is identical to every other unit.

price taker A firm that can alter its output and sales without affecting the market price of its product.

The first three assumptions imply that each firm in a perfectly competitive industry is a **price taker**, meaning that the firm can alter its output and sales without affecting the market price of its product. Thus, a firm operating in a perfectly competitive market has no market power. It must passively accept whatever happens to be the market price, but it can sell as much as it wants at that price.

Our Saskatchewan and Manitoba wheat farmers provide us with good illustrations of firms that are operating in a perfectly competitive market. Because each individual wheat farmer is just one of thousands of producers who are all growing the same product, one firm's contribution to the industry's total production is a tiny drop in an extremely large bucket.

A wheat farmer in Saskatchewan does not "compete" in any real way with a wheat farmer elsewhere in the world. However, both exist in what economists call a perfectly competitive market.

Each firm will correctly assume that realistic variations in its output have no effect on the price of wheat. Thus, each firm, knowing that it can sell as much or as little as it chooses at that price, adapts its behaviour to a given market price of wheat. Furthermore, there is nothing that any one farmer can do to stop another farmer from growing wheat, and there are no legal deterrents to becoming a wheat farmer. Anyone who has enough money to buy or rent the necessary land, labour, and equipment can become a wheat farmer.

The difference between the wheat farmers and MasterCard or Visa is the *degree of market power*. Each firm that is producing wheat is an insignificant part of the whole market and thus has no power to influence the price of wheat. MasterCard and Visa, on the other hand, have power to influence the credit-card market because each firm's sales represent a significant part of the total sales of credit-card services.

The Demand Curve for a Perfectly Competitive Firm

A major distinction between firms in perfectly competitive markets and firms in any other type of market is the shape of the demand curve facing the firm.

> **Even though the demand curve for the entire industry is negatively sloped, each firm in a perfectly competitive industry faces a horizontal demand curve because variations in the firm's output have no significant effect on market price.**

The horizontal (perfectly elastic) demand curve does not indicate that the firm could actually sell an infinite amount at the going price. It indicates, rather, that any realistic variations in that firm's production will leave price unchanged because the effect on total industry output will be negligible.

Figure 9-1 contrasts the market demand curve for the product of a competitive industry with the demand curve that a single firm in that industry faces. *Applying Economic Concepts 9-1* provides an example of the important difference between the

FIGURE 9-1 **The Demand Curve for a Competitive Industry and for One Firm in the Industry**

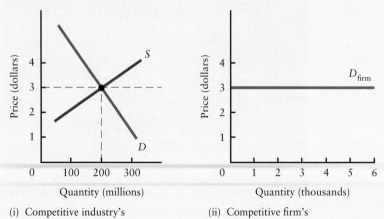

(i) Competitive industry's demand curve

(ii) Competitive firm's demand curve

The industry's demand curve is negatively sloped; the competitive firm's demand curve is horizontal. Notice the difference in the quantities shown on the horizontal scale in each part of the figure. The competitive industry has an output of 200 million units when the price is $3. The individual firm takes that market price as given and considers producing up to, say, 6000 units. The firm's demand curve in part (ii) is horizontal because any change in output that this single firm could manage would leave price virtually unchanged at $3. The firm's realistic output variation has an imperceptible effect on industry output and thus market price.

APPLYING ECONOMIC CONCEPTS 9-1

Why Small Firms Are Price Takers

Consider an individual wheat farmer and the world market for wheat. Since products have negatively sloped market demand curves, any increase in the industry's output (caused by a shift in supply) will cause some fall in the market price. However, as the calculations here show, any conceivable increase that one wheat farm could make in its output has such a negligible effect on the industry's price that the farmer correctly ignores it—the individual wheat farmer is thus a price taker.

The *market* elasticity of demand for wheat is approximately 0.25. (Recall from Chapter 4 that an elasticity of 0.25 means that a 10 percent decline in market price is associated with only a 2.5 percent increase in quantity demanded.) Thus, if the quantity of wheat supplied in the world were to increase by 1 percent, the price of wheat would have to fall by roughly 4 percent to induce the world's wheat buyers to purchase the extra wheat.

The total world production of wheat in 2014 was approximately 710 million tonnes, of which 37 million tonnes were produced in Canada. In that year there were approximately 20 000 wheat farms in Canada. Thus, the average crop size for a Canadian wheat farmer in 2014 was about 1850 tonnes (= 37 million/20 000), only 0.0003 percent of the world wheat crop.

As a result of being such a small fraction of the overall market, individual wheat farmers face a horizontal demand curve. To see this, suppose an individual farmer on an average-sized farm decided in one year to produce nothing and in another year managed to produce twice the average output of 1850 tonnes. This is an extremely large variation in one farm's output. The increase in output from 0 to 3700 tonnes represents a 200 percent variation measured around the farm's average output. Yet the percentage increase in world output is only (3700/710 million) × 100 = 0.0005 percent. Given that the world's demand for wheat has a price elasticity of about 0.25, this increase in output would lead to a decrease in the world price of 0.002 percent.

This very small decline in price, together with the 200 percent increase in the farm's own output, implies that the farm's own demand curve has an elasticity of 100 000 (= 200/0.002). This enormous elasticity of demand means that the farm would have to increase its output by 100 000 percent to bring about a 1 percent decrease in the world price of wheat. Because the farm's output cannot be varied this much, it is not surprising that the farmer regards the price of wheat as unaffected by any change in output that he or she could conceivably make. For all intents and purposes, the individual farmer faces a perfectly elastic—horizontal—demand curve for the product and is thus a *price taker*.

firm's demand curve and the market demand curve. It uses a numerical example to show why the demand curve facing any individual wheat farmer is very nearly perfectly elastic, even though the *market* demand for wheat is quite inelastic.

Total, Average, and Marginal Revenue

To study the revenues that firms receive from the sale of their products, economists define three concepts called *total, average*, and *marginal revenue*.

Total revenue (*TR*) is the total amount received by the firm from the sale of a product. If Q units are sold at p dollars each,

$$TR = p \times Q$$

total revenue (*TR*) Total receipts from the sale of a product; price times quantity.

Average revenue (*AR*) is the amount of revenue per unit sold. It is equal to total revenue divided by the number of units sold and is thus equal to the price at which the product is sold:

$$AR = \frac{TR}{Q} = \frac{(p \times Q)}{Q} = p$$

average revenue (*AR*) Total revenue divided by quantity sold; this is the market price when all units are sold at the same price.

marginal revenue (MR) The change in a firm's total revenue resulting from a change in its sales by one unit.

Marginal revenue (*MR*) is the *change* in a firm's total revenue resulting from a *change* in its sales by 1 unit. Whenever output changes by more than 1 unit, the change in revenue must be divided by the change in output to calculate the approximate marginal revenue. For example, if an increase in output of 3 units is accompanied by an increase in revenue of $1500, the marginal revenue is $1500/3, or $500. [21]

$$MR = \frac{\Delta TR}{\Delta Q}$$

To illustrate each of these revenue concepts, consider a farmer who is selling barley in a perfectly competitive market at a price of $3 per bushel. Total revenue rises by $3 for every bushel sold. Because every bushel brings in $3, the average revenue per bushel sold is clearly $3. Furthermore, because each *additional* bushel sold brings in $3, the marginal revenue of an extra bushel sold is also $3. The table in Figure 9-2 shows calculations of these revenue concepts for a range of outputs between 10 and 13 bushels. The figure plots the various revenue curves.

The important point illustrated in the table is that as long as the firm's own level of output cannot affect the price of the product it sells, then the firm's marginal revenue is equal to its average revenue. Thus, for a price-taking firm, *AR* = *MR* = price. Graphically, as shown in part (i) of Figure 9-2, average revenue and marginal revenue are the same horizontal line drawn at the level of market price. Because the firm can sell any quantity it chooses at this price, the horizontal line is also the firm's demand curve; it shows that any quantity the firm chooses to sell will be associated with this same market price.

FIGURE 9-2 Revenues for a Price-Taking Firm

Revenue Concepts				
Price p	Output Q	$TR = p \times Q$	$AR = TR/Q$	$MR = \Delta TR/\Delta Q$
$3	10	$30	$3	
3	11	33	3	$3
3	12	36	3	3
3	13	39	3	3

(i) Average and marginal revenue

(ii) Total revenue

When the firm is a price taker, *AR* = *MR* = *p*. Because price does not change as a result of the firm changing its output, neither marginal revenue nor average revenue varies with output. In the table, marginal revenue is shown between the rows because it represents the *change* in total revenues in response to a *change* in quantity. When price is constant, total revenue (which is price times quantity) is an upward-sloping straight line starting from the origin.

> For a competitive price-taking firm, the market price is the firm's marginal (and average) revenue.

9.3 SHORT-RUN DECISIONS

We learned in Chapter 7 how each firm's costs vary with its output in the short run. Recall that in the short run, the firm has one or more fixed factors, and the only way it can change its output is by changing the amount of its variable factor inputs. In this chapter, we have seen how the firm's total, average, and marginal revenues vary as the firm changes its level of output. The next step is to put the cost and revenue information together to determine the level of output that will maximize the firm's economic profits. Recall also from Chapter 7 that economic profit is the difference between total revenue and total cost,

$$\pi = TR - TC$$

where all costs are measured as economic (as opposed to accounting) costs. If total revenues are not enough to cover total costs, economic profits will be negative—in this case we say that the firm is making *losses*.

We need to ask and answer two questions for a competitive firm. First, should the firm produce any output at all, or would it be better to shut down and produce nothing? Second, if it makes economic sense for the firm to remain in business and produce some output, *what level* of output should it produce? To answer both questions, we assume the firm's objective is to maximize its profits.

Should the Firm Produce at All?

The firm always has the option of producing nothing. If it produces nothing, it will have an operating loss that is equal to its fixed costs. If it decides to produce, it will add the variable cost of production to its costs and the receipts from the sale of its product to its revenue. Since it must pay its fixed costs in any event, it will be worthwhile for the firm to produce as long as it can find some level of output for which revenue exceeds *variable* cost. However, if its revenue is less than its variable cost at every level of output, the firm will actually lose more by producing than by not producing at all.

Table 9-1 shows an example of a firm that decides to minimize its losses by producing no output when it faces a low market price. The table shows the firm's variable and fixed costs for each level of output. (If you were to graph the *TVC, TFC,* and *TC* curves from this table, you would find that they look like the curves we studied in Chapter 7.) The table also shows the firm's total revenues and profits at every level of output. When the market price is $2 per unit, the firm's profits are negative *at every level of output*—the firm's revenues *never* cover its costs. At this low market price, the firm's revenues don't even cover its variable costs and, in fact, the negative profits (losses) only grow larger as output increases. In this situation, the firm is better off to produce no output at all. In this case, the firm is maximizing its profits by *minimizing its losses*. (The table also presents a situation in which the price is $5 per unit; for reasons that we will soon see, the firm's best option in this case is to produce some output even though its profits are still negative.)

> **Rule 1: A firm should not produce at all if, for all levels of output, total revenue (*TR*) is less than total variable cost (*TVC*). Equivalently, the firm should not produce at all if, for all levels of output, the market price (*p*) is less than average variable cost (*AVC*). [22]**

We have been looking at the firm's decision about whether to produce at all by comparing total revenues with total variable costs. Equivalently, we can examine this decision by comparing the market price with average variable cost.

TABLE 9-1 Negative Profits and the Firm's Shut-Down Decision

				Low Price ($2)		High Price ($5)	
Q	TVC	TFC	TC	TR	Profit (TR − TC)	TR	Profit (TR − TC)
0	0	200	200	0	−200	0	−200
10	50	200	250	20	−230	50	−200
20	80	200	280	40	−240	100	−180
30	100	200	300	60	−240	150	−150
40	110	200	310	80	−230	200	−110
50	130	200	330	100	−230	250	−80
60	160	200	360	120	−240	300	−60
70	200	200	400	140	−260	350	−50
80	260	200	460	160	−300	400	−60
90	320	200	520	180	−340	450	−70
100	380	200	580	200	−380	500	−80

A competitive firm may maximize its profits (or minimize its losses) by producing zero output. The data in the table show costs and revenues at various levels of output. The firm must pay its fixed costs even if it produces no output and earns no revenue. At a price of $2, there is no level of output at which the firm's revenues cover its variable costs. In this situation, the firm can minimize its losses by choosing to produce zero output.

At a higher price of $5, the profit-maximizing firm should choose to produce 70 units of output even though its profits are negative. At this level of output, the firm's revenues more than cover its variable costs and help to pay some portion of the fixed costs. Since the firm must pay its fixed costs no matter what level of output is produced, its profits would be even lower if it chose to produce zero output.

shut-down price The price that is equal to the minimum of a firm's average variable costs. At prices below this, a profit-maximizing firm will produce no output.

The price at which the firm can just cover its average variable cost, and so is indifferent between producing and not producing, is called the **shut-down price**. Such a price is shown in Figure 9-3. At a price of p_0, the firm can just cover its variable cost by producing Q_0 units. For any price *below* p_0, there is no level of output at which variable costs can be covered, and thus the firm will choose to produce nothing. The price p_0 is therefore the firm's shut-down price. At any price above p_0, there are many levels of output that cover average variable costs (but for each price above p_0 there is only a single level of output that *maximizes* the firm's profit, which we will see shortly).

How Much Should the Firm Produce?

If a firm decides that, according to Rule 1, production is worth undertaking, it must then decide *how much* to produce. The key to understanding how much a profit-maximizing firm should produce is to think about it on a unit-by-unit basis. If any unit of production adds more to revenue than it does to cost, producing and selling that unit will increase profits. According to the terminology introduced earlier, a unit of production raises profits if the *marginal* revenue obtained from selling it exceeds the *marginal* cost of producing it.

Now let's consider a firm already producing some level of output and see what happens if it increases or decreases its output. If an extra unit of output will increase the firm's revenues by more than it increases costs ($MR > MC$), the firm should expand its output. However, if the last unit produced increases revenues by less than it increases costs ($MR < MC$), the profit-maximizing firm should reduce its output. From this logic we get our profit-maximizing rule.

Rule 2: If it is worthwhile for the firm to produce at all, the profit-maximizing firm should produce the output at which marginal revenue equals marginal cost. [23]

The two rules that we have stated refer to each firm's own costs and revenues, and they apply to all profit-maximizing firms, whatever the market structure in which they operate. However, we have already seen that for price-taking firms, marginal revenue is equal to the market price. Combining these two results gives us an important conclusion:

A profit-maximizing firm that is operating in a perfectly competitive will produce the output that equates its marginal cost of production with the market price of its product (as long as price exceeds average variable cost).

If you look back to Table 9-1, when the market price is $5 the application of this rule is evident after doing a few calculations. Since price is $5, and the firm is a price taker, the firm's MR is also $5. If you compute the firm's MC between output levels $Q = 60$ and $Q = 80$, you see that the firm's $MC = \Delta TC/\Delta Q = \$100/20 = \$5$. Thus, the highlighted row which indicates the firm's maximum profits (or minimum losses) also shows the level of output where $MR = MC$.

In a perfectly competitive industry, the market forces of demand and supply determine the price at which the firm sells its product. The firm then picks the quantity of output that maximizes its own profits. We have seen that this is the output for which price equals marginal cost. When the firm has reached a position in which its profits are maximized, it has no incentive to change its output. Therefore, unless prices or

FIGURE 9-3 Shut-Down Price for a Competitive Firm

When the market price is less than the minimum average variable cost, the competitive firm will choose to produce no output. If the price is exactly p_0, the firm can just cover its variable costs by producing Q_0 units of output (and so is indifferent between producing Q_0 units or nothing). At any price below p_0, the firm is better off shutting down and producing no output. At any price above p_0, there are many output levels that cover variable costs. For example, at price p_1, any level of output between Q_1 and Q_1' will cover variable costs.

FIGURE 9-4   Profit Maximization for a Competitive Firm

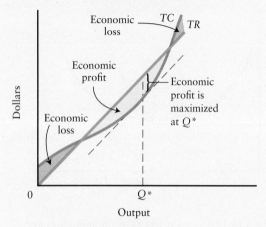

(i) Total costs and total revenues

(ii) Marginal cost and marginal revenue

The firm chooses the level of output at which profits are maximized. If it is profitable to produce at all (that is, if $p >$ minimum of AVC), the firm chooses the level of output where marginal revenue equals marginal cost. In part (i), this is shown as the level of output where the vertical distance between TR and TC is largest (and thus where the slopes of the TR and TC curves are the same). In part (ii), price is equal to marginal revenue since the firm is a price taker, and so the profit-maximizing level of output is the point at which price (marginal revenue) equals marginal cost. For each of the Q^* units sold, the firm earns revenue of p and the average total cost is c; therefore, total profit is $(p - c)Q^*$, which is the shaded area.

costs change, the firm will continue to produce this output because it is doing as well as it can do, given the market situation. This profit-maximizing behaviour is illustrated in Figure 9-4.

> **The perfectly competitive firm adjusts its level of output in response to changes in the market-determined price.**

Figure 9-4 shows the profit-maximizing choice of the firm in two different ways. In part (i), the firm's total cost and total revenue curves are shown, and the profit-maximizing level of output, Q^*, is the level that shows the largest positive gap between total revenues and total costs. In part (ii), the firm's average and marginal cost curves are shown together with the market price (which for a price-taking firm equals average and marginal revenue) and the profit-maximizing level of output, Q^*, is the level at which price equals marginal cost. These are two different ways of viewing the same profit-maximization problem; the value of Q^* in part (i) must be the same as the value of Q^* in part (ii).

Short-Run Supply Curves

Now that we know how a perfectly competitive firm determines its profit-maximizing level of output, we can derive its supply curve. Once we have derived the individual firm's supply curve, we can derive the supply curve for the entire market.

The Supply Curve for One Firm   A competitive firm's supply curve is derived in part (i) of Figure 9-5, which shows a firm's marginal cost curve and four alternative prices. What we are trying to derive is a supply curve that shows the quantity of output that the firm will supply at each price. For prices below average variable cost, the firm will supply zero units (Rule 1). For prices above the minimum of average variable cost, the competitive firm will choose its level of output to equate price and marginal cost (Rule 2). This behaviour leads to the following conclusion:

> **A competitive firm's supply curve is given by the portion of its marginal cost curve that is above its average variable cost curve.**

FIGURE 9-5 **The Derivation of the Supply Curve for a Competitive Firm**

(i) Marginal cost and average variable cost curves

(ii) Firm's supply curve

The supply curve for a competitive firm is the portion of its *MC* curve above the *AVC* curve. For prices below $20, output is zero because there is no output at which variable costs can be covered. The point *A*, at which the price of $20 is just equal to the minimum of *AVC*, is the firm's shut-down point. As price rises to $30, $40, and $50, the profit-maximizing point changes to *B*, *C*, and *D*, taking output to Q_1, Q_2, and Q_3. At any of these prices, the firm's revenue exceeds its variable costs of production and thus can help to cover some part of its fixed costs.

The Supply Curve for an Industry   Figure 9-6 shows the derivation of an industry supply curve for an industry containing only two firms. The general result is as follows:

> **In perfect competition, the industry supply curve is the horizontal sum of the marginal cost curves (above the level of average variable cost) of all firms in the industry.**

Each firm's marginal cost curve shows how much that firm will supply at each given market price, and the industry supply curve shows what all firms together will supply. Notice in Figure 9-6 the "kink" in the industry supply curve, which occurs at the price of $2; at any lower price the second firm chooses not to produce any output.

This supply curve, based on the short-run marginal cost curves of all the firms in the industry, is the industry's supply curve that we first encountered in Chapter 3. We have now established the profit-maximizing behaviour of individual firms that lies behind that curve. It is sometimes called a *short-run supply curve* because it is based on the short-run, profit-maximizing behaviour of all the firms in the industry.

Short-Run Equilibrium in a Competitive Market

The price of a product sold in a perfectly competitive market is determined by the interaction of the market supply curve and demand curve. Although no single firm can influence the market price significantly, the collective actions of all firms in the industry (as shown by the market supply curve) and the collective actions of households (as shown by the market demand curve) together determine the equilibrium price. This occurs at the point at which the market demand and supply curves intersect.

FIGURE 9-6 **The Derivation of a Competitive Industry's Supply Curve**

(i) Firm A's supply curve   (ii) Firm B's supply curve   (iii) Industry supply curve

The industry's supply curve is the horizontal sum of the supply curves of each of the firms in the industry. At a price of $3, Firm A would supply 4 units and Firm B would supply 3 units. Together, as shown in part (iii), they would supply 7 units. If there are hundreds of firms, the process is the same. In this example, because Firm B does not enter the market at prices below $2, the supply curve S_{A+B} is identical to S_A up to the price $2 and is the horizontal sum of S_A and S_B above $2.

short-run equilibrium For a competitive industry, the price and output at which industry demand equals short-run industry supply, and all firms are maximizing their profits. Either profits or losses for individual firms are possible.

When a perfectly competitive industry is in **short-run equilibrium**, each firm is producing and selling a quantity for which its marginal cost equals the market price. No firm is motivated to change its output in the short run. Because total quantity demanded equals total quantity supplied, there is no reason for market price to change in the short run.

> **When an industry is in short-run equilibrium, quantity demanded equals quantity supplied, and each firm is maximizing its profits given the market price.**

Figure 9-7 shows the relationship between the market equilibrium, determined by the intersection of demand and supply, and a typical profit-maximizing firm within that market. The individual firm is shown to have positive (economic) profits in the short-run equilibrium. We can see that the firm's profits are positive because the market price exceeds average total costs when the firm is producing its profit-maximizing level of output. But such positive profits need not always occur in the short run. In general, we do not know whether firms in the short-run competitive equilibrium will be earning positive, zero, or negative profits. We *do* know that each firm is maximizing its profits; we just don't know how large those profits are.

Figure 9-8 shows three possible positions for a firm when the industry is in short-run equilibrium. In all cases, the firm is maximizing its profits by producing where price equals marginal cost, but in part (i) the firm is suffering losses, in part (ii) it is just covering all of its costs (breaking even), and in part (iii) it is making positive profits. In all three cases, the firm is doing as well as it can, given its costs and the market price.

Note that the competitive firm's profit per unit is shown by the difference between price and average total cost. To see this algebraically, note that the firm's total profits are

$$\text{Profits} = TR - TC$$
$$= (p \times Q) - (ATC \times Q)$$
$$= (p - ATC) \times Q$$

FIGURE 9-7 **A Typical Firm When the Competitive Market Is in Short-Run Equilibrium**

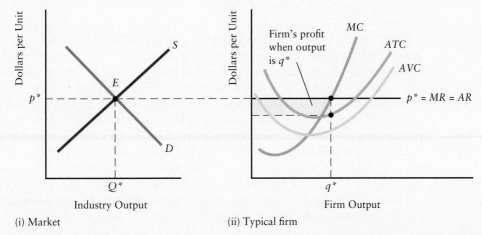

(i) Market   (ii) Typical firm

Short-run equilibrium in a competitive market has a market-clearing price and each firm is maximizing its profits. Part (i) shows the overall market. The equilibrium price and quantity (p^*, Q^*) are determined at the intersection of the market demand and supply curves at point E. Part (ii) shows a typical firm in the market. Notice that the horizontal scales are different in the two parts of the figure—total market output is designated by Q, whereas firm-level output is designated by q. The equilibrium price in part (i) becomes the MR curve for each firm in the market. Given its MC curve, the firm's profit-maximizing level of output is q^*. In the case shown, the firm is making positive profits equal to the shaded area.

FIGURE 9-8 **Alternative Short-Run Profits of a Competitive Firm**

(i) Losses (Negative profit)   (ii) Zero profit   (iii) Positive profit

When the industry is in short-run equilibrium, a competitive firm may be making losses, breaking even, or making profits. The diagrams show a firm with given costs that face three alternative short-run equilibrium market prices: p_1, p_2, and p_3. Because in all three cases price exceeds the minimum of AVC, the firm produces positive output in each case.

In part (i), price is p_1 and the firm is making losses, shown by the shaded area, because price is below average total cost. Because price exceeds average variable cost, it is worthwhile for the firm to keep producing. In part (ii), price is p_2 and the firm is just covering its total costs. In part (iii), price is p_3 and the firm is earning profits, shown by the shaded area.

So, profit *per unit* is given by $p - ATC$, whereas the firm's *total* profit (or loss) associated with the production of all Q units is $(p - ATC) \times Q$, and is illustrated by the shaded rectangles in Figure 9-8.

It is worth repeating that some firms will choose to continue producing even though they are making losses. The firm shown in part (i) of Figure 9-8 is incurring losses every period that it remains in business, but it is still better for it to carry on producing than to temporarily halt production. If the firm produces nothing this period, it still must pay its fixed costs, so it makes sense to continue producing as long as its revenues more than cover its variable costs or, equivalently, as long as price exceeds *AVC*. Any amount of money left over after the variable costs have been paid can then go toward paying some of the fixed costs. This is more than the firm would have if it simply produced nothing and hence earned no revenue whatsoever. (Look back to Table 9-1 to see an example of this situation, in the case where market price is $5 per unit.) *Applying Economic Concepts 9-2* discusses an interesting example of a firm that remains in operation even though it is making losses. You would probably see many firms like this one if you drove through small towns in any part of Canada.

9.4 LONG-RUN DECISIONS

In Chapters 7 and 8, we described the short run as the span of time for which individual firms have a fixed factor of production (typically capital), and the long run as the span of time for which all of the firm's factors are variable. When we look at the entire industry, the distinction is very similar. In the short run, there is a given number of firms and each has a given plant size. In the long run, both the number of firms and the size of each firm's plant are variable.[1]

We begin our discussion of the long run by assuming that all firms in the industry have the same technology and therefore have the same set of cost curves. Thus, the short-run equilibrium in the industry will have *all* firms in the industry being equally profitable (or making equal losses). Toward the end of the chapter we relax this assumption when we allow new firms to have better technologies and thus lower costs than older firms already in the industry.

Entry and Exit

The key difference between a perfectly competitive industry in the short run and in the long run is the entry or exit of firms. We have seen that all the firms in the industry may be making profits, suffering losses, or just breaking even when the industry is in short-run equilibrium. Because economic costs include the opportunity cost of capital, if the firms are just breaking even they are doing as well as they could do by investing their capital elsewhere. Hence, there will be no incentive for firms to leave the industry if economic profits are zero. Similarly, if new entrants expect just to break even, there will be no incentive for firms to enter the industry because capital can earn the same return elsewhere in the economy. If, however, the existing firms are earning revenues in excess of all costs, including the opportunity cost of capital, new capital will eventually enter the

---

[1] For four examples of what we mean by a firm's plant size, consider the following: the amount of land for a farmer; the number of trucks for a trucking company; the number of sewing machines for a clothes manufacturer; or the number of rooms for a motel.

APPLYING ECONOMIC CONCEPTS 9-2

The Parable of the Seaside Inn

Why do some resort hotels stay open during the off-season, even though they must offer bargain rates that do not even cover their "full costs"? Why do the managers of other hotels allow them to fall into disrepair even though they are able to attract enough customers to stay in business? Are the former being overly generous, and are the latter being irrational penny-pinchers?

To illustrate what is involved, consider an imaginary hotel called the Seaside Inn. Its revenues and costs of operating during the four months of the high-season and during the eight months of the off-season are shown in the accompanying table. When the profit-maximizing price for its rooms is charged in the high-season, the hotel earns revenues of $58 000 and incurs variable costs equal to $36 000. Thus, there is an "operating profit" of $22 000 during the high-season. This surplus goes toward meeting the hotel's annual fixed costs of $24 000. Thus, $2000 of the fixed costs are not yet paid.

The Seaside Inn: Total Costs and Revenues ($)

Season	Total Revenue (*TR*)	Total Variable Cost (*TVC*)	Contribution to Fixed Costs (*TR – TVC*)	Total Fixed Costs
High-Season	58 000	36 000	22 000	
Off-Season	20 000	18 000	2 000	
Total	78 000	54 000	24 000	24 000

If the Seaside Inn were to charge the same rates during the off-season, it could not attract enough customers even to cover its costs of maids, receptionists, and managers. However, the hotel discovers that by charging lower rates during the off-season, it can rent some of its rooms and earn revenues of $20 000. Its costs of operating (variable costs) during the off-season are $18 000. So, by operating at reduced rates in the off-season, the hotel is able to contribute another $2000 toward its annual fixed costs, thereby eliminating the shortfall.

Therefore, the hotel stays open during the whole year by offering off-season bargain rates to grateful guests. Indeed, if it were to close during the off-season, it would not be able to cover its total fixed and variable costs solely through its high-season operations.

We have not yet discussed firms' long-run decisions, but you can get a feel for the issues by considering the following situation. Suppose the off-season revenues fall to $19 000 (but everything else remains the same). The short-run condition for staying open, that total revenue (*TR*) must exceed total variable cost (*TVC*), is met for both the high-season and the off-season. However, since the *TR* over the whole year of $77 000 is less than the total costs of $78 000, the hotel is now making losses for the year as a whole. The hotel will remain open as long as it can do so with its present capital—it will produce in the short run. However, it will not be worthwhile for the owners to replace the capital as it wears out.

If the reduction in revenues persists, the hotel will become one of those run-down hotels about which guests ask, "Why don't they do something about this place?" But the owners are behaving quite sensibly. They are operating the hotel as long as it covers its variable costs, but they are not putting any more investment into it because it cannot fully cover its fixed costs. Sooner or later, the fixed capital will become too old to be run, or at least to attract customers, and the hotel will be closed.

Hotels and other resorts often charge low prices in the off-season, low enough that they do not cover their total costs. But as long as the price more than covers the variable costs, it is better than shutting down during the off-season.

industry to share in these profits. Conversely, if the existing firms are suffering economic losses, capital will eventually leave the industry because a better return can be obtained elsewhere in the economy. Let us now consider this process in a little more detail.

An Entry-Attracting Price First, suppose there are 100 firms in a competitive industry, all making positive profits like the firm shown in part (iii) of Figure 9-8. New firms, attracted by the profitability of existing firms, will enter the industry. Suppose that in response to the high profits, 20 new firms enter. The market supply curve that formerly added up the outputs of 100 firms must now add up the outputs of 120 firms. At any price, more will be supplied because there are more producers. This entry of new firms into the industry causes a rightward shift in the industry supply curve.

With an unchanged market demand curve, this rightward shift in the industry supply curve will reduce the equilibrium price. In order to maximize profits, both new and old firms will have to adjust their output to this new price. New firms will continue to enter, and the equilibrium price will continue to fall, until all firms in the industry are just covering their total costs. The industry has now reached what is called a *zero-profit equilibrium*. The entry of new firms then ceases. The effect of entry is shown in Figure 9-9.

> **Profits in a competitive industry are a signal for the entry of new firms; the industry will expand, pushing price down until economic profits fall to zero.**

FIGURE 9-9 The Effect of New Entrants Attracted by Positive Profits

(i) Market   (ii) Typical firm

Positive profits lead to the entry of new firms; this entry reduces the equilibrium market price and reduces the profits of all firms. The initial short-run equilibrium is E_0 in part (i) with equilibrium price p_0^*. At this price, a typical firm in the industry is producing q_0^* units of output and is earning positive profits (since $p_0^* > ATC$ at q_0^*). These positive profits attract other firms who then enter the industry, causing the supply curve to shift to the right and reducing the market price. The process of entry will continue until profits are driven to zero. S_1 is the final supply curve and the equilibrium market price has fallen to p_1^*. At the new market price, firms have each reduced their output to q_1^* and are now just covering their total costs. Notice that each of the original firms is producing less than before, but because of the new entrants total industry output has increased from Q_0^* to Q_1^*.

FIGURE 9-10 **The Effect of Exit Caused by Losses**

(i) Market

(ii) Typical firm

Negative profits lead to the eventual exit of some firms as their capital becomes obsolete or becomes too costly to oper- ate; this exit increases the equilibrium price and increases profits for those firms remaining in the market. The initial market equilibrium is E_0 in part (i), with equilibrium price p_0^*. At this market price, a typical firm is producing q_0^* units and is making negative profits but, because price exceeds AVC, the firm remains in business. Since firms are earning less than the opportunity cost on their capital, they do not replace their capital as it becomes obsolete. Eventually, some firms close down. As firms exit the industry, the industry supply curve shifts to the left and the market price increases to p_1^*. For the remaining firms, this price increase leads them to increase their output from q_0^* to q_1^*, the level of output at which they are just covering their total costs. Notice that the remaining firms are producing more than before, but because of the exit of firms total industry output has fallen from Q_0^* to Q_1^*.

An Exit-Inducing Price We have seen that the firm's supply curve is the section of its marginal cost curve above the average variable cost curve. If the market price falls below the minimum of average variable cost, the firm will produce no output. If the low price is expected to persist, the firm will likely exit the industry altogether.

If firms are making losses but the market price is *above* the shut-down point, there will still be exit from the industry, but it will be gradual. Although in this situation the firms are covering their variable costs, they are not earning enough to cover their fixed costs. The return of the owners' capital is therefore less than the opportunity cost of their capital, which is a signal for the gradual exit of firms. Old plants and equipment will not be replaced as they wear out. As a result, the industry's supply curve eventually shifts leftward, and the market price rises. Firms will continue to exit, and the market price will continue to rise, until the remaining firms can cover all their costs. Once again the market reaches a zero-profit equilibrium. The exit of firms then ceases. This gradual process of exit is shown in Figure 9-10.

> **Losses in a competitive industry are a signal for the exit of firms; the industry will contract, driving the market price up until the remaining firms are just covering their total costs.**

The Speed of Exit The process of exit is not always quick and is sometimes painfully slow for the loss-making firms in the industry. The rate at which firms leave unprofitable

Oil tankers take a long time to become economically obsolete. A perfectly competitive shipping company that is incurring losses may choose to remain in operation for many years rather than shutting down operations.

industries depends on how quickly their capital becomes obsolete or becomes too costly to operate because of rising maintenance costs as it ages. In many professional service industries, such as graphic design or consulting, the physical capital is mostly office equipment, such as computers, printers, and so on. This equipment becomes obsolete in just a few years, and thus loss-making firms will tend to exit the industry very quickly. In other industries, such as railways or shipping, the physical capital takes much longer to wear out or become obsolete. The result is that loss-making firms in these industries will remain in operation for many years.

> **The longer it takes for firms' capital to become obsolete or too costly to operate, the longer firms will remain in the industry while they are earning economic losses.**

Long-Run Equilibrium

Because sooner or later firms exit when they are making losses, and enter in pursuit of profits, we get the following conclusion:

> **The long-run equilibrium of a competitive industry occurs when firms are earning zero profits.**

When a perfectly competitive industry is in long-run equilibrium, each firm will be like the firm in part (ii) of Figure 9-8, earning zero economic profit. For such firms, the price p_2 is sometimes called the **break-even price**. It is the price at which all economic costs, including the opportunity cost of capital, are being covered. Any firm that is just breaking even is willing to stay in the industry. It has no incentive to leave, nor do other firms have an incentive to enter.

break-even price The price at which a firm is just able to cover all of its costs, including the opportunity cost of capital.

Conditions for Long-Run Equilibrium The previous discussion suggests four conditions for a competitive industry to be in long-run equilibrium.

1. Existing firms must be maximizing their profits, given their existing capital. Thus, short-run marginal costs of production must be equal to market price.

2. Existing firms must not be suffering losses. If they are suffering losses, they will not replace their capital and the size of the industry will decline over time.

3. Existing firms must not be earning profits. If they are earning profits, then new firms will enter the industry and the size of the industry will increase over time.

4. Existing firms must not be able to increase their profits by changing the size of their production facilities. Thus, each existing firm must be at the minimum point of its *long-run* average cost (*LRAC*) curve.

This last condition is new to our discussion. Figure 9-11 shows that if the condition does not hold—that is, if the firm is *not* at the minimum of its *LRAC* curve—a firm can increase its profits. In the case shown, although the firm is maximizing its profits with its existing production facilities, there are unexploited economies of scale. By building a larger plant, the firm can move down its *LRAC* curve and reduce its average cost. Alternatively, if the firm were producing at an output that put it beyond the lowest point on its *LRAC* curve, it could raise its profits by reducing its plant size. Because in either situation average cost is just equal to the market price, any reduction in average cost must yield profits.

> **For a competitive firm to be maximizing its long-run profits, it must be producing at the minimum point on its *LRAC* curve.**

As we saw in Chapter 8, the level of output at which *LRAC* reaches a minimum is known as the firm's *minimum efficient scale (MES)*. When each firm in the industry is producing at the minimum point of its long-run average cost curve and just covering its costs, as in Figure 9-12, the industry is in long-run equilibrium. Because marginal cost equals price, no firm can improve its profits by varying its output in the short run. Because each firm is at the minimum point on its *LRAC* curve, there is no incentive for any existing firm to alter the scale of its operations. Because there are neither profits nor losses, there is no incentive for entry into or exit from the industry.

> **In long-run competitive equilibrium, each firm's average cost of production is the lowest attainable, given the limits of known technology and factor prices.**

FIGURE 9-11 **Short-Run Versus Long-Run Profit Maximization for a Competitive Firm**

A competitive firm that is not at the minimum point on its *LRAC* curve is not maximizing its long-run profits. A competitive firm with short-run cost curves *SRATC* and *MC* faces a market price of p_0. The firm produces Q_0, where *MC* equals price and total costs are just being covered. However, the firm's long-run average cost curve lies below its short-run curve at output Q_0. The firm could produce output Q_0 at cost c_0 by building a larger plant so as to take advantage of economies of scale. Profits would rise, because average total costs of c_0 would then be less than price p_0. The firm cannot be maximizing its long-run profits at any output below Q_m because, with any such output, average total costs can be reduced by building a larger plant. The output Q_m is the minimum efficient scale of the firm.

Changes in Technology

Our discussion of firms' long-run decisions has assumed that all firms in the industry have the same technology and thus the same cost curves. We now relax that assumption and consider how a competitive industry responds to technological improvements *by new firms*.

Consider a competitive industry in long-run equilibrium. Because the industry is in long-run equilibrium, each firm must be earning zero profits. Now suppose that some technological development lowers the cost curves of *newly built plants* but no further advances are anticipated. Because price is just equal to the average total cost for the *existing plants*, new plants will be able to earn profits, and some of them will now be

FIGURE 9-12 A Typical Competitive Firm When the Industry Is in Long-Run Equilibrium

In long-run competitive equilibrium, each firm is operating at the minimum point on its *LRAC* curve. In long-run equilibrium, each firm must be (1) maximizing short-run profits, $MC = p$; (2) earning profits of zero on its existing plant, $SRATC = p$; and (3) unable to increase its profits by altering the scale of its operations. These three conditions can be met only when the firm is at the minimum point on its *LRAC* curve, with price p^* and output Q_m.

built. The resulting expansion in capacity shifts the short-run supply curve to the right and drives price down.

The expansion in industry output and the fall in price will continue until price is equal to the short-run average total cost of the *new* plants. At this price, old plants will not be covering their long-run costs. As long as price exceeds their average variable cost, however, such plants will continue in production. As the outmoded plants wear out or become too costly to operate, they will gradually be closed. Eventually, a new long-run equilibrium will be established in which all plants will use the new technology; market price will be lower and output higher than under the old technology.

What happens in a competitive industry in which technological change does not occur as a single isolated event but instead happens more or less continuously? Plants built in any one year will tend to have lower costs than plants built in any previous year. This common occurrence is illustrated in Figure 9-13.

Industries subject to continuous technological change have three common characteristics. The first is that plants of different ages and with different costs exist side by side. In the steel and newsprint industries, for example, there are ongoing and gradual technological improvements, and thus it is common for new plants to have considerably

FIGURE 9-13 Plants of Different Vintages in an Industry with Continuous Technological Progress

(i) Plant 1: High costs   (ii) Plant 2: Medium costs   (iii) Plant 3: Low costs

Entry of progressively lower-cost firms forces price down, but older plants with higher costs remain in the industry as long as price covers their average variable costs. Plant 3 is the newest plant with the lowest costs. Long-run equilibrium price will be determined by the average total costs of plants of this type because entry will continue as long as the owners of the newest plants expect to earn profits from them. Plant 1 is the oldest plant in operation. It is just covering its *AVC*, and if the price falls any further, it will be closed down. Plant 2 is a plant of intermediate age. It is covering its variable costs and earning some contribution toward its fixed costs. Losses at all but the newest plants, in parts (i) and (ii), are shown by the shaded areas.

lower costs than the plants built several years earlier. Most of us do not see these differences, however, because we rarely if ever visit production facilities in these industries. But the same characteristic is dramatically displayed in an industry that most of us observe casually through our car windows—agriculture. You will probably have noticed different farms with different vintages of agricultural machinery; some farms have much newer and better equipment than others. Indeed, even any individual farm that has been in operation for a long time will have various vintages of equipment, all of which are in use. Older models are not discarded as soon as a better model comes on the market.

Critics who observe the continued use of older, higher-cost plants and equipment often urge that something be done to "eliminate these wasteful practices." These critics miss an important aspect of profit maximization. If the plant or piece of equipment is already there and has little or no resale value, it can be profitably operated as long as its revenues more than cover its *variable* costs. As long as a plant or some equipment can produce goods that are valued by consumers at an amount above the value of the resources currently used up for their production (variable costs), the value of society's total output is increased by using it.

> In industries with continuous technological improvement, low-cost plants will exist side by side with older high-cost plants. The older plants will continue operating as long as their revenues cover their variable costs.

A second characteristic of a competitive industry subject to continuous technological improvement is that price is eventually governed by the minimum *ATC* of the *lowest-cost* (i.e., the newest) plants. New firms using the latest technologies will enter the industry until their plants are just expected to earn normal profits over their lifetimes. The benefits of the new technology are passed on to consumers because all the units of the product, whether produced by new or old plants, are sold at a price that is related solely to the *ATCs* of the new plants. Owners of older plants find that their returns over variable costs fall steadily as newer plants drive the price of the product down.

A third characteristic is that old plants are discarded (or "mothballed") when the price falls below their *AVCs*. This may occur well before the plants are physically worn out. In industries with continuous technological progress, capital is usually discarded because it is *economically obsolete*, not because it is physically worn out. Old capital is obsolete when the market price of output does not cover its average variable cost of production. Thus, a steel mill that is still fully capable of producing top-quality steel may be shut down for perfectly sensible reasons; if the price of steel cannot cover the average variable cost of the steel produced, then profit-maximizing firms will shut down the plant.

Declining Industries

What happens when a competitive industry in long-run equilibrium experiences a continual decrease in the demand for its product? One example of this might be a long-term reduction in demand for in-store video rentals driven by the availability of online movies. Another example is the ongoing substitution away from glass soft-drink bottles to plastic ones. As market demand for these products declines, market price falls, and firms that were previously covering average total costs are no longer able to do so. They find themselves suffering losses instead of breaking even; the signal for the exit of capital is given, but exit takes time.

The Response of Firms   The profit-maximizing response to a steadily declining demand is to continue to operate with existing equipment as long as revenues can cover the variable costs of production. As equipment becomes obsolete because the firm cannot cover even its variable cost, it will not be replaced unless the new equipment can cover its total cost. As a result, the capacity of the industry will shrink. If demand keeps declining, capacity will continue shrinking.

Declining industries typically present a sorry sight to the observer. Revenues are below long-run total costs and, as a result, new equipment is not brought in to replace old equipment as it wears out. The average age of equipment in use rises steadily. The untrained observer, seeing the industry's plight, is likely to blame it on the old equipment.

> **The antiquated equipment in a declining industry is typically the effect rather than the cause of the industry's decline.**

The Response of Governments   Governments are often tempted to support declining industries because they are worried about the resulting job losses. Experience suggests, however, that propping up genuinely declining industries only delays their demise—at significant cost to the taxpayers. When the government finally withdraws its support, the decline is usually more abrupt and, hence, the required adjustment is more difficult than it would have been had the industry been allowed to decline gradually under the natural market forces.

Once governments recognize that the decay of certain industries and the collapse of certain firms are an inevitable part of a changing and evolving economy, a more effective response is to provide retraining and temporary income-support schemes that cushion the impacts of change. These can moderate the effects on the incomes of workers who lose their jobs and make it easier for them to transfer to expanding industries. Intervention that is intended to increase mobility while reducing the social and personal costs of mobility is a viable long-run policy; trying to freeze the existing industrial structure by shoring up an inevitably declining industry is not.

SUMMARY

9.1 MARKET STRUCTURE AND FIRM BEHAVIOUR   LO 1

- A competitive market structure is one in which individual firms have no market power—that is, they have no power to influence the price at which they sell their product.
- Competitive behaviour exists when firms actively compete against one another, responding directly to other firms' actions.

- Perfectly competitive firms *do not* have competitive behaviour because the actions of any one firm would have no effect on any other firm.

9.2 THE THEORY OF PERFECT COMPETITION

- Four key assumptions of the theory of perfect competition are as follows:
  1. All firms produce a homogeneous product.
  2. Consumers know the nature of the product and the price charged for it.
  3. Each firm's minimum efficient scale occurs at a level of output that is small relative to the industry's total output.
  4. The industry displays freedom of entry and exit.

- Each firm in perfect competition is a price taker. It follows that each firm faces a horizontal demand curve at the market price (even though the market demand curve is downward sloping).

9.3 SHORT-RUN DECISIONS

- Any profit-maximizing firm will produce at a level of output at which (a) price is at least as great as average variable cost and (b) marginal cost equals marginal revenue.
- In perfect competition, firms are price takers, so marginal revenue is equal to price. Thus, a profit-maximizing competitive firm chooses its output so that its marginal cost equals the market price.
- Under perfect competition, each firm's short-run supply curve is identical to its marginal cost curve above the minimum of average variable cost. The perfectly competitive industry's short-run supply curve is the horizontal sum of the supply curves of the individual firms.
- In short-run equilibrium, each firm is maximizing its profits. However, any firm may be making losses, making profits, or just breaking even.

9.4 LONG-RUN DECISIONS

- In the long run, profits or losses will lead to firms' entry into or exit out of the industry. This pushes any competitive industry to a long-run, zero-profit equilibrium and moves production to the level that minimizes average cost.
- The long-run response of an industry to steadily changing technology is the gradual replacement of less efficient plants by more efficient ones. Older plants will be discarded and replaced by more modern ones only when price falls below average variable cost.
- The long-run response of a declining industry will be to continue to satisfy demand by employing its existing plants as long as price exceeds short-run average variable cost.

KEY CONCEPTS

Competitive behaviour and competitive market structure
Perfect competition
Price taking and a horizontal demand curve

Average revenue, marginal revenue, and price under perfect competition
Rules for maximizing profits
The relationship of supply curves to marginal cost curves

Short-run and long-run equilibrium of competitive industries
Entry and exit in achieving long-run equilibrium

STUDY EXERCISES

MyEconLab Make the grade with MyEconLab: Study Exercises marked in ● can be found on MyEconLab. You can practise them as often as you want, and most feature step-by-step guided instructions to help you find the right answer.

① Fill in the blanks to make the following statements correct.

a. The demand curve faced by a single firm in a perfectly competitive market is _____.

b. The demand curve faced by a single firm in a perfectly competitive industry coincides with the firm's _____ curve and its _____ curve.

c. Total revenue is calculated by multiplying _____ and _____. Average revenue is calculated by dividing _____ by _____. Marginal revenue is calculated by dividing _____ by _____.

d. A firm's loss when it produces *no* output is equal to its _____.

② Fill in the blanks to make the following statements correct.

a. The shut-down price is the price at which the firm can just cover its _____.

b. If the average variable cost of producing any given level of output exceeds the price at which it can be sold, then the firm should _____.

c. If a firm is producing a level of output such that $MC > MR$, that firm should _____ output.

d. The profit-maximizing level of output for a price-taking firm is the output at which MR and MC are _____ and the gap between TR and TC is _____.

e. If a perfectly competitive firm is producing its profit-maximizing level of output and the price of its output rises, then MR will be _____ MC and the firm should _____ output.

③ Fill in the blanks to make the following statements correct.

a. The short-run supply curve for a perfectly competitive firm is that firm's marginal cost curve for levels of output where marginal cost exceeds _____.

b. If a firm is producing a level of output where $MR = MC$ but is suffering losses, we know that price is below _____. This firm should continue to produce as long as price exceeds _____.

c. If a firm is earning profits, we know that price is above its _____. There is an incentive for other firms to _____ this industry.

④ In Figure 9-1, we explain the difference between the demand curve for a competitive industry and the demand curve facing an individual firm in that industry. Review that figure and answer the following questions.

a. Explain what would happen if the individual firm tried to charge a higher price for its product.

b. Explain why the individual firm has no incentive to charge a lower price for its product.

c. Explain why the demand curve for an individual firm is horizontal at the current market price.

⑤ Consider the following table showing the various revenue concepts for DairyTreat Inc., a perfectly competitive firm that sells milk by the litre. Suppose the firm faces a constant market price of $2 per litre.

Price (p)	Quantity	Total Revenue (TR)	Average Revenue (AR)	Marginal Revenue (MR)
$2	150	—	—	
2	175	—	—	—
2	200	—	—	—
2	225	—	—	—
2	250	—	—	—

a. Compute total revenue for each level of output. Fill in the table.

b. Compute average and marginal revenue for each level of output. Fill in the table. (Remember to compute marginal revenue *between* successive levels of output.)

c. Explain why for a perfectly competitive firm, $AR = MR = p$.

d. Plot the TR, MR, and AR curves on a scale diagram. What is the slope of the TR curve?

⑥ The diagram below shows the various short-run cost curves for a perfectly competitive firm.

Market Price ($)	Firm's Output	Is Price > ATC?	Is Price > AVC?	Are Profits Positive?
$3	—	—	—	—
4	—	—	—	—
5	—	—	—	—
6	—	—	—	—
7	—	—	—	—
8	—	—	—	—
9	—	—	—	—
10	—	—	—	—

a. Based on the diagram, and the assumption that the firm is maximizing its profit, fill in the table. The last three columns require only a "yes" or "no."
b. What is this firm's shut-down price? Explain.
c. What is this firm's supply curve? Explain.

7 Consider the table below showing the supply schedules for three competitive firms, each producing honey. These three firms make up the entire industry.

Market Price ($/kg)	Output (kg)			
	Firm A	Firm B	Firm C	Industry
2.50	100	0	0	—
3.00	125	0	0	—
3.50	150	100	0	—
4.00	175	150	0	—
4.50	200	200	100	—
5.00	225	250	175	—
5.50	250	300	250	—
6.00	275	350	325	—

a. Compute the total industry supply at each price and fill in the table.
b. On a scale diagram similar to Figure 9-6, plot the supply curve for each firm and for the industry as a whole.
c. Can you provide a likely explanation for why Firm B produces no output at prices $3 and lower, and why Firm C produces no output at prices $4 and lower?

8 Larry's Linens produces white cloth napkins for restaurants in a perfectly competitive market. The table below shows output and total costs for one day of production.

Output	TVC	TFC	TC	MC	ATC	AVC
0	0	100	—	—	—	—
100	40	100	—	—	—	—
200	70	100	—	—	—	—
300	120	100	—	—	—	—
400	180	100	—	—	—	—
500	250	100	—	—	—	—
600	330	100	—	—	—	—
700	420	100	—	—	—	—
800	520	100	—	—	—	—
900	630	100	—	—	—	—

a. Complete the cost schedule for this firm by calculating TC, MC, ATC, and AVC. Remember to record the MC figures *between* the rows of output and total cost.
b. Draw a scale diagram and plot ATC, AVC, and MC.
c. Below which price should this firm choose to produce zero output?
d. If the market price per napkin is $0.80, what is this firm's profit-maximizing level of output? Since MC is calculated between the rows of the output levels given, state the *range* of output in which the profit-maximizing level of output will fall. Do the same for market prices of $0.60 and $1.00.
e. Calculate the firm's profit per unit and total profit per day at an output level of 450 napkins per day and at a market price of $0.70.

9 Consider each of the following scenarios for profit-maximizing firms operating in perfectly competitive markets. For each firm, state whether the firm should produce nothing, or increase, decrease, or maintain its output level.

a. XYZ Corp. has output of 2000 units, market price = $64, average total cost = $62, average variable cost = $48, and marginal cost = $67.
b. XYZ Corp. has output of 2000 units, market price = $64, average total cost = $70, average variable cost = $66, and marginal cost = $64.
c. XYZ Corp. has output of 2000 units, market price = $64, average total cost = $62, average variable cost = $58, and marginal cost = $60.
d. XYZ Corp. has output of 2000 units, market price = $64, average total cost = $64, average variable cost = $62, and marginal cost = $64.
e. UVW Corp. has output of 6000 units, market price = $10, total costs = $72 000, total variable costs = $66 000, and marginal cost = $9.

f. UVW Corp. has output of 10 000 units, market price = \$4, total costs = \$50 000, total variable costs = \$30 000, and marginal cost = \$4.

10 Consider the perfectly competitive barley industry. It is initially in long-run equilibrium at quantity Q_0 and price p_0.

a. Draw a supply-and-demand diagram for the barley market, showing the initial long-run equilibrium.

b. Draw a diagram for a typical firm when the industry is in its initial long-run equilibrium, showing its MC, ATC, and $LRAC$ curves. Are any profits being earned by the typical barley farmer?

c. Now suppose there is an increase in demand (caused by an increase in demand for beer, which uses barley as an input). The price for barley rises to p_1. In your diagram, show the effects on the supply and demand diagram for the entire industry and the typical firm's short-run response to the increase in market price from p_0 to p_1. Show the area that represents the typical firm's profits at this new price.

d. Explain how this industry adjusts to its new long-run equilibrium. Illustrate this adjustment both in the demand-and-supply diagram and in the diagram of the typical firm. (You may assume that the cost curves for barley firms are unaffected by this change.)

11 The diagrams below show short-run cost curves for four perfectly competitive firms. Assume that each firm faces a market price of p_0.

a. Which firms could earn positive profits at some level of output?

(i) Firm 1

(ii) Firm 2

(iii) Firm 3

(iv) Firm 4

b. Which firms would be incurring losses at their profit-maximizing level of output, but will continue producing in the short run?

c. Which firms will choose not to produce at price p_0?

12 Which of the following observed facts about an industry are inconsistent with its being a perfectly competitive industry?

a. Different firms use different methods of production.

b. The industry's product is extensively advertised by a trade association.

c. Individual firms devote a large fraction of their sales receipts to advertising their own product brands.

d. There are 24 firms in the industry.

e. The largest firm in the industry makes 40 percent of the sales, and the next largest firm makes 20 percent of the sales, but the products are identical, and there are 61 other firms.

f. All firms made large profits last year.

13 What, if anything, does each one of the following tell you about ease of entry into or exit from an industry?

a. Profits have been very high for two decades.

b. No new firms have entered the industry for 20 years.

c. The average age of the firms in the 40-year-old industry is less than seven years.

d. Most existing firms are using old-technology equipment alongside newer, more modern equipment.

e. Profits are low or negative; many firms are still producing, but from steadily aging equipment.

10

Monopoly, Cartels, and Price Discrimination

CHAPTER OUTLINE	LEARNING OBJECTIVES (LO)
	After studying this chapter you will be able to
10.1 A SINGLE-PRICE MONOPOLIST	**1** explain why marginal revenue is less than price for a profit-maximizing monopolist.
	2 understand how entry barriers can allow monopolists to maintain positive profits in the long run.
10.2 CARTELS AND MONOPOLY POWER	**3** describe why firms would form a cartel to restrict industry output and how this would increase their profits.
10.3 PRICE DISCRIMINATION	**4** explain how some firms can increase their profits through price discrimination.

PERFECT competition is at one end of the spectrum of market structures. At the other end is **monopoly**. When the output of an entire industry is produced by a single firm, we call that firm a **monopolist** or a *monopoly firm*. A perfectly competitive firm has no market power, which means it has no ability to influence the market-determined price. A monopolist, on the other hand, has the maximum possible market power because it is the only firm in its industry. These two extremes of behaviour are useful for economists in their study of market structures.

Examples of monopoly are quite rare, partly because when they do exist their high profits attract entry by rival firms, at which point they cease to be monopolists. When a monopoly is able to persist, it is often because it has been granted some special protection by government,

as in the case of electric utilities (often owned by provincial governments) or prescription drugs (which often are protected by patents). Even though monopolies are rare, some monopoly behaviour extends to other market structures that we will study in later chapters.

In this chapter we examine how a profit-maximizing monopolist determines its price and quantity. We begin by considering a monopolist that sells all its output at a single price. We then consider *cartels* that are formed when several firms band together in order to behave more like a monopolist. We end the chapter by examining situations in which monopolists and other firms with market power are able to charge different prices to different customers—something you have probably observed with airline tickets, subway and bus passes, movie tickets, and even some products at your local grocery store.

10.1 A SINGLE-PRICE MONOPOLIST

monopoly A market containing a single firm.

monopolist A firm that is the only seller in a market.

We look first at a monopolist that charges a single price for its product. This firm's profits, like those of all firms, will depend on the relationship between its costs and its revenues.

Revenue Concepts for a Monopolist

We saw in Chapter 7 that the shape of a firm's short-run cost curves arises from the conditions of production rather than from the market structure in which the firm operates. The same forces that lead perfectly competitive firms to have U-shaped cost curves apply equally to monopolists. Therefore we do not need to introduce any new cost concepts to analyze a monopoly firm—everything we saw in Chapter 7 applies equally to firms in *all* market structures. We can therefore focus our attention on a monopolist's revenues.

Because a monopolist is the sole producer of the product that it sells, the demand curve it faces is simply the market demand curve for that product. The market demand curve, which shows the total quantity that buyers want to purchase at each price, also shows the quantity that the monopolist will be able to sell at each price.

Unlike a perfectly competitive firm, a monopolist faces a negatively sloped demand curve.

A monopolist therefore faces a tradeoff between the price it charges and the quantity it sells. For a monopolist, sales can be increased only if price is reduced, and price can be increased only if sales are reduced.

Average Revenue Starting with the market demand curve, we can readily derive the monopolist's average and marginal revenue curves. When the monopolist charges the same price for all units sold, its total revenue (*TR*) is simply equal to the single price times the quantity sold:

$$TR = p \times Q$$

Since average revenue is total revenue divided by quantity, it follows that average revenue is equal to the price:

$$AR = \frac{TR}{Q} = \frac{p \times Q}{Q} = p$$

And since the demand curve shows the price of the product, it follows that the demand curve is also the monopolist's average revenue curve.

Marginal Revenue Now let's consider the monopolist's *marginal revenue*—the revenue resulting from the sale of one more unit of the product. Because its demand curve is negatively sloped, the monopolist must reduce the price that it charges on *all* units in order to sell an extra unit. But this implies that the price received for the extra unit sold is *not* the firm's marginal revenue because, by reducing the price on all previous units, the firm loses some revenue. Marginal revenue is therefore equal to the price *minus* this lost revenue. It follows that the marginal revenue resulting from the sale of an extra unit is less than the price that the monopolist receives for that unit.

FIGURE 10-1 A Monopolist's Average and Marginal Revenue

Computing Average and Marginal Revenue

Price (Average Revenue) (1)	Quantity Sold Q (2)	Total Revenue $(p \times Q)$ (3)	Change in Total Revenue (ΔTR) (4)	Marginal Revenue $(\Delta TR/\Delta Q)$ (5)
10	0	0		
			90	9
9	10	90		
			70	7
8	20	160		
			50	5
7	30	210		
			30	3
6	40	240		
			10	1
5	50	250		
			−10	−1
4	60	240		
			−30	−3
3	70	210		
			−50	−5
2	80	160		
			−70	−7
1	90	90		
			−90	−9
0	100	0		

Average and Marginal Revenue Curves

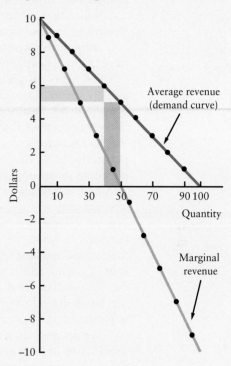

Marginal revenue is less than price because the price must be reduced on all units in order to sell an additional unit. Our example shows that every time the firm lowers its price by $1, its sales increase by 10 units. At a price of $6, the firm sells 40 units for a total revenue of $240. If it lowers its price to $5 *on all units,* total sales rise to 50 units and total revenue rises to $250. The purple rectangle shows the $50 gain in revenue associated with the 10 extra units sold at $5 each. The green rectangle shows the $40 *loss* in revenue associated with reducing the price by $1 on the original 40 units. Thus, the firm's marginal revenue when it reduces its price from $6 to $5 is the change in total revenue ($250 − $240 = $10) divided by the change in quantity (50 − 40 = 10). *MR* = $10/10 = $1.

The monopolist's marginal revenue is less than the price at which it sells its output. Thus the monopolist's *MR* curve is below its demand curve. [24]

The relationship between marginal revenue and price for a numerical example is shown in detail in Figure 10-1. Consider the table first. Notice that the numbers in columns 4 and 5 are plotted between the rows that refer to specific prices and quantities, because the numbers refer to what happens when we move from one row to the next. As price declines and quantity sold increases, marginal revenue is calculated as the change in total revenue divided by the change in quantity:

$$MR = \frac{\Delta TR}{\Delta Q}$$

Now look at the figure. It plots the demand curve described by the price and quantity values shown in the first two columns of the table. It also plots the marginal revenue curve and locates the specific points on it that were calculated in the table. For purposes of illustration, a straight-line demand curve has been chosen.[1]

Notice that marginal revenue is positive up to 50 units of sales, indicating that reductions in price between $10 and $5 increase total revenue. Notice also that marginal revenue is *negative* for sales greater than 50 units, indicating that reductions in price below $5 cause total revenue to fall even though total quantity sold increases.

The figure also illustrates the two opposing forces that are present whenever the monopolist considers changing its price. As an example, consider the reduction in price from $6 to $5. First, the 40 units that the firm was already selling bring in less money at the new lower price than at the original higher price. This loss in revenue is the amount of the price reduction multiplied by the number of units already being sold (40 units × $1 per unit = $40). This is shown as the green shaded area in the figure. The second force, operating in the opposite direction, is that new units are sold, which adds to revenue. This gain in revenue is given by the number of new units sold multiplied by the price at which they are sold (10 units × $5 = $50). This is shown as the purple shaded area. The *net change* in total revenue is the *difference* between these two amounts. In the example shown in the figure, the increase resulting from the sale of new units exceeds the decrease resulting from existing sales now being made at a lower price. Since total revenue has increased as a result of the price reduction, we know that marginal revenue is positive. To calculate the marginal revenue, remember that $MR = \Delta TR/\Delta Q$. In this example the change in total revenue is $10 and the change in quantity is 10 units, so $\Delta TR/\Delta Q = \$1$, as plotted in the figure at a quantity of 45 units (halfway between $Q = 40$ and $Q = 50$).

The proposition that marginal revenue is always less than price for a monopolist provides an important contrast with perfect competition. Recall that in perfect competition, the firm's marginal revenue from selling an extra unit of output is equal to the price at which that unit is sold. The reason for the difference is not difficult to understand. The perfectly competitive firm is a price taker; it can sell all it wants at the given market price. In contrast, the monopolist faces a negatively sloped demand curve; it must reduce its price in order to increase its sales.

If you plot the data on TR from the table in Figure 10-1, you will notice that TR rises (MR is positive) as price falls, reaching a maximum where $p = \$5$ and $MR = 0$. Then, as price continues to fall, TR falls (MR is negative). Using the relationship between elasticity and total revenue that we first saw in Chapter 4, it follows that demand is elastic ($\eta > 1$) when MR is positive and demand is inelastic ($\eta < 1$) when MR is negative. The value of elasticity (η) declines steadily as we move down the demand curve. As we will see shortly, a profit-maximizing monopolist will always produce on the *elastic* portion of its demand curve (that is, where MR is positive).

Short-Run Profit Maximization

We began this chapter by noting that the cost concepts from Chapter 7 apply equally to a monopolist as to a competitive firm. We have now examined a monopolist's average

---

[1] When drawing these curves, note that if the demand curve is a negatively sloped straight line, the MR curve is also a negatively sloped straight line but is exactly twice as steep as the demand curve. The MR curve's vertical intercept (where $Q = 0$) is the same as that of the demand curve, and its horizontal intercept (where $p = 0$) is one-half that of the demand curve. [25]

and marginal revenues and are therefore ready to combine the cost and revenue information to determine the monopolist's profit-maximizing price and level of output.

Recall the two general rules about profit maximization from Chapter 9:

Rule 1: The firm should produce only if price (average revenue) exceeds average variable cost.

Rule 2: If the firm does produce, it should produce a level of output such that marginal revenue equals marginal cost.

Figure 10-2 illustrates a monopolist's choice of output to equate its marginal cost with its marginal revenue. Recall that it is the intersection of the *MR* and *MC* curves that determines the firm's profit-maximizing *quantity*. For the monopolist, the price is then determined by the demand curve. With the firm's costs given by the *ATC* curve shown in the figure, the monopolist is making positive profits, as shown by the red shaded area.

The firm depicted in Figure 10-2 is earning positive profits. But you can easily imagine other possibilities. If the firm's *ATC* curve was higher (perhaps because of higher fixed costs), the firm with the same level of output and charging the same price could be breaking even (zero profits) or even making negative profits (losses). (You can create your own diagrams like Figure 10-2 and draw in the appropriate *ATC* curves to illustrate these two possibilities.)

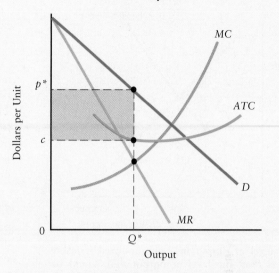

FIGURE 10-2 Short-Run Profit Maximization for a Monopolist

The profit-maximizing output is Q^*, where $MR = MC$; price is p^*. The rules for profit maximization require $MR = MC$ and $p > AVC$. (*AVC* is not shown in the graph, but it must be below *ATC*.) With average costs given by *ATC*, unit costs at Q^* are given by c and the monopolist makes positive profits shown by the shaded rectangle.

Nothing guarantees that a monopolist will make positive profits in the short run, but if it suffers persistent losses, it will eventually go out of business.

An important aspect of monopoly is shown by the outcome in Figure 10-2. The profit-maximizing level of output is determined where $MR = MC$ (Rule 2); and since MR is less than price for a monopolist, it must follow that price exceeds marginal cost.

For a profit-maximizing monopolist, price is greater than marginal cost.

We come back to this important point shortly when we address the *efficiency* of monopoly and compare the monopoly outcome to that in a perfectly competitive market.

No Supply Curve for a Monopolist In describing the monopolist's profit-maximizing behaviour, we did not introduce the concept of a supply curve, as we did in the discussion of perfect competition. In perfect competition, each firm is a price taker and its supply curve is given by its own *MC* curve. An increase in the market price leads to an increase in quantity supplied as the firm moves along its *MC* curve. There is no such relationship in monopoly.

FIGURE 10-3   The Inefficiency of Monopoly

The level of output in a monopolized industry is less than the level of output that would be produced if the industry were perfectly competitive. If the industry is made up of many price-taking firms, the industry supply curve S is the horizontal sum of the many individual marginal cost curves. Given the market demand curve D, the competitive equilibrium quantity is Q_c and the price is p_c. Now suppose the industry has a monopolist with marginal costs given by the MC curve shown. In this case, MR is the monopolist's marginal revenue curve. The profit-maximizing monopolist produces Q_m units of output and charges a price of p_m.

Notice in the monopoly outcome that for the units of output between Q_m and Q_c, the marginal value to society of extra units of the good (as shown by the demand curve) exceeds the marginal cost of producing extra units, and thus society would benefit from having these units produced. The monopolist's restriction of output below Q_c creates a deadweight loss for society shown by the shaded area. The monopoly outcome is therefore *inefficient*.

A monopolist does not have a supply curve because it is not a price taker; it chooses its profit-maximizing price–quantity combination from among the possible combinations on the market demand curve.

Like a perfectly competitive firm, a monopolist has a marginal cost curve. But unlike a competitive firm, a monopolist does not face a given market price. The monopolist *chooses* the price-quantity combination on the market demand curve that maximizes its profits. Following Rule 2, the profit-maximizing level of output is determined where the MC and MR curves intersect.

Firm and Industry   Because the monopolist is the only producer in an industry, there is no need for a separate discussion about the firm and the industry, as is necessary with perfect competition. The monopolist *is* the industry. Thus, the short-run, profit-maximizing position of the firm, as shown in Figure 10-2, is also the short-run equilibrium of the industry.

Competition and Monopoly Compared   The comparison of monopoly with perfect competition is important. For a perfectly competitive industry, the equilibrium is determined by the intersection of the industry demand and supply curves. Since the industry supply curve is simply the sum of the individual firms' marginal cost curves, the equilibrium output in a perfectly competitive industry is such that price equals marginal cost (such as price p_c and quantity Q_c in Figure 10-3). As shown in Figures 10-2 and 10-3, however, the monopolist produces a *lower* level of output and, at that output level, price is greater than marginal cost.

In Chapter 5 we briefly discussed the meaning of *market efficiency* and how it relates to the amount of *economic surplus* generated in the market. We will examine these concepts in more detail in Chapter 12. For now we can observe why the decisions of the monopolist—though perhaps very profitable for the firm—lead to an inefficient outcome for society as a whole.

Since price exceeds marginal cost for a monopolist, society as a whole would benefit if more units of the good were produced—because the marginal value to society of extra units, as reflected by the price, exceeds the marginal cost of producing the extra units. In the terminology we introduced in Chapter 5, more *economic surplus* would be generated for society if the monopolist increased its level of output. The monopolist's profit-maximizing decision to restrict output below the competitive level creates a loss of economic surplus for society—a deadweight loss. In other words, it leads to market *inefficiency*.

A monopolist restricts output below the competitive level and thus reduces the amount of economic surplus generated in the market. The monopolist therefore creates an inefficient market outcome.

Why Are Monopolies So Rare?

Very few of the firms that sell the goods and services you buy are monopolists. Some may be very large in their respective industries—such as the companies that sell you Internet services or publish the textbooks you buy or sell the breakfast cereal you eat—but they are not pure monopolists, with 100 percent of the market.

The main reason monopolists are so rare is that when they do exist they tend to earn very large profits, and this profitability quickly attracts other firms into the industry. When those other firms enter the industry, the first firm is no longer a monopolist. As a result, it is far more common for an industry to contain a few large firms (an "oligopoly", discussed in Chapter 11) than it is to have one monopoly firm.

In the rare circumstances where a monopolist is able to persist, it is usually either heavily regulated by government or, as in the case of Canadian electric utilities, owned outright by government. The government involvement is usually motivated by a desire to ensure that the monopolist is not able to set a high price and restrict output in such a way as to significantly reduce market efficiency, as we see in Figure 10-3.

Entry Barriers

If monopoly profits are to persist, the entry of new firms must be prevented. Anything that prevents the entry of new firms is called an **entry barrier**. Such barriers may be *natural* or *created*.

> **entry barrier** Any barrier to the entry of new firms into an industry. An entry barrier may be natural or created.

Natural Entry Barriers   Natural barriers most commonly arise as a result of economies of scale. When the long-run average cost curve is negatively sloped over a large range of output, big firms have significantly lower average total costs than small firms. Recall from Chapter 8 that the *minimum efficient scale (MES)* is the smallest-size firm that can reap all the economies of large-scale production. It occurs at the level of output at which the firm's long-run average cost curve reaches a minimum.

To see how economies of scale can act as an entry barrier, consider the production of newsprint. Suppose the technology of newsprint production is such that a firm's *MES* is 10 000 tonnes per year at an average total cost of $500 per tonne. Further suppose that at a price of $600, the quantity demanded in the entire market is 11 000 tonnes per year. Under these circumstances, only one firm could operate at or near its *MES*. Any potential entrant would have unit costs significantly higher than those of the existing firm and so could not compete successfully.

A **natural monopoly** occurs when the industry's demand conditions allow no more than one firm to cover its costs while producing at its minimum efficient scale. Electrical power transmission is a natural monopoly—with current technology it is cheaper to have only one set of power lines (rather than two or more) serving a given region.

> **natural monopoly** An industry characterized by economies of scale sufficiently large that only one firm can cover its costs while producing at its minimum efficient scale.

Another example of a natural entry barrier is limited access to key natural resources. For example, in order to produce diamonds or gold or copper, it is necessary to possess a mine that is rich enough in its deposits and large enough in scale that the

The six large Canadian banks have extensive country-wide networks of retail branches. In order to compete effectively in this market, any new entrant would need to build a similar network, at enormous cost. The established network of retail branches is therefore an effective entry barrier.

production costs are reasonably close to those of existing mining firms. Such deposits are only found after hundreds of millions of dollars are spent on quite risky exploration; and even then there is considerable luck involved in the discovery of the mine. The result is that entry by new firms is difficult and incumbent firms often possess market power for extended periods of time.

Created Entry Barriers   Many entry barriers are created by conscious government action. Patent laws, for instance, prevent entry by conferring on the patent holder the sole legal right to produce a particular product for a specific period of time. A firm may also be granted a charter or a franchise that prohibits competition by law. Canada Post, for example, has a government-sanctioned monopoly on the delivery of first-class mail. In other cases the regulation and/or licensing of firms severely restricts entry. Professional organizations for dentists or engineers, for example, often restrict the number of places in accredited dental or engineering schools and thus restrict entry into those industries.

Other barriers can be created by the firm or firms already in the market. In extreme cases, the threat of force or sabotage can deter entry. The most obvious entry barriers of this type are encountered in organized crime, where operation outside the law makes available an array of illegal but potent barriers to new entrants. But law-abiding firms must use legal tactics in an attempt to increase a new entrant's costs and thereby deter their entry. Such tactics range from the threat of price cutting—designed to impose unsustainable losses on a new entrant—to heavy brand-name advertising. (These and other created entry barriers will be discussed in more detail in Chapter 11.)

The Very Long Run and Creative Destruction

In the very long run, technology changes. New ways of producing old products are invented, and new products are created to satisfy both familiar and new wants. These are related to the concept of entry barriers; a monopoly that succeeds in preventing the entry of new firms capable of producing its product will sooner or later find its barriers circumvented by innovations.

A firm may be able to develop a new production process that circumvents a patent upon which a monopolist relies to bar the entry of competing firms.

A firm may compete by producing a somewhat different product satisfying the same need as the monopolist's product. An example is the courier services provided by United Parcel Service or Federal Express that compete with the package delivery of Canada Post. Canada Post still has a government-granted monopoly on the delivery of first-class mail, but it has no monopoly on the delivery of packages, whatever their size.

Finally, a firm may get around a natural monopoly by inventing a technology that produces at a low minimum efficient scale (*MES*) and allows it to enter the industry and still cover its full costs. Cell-phone technology, for example, allows the provider of cell-phone services to compete with the provider of local land-line telephone services without having to establish an expensive network of wires, thus allowing successful competition at a much smaller scale of operations. In addition, Skype, Facetime, and other Internet-based substitutes to land-line telephone services are further eroding the market power of the traditional phone companies.

> **Entry barriers are often circumvented by the innovation of production processes and the development of new goods and services. Such innovation explains why monopolies rarely persist over long periods.**

The distinguished economist Joseph Schumpeter (1883–1950) took the view that entry barriers were not a serious obstacle in the very long run. He argued that the short-run profits of a monopoly provide a strong incentive for others, through their own innovations and product development, to try to usurp some of these profits for themselves. If a frontal attack on the monopolist's entry barriers is not possible, the barriers will be circumvented by such means as the development of similar products against which the monopolist will not have entry protection. Schumpeter called the replacement of one product by another the process of *creative destruction*. "Creative" referred to the rise of new products; "destruction" referred to the demise of the existing products and perhaps the firms that produced them. Some old and current examples are presented in *Applying Economic Concepts 10-1*.

Schumpeter argued that this process of creative destruction reflects new firms' abilities to circumvent entry barriers that would otherwise permit firms to earn high profits in the long run. He also argued that because creative destruction thrives on innovation, the existence of high profits is a major incentive to economic growth. Schumpeter was writing during the 1940s, when the two dominant market structures studied by economists were perfect competition and monopoly. His argument easily extends, however, to any market structure that allows profits to exist in the long run. Today, pure monopolies are few, but there are many industries in which high profits can be earned for long periods of time. Such industries, which are called oligopolies, are conducive to the process of creative destruction. We study these industries in detail in Chapter 11.

10.2 CARTELS AND MONOPOLY POWER

So far in our discussion, a monopoly has meant that there is only one firm in an industry. A second way a monopoly can arise is for several firms in an industry to agree to cooperate with one another, eliminating competition among themselves. In this case, they would band together and behave as if they were a single seller with the objective of maximizing their joint profits. Such a group of firms is called a **cartel**. The firms can agree among themselves to restrict their total output to the level that maximizes their joint profits.

cartel An organization of producers who agree to act as a single seller in order to maximize joint profits.

Some of the best examples of cartels come from history. In the United States in the last half of the nineteenth century, cartels existed in the steel and oil industries. These cartels were so successful in restricting output and elevating prices that much of current U.S. anti-trust policy dates from that time. As we will see in Chapter 12, U.S. and Canadian policy has been quite effective at preventing the creation of large cartels that would otherwise possess considerable market power.

As a result of successful policies aimed at preventing the creation of *domestic* cartels, the best current examples of cartels are ones that operate in global markets and are supported by national governments. The Organization of the Petroleum Exporting Countries (OPEC) is perhaps the best-known cartel in the world. This cartel first came

APPLYING ECONOMIC CONCEPTS 10-1

Disruptive Technologies and Creative Destruction

Seventy-five years ago, Joseph Schumpeter coined the phrase "creative destruction" to describe the elimination of one product by a superior one—and argued that economic growth in all advanced economies relied on this process. This term is still used today, although it is now becoming more common to hear about the economic effects of "disruptive technologies." But the idea is the same: new firms and their products are developed that compete against and often displace old firms and their products. There are countless examples of this process, both old and new. Here are just a few.

Steel-nibbed pens eliminated the quill pen with its sharpened bird's feather nib. Fountain pens eliminated the steel pen and its accompanying inkwell. Ballpoint pens virtually eliminated the fountain pen.

Silent films eliminated vaudeville. The talkies eliminated silent films and colour films have all but eliminated black and white. Television seriously reduced the demand for films (and radio) while not eliminating either of them. Cable greatly reduced the demand for direct TV reception by offering a better picture and a more varied selection. Access to movies and programs that can be live-streamed on the Internet is now challenging the dominance of cable TV.

For long-distance passenger travel by sea, the steamship eliminated the sailing vessel around the beginning of the twentieth century. In the 1960s the airplane eliminated the ocean liner as a means of long-distance travel (but not for holiday cruises). For passenger travel on land, the train eliminated the stagecoach, while the bus competed with the train without eliminating it. The airplane is now the dominant form of travel for long distances, leaving trains and buses to be used mainly for short distances.

These examples all involve the elimination of a product by the development of a new, preferred product. But

DeBeers *controls approximately 40 percent of the world's supply of diamonds through its Diamond Trading Company.*

to prominence when, in 1973, its members collectively agreed to restrict their output of crude oil and thereby increased the world price of oil by nearly 300 percent. In 1979, further output restrictions led the price to increase by another 120 percent. During the 1980s and 1990s, as oil production by non-OPEC countries increased significantly, OPEC found it difficult to maintain such a controlling influence on the oil market. OPEC also ran into problems enforcing the agreements among its members. As we will see in this section, these are typical challenges that all cartels face.

Another well-known example of a cartel that was successful over many years is the diamond cartel controlled by the South African company DeBeers. DeBeers produces a significant share of the world's annual output of rough diamonds but also purchases diamonds from smaller producers worldwide. The result is that about 40 percent of the world's annual diamond supply is marketed through the DeBeers-controlled Diamond Trading Company (DTC). In years when demand is slack, DeBeers restricts the output of diamonds through the DTC to keep prices from falling.

A third, less familiar example has recently gained prominence. In 1970, three Canadian companies that produce potash in Saskatchewan—a mineral used to produce fertilizer—created a special company to sell their product in world markets. Canpotex (named for *Can*adian *pot*ash *ex*ports) now sells about one-third of creative destruction also occurs with the development of better *processes*. The laborious hand-setting of metal type for printing was replaced by linotype that allowed the type to be set by a keyboard operator. The linotype was swept away by computer typesetting and much of the established printing shop operations have now been replaced by low-cost laser printing.

A century ago, automobiles were produced with skilled craftsmen operating relatively unsophisticated equipment. When Henry Ford perfected the techniques of mass production in the early 1920s, masses of less-skilled workers operated specialized and inflexible equipment. Today, relatively few highly skilled workers operate very sophisticated robotics equipment to produce today's vehicles.

Very recently, the Internet has permitted some services to be delivered to customers in ways that seriously challenge the market power of incumbent firms. Online apps that match customers to drivers, for example, are threatening to disrupt established taxicab companies in many cities. Similarly, other apps match customers with overnight rental accommodations and threaten to disrupt the established hotel industry. In both cases, debate currently rages as to whether and to what extent the "disrupters" in each case should be regulated—or perhaps even prevented from conducting their businesses altogether.

These cases all illustrate the same general message. Technological change transforms the products we consume, and also how we make those products. It continually sweeps away positions of high income and economic power established by firms that were in the previous wave of technological change. It is an agent of dynamism in our economy, an agent of change and economic growth, but it is not without its dark side in terms of the periodic loss of privileged positions on the part of the displaced firms and their workers.

the world's potash, and the three companies restrict their combined annual production in an attempt to influence the world price. In recent years, Canpotex has also devised special grades of potash designed to suit specific crops, and in doing so the company has secured a much larger market share in countries such as South Korea, Japan, and Taiwan.

Notice in all three examples that there are firms *outside* the cartel. There are many oil producers (including all those in Canada and the United States) that are not part of OPEC; there are many diamond mines that are not owned or controlled by DeBeers (two of which are the Ekati and Diavik mines in the Northwest Territories that together make up approximately nine percent of total world diamond production); and there are other large potash producers in Belarus, Russia, Germany, and Israel that do not sell their potash through Canpotex. Indeed, this type of cartel is much more common than one in which *all* firms in the industry successfully band together.

In this chapter, however, we simplify the analysis by considering the case in which *all* firms in the industry form a cartel. This is the easiest setting in which to see the central point—that cartels are inherently unstable.

The Effects of Cartelization

If all firms in a competitive industry come together to form a cartel, they must recognize the effect their *joint* output has on price. That is, like a monopolist they must recognize that they face a downward-sloping demand curve and, as a result, an increase in the total volume of their sales requires a reduction in price. They can agree to restrict industry output to the level that maximizes their joint profits (where the industry's marginal

FIGURE 10-4 **The Effect of Cartelizing a Competitive Industry**

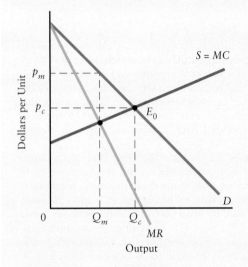

Cartelization of a competitive industry can always increase that industry's profits. Equilibrium for a competitive industry occurs at E_0. Equilibrium price and output are p_c and Q_c.

If all the firms in the industry form a cartel, profits can be increased by reducing output. All units between Q_m and Q_c add less to revenue than to cost—the MR curve lies below the MC curve—and therefore will not be produced by a profit-maximizing cartel. The cartel maximizes its joint profits by producing output of Q_m and setting price equal to p_m (the same as the monopoly outcome).

cost is equal to the industry's marginal revenue). The incentive for firms to form a cartel lies in the cartel's ability to restrict output, thereby raising price and increasing profits. This is shown in Figure 10-4.

> The profit-maximizing cartelization of a competitive industry will reduce output and raise price from the perfectly competitive levels.

Problems That Cartels Face

Cartels encounter two characteristic problems. The first is ensuring that members follow the behaviour that will maximize the cartel members' *joint* profits. The second is preventing these profits from being eroded by the entry of new firms.

Enforcement of Output Restrictions The managers of any cartel want the industry to produce its profit-maximizing output. Their job is made more difficult if individual firms either stay out of the cartel or join the cartel and then "cheat" by producing too much output. Any one firm, however, has an incentive to do just this—to be either the one that stays out of the organization or the one that enters and then cheats. For simplicity, assume that all firms enter the cartel; thus enforcement problems are concerned strictly with cheating by its members.

If Firm X is the only firm to cheat, it is then in the best of all possible situations. Other firms have restricted their output and the industry price is near its monopoly level, allowing all cartel members to jointly share the monopoly profits. Firm X can then earn extra profits by violating the cartel agreement and selling additional output at the high monopoly price. However, if all firms cheat, the total level of output will rise and the price will be pushed back to the competitive level. All the firms will then be back to their competitive position. This conflict between the interests of the group as a whole and the interests of each individual firm is the cartel's main dilemma and is illustrated in Figure 10-5.

> Cartels tend to be unstable because of the incentives for individual firms to violate the output restrictions needed to sustain the joint-profit-maximizing (monopoly) price.

The predicted instability of cartels is evident in the data. After the tremendous successes in 1973 and 1979 in restricting the output of crude oil and significantly elevating its world price, the members of the OPEC cartel began to encounter difficulties in enforcing their agreements. After several years of sluggish world demand for oil, the cartel almost collapsed in 1986 as several OPEC members increased their output in efforts to generate more income. Throughout the 1990s, however, OPEC members learned the important lesson that their attempts to push oil prices very high attract entry, encourage

FIGURE 10-5   A Cartel Member's Incentive to Cheat

(i) Market equilibrium   (ii) Firm incentives

Cooperation leads to the monopoly price, but individual self-interest can lead to production in excess of the monopoly output. Market conditions are shown in part (i), and the situation of a typical firm is shown in part (ii). (The change of scale between the two graphs is reflected by the upper case Q in part (i) and the lower case q in part (ii).) Initially, the market is in competitive equilibrium with price p_0 and quantity Q_0. The individual firm is producing output q_0 and is just covering its total costs.

A successful cartel reduces total output to Q_1 and elevates price to p_1. Q_1 is the joint-profit-maximizing level of output because industry MR equals industry MC. A typical firm in the cartel bound to the output restriction is then producing output q_1 in part (ii). The firm's profits rise from zero to the amount shown by the shaded area in part (ii). Once price is raised to p_1, however, the individual firm would like to increase output to q_2, where its marginal cost is equal to the price set by the cartel. This would allow the firm to earn much larger profits, shown by the diagonally striped area. However, if all firms increase their output in such a manner, industry output will increase far beyond Q_1, and the resulting fall in price will reduce the joint profits of the cartel.

the development of alternative oil supplies, and undermine their output restrictions. As a result, OPEC members avoided the large output restrictions and price increases of the 1970s, instead trying to keep oil prices relatively stable at more moderate levels.

Over time, however, OPEC's market power declined considerably as its share of global oil production fell to just over 30 percent (down from 55 percent in the 1970s). While OPEC countries still meet regularly and have agreements regarding each member's annual output, the cartel's ability to influence the world price of oil is much smaller than it was 40 years ago.

Another example of a cartel's instability involves the world coffee market. In 2000, the Association of Coffee Producing Countries (ACPC), a cartel of 15 countries that produced approximately 75 percent of the world's coffee, agreed to restrict coffee output to keep coffee prices between U.S.$0.95 and U.S.$1.05 per pound. Within two years, however, a bumper crop in Brazil, the world's largest coffee producer, led to the inevitable pressure to cheat. Brazil had the incentive to sell its new production rather than incur storage costs. Other countries, facing low prices, had the incentive to increase their sales to bolster their incomes. By 2003, the ACPC had closed down its operations. Perhaps the cartel will be re-established at some point in the future when it has improved its ability to enforce its members' behaviour.

Restricting Entry   A successful cartel not only must police the behaviour of its members but also be able to prevent the entry of new producers. An industry that is able to support a number of individual firms presumably has no overriding natural entry barriers. Thus, if it is to maintain its profits in the long run, a cartel of many separate firms must create barriers that prevent the entry of new firms that are attracted by the cartel's profits. Successful cartels are often able to license the firms in the industry and to control entry by restricting the number of licences. This practice is often used by doctors, lawyers, dentists, and engineers, whose professional organizations restrict entry to those individuals who meet certain qualifications. At other times, the government has operated a quota system and has given it the force of law. If no one can produce without a quota and the quotas are allocated among existing producers, entry is successfully prevented. This approach is used to limit the number of taxicabs in many cities as well as the quantity of milk produced by Canada's dairy farmers. Governments also directly own some firms and prohibit competition from the private sector. In most Canadian provinces, for example, retail liquor sales are permitted only by government-owned establishments.

As we mentioned earlier, for many years DeBeers was successful at preventing the entry of new diamond producers and was able to control a large fraction of the world's annual sales of rough diamonds. But restricting entry into the diamond industry has become more challenging. In the diamond industry, of course, "entry" means the development of new diamond mines. In 2004, two new mines in the Northwest Territories reached full-scale production. The combined annual output of rough diamonds from the Ekati and Diavik mines is about nine percent of total world production. The owners of the Ekati and Diavik mines, however, market their diamonds independently rather than going through DeBeers. With entries such as this, combined with some Russian and Australian producers also choosing to sell their diamonds independently, DeBeers is faced with the challenge of keeping diamond prices supported above competitive levels. The challenges faced by cartels— both for enforcing output restrictions and for restricting entry—involve conflicting incentives between individual firms. To analyze these sorts of problems more completely, economists use *game theory*, a tool that we introduce and discuss in detail in Chapter 11.

10.3 PRICE DISCRIMINATION

So far in this chapter, we have assumed that the monopolist charges the same price for every unit of its product, no matter where or to whom it sells that product. But as we will soon see, a monopolist always finds it profitable to sell different units of the same product at different prices whenever it gets the opportunity. In principle, the same is true for *any* firm that faces a negatively sloped demand curve. Because this practice is prevalent both for monopoly and for markets in which there are a few large sellers, the range of examples we will discuss covers both types of market structure.

Airlines often charge less to people who stay over a Saturday night than to those who come and go within the week. In countries in which medical services are provided by the market, physicians in private practice often charge for their services according to the incomes of their patients. Movie theatres often have lower admission prices for seniors and children (and for everyone on Tuesdays). Bus and transit passes are usually cheaper for students than for others. Electric companies typically sell electricity at one rate to homes and at a different rate to firms.

Price discrimination occurs when a producer charges different prices for different units of the same product *for reasons not associated with differences in cost.* Not all price differences represent price discrimination. Quantity discounts, differences between wholesale and retail prices, and prices that vary with the time of day or the season of the year may not represent price discrimination because the same product sold at a different time, in a different place, or in different quantities may have different costs. An excellent example is electricity. If an electric power company has unused capacity at certain times of the day, it may cost less for the company to provide service at those hours than at peak demand hours.

> If price differences reflect cost differences, they are not discriminatory. When price differences are based on different buyers' valuations of the same product, they are discriminatory.

It does not cost a movie-theatre operator less to fill seats with senior citizens than with non-seniors, but it is worthwhile for the movie theatre to let the seniors in at a discriminatory low price if few of them would attend at the full adult fare and if they take up seats that would otherwise be empty. Similarly, it does not cost VIA Rail any less to sell a ticket to a student than to a non-student. But since few students may be inclined to buy tickets at the full price, it is profitable for VIA Rail to attract more students with a lower price and, in that manner, fill up seats that would otherwise be empty.

When Is Price Discrimination Possible?

Price discrimination is profitable for firms, but is not always possible. Three conditions must be satisfied before a firm can successfully price discriminate.

Market Power   Any firm that is a price taker cannot discriminate because it has no power to influence the price at which it sells its product. Our entire discussion about price discrimination therefore applies only to firms with some amount of market power. For simplicity, we will consider the case of a monopoly firm, although *any* firm with market power will, in general, be interested in the greater profits that are possible through price discrimination.

Different Valuations of the Product   Price discrimination is possible if the firm is able to determine the willingness of its various consumers to pay. Consider two situations. First, any given consumer might be prepared to pay a different price for different units of the good. Second, some consumers might be prepared to pay more for the same good than other consumers are. In this second situation, if the firm is able to determine which consumers are prepared to pay a high price and which are prepared to pay only a low price, the firm is able to *segment* the market.

The Internet and online shopping have provided firms with access to huge amounts of information about consumers' buying habits. Firms can now collect data on who visits their websites, what products they look at, and which combinations of products are often purchased together. Analysis of these data allows firms to know much more about consumers' preferences, much more quickly, than was true even 10 years ago. Not surprisingly, perhaps, the Internet has facilitated firms' ability to price discriminate.

price discrimination The sale by one firm of different units of a product at two or more different prices for reasons not associated with differences in cost.

Paul Springett B/Alamy

In markets like this in which bargaining takes place, the sellers tend to be very good at determining each consumer's genuine willingness to pay. As a result, different consumers end up paying different prices for the same products. This is effective price discrimination.

Prevent Arbitrage   Whenever the same product is being sold at different prices, there is an incentive for buyers to purchase the product at the lower price and re-sell it at the higher price, thereby making a profit on the transaction. This is called *arbitrage*. A price-discriminating firm must be able to prevent people from conducting such transactions. Otherwise the firm will end up selling only at the low price and all the profits that the strategy of price discrimination was designed to produce will accrue to those who do the arbitrage. As we will soon see, the successful prevention of this arbitrage depends crucially on the nature of the product being sold.

Different Forms of Price Discrimination

Now that we have seen the conditions that make price discrimination possible, let's examine the two general forms that it can take: price discrimination among *units of output* and price discrimination among *market segments*.

Price Discrimination Among Units of Output   Recall our discussion in Chapter 6 where we noted that the demand curve can be viewed as a *willingness to pay* curve. We also discussed the concept of *consumer surplus*, the difference between the price the consumer is *willing* to pay and the price that the consumer *actually* pays.

A firm that charges different prices for different units of a product is trying to capture some of this consumer surplus. Figure 10-6 shows a monopolist's profits in two situations. In the first, the monopolist is only able to charge a single price per unit. In the second, the monopolist is able to charge different prices on different units of output and it increases its profits by doing so. Notice that even in the case where the firm charges several prices, consumers still earn some consumer surplus.

Price discrimination among units of output sold to the *same* consumer requires that the firm be able to keep track of the units that a buyer consumes in each period. Thus, the tenth unit purchased by a given consumer in a given month can be sold at a price that is different from the fifth unit *only* if the firm can keep track of that consumer's purchases. This can be done, for example, by an electric company through its meter readings or by a coffee shop by using a "loyalty card," whereby after paying for seven coffees the customer gets the eighth for free.

Price Discrimination Among Market Segments   It is usually much easier for firms to distinguish between different groups of consumers of a product—different market segments—than it is to detect an individual consumer's willingness to pay for different units of that product. As a result, price discrimination among market segments is more common than price discrimination among units.

Suppose a firm with market power faces a market demand curve that is made up of distinct market segments. These segments may correspond to the age of consumers, such as children, adults, and seniors. Or the segments may correspond to different regions in

FIGURE 10-6 Price Discrimination Among Units of Output

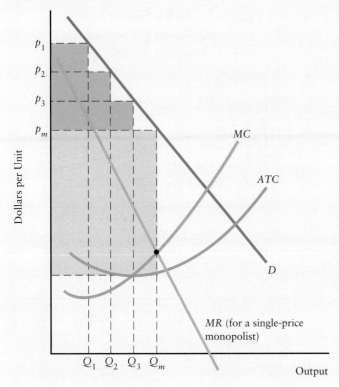

Profits can be increased by price discriminating. A single-price monopolist produces where $MR = MC$, output is Q_m, and price is p_m. In this case, profits are the light shaded area, and consumers receive consumer surplus given by the entire area above p_m and below the demand curve.

Price discrimination transfers some of this consumer surplus to the firm. Suppose the firm keeps output constant at Q_m but is able to charge different prices for different blocks of units. For example, it might charge p_1 for the first Q_1 units, p_2 for the next block of units up to Q_2, p_3 for the next block of units up to Q_3, and p_m for the remaining units up to Q_m. (The firm would expand output beyond Q_m if it could offer even more prices, but we simplify here to focus on the transfer of surplus with unchanged output.) In this case, the firm's costs have not changed but its revenues have increased by the dark shaded area. Since costs have not changed, the increase in revenue earned by price discrimination also represents an increase in profits for the firm. Consumer surplus has been reduced to the unshaded triangles just below the demand curve.

which the consumers live, such as the North American automobile market being segmented into the Canadian and U.S. segments. Whatever the nature of the market segmentation, suppose the firm recognizes the distinct market segments and is able to prevent any purchase-and-resale between them. What is the firm's profit-maximizing pricing policy?

The answer is for the firm to charge a higher price in the market segment with the *less elastic demand*, as shown in the numerical example in Figure 10-7. To understand this result, recall our discussion from Chapter 4 regarding elasticity. The elasticity of demand reflects consumers' ability or willingness to substitute between this product and other products. The market segment with less elastic demand therefore contains consumers that are more "committed" to this product than are the consumers in the market segment with more elastic demand. To put it differently, the consumers with less elastic demand represent a more "captive" market for the firm. It should not be surprising, therefore, that the profit-maximizing firm will charge a higher price to the more captive consumers and a lower price to those consumers who can more easily substitute away to other products.

A firm with market power that can identify distinct market segments will maximize its profits by charging higher prices in those segments with less elastic demand.

FIGURE 10-7 A Numerical Example of Profitable Price Discrimination

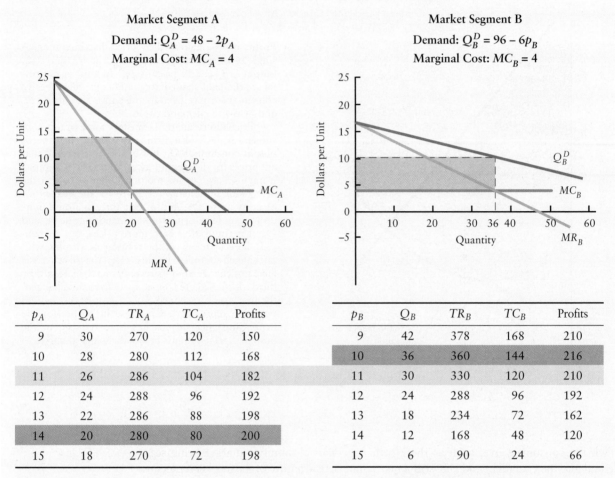

Market Segment A

Demand: $Q_A^D = 48 - 2p_A$

Marginal Cost: $MC_A = 4$

Market Segment B

Demand: $Q_B^D = 96 - 6p_B$

Marginal Cost: $MC_B = 4$

p_A	Q_A	TR_A	TC_A	Profits
9	30	270	120	150
10	28	280	112	168
11	26	286	104	182
12	24	288	96	192
13	22	286	88	198
14	20	280	80	200
15	18	270	72	198

p_B	Q_B	TR_B	TC_B	Profits
9	42	378	168	210
10	36	360	144	216
11	30	330	120	210
12	24	288	96	192
13	18	234	72	162
14	12	168	48	120
15	6	90	24	66

Profit-maximizing price discrimination results in higher prices in those market segments with less elastic demand. The figure shows two market segments, each with a different demand curve. At any given price, demand in segment A is less elastic than demand in segment B. Profit-maximizing price discrimination requires that $MC = MR$ in each market segment.

For each market segment, the table shows different possible prices, and the associated quantities, revenues, costs, and profits. Marginal costs are assumed to be $4 for each unit produced. Suppose first that the firm is unable to price discriminate and thus charges the same price in each segment. By comparing the total profit in the two segments *along any single row of the table*, it is apparent that the single profit-maximizing price is $11, total output is 56 units, and the resulting total profit is $392, as shown by the green shaded row. The firm can increase its profits, however, if it can charge different prices in the two market segments. By charging $14 in segment A and only $10 in segment B, the firm's total output is unchanged at 56 units, but the allocation of that output across the market segments is changed, and the firm's total profit increases to $416, as shown by the two red shaded rows.

Price discrimination among market segments is very common. When the different segments occur in different regions or countries, distance and transportation costs keep the markets separate, but sometimes those impediments are not enough. For example, new cars in the United States typically sell at a tax-inclusive price between 10 percent and 20 percent below the price for the same car in Canada. For several years it was common to hear of Canadians crossing the border to purchase their cars, paying the necessary Canadian sales taxes when they returned to Canada, and still saving several thousand dollars on the purchase. When such behaviour became widespread enough to present a serious problem to the Canadian dealers who were losing sales to those enterprising customers, the car companies effectively put an end to the practice by requiring their Canadian dealers to not honour service warranties for cars purchased in the United States. In this way, the car companies successfully maintain their strategy of market segmentation and price discrimination.

A more local example of price discrimination among market segments is the different prices charged by movie theatres for adults and seniors. The cost to the theatre of providing a seat to any customer is independent of the customer's age. But the two market segments contain consumers who are thought to have different elasticities of demand, the adults with the less elastic demand than seniors. The profit-maximizing pricing policy by the theatre is therefore to charge a higher price to adults than to seniors. This same logic applies to many goods and services for which there are "seniors' discounts."

The example of seniors' discounts at theatres also illustrates an important point about how the firm prevents arbitrage when price discriminating. When you buy a ticket to see a movie, you are buying a service rather than a tangible good. You don't take anything away with you after the movie—you are really just paying for the right to see the movie. This aspect of the product makes price discrimination easier to enforce. A young adult trying to circumvent the price discrimination could buy a senior's ticket, but upon entry to the theatre that person would be stopped and easily recognized as ineligible for the seniors' discount.

> **Price discrimination is easier for services than for tangible goods because for most services the firms transact directly with the final customer and thus can more easily prevent arbitrage.**

That price discrimination is often more difficult to sustain with tangible goods explains another familiar observation. Grocery stores and drugstores often have promotions with widely used products (toilet paper and paper towels, for example) on sale at heavily discounted prices. What prevents entrepreneurial shoppers in these situations from buying a large number of units at the special price and re-selling them to others at a higher price? The answer is that firms usually place quantity limits on special deals, thus preventing any large-scale arbitrage that would undermine their pricing policy.

Hurdle Pricing   Market segments are often well defined but very difficult for the firm to detect. For example, we all know people who are sufficiently impatient that they *must* buy the latest Hollywood movie available for purchase on DVD or from iTunes. Whereas many other people are prepared to wait several months until it is available at a considerably lower price. This pricing strategy is intentional and is an example of *hurdle pricing*. The firms producing these goods know that some people are patient and others are impatient. By setting a high initial price and a lower price only after several months, the firms are setting a "hurdle" that consumers must "jump over" in order to get the low price. In this case, the hurdle is that consumers must wait several months. This same type of hurdle exists in the pricing of high-priced hardcover books and lower-priced paperback books that are released several months later. In this case, the slightly altered products do have different costs, although the cost differences are considerably smaller than the differences in prices.

> **Hurdle pricing exists when firms create an obstacle that consumers must overcome in order to get a lower price. Consumers then assign themselves to the various market segments—those who don't want to jump the hurdle and are willing to pay the high price, and those who choose to jump the hurdle in order to benefit from the low price.**

Another familiar example of hurdle pricing involves coupons for discounts at grocery stores. Most of us receive grocery-store flyers in the mail every week. Many people ignore grocery store coupons because they can't be bothered to look through them and clip out their chosen ones, while others do so studiously. In this case, the price discrimination is between those people who can't be bothered to deal with the coupons (less elastic demand) and those people who care enough about the discounts to clip the coupons (more elastic demand). Everyone is presented with the option between higher prices and lower prices, and the hurdle of clipping coupons is designed to have people assign themselves to the two market segments.

The Consequences of Price Discrimination

We can examine the consequences of price discrimination for firm profits, output, and consumer surplus.

Price Discrimination and Firm Profits Our first proposition is about the consequences of price discrimination for firm profits:

> **For any given level of output, the most profitable system of discriminatory prices will always provide higher profits to the firm than the profit-maximizing single price.**

This proposition, which was illustrated in Figure 10-6, requires only that the demand curve have a negative slope. To see that the proposition is correct, remember that a monopolist with the power to discriminate could produce exactly the same quantity as a single-price monopolist and charge everyone the same price. Therefore, it need never receive less revenue, and it can do better if it can raise the price on even one unit sold, so long as the price need not be reduced on any other. This proposition is also illustrated in Figure 10-7 in which the firm faces two market segments and increases its profits by charging a different price in each segment.

Price Discrimination and Output Our second proposition relates to how price discrimination affects the level of output.

> **A monopolist that price discriminates among units will produce more output than will a single-price monopolist.**

To understand this second proposition, remember that a single-price monopolist will produce less than would all the firms in a perfectly competitive industry (recall Figure 10-3). It produces less because it knows that selling more depresses the price. Price discrimination allows it to reduce this disincentive. If the firm can sell its output in separate blocks, it can sell another block without spoiling the market for blocks that are already sold. If each unit can be sold at a separate price, the profit-maximizing monopolist will produce every unit for which the price charged is greater than or equal to its marginal cost. In general, therefore, a price discriminating monopolist will sell more output than a single-price monopolist.

This second proposition has implications for *market efficiency*, a concept we introduced in Chapter 5 and reviewed earlier in this chapter. Recall that a single-price monopolist produces at a level of output at which price exceeds marginal cost. Thus, society would benefit from having more of the good produced because the marginal value of the good to society (as reflected by its price) exceeds the marginal cost of the good. Put differently, a higher level of output would lead to more economic surplus being generated in the market and thus a more efficient outcome for society as a whole.

For a monopolist that price discriminates among units, however, there are several prices rather than just a single price. As you can see in Figure 10-6, if the firm sold another block of output beyond Q_m at a price below p_m it would increase its profits further (because the new price would still be above MC). And the more output it produces, the more economic surplus is generated in the market.

> If price discrimination leads the firm to increase total output, the total economic surplus generated in the market will increase, and the outcome will be more efficient.

Price Discrimination and Consumer Surplus   The final aspect of price discrimination is its effect on consumers, and this is where we often witness strong emotional reactions to price discrimination. But one's view will depend on who benefits and who loses.

For instance, when railways discriminate against small farmers, the results arouse public anger. It seems acceptable to many people, however, that doctors practise price discrimination in countries where medical services are provided by the market, charging lower prices to poor patients than to wealthy ones. And few people disapprove when airlines discriminate by giving senior citizens and vacationers lower fares than business travellers.

By increasing the seller's profits, price discrimination transfers income from buyers to sellers. When buyers are poor and sellers are rich, this transfer may seem undesirable. However, as in the case of doctors' fees and senior citizens' discounts, discrimination sometimes allows lower-income people to buy a product that they would otherwise be unable to afford if it were sold at the single price that maximized the producer's profits. In this case some consumers are made better off by the firm's decision to price discriminate.

> There is no general relationship between price discrimination and consumer welfare. Price discrimination usually makes some consumers better off and other consumers worse off.

SUMMARY

10.1 A SINGLE-PRICE MONOPOLIST

LO 1, 2

- Monopoly is a market structure in which an entire industry is supplied by a single firm. The monopolist's own demand curve is identical to the market demand curve for the product. The market demand curve is the monopolist's average revenue curve, and its marginal revenue curve always lies below its demand curve.
- A single-price monopolist is maximizing its profits when its marginal revenue is equal to marginal costs.
- A monopolist produces such that price exceeds marginal cost, whereas in a perfectly competitive industry, price equals marginal cost. By restricting output below the competitive level, the monopolist imposes

a deadweight loss on society; this is the inefficiency of monopoly.
- The profits that a monopoly earns may be positive, zero, or negative in the short run, depending on the relationship between demand and cost.
- For monopoly profits to persist in the long run, there must be effective barriers to the entry of other firms. Entry barriers can be natural or created.
- In the very long run, it is difficult to maintain entry barriers in the face of the process of creative destruction—the invention of new processes and new products to attack the entrenched position of existing firms.

10.2 CARTELS AND MONOPOLY POWER

LO 3

- A group of firms may form a cartel by agreeing to restrict their joint output to the monopoly level. Total profits at this reduced level of output exceed total profits in the competitive equilibrium.

- Cartels tend to be unstable because of the strong incentives for each individual firm to cheat by producing more than its agreed-upon level of output.

10.3 PRICE DISCRIMINATION

LO 4

- Any firm that faces a downward-sloping demand curve can increase its profits if it can price discriminate.
- Successful price discrimination requires that the firm be able to control the supply of the product offered to particular buyers and to prevent the resale of the product.
- A firm that price discriminates among units will produce more output than if it sets only a single price. Price discrimination of this type is possible only if it can monitor use of the product by consumers.
- A firm that discriminates between different market segments will equate MC and MR in each market. The

market with the less elastic demand will have the higher price.
- Hurdle pricing is a common form of price discrimination that requires customers to overcome some obstacle in order to benefit from a lower price. This method of price discrimination leads customers to reveal through their actions which market segment they are in.
- If price discrimination leads the firm to increase output, market efficiency is improved. In general, some consumers will benefit and others will be made worse off by price discrimination.

KEY CONCEPTS

The relationship between price and
  marginal revenue for a monopolist
Short-run monopoly profits
Natural and created entry barriers

The process of creative destruction
Cartels as monopolies
The instability of cartels
Price discrimination

Arbitage
Market segmentation
Hurdle pricing

STUDY EXERCISES

MyEconLab Make the grade with MyEconLab: Study Exercises marked in ● can be found on MyEconLab. You can practise them as often as you want, and most feature step-by-step guided instructions to help you find the right answer.

① Fill in the blanks to make the following statements correct.

a. A perfectly competitive firm faces a _____ demand curve, whereas a single-price monopolist faces a _____ demand curve.

b. A single-price monopolist that maximizes profits will produce at the output where _____ equals _____. A perfectly competitive firm (and industry) produces a level of output such that price _____ marginal cost. The monopolist produces a level of output such that price _____ marginal cost.

c. A monopolist will be earning profits as long as price is _____ average total cost.

d. At its profit-maximizing level of output, marginal cost for a single-price monopolist is always _____ the price it charges for its output.

② The following table shows data for a monopolist. The first two columns provide all the data necessary to plot the monopolist's demand curve.

Price	Quantity Demanded	Total Revenue (TR)	Average Revenue (AR)	Marginal Revenue (MR)
$20	100	—	—	—
18	125	—	—	—
16	150	—	—	—
14	175	—	—	—
12	200	—	—	—
10	225	—	—	—
8	250	—	—	—
6	275	—	—	—
4	300	—	—	—

a. Compute total and average revenue for each level of output and fill in the third and fourth columns in the table. Explain why average revenue is equal to price.

b. Compute marginal revenue for each successive change in output and fill in the last column. Explain why MR is less than price.

c. On a scale diagram, plot the demand (average revenue) curve and the marginal revenue curve.

d. On a second scale diagram, with dollars on the vertical axis and output on the horizontal axis, plot the TR curve. What is the value of MR when TR reaches its maximum?

③ The diagram below shows the demand curve facing a single-price monopolist. The firm is currently at point A on the demand curve, selling 20 units of output at a price of $160 per unit.

a. Calculate TR at each point along the demand curve, A through H.

b. Suppose the firm reduces the price from $160 to $140. Calculate the revenue it will give up on the units it was already selling. Calculate the revenue it will gain on the new units it will sell. What is the firm's marginal revenue by moving from point A to point B?

c. Calculate the marginal revenue for each increment of 10 additional units the firm sells, from B to C, C to D, and so on. Plot the MR curve on the diagram.

d. Explain in words why the MR curve facing a single-price monopolist is different than the MR curve facing a perfectly competitive firm.

④ The diagram below shows the demand curve, marginal revenue curve, and cost curves for a monopolist that owns the only golf course on Eagle Island. The monopolist's product is 18-hole golf games.

a. What is the profit-maximizing price and output (number of rounds of golf per week) for the monopolist on ?
b. What is the average total cost per round of golf at the profit-maximizing level of output?
c. Calculate the profit, in dollars per week, to this monopolist.

⑤ Each scenario below provides the price and output level at which a single-price monopolist is currently operating. In each case, determine the firm's profit per unit, the firm's total profit, and whether the firm should increase or decrease its output in order to maximize profits. (Drawing diagrams may help you to answer these questions. Prices and costs are in dollars.)

a. $p = 15$, $Q = 600$, $MR = 7$, $ATC = 5$, $MC = 7$
b. $p = 18$, $Q = 300$, $MR = 13$, $ATC = 5.50$, $MC = 3.50$
c. $p = 11$, $Q = 680$, $MR = 2$, $ATC = 6$, $MC = 9$
d. $p = 15$, $Q = 600$, $MR = 7$, $ATC = 17$, $MC = 7$
e. $p = 13$, $Q = 700$, $MR = 1.75$, $ATC = 12.50$, $MC = 9$

⑥ The diagram below shows a monopolist's MC and ATC curves as well as the industry demand and MR curves.
a. What is the profit-maximizing price and level of output for the monopolist?
b. What area in the figure shows the level of profits for the monopolist? Are profits positive or negative?

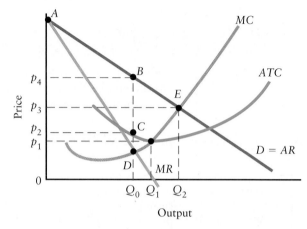

c. What area shows the deadweight loss to society resulting from the monopolist's output decision?
d. Now suppose the industry is made up of many small, price-taking firms (with the same technology). What are the equilibrium price and level of output in this case?

⑦ Imagine a monopolist that has fixed costs but no variable costs (thus there are no marginal costs, so $MC = 0$). For example, consider a firm that owns a spring of water that can produce indefinitely once it installs certain pipes, in an area where no other source of water is available.

a. Draw a downward-sloping demand curve for water, its associated MR curve, and the monopolist's MC curve.
b. On your diagram, show the monopolist's profit-maximizing price and level of output.
c. At the monopolist's profit-maximizing level of output, what is the marginal value of this good to society, and how does it compare with the marginal cost?

⑧ In this chapter we discuss several types of entry barriers that could allow a firm to maintain some monopoly power. For each of the cases below, describe the type of entry barrier that appears to be most relevant and the kinds of innovation that are or could be circumventing these entry barriers. If you are unfamiliar with these industries you may need to do a little research.

- a patented blood pressure medication
- legal services
- electricity transmission
- municipal sewage services
- copyrighted songs and music
- delivery of first class mail in Canada
- taxicabs
- hotels

⑨ Consider the market for corn. Suppose this is a competitive industry, made up of many price-taking farmers. We begin in a situation where market price is p_0, industry output is Q_0, and the typical farm is producing q_0 and earning zero profit.

a. Draw the two diagrams below.

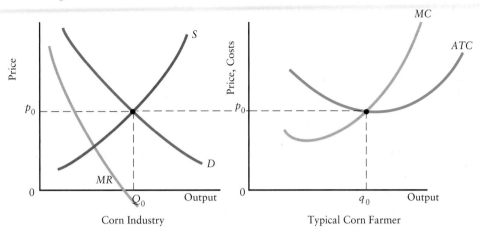

Corn Industry

Typical Corn Farmer

b. Now suppose that the farmers in this industry form a cartel and collectively agree to restrict the industry output of corn to the level that a monopolist would produce. Call this level of output Q^M and call the new price p^M. Each firm now produces output of $q^M < q_0$. (Hint: Assume that q^m will be the same proportion of q_0 as Q^M is of Q_0.) Show this outcome in the two diagrams.

c. Show how the cartel raises the profits for the typical farmer.

d. Now consider the incentives for an individual farm to cheat on its fellow cartel members. Would it be profitable to produce an extra unit and sell it at the cartel price? How is this incentive illustrated in your diagram?

e. Show how the typical farm's profits would rise if it were the only farm to cheat. What level of output would the cheating farm produce?

f. Explain what would happen if *all* farms tried to cheat in this way.

⑩ Consider each of the following examples in which a firm sells the same product to different customers at different prices. Identify in each case whether price discrimination is likely to be taking place. If there is unlikely to be price discrimination occurring, what explains the different prices?

a. Weekend airline fares that are less than weekday fares.

b. Business-class airline fares that are 150 percent higher than economy-class fares. (Recognize that two business-class seats take the same space inside the plane as three economy-class seats.)

c. Discounts on furniture negotiated from the "suggested retail price" for which sales personnel are authorized to bargain and to get as much in each transaction as the customer is prepared to pay.

d. Higher tuition for MBA students than for graduate students in economics.

⑪ Look back to the diagram of the monopolist on Eagle Island in Question 4.

a. Suppose the monopolist is able to charge a different price on each different unit sold. What would be the total number of rounds of golf sold per week? What would be the price on the last round sold?

b. What is the area representing consumer surplus in the absence of any price discrimination?

c. What is the area representing consumer surplus when the monopolist is practising this "perfect" price discrimination?

d. Could this monopolist realistically engage in such perfect price discrimination? Describe a more likely form of price discrimination that this monopolist could achieve on Egale Island.

⑫ When selling its famous Levi 501 jeans, Levi Strauss price discriminates between the European and U.S. markets, selling the product at a higher price in Europe than in the United States. The following equations are hypothetical demand curves for Levi 501s in Europe and in the United States. We have expressed the price in dollars in both markets, and quantity is thousands of units per year.

$$\text{European Demand: } Q^D{}_E = 150 - p$$

$$\text{U.S. Demand: } Q^D{}_A = 250 - 4p$$

a. On separate scale diagrams, one for Europe and one for the United States, plot the two demand curves.

b. Recalling that a straight-line demand curve has an associated *MR* curve that has twice its slope, plot the two *MR* curves.

c. Suppose Levi Strauss has a constant marginal cost of $15 per unit. Plot the *MC* curve in both diagrams.

d. What is the profit-maximizing price in each market? Explain why profit maximization requires that *MC* be equated to *MR* *in each market segment.*

e. Compute the price elasticity of demand (at the profit-maximizing points) in each market segment. (You may want to review Chapter 4 on elasticity at this point.) Does the market segment with less elastic demand have the higher price?

13 Consider each of the following examples of price discrimination. For each case, explain how the price discrimination works. Also explain which consumers would be worse off and which consumers would be better off if the firm were *unable* to price discriminate in this way.

a. Seniors pay lower prices for theatre tickets than do other adults.

b. Consumers pay less for paperback books than for hardcover books, but must wait 6 to 12 months before the paperbacks are made available.

c. Customers of smartphone packages pay a lower price if they ask for one—that is, if they reveal that they are prepared to consider shopping elsewhere for their phone package.

d. Airline customers get a discount fare if they are prepared to stay over a Saturday night at their destination.

14 Consider the following industries:

- chocolate bars
- copper wire
- outboard motors
- coal
- local newspaper

a. Which of these industries would it be most profitable to monopolize, and why?

b. Does your answer to part (a) depend on several factors or just one or two?

c. As a consumer, which of these industries would you least like to have monopolized by someone else?

d. If your answers to parts (a) and (c) are different, explain why.

11 Imperfect Competition and Strategic Behaviour

CHAPTER OUTLINE	LEARNING OBJECTIVES (LO)
	After studying this chapter you will be able to
11.1 IMPERFECT COMPETITION	1 recognize that Canadian industries typically have either a large number of small firms or a small number of large firms.
	2 explain why imperfectly competitive firms have differentiated products and often engage in non-price competition.
11.2 MONOPOLISTIC COMPETITION	3 describe the key elements of the theory of monopolistic competition.
11.3 OLIGOPOLY AND GAME THEORY	4 use game theory to explain the difference between cooperative and non-cooperative outcomes among oligopolists.
11.4 OLIGOPOLY IN PRACTICE	5 provide examples of the nature of the competition among oligopolists and the most common entry barriers.

THE two market structures that we have studied so far—perfect competition and monopoly—are polar cases; they define the two extremes of a firm's market power within an industry. Under perfect competition, firms are price takers, price is equal to marginal cost, and economic profits in the long run are zero. Under monopoly, the firm is a price setter, it sets price above marginal cost, and it can earn positive profits in the long run if there are sufficient entry barriers.

Although they provide crucial insights for understanding some industries, these two polar cases are insufficient for understanding the behaviour of *all*

firms. Indeed, most of the products that we easily recognize—swimsuits, cell phones, jeans, cameras, hamburgers, sunglasses, perfume, running shoes, computers, breakfast cereals, and cars, to name just a few—are produced by firms that have considerable market power yet are not monopolists.

This chapter discusses market structures that lie between these two polar cases of perfect competition and monopoly. Before discussing the theory, however, we turn to a brief discussion of the prevalence of these "intermediate" market structures in the Canadian economy.

11.1 IMPERFECT COMPETITION

Most firms in Canada fall somewhere between the two ends of the spectrum of market structures—they are neither perfectly competitive nor monopolistic. We refer to the market structures between these two extremes as *imperfectly competitive*. There is, of course, a wide range of firm behaviour between these two extremes. Consider, for example, how differently your local hair salon behaves compared to your cell-phone service provider. The theories of monopolistic competition and oligopoly have been developed to understand and explain the behaviour of these many firms "in the middle." Much of the difference among these firms in the middle involves the extent of their market power.

Between the Two Extremes

Between the two extreme market structures of perfect competition and monopoly are two common types of industries—those with many small firms and those with a few large firms.

Industries with Many Small Firms The majority of Canada's output each year is produced in industries where the firms are small relative to the size of their industry. The perfectly competitive model does well in explaining the behaviour of individual firms that produce more-or-less identical products and are price takers. Forest and fish products, agricultural products, and commodities such as iron ore, tin, and copper are sold in markets where most individual firms do not possess market power. Many other Canadian industries, however, contain many small firms but are not well described by the perfectly competitive model.

The theory of *monopolistic competition* was originally developed to help explain economic behaviour and outcomes in industries in which there are many small firms, but where each firm has some degree of market power. Consider your local hair salon, car mechanic, or neighbourhood pub, each of which has some ability to influence the prices of their products. They probably spend some money on advertising, which they would not do if they were price takers. Nor are these firms selling identical products. A hair salon can easily distinguish itself from its competitors, as can a neighbourhood pub. Even the car mechanic can offer different levels of service and speed to differentiate its product. Each of these firms also differentiates itself simply by being in a different location, which itself gives it some degree of market power, unlike a perfectly competitive firm.

Industries with a Few Large Firms About one-third of Canada's total output is produced in industries dominated by either a single firm or a few large ones. As we saw in Chapter 10, cases of true monopoly in Canada are rare, and the provincial hydro-electric utilities are the most striking example of an industry where a single firm dominates the market. However, these are typically owned by provincial governments. Local telephone, cable, and Internet providers may have some local monopoly power, but are subject to significant government regulation. More common in advanced economies like Canada's are industries where a few very large firms dominate the market. This is certainly true in Canada, where many such industries form a significant part of the economy and are not well described by the model of monopoly.

The theory of *oligopoly* helps us to understand these industries in which there are a small number of large firms, each with considerable market power, and that compete actively with each other. These firms are well known to most of us. The grocery business is dominated by a few large firms—Loblaws, Metro, Sobeys, and Walmart.

The life insurance business is dominated by Sun Life, Great West Life, and Manulife; the railway industry has two dominant firms—Canadian Pacific Railways and Canadian National. Many industries that used to be dominated by small, independent firms have been transformed in recent years by the development of large, world-wide firms. This is especially true in the accounting, engineering, management consulting, and law professions. All of these firms have market power but still compete actively with their rivals.

Industrial Concentration   An industry with a small number of relatively large firms is said to be highly *concentrated*. A formal measure of such industrial concentration is given by the *concentration ratio*.

> **concentration ratio** The fraction of total market sales controlled by a specified number of the industry's largest firms.

Concentration Ratios.   When we measure whether an industry has power concentrated in the hands of only a few firms or dispersed over many, it is not sufficient to count the firms. For example, an industry with one enormous firm and 29 very small ones is more concentrated in any meaningful sense than an industry with only five equal-sized firms. One approach to this problem is to calculate what is called a **concentration ratio**, which shows the fraction of total market sales controlled by the largest sellers, often taken as the largest four or eight firms.

Figure 11-1 shows the four-firm concentration ratios in several Canadian manufacturing industries. As is clear, the degree of concentration is quite varied across these industries. In the petroleum industry, for example, the largest four firms account for about 65 percent of total sales. At the other extreme, the largest four firms in the fabricated metals industry account for less than 10 percent of sales. These largest firms may be large in some absolute sense, but the low concentration ratios suggest that they have quite limited market power.

Defining the Market.   The main problem associated with using concentration ratios is to *define the market* with reasonable accuracy. On the one hand, the market may be much smaller than the whole country. For example, concentration ratios in national cement sales are low, but they understate the market power of cement companies because high transportation costs divide the cement *industry* into a series of *regional*

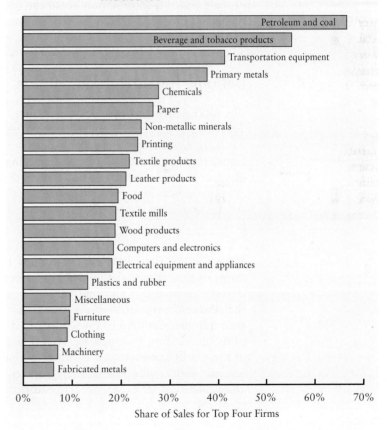

FIGURE 11-1   Concentration Ratios in Selected Canadian Industries

Concentration ratios vary greatly among manufacturing industries. These data show the share of total annual sales (in dollar terms) accounted for by the four largest firms in the industry.

(*Source*: Author's calculations based on data provided by Statistics Canada.)

markets, with each having relatively few firms. On the other hand, the market may be larger than one country, as is the case for most internationally traded commodities. This is particularly important for Canada.

The globalization of competition brought about by the falling costs of transportation and communication has been one of the most significant developments in the world economy in recent decades. As the world has "become smaller" through the advances in transportation and communication technologies, the nature of domestic markets has changed dramatically. For example, the presence of only a single firm in one industry in Canada in no way implies monopoly power when it is in competition with several foreign firms that can easily sell in the Canadian market. This is the situation faced by many Canadian companies producing raw materials, such as Cameco, Encana, Suncor, Canfor, Rio Tinto Alcan, and Barrick. These companies may be large relative to the *Canadian* market, but the relevant market in each case (uranium, natural gas, oil, forest products, aluminum, and gold) is the *global* one in which these firms have no significant market power.

In the cases of markets for internationally traded products, concentration ratios (appropriately adjusted to define the relevant market correctly) can still be used to provide valuable information about the degree to which production in a given market is concentrated in the hands of a few firms.

Defining Imperfect Competition

The market structures we are now going to study are called *imperfectly competitive.* The word *competitive* emphasizes that we are not dealing with monopoly, and the word *imperfect* emphasizes that we are not dealing with perfect competition (in which firms are price takers). Let's begin by noting a number of characteristics that are typical of imperfectly competitive firms. To help organize our thoughts, we classify these under three main headings. First, firms choose the *variety* of the product they produce and sell. Second, firms choose the *price* at which they sell that product. Third, firms engage in *non-price* competition.

Firms Choose Their Products   If a new farmer enters the wheat industry, the full range of products that the farmer can produce is already in existence. In contrast, if a new firm enters the smartphone or tablet industry, that firm must decide on the characteristics of the new products it is to design and sell. It will not produce smartphones identical to those already in production. Rather, it will develop variations on existing products or even a product with a whole new capability. Each of these will have its own distinctive characteristics including colour, size, shape, screen quality, video capability, and so on. As a result, firms in the smartphone and tablet industries sell an array of differentiated products, no two of which are identical.

The term **differentiated product** refers to a group of products similar enough to be called the same product but dissimilar enough that they can be sold at different prices. For example, although one brand of shampoo is similar to most others, shampoos differ from each other in chemical composition, colour, smell, brand name, packaging, and reputation. All shampoos taken together can be regarded as one differentiated product.

differentiated product A group of products similar enough to be called the same product but dissimilar enough that all of them do not have to be sold at the same price.

Most firms in imperfectly competitive markets sell differentiated products. In such industries, the firm itself must choose its product's characteristics.

Firms Choose Their Prices   Whenever different firms' products are not identical, each firm must decide on a price to set. For example, a single price is not established for cars or TVs or jeans by equating overall demand with overall supply. What is true for cars and TVs is true for virtually all consumer goods. Any one manufacturer will typically have several product lines that differ from each other and from the competing product lines of other firms. Each product has a price that must be set by its producer.

Firms that choose their prices are said to be **price setters**. Each firm has expectations about the quantity it can sell at each price that it might set. Unexpected demand fluctuations then cause unexpected variations in the quantities sold at these prices.

price setter A firm that faces a downward-sloping demand curve for its product. It chooses which price to set.

In market structures other than perfect competition, firms set their prices and then let demand determine sales. Changes in market conditions are signalled to the firm by changes in the firm's sales.

One striking contrast between perfectly competitive markets and markets for differentiated products concerns the behaviour of prices. In perfect competition, prices change continually in response to changes in demand and supply. In markets where differentiated products are sold, prices change less frequently.

Firms that sell differentiated products typically have many distinct products on their price lists. Changing such a long list of prices is often costly enough that it is done only infrequently. The costs of changing the prices include the costs of printing new list prices and notifying all customers, the difficulty of keeping track of frequently changing prices for accounting purposes and the loss of customer and retailer goodwill caused by frequent changes in prices. As a result, imperfectly competitive firms often respond to fluctuations in demand by changing output and holding prices constant. Only after changes in demand are expected to persist will firms adjust their entire list of prices.

There are important exceptions to this behaviour, however, especially for firms that rely to a large extent on their online sales. For example, airlines have websites on which they post their prices, which change very frequently, even hourly. And for retailers who use the Internet or social networking to contact their customers, "flash sales" are now common, whereby the store advertises special sale prices that last for one day or even one hour.

These breakfast cereals are different enough that each can have its own price, but they are similar enough to be called the same product—they are a differentiated product.

Non-Price Competition   Firms in imperfect competition behave in other ways not observed under either perfect competition or monopoly.

First, many firms spend large sums of money on advertising. They do so in an attempt both to shift the demand curve for the industry's products and to attract customers from competing firms. A firm in a perfectly competitive market would not engage in advertising because the firm faces a perfectly elastic (horizontal) demand curve at the market price and so advertising would involve costs but would not increase the firm's revenues. A monopolist has no competitors in the industry and so will not advertise to attract customers away from other brands. However, in some cases a monopolist will still advertise in an attempt to convince consumers to shift their spending away from other types of products and toward the monopolist's product.

Second, many firms engage in a variety of other forms of non-price competition, such as offering competing standards of quality and product guarantees. In the car industry, for example, Toyota and GM compete actively in terms of the duration of their "bumper-to-bumper" warranties. Many firms also compete through the services they offer along with their products. The car industry is again a good example, with manufacturers and dealers competing in their "after-sales" services provided to the customer, ranging from oil changes and car washes to emergency on-road assistance.

Third, firms in many industries engage in activities that appear to be designed to hinder the entry of new firms, thereby preventing the erosion of existing profits. For example, a retailer's public commitment to match any price offered by a competing retailer may convince potential entrants not to enter the industry.

Two In-Between Market Structures   Our discussion in this section has been a general one concerning firms in imperfectly competitive market structures. We now go into a little more detail and make a distinction between industries with a large number of small firms and industries with a small number of large firms.

Behaviour in the first group of industries can be understood with the theory of *monopolistic competition*. To understand behaviour in the second group we use the theory of *oligopoly*, in which *game theory* plays a central role. As you will see in the remainder of this chapter, a key difference between these two market structures is the amount of *strategic behaviour* displayed by firms.

11.2 MONOPOLISTIC COMPETITION

monopolistic competition
Market structure of an industry in which there are many firms and freedom of entry and exit but in which each firm has a product somewhat differentiated from the others, giving it some control over its price.

The theory of **monopolistic competition** was originally developed to deal with the phenomenon of product differentiation. This theory was first developed by U.S. economist Edward Chamberlin in his pioneering 1933 book *The Theory of Monopolistic Competition*.

This market structure is similar to perfect competition in that the industry contains many firms and exhibits freedom of entry and exit. It differs, however, in one important respect: Whereas firms in perfect competition sell an identical product and are price takers, firms in monopolistic competition sell a differentiated product and thus have some power over setting price.

Product differentiation leads to the establishment of brand names and advertising, and it gives each firm a degree of market power over its own product. Each firm can raise its price, even if its competitors do not, without losing all its sales. This is the *monopolistic* part of the theory. However, each firm's market power is severely restricted in both the short run and the long run. The short-run restriction comes from the presence of similar products sold by many competing firms; this causes the demand curve faced by each firm to be very elastic. The long-run restriction comes from free entry into the industry, which permits new firms to compete away the profits being earned by existing firms. These restrictions comprise the *competition* part of the theory.

Many of the small, service-based businesses located in your neighbourhood are monopolistic competitors—corner stores, dry cleaners, hair stylists, restaurants, auto mechanics, shoe-repair shops, grass-cutting and snow-removal services, home-renovation firms, plumbers, electricians, and painters. In each case, the firm tries to differentiate its product by offering more convenient hours, better workmanship, guarantees of some kind, or perhaps just nicer people. And in each case the firm has some ability to set its own price—but its market power is limited by the nearby presence of other firms selling similar products.

The Assumptions of Monopolistic Competition

The theory of monopolistic competition is based on four key simplifying assumptions.

1. Each firm produces its own version of the industry's differentiated product. Each firm thus faces a demand curve that, although negatively sloped, is highly elastic because competing firms produce many close substitutes.

2. All firms have access to the same technological knowledge and so have the same cost curves.

3. The industry contains so many firms that each one ignores the possible reactions of its many competitors when it makes its own price and output decisions. In this respect, firms in monopolistic competition are similar to firms in perfect competition.

4. There is freedom of entry and exit in the industry. If profits are being earned by existing firms, new firms have an incentive to enter. When they do, the demand for the industry's product must be shared among the increased number of firms.

Predictions of the Theory

Product differentiation, which is the *only* thing that makes monopolistic competition different from perfect competition, has important consequences for behaviour in both the short and the long run.

The Short-Run Decision of the Firm   In the short run, a firm that is operating in a monopolistically competitive market structure is similar to a monopoly. It faces a negatively sloped demand curve and maximizes its profits by choosing its level of output such that marginal costs equal marginal revenue. The firm shown in part (i) of Figure 11-2 makes positive profits, although in the short run it is possible for a monopolistically competitive firm to break even or even to make losses.

Most of the service-based businesses in your neighbourhood, such as hair salons, exist in monopolistically competitive markets.

The Long-Run Equilibrium of the Industry   Profits, as shown in part (i) of Figure 11-2, provide an incentive for new firms to enter the industry. As they do so, the total

FIGURE 11-2   Profit Maximization for a Firm in Monopolistic Competition

(i) A typical firm in the short run   (ii) A typical firm when the industry is in long-run equilibrium

The short-run position for a monopolistically competitive firm is similar to that of a monopolist—profits can be positive, zero, or negative. In the long run, firms in a monopolistically competitive industry have zero profits and excess capacity. Note the very elastic demand curve—this reflects the fact that each firm produces a good for which there are many close (but not perfect) substitutes. Short-run profit maximization occurs in part (i) at E_S, the output for which $MR = MC$. Price is p_S and quantity is Q_S. Profits or losses may exist in the short run; in this example profits are positive and are shown by the shaded area. Starting from the short-run position shown in part (i), entry of new firms shifts each firm's demand curve to the left until profits are eliminated. In part (ii), point E_L, where demand is tangent to $LRAC$, is the position of each firm when the industry is in long-run equilibrium. Price is p_L and quantity is Q_L. In such a long-run equilibrium, each monopolistically competitive firm has zero profits and excess capacity of $Q_L Q_C$.

demand for the industry's product must be shared among this larger number of firms; thus, each firm gets a smaller share of the total market. Such entry shifts to the left the demand curve faced by each existing firm. Entry continues until profits are eliminated. When this has occurred, each firm is in the position shown in part (ii) of Figure 11-2. Its demand curve has shifted to the left until the curve is *tangent* to the long-run average cost (*LRAC*) curve. Each firm is still maximizing its profit, but its profit is now equal to zero.

To see why this "tangency solution" provides the only possible long-run equilibrium for an industry that fulfills all of the theory's assumptions, consider the two possible alternatives. First, suppose the demand curve for each firm lies below and never touches its *LRAC* curve. There would then be no output at which costs could be covered, and firms would leave the industry. With fewer firms to share the industry's demand, the demand curve for each *remaining* firm shifts to the right. Exit will continue until the demand curve for each remaining firm touches and is tangent to its *LRAC* curve. Second, suppose the demand curve for each firm *cuts* its *LRAC* curve. There would then be a range of output over which positive profits could be earned. Such profits would lead firms to enter the industry, and this entry would shift the demand curve for each existing firm to the left until it is just tangent to the *LRAC* curve, where each firm earns zero profit.

The Excess-Capacity Theorem   Part (ii) of Figure 11-2 makes it clear that monopolistic competition results in a long-run equilibrium of zero profits, even though each individual firm faces a negatively sloped demand curve. It does this by forcing each firm into a position in which it has *excess capacity*; that is, each firm is producing an output less than that corresponding to the lowest point on its *LRAC* curve. If the firm were to increase its output, it would reduce its cost per unit, but it does not do so because selling more would reduce revenue by more than it would reduce cost. This result is often called the **excess-capacity theorem**.

> **In long-run equilibrium in monopolistic competition, goods are produced at a point where average total costs are not at their minimum.**

In contrast, the long-run equilibrium under perfect competition has price equal to the minimum of long-run average costs. In part (ii) of Figure 11-2, this is shown as point E_C, with price p_C and output Q_C. (Recall that with perfect competition, each firm faces a horizontal demand curve at the market price, so at price p_C each firm would be on its *MC* curve at point E_C.)

The excess-capacity theorem once aroused passionate debate among economists because it seemed to show that all industries selling differentiated products would produce them at a higher cost than was necessary. Because product differentiation is a characteristic of virtually all modern consumer goods and many service industries, this theorem seemed to suggest that modern market economies were systematically inefficient. In time, however, it was generally accepted that the excess capacity of monopolistic competition does not necessarily indicate a waste of resources because benefits accrue to consumers who can choose among the variety of products.

Saying that consumers value variety is not saying that *each* consumer necessarily values variety. You might like only one of the many brands of toothpaste and be better off if only that one brand were sold at a lower price. But other consumers would prefer one of the other brands. Thus, it is the differences in tastes *across many consumers* that give rise to the social value of variety, and the cost of achieving that greater variety is the higher price per unit that consumers pay.

> **From society's point of view, there is a tradeoff between producing more brands to satisfy diverse tastes and producing fewer brands at a lower cost per unit.**

excess-capacity theorem The property of long-run equilibrium in monopolistic competition that firms produce on the falling portion of their long-run average cost curves. This results in excess capacity, measured by the gap between present output and the output that coincides with minimum average cost.

11.3 OLIGOPOLY AND GAME THEORY

Industries that are made up of a small number of large firms have a market structure called *oligopoly*, from the Greek words *oligos polein*, meaning "few to sell." An **oligopoly** is an industry that contains two or more firms, at least one of which produces a significant portion of the industry's total output. Whenever there is a high concentration ratio for the firms serving one particular market, that market is oligopolistic. The market structures of oligopoly, monopoly, and monopolistic competition are similar in that firms in all these markets face negatively sloped demand curves.

oligopoly An industry that contains two or more firms, at least one of which produces a significant portion of the industry's total output.

Profit Maximization Is Complicated

Like firms in other market structures, an oligopolist that wants to maximize its profits produces the level of output where its marginal revenue equals its marginal cost. But determining this level of output is more complicated for an oligopolist than it is for any other kind of firm because the firm's marginal revenue depends importantly on what its rivals do. For example, if Toyota decides to increase its production of compact cars in an attempt to equate its *MR* with its *MC*, Ford and Nissan may respond by aggressively increasing their output of compacts—thus reducing Toyota's marginal revenue. Alternatively, Ford and Nissan might *reduce* their output of compacts and instead focus their attention on market niches in which Toyota plays a smaller role. Or they might leave their output levels unchanged and introduce new options on their compact cars in an attempt to attract consumers to their products.

The general point is that determining the level of output that maximizes profits is complicated for an oligopolistic firm because it must consider its rivals' likely responses to its actions. Economists say that oligopolists exhibit **strategic behaviour**, which means that they take explicit account of the impact of their decisions on competing firms and of the reactions they expect them to make. In the remainder of this section we examine the strategic behaviour practised by oligopolistic firms.

strategic behaviour Behaviour designed to take account of the reactions of one's rivals to one's own behaviour.

> **Oligopolistic firms often make strategic choices; they consider how their rivals are likely to respond to their own actions.**

The Basic Dilemma of Oligopoly

The basic dilemma faced by oligopolistic firms is very similar to the dilemma faced by the members of a cartel, which we studied in Chapter 10. There we saw that the cartel as a whole had an incentive to form an agreement to restrict total output (and raise price), but each individual member of the cartel had the incentive to cheat on the agreement and increase its own level of output.

For the small number of firms in an oligopoly, the incentives are the same. Firms can either *cooperate* (or *collude*) in an attempt to maximize joint profits, or they can *compete* in an effort to maximize their individual profits. Not surprisingly, the decision by one firm to cooperate or to compete will depend on how it thinks its rivals will respond to its decision.

How do these decisions by firms affect price and output in the markets in which they operate? To answer this question, we first make a distinction between *cooperative* and *non-cooperative* behaviour. If the firms cooperate to produce among themselves the monopoly output, they can maximize their joint profits. If they do this, they will reach what is called a **cooperative (or collusive) outcome**, which is the position that a single monopoly firm would reach if it owned all the firms in the industry.

cooperative (collusive) outcome A situation in which existing firms cooperate to maximize their joint profits.

If the firms are at the cooperative outcome, it will usually be worthwhile for any one of them to cut its price or to raise its output, so long as the others do not do so. However, if every firm does the same thing, they will be worse off as a group and may all be worse off individually. An industry outcome that is reached when firms proceed by calculating only their own gains without cooperating with other firms is called a **non-cooperative outcome**.

non-cooperative outcome An industry outcome reached when firms maximize their own profit without cooperating with other firms.

The behaviour of firms in an oligopoly is complex. As in other market structures, it is necessary to think about how individual firm behaviour affects the overall market outcome. Unlike other market structures, however, in oligopoly each firm typically thinks about how the other firms in the industry will react to its own decisions. Then, of course, the other firms may respond to what the first firm does, and so on. This behaviour resembles a game of strategy. Economists use *game theory* to better understand how these firms behave.

Some Simple Game Theory

Game theory is used to study decision making in situations in which there are a number of players, each knowing that others may react to their actions and each taking account of others' expected reactions when making moves. For example, suppose a firm is deciding whether to raise, lower, or maintain its price. Before arriving at an answer, it asks, "What will the other firms do in each of these cases, and how will their actions affect the profitability of whatever decision I make?"

game theory The theory that studies decision making in situations in which one player anticipates the reactions of other players to its own actions.

> When game theory is applied to oligopoly, the players are firms, their game is played in the market, their strategies are their price or output decisions, and the payoffs are their profits.

An illustration of the basic dilemma of oligopolists, to cooperate or to compete, is shown in Figure 11-3 for the case of a two-firm oligopoly, called a *duopoly*. In this simplified game, we assume that both firms are producing an identical product, and so there is a single market price. The only choice for each firm is how much output to produce. If the two firms "cooperate" to jointly act as a monopolist, each firm produces one-half of the monopoly output and each earns large profits. If the two firms "compete," they each produce more than half (say two-thirds) of the monopoly output, and in this case both firms earn low profits. As we will see, even this very simple example is sufficient to illustrate several key ideas in the modern theory of oligopoly.

A Payoff Matrix   Figure 11-3 shows a *payoff matrix* for this simple game. It shows the profits that each firm earns in each possible combination of the two firms' actions. The upper-left cell in this example shows that if each firm produces one-half of the monopoly output, each firm will earn profits of 20. The lower-right cell shows that if each firm produces two-thirds of the monopoly output, each firm will earn a profit of 17. Since *joint* profits must be maximized at the monopoly output, the total profit in the upper-left cell (40) is greater than the total profit in the lower-right cell (34).

The upper-right and lower-left cells show the profits in the case where one firm produces one-half of the monopoly output and the other firm produces two-thirds of the monopoly output. Note that in these cells, the firm that produces more earns the greater profit. The firm that produces one-half of the monopoly output is helping to restrict output and keep prices high. The firm that produces two-thirds of the monopoly output then benefits from the first firm's output restrictions.

FIGURE 11-3   The Oligopolist's Dilemma: To Cooperate or to Compete?

Cooperation to determine the overall level of output can maximize joint profits, but it leaves each firm with an incentive to cheat. The figure shows a payoff matrix for a two-firm game. Firm A's production is indicated across the top, and its payoffs are shown in the green circles within each cell. Firm B's production is indicated down the left side, and its payoffs are shown in the red circles within each cell.

If A and B cooperate, each produces one-half the monopoly output and receives a payoff of 20. If A and B do not cooperate, they each end up producing two-thirds of the monopoly output and receiving a payoff of 17. In this example, this non-cooperative outcome is a Nash equilibrium.

Strategic Behaviour   The payoff matrix shows the profit each player earns with each combination of the two players' moves. But what will actually happen? To answer this question, we must first know whether the game being played is *cooperative* or *non-cooperative*.

Cooperative Outcome.   If the two firms in this duopoly can cooperate, the payoff matrix shows that their highest *joint* profits will be earned if each firm produces one-half of the monopoly output. This is the cooperative outcome. The payoff matrix also shows, however, that if each firm thinks the other will cooperate (by producing half of the monopoly output), then it has an incentive to cheat and produce two-thirds of the monopoly output. Thus, the cooperative outcome can only be achieved if the firms have some effective way to enforce their output-restricting agreement. As we will see in Chapter 12, explicit output-restricting agreements are usually illegal.

Non-Cooperative Outcome.   Now suppose the firms believe cooperation to be impossible because they have no legal way of enforcing an agreement. What will be the non-cooperative outcome in this duopoly game? To answer this question, we must examine each player's incentives, given the possible actions of the other player.

Firm A reasons as follows: "If B produces one-half of the monopoly output (upper row of the matrix), then my profit will be higher if I produce two-thirds of the monopoly output. Moreover, if B produces two-thirds of the monopoly output (bottom row of the matrix), my profit will be higher if I also produce two-thirds of the monopoly output. Therefore, no matter what B does, I will earn more profit if I produce two-thirds of the monopoly output." A quick look at the payoff matrix in Figure 11-3 reveals that this game is *symmetric,* and so Firm B's reasoning will be identical to A's: It will conclude that its profit will be higher if it produces two-thirds of the monopoly output no matter what A does.

The final result is therefore clear. Each firm will end up producing two-thirds of the monopoly output and each firm will receive a profit of 17. This is the non-cooperative outcome. Note that each firm will be worse off than it would have been had they been able to enforce an output-restricting agreement and thus achieve the cooperative outcome. This type of game, in which the non-cooperative outcome makes *both* players worse off than if they had been able to cooperate, is called a *prisoners' dilemma*. The reason for this curious name is discussed in *Extensions in Theory 11-1*.

Nash Equilibrium.   The non-cooperative outcome shown in Figure 11-3 is called a **Nash equilibrium**, after the U.S. mathematician John Nash, who developed the concept in the 1950s and received the Nobel Prize in economics in 1994 for this work. (The 2002 movie *A Beautiful Mind* is about John Nash's life and contains a few fascinating bits of game theory!) In a Nash equilibrium, each player's best strategy is to maintain its current behaviour *given the current behaviour of the other players.*

It is easy to see that there is only one Nash equilibrium in Figure 11-3.[1] In the bottom-right cell, the best decision for each firm, given that the other firm is producing two-thirds of the monopoly output, is to produce two-thirds of the monopoly output itself. Between them, they produce a joint output of 1.33 times the monopoly output. Neither firm has an incentive to depart from this position (except through enforceable cooperation with the other). In any other cell, each firm has an incentive to change its output *given the output of the other firm.*

Nash equilibrium An equilibrium that results when each player is currently doing the best it can, given the current behaviour of the other players.

---

[1] In general, an economic "game" may have zero, one, or more Nash equilibria. For an example of an economic setting in which there are two Nash equilibria, see Study Exercise #12 at the end of this chapter.

EXTENSIONS IN THEORY 11-1

The Prisoners' Dilemma

The game shown in Figure 11-3 is often known as a prisoners' dilemma game. This is the story behind the name:

Two men, John and William, are arrested on suspicion of jointly committing a crime and, in the absence of witnesses, are interrogated separately. They know that if they both plead innocence, they will get only a light sentence, and if they both admit guilt they will both receive a medium sentence. Each is told, however, that if either protests innocence while the other admits guilt, the one who claims innocence will get a severe sentence while the other will be released with no sentence at all.

Here is the payoff matrix for that game:

		John's Plea	
		Innocent	**Guilty**
William's Plea	**Innocent**	J light sentence / W light sentence	J no sentence / W severe sentence
	Guilty	J severe sentence / W no sentence	J medium sentence / W medium sentence

John reasons as follows: "William will plead either guilty or innocent. If he pleads innocent, I will get a light sentence if I also plead innocent but no sentence at all if I plead guilty, so guilty is my better plea. If he pleads guilty, I will get a severe sentence if I plead innocent and a medium sentence if I plead guilty. So once again guilty is my preferred plea."

William reasons in the same way and, as a result, they both plead guilty and get a medium sentence. Note, however, that if they had been able to communicate and coordinate their pleas, they could both have agreed to plead innocent and get off with a light sentence.

The prisoners' dilemma arises in many economic situations. We have already seen an example of a two-firm oligopoly. Economists use the basic structure of this simple game to think about how firms compete in their decisions to build new factories, launch advertising campaigns, and adjust the prices of their differentiated products.

Simple game theory and the prisoners' dilemma also figure prominently in the study of political science. Robert Axelrod's 1984 book *The Evolution of Cooperation* discusses how the key insights from the prisoners' dilemma have been used in the analysis of elections (where candidates' choices are their electoral platforms) and the nuclear arms race (in which national governments' choices are their decisions to build and stockpile weapons).*

*For those interested in a very readable treatment of game theory applied to many aspects of life, see *Thinking Strategically* (Norton, 1993) by Avinash Dixit and Barry Nalebuff, two leading economists.

The basis of a Nash equilibrium is rational decision making in the absence of cooperation. Its particular importance in oligopoly theory is that it is a self-policing equilibrium, in the sense that there is no need for group behaviour to enforce it. Each firm has a self-interest to maintain it because no move will improve its profits, given what other firms are currently doing.

If a Nash equilibrium is established by any means whatsoever, no firm has an incentive to depart from it by altering its own behaviour.

Extensions in Game Theory

The simple game that we have just described helps us understand the dilemma faced by oligopolists producing identical products, such as steel, aluminum, cement, newsprint, and copper pipe. But game theory can also be used in other settings, such as examining how oligopoists interact when:

- they charge different prices for their differentiated products, such as Nike and Reebok for running shoes, Coke and Pepsi for soft drinks, or Toshiba and Dell for personal computers;
- the decision is not about how much to produce or what price to charge, but rather whether to develop a new product, such as GM's and Toyota's decisions to introduce an electric car, or Samsung's and Apple's decisions to introduce a new personal mobile device.

For almost any oligopolistic business decision you can imagine, it is possible to describe and analyze the firms' decisions by using game theory. Sometimes the game and the solution are relatively simple, as in Figure 11-3. Often, however, the game and solution are much more complicated. If you take an advanced course in industrial organization you will encounter some of these situations, but the straightforward intuition developed in our simple game can nonetheless help explain a great deal of real-world behaviour.

11.4 OLIGOPOLY IN PRACTICE

We have examined the incentives for firms in an oligopoly to cooperate and the incentives for firms to cheat on any cooperative agreement. We can now look at the behaviour that we actually observe among oligopolists. How do they cooperate? How do they compete?

Cooperative Behaviour

When firms agree to cooperate in order to restrict output and raise prices, their behaviour is called **collusion**. Collusive behaviour may occur with or without an explicit agreement. Where explicit agreement occurs, economists speak of *overt* or *covert collusion*, depending on whether the agreement is open or secret. Where no explicit agreement actually occurs, economists speak of *tacit collusion*. In this case, all firms behave cooperatively without an explicit agreement to do so. They merely understand that it is in their mutual interest to restrict output and to raise prices.

collusion An agreement among sellers to act jointly in their common interest. Collusion may be overt or covert, explicit or tacit.

Explicit Collusion   The easiest way for firms to ensure that they will all maintain their joint profit-maximizing output is to make an explicit agreement. Such collusive agreements have occurred in the past, although they have been illegal among privately owned firms in Canada for a long time (with some exceptions made for firms exporting their product). When they are discovered today, they are rigorously prosecuted. We will see, however, that such agreements are not illegal everywhere in the world, particularly when they are supported by national governments.

We saw in Chapter 10 that when several firms get together to act in this way, they create a *cartel*. Cartels show in stark form the basic conflict between cooperation and competition that we just discussed. Cooperation among cartel members allows them to restrict output and raise prices, thereby increasing the cartel members' profits. But it also presents each cartel member with the incentive to cheat. The larger the number of firms, the greater the temptation for any one of them to cheat. After all, cheating by only one firm may not be noticed because it will have a small effect on price. Conversely, a cartel made up of a small number of firms is more likely to persist because cheating by any one member is more difficult to conceal from the other members.

As we mentioned in Chapter 10, DeBeers is an example of a firm that has been able to assemble a cartel in the world's diamond industry. Through its own Diamond Trading Company (DTC), DeBeers markets approximately 40 percent of the world's annual diamond production. With such influence over the market, it is able to manage the flow of output, in response to changes in world demand, to keep prices high. In recent years, however, the discovery of large diamond mines by firms that wanted to remain independent of DeBeers has led to a reduction in DeBeers' ability to set the market price. In fact, the independent producers—in particular, Canadian producers—have been successful at establishing their own "brand" of diamonds. This has led DeBeers to reduce its efforts through the DTC to manage market prices and instead focus more of its efforts on creating its own brand of diamonds and other luxury products.

The most famous example of a cartel—and the one that has had the most dramatic effect on the world economy—is the Organization of the Petroleum Exporting Countries (OPEC). OPEC first attracted world attention in 1973, when its members agreed to restrict their output of oil. At the time, the OPEC members' collective output represented about 55 percent of total world oil output, and their actions caused the world price of oil to rise by about 300 percent. In 1979–1980, similar actions led to a further doubling of the world price. The next 30 years, however, presented serious challenges to OPEC. First, the incentives for individual cartel members to cheat became unavoidable, and the cartel almost collapsed in the mid-1980s, with large increases in output and dramatic declines in the world price. Second, many discoveries of new oil reserves around the world led to large declines in OPEC's market share, with an associated reduction in the cartel's ability to influence the world price. Today, OPEC controls less than one-third of the world's supply of oil. While the cartel still exists and its members still meet regularly to discuss their output levels, the cartel no longer has the significant effect it once had on the world oil market.

Tacit Collusion   Firms may behave cooperatively without any explicit agreement to do so, simply because each firm recognizes that maximizing their joint profits is in its own interest. This is called *tacit* collusion. However, the same incentive exists for any one firm to behave competitively in an effort to further increase its own profits.

In many industries there is suggestive evidence of tacit collusion, although it is very difficult to prove rigorously. For example, when one large steel company announces that it is raising its price for a specific quality of steel, other steel producers will often announce similar price increases within a day or two. Or when one Canadian bank announces an increase in its interest rate for five-year mortgages, other banks usually increase their rates within a few days. These seemingly coordinated actions may be the result of a secret explicit agreement or of tacit collusion. However, the firms that followed the first firm's price or interest-rate increase could easily argue (and usually do in such cases) that with their competitor raising prices, and thereby driving some customers toward them, the natural response is to raise their own prices.

Competitive Behaviour

Firms in an oligopoly often choose to compete actively with each other in an attempt to attract consumers away from their rivals, to increase their overall share of the market, and to increase their profits. Such actions are generally good for consumers because they result in lower prices, better products, or better service. For the firms engaged in such competition, however, it can be a real challenge.

Oligopolistic firms producing differentiated products often compete very little through prices. Sometimes the most aggressive competition takes place through their continual processes of innovation, as well as the introduction of new products.

Winners find their profits rising and their business expanding; losers see their business shrinking and profits falling.

Three major types of competitive behaviour are worth noting. First, firms with differentiated products may compete by reducing their prices and hoping to attract customers away from their rivals. This behaviour is common among car makers, cell-phone service providers, and commercial banks.

Second, firms often actively engage in non-price competition, especially through advertising campaigns and variations in product quality. The markets for fast food, consumer electronics, laundry detergent, disposable diapers, and a whole range of familiar consumer products display this kind of competition.

Finally, many firms find that they can keep a step ahead of their rivals by developing new products or by making significant improvements in existing ones. As we saw in Chapter 10, the Austrian economist Joseph Schumpeter emphasized the process of "creative destruction" as a crucial means by which one firm tries to usurp another firm's market power. Such competition through innovation is an important force driving improvements in our long-run living standards.

> There are strong incentives for oligopolists to compete with each other through pricing, advertising, product quality, and innovation. Consumers usually gain from such competition.

An obvious example of oligopolistic competition through innovation is Apple's ongoing development of new products. In the last decade, Apple has been highly successful with its iPod, iPhone, and iPad and is currently developing an iTV. In each case, the features and remarkable consumer appeal of the products not only took sales away from Apple's rivals (such as Samsung and Nokia) but also expanded the total market by attracting consumers who previously owned no such products. But Apple's enormous success has attracted the entry of rivals, as is so often the case. Microsoft, which for many years focused only on the development of software, has now entered the market for electronic devices and is building a network of retail stores to compete against the iconic Apple stores. The next few years should see some fascinating rivalry between these two technology titans.

The Importance of Entry Barriers

Suppose firms in an oligopolistic industry succeed in raising prices above long-run average costs and earn substantial profits that are not completely eliminated by competition among them. Without significant entry barriers, new firms will enter the industry and erode the profits of existing firms, as they do in monopolistic competition. Natural barriers to entry were discussed in Chapter 10, the most important being a large minimum efficient scale. This type of entry barrier is an important part of the explanation of the persistence of profits in many oligopolistic industries.

Where such natural entry barriers do not exist, however, oligopolistic firms can earn profits in the long run only if they can *create* entry barriers. To the extent this is done, existing firms can continue to enjoy high profits without fear that new firms will enter the industry. We now discuss three important types of *firm-created* entry barriers.

1. Brand Proliferation as an Entry Barrier   By altering the characteristics of a differentiated product, it is possible to produce a vast array of variations on the general theme of that product, each with its unique identifying brand. Think, for example, of the many different brands of soap or shampoo, breakfast cereals or cookies, and even cars or motorcycles. In these cases, each firm in the industry produces *several* brands of the differentiated product.

Although such brand proliferation is no doubt partly a response to consumers' tastes, it can also have the effect of discouraging the entry of new firms. To see why, suppose the product is the type for which there is a substantial amount of brand switching by consumers. In this case, the larger the number of brands sold by existing firms, the smaller the expected sales of a new entrant.

Suppose, for example, that an industry contains three large firms, each selling one brand of beer, and say that 30 percent of all beer drinkers change brands in a random fashion each year. If a new firm enters the industry, it can expect to pick up one-third of the customers who change brands (a customer who switches brands now has three *other* brands among which to choose). The new firm would get 10 percent (one-third of 30 percent) of the total market the first year merely as a result of picking up its share of the random switchers, and it would keep increasing its share for some time thereafter. If, however, the existing three firms have five brands each, there would be 15 brands already available, and a new firm selling one new brand could expect to pick up only one-fifteenth of the brand switchers, giving it only 2 percent of the total market the first year, with smaller gains also in subsequent years. This is an extreme case, but it illustrates a general result.

> The larger the number of differentiated products that are sold by existing oligopolists, the smaller the market share available to a new firm that is entering with a single new product. Brand proliferation therefore can be an effective entry barrier.

2. Advertising as an Entry Barrier   In addition to producing useful information about existing products, advertising can operate as a potent entry barrier by increasing the costs of new entrants. Where heavy advertising has established strong brand images for existing products, a new firm may have to spend heavily on advertising to create its own brand images in consumers' minds. If the firm's sales are small, advertising costs *per unit* will be large, and price will have to be correspondingly high to cover those costs. Consider Nike, Reebok, and their competitors. They advertise not so much the quality of their athletic shoes as images that they want consumers to associate with the shoes. The same is true for cosmetics, beer, cars, hamburgers, and many more consumer goods. Successful ads are usually expensive to produce and can constitute a formidable entry barrier for a new producer.

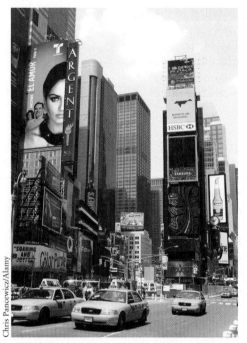

Chris Pancewicz/Alamy

Advertising can be very informative for consumers. But by raising the costs of new entrants, advertising can also act as a potent entry barrier.

A new entrant with small sales but large required advertising costs finds itself at a substantial cost disadvantage relative to its established rivals.

The combined use of brand proliferation and advertising also creates a powerful entry barrier. The soap and beer industries provide classic examples of this behaviour. Because all available scale economies can be realized by quite small plants, both industries have few natural barriers to entry. Both contain a few large firms, each of which produces an array of heavily advertised products. The proliferation of brands makes it harder for a new entrant to obtain a large market niche with a single new product. The heavy advertising, although directed against existing products, creates an entry barrier by increasing the average costs of any new firm trying to establish its own brand image.

3. Predatory Pricing as an Entry Barrier   A firm will not enter a market if it expects continued losses after entry. An existing firm can create such an expectation by cutting prices below costs whenever entry occurs and keeping them there until the entrant goes bankrupt. The existing firm sacrifices profits while doing this, but it sends a discouraging message to potential future rivals, as well as to present ones. Even if this strategy is costly in terms of lost profits in the short run, it may pay for itself in the long run by creating *reputation effects* that deter the entry of new firms at other times or in other markets that the firm controls. Predatory pricing is illegal in Canada and a number of firms have been convicted of using it as a method of restricting entry.

Oligopoly and the Economy

Oligopoly is found in many industries and in all advanced economies. It typically occurs in industries with significant economies of scale. In such industries, there is simply not enough room for a large number of firms all operating at or near their minimum efficient scales.

Two questions are important for assessing the extent to which oligopoly is beneficial for society. First, in their short-run and long-run outcomes, where do oligopolistic firms typically settle between the extreme outcomes of earning zero profits and earning monopoly profits? Second, how much do oligopolists contribute to economic growth by encouraging innovative activity in the very long run?

Profits Under Oligopoly   Some firms in some oligopolistic industries succeed in coming close to joint profit maximization in the short run. In other oligopolistic industries, firms compete so intensely among themselves that they come close to achieving competitive prices and outputs. To the extent that price remains above competitive levels (and output below), oligopoly will be less efficient than perfect competition, with implied welfare losses for society as a whole.

In the long run, those profits that do survive competitive behaviour among existing firms will tend to attract entry. Profits will persist only insofar as entry is restricted either by natural barriers, such as large minimum efficient scales for potential entrants, or by barriers created, and successfully defended, by the existing firms or, perhaps, created by government regulations.

Oligopoly and Innovation   Is oligopoly conducive to innovation? As we discussed in Chapter 8, innovation and productivity improvements are the driving force of the economic growth that has so greatly raised living standards over the past two centuries. They are intimately related to Schumpeter's concept of creative destruction, which we first encountered in our discussion of entry barriers in Chapter 10.

Examples of creative destruction abound. In the nineteenth century, railways began to compete with wagons and barges for the carriage of freight. In the twentieth century, trucks operating on newly constructed highways began competing with trains. During the 1950s and 1960s, airplanes began to compete seriously with both trucks and trains. Cellphones have significantly weakened the monopoly power that telephone companies had for the provision of local phone service. The ability of consumers to easily download or stream all types of news and entertainment has dramatically reduced the market power of firms in the newspaper, publishing, television, and music industries.

An important defence of oligopoly is based on Schumpeter's idea of creative destruction. Some economists argue that oligopoly leads to more innovation than would occur in either perfect competition or monopoly. They argue that the oligopolist faces strong competition from existing rivals and cannot afford the more relaxed life of the monopolist. Moreover, oligopolistic firms expect to keep a good share of the profits they earn from their innovative activity and thus have considerable incentive to innovate.

Everyday observation provides support for this view. Leading North American firms that operate in highly concentrated industries, such as Alcoa, Amazon, Apple, Canfor, Bombardier, DuPont, General Electric, Google, Canadian National, Microsoft Xerox, and Boeing, have been highly innovative over many years.

This observation is not meant to suggest that *only* oligopolistic industries are innovative. Much innovation is also done by very small, new firms. If today's small firms are successful in their innovation, they may become tomorrow's corporate giants. For example, Microsoft, Amazon, Apple, and Intel, which are enormous firms today, barely existed 40 years ago; their rise from new start-up firms to corporate giants reflects their powers of innovation.

Oligopoly is an important market structure in modern economies because there are many industries in which the minimum efficient scale is simply too large to support many competing firms. The challenge to public policy is to keep oligopolists competing, rather than colluding, and using their competitive energies to improve products and to reduce costs, rather than merely to erect entry barriers.

SUMMARY

11.1 IMPERFECT COMPETITION

- Most industries in the Canadian economy lie between the two extremes of monopoly and perfect competition. Within this spectrum of market structure we can divide Canadian industries into two broad groups: those with a large number of relatively small firms and those with a small number of relatively large firms. Such intermediate market structures are called imperfectly competitive.
- When measuring whether an industry has power concentrated in the hands of only a few firms or dispersed over many, it is not sufficient to count the firms.

Instead, economists consider the concentration ratio, which shows the fraction of total market sales controlled by a group of the largest sellers.
- Most firms operating in imperfectly competitive market structures sell differentiated products whose characteristics they choose themselves.
- Imperfectly competitive firms usually choose their prices and engage in non-price competition, including advertising and varying product qualities.

11.2 MONOPOLISTIC COMPETITION

- Monopolistic competition is a market structure that has the same characteristics as perfect competition except that the many firms each sell a differentiated product rather than all selling a single homogeneous product. Firms face negatively sloped demand curves and may earn profits in the short run.
- As in a perfectly competitive industry, the long run in the theory of monopolistic competition sees new firms enter the industry whenever profits can be made.

Long-run equilibrium in the industry requires that each firm earn zero profits.
- In long-run equilibrium in the theory of monopolistic competition, each firm produces less than its minimum-cost level of output. This is the excess-capacity theorem associated with monopolistic competition.
- Even though each firm produces at a cost that is higher than the minimum attainable cost, the resulting product variety is valued by consumers and so may be worth the extra cost.

11.3 OLIGOPOLY AND GAME THEORY

- Oligopolies are dominated by a few large firms that have significant market power. They can maximize their joint profits if they cooperate to produce the monopoly output. By acting individually, each firm has an incentive to depart from this cooperative outcome.
- Oligopolists have difficulty cooperating to maximize joint profits unless they have a way of enforcing their output-restricting agreement.

- Economists use game theory to analyze the strategic behaviour of oligopolists—that is, how each firm will behave when it recognizes that other firms may respond to its actions.
- A possible non-cooperative outcome is a Nash equilibrium in which each player is doing the best it can, given the actions of all other players.

11.4 OLIGOPOLY IN PRACTICE

- Explicit collusion between oligopolists is illegal in domestic markets. But it can take place in situations where firms in global markets are supported by national governments, as is the case for OPEC.
- Tacit collusion is possible but may break down as firms struggle for market share, indulge in non-price competition, and seek advantages through the introduction of new technology.

- Oligopolistic industries will exhibit profits in the long run only if there are significant barriers to entry. Natural barriers are most commonly due to economies of scale. Firm-created barriers can be formed by brand proliferation, advertising, and the threat of predatory pricing when new entry occurs.
- Evaluation of oligopoly depends on how much interfirm competition (a) drives the firms away from the cooperative, profit-maximizing solution and (b) leads to innovations in the very long run.

KEY CONCEPTS

Concentration ratios
Product differentiation
Monopolistic competition
The excess-capacity theorem
Oligopoly

Strategic behaviour
Game theory
Cooperative and non-cooperative
  outcomes
Nash equilibrium

Explicit and tacit collusion
Natural and firm-created entry
  barriers
Oligopoly and creative destruction

STUDY EXERCISES

MyEconLab Make the grade with MyEconLab: Study Exercises marked in ⬤ can be found on MyEconLab. You can practise them as often as you want, and most feature step-by-step guided instructions to help you find the right answer.

❶ Fill in the blanks to make the following statements correct.

a. Suppose the four largest steel producers in Canada among them control 85 percent of total market sales. We would say that this industry is highly _____. We say that 85 percent is the _____ in this industry.

b. A firm that has the ability to set prices faces a _____ demand curve.

c. The theory of monopolistic competition helps explain industries with a _____ number of _____ firms. The theory of oligopoly helps explain industries with a _____ number of _____ firms.

d. A firm operating in a monopolistically competitive market structure maximizes profits by equating _____ and _____. A firm that is operating in an oligopolistic market structure maximizes profit by equating _____ and _____ although its rivals' responses to its actions will affect its _____.

e. In long-run equilibrium, and in comparison to perfect competition, monopolistic competition produces a _____ range of products but at a _____ cost per unit.

❷ Fill in the blanks to make the following statements correct.

a. Economists say that oligopolistic firms exhibit _____ behaviour. These firms are aware of and take account of the decisions of _____.

b. The firms in an oligopoly have a collective incentive to _____ in order to maximize joint _____; individually, each firm has an incentive to _____ in order to maximize individual _____.

c. Oligopolistic firms exhibit profits in the long run only if there are significant _____.

d. Three examples of entry barriers that firms with market power can create are _____, _____, and _____.

e. An important defence of oligopoly is the idea that it leads to more _____ than would occur in either perfect competition or monopoly. The oligopolistic firm has an incentive to _____ because it can expect to keep a good share of the resulting profit.

❸ Each of the statements below describes a characteristic of the following market structures: perfect competition, monopolistic competition, oligopoly, and monopoly. Identify which market structure displays each of the characteristics. (There may be more than one.)

a. Each firm faces a downward-sloping demand curve.

b. Price is greater than marginal revenue.

c. Each firm produces at *MES* in long-run equilibrium.

d. Firms earn profit in long-run equilibrium.

e. Firms produce a homogeneous product.

f. Firms advertise their product.

g. Each firm produces output where $MC = MR$.

h. Each firm produces output where $P = MC$.

i. There is free entry to the industry.

j. Firms produce a differentiated product.

❹ Do you think any of the following industries might be monopolistically competitive? Why or why not?

a. Textbook publishing (approximately 10 introductory economics textbooks are in use on campuses in this year)

b. Post-secondary education

c. Cigarette manufacturing

d. Restaurant operation

e. Automobile retailing

f. Landscaping services

g. Home renovation firms

5 The following table provides annual sales for the four largest firms in four industries in Canada. Also provided are total Canadian and total world sales for the industry. (All figures are hypothetical and are in millions of dollars.)

a. Suppose Canada does not trade internationally any of the goods produced in these industries. Compute the four-firm Canadian concentration ratio for each industry.

b. Rank the industries in order from the most concentrated to the least concentrated.

c. Now suppose goods in these industries are freely traded around the world. Are the concentration ratios from part (a) still relevant? Explain.

	Firm 1	Firm 2	Firm 3	Firm 4	Total Sales (Canada)	Total Sales (World)
Forestry products	185	167	98	47	550	1368
Chemicals	27	24	9	4	172	2452
Women's clothing	6	5	4	2	94	3688
Pharmaceuticals	44	37	22	19	297	2135

6 The table below provides price, revenue, and cost information for a monopolistically competitive firm selling drive-through car washes in a large city.

a. Complete the table.
b. Plot the demand, marginal revenue, marginal cost, and average cost curves for the firm. (Be sure to plot MR and MC at the midpoint of the output intervals.)

c. What is the profit-maximizing number of car washes (per month)?
d. What is the profit-maximizing price?
e. Calculate the total maximum profit (per month).
f. How can this firm differentiate its product from other car washes?

Quantity (number of car washes per month)	Price	Total Revenue	Marginal Revenue	Total Cost	Average Total Cost	Marginal Cost	Total Profit
1000	30	___		25 000	___		___
1100	29	___	___	26 000	___	___	___
1200	28	___	___	27 200	___	___	___
1300	27	___	___	28 500	___	___	___
1400	26	___	___	30 000	___	___	___
1500	25	___	___	32 200	___	___	___
1600	24	___	___	35 000	___	___	___
1700	23	___	___	38 500	___	___	___
1800	22	___	___	43 000	___	___	___

7 Draw two diagrams of a monopolistically competitive firm. In the first, show the firm earning profits in the short run. In the second, show the firm in long-run equilibrium earning zero profits. What changed for this firm between the short run and the long run?

8 The following figure shows the revenue and cost curves for a typical monopolistically competitive firm in the short run.

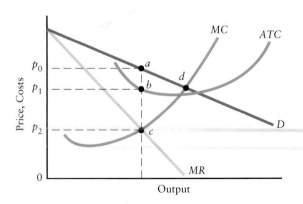

a. Note that the firm's demand curve is shown to be quite flat. Explain which assumption of monopolistic competition suggests a relatively elastic demand curve for each firm.

b. Show the profit-maximizing level of output for the firm on the diagram.

c. At the profit-maximizing level of output, are profits positive or negative? What area in the diagram represents the firm's profits?

d. Will firms enter or exit the industry? Explain.

9 The diagram below shows a typical monopolistically competitive firm when the industry is in long-run equilibrium.

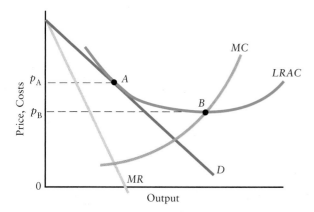

a. Explain why free entry and exit implies that the long-run equilibrium is at point A.

b. What is the significance of point B and price p_B?

c. Explain why long-run equilibrium in monopolistic competition can be considered to be less efficient than in perfect competition. Explain why that may not be the case.

10 In the text we argued that a key difference between monopolistic competition and oligopoly is that in the former firms do not behave *strategically* whereas in the latter they do. For each of the goods or services listed below, state whether the industries are likely to be best described by monopolistic competition or oligopoly. Explain your reasoning.

a. Car repair
b. Haircuts
c. Dry cleaning
d. Soft drinks
e. Breakfast cereals
f. Restaurant (not fast food) meals
g. Automobiles

11 Consider the following industries in Canada that have traditionally been oligopolistic:
- Brewing
- Airlines
- Railways
- Banking
- Internet service providers
- Grocery stores

a. What are the barriers to entry in each of these industries that might explain persistently high profits?

b. Explain in each case how technology is changing in ways that circumvent these entry barriers.

12 The table below is the payoff matrix for a simple two-firm game. Firms A and B are bidding on a government contract, and each firm's bid is not known by the other firm. Each firm can bid either $10 000 or $5000. The cost of completing the project for each firm is $4000. The low-bid firm will win the contract at its stated price; the high-bid firm will get nothing. If the two bids are equal, the two firms will split the price and costs evenly. The payoffs for each firm under each situation are shown in the matrix.

	A bids $10 000	A bids $5000
B bids $10 000	Firms share the contract	A wins the contract
	Payoff to A = $3000	Payoff to A = $1000
	Payoff to B = $3000	Payoff to B = $0
B bids $5000	B wins the contract	Firms share the contract
	Payoff to A = $0	Payoff to A = $500
	Payoff to B = $1000	Payoff to B = $500

a. Recall from the text that a Nash equilibrium is an outcome in which each player is maximizing his or her own payoff *given the actions of the other players.* Is there a Nash equilibrium in this game?

b. Is there more than one Nash equilibrium? Explain.

c. If the two firms could cooperate, what outcome would you predict in this game? Explain.

13 The table below shows the payoff matrix for a game between Toyota and Honda, each of which is contemplating building a factory in a new market. Each firm can either build a small factory (and produce a small number of cars) or build a large factory (and produce a large number of cars). Suppose no other car manufacturers are selling in this market.

		Toyota's Decision	
		Small Factory	Large Factory
Honda's Decision	Small Factory	*High Industry Price*	*Medium Industry Price*
		Honda profits: $20 million	Honda profits: $12 million
		Toyota profits: $20 million	Toyota profits: $25 million
	Large Factory	*Medium Industry Price*	*Low Industry Price*
		Honda profits: $25 million	Honda profits: $14 million
		Toyota profits: $12 million	Toyota profits: $14 million

a. Assuming that the demand curve for cars in this new market is negatively sloped and unchanging, explain the economic reasoning behind the prices and profits shown in each cell in the payoff matrix.

b. What is the cooperative outcome in this game? Is it likely to be achievable? Explain.

c. What is Honda's best action? Does it depend on Toyata's action?

d. What is Toyata's best action? Does it depend on Honda's action?

e. What is the non-cooperative outcome in this game? Is it a Nash equilibrium?

12

Economic Efficiency and Public Policy

CHAPTER OUTLINE	LEARNING OBJECTIVES (LO)
	After studying this chapter you will be able to
12.1 PRODUCTIVE AND ALLOCATIVE EFFICIENCY	**1** distinguish between productive efficiency and allocative efficiency.
	2 explain why perfect competition is allocatively efficient, whereas monopoly is allocatively inefficient.
12.2 ECONOMIC REGULATION TO PROMOTE EFFICIENCY	**3** describe alternative methods for regulating a natural monopoly.
12.3 CANADIAN COMPETITION POLICY	**4** discuss some details about Canadian competition policy.

IN the previous three chapters we examined various market structures, from perfect competition at one end of the spectrum to monopoly at the other end. In the middle were two forms of imperfect competition: monopolistic competition and oligopoly. We have considered how firms behave in these various market structures, and we are now able to evaluate the *efficiency* of the market structures. Then we will see why economists are suspicious of monopolistic practices and seek to encourage competitive behaviour. Table 12-1 provides a review of the four market structures and the industry characteristics relevant to each.

We begin our discussion in this chapter by examining the various concepts of efficiency used by economists. This discussion will develop more fully the concept of efficiency we first saw at the end of Chapter 5. We then discuss how public policy deals with the challenges of monopoly and oligopoly in an effort to improve the efficiency of the economy.

12.1 PRODUCTIVE AND ALLOCATIVE EFFICIENCY

Efficiency requires that factors of production be fully employed. However, full employment of resources is not enough to prevent the *waste* of resources. Even when resources are fully employed, they may be used inefficiently. Here are three examples of inefficiency in the use of fully employed resources.

1. If firms do not use the least-cost method of producing their chosen outputs, they are being inefficient. For example, a firm that produces 30 000 pairs of shoes at a resource cost of $400 000 when it could have been done at a cost of only $350 000 is using resources inefficiently. The lower-cost method would allow $50 000 worth of resources to be transferred to other productive uses.

2. If the marginal cost of production is not the same for every firm in an industry, the industry is being inefficient. For example, if the cost of producing the last tonne of steel is higher for some firms than for others, the industry's overall cost of producing a given amount of steel is higher than necessary. The same amount of steel could be produced at lower total cost if the total output were distributed differently among the various producers.

3. If too much of one product and too little of another product are produced, the economy's resources are being used inefficiently. To take an extreme example, suppose so many shoes are produced that every consumer has all the shoes he or she could possibly want and thus places a zero value on obtaining an additional pair of shoes. Suppose also that so few coats are produced that consumers place a high value on obtaining an additional coat. In these circumstances, consumers can be made better off if resources are reallocated from shoe production, where the last shoe produced has a low value in the eyes of each consumer, to coat production, where one more coat produced would have a higher value to each consumer.

These three examples illustrate inefficiency in the use of resources. But the *type* of inefficiency is different in each case. The first example considers the cost for a single firm producing some level of output. The second example is related, but the focus is on the total cost for all the firms in an industry. The third example relates to the level of output of one product compared with another. Let's explore these three types of inefficiency in more detail.

TABLE 12-1	Review of Four Market Structures
Market Structure	Industry Characteristics
Perfect competition	• Many small firms • Firms sell identical products • All firms are price takers • Free entry and exit • Zero profits in long-run equilibrium • Price = MC
Monopolistic competition	• Many small firms • Firms sell differentiated products • Each firm has some power to set price • Free entry and exit • Zero profits in long-run equilibrium • Price > MC; less output than in perfect competition; excess capacity
Oligopoly	• Few firms, usually large • Strategic behaviour among firms • Firms often sell differentiated products and are price setters • Often significant entry barriers • Usually economies of scale • Profits depend on the nature of firm rivalry and on entry barriers • Price usually > MC; output usually less than in perfect competition
Monopoly	• Single firm faces the entire market demand • Firm is a price setter • Profits persist if sufficient entry barriers • Price > MC; less output than in perfect competition

Productive Efficiency

Productive efficiency has two aspects, one concerning production within each firm and one concerning the allocation of production among the firms in an industry. The first two examples above relate to these two different aspects of productive efficiency.

Productive efficiency for the firm requires that the firm produce any given level of output at the lowest possible cost. In the short run, with at least one fixed factor, the firm merely uses enough of the variable factors to produce the desired level of output. In the long run, however, more methods of production are available. Productive efficiency requires that the firm use the least costly of the available methods of producing any given output—that is, firms are located on, rather than above, their long-run average cost curves.

> **productive efficiency for the firm** When the firm chooses among all available production methods to produce a given level of output at the lowest possible cost.

> Productive efficiency for the firm requires the firm to be producing its output at the lowest possible cost.

Any firm that is not being productively efficient is producing at a higher cost than is necessary and thus will have lower profits than it could have. It follows that any profit-maximizing firm will seek to be productively efficient no matter the market structure within which it operates—perfect competition, monopoly, oligopoly, or monopolistic competition.

Productive efficiency for the industry requires that the industry's total output be allocated among its individual firms in such a way that the total cost in the industry is minimized. If an industry is productively *inefficient*, it is possible to reduce the industry's total cost of producing any given output by reallocating production among the industry's firms.

> **productive efficiency for the industry** When the industry is producing a given level of output at the lowest possible cost. This requires that marginal cost be equated across all firms in the industry.

> Productive efficiency for the industry requires that the marginal cost of production be the same for each firm.

To see why marginal costs must be equated across firms, consider a simple example that is illustrated in Figure 12-1. Aslan Widget Company has a marginal cost of $80 for the last widget of some standard type it produces. Digory Enterprises has a marginal cost of only $40 for its last widget of the same type. If Aslan were to produce one fewer widget and Digory were to produce one more widget, total production would be unchanged. Total industry costs, however, would be lower by $40.

Clearly, this cost saving can go on as long as the two firms have different marginal costs. However, as Aslan produces fewer widgets, its marginal cost falls, and as Digory produces more widgets, its marginal cost rises. Once marginal cost is equated across the two firms, at a marginal cost of $60 in the figure, there are no further cost savings to be obtained by reallocating production. Only at this point is the industry productively efficient.

Over the next few pages we will see how such an efficient allocation of output across firms is achieved, but for now the point is simply that if marginal costs are not equated across firms, then a reallocation of output is necessary in order for the industry to become productively efficient.

Productive Efficiency and the Production Possibilities Boundary   If firms are productively efficient, they are minimizing their costs; there is no way for them to increase output without using more resources. If an industry is productively efficient, the industry as a whole is producing its output at the lowest possible cost; the industry could not increase its output without using more resources.

FIGURE 12-1 **Productive Efficiency for the Industry**

Aslan Widget Co.   Digory Enterprises

Productive efficiency for the industry requires that marginal costs for the production of any one product be equated across firms. At the initial levels of output, Q_A and Q_D, marginal costs are $80 for Aslan and $40 for Digory. If Digory increases output by ΔQ to Q'_D and Aslan reduces output by the same amount ΔQ to Q'_A, total output is unchanged. Aslan's total costs have fallen by the green shaded area, whereas Digory's total costs have increased by the smaller purple shaded area. Total industry costs are therefore reduced when output is reallocated between the firms. When marginal costs are equalized, at $60 in this example, no further reallocation of output can reduce costs—productive efficiency will have been achieved.

Now think about the economy's production possibilities boundary (PPB), which we first saw in Chapter 1 and which is shown again in Figure 12-2. The PPB shows the combinations of output of two products that are possible when the economy is using its resources *efficiently.* An economy that is producing at a point inside the PPB is being productively inefficient—it could produce more of one good without producing less of the other. This inefficiency may occur because individual firms are not minimizing their costs or because, within an industry, marginal costs are not equalized across the various firms. Either situation would lead the economy to be inside its production possibilities boundary.

> **If firms and industries are productively efficient, the economy will be on, rather than inside, the production possibilities boundary.**

In Figure 12-2, every point on the PPB is productively efficient. Is there one point on the PPB that is "better" in some way than the others? The answer is yes, and this brings us to the concept of *allocative efficiency.*

Allocative Efficiency

allocative efficiency A situation in which the output of each good is such that its market price and marginal cost are equal.

Allocative efficiency concerns the quantities of the various products to be produced. When the combination of goods produced is allocatively efficient, economists say that the economy is *Pareto efficient,* in honour of nineteenth-century Italian economist Vilfredo Pareto (1843–1923), who developed this concept of efficiency.

How do we find the allocatively efficient point on the production possibilities boundary? The answer is as follows:

> The economy is allocatively efficient when, for each good produced, its marginal cost of production is equal to its price.

To understand this answer, recall our discussion in Chapters 5 and 6 about the marginal value that consumers place on the next unit of some good. When utility-maximizing consumers face the market price for some good, they adjust their consumption of the good until their marginal value is just equal to the price. Since price then reflects the marginal value of the good to consumers, we can restate the condition for allocative efficiency to be that for each good produced, marginal cost must equal marginal value.[1]

If the level of output of some product is such that marginal cost to producers exceeds marginal value to consumers, too much of that product is being produced, because the cost to society of the last unit produced exceeds the benefits of consuming it. Conversely, if the level of output of some good is such that the marginal cost is less than the marginal value, too little of that good is being produced, because the cost to society of producing the next unit is less than the benefits that would be gained from consuming it.

Allocative Efficiency and the Production Possibilities Boundary

Figure 12-3 shows a production possibilities boundary in an economy that can produce wheat and steel, and also shows the individual supply-and-demand diagrams for the two markets. Notice that the vertical axis in each of the supply-and-demand diagrams shows the *relative* price of the appropriate good. For example, in the market for wheat, the relevant price is the price of wheat *relative to the price of steel*. This is consistent with our initial treatment of supply and demand in Chapter 3, in which we held constant all other prices and then examined how the price of any specific product was determined.

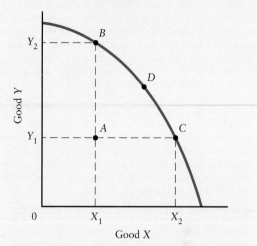

FIGURE 12-2 **Productive Efficiency and the Production Possibilities Boundary**

Any point on the production possibilities boundary is productively efficient. The boundary shows all combinations of two goods X and Y that can be produced when the economy's resources are fully employed and productively efficient.

Any point inside the curve, such as A, is productively inefficient. If the inefficiency exists in industry X, then either some producer of X is productively inefficient or industry X as a whole is productively inefficient. In either case, it is possible to increase total production of X without using more resources, and thus without reducing the output of Y. This would take the economy from point A to point C. Similarly, if the inefficiency exists in industry Y, production of Y could be increased, moving the economy from point A to point B.

Figure 12-3 illustrates how the allocation of resources in the economy changes as we move along the production possibilities boundary. For example, as the economy moves from point A to point B to point C along the PPB, resources are being transferred from the steel sector to the wheat sector, so steel output is falling and wheat output is rising.

What is the allocatively efficient combination of steel and wheat output in this economy? Allocative efficiency will be achieved when in each market the marginal cost of producing the good equals the marginal value of consuming the good. In Figure 12-3, allocative efficiency is achieved at point B, with S_B steel being produced and W_B wheat being produced.

---

[1]Allocative efficiency is exactly the same concept as market efficiency that we discussed in Chapter 5. Now that we have introduced the distinction between productive and allocative efficiency, we will continue to use these two terms only.

FIGURE 12-3 Allocative Efficiency and the Production Possibilities Boundary

Allocative efficiency requires that all goods be produced to the point where the marginal cost to producers equals the marginal value to consumers. The production possibilities boundary shows the combinations of wheat and steel that are possible if firms and industries are productively efficient. The lower diagrams show the marginal cost (supply) and marginal value (demand) curves in each industry.

At point A, steel output is S_A and wheat output is W_A. As the lower figures show, however, at W_A the marginal value of wheat consumption exceeds its marginal cost of production. Thus, society would be better off if more wheat were produced. Similarly, at S_A the marginal cost of steel production exceeds its marginal value to consumers, and thus society would be better off with less steel being produced.

Point A is therefore not allocatively efficient; there is too little wheat and too much steel being produced. The argument is similar at point C, at which there is too much wheat and too little steel being produced. Only at point B is each good produced to the point where the marginal cost to producers is equal to the marginal value to consumers. Only point B is allocatively efficient.

Which Market Structures Are Efficient?

We now know that for productive efficiency, all firms must be minimizing their costs and marginal cost should be the same for all firms in any one industry. For allocative efficiency, marginal cost should be equal to price in each industry. Do the market structures we have studied in earlier chapters lead to productive and allocative efficiency? Here is a brief point-form assessment.

Perfect Competition

- In long-run equilibrium, each perfectly competitive firm is producing at the lowest point on its *LRAC* curve. Therefore, every profit-maximizing firm is productively efficient.
- All firms face the same market price and equate their own marginal cost to that price, so marginal cost is equated across all firms. Therefore, in a perfectly competitive industry with profit-maximizing firms, the industry as a whole is productively efficient.
- If perfect competition were the market structure for the whole economy, price would be equal to marginal cost in each industry, resulting in allocative efficiency across the entire economy.
- While specific industries may be perfectly competitive and allocatively efficient, entire modern economies are neither perfectly competitive nor allocatively efficient.

Monopoly

- A monopolist's profits will be maximized when it adopts the lowest-cost production method, which means that a profit-maximizing monopolist will operate on its *LRAC* curve, and will therefore be productively efficient. Since the firm is alone in the industry, it follows that the industry is also productively efficient.
- For a profit-maximizing monopolist, price is greater than marginal cost. The marginal value to consumers therefore exceeds the marginal cost of production, and so monopoly is not allocatively efficient.

Monopolistic Competition and Oligopoly

- Monopolistic competitors and oligopolists maximize their profits when they adopt the lowest-cost method of production. Profit-maximizing firms in each of these market structures operate on their *LRAC* curves and are therefore productively efficient.
- It is not possible to say whether the *industry* in either of these market structures will be productively efficient. Since these firms sell differentiated products and there is no single industry-wide price, it is impossible to conclude that marginal costs will be equated across all firms.
- For both oligopoly and monopolistic competition, price exceeds marginal cost, so neither market structure is allocatively efficient. For oligopoly, however, there are some situations where rivalry between firms drives price *toward* marginal cost, improving efficiency.

Allocative Efficiency and Total Surplus

By using the concepts of marginal value to consumers and the marginal cost of production, we have established the basic points of productive and allocative efficiency. A different way of thinking about allocative efficiency—though completely consistent with the first approach—is to use the concepts of consumer and producer surplus, both of which are part of the economic surplus that we first introduced in Chapter 5.

Consumer and Producer Surplus   Recall from Chapter 6 that consumer surplus is the difference between the value that consumers place on a product and the payment that they actually make to buy that product. In Figure 12-4, if the competitive market price is p_0 and consumers buy Q_0 units of the product, consumer surplus is the blue shaded area.

Producer surplus is an analogous concept to consumer surplus. **Producer surplus** is the difference between the actual price that the producer receives for a product and the lowest price that the producer would be willing to accept for the sale of that product. By producing one more unit, the producer's costs increase by the marginal cost, and this is the lowest amount that the producer will accept for the product. To accept any amount less than the marginal cost would *reduce* the firm's profits.

producer surplus The price of a good minus the marginal cost of producing it, summed over the quantity produced.

> For each unit sold, producer surplus is the difference between price and marginal cost.

For a producer that sells many units of the product, total producer surplus is the difference between price and marginal cost summed over all the units sold. So, for an individual producer, total producer surplus is the area above the marginal cost curve and below the price line.

For the industry as a whole, we need to know the industry supply curve in order to compute overall producer surplus. Since in perfect competition the industry supply curve is simply the horizontal sum of all firms' *MC* curves, producer surplus in a perfectly competitive market is the area above the market supply curve and below the price line, as shown in Figure 12-4.

The Allocative Efficiency of Perfect Competition Revisited   In Chapter 5 we said that (allocative) efficiency exists in a market if the total economic surplus is maximized. At that point, we did not make the distinction between the two parts of total surplus—consumer surplus and producer surplus. Now that we have identified these different parts of total surplus, we can restate the conditions for allocative efficiency in a slightly different way.

> Allocative efficiency occurs at the level of output where the sum of consumer and producer surplus is maximized.

In a perfectly competitive market, the allocatively efficient level of output occurs where the demand and supply curves intersect—that is, at

FIGURE 12-4   Consumer and Producer Surplus in a Competitive Market

Consumer surplus is the area under the demand curve and above the market price line. Producer surplus is the area above the supply curve and below the market price line. The total value that consumers place on Q_0 of the commodity is given by the area under the demand curve up to Q_0. The amount they pay is the rectangle p_0Q_0. The difference, shown as the blue shaded area, is consumer surplus.

The revenue to producers from the sale of Q_0 units is p_0Q_0. The area under the supply curve is the minimum amount producers require to supply the output. The difference, shown as the red shaded area, is producer surplus.

equilibrium. This level of output is shown at Q^* in Figure 12-5. For any level of output below Q^*, the demand curve lies above the supply curve, which tells us (1) that consumers value an extra unit of the product *more* than it costs to produce it, and (2) that society is better off if more of that product is produced. Notice that if output is only Q_1 there is no consumer or producer surplus earned on the units between Q_1 and Q^*. Thus, the areas 1 and 2 in Figure 12-5 represent a loss to the economy. Total surplus—consumer plus producer surplus— is lower at Q_1 than at Q^*.

For any level of output above Q^*, the demand curve lies below the supply curve, which tells us (1) that consumers value an extra unit of the product *less* than it costs to produce it, and (2) that society is better off if less of that product is produced. If output is Q_2, total surplus is less than it is at Q^*. To see this, suppose that the price is p^*. Producers would earn *negative* producer surplus on the units above Q^* because the marginal cost on those units exceeds p^*. Similarly, consumers would earn *negative* consumer surplus on the units above Q^* because their marginal value of the product is less than p^*. (You should be able to convince yourself that for *any* price, the total surplus earned on the units above Q^* is negative.) From the figure, we conclude that at any level of output above Q^*, total surplus is less than it is at Q^*.

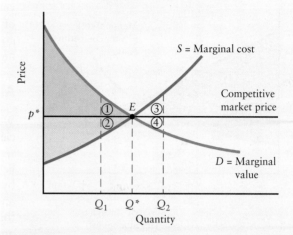

FIGURE 12-5   The Allocative Efficiency of Perfect Competition

Competitive equilibrium is allocatively efficient because it maximizes the sum of consumer and producer surplus. The competitive equilibrium occurs at the price–output combination of p^* and Q^*. At this equilibrium, consumer surplus is the shaded area above the price line, while producer surplus is the shaded area below the price line.

For any output that is less than Q^*, the sum of the two surpluses is less than at Q^*. For any output that is greater than Q^*, the sum of the surpluses is also less than at Q^*. Thus, total surplus is maximized when output is Q^*.

The sum of producer and consumer surplus is maximized only at the perfectly competitive level of output. This is the only level of output that is allocatively efficient.

The Allocative Inefficiency of Monopoly Revisited   We have just seen in Figure 12-5 that the output in perfectly competitive equilibrium maximizes the sum of consumer and producer surplus. It follows that the lower monopoly output must result in a smaller total of consumer and producer surplus.

The monopoly equilibrium is not the outcome of a voluntary agreement between the one producer and the many consumers. Instead, it is imposed by the monopolist by virtue of the power it has over the market. When the monopolist chooses an output below the competitive level, market price is higher than it would be under perfect competition. As a result, consumer surplus is diminished, and producer surplus is increased. In this way, the monopolist gains at the expense of consumers. This is not the whole story, however.

When output is below the competitive level, there is always a *net loss* of total surplus: More surplus is lost by consumers than is gained by the monopolist. Some surplus is lost because output between the monopolistic and the competitive levels is not produced.

FIGURE 12-6 The Deadweight Loss of Monopoly

Monopoly restricts output and reduces total surplus, thereby imposing a deadweight loss on society. If this market were perfectly competitive, output would be Q_c and price would be p_c. Total surplus would be the total shaded area. Consumer surplus would be the sum of areas 1, 2, and 3. Producer surplus would be the sum of areas 4 and 5.

When the industry is monopolized, and the monopolist has the same marginal costs as the competitive industry, output is restricted to Q_m and price rises to p_m. Consumer surplus is reduced to the blue area. Producer surplus rises by area 2 but falls by area 5. (Since p_m must maximize the producer's profit, we know that area 2 is larger than area 5.) Total producer surplus for the monopolist is therefore the red area.

The deadweight loss of monopoly is the sum of areas 3 and 5. This area represents the additional surplus that would be earned if the market were competitive. Since the monopolist restricts output to Q_m, the units between Q_m and Q_c are not produced and therefore they generate neither consumer nor producer surplus.

This loss of surplus is called the *deadweight loss of monopoly*. It is illustrated in Figure 12-6.

It follows that there is a conflict between the private interest of the monopolist and the public interest of all the nation's consumers. This creates grounds for government intervention to prevent the formation of monopolies or at least to regulate their behaviour.

Allocative Efficiency and Market Failure

We have seen that perfect competition is allocatively efficient and that monopoly, in general, is not. Most of the remainder of this chapter presents ways in which public policy has attempted to deal with problems raised by monopoly. Before we go on, however, it is important to re-emphasize that perfect competition is an ideal that exists in a small number of industries, is at best only approximated in some others, and is not even closely resembled in most. Hence, to say that perfect competition is allocatively efficient is not to say that real-world market economies are ever allocatively efficient.

In Chapter 16, we discuss the most important ways (other than monopoly) in which market economies may fail to produce efficient outcomes. In Chapters 17 and 18, we discuss and evaluate the most important public policies that have been used to try to correct for these *market failures*. One of the most important problems arises when market transactions—production or consumption or both—impose costs or confer benefits on economic agents who are not involved in the transaction. Cases like these, which are called *externalities* because they involve economic costs or benefits for parties that are "external" to the transaction, generally raise the possibility that market outcomes will be allocatively inefficient.

A simple example illustrates the problem. We know that markets for most agricultural commodities are highly competitive, with many small producers who are unable to affect the price of the goods they are producing. At the same time, the technology of agricultural production involves the extensive use of fertilizers that pollute nearby rivers and lakes. This pollution imposes costs on households who use the water for drinking and also on the health of local fish populations. Because these costs are not taken into account in the market for the agricultural products, they will be external to transactions in those markets. Generally, when production of a good or service causes pollution, the quantity produced in a perfectly competitive industry will exceed the efficient amount.

One of the most important issues in public policy is determining the circumstances in which government action can increase the allocative efficiency of market outcomes.

As we will see later in this book, there are many circumstances in which there is room for public policy to increase the efficiency of market outcomes, but there are also many cases in which the cure is worse than the disease. In the remainder of this chapter we examine economic regulation and competition policy, both of which are designed to promote allocative efficiency.

12.2 ECONOMIC REGULATION TO PROMOTE EFFICIENCY

Monopolies, cartels, and price-fixing agreements among oligopolists, whether explicit or tacit, have met with public suspicion and official hostility for more than a century. These and other non-competitive practices are collectively referred to as *monopoly practices.* The laws and other instruments that are used to encourage competitive behaviour and discourage monopoly practices make up *competition policy* (referred to as *anit-trust* policy in the United States). Canadian competition policy has sought to create more competitive market structures where possible, to discourage monopolistic practices, and to encourage competitive behaviour where competitive market structures cannot be established.

Federal, provincial, and local governments also employ *economic regulations,* which prescribe the rules under which firms can do business and in some cases determine the prices that businesses can charge for their output. For example, the Canadian Radio-television and Telecommunications Commission (CRTC) is a federal agency that regulates many aspects of the radio, television, and telecommunications industries, including the price you pay for cellphone and Internet services. Another federal agency is the Office of the Superintendent of Financial Institutions (OSFI), which oversees the regulation of Canada's banks and insurance companies. Provincial governments regulate the extraction of fossil fuels and the harvesting of forests within their provincial boundaries, and charge royalties to the firms who develop these natural resources. Local governments regulate the zoning of land and thus have an important influence on where firms can and cannot operate their businesses; they also regulate the operation of restaurants and taxicabs, and issue licences for retail businesses.

The quest for allocative efficiency provides rationales both for competition policy and for economic regulation. Competition policy is used to promote allocative efficiency by increasing competition in the marketplace. Where competitive behaviour is not possible (as in the case of natural monopolies, such as natural gas or electricity distribution companies), public ownership or economic regulation of privately owned firms can be used as a substitute for competition. Consumers can then be protected from the high prices and restricted output that would likely result from the unregulated use of monopoly power.[2]

In the remainder of this chapter, we look at a variety of ways in which policymakers have chosen to intervene in the workings of the market economy using economic regulation and competition policy.

Regulation of Natural Monopolies

The clearest case for public intervention arises with a **natural monopoly**—an industry in which economies of scale are so dominant that there is room for *at most* one firm

natural monopoly An industry characterized by economies of scale sufficiently large that one firm can most efficiently supply the entire market demand.

---

[2]A second kind of regulation involves the legislated rules that require firms to consider the environmental and other consequences of their behaviour. Environmental regulation is discussed in Chapter 17.

to operate at the minimum efficient scale. (In other words, the firm's *LRAC* curve is declining over the entire range of the market demand curve.) Natural monopolies are found mainly in public utilities, such as electricity transmission and natural gas distribution. These industries require the establishment of large and expensive distribution networks (transmission lines and pipelines) and the size of the market is such that only a single firm can achieve its minimum efficient scale while still covering these fixed costs. Local telephone service and cable TV were also natural monopolies for many years. Recent technological change, however, has now allowed other firms to compete effectively in these markets.

Crown corporations In Canada, business concerns owned by the federal or provincial government.

One response to natural monopoly is for government to assume ownership of the single firm. In Canada, such government-owned firms are called **Crown corporations**. In these cases, the government appoints managers and directors who are supposed to set prices in the public interest. Another response to the problem of natural monopoly is to allow private ownership but to *regulate* the monopolist's behaviour. In Canada, both government ownership (e.g., Canada Post and most of the provincial hydro authorities) and regulation (e.g., cable television and local Internet service providers) are used actively. In the United States, with a few notable exceptions, private ownership with regulation has been the preferred alternative.

Whether the government owns or merely regulates natural monopolies, the industry's pricing policy is determined by the government. The industry is typically required to follow some pricing policy that *conflicts* with the goal of profit maximization. We will see that such government intervention must deal with problems that arise in the short run, the long run, and the very long run.

Short-Run Price and Output Three general types of pricing policies exist for regulated natural monopolies: *marginal-cost pricing, two-part tariffs,* and *average-cost pricing.* We discuss each in turn.

1. Marginal-Cost Pricing. Sometimes the government dictates that the natural monopoly set a price where the market demand curve and the firm's marginal cost curve intersect. This policy, called *marginal-cost pricing,* leads to the allocatively efficient level of output. This is not, however, the profit-maximizing output, which is where marginal cost equals marginal revenue. Thus, marginal-cost pricing sets up a tension between the regulator's desire to achieve the allocatively efficient level of output and the firm's desire to maximize profits.

Figure 12-7 illustrates a natural monopoly and shows that the firm's *LRAC* curve is declining over the entire range of the market demand curve. Since *LRAC* is declining, *MC* is less than long-run average cost. It follows that when price is set equal to marginal cost, price will be less than average cost, and marginal-cost pricing will lead to losses.

When a natural monopoly with falling average costs sets price equal to marginal cost, it will suffer losses.

If regulations impose marginal-cost pricing, and the firm ends up incurring economic losses, this situation cannot be sustained for long. This problem provides the motivation for two alternative pricing policies.

2. Two-Part Tariff. One pricing policy that permits the natural monopoly to cover its costs is to allow it to charge a two-part tariff in which customers pay one price to gain access to the product and a second price for each unit consumed. Consider the

case of a regulated cable TV company or Internet service provider (ISP). In principle, the hook-up fee covers fixed costs, and then each unit of output can be priced at marginal cost. Indeed, many new subscribers to cable TV or Internet service are surprised at how high the hook-up fee is—clearly much higher than the cost of the cable guy's half-hour to complete the job! Yet if this fee also includes that household's share of the firm's fixed costs (spread over many thousands of households), then the large hook-up fee is more understandable.

3. Average-Cost Pricing. Another method of regulating a natural monopoly is to set prices just high enough to cover total costs, thus generating neither profits nor losses. This is called *average-cost pricing*. The firm produces the level of output at which the demand curve cuts the *LRAC* curve. Figure 12-7 shows that for a firm with declining long-run average costs, this pricing policy requires producing at less than the allocatively efficient output. The firm's financial losses that would occur under marginal-cost pricing are avoided by producing less output (and having higher prices) than what is socially optimal.

> **For a natural monopoly with falling average costs, a policy of average-cost pricing will not result in allocative efficiency because price exceeds marginal cost.**

On what basis do we choose between marginal-cost pricing and average-cost pricing? Marginal-cost pricing generates allocative efficiency, but the firm incurs losses. In this case, the firm will eventually go out of business unless someone is prepared to cover the firm's losses. If the government is unwilling to do so, seeing no reason why taxpayers should subsidize the users of the product in question, then average-cost pricing may be preferable. It provides the lowest price that can be charged and the largest output that can be produced, given the requirement that revenue must cover the total cost of producing the product.

Long-Run Investment We have seen why regulators may choose average-cost pricing rather than marginal-cost pricing. What is the implication of this choice in the long run? Since marginal cost for a natural monopoly is below average cost, average-cost pricing will generally lead to inefficient patterns of long-run investment. For example, consider the situation depicted in part (ii) of Figure 12-7—a natural monopoly required to set price equal to average cost. The firm will be just breaking even. If it expanded its capacity (and moved downward along its *LRAC* curve) the regulated price would fall and so the firm would still be

FIGURE 12-7 Pricing Policies for Natural Monopolies

(i) Marginal-cost pricing

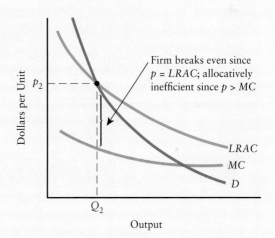

(ii) Average-cost pricing

A natural monopoly has falling long-run average costs; marginal-cost pricing leads to losses, whereas average-cost pricing leads to allocative inefficiency. In both parts, average costs are falling as output rises, and thus the *MC* curve is below the *LRAC* curve.

In part (i), a policy that requires setting price equal to *MC* leads to output Q_1 and price p_1. This outcome is allocatively efficient but the firm cannot cover its full unit costs of c_1. In part (ii), a policy that requires setting price equal to average cost results in output Q_2 and price p_2. The firm can cover its full costs but the outcome is allocatively inefficient because price exceeds marginal cost.

breaking even. Thus, it has no incentive to undertake such investment. Note, however, that the price in this case must exceed the marginal cost (because marginal cost must be below average cost if average cost is falling). As a result, society would benefit by having a larger amount of fixed capital allocated to producing this good.

A government-owned natural monopoly may be prepared to make such investments, as it presumably has a mandate to protect society's overall interests. A regulated but privately owned firm, on the other hand, has little or no financial incentive to undertake investment if it will only break even. As a result, socially desirable investment will not likely occur when the firm is required to use average-cost pricing.

Average-cost pricing often leads to inefficient long-run investment decisions.

Very Long-Run Innovation   In many places in the last few chapters we have discussed the importance of innovation and technological change. In particular, we mentioned how innovation can lead to the erosion of market power through Schumpeter's process of "creative destruction." Technological changes have led to the evolution of many natural monopolies into more competitive industries.

A striking example is found in the telecommunications industry. Thirty years ago, hard-copy message transmission in Canada was close to a natural monopoly belonging to Canada Post, a Crown corporation. Today, technological developments, such as efficient courier services, email, scanners, and the Internet, have made this activity highly competitive. Canada Post still has a legislated monopoly over delivery of first-class mail, but this segment of the overall "package delivery" market is now much smaller than it once was. As a result, the demand for Canada Post's services is gradually shrinking with each passing year.

Other examples of industries that used to be natural monopolies but are now much more competitive include airlines, long-distance telephone service, and the generation of electricity (the *distribution* of electricity continues to be a natural monopoly).

The case of electricity is particularly interesting. The combined production and distribution of electricity was once viewed as a natural monopoly, and the policy response was either to establish publicly owned power authorities (as happened in Canadian provinces) or to regulate privately owned power companies (as occurred in the United States). The source of the natural monopoly was twofold. First, the generation of electricity at low unit cost required large and expensive generating stations. Second, the transmission of power required the establishment of power grids, with networks of wires running from the generating stations to the users.

In recent years, however, the technology of electricity *generation* has changed. Though nuclear and hydro stations are still very expensive to build, it is now possible to build small and relatively inexpensive natural gas–powered generating stations that produce electricity at low unit costs. These technological changes have led to the realization that the generation of electricity is no longer a natural monopoly even though the distribution of electricity still is. This realization led several jurisdictions in Canada and the United States to embark on a path of privatization or deregulation of electricity markets.

Problems With Regulations   Many practical problems arise with regulations designed to prevent natural monopolies from charging profit-maximizing prices. These problems begin with the fact that regulators usually do not have enough data to determine demand and cost curves precisely. In the absence of accurate data, regulators have tended to judge prices according to the level of the regulated firm's profits. Regulatory agencies tend to permit price increases only when profits fall below "fair" levels and require price reductions if profits exceed such levels. What started as price regulation becomes instead profit regulation, which is often called *rate-of-return regulation*. Concepts of marginal cost and allocative efficiency are often ignored in such regulatory decisions.

If average-cost regulation is successful, only a normal rate of return will be earned; that is, economic profits will be zero. Unfortunately, the reverse is not necessarily true. Profits can be zero for any of a number of reasons, including inefficient operation, excessive salaries or employee benefits, and misleading accounting. Thus, regulatory commissions that rely on rate of return as their guide to pricing must monitor a number of other aspects of the regulated firm's behaviour in order to limit the possibility of wasting resources. This monitoring itself requires a considerable expenditure of resources.

Canada Post has long held a legislated monopoly for the delivery of first-class mail, but technological change has provided an expanding set of alternatives to its services, thereby eroding its monopoly power.

Regulation of Oligopolies

Governments have also intervened in industries that were oligopolies (rather than natural monopolies), seeking to enforce the type of price and entry behaviour that was thought to be in the public interest. Such intervention has typically taken two distinct forms. In the period following the Second World War, many European countries, including Britain, nationalized entire oligopolistic industries, such as railways, steel, and coal mining, which were then run by government-appointed boards. In the United States, airlines and railways, for example, were left in private hands, but their decisions were regulated by government-appointed bodies that set prices and regulated entry. As often happens, Canada followed a mixture of British and American practices. Many Canadian Crown corporations were established, and many firms that remained in private hands were regulated. For example, Canadian Pacific Railway was privately owned and regulated while Canadian National Railway, until it was privatized in 1995, was a Crown corporation.

Skepticism About Government Direction Policymakers have become increasingly skeptical of their ability to improve the behaviour of oligopolistic industries by having governments direct the details of their behaviour through either ownership or regulation. Two main experiences were important in developing this skepticism.

Oligopolies and Innovation. During the twentieth century and into the present, new products and production methods have followed each other in rapid succession, leading to higher living standards and higher productivity. Many of these innovations have been provided by firms in oligopolistic industries, such as cars, agricultural machinery, petroleum refining, chemicals, electronics, computing, and telecommunications. As long as oligopolists continue to compete with one another, rather than cooperating to produce monopoly profits, most economists see no need to regulate the prices at which oligopolists sell their products and the conditions of entry into oligopolistic industries.

Protection from Competition. Postwar government intervention in regulated industries did not prove as successful as its supporters had predicted. Research by the University of Chicago's George Stigler (1911–1991) and others showed that in many industries the regulatory bodies get "captured" by the very firms they are supposed to be regulating. This capture is unsurprising because regulatory agencies, in an attempt to hire people knowledgeable about the industry, often hire many former employees of the regulated firms. These people naturally tend to be sympathetic to the firms in the industry, and as a result, the regulatory agencies that are meant to ensure competition often act to enforce monopoly practices that would be illegal if instituted by the firms themselves. As a result, the process of regulation, rather than protecting consumers from anti-competitive behaviour by the firms, often ends up protecting firms from the forces of competition.

Deregulation and Privatization In the 1980s many industrialized economies began to reduce the level of government control over industry. This was especially true in the United States under President Ronald Reagan and in the United Kingdom under Prime Minister Margaret Thatcher. But it also occurred in many other countries, including Canada. Various experiences were pushing in this direction:

- The realization that the actions of regulatory bodies often reduced, rather than increased, competition;
- The dashing of the hopes that publicly owned firms would work better than privately owned firms in the areas of efficiency, productivity growth, and industrial relations; and
- The awareness that falling costs for transportation, communications, and data processing exposed local industries to much more widespread international competition than they had previously experienced domestically.

Two policy responses ensued. The first was deregulation—intended to leave prices and entry to be determined by private decisions. The second was privatization of publicly owned firms.

In the United States, where regulation rather than government ownership had been the adopted policy, many industries were deregulated. In the United Kingdom, virtually all of the formally nationalized industries were privatized. The level of public ownership in that country now compares with that in the United States. In Canada, hundreds of Crown corporations that the government had acquired for a variety of reasons (but were neither natural monopolies nor operating in highly concentrated industries) were sold off. Many large Crown corporations operating in oligopolistic industries, such as Air Canada, Petro-Canada, and Canadian National Railway, were privatized. Also, many industries, such as airlines and gas and oil, were deregulated. Prices were freed, to be set by the firms in the industries, and entry was no longer restricted by government policy.

A Return to Government Control? With the onset of a global financial crisis in 2008 followed immediately by a severe global recession, governments found themselves faced with a tough choice. Many large U.S. financial institutions were threatened with collapse, as were General Motors and Chrysler. Should these companies be allowed to fail, as was likely to happen without government action? Or should the government intervene to support these firms in an attempt to dampen the reduction in output and rise in unemployment that were already occurring? As it happened, the U.S. government intervened aggressively to support U.S. financial institutions and the U.S. and Canadian (and Ontario) governments intervened to support operations of the two major car companies on both sides of the border. In all cases, however, the government support was designed to be temporary. The intervention was not designed to be a return to the government control of private firms, but rather it was seen as a temporary but pragmatic government response to extraordinary problems during extraordinary times.

Applying Economic Concepts 12-1 discusses a different kind of regulation for an important Canadian industry. The Canadian banking industry is oligopolistic, containing a small number of very large banks. Some of the most important regulations in the banking industry, however, are aimed at promoting confidence and reducing risk-taking behaviour rather than at encouraging competition.

12.3 CANADIAN COMPETITION POLICY

The least stringent form of government intervention is designed neither to force firms to sell at particular prices nor to regulate the conditions of entry and exit; it is designed, instead, to create conditions of competition by preventing firms from merging unnecessarily or from engaging in anticompetitive practices, such as colluding to set monopoly prices. This is referred to as **competition policy**.

competition policy Policy designed to prohibit the acquisition and exercise of monopoly power by business firms.

The Evolution of Canadian Policy

Canadian competition policy began in the late 1890s and evolved gradually over the next half-century. By the 1950s, the following three broad classes of activity were illegal:

- Price-fixing agreements that unduly lessen competition;
- Mergers or monopolies that operate to the detriment of the public interest; and
- "Unfair" trade practices.

After various revisions to the policies, the *Competition Act* of 1986 came into effect. The *Act* allowed *civil* rather than *criminal* actions to be brought against firms for alleged offences in the three categories listed above. This change was important because in civil cases the standard of proof is less strict than in criminal cases, in which convictions require proof "beyond a reasonable doubt."

In order to adjudicate such civil cases, a Competition Tribunal was established. The Commissioner of the Competition Bureau now acts as a "watchdog" for the economy, looking out for mergers or trade practices that are likely to have detrimental effects on overall welfare. In such cases, the Commissioner sends the alleged violations to the Competition Tribunal for adjudication.

In the case of a large merger that might substantially lessen competition, the firms are required to notify the Competition Bureau of their intention to merge. The Bureau then reviews the proposed merger, evaluates its probable effect on the economy, and then allows or disallows it.

Another important aspect of the *Competition Act* is that economic effects are considered to be directly relevant in judging the acceptability of a proposed merger. When reviewing a merger, the Competition Bureau is obliged to consider such things as effective competition after the merger, the degree of foreign competition, barriers to entry, the availability of substitutes, and the financial state of the merging firms.

APPLYING ECONOMIC CONCEPTS 12-1

Confidence, Risk, and Regulation in Canadian Banking

Credit is crucial for any modern economy. Most consumers borrow to buy a house and car, and many have lines of credit which allow them to finance other purchases. Most firms borrow to expand their facilities, but also to pay their workers on a regular basis when their revenues arrive in a less predictable way. In short, credit is a crucial input, and without a well-functioning credit market it would be difficult if not impossible to maintain our current high level of economic activity.

Banks play a vital role as *intermediaries* in the credit market. They accept deposits from millions of households and firms who want to save, and then channel those funds to other firms and households who want to borrow. The business model for banks is actually quite simple: pay a relatively low interest rate on deposits, charge a higher interest rate on loans, and the bank then earns a profit based on the *spread* in interest rates.

At the core of the banking system lies both *confidence* and *risk*. The banks' depositors require confidence that they can access their funds when they want and that the bank will not collapse. Without such confidence, few would deposit their money in the bank, and without deposits the bank would not be able to make loans. The loans that the bank makes are inherently risky because firms and households may fail to repay what they owe.

Given the role of banks as intermediaries in the credit market and the need to maintain confidence in an industry that is inherently about risk-taking, several government regulations apply to Canadian banks (and those in most other countries as well). Examples of such regulations are:

- All Canadian banks are members of the Canada Deposit Insurance Corporation (CDIC). CDIC is a Crown corporation that uses fees paid by the member banks to provide insurance to depositors against the risk of bank failure. This insurance is central in providing individuals confidence that their deposits are safe (up to a limit of $100 000 per deposit.)

- Banks are limited in the amount of their assets (loans) that can be financed by customer deposits. Some fraction of their assets must be financed by the financial capital provided by the banks' owners. Such restrictions permit the banks' assets to fall in value by a modest amount (as occasionally happens) without leading to bank insolvency and failure.

- Banks that extend home mortgages to customers are required to purchase mortgage insurance if the value of the loan exceeds 80 percent of the value of the home (i.e., if the borrower's down payment is less than 20 percent). With such insurance, the bank is protected from loss in the event that the borrower defaults on the loan. The bank can purchase mortgage insurance from the Canada Mortgage and Housing Corporation (CMHC), a Crown corporation, or from private-sector insurers.

This is just a small sample of the many regulations that apply to Canadian banks. Given the nature of the industry it is not surprising that many regulations are aimed at promoting confidence and limiting the amount and nature of risks to which banks are exposed.

This aspect of Canadian bank regulation came to the attention of international observers during the global financial crisis of 2008–2009. While several large banks in other developed economies collapsed, and many others required significant government assistance in order to avoid collapse, no Canadian banks experienced equivalent strains. Some argue that Canadian bankers have traditionally been more prudent than bankers in other countries; others argue that Canada was just lucky. Most economists agree, however, that Canadian bank regulation prevented some of the extreme risk-taking behaviour that occurred elsewhere and was partly responsible for the better performance of the Canadian banking industry.

The Competition Bureau also considers any reduction in costs that a merger might generate. Even in a situation where there are considerable entry barriers to an industry, a merger may bring benefits to consumers even though it raises the industry's measured concentration. If, by merging, two firms can achieve scale economies that were not achievable separately, reductions in average total costs may get passed on to consumers in the form of lower prices.

This possibility presents a significant challenge to competition policy. The challenge is to prevent those mergers that mostly lead to less competition, producing only small cost reductions, but to allow those mergers that mostly lead to cost reductions, with only small reductions in competition. The practical problem for the authorities is to identify the likely effects of each merger.

Recent Reforms

For many years, Canadian legislation provided substantial protection to consumers against the misuse of market power by large firms. With the 1986 *Competition Act* it also provides substantial protection against the creation, through mergers, of market power that is not justified by gains to efficiency or international competitiveness.

Canadian competition policy continues to evolve. In 2009, the *Competition Act* was amended to:

- increase the penalties for deceptive marketing and empower the courts to award restitution to victims of false advertising;
- create a more effective mechanism for the criminal prosecution of significant cartel agreements;
- introduce a two-stage merger review process to improve efficiency and effectiveness; and
- allow the Competition Tribunal to assign monetary penalties to companies who abuse a dominant position in the marketplace.

A recent example illustrates the kind of market developments that attract the attention of the Competition Bureau. In 2011 Air Canada and a U.S. airline, United Continental, announced their plans to create a "joint venture" on a number of air routes between major U.S. and Canadian cities. The joint venture would allow the two airlines to share costs and revenues on a total of 19 routes. The Competition Bureau saw this venture as a clear effort to create monopoly power that would raise prices to consumers. Of the 19 routes included in the proposed joint venture, the Competition Bureau estimated that the market share of the joint venture would be 100 percent on 10 of the routes, and would average 68 percent on the remaining 9 routes. The Competition Bureau filed an application with the Competition Tribunal to block the joint venture. After a series of discussions between the two airlines and the Competition Bureau, the airlines agreed to suspend their joint venture, at least temporarily.

Future Challenges

What other types of reforms might we expect in the years ahead? The ongoing process of globalization poses two challenges for Canadian competition policy. First, as the flow of goods and services across national boundaries increases, it becomes more important to define markets on an international rather than a national basis. For example, consider the Canadian banking industry. With the continuing development of the Internet, it becomes possible for foreign-based banks to sell some financial services to Canadians without establishing a costly *physical* presence in Canada—such as a network of branches. In this case, the appropriate definition of the market (for the case of assessing the impact of a merger) is larger than just the one defined by Canada's borders.

The second challenge posed by globalization is the desirability of standardizing competition policy across countries. Firms that are mobile and have considerable market power may tend to locate their firms where competition policy is the most lax, exporting into other countries. To avoid such socially inefficient locational choices, countries have an incentive to standardize their competition policy—in this case, firms would choose their locations on the basis of economic rather than legal forces.

These are challenges for the near future. Time will tell how Canadian competition authorities respond.

SUMMARY

12.1 PRODUCTIVE AND ALLOCATIVE EFFICIENCY   LO 1, 2

- Productive efficiency for the firm requires that the firm be producing its output at the lowest possible cost. Productive efficiency for the industry requires that all firms in the industry have the same marginal cost.
- Allocative efficiency in an individual industry exists when the level of output is such that the marginal cost of production equals the market price. The overall economy is allocatively efficient when price equals marginal cost in all industries simultaneously.
- Productive efficiency and allocative efficiency are both achieved in perfect competition.
- Monopoly is allocatively inefficient because price exceeds marginal cost. Monopoly leads to a deadweight loss for the economy.

12.2 ECONOMIC REGULATION TO PROMOTE EFFICIENCY   LO 3

- Two broad types of policies are designed to promote allocative efficiency in imperfectly competitive markets. These can be divided into *economic regulations* and *competition policy*. Economic regulation is used both in the case of a natural monopoly and in the case of an oligopolistic industry. Competition policy applies more to the latter.
- For a natural monopoly (with a declining *LRAC* curve), marginal-cost pricing is allotively efficient but will lead the firm to make economic losses.
- Average-cost pricing allows the natural monopoly to break even but leads to allocative inefficiency (because price is not equal to marginal cost).
- The deregulation of oligopolistic industries has been based on the observations that (1) oligopolistic industries are major engines of growth, and (2) direct control of such industries has produced disappointing results in the past.

12.3 CANADIAN COMPETITION POLICY   LO 4

- Canadian competition policy is designed to restrict mergers and trade practices that unduly lessen competition.
- In the past, mergers harmful to the public interest were criminal offences and difficult to prosecute. The current legislation allows civil cases to be brought against firms, making prosecution less difficult.
- The *Competition Act* of 1986 established a Competition Tribunal to adjudicate cases brought to it by the Competition Bureau.
- In the case of mergers, the Competition Bureau and Tribunal must consider whether the merger will generate cost reductions that will offset the effects of any lessening of competition.

KEY CONCEPTS

Productive and allocative efficiency
Consumer and producer surplus
The allocative efficiency of
  competition

The allocative inefficiency of
  monopoly
Regulation of natural monopolies
Marginal- and average-cost pricing

Two-part tariffs
Regulation of oligopolies
Deregulation and privatization
Canadian competition policy

STUDY EXERCISES

MyEconLab Make the grade with MyEconLab: Study Exercises marked in ⊕ can be found on MyEconLab. You can practise them as often as you want, and most feature step-by-step guided instructions to help you find the right answer.

❶ Summer Tees and Fancy Tees make up an industry of two firms producing T-shirts. The table below shows the average cost of producing T-shirts for the two companies.

	Summer Tees				Fancy Tees		
Quantity	ATC	TC	MC	Quantity	ATC	TC	MC
5	$8	—	—	5	$9	—	—
10	7	—	—	10	7	—	—
15	6	—	—	15	6	—	—
20	6	—	—	20	5	—	—
25	7	—	—	25	5.50	—	—
30	9	—	—	30	6.50	—	—
35	11	—		35	8	—	

a. Calculate *TC* and *MC* for both companies and fill in the table.
b. Draw, in separate diagrams, the *ATC* and *MC* curves for each firm.
c. Summer Tees is initially producing 30 shirts; Fancy Tees is initially producing 15 shirts. What is the total industry production cost?
d. Now suppose that Summer Tees produces 10 fewer shirts. By how much do its costs fall?
e. Suppose that Fancy Tees produces 10 more shirts. By how much do its costs rise?
f. If the two firms are to produce 45 shirts in total, what is the cost-minimizing way to allocate production between the two firms? (Assume that production must be changed by increments of five shirts, as shown in the table.)
g. Explain how this question relates to the concept of productive efficiency.

❷ Fill in the blanks to make the following statements correct.

a. If the marginal cost of producing the last unit of a product is the same for all firms in an industry, we can say that the industry is _____ efficient, but we do not know enough to say that the industry is _____ efficient.
b. If the marginal cost of some product is $12, and the market price of that product is $15, then to achieve allocative efficiency, the economy should produce_____ of this product and therefore _____ of other products.
c. The market structure that leads to both productive and allocative efficiency is _____.
d. A monopolistic industry may be productively efficient but will not be allocatively efficient because _____.
e. The sum of consumer surplus and producer surplus is _____ at the competitive equilibrium.
f. At the monopolist's profit-maximizing output there is _____ total surplus than at the competitive output. Some surplus is transferred from _____ to _____. The surplus lost because the output is not produced is called _____.

❸ Firms A, B, and C all produce roof shingles in a perfectly competitive market. The diagrams below show marginal cost curves for each of the three firms.

a. Suppose each firm is producing 1000 bundles per day. Is this industry productively efficient?
b. If the industry's total output is to be maintained at 3000 bundles, how should the production be allocated among the firms in order to minimize the total cost of production?

c. If the market price of a bundle of roof shingles is $20, how many bundles should each firm produce if it wants to maximize its profits? Is this outcome also productively efficient? Explain.

d. Is the outcome from part (c) also allocatively efficient in this industry? Explain.

④ Assume that the market for eggs is perfectly competitive. The diagram shows the demand for and the supply of eggs.

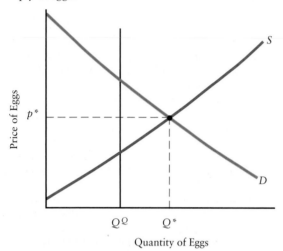

a. At the free-market equilibrium, p^* and Q^*, show what areas represent consumer and producer surplus.

b. Now suppose the egg producers organize themselves and establish a system of quotas. Each farmer's output is restricted by an amount to keep aggregate output at Q^Q. What happens to industry price?

c. In the quota system in part (b), what areas now represent consumer and producer surplus? Is the quota system allocatively efficient? Explain.

⑤ The diagram below shows supply and demand in a perfectly competitive labour market.

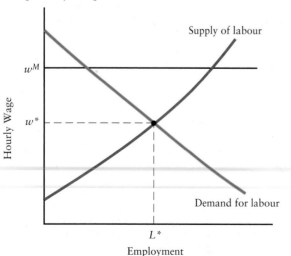

a. At the free-market equilibrium, w^* and L^*, show what areas represent consumer and producer surplus.

b. Describe in words what consumer and producer surplus means in this case.

c. Now suppose the government establishes a minimum wage at w^M. Show on the diagram and label the new level of employment in this case.

d. In the situation of part (c), what areas now represent consumer and producer surplus? Is the outcome allocatively efficient? Explain.

⑥ The diagram below shows supply and demand in a perfectly competitive local market for cubic metres (m^3) of garden soil.

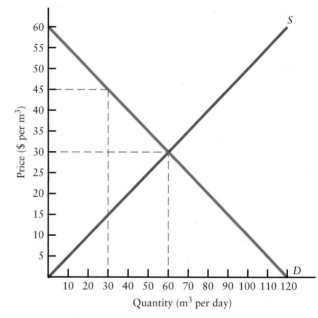

a. At the equilibrium market price, determine the following values:

- total revenue received by sellers

- consumer surplus

- producer surplus

- total economic surplus

b. Now suppose that sellers in this market cooperate and restrict their total output to 30 m^3 per day. At the resulting price of $45 per m^3, determine each of the same values as in part (a).

c. What is the change in consumer surplus when output is restricted? What is the change in producer surplus?

d. What is the deadweight loss to the economy in this market when output is restricted?

⑦ The diagram below shows the demand, marginal cost, and marginal revenue curves for a monopolist. Redraw the diagram for yourself to be able to answer the following questions.

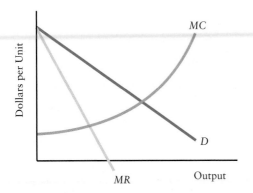

a. If the monopolist charges its single profit-maximizing price, show what areas are consumer surplus and producer surplus.
b. Now suppose the industry is perfectly competitive and the industry supply curve is given by the *MC* curve. What areas would be consumer and producer surplus in this case?
c. Use the concept of surplus to explain the economic argument against monopoly and in favour of competition.
d. Consider again the situation of monopoly, but now assume the firm can *perfectly* price discriminate—that is, it can charge a different price for every unit of the good. What areas now represent consumer and producer surplus?
e. Does the possibility of "perfect" price discrimination lead you to change your argument from part (c)? Are there considerations other than allocative efficiency that might be important here?

❽ The diagram below shows the production possibilities boundary for a country that produces only two goods: limes and coconuts. Assume that resources are fully employed at points *A, B, C,* and *D*.

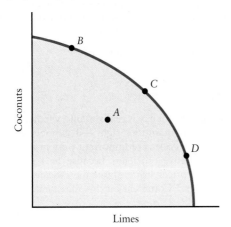

a. Suppose individual firms in the lime industry are not producing at their minimum possible cost. Which point(s) could represent this situation?

b. Suppose all firms and both industries are productively efficient. Which points could represent this situation?
c. Suppose point *B* occurs when the lime industry is monopolized but the coconut industry is perfectly competitive. Is point *B* allocatively efficient? Is it productively efficient?
d. Suppose point *D* occurs when the coconut industry is monopolized but the lime industry is perfectly competitive. Is point *D* allocatively efficient? Is it productively efficient?
e. Suppose point *C* is allocatively efficient. What do we know about each industry in this case?

❾ Fill in the blanks to make the following statements correct.

a. The term *natural monopoly* refers to an industry in which only a single firm can operate at its _____.
b. A regulated natural monopoly that is forced to set its price equal to marginal cost will earn _____ if its long-run average costs are falling.
c. A regulated natural monopoly that is subject to average-cost pricing and operating on the downward-sloping portion of its *LRAC* curve will earn _____ profits. Since price _____ marginal cost, this outcome will not be allocatively efficient.
d. Marginal-cost pricing for a natural monopoly is an efficient pricing system, but it leads to _____ for the firm if average costs are falling.

❿ The following diagram shows the *LRAC* and *MC* curves for a natural monopoly—long-run average costs are falling over the entire range of the demand curve.

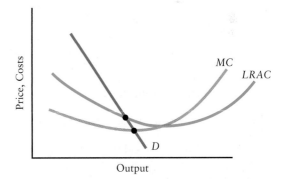

a. Show on the diagram the price and quantity that would exist if the firm were required by regulators to set price equal to average cost.
b. In the diagram, show the profits (or losses) in this case.
c. Would the outcome be allocatively efficient? Explain why or why not.
d. Suppose now that the firm were required by regulators to set price equal to marginal cost. Show on the graph what the price and quantity would be in this case.
e. In the diagram, show the profits (or losses) in this case.
f. Would the outcome be allocatively efficient? Explain why or why not.

⑪ The distribution of natural gas for residential use is often a natural monopoly. The diagram below shows the cost and revenue curves for a profit-maximizing gas distribution firm. Price is given in dollars per cubic metre (m³) and quantity is the number of cubic metres per month.

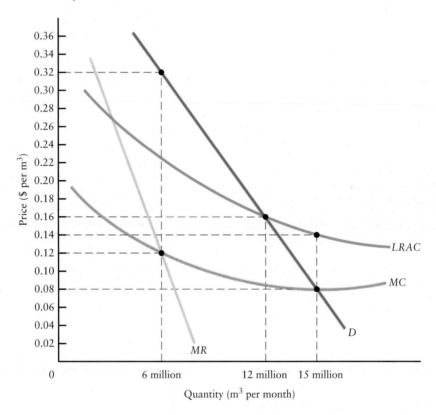

a. Explain how you know that this firm is a natural monopoly.
b. If the firm is unregulated, what do you predict its price, output, and profits to be?
c. If the firm is regulated and required to use marginal-cost pricing, what is the predicted price, output, and profits?
d. If the firm is regulated and required to use average-cost pricing, what is the predicted price, output, and profits?
e. What is an important problem with the regulatory policy in part (c)?
f. What is an important problem with the regulatory policy in part (d)?

⑫ One important factor that the Canadian Competition Bureau must consider when assessing the likely effects of a merger is the definition of the market. Discuss how geography is likely to affect the definition of the market for the following products:

a. Fresh-baked breads and cakes
b. Cement
c. Gold jewellery
d. Computer hardware

⑬ "Allocative efficiency is really about whether the economy 'has the quantities right'—it is not really about prices at all. Prices are important only in a discussion about allocative efficiency because *in a free market* changes in prices bring about the efficient allocation of resources." Comment on this statement.

13 How Factor Markets Work

CHAPTER OUTLINE	LEARNING OBJECTIVES (LO)
	After studying this chapter you will be able to
13.1 THE DEMAND FOR FACTORS	**1** determine a profit-maximizing firm's demand for a factor of production.
13.2 THE SUPPLY OF FACTORS	**2** examine the role of factor mobility in determining factor supply.
13.3 THE OPERATION OF FACTOR MARKETS	**3** distinguish between temporary and equilibrium factor-price differentials.
	4 discuss "economic rent" and how it relates to factor mobility.

WHAT determines the wages that individuals earn? What explains why neurosurgeons usually are paid more than family doctors, or why movie stars are paid more than "extras"? Labour is not the only factor of production, of course. Physical capital and land are also important. Why does a hectare of farmland in Northern Saskatchewan rent for much less than a hectare of land in downtown Toronto? Not surprisingly, understanding why different factors of production earn different payments requires us to understand both demand-side and supply-side aspects of the relevant factor markets.

In this chapter we examine the issue of factor pricing and the closely related issue of factor mobility. We confine ourselves to factor markets that are perfectly competitive. As a result, the firms we study face a given price of each factor that they buy. Similarly, owners of factors face a given price for the factor services that they sell.

Dealing first with competitive factor markets allows us to study the principles of factor-price determination in the simplest context. Once these principles are understood, it is relatively easy to extend the theory to more complicated settings, which we do in the next chapter.

13.1 THE DEMAND FOR FACTORS

Firms require the services of land, labour, and capital to be used as inputs. Firms also use as inputs the products of other firms, such as steel, legal services, computer software, and electricity.

Firms require inputs not for their own sake but as a means to produce goods and services. For example, the demand for software engineers and technicians is growing as more and more computers and software are produced. The demand for carpenters and building materials rises and falls as the amount of housing construction rises and falls. The demand for any input is therefore *derived from the demand* for the goods and services that it helps to produce; for this reason, the demand for a factor of production is said to be a **derived demand**.

derived demand The demand for a factor of production that results from the demand for the products that it is used to make.

Marginal Revenue Product

What determines whether an individual firm will choose to hire one extra worker, or whether the same firm will decide to use one extra machine, or an extra kilowatt-hour of electricity? Just as a firm makes a profit-maximizing decision to produce a level of output where the last unit produced adds as much to revenue as to cost (where $MR = MC$), the firm makes a similar decision about the quantity of a factor to employ. A profit-maximizing firm will increase its use of any factor of production until the last unit of the factor adds as much to revenue as it does to costs.

> **Profit-maximizing firms will hire units of a variable factor up to the point at which the marginal revenue generated by the factor equals the marginal cost of employing the factor.**

This result is true of all profit-maximizing firms, whether they are selling under conditions of perfect competition, monopolistic competition, oligopoly, or monopoly.

Now we introduce a new term to help us state this profit-maximizing condition more clearly. The **marginal revenue product** (*MRP*) is the extra revenue generated by hiring one more unit of a variable factor. How is it computed? Recall that marginal revenue (*MR*) is the change in revenue resulting from the sale of one additional unit of output. Also recall that the marginal product (*MP*) of a factor is the additional output that results from the use of one additional unit of that factor. By multiplying marginal revenue and marginal product we determine the marginal revenue product of the factor. [26] For example, if the factor's marginal product is 2 units and the firm's marginal revenue is $7.50, the factor's marginal revenue product is $15 (2 × $7.50).

marginal revenue product (*MRP*) The extra revenue that results from using one more unit of a variable factor.

We can now restate the condition for a firm to be maximizing its profits:

$$\underset{\text{of the factor}}{\text{Marginal cost}} = \underset{\underset{MP \times MR}{\underbrace{\text{of the factor}}}}{\text{Marginal revenue product}} \qquad (13\text{-}1)$$

This condition applies to *any* firm and any factor, in any market structure. In the special case of competitive goods and factor markets, however, we can simplify the condition. In competitive factor markets the marginal cost of the factor is simply the factor's price, since the firm can hire any amount of the factor at a given price. Call this factor price w. Also, we know that in competitive goods markets, the firm's MR is just the market price of the product, p. It follows that MRP is equal to $MP \times p$. Thus, the condition for profit maximization for a competitive firm is

$$w = MP \times p \qquad (13\text{-}2)$$

To check your understanding of Equation 13-2, consider an example. Suppose labour is available to the firm at a cost of $10 per hour ($w = \$10$). Suppose also that employing another hour of labour adds 3 units to output ($MP = 3$) and that any amount of output can be sold for $5 per unit ($p = \$5$). Thus, the additional hour of labour adds $15 to the firm's revenue but only $10 to its costs. In this case, the firm will increase profits by hiring more hours of labour. The firm will stop hiring additional labour only when the marginal cost of hiring (w) is equal to the marginal revenue product ($MP \times p$).

> To maximize its profits, any firm must hire each factor of production to the point where the factor's marginal revenue product just equals the factor's price.

In Chapters 9 and 10, we saw the firm varying its output until the marginal cost of producing another unit was equal to the marginal revenue derived from selling that unit. Now we see the same profit-maximizing behaviour in terms of the firm's varying its inputs until the marginal cost of another unit of input is just equal to the extra revenue derived from selling that unit's marginal product.

The Firm's Demand Curve for a Factor

Now that we have determined the firm's profit-maximizing decision about how much of a factor to employ given a specific factor price (w) and a specific output price (p), we can derive the firm's *entire* demand curve for the factor. How much will the firm hire at *each* factor price?

The *MRP* Curve Is the Factor Demand Curve

Part (i) of Figure 13-1 shows a marginal product curve, just as we saw in Chapter 7. The curve is downward sloping because of the law of (eventually) diminishing returns; as the firm adds further units of the variable factor to a given quantity of the fixed factor, the marginal product of the variable product will decrease. (Note that for simplicity we show only the downward-sloping portion of the MP curve—the portion *after* diminishing returns set in.)

Part (ii) of Figure 13-1 converts the marginal product curve to a marginal revenue product (MRP) curve. Recall that $MRP = MP \times MR$. Also recall that for a competitive firm, marginal revenue is equal to the price of the product, p. In the figure the market price (and thus the firm's MR) is $5 per unit. The MRP curve, therefore, has the same shape as the MP curve. Notice that on the vertical axis, the MRP is simply the MP from part (i) multiplied by $5.

Equation 13-2 states that a profit-maximizing competitive firm will employ additional units of the factor up to the point at which the MRP equals the price of the factor. For example, in Figure 13-1, if the price of hiring one unit of the factor were $2000 per month, the profit-maximizing firm would employ 60 units of the factor. However, if hiring an extra unit of the factor cost $3000 per month, the firm would only choose to hire 45 units. It should be clear that since the MRP curve shows how many units of

FIGURE 13-1 From Marginal Product to Demand Curve

(i) The *MP* curve   (ii) The *MRP* curve (the demand curve)

The law of diminishing marginal returns implies that firms have a negatively sloped demand curve for factors of production. In part (i), the *MP* curve for a factor is downward sloping because of the law of diminishing marginal returns. If the firm uses 60 units of the factor per month, the factor's *MP* will be 400 units of output per month. In part (ii), it is assumed that each unit of the firm's output can be sold at $5. If the firm uses 60 units of the factor per month, the factor's *MRP* is $2000 (400 units per month × $5 per unit). Since the *MRP* curve shows, for each separate factor price, how many units of the factor will be hired by a profit-maximizing firm, the *MRP* curve is the firm's demand curve for the factor.

the factor will be hired at different factor prices, the factor's *MRP* curve is the firm's demand curve for the factor.

> **A competitive firm's demand curve for a factor is given by that factor's *MRP* curve.**

This logic applies equally to any factor of production. A profit-maximizing farmer will rent land up to the point where the marginal revenue product from an extra hectare of land is just equal to the rental price for that hectare of land. A profit-maximizing machine-tools manufacturer will use extra machines (capital) until the marginal revenue product from an extra machine just equals the price of using that machine. And a profit-maximizing paper mill will hire workers up to the point where the marginal revenue product of an extra worker is just equal to that worker's wage.

Elasticity of the Firm's Factor Demand Curve The elasticity of demand for a factor is the same basic concept as the elasticity of demand for any product that we first saw in Chapter 4. The more elastic the demand for a factor, the greater is the change in quantity demanded in response to a change in the price of that factor. The price elasticity of demand for a factor depends on:

1. The Elasticity of Demand for the Final Product. A tomato farmer facing a highly elastic demand curve (almost horizontal) for her tomatoes will have very little ability to pass on, in the form of higher prices, the additional costs associated with paying a higher wage to her workers. This farmer is therefore quite sensitive to changes in the prices of the factors of production that she uses to grow tomatoes. Any increase in the wage, for example, will thus have a relatively large decrease in her quantity demanded for workers. In contrast, a farmer with a special piece of land growing a rare type of mushrooms might have considerable power in his product market; in this case, the farmer could pass some part of cost increases on to consumers and would thus have a less elastic demand for the factors of production he uses.

2. The Ability to Substitute Between Factors.   As we saw in Chapter 8, when the price of one factor rises, a profit-maximizing firm will substitute away from the factor whose price has risen and toward a cheaper factor. The ease with which this substitution can take place affects the elasticity of demand for the factor whose price has increased. For example, a clothing manufacturer may be able to adjust its designs and easily switch between fabrics as their prices change. In contrast, a firm producing aluminum will find it difficult to substitute any other factors for its two primary inputs, bauxite and electricity. The clothing firm's elasticity of demand for its factors of production will be much greater than that of the aluminum producer.

The Market Demand Curve for a Factor

We saw in Chapter 6 that the market demand curve for any good or service is simply the horizontal summation of all the individual consumers' demand curves. With factor demand curves, the same basic logic applies except for one complication, which we discuss in a moment. For now, we examine reasons for *shifts* in the market demand curve for any factor of production.

Shifts of the Market Factor Demand Curve   To examine shifts in the demand curve for a factor, let's go back and think about what is happening at the level of the individual firms. If we know why individual firms' factor demand curves shift, we will also know why the *market* factor demand curve shifts.

Figure 13-1 illustrated a firm's demand curve for a factor of production and showed that the factor's *MRP* curve was also the firm's demand curve for that factor. Since *MRP* is equal to *MP* times *MR*, there are two reasons why the demand curve for a factor can shift—because of a shift in the factor's *MP* curve or because of a change in firms' *MR*.

A Change in the Factor's Marginal Product.   Anything that changes the marginal product of a factor will change the *MP* curve and therefore the *MRP* curve in Figure 13-1. Improvements in technology often increase the marginal product of factors of production, and thus lead to a rightward shift of the *MP* curve. For labour, for example, one kind of "better technology" is better-educated workers. If better education increases the marginal product of labour, the *MP* curve for labour will shift to the right, firms' demand for labour will increase, and firms will hire more labour at any given wage.

A second way in which the marginal product of a factor can increase is if there are more units of *other factors* with which to work. An increase in the amount of physical capital, for example, will generally increase the marginal product of any given amount of labour. Suppose that Figure 13-1 shows the marginal product (and *MRP*) for labour under the assumption that the firm has a given stock of capital. If the firm now expands its capital stock by building a larger factory, the marginal product of any given amount of labour will increase, thus shifting the *MP* curve in part (i) to the right. The result will be that the *MRP* curve in part (ii) also shifts to the right, thus increasing the firm's demand for labour.

> Any increase in a factor's marginal product will lead to an increase in demand for that factor. Such an increase can come about through improvements in the quality of the factor or an increase in the amount of other factors of production.

A Change in Firms' Marginal Revenue.   Anything that increases firms' marginal revenue will increase the *MRP* of a factor and thus lead to an increase in demand for that factor. For firms that operate in a competitive product market, an increase in marginal revenue is simply an increase in the market price of the product. In Figure 13-1, if the product price rises from $5 to $10, the *MRP* curve shifts to the right (even though the *MP* curve does not move). For imperfectly competitive firms, an increase in *MR* occurs if the demand curve faced by those firms shifts to the right. In both cases, the increase in *MR* leads to an increase in the demand for the factor.

> Anything that leads to an increase in demand for a product will lead to an increase in demand for the factors used to produce that product.

A Complication.   As we said earlier, the market demand curve for a factor is not *simply* the horizontal summation of all firms' factor demand curves. As all firms hire more of any specific factor of production, the supplies of the goods produced by that factor increase and the prices of these products fall. This decline in product prices leads firms to increase their hiring of the factors by less than would otherwise occur. The result is that the *market* demand curve for any specific factor of production is *less elastic* than would be the case if we took a simple horizontal summation of the individual firms' factor demand curves.

An example will clarify this point. Consider a competitive furniture-building industry and the individual firms' demand for carpenters. Any one firm's production of furniture will have no significant effect on the equilibrium price of furniture, and so its hiring of carpenters similarly has no effect on the market price of furniture. But all furniture-building firms taken together *do* have an effect on the equilibrium price of furniture. As *all* such firms increase their hiring of carpenters, the total supply of furniture increases and the equilibrium price of furniture declines. As the price falls, each firm will reduce its hiring of carpenters, offsetting to some extent the initial increase in hiring.

> The market demand curve for any factor of production is less elastic than what would result from a simple horizontal summation of all the firms' demand curves for that factor.

13.2 THE SUPPLY OF FACTORS

When we consider the supply of any factor of production, we can consider supply at three different levels of aggregation:

- The amount supplied to the economy as a whole
- The amount supplied to a particular industry
- The amount supplied to a particular firm

To illustrate, consider your decision to seek employment—to supply your labour services to the labour market. You must make three general decisions. First, you must decide whether to supply your labour services at all, the alternative being not to seek any kind of employment. Your decision will influence the overall supply of labour to the economy (though only by a tiny amount). Second, once you have decided to supply your labour services, you must choose an industry and occupation. Your decision to seek employment in the telecommunications industry rather than the auto manufacturing industry influences the economy's allocation of labour across industries. Third, once you have decided to seek employment in a particular industry, you must choose which firms in that industry appeal to you. Your decision influences the allocation of labour across firms.

The elasticity of supply of a factor will normally be different at each of these levels of aggregation because the amount of *factor mobility* is different in each case. A given factor of production is often very mobile between firms within a given industry, less mobile between different industries, and even less mobile from the perspective of the entire economy. For example, an electrician may be very mobile between firms and industries within a given city, and reasonably mobile between provinces, but it may be very difficult for that electrician to move to another country to find a job. In this section, we examine the relationship between factor mobility and the supply of factors of production. We start with the highest level of aggregation.

The Supply of Factors to the Economy

At any one time, the total supply of each factor of production is given. For example, in each country, the labour force is of a certain size, so much arable land is available, and there is a given stock of physical capital. However, these supplies can and do change. Sometimes the change is very gradual, as when climate change slowly turns arable land into desert or when medical advances reduce the rate of infant mortality and increase the rate of population growth, thereby eventually increasing the supply of adult labour. Sometimes the changes can be more rapid, as when a boom in business activity brings retired persons back into the labour force.

Physical Capital   The capital stock in a country is the existing machines, factories, and equipment. Capital is a manufactured factor of production, and its total supply changes slowly. Each year, the stock of capital goods is diminished by the amount that becomes physically or economically obsolete and is increased by the amount of new investment by firms. But the stock of capital is so large that even when there is an investment boom the percentage change in the stock of capital will be tiny. On balance, the trend has been for the capital stock to grow from decade to decade over the past few centuries. We will consider the determinants of investment in physical capital in Chapter 15.

Land   The total area of dry land in a country is almost completely fixed, but the supply of *arable* land is not. Considerable care and effort are required to sustain the productive power of land. If farmers earn low incomes, they may not provide the necessary care, and the land's suitability for growing crops may be destroyed within a short time. In contrast, high earnings from farming may provide the incentive to increase the supply of arable land by irrigation and other forms of reclamation.

Labour   The number of people willing to work is called the labour force; the total number of hours they are willing to work is called the *supply of labour*. The supply of labour depends on three influences: the size of the population, the proportion of the population willing to work, and the number of hours that each individual wants to work. Each of these is partly influenced by economic forces.

Stockbyte/Getty Images

The significant increase in female labour-force participation that occurred between the 1960s and the 1990s had a significant effect on the growth of Canada's aggregate labour supply.

Population. The population of a country varies over time, and these variations are influenced by economic forces. There is evidence, for example, that the birthrate and the net immigration rate (immigration minus emigration) are higher in good economic times than in bad.

Labour-Force Participation. The proportion of the total population that is willing to work is called the *labour-force participation rate*. Economists also define participation rates for subgroups, such as men, women, or youths. Participation rates vary in response to many influences, including changes in attitudes and preferences. The enormous rise in female participation rates between the 1960s and 1990s for example, had a significant effect on the Canadian labour force.

Changes in real wages also play a role in determining the labour-force participation rate. A rise in the demand for labour, and an accompanying rise in the real wage, will lead to an increase in the proportion of the population willing to work. For example, for the decade after 2003 in Alberta, a booming economy driven by high energy prices increased real wages up to the point that there was a notable increase in high-school dropout rates as some students chose instead to pursue employment in the labour market. With the massive decline in world oil prices in late 2014, however, these pressures were reversed.

Hours per Person. The wage rate influences not only the number of people who want to work but also the number of hours that each person wants to work. When workers sell their labour services to employers, they are giving up leisure in order to gain income with which to buy goods. They can therefore be thought of as trading leisure for goods. A rise in the wage implies a change in the relative price of goods and leisure. An increase in the wage means that leisure becomes more expensive relative to goods, because each hour of leisure consumed is at the cost of more goods forgone.

It is not necessarily the case, however, that an increase in the wage increases the amount of hours worked. In fact, an increase in the wage generates both income and substitution effects (see Chapter 6). As the wage rises, the substitution effect leads the individual to work more hours (consume less leisure) because leisure is now relatively more expensive. The income effect of a higher wage, however, leads the individual to work fewer hours (consume more leisure). Because the two effects work in the opposite direction we are, in general, unsure how a rise in the wage will affect the number of hours an individual chooses to work.

Over the past century, the Canadian data show a clear increase in the average real wage and a clear reduction in the average number of hours worked per week. These observations are consistent with the idea that, at some relatively high level of wages, the income effect of wage increases dominates the substitution effect. In other words, workers at some point choose to "spend" their higher wages on more leisure rather than just on more goods and services.

The economy's total supplies of land, labour, and capital each respond to economic forces, but tend to change only gradually.

The Supply of Factors to a Particular Industry

Most factors have many uses. A given piece of land can be used to grow any one of several crops, or it can be subdivided for a housing development. A computer engineer living in the Ottawa Valley can work for one of many firms, for the government, or for Carleton University. A lathe can be used to make many different products, and it requires no adaptation when it is turned for one use or another.

> One industry can attract a factor away from another industry, even though the economy's total supply of that factor may be fixed. Thus, a factor's elasticity of supply to a particular industry is larger than its elasticity of supply to the entire economy.

When we consider the supply of a factor for a particular use, the most important concept is **factor mobility**. A factor that shifts easily between uses in response to small changes in incentives is said to be *mobile*. Its supply to any one use will be elastic because a small increase in the price offered will attract many units of the factor from other uses. A factor that does not shift easily from one use to another, even in response to large changes in remuneration, is said to be *immobile*. It will be in inelastic supply in any one use because even a large increase in the price offered will attract only a small inflow from other uses. Generally, a factor is less mobile in the short run than in the long run.

factor mobility The ease with which a factor of production can move between firms, industries, occupations, or regions.

> An important determinant of factor mobility is time: The longer the time interval, the easier it is for a factor to convert from one use to another.

Consider the factor mobility among particular uses for each of the three key factors of production.

The Mobility of Capital   Some kinds of capital equipment—lathes, trucks, and computers, for example—can be shifted readily among firms, among industries, and even across different regions of the country. These are considered *mobile* capital. Other kinds of capital are quite immobile. For example, some plants and machinery are built for a specific purpose and are difficult, if not impossible, to modify for other purposes. Equipment of this type is immobile across uses, although it might be mobile in the sense that one firm could sell it to another. Factories designed for a specific purpose are immobile both across uses and across regions, though they could still be transferred from one owner to another.

The Mobility of Land   Land, which is physically the least mobile of factors, is one of the *most* mobile in an economic sense. Consider agricultural land. In a given year, one crop can be harvested and a totally different crop can be planted. A farm on the outskirts of a growing city can be sold for subdivision and development on short notice. Once land is built on, however, its mobility is much reduced.

Although land is highly mobile among alternative uses, it is completely immobile as far as location is concerned. There is only so much land within a given distance of the centre of any city, and no increase in the price paid can induce further land to be located within that distance. This locational immobility has important consequences, including high prices for desirable locations and the tendency to build tall buildings to economize on the use of scarce land. It is no accident that the downtown cores of New York, Hong Kong, Toronto, Shanghai, and many other large cities contain so many tall buildings.

Andrew Zarivny/Shutterstock

The high prices paid for land in the centre of large cities, where demand for land is highest, cannot lead to an increase in the quantity of land supplied because it is an immobile factor. The natural market response is the construction of very tall buildings, increasing the amount of office space supplied per unit of land.

The Mobility of Labour The supply of labour services usually requires the physical presence of the person who supplies it. Absentee landlords, while continuing to live in the place of their choice, can obtain income from land that is located in remote parts of the world. Similarly, investment can be shifted from iron mines in South Africa to mines in Labrador while the mine owners commute between Calgary and Hawaii. The same is true for some workers, such as designers or bookkeepers, who can work in one location and submit their work to clients in other locations. But almost all workers involved in manufacturing and most of those involved in serving the public in stores, restaurants, and so on must actually be present to supply their labour services to an employer. When a worker who is employed by a firm producing men's suits in Montreal decides instead to supply his or her labour services to a firm producing women's shoes in Winnipeg, the worker must physically travel to Winnipeg. This has an important consequence.

> **Because of the need for labour's physical presence when its services are provided for the production of most goods and services, non-monetary considerations are much more important for the supply of labour than for other factors of production.**

People may be satisfied with or frustrated by the kind of work that they do, where they do it, the people with whom they do it, and the social status of their occupations. Because these considerations influence their decisions about what they will do with their labour services, they will not always move just because they could earn a higher wage.

Nevertheless, labour is mobile among industries, occupations, and regions in response to changes in the signals provided by wages and opportunities for employment. The ease with which such mobility occurs depends on many forces. For example, it is not difficult for a travel agent to shift from one company to another in order to take a job in Edmonton instead of Regina, but it can be difficult for the same travel agent to become an editor, a model, a machinist, or a doctor within a short period of time. Workers who lack ability, training, or inclination find certain kinds of mobility difficult or impossible.

Some barriers to movement may be virtually insurmountable once a person's training has been completed. For example, it may be impossible for a farmer to become a surgeon or for a truck driver to become a professional athlete, even if the relative wage rates change greatly. However, the children of farmers, doctors, truck drivers, and athletes, when they are deciding how much education or training to obtain, are not nearly as limited in their choices as their parents, who have already completed their education and are settled in their occupations.

> **The labour force as a whole is mobile, even though many individual members in it are not.**

The Supply of Factors to a Particular Firm

Most firms employ only a very small proportion of the economy's total supply of each factor. As a result, they can usually obtain their factors at the going market price. This is true for labour, capital, and land. For example, a commercial bank that is hoping to expand its economics department can hire an extra economist and it will need to pay the going wage (or salary) to attract that economist. A car manufacturer can purchase new robotics equipment and will pay the market price to get it. And a rancher can buy more land at the going market price. In each case the firm's actions will have no effect on the market price for the factors of production.

Individual firms generally face perfectly elastic supply curves for factors, even though the supply for the economy as a whole may be quite inelastic.

13.3 THE OPERATION OF FACTOR MARKETS

Once you have mastered the basic analysis of demand and supply in Chapters 3, 4, and 5, the determination of the price, quantity, and income of a factor in a single market poses no new problems. Figure 13-2 shows a competitive market for a factor. In both parts of the figure, the intersection of the demand and supply curves determines the factor's price and the quantity of the factor employed. The total market income earned by the factor is given by the equilibrium price times the equilibrium quantity.

Changes in factor markets can occur either because of a change in demand for the factor or because of a change in the supply of the factor, or both. Part (i) of Figure 13-2 illustrates a case in which an increase in demand for a factor leads to a rise in that factor's price and an increase in total income earned by that factor. What could cause such a change? Recall that the market demand curve for any factor comes from the many firms' *MRP* curves for that factor. An increase in the productivity of that factor (or an increase in demand for the products using that factor) would lead to a rightward shift in the *MRP* curves and thus to an increase in the market demand for the factor. Indeed, increases in productivity account for a gradual but ongoing increase in the demand for most factors of production.

Part (ii) of Figure 13-2 shows that an increase in the supply of some factor of production leads to a decline in that factor's equilibrium price and an increase in the quantity of the factor employed. (The total income earned by the factor may rise or fall, depending on the elasticity of demand for the factor.) Though the supply of any factor to a specific firm may change suddenly, the supply to the economy as a whole tends to change very gradually.

We now go on to explore two issues relating to factor pricing. First, what explains the differences in payments received by different units of the same factor, and can these differences be eliminated? Second, we explore the important concept of *economic rent*.

Differentials in Factor Prices

Airline pilots typically get paid more than auto mechanics, and a hectare of land in downtown Calgary rents for much more than a hectare of land 150 kilometres away in the Crowsnest Pass. Are such *factor-price differentials* to be expected in well-functioning factor markets?

FIGURE 13-2   Demand and Supply Shifts in a Competitive Factor Market

(i) An increase in factor demand

(ii) An increase in factor supply

Equilibrium factor prices and quantities are determined by the demand for and supply of factors. In both parts of the figure, the initial equilibrium is determined by D_0 and S_0. The equilibrium factor price is w_0, the equilibrium quantity of the factor is Q_0, and total factor income is the area w_0Q_0.

In part (i), an increase in demand for the factor shifts the demand curve to D_1. The equilibrium factor price rises to w_1 and quantity increases to Q_1. Since both price and quantity have increased, the total income earned by the factor clearly increases.

In part (ii), an increase in the supply of the factor shifts the supply curve to S_1. The equilibrium factor price falls to w_1 but the quantity increases to Q_1. Since price falls but quantity rises, the effect on total factor income is unclear. If demand for the factor is inelastic, total factor income will fall; if demand is elastic, total factor income will rise.

If all workers were the same, if the attractiveness of all jobs were the same, and if workers moved freely among markets, all workers would earn the same wage. Imagine what would happen if wages were different across jobs that were very similar. Workers would move from low-wage to high-wage jobs. The supply of labour would fall in low-wage occupations and the resulting labour shortage would tend to force those wages up. Conversely, the supply of labour would increase in high-wage occupations and would force those wages down. The movement would continue until there were no further incentives to change occupations—that is, until wages were equalized in all uses.

In fact, however, wage differentials obviously occur. As it is with labour, so it is with other factors of production. Factor-price differentials can be divided into two types: those that exist only temporarily and those that exist in long-run equilibrium.

Temporary factor-price differentials lead to, and are eroded by, factor mobility. Equilibrium differentials in factor prices are not eliminated by factor mobility.

Temporary Differentials   Some factor-price differentials reflect temporary disturbances, such as the growth of one industry or the decline of another. The differentials themselves lead to the movement of factors, and such movements in turn act to eliminate the differentials.

Consider the effect on factor prices of a rise in the demand for air transport when there is no change in the demand for rail transport. Specifically, consider the wages for the individuals who organize and handle freight shipments in the two industries. The airline industry's demand for workers increases while there is no change in demand for workers in the railway industry. Wages will rise in the airline industry and create a factor-price differential. The differential in wages causes a net movement of workers away from the railway industry and toward the airline industry, and this movement causes the wage differentials to lessen and eventually to disappear. This adjustment process is illustrated in Figure 13-3. How long this process takes depends on how easily workers can be reallocated from one industry to the other—that is, on the degree of factor mobility.

The behaviour that causes the erosion of temporary differentials is summarized in the hypothesis of the *maximization of net advantage*: The owners of factors of production will allocate those factors to uses that maximize the net advantages to themselves, taking both monetary and non-monetary rewards into consideration. If net advantages were higher in occupation A than in occupation B, factors would move from B to A. The increased supply in A and the reduced supply in B would drive factor

FIGURE 13-3 **The Creation and Erosion of Temporary Factor-Price Differentials**

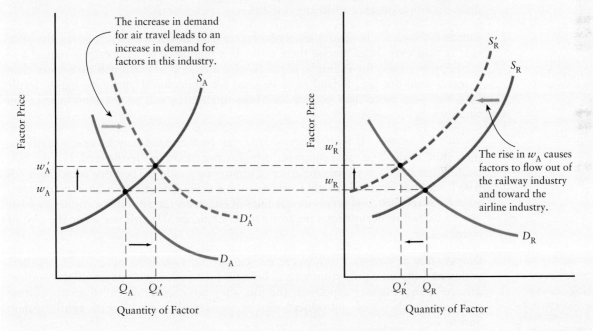

(i) Airline industry   (ii) Railway industry

The mobility of factors leads to the erosion of temporary differentials in factor prices. The two figures show the markets for some factor of production (land, labour, or capital) in the airline and railway industries. Suppose the initial equilibrium has the factor receiving the same price in both industries ($w_A = w_R$). Q_A units are employed in the airline industry and Q_R units are employed in the railway industry.

An increase in demand for air travel leads to an increase in demand for factors in the airline industry. The demand curve shifts to D_A' and factor prices in that industry rise to w_A'. As factor prices in the airline industry rise, factors leave the railway industry and enter the airline industry. This flow of factors is a leftward shift of S_R to S_R' and a movement upward along S_A. There is a reduction of factors employed in the railway industry and an increase in factors employed in the airline industry. The flow of factors stops when factor prices are again equalized, $w_A' = w_R'$.

The long and costly training required to become a surgeon reduces the supply of surgeons relative to many other occupations and is one reason surgeons typically earn very high incomes. This is an equilibrium wage differential.

earnings down in *A* and up in *B* until net advantages would be equalized, after which no further movement would occur. This analysis gives rise to the prediction of *equal net advantage*: In equilibrium, units of each kind of factor of production will be allocated among alternative possible uses in such a way that the net advantages in all uses are equalized.

> **A change in the relative price of a factor between two uses will lead to a shift of some units of that factor to the use for which relative price has increased. This factor mobility will, in turn, tend to reduce the differential in relative prices.**

Equilibrium Differentials   Some factor-price differentials persist without generating any forces that eliminate them. These equilibrium differentials can be explained by intrinsic differences in the factors themselves and, for labour, by differences in the cost of acquiring skills and by different non-monetary advantages of different occupations.

Intrinsic Differences.   If various units of a factor have different characteristics, the price that is paid may differ among these units. If a high level of numeracy is required to accomplish a task, for example, workers who are good at math will earn more than workers who are not. If land is to be used for agricultural purposes, highly fertile land will earn more than poor land. These differences will persist even in long-run equilibrium.

Acquired Differences.   If the fertility of land can be increased only by costly methods, then more fertile land must command a higher price than less fertile land. If it did not, landowners would not incur the costs of improving fertility. The same principle holds true for labour since it is costly to acquire most skills. For example, an engineer must train for some time, and unless the earnings of engineers remain sufficiently above what can be earned in occupations requiring fewer skills, people will not incur the cost of training.

Compensating Differentials.   Whenever working conditions differ across jobs, workers will earn different equilibrium wages. Because such factor-price differentials *compensate* for non-monetary aspects of the job, they are commonly called **compensating differentials**; they were introduced into economics almost 250 years ago by Adam Smith.

compensating differential
A difference in the payment to a factor of production (usually labour) across two jobs to compensate the factor for differences in non-monetary aspects of the two jobs.

Academic researchers commonly earn less than they could earn in the world of commerce and industry because of the substantial non-monetary advantages of academic employment. If chemists were paid the same in both sectors, many chemists would prefer academic to industrial jobs. Excess demand for industrial chemists and excess supply of academic chemists would then force chemists' wages up in industry and down in academia until the two types of jobs seemed equally attractive on balance.

Compensating differentials also exist in the regional earnings of otherwise identical factors. People who work in remote logging or mining areas are paid more than people who do jobs requiring similar skills in large cities. Without higher pay, not enough people would be willing to work at sometimes dangerous jobs in unattractive or remote locations.

Can Differentials Be Eliminated?   The distinction between temporary and equilibrium factor-price differentials raises an important consideration for policy. Trade unions and governments sometimes have explicit policies about earnings differentials and seek to eliminate them in the name of equity. The success of such policies depends to a great extent on the kind of differential that is being attacked. An important general lesson from this experience is the following: Policies that attempt to eliminate *temporary* differentials may be successful in speeding up what may otherwise be a slow adjustment process. But policies aimed at eliminating *equilibrium* differentials will encounter difficulties.

Canadian governments have introduced legislation to redress male–female wage differentials that appear to exist *only* because of discrimination in the labour market. As the social norms that sustain these discriminatory forces change, so too will the wage differentials. But the adjustment may be very gradual. Canadian *pay-equity* legislation has been designed to speed this adjustment and, in the process, reduce the underlying discriminatory forces. These policies have been successful in reducing male–female wage differentials in situations where the men and women concerned are equally qualified and are in the same jobs.

Other government pay-equity legislation is less successful because it attempts to reduce or eliminate *equilibrium* wage differentials. Such policy is designed to eliminate the wage differentials that exist between workers *in different jobs* but who are deemed to have approximately the same skills and responsibilities.

Jobs with unpleasant working conditions usually pay higher wages than more pleasant jobs requiring the same skills. Such differences in wages are called "compensating differentials." Any policy that attempts to eliminate these differentials is likely to be ineffective.

To illustrate the nature of the problem encountered by such legislation, consider the example of two types of construction workers—those who work mostly indoors doing home and building renovations, and those who work mostly outdoors on bridges or the exteriors of buildings. Suppose these two jobs demand equal skills and training. But in a city with a harsh climate, the outside construction job is less pleasant than the inside construction job. In the absence of pay-equity legislation, the wage for outside workers would exceed that for inside workers—an equilibrium wage differential. If legislation now requires equal pay for both jobs, there will be a shortage of people willing to work outside and an excess of people willing to work inside. Employers will seek ways to attract outside workers. Higher pensions, shorter hours, and longer holidays may be offered. If these are allowed, they will achieve the desired result but will defeat the original purpose of equalizing the monetary benefits of the inside and outside jobs. If the jobs are unionized or if the government prevents such "cheating," the shortage of workers for outside jobs will remain.

> **Policies that seek to eliminate equilibrium factor-price differentials without consideration of what causes them or how they affect the supply of the factor often have perverse results.**

Economic Rent

One of the most important concepts in economics is that of *economic rent*.

A mobile factor must earn a certain amount in its present use to prevent it from moving to another use—the great nineteenth-century economist Alfred Marshall called

transfer earnings The minimum payment required by a factor in order to prevent it from leaving its current use.

economic rent The excess of total earnings over the minimum necessary to prevent a factor from moving to another use.

this amount the factor's **transfer earnings,** but most economists today would simply call it the factor's opportunity cost. Any amount that the factor earns *above* its transfer earnings is called **economic rent.** Economic rent is analogous to economic profit as a surplus over the opportunity cost of capital. Here are three examples:

1. Consider a farmer who grows wheat and earns $1000 per hectare. She has calculated that if her earnings fall to $900 per hectare, she will switch to growing barley instead, her next best alternative. In this case, each hectare of land growing wheat is earning $100 of economic rent.

2. A famous actor earns $15 million per year. He decides that his next best alternative to acting is appearing in TV commercials, in which case he would earn $5 million per year. He is earning $10 million per year of economic rent.

3. An individual has invested $300 000 of financial capital into a restaurant and currently earns a 20 percent annual return—investment income of $60 000 annually. The next best alternative investment (with similar risk) can earn a 15 percent return, or $45 000 annually. The $300 000 of capital is thus earning economic rent equal to $15 000 per year. In this case, rent is just another name for profit in the economist's sense of the term.

The concept of economic rent is crucial for predicting the effects that changes in earnings have on the movement of factors among alternative uses. However, the terminology is confusing because economic rent is often simply called rent, which can of course also mean the price paid to hire something, such as a machine, a piece of land, or an apartment. How the same term came to be used for these two different concepts is explained in *Lessons from History 13-1.*

How Much of Factor Earnings Is Rent?   In most cases, as in the three previous examples, economic rent makes up part of the factor's total earnings. From the definitions just given, however, note that total earnings for any factor are the sum of its transfer earnings and its economic rent.

A factor's transfer earnings plus its economic rent equals its total earnings.

But *how much* of total earnings is economic rent? A different but related question is, How much would the factor price have to fall before the factor left its current use?

The possibilities are illustrated in Figure 13-4. When supply is perfectly elastic, as in part (i), the factor is extremely mobile between various uses. In this case, all of the factor's income is transfer earnings and so none of it is economic rent. If any lower price is offered, nothing whatsoever will be supplied since all units of the factor will transfer to some other use.

When supply is perfectly inelastic, as in part (iii), the same quantity is supplied whatever the price. Evidently, the quantity supplied does not decrease, no matter how low the price goes. This inelasticity indicates that the factor has no alternative use, and thus requires no minimum payment to keep it in its present use. In this case, there are no transfer earnings and so the whole of the payment is economic rent.

The more usual situation is that of an upward-sloping supply curve, as shown in part (ii) of Figure 13-4. A rise in the factor's price serves the allocative function of attracting

LESSONS FROM HISTORY 13-1

David Ricardo and "Economic Rent"

In the early nineteenth century, there was a public debate about the high price of wheat in England. The high price was causing great hardship because bread was a primary source of food for the working class. Some people argued that wheat had a high price because landlords were charging high rents to tenant farmers. Some of those who held this view advocated restricting the rents that landlords could charge.

David Ricardo (1772–1823), a great British economist who was one of the originators of Classical economics, argued that the situation was exactly the reverse. The price of wheat was high, he said, because there was a shortage, caused by the Napoleonic Wars. Because wheat was profitable to produce, there was keen competition among farmers to obtain land on which to grow wheat. This competition in turn forced up the rental price of wheat land. Ricardo advocated removing the existing tariff on wheat so that plentiful imported wheat could come into the country. The increase in imports would then increase the supply of wheat in England and lower its price. This would then reduce the rent on land.

The essentials of Ricardo's argument were these: The supply of land was fixed. Land was regarded as having only one use, the growing of wheat. Nothing had to be paid to prevent land from transferring to a different use because it had no other use. No landowner would leave land idle as long as some return could be obtained by renting it out. Therefore, all the payment to land—that is, rent in the ordinary sense of the word—was a surplus over and above what was necessary to keep it in its present use.

Given a fixed supply of land, the price of land depended on the demand for land, which depended in turn on the price of wheat. Rent, the term for the payment for the use of land, thus became the term for a surplus payment to a factor over and above what was necessary to keep it in its present use.

Later, two facts were realized. First, land often had alternative uses, and, from the point of view of any one use, part of the payment made to land would necessarily have to be paid to keep it in that use. Second, factors of production other than land also often earned a surplus over and above what was necessary to keep them in their present use. This surplus is now called *economic rent*, whether the factor is land, labour, or a piece of capital equipment.

David Ricardo was the first economist to clarify the connection between factor earnings and economic rent.

more units of the factor into the market in question, but the same rise provides additional economic rent to all units of the factor that are *already employed*. We know that the extra pay that is going to the units already employed is economic rent because the owners of these units were willing to supply them at the previous lower price.

The production and sale of oil provides a good example of the relationship between economic rent and market price. Oil is extracted and refined in various parts of the world at vastly different costs of production, but is typically sold at a common world price. Suppose a producer in Alberta's oil sands incurs costs of production of $60 per barrel while a producer in Saudi Arabia incurs costs of only $20 per barrel. At a world oil price of $60, the Alberta producer is *marginal* and is earning transfer earnings only; any decrease in the world price would lead the Alberta producer to reduce output. The

FIGURE 13-4 The Determination of Rent in Factor Markets

(i) Perfectly elastic supply   (ii) Positively sloped supply   (iii) Perfectly inelastic supply

The amount of a factor's earnings that is economic rent depends on the mobility (and thus on the elasticity of supply) of the factor. In each case, the equilibrium is determined by the intersection of the demand and supply curves, and total factor earnings are given by factor price times quantity, wQ.

In part (i), supply is perfectly elastic, indicating that even a slightly lower factor price would cause the factor to leave. None of the earnings are economic rent; all are the factor's transfer earnings.

In part (ii), supply is positively sloped, indicating that more units of the factor will be supplied at a higher price. The area below the supply curve is the amount needed to keep Q_2 units of the factor in its current use—this area is the factor's transfer earnings. The red shaded area above the supply curve is economic rent.

In part (iii), supply is perfectly inelastic, indicating that the factor has no other uses. In this case, transfer earnings are zero and all of the factor's earnings are economic rent.

producer in Saudi Arabia, however, is earning significant rent on each barrel of oil produced; the world price would have to fall below $20 before output was reduced below current levels. In terms of Figure 13-4, the world supply of oil is as depicted in part (*ii*), with the Saudi Arabian producer farther to the left along the supply curve and the Alberta producer closer to the market equilibrium.

Various Perspectives on Economic Rent The proportion of a given factor payment that is economic rent varies from situation to situation. We cannot point to a factor of production and assert that some fixed fraction of its income is always its economic rent. The proportion of its earnings that is rent depends on its alternatives.

Consider first a narrowly defined use of a given factor—say, its use by a particular firm. From that firm's point of view, the factor will be highly mobile, as it could readily move to another firm in the same industry. The firm must pay the going wage or risk losing that factor. Thus, only a small portion of its payment is rent.

Now consider a more broadly defined use—for example, the factor's use in an entire industry. From the industry's point of view, the factor is less mobile because it would be more difficult for it to gain employment quickly outside the industry. From the perspective of the particular *industry* (rather than the specific *firm* within the industry), a larger proportion of the payment to a factor is economic rent.

From the even more general perspective of a particular *occupation*, mobility is likely to be even less, and the proportion of the factor payment that is economic rent is likely to be more. It may be easier, for example, for a carpenter to move from the construction industry to the furniture industry than to retrain to be a software engineer.

> As the perspective moves from a narrowly defined use of a factor to a more broadly defined use of a factor, the mobility of the factor decreases; as mobility decreases, the share of the factor payment that is economic rent increases.

Consider how this relationship applies to the often controversial large salaries that are received by some highly specialized types of workers, such as movie stars and professional athletes. These performers have a unique style and a talent that cannot be duplicated, whatever the training. The earnings that they receive are mostly economic rent from the viewpoint of the occupation: These performers generally enjoy their occupations and would pursue them for much less than the high remuneration that they actually receive.

Increases in the price of oil that are not needed to increase the quantity supplied generate economic rents for producers. For example, if the owner of this well is only willing to operate it when the price of oil is $35 per barrel or higher, then any price above that level generates some economic rent for the producer.

For example, Sidney Crosby would probably have chosen hockey over other alternatives even at a much lower salary. However, because of Crosby's superior skills as a hockey player, most hockey teams would pay handsomely to have him on their rosters, and he is able to command a high salary from the team for which he does play. From the perspective of the individual firm, the Pittsburgh Penguins, most of Crosby's salary is required to keep him from switching to another team and hence is not economic rent. From the point of view of the hockey "industry," however, much of his salary is economic rent.

Notice also that Sidney Crosby's salary is largely determined by the demand for his services. The supply is perfectly inelastic—no one else has his particular combination of skills. So the market-clearing price is determined by the position of the demand curve.

A Final Word

This chapter has examined the operation of factor markets. You should now be able to answer the questions we posed in the opening paragraph. Here are some of the key points for two of those questions.

What explains why neurosurgeons are usually paid more than family doctors? Part of the answer is that to be a neurosurgeon requires more years of costly specialized training than that needed to be a family doctor. Since that extra training is costly and time-consuming, it is not surprising that fewer people are willing or able to become neurosurgeons than family doctors. This lower supply for neurosurgeons, other things being equal, leads to a higher wage.

Why does a hectare of farmland in Northern Saskatchewan rent for far less than a hectare of land in downtown Toronto? To answer this, just think about the alternative uses for the farm land, and compare them with the alternative uses for the hectare in downtown Toronto. The hectare of farmland has very few alternative uses. Or, more correctly, it has many alternative uses, but there is little demand to use that particular piece of land to build a skyscraper, shopping mall, or baseball stadium. But one hectare of land in downtown Toronto has many alternative uses—there is almost always demand for additional space for parking garages, office buildings, retail stores, and many other things. Since the piece of farmland in Saskatchewan must stay where it is, its rental price is determined by demand. Since there is little demand for the land, its rental price is low. Similarly, the land in downtown Toronto cannot move anywhere, and so its rental price is determined by demand. And since there is lots of demand for a hectare in downtown Toronto, its rental price is high.

Having learned about factor markets in general, we are now ready to examine some specific factor markets. In Chapter 14, we examine some details about labour markets, such as minimum wages, discrimination, labour unions, and income inequality. In Chapter 15, we examine capital markets and the interest rate.

SUMMARY

13.1 THE DEMAND FOR FACTORS
LO 1

- A firm's decisions on how much to produce and how to produce it imply demands for factors of production, which are said to be derived from the demand for goods they are used to produce.
- A profit-maximizing firm will hire units of a factor until the last unit adds as much to revenue as it does to cost. Thus, the marginal revenue product of the factor will be equated with that factor's marginal cost.
- When the firm is a price taker in factor markets, the marginal cost of the factor is its price per unit. When the firm sells its output in a competitive market, the marginal revenue product is the factor's marginal product multiplied by the market price of the output.
- A price-taking firm's demand curve for a factor is negatively sloped because the law of diminishing returns implies that the marginal product of a factor declines as more of that factor is employed (with other inputs held constant).
- The demand for a factor will increase if the factor becomes more productive or if the price of the product increases.

13.2 THE SUPPLY OF FACTORS
LO 2

- The total supply of each factor is fixed at any moment but varies over time. The supply of labour depends on the size of the population, the participation rate, and the number of hours that people want to work.
- A rise in the wage rate has a substitution effect, which tends to induce more work, and an income effect, which tends to induce less work (more leisure consumed).
- The supply of a factor to a particular industry or occupation is more elastic than its supply to the whole economy because one industry can bid units away from other industries.
- The elasticity of supply to a particular use depends on factor mobility, which tends to be greater the longer the time allowed for a reaction to take place.

13.3 THE OPERATION OF FACTOR MARKETS
LO 3, 4

- Factor-price differentials often occur in competitive markets. Temporary differentials in the earnings of different units of factors of production induce factor movements that eventually remove the differentials. Equilibrium differentials reflect differences among units of factors as well as non-monetary benefits of different jobs; they can persist indefinitely.
- Factors will be allocated between uses to generate the greatest net advantage to their owners, allowing for both the monetary and non-monetary advantages of a particular employment.
- Some amount must be paid to a factor to prevent it from moving to another use. This amount is the factor's transfer earnings. Economic rent is the difference between that amount and a factor's total earnings.
- Whenever the supply curve is positively sloped, part of the total payment going to a factor is needed to prevent it from moving to another use, and part of it is economic rent. The more narrowly defined the use, the larger the fraction that is transfer earnings and the smaller the fraction that is economic rent.

KEY CONCEPTS

Derived demand for a factor
Marginal product (*MP*)
Marginal revenue product (*MRP*)

The determinants of elasticity of factor
  demand
Factor mobility
Temporary versus equilibrium factor-
  price differentials

Equal net advantage
Transfer earnings
Economic rent

STUDY EXERCISES

MyEconLab   **Save Time. Improve Results Make the grade with MyEconLab: Study Exercises marked in ⊕ can be found on MyEconLab. You can practise them as often as you want, and most feature step-by-step guided instructions to help you find the right answer.**

① According to a recent article in *The Globe and Mail*, the fastest-growing small businesses in Canada were

  a. specialty clothes manufacturing
  b. health practitioners
  c. accounting and bookkeeping
  d. computer-software design
  e. machinery and equipment repair
  f. architectural services

In each case, list two derived demands that you predict will be increasing as a result, and explain your reasoning.

② Fill in the blanks to make the following statements correct.

  a. Marginal revenue product is calculated by multiplying _____ and _____.
  b. Marginal revenue product represents the addition to a firm's total revenue as a result of _____.
  c. To maximize its profits, a firm will hire all units of a factor that have a(n) _____ greater than or equal to its _____.
  d. To maximize its profits, any firm will hire each factor of production to the point where the factor's _____ equals the _____.

③ Fill in the blanks to make the following statements correct.

  a. The *MRP* curve for a factor is the same as the firm's _____ for that factor.
  b. If the marginal product for a factor declines rapidly as more of that factor is used, demand for that factor will be relatively _____.

  c. Other things being equal, if the demand for a product that a factor is used to produce is relatively inelastic, the demand for that factor will be relatively _____.
  d. An increase in the price at which a competitive firm sells its product leads the firm's demand curve for its factor to _____.
  e. If a technological improvement leads every unit of a given factor to produce 10 percent more output than previously, the _____ curve will _____ and thus the firm's demand curve for the factor will _____.

④ The Apple Pie Factory produces apple pies. The firm sells its product and hires its workers in competitive markets. The market price (*p*) for a pie is $4 and the wage rate (*w*) is $10 per hour. The table below shows the total hourly production (*Q*) for varying amounts of workers (*L*). (Remember that for a price-taking firm, *p* = *MR*.)

L	Q	w	p	MP	MRP
4	40	——	——		
				——	——
5	48	——	——		
				——	——
6	55	——	——		
				——	——
7	61	——	——		
				——	——
8	66	——	——		
				——	——
9	70	——	——		
				——	——
10	73	——	——		
				——	——
11	75	——	——		
				——	——
12	76	——	——		

a. Fill in the *p* and *w* columns.
b. Calculate the *MP* and the *MRP* for each amount of labour employed. Put the numbers between the rows.
c. What is the logic of the firm's profit-maximizing condition for hiring labour?
d. How many workers should this profit-maximizing firm hire?

5 Refer back to the production schedule for the Apple Pie Factory in Question 4. In this question we will derive the firm's demand curve for labour.

a. On a diagram, with *MRP* on the vertical axis and the number of workers on the horizontal axis, plot the *MRP* curve.
b. If the wage is $10 per hour, how many workers will be hired? Why?
c. If the wage is $5 per hour, how many workers will be hired? Why?
d. If the wage is $20 per hour, how many workers will be hired? Why?
e. Explain why the *MRP* curve is the firm's factor demand curve.

6 Fill in the blanks to make the following statements correct. Each firm is assumed to be hiring factors in competitive markets.

a. A tax-preparation firm produces completed tax returns (one unit of output) which produce revenue of $50 per unit. The firm hires labour for $22 per hour. If the last hour of labour hired produces 0.25 units of output, that hour's MRP is _____. The last hour contributes _____ to the firm's profits. The firm should hire (more/fewer/the same) hours of labour in order to maximize its profits.
b. An excavation company digs holes (one unit of output) which produce revenue of $100 per unit. The firm pays a rental price of $200 per day for a backhoe. The last day hired of this machine produces three units of output. This factor's MRP is _____. The last day rented contributes _____ to the firm's profits. The firm should hire (more/fewer/the same) day-rentals of the backhoe in order to maximize its profits.
c. A software developer produces software programs (one unit of output) which produce revenue of $12 000 per unit. The firm hires programmers for $6000 per month. If the last month of labour hired produces 0.5 units of output, the MRP for the last month hired is _____. This last unit of the factor contributes _____ to the firm's profits. This firm should hire (more/fewer/the same) months of labour in order to maximize its profits.

7 The following diagram shows the market for fast-food workers in British Columbia. Assume there is no legislated minimum wage.

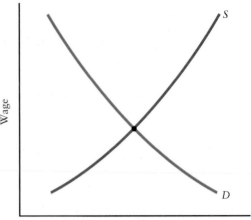

Quantity of Labour

a. The supply curve is upward sloping. If the wage in this industry rises, where do the extra workers come from?
b. Suppose there is a significant decrease in demand for fast food. How is this likely to affect the earnings of fast-food workers? Show this in the diagram.
c. Now suppose new legislation bans the assignment of homework to high school students. As a result, more students look for jobs in the fast-food industry. How will this affect the labour market for fast-food workers? Show this in the diagram.
d. What will be the effect on total earnings in the fast-food industry from the change in part (c)? On what does the answer depend?

8 The three following diagrams show the supply of luxury ocean liners at three different levels of aggregation—the entire world, a particular country, and a particular firm.

Diagram 1   Diagram 2

Diagram 3

a. Which diagram shows the supply of ocean liners to the world as whole? Explain its elasticity.

b. Which diagram shows the supply of ocean liners to Canada? Explain its elasticity.

c. Which diagram shows the supply of ocean liners to an individual Canadian firm? Explain its elasticity.

d. What is the general relationship between factor mobility and the elasticity of factor supply?

9 In the text we argued that temporary factor-price differentials tend to be eroded by factor mobility. This question requires you to think about this process. Consider the two markets for sheet-iron workers and steel-pipe workers in the same region. Suppose both markets are competitive. We begin in a situation in which both sheet-iron workers and steel-pipe workers earn $20 per hour. Assume that workers can switch easily between the two jobs.

a. Draw diagrams showing the supply and demand for labour in each market.

b. Now suppose there is a sharp increase in the demand for steel pipe. Explain what happens in the market for steel-pipe workers.

c. If the employment of steel-pipe workers increased in part (b), explain where the extra workers came from.

d. What effect does the event in part (b) have on the market for sheet-iron workers?

e. What is the long-run effect of the shock on the relative wages in the two types of jobs?

10 The diagram below shows the competitive market for landscaping workers in a particular region.

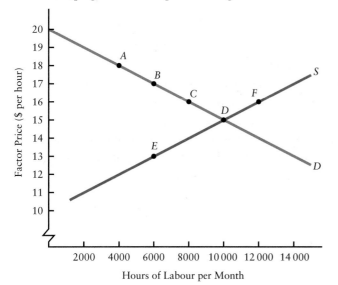

a. What is the marginal revenue product of the 10 000th hour of labour?

b. Suppose the wage is $16 per hour. Explain the forces that would push the market's outcome back toward equilibrium at point D.

c. Assuming this market is in equilibrium, determine each of the following:

- total factor earnings
- transfer earnings of the 10 000th hour of labour employed
- economic rent for the 10 000th hour of labour employed
- transfer earnings of the 6000th hour of labour employed
- economic rent for the 6000th hour of labour employed

d. Provide two reasons why this demand curve could shift to the right toward a new equilibrium at point F.

11 How much of the following payments for factor services is likely to be economic rent?

a. The $750 per month that a landlord receives for renting an apartment

b. The salary of the Canadian prime minister

c. The annual income of Tiger Woods or Katy Perry

d. The salary of a window cleaner who says, "It's dangerous work, but it beats driving a truck."

e. An engineer at Google headquarters who loves going to work every day

12 It is common to hear comments like "Why do baseball players earn millions of dollars a year for their negligible contribution to society while major contributors—such as schoolteachers, police officers, firefighters, and ambulance drivers—earn barely enough to survive?" Can you offer an answer based on what was discussed in this chapter?

13 Using the concepts of transfer earnings and economic rent, can you derive a form of taxation—of the earnings by oil companies, for example—that would generate tax revenue but not influence the companies' supply decisions? Is your approach consistent with that followed by Canada's provincial governments when they collect royalties on natural-resource revenues?

14 Labour Markets and Income Inequality

CHAPTER OUTLINE	LEARNING OBJECTIVES (LO)
	After studying this chapter you will be able to
14.1 WAGE DIFFERENTIALS	1 explain wage differentials in both competitive and non-competitive labour markets.
	2 describe the possible effects of legislated minimum wages.
14.2 LABOUR UNIONS	3 discuss the tradeoff that unions usually face between wages and employment.
14.3 INCOME INEQUALITY	4 understand some possible explanations for the recent trend toward rising income inequality.

THE competitive theory of factor-price determination, presented in Chapter 13, tells us a great deal about the determinants of factor incomes and factor movements. In this chapter, we look specifically at labour markets. We begin by discussing why some workers get high wages and others get low wages. We then look beyond our theory of competitive labour markets to examine situations where either firms or workers have some market power. We also discuss the effects of legislated minimum wages, as well as the debate surrounding this contentious policy. The chapter then discusses labour unions, and the tradeoff they face between increasing their membership and increasing their members' wages. Finally, we examine measures of the distribution of income within a country and discuss the rising income inequality that is occurring in many countries, including Canada.

Before getting to these topics, however, we can set the stage by examining the broad patterns of employment in Canada over the past century, as shown in Figure 14-1. The share of total employment in agriculture fell from 45 percent in 1891 to just under 2 percent today, while the share of total employment in services (including government) increased from 20 percent in 1891 to 80 percent today. The combined share for manufacturing, construction, and natural resources (forestry, mining, oil and gas, etc.) has been more stable over the last century, but has been on a gradual downward trend for the past 50 years, falling from about 35 percent in 1951 to about 20 percent today.

The dramatic rise in service-sector employment, and the decline in the relative importance of agriculture and manufacturing, is not just a Canadian phenomenon. The same pattern is evident in all developed countries. In general, this increased importance of services reflects our spending patterns as our incomes increase—spending relatively less on tangible goods and relatively more on services such as education, healthcare, entertainment, and so on.

The service sector contains an enormous variety of occupations. Many jobs in the service sector require considerable education and training, and thus the workers in these jobs are highly paid. Obvious examples include lawyers, doctors, architects, design engineers, accountants, management consultants, and professors. On the other hand, the service sector also contains many jobs that require much less training and whose workers receive much lower wages. Examples of these occupations include restaurant servers, fast-food employees, store clerks, flight attendants, telephone solicitors, janitors, and hotel maids.

The changing pattern of Canadian employment evident in Figure 14-1 provides some of the context for the main issues we examine in this chapter—wage differentials, minimum wages, labour unions, and income inequality.

FIGURE 14-1 A Century of Change in the Composition of Canadian Employment

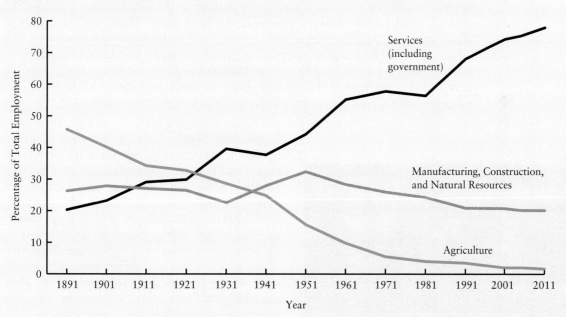

Over the past century, major shifts in employment have taken place between sectors of the economy. In 1891, more than 45 percent of Canadian employment was in agriculture, and only 20 percent in services (including government). By 2011, agriculture accounted for only 1.8 percent of employment, while services had increased to 78 percent. The share of employment in manufacturing increased from 26 percent in 1891 to 32 percent just after the Second World War, and then declined to 20 percent by 2011.

(*Source:* Based on *Canadian Census*, various years, and author's calculations. The most recent data are available on the Statistics Canada website at www.statcan.gc.ca. Choose "Summary Tables" and then type in "employment by industry.")

14.1 WAGE DIFFERENTIALS

We argued in the last chapter that if all workers were identical, all jobs had the same working conditions, and labour markets were perfectly competitive, all workers would earn the same wage. In reality, however, wages vary enormously across such dimensions as occupations, skills, amounts of education, and geographical areas. Generally, the more education and experience a worker has, the higher are his or her wages. Given equal education and experience, women on average earn less than men. Workers in highly unionized industries tend to be paid more than workers with similar skills and experience in non-unionized industries. Such differentials arise because workers are not all identical, jobs are not all identical, and important non-competitive forces sometimes operate in labour markets. We now look more systematically at some of the main reasons that different workers earn different wages.

Wage Differentials in Competitive Markets

Wage differentials exist in competitive labour markets because workers are not all identical and jobs are not all identical. We examine four main reasons for existing wage differentials.

1. Working Conditions   Given identical skills, those working under relatively onerous or risky conditions earn more than those working in pleasant or safe conditions. For example, construction workers who work the "high iron," assembling the frames for skyscrapers, are paid more than workers who do similar work at ground level. The reason is simple: Risk and unpleasantness reduce the supply of labour, thus raising the wage above what it would otherwise be. Different working conditions in different jobs thus lead to *compensating differentials* as we discussed in Chapter 13. These wage differentials are not temporary—they are *equilibrium* wage differentials.

2. Inherited Skills   Large incomes will be earned by people who have scarce skills that cannot be taught and that are in high demand—for example, an NBA basketball player, an opera singer, or a movie star. In these cases, the combination of a small and inelastic supply and a large enough demand for the relevant kind of labour cause the market-clearing wage to be high. Wage differentials of this kind are also equilibrium wage differentials. Later in the chapter we have more to say about the salaries of "superstars" and how modern communications technology has dramatically increased their earnings in the last few decades.

Many jobs involve dangerous or unpleasant working conditions. Wages in such jobs are generally higher than in other jobs requiring comparable skills. These are called compensating wage differentials.

© Sergio Azenha/Alamy

3. Human Capital   A machine is physical capital. It requires an investment of time and money to create it, and once created, it yields valuable services over a long time. In the same way, labour skills require an investment of time and money to acquire, and once acquired, they may yield an increased income for their owner over a long time. Since investment in labour skills is similar to investment in physical capital, acquired skills are called **human capital**. The more costly it is to acquire the skill required for a particular job, the higher its pay must be to attract people to train for it.

human capital The acquired skills that Individuals have, usually from formal education or on-the-job training.

> **Investment in human capital is costly, and the return is usually in terms of higher future wages.**

The two main ways in which human capital is acquired are through formal education and on-the-job training.

Formal Education.   Compulsory primary and secondary education provides some minimum human capital for all citizens. People who decide to stay on in school are deciding to invest in acquiring further human capital. The opportunity cost is measured by the income that you could have earned if you had entered the labour force immediately, in addition to the direct costs for such items as tuition fees and books and equipment. The financial return is measured by the higher income earned when a better job is obtained.

How large is the payoff from higher education? Figure 14-2 shows how average employment income varies with years of schooling. In 2007, the last year these data were made available, the average employment income for Canadians with a university degree was more than $61 400; in contrast, someone who failed to complete high school had an average employment income of less than $21 000.[1] It is worth emphasizing that the data in Figure 14-2 are *averages*; there are many individuals who earn more, and many others who earn less, than the incomes shown in the figure.

Evidence suggests that in recent years the demand for workers with more skills and education has been rising relative to the demand for those with less. As a result, earnings of high-skilled workers have been rising relative to those of low-skilled workers. As we will see in this chapter's final section, such changes in the structure of labour demand offer a partial explanation of rising income inequality.

On-the-Job Training.   Wage differentials according to experience are readily observable in most firms

FIGURE 14-2 Education and Employment Income

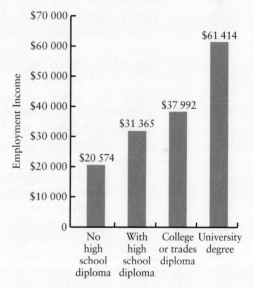

Canadians with more years of education earn more than those with less education. With each increase in the level of educational achievement there is a considerable increase in average income; the largest is for a university degree.

(*Source:* Based on the data from Statistics Canada's website, www.statcan.gc.ca. See *Income Trends in Canada 1976 to 2007*, publication 13-F0022X.)

[1] Figure 14-2 shows only the *correlation* between education and earnings; these raw data do not indicate a *causal* relationship. More advanced statistical studies, however, show that there is a clear financial payoff from additional years of education.

and occupations. To a significant extent, these differentials are a response to human capital acquired on the job. For example, a civil engineer with 20 years' experience in bridge design will generally earn more than a newly graduated civil engineer, even though they both have the same formal education.

On-the-job training is important in creating rising wages for employees and for making firms competitive. Evidence suggests that people who miss on-the-job training early in life are handicapped relative to others throughout much of their later working careers.

4. Discrimination   Wage differentials can also exist due to *discrimination* in the labour market, but care must be taken when interpreting the data. For example, in 2011 the average female full-time worker in Canada earned almost 25 percent less than the average full-time male worker. More detailed studies suggest that a significant part of these differences can be explained by such considerations as the nature of the job and the amount of human capital acquired through both formal education and on-the-job experience. When all such explanations are taken into account, however, there still appears to be a gap between male and female wages that reveals gender-based discrimination.

To understand the effects of labour-market discrimination, we begin by building a simplified model of a non-discriminating labour market and then introduce discrimination between two sets of equally qualified workers. The discussion here is phrased in terms of males and females but the analysis applies equally well to any situation in which workers are distinguished on grounds *other than* their ability, such as race or skin colour, citizenship, religion, sexual orientation, or political beliefs.

Suppose half of the people in the labour force are male and the other half are female. Each group has the same proportion who are educated to various levels, identical distributions of talent, and so on. Suppose also that there are two occupations. Occupation E (*elite*) requires people of above-average education and skills, and occupation O (*ordinary*) can use anyone. Finally, suppose the non-monetary aspects of the two occupations are the same.

In the absence of discrimination, the theory of competitive factor markets that we have developed suggests that the wages in E occupations will be bid up above those in O occupations in order that the E jobs attract the workers of above-average skills. Men and women of above-average skill will take the E jobs, while the others, both men and women, will have no choice but to seek O jobs. Because skills are equally distributed between both sexes, each occupation will employ one-half men and one-half women.

Now suppose discrimination enters in an extreme form. All E occupations are hereafter open only to men, but O occupations are open to either men or women. The immediate effect is to reduce by 50 percent the supply of job candidates for E occupations; all previously qualified female candidates are no longer eligible because candidates must now be *both* men and above average. The discrimination also increases the supply of applicants for O jobs because the women who cannot be employed in E jobs move instead to get O jobs. The new group of O-job candidates now includes all women and the below-average men. As shown in Figure 14-3, wages rise in E occupations and fall in O occupations.

> **Labour-market discrimination, by changing supply, decreases the wages of a group that is discriminated against and increases the wages of the "favoured" group.**

FIGURE 14-3 The Effect of Discrimination on Wages

(i) Elite market (E)   (ii) Ordinary market (O)

If market E discriminates against one group and market O does not, wages will rise in E and fall in O. Market E requires above-average skills, while market O requires only ordinary skills. When there is no discrimination, demand and supply are D_E and S_E in market E and D_O and S_O in market O. Initially, the wage rate is w_0 and employment is L_0 in each market. (w_0 in market E is higher than w_0 in market O because the workers in E have higher skills than those in O. This is an equilibrium wage differential.) When discrimination excludes women from E occupations, the supply curve shifts to S'_E, and the wage earned by the remaining workers, all of whom are men, rises to w_1. Women ineligible for work in the E occupations now seek work in the O occupations. The resulting shift in the supply curve to S'_O reduces the wage to w_2 in the O occupations. Because all women are in O occupations, they have a lower wage rate than many men. The average male wage in the economy is higher than the average female wage.

In the longer run, further changes may occur. Employers that continue to discriminate against women may find ways to attract the slightly below-average male workers away from the O occupations. Although this will raise O wages slightly, it will also make these occupations increasingly "female occupations." If discrimination has been in place for a sufficient length of time, women will learn that it does not pay to acquire above-average skills because even with such skills they cannot get the best jobs. Regardless of ability, women are forced by discrimination to work in unskilled jobs.

The final point to address regarding labour-market discrimination is whether discriminatory wage differentials are equilibrium or temporary differentials. The simple answer is that the differentials will persist as long as the discrimination itself persists. Consider three general cases.

In the first case, the discrimination is supported by government policy, as in the South African apartheid system in which blacks were prohibited by law from holding prestigious and high-paying jobs. In such cases, as long as the law remains in place, so too will the discriminating wage differentials. If political pressure forces a change in the law, as happened in South Africa in the 1980s and 1990s, the effects of the discrimination will be reversed, but it may take some time. In particular, it will take time for the once-discriminated-against individuals, who had little incentive to invest in their own human capital, to acquire the human capital necessary for them to qualify for the prestigious jobs. The effects of the legislated discrimination are likely to linger long after the policy itself.

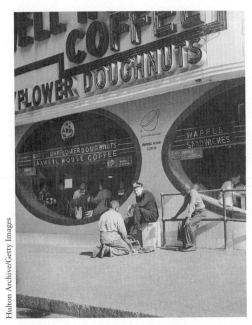

The attitudes of many white customers were responsible for much discrimination against black people in the United States in the first few decades of the twentieth century. As long as these attitudes persist, so will the discrimination, unless legislation forces a change.

In the second case, discrimination is not supported by official government policy but instead reflects the views of the firms' managers. In this case, there are economic pressures opposing the discrimination. For example, if some firms discriminate against even well-qualified women, our analysis in Figure 14-3 suggests there will be well-qualified women who can only find low-wage jobs. There is an incentive for other, non-discriminating firms to hire these well-qualified women and thereby benefit from lower costs. If enough firms see this advantage, there will be an increase in demand for well-qualified women, eventually reversing the effects of the initial discrimination.

In the third case, the cause of the discrimination is the preferences of the *customers*. Unlike the second case where the discrimination reflects the views of the firms' managers, there are no economic forces working to offset this customer-driven discrimination. As long as such discriminatory views persist, the discriminatory wage differentials will be sustained—only legislation or fundamental changes in customers' attitudes will reverse the situation. For many years, this was an important aspect of racial discrimination in the southern U.S. states, where many white customers were not prepared to have some services, such as haircuts, provided to them by blacks.

Wage Differentials in Non-competitive Markets

We have examined several explanations for why wage differentials exist in competitive labour markets. Another explanation for wage differentials is a non-competitive labour market. To study the influence of different labour-market structures on wages, we will consider the case of an industry in which all workers are identical and there is only one kind of job. In this way, we eliminate the possibility that any wage differentials are caused by differences between workers or differences between jobs.

Let's examine two general cases. First, workers form a labour union and exercise market power over setting the wage; that is, the labour union acts as a *monopoly* seller of labour services. Second, a single firm is the sole buyer of labour services; that is, the firm is a *monopsony* in the labour market.

A Union in a Competitive Labour Market For the purposes of our discussion of labour markets, a **labour union** is an association that is authorized to represent workers in negotiations with their employers; we will view the labour union as a single supplier of labour.

Labour union An association authorized to represent workers in bargaining with employers.

As the single seller of labour for many buyers, the union is a monopolist, and it can establish a wage below which no one will work, thus changing the supply curve of labour. Firms can hire as many units of labour as are prepared to work at the union wage but no one at a lower wage. Thus, all firms in the industry face a supply curve that is horizontal at the level of the union wage up to the maximum quantity of (union) labour that is willing to work at that wage.

If the union uses its monopoly power, it will negotiate a wage above the competitive level. This situation is shown in Figure 14-4, in which the intersection of this horizontal supply curve and the demand curve establishes a higher wage rate and a lower level of employment than the competitive equilibrium. In this case, there will be some workers who would like to work in the unionized industry or occupation but cannot. A conflict of interest has been created between serving the interests of the union's employed members and members who are unemployed or who must seek employment in less preferred jobs.

An alternative way to achieve the higher wage is to shift the supply curve to the left, thereby securing the higher wage without creating unemployment among the union's membership. The union may do this by restricting entry into the occupation by methods such as lengthening the required period of apprenticeship and reducing openings for trainees. The union could also shift the supply curve to the left by persuading the government to impose restrictive licensing or certification requirements on people who wish to work in certain occupations. The union might even lobby the government to implement restrictive immigration policies in an attempt to reduce the supply of labour to specific industries.

FIGURE 14-4　A Union in a Competitive Labour Market

A union operating in a competitive market can raise the wages of people who continue to be employed but only by reducing the number of people employed. The competitive equilibrium is at E_0, the wage is w_0, and employment is L_0. If a monopoly union enters this market and sets a wage of w_1, a new equilibrium will be established at E_1. The supply curve has become w_1xS_0. At the new wage w_1, employment will be L_1, and there will be L_1L_2 workers who would like to work but whom the industry will not hire.

The wage w_1 can be achieved without generating a pool of unemployed persons. To do so, the union must restrict entry into the occupation and thus shift the supply curve to the left to S_1. Employment will again be L_1.

> By restricting entry into the occupation or industry, unions can drive the wage above the competitive level. As a result, the level of employment will fall.

Raising wages by restricting entry is not limited to unions. It occurs, for example, with many professional groups, including doctors, architects, engineers, and lawyers. By limiting enrollments in professional programs at universities, the restricted supply of labour drives wages in these occupations higher than they would otherwise be.

A Monopsony Firm in the Labour Market　A **monopsony** is a market in which there is only one buyer; monopsony is to the buying side of the market what monopoly is to the selling side. Examples are rarer today, but historically in both Canada and the United States many small towns were dominated by a single employer, such as a factory, a lumber mill, or a coal mine. Other examples of monopsony include cities in which a single school board is the sole employer of teachers or a regional health authority that is the sole employer of nurses. For concreteness, we consider a case in which the few firms operating in one labour market form an employers' hiring association in order to act as a single buying unit. We therefore refer to a single monopsonist, and assume that workers are not members of a labour union.

The monopsonist can offer any wage rate that it chooses, and the workers must either accept employment at that rate or find a different job. Suppose the monopsonist decides to hire some specific quantity of labour. The labour supply

monopsony A market structure in which there is a single buyer.

FIGURE 14-5 Monopsony in a Labour Market

Quantity of Labour

A profit-maximizing monopsonist lowers both the wage rate and employment below their competitive levels. MRP and S are the competitive demand and supply curves, respectively. The competitive equilibrium is E_0. The marginal cost of labour (MC) to the monopsonist is above the average cost. The monopsonistic firm maximizes profits at E_1. It hires only L_1 units of labour. At L_1, the marginal cost of the last worker is just equal to the amount that the worker adds to the firm's revenue, as shown by the MRP curve. The wage that must be paid to get L_1 workers is only w_1.

curve shows the wage that it must offer. To the monopsonist, each point on the supply curve shows the *average* cost of labour for a given quantity of labour employed. In deciding how much labour to hire, however, the monopsonist trying to maximize its profits is interested in the *marginal cost* of hiring additional workers. The monopsonist wants to know how much its total costs will increase as it takes on additional units of labour.

The marginal cost exceeds the wage paid (the average cost) because the increased wage rate necessary to attract an extra worker must also be paid to *everyone already employed*. [27] For example, assume that 100 workers are employed at $15.00 per hour and that to attract an extra worker, the wage must be raised to $15.25 per hour. The marginal cost of that 101st worker is not the $15.25 per hour paid to the worker but $40.25 per hour—equal to the extra 25 cents per hour paid to the 100 existing workers plus the $15.25 paid to the new worker. Thus, the marginal cost is $40.25, whereas the average cost is $15.25.

The profit-maximizing monopsonist will hire labour up to the point at which the marginal cost of labour just equals labour's marginal revenue product (MRP). The quantity of labour hired is thus determined by the intersection of the firm's marginal cost of labour curve and the MRP curve, as illustrated in Figure 14-5. The wage rate for that quantity of labour, however, is determined by the supply of labour curve.

> The full exercise of monopsony power in a labour market will result in a lower level of employment and lower wages than would exist in a competitive labour market.

The intuitive explanation is that the monopsonistic employer is aware that by trying to purchase more, it is responsible for driving up the wage. If it wants to maximize its profits it will therefore stop short of the point that is reached when workers are hired by many competitive firms, no one of which can exert a significant influence on the wage rate.

Bilateral Monopoly   What happens when a firm with monopsony power confronts a labour union with monopoly power? This situation is quite common, as when the provincial Ministry of Health negotiates with a large nurses' union or when an association of NHL players negotiates with an organized group of team owners. This situation is referred to as *bilateral monopoly* because there is considerable market power on both sides of the market.

In situations of bilateral monopoly, the market outcome depends importantly on the negotiating ability of the two parties. The firm (or association of firms) would like to push the wage and employment below the competitive levels, as shown in Figure 14-5. In contrast, the labour union would like to raise the wage above the competitive level, as shown in Figure 14-4. However, without knowing more about how the two parties negotiate, and which things *other than* the wage are part of the negotiation (such as benefits, hours, overtime, etc.), it is impossible to make a clear prediction of the result. We address labour unions and the process of *collective bargaining* later in the chapter.

Legislated Minimum Wages

We have examined wage differentials arising in competitive and non-competitive labour markets. Government can also affect observed wage differentials by legislating minimum wages. Governments in Canada and many other countries legislate specific **minimum wages**, which define the lowest wage rates that may legally be paid. In 2015, minimum wages ranged from $10.30 per hour in New Brunswick to $12.50 per hour in the Northwest Territories.

minimum wages Legally specified minimum rate of pay for labour.

Although legislated minimum wages are now an accepted part of the labour scene in Canada and many other industrialized countries, there is significant debate among economists about the benefits from such a policy. As our analysis in Chapter 5 indicated, a binding price floor in a competitive market leads to a market surplus of the product—in this case, an excess supply of labour, or unemployment. Thus, theory predicts that a policy that legislates minimum wages in an otherwise competitive market will benefit some workers only by hurting others. In the cases of non-competitive labour markets, however, the analysis is a little more complicated.

Predicted Effects of a Minimum Wage   Minimum-wage laws usually apply uniformly to almost all occupations, but they will be *binding* only in the lowest-paid occupations and industries, which often involve unskilled or semi-skilled workers. These workers are usually not members of labour unions. Thus, the situations in which minimum wages will affect labour-market outcomes include competitive labour markets and those in which employers exercise some monopsony power. The effects on employment are different in the two cases.

Competitive Labour Markets.   The predicted consequences for employment of a binding minimum wage are unambiguous when the labour market is competitive. By raising the wage that employers must pay, minimum-wage legislation leads to a reduction in the quantity of labour that is demanded and an increase in the quantity of labour that is supplied. As a result, the actual level of employment falls, and unemployment rises. The excess supply of labour at the minimum wage also creates incentives for people to evade the law by working "under the table" at wages below the legal minimum wage. The predicted effect of a minimum wage in a competitive labour market is shown in part (i) of Figure 14-6.

Firms with Monopsony Power.   Our theory predicts that the minimum-wage law can simultaneously increase both wages and employment in markets in which firms have monopsony power. In part (ii) of Figure 14-6, the monopsony wage is w_1. If the minimum wage pushes the wage up to w_2, both employment and wages will rise. But beyond the competitive wage (w^*), further increases in the minimum wage will begin to decrease employment and create a pool of unemployed workers.

FIGURE 14-6 The Predicted Effects of Minimum Wages

(i) Competitive labour market

(ii) Firms have monopsony power

Minimum wages are predicted to reduce employment in competitive labour markets; the predicted effects on employment in monopsonistic labour markets are less clear. Part (i) shows a competitive labour market with the competitive equilibrium at w^* and L^*. A binding minimum wage raises the wage to w_{min}. Firms respond by reducing employment to L_1. The quantity of labour supplied by workers increases to L_2. Unemployment is equal to L_1L_2 workers.

Part (ii) shows a labour market in which firms behave as a monopsonist. The monopsony equilibrium is w_1 and L_1. If the minimum wage is set at w_2, employment will rise to L_2. If the minimum wage is set as high as the competitive wage w^*, employment rises to the competitive level L^*. But if the minimum wage rises above w^*, employment will fall below L^*. If the minimum wage were set above w_3, employment would fall below the monopsony level, L_1.

Evidence on the Effects of Minimum Wages Empirical research on the effects of minimum-wage laws reflects these mixed theoretical predictions. There is some evidence that people who keep their jobs gain when the minimum wage is raised. There is some evidence that some groups suffer a decline in employment consistent with raising the wage in a fairly competitive market. At other times and places, there is evidence that both wages and employment *rise* when the minimum wage rises, consistent with labour markets in which employers have monopsony power.

Some widely discussed research in the United States has produced hotly debated results. David Card, from Berkeley, and Alan Krueger, from Princeton University, traced the effects of minimum-wage increases in California and New Jersey and found that substantial rises in these states' minimum wages not only increased wages but also were associated with small employment *gains* for teenagers. Card and Krueger argue that these findings are inconsistent with a competitive labour market and thus take the results as evidence in support of the view that firms have some monopsony power in the labour market.

The Card and Krueger results have been criticized by many economists. One criticism relates to the short span of time covered by their study. The argument is that firms will not immediately reduce the level of employment in response to an increase in the minimum wage—they will instead choose *not to* replace workers who leave their jobs in the natural turnover process that occurs in labour markets. But workers who are receiving the minimum wage may be more reluctant to leave their job after an increase in their wages, thereby reducing this natural turnover. Thus, it is not surprising to see few employment losses (or slight gains) when one examines the labour market immediately before and immediately after the change in legislation. Proponents of this view argue that the total employment effects of minimum wages can be detected only by examining the data over longer periods of time.

Several Canadian studies have examined the relationship between minimum wages and employment (or unemployment). Though the studies differ in their approaches and data used, there is a broad consensus that minimum wages decrease the level of employment (and raise unemployment), particularly for low-skilled workers. Since workers with few skills often earn only low wages, a binding minimum wage has a larger impact on the employment prospects of these workers than it does for higher-skilled, higher-wage workers. In this sense, the Canadian results confirm the theoretical predictions of the effects of minimum wages in competitive labour markets. In these cases, the wage gains by the majority of workers who retain their jobs must be set against the loss of employment by a smaller group of workers.

14.2 LABOUR UNIONS

Unions currently represent about 25 percent of the labour force in Canada. Of those workers employed in the public sector, however, approximately 73 percent are unionized or covered by a union contract. Figure 14-7 shows how union membership has changed in Canada over the past several decades. For various industries, Table 14-1 shows the percentage of workers whose wages and salaries are covered by a union contract (even though they may not be members of a union). As is clear from the table, unionization is most common in the public, educational, and utilities sectors and least common in agriculture, finance, and retail trade.

Despite the relatively low degree of unionization among Canada's private-sector workers, unions have a considerable influence in the private sector. One reason is the impact that union wage contracts have on other labour markets. When, for example, Unifor negotiates a new contract with an automobile producer in Oshawa, its provisions set a pattern that directly

FIGURE 14-7   Union Membership in Canada, 1921–2015

As a share of the labour force, the number of union members has increased significantly over the past century, but has declined gradually since the mid-1980s. The large increases in Canadian unionization occurred during and after the Second World War, and during the 1960s. (Data are missing for 1950 and 1996.)

(*Source:* Based on author's calculations, using data from Statistics Canada. Labour force data can be found in Statistics Canada Series (D124-133, D134-145) and Cansim Tables (282-0001); union membership data can be found at Statistics Canada Series (E175-177) and Cansim Tables (279-0025, 282-0078, 282-0077.)

TABLE 14-1   Union Coverage by Industry, 2015

Industry	Percentage of workers covered by unions	
Goods-producing sector		27%
Agriculture	6%	
Forestry, fishing, mining, quarrying, oil and gas	23%	
Utilities	65%	
Construction	29%	
Manufacturing	24%	
Services-producing sector		32%
Retail trade	13%	
Transportation and warehousing	40%	
Finance, insurance, real estate and leasing	9%	
Educational services	72%	
Health care and social assistance	55%	
Public administration	73%	
Total employees		31%

There is considerable variation across Canadian industries in the extent of union coverage. The public sector and the educational services sector are the most unionized; agriculture, finance, and retail trade are the least unionized.

(*Source:* Adapted from Statistics Canada, Labour Force Survey, Table 282-0077.)

collective bargaining The process by which unions and employers arrive at and enforce agreements.

or indirectly affects other labour markets, both in Ontario and in other provinces. A second reason is the major leadership role that unions have played in the past 50 years in the development of labour market practices and in lobbying for legislation that applies to all workers.

In this section, we discuss the process of *collective bargaining* and, in particular, examine the inherent conflict that unions face between striving for higher wages and for increasing employment.

Collective Bargaining

The process by which unions and employers reach an agreement is known as **collective bargaining**. This process has an important difference from the theoretical models that we discussed in the previous section. In those models, we assumed that the union had the power to set the wage unilaterally; the employer then decided how much labour to hire. In actual collective bargaining, however, the firm and union typically bargain over the wage (as well as other aspects of the employment relationship, such as benefits, pensions, working conditions, overtime conditions, and flexibility in scheduling). The actual result of the bargain depends on the strengths of the two bargaining parties, the skill of their negotiators, and the overall business environment. Note that while actual collective bargaining has the firm and union bargaining over the wage, it is typically the case that the firm retains the "right to manage"—meaning that the firm can decide how much labour it wants to employ at the negotiated wage.

Wages Versus Employment   Unions seek many goals when they bargain with management. They may push for higher wages, more generous benefits, or less onerous working conditions. Many unions in Canada also emphasize the importance of "job security," meaning a commitment by the firm not to lay workers off in the event of a downturn in business conditions. Firms, however, are understandably reluctant to promise such security since reducing their workforce is an effective way to reduce costs when business conditions deteriorate.

Whatever unions' specific goals, they must deal with a fundamental dilemma.

An inherent conflict exists between the level of wages and the size of the union itself.

The more successful a union is in raising wages, the more management will reduce the size of its workforce, substituting capital for labour. This will lead to lower union membership. However, if the union is unable to offer better wages or benefits to its members, they have little incentive to remain with the union and will eventually seek employment elsewhere.

The Union Wage Premium   Despite the costs to unions (i.e., reduced membership) of pushing for higher wages, there is clear evidence in Canada of a *union wage premium*— that is, a higher wage attributed only to the union status of the job. It is not easy to measure this wage premium, however, because it is not appropriate simply to compare the average wage of unionized workers with the average wage of non-unionized workers. After all, unions may occur mainly in industries where workers have higher skills or where working conditions are less pleasant. And we know from the first section of this chapter that differences in skills or working conditions can lead to equilibrium wage differentials. Economists therefore rely on advanced statistical techniques to identify this union wage premium.

For 2015, the raw data show that average hourly wages are about 23 percent greater for union workers than for non-union workers. After controlling for the observable attributes of the workers and jobs, however, the evidence suggests that the union wage premium in Canada is between 10 and 15 percent—that is, unionized workers with a particular set of skills in particular types of jobs get paid 10 to 15 percent more than *otherwise identical workers* who are not members of unions.

On average, unionized workers earn between 10 and 15 percent higher wages than non-unionized workers with similar characteristics.

Employment Effects of Unions   We said earlier that unions face an inherent conflict between the level of wages they negotiate and the level of employment experienced by their membership. This conflict simply reflects the firm's profit-maximizing behaviour as embodied in its negatively sloped demand curve for labour. As the union pushes for higher wages, the firm naturally chooses to hire fewer workers.

What continues to puzzle economists, however, is how the clear evidence of a 10 to 15 percent union wage premium can be consistent with a second empirical result—the *absence* of any clear effect on employment in unionized industries. One possible explanation for the absence of an employment effect is that unions use the collective bargaining process to pressure firms to hire more workers than they otherwise would. This practice is known as *featherbedding* and for years was infamous in the railways, where union contracts required the railways to hire firemen (whose job was to keep the coal fires burning) long after the widespread adoption of diesel locomotives.

If such featherbedding is pervasive in unionized firms, it may be the explanation for the absence of an observable union effect on employment. The employment reduction caused by the higher wage may be offset by the employment increase due to featherbedding.

FIGURE 14-8 The Union Wage Premium and the Union Employment Effect

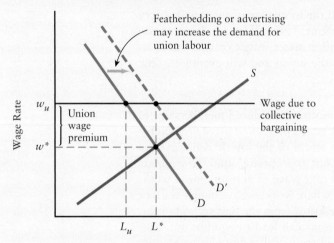

Featherbedding and advertising may explain the absence of a union employment effect even though there is a clear union wage premium. If the labour market is competitive, wages and employment will be given by w^* and L^*. The collective bargaining between firms and unions results in a wage of w_u, showing a clear premium above the competitive wage. If the demand for labour remains at D, employment would fall to L_u and there would be a reduction in employment caused by the higher negotiated wage. If the collective agreement requires firms to use more labour, however, or if the union successfully promotes union-made products, the demand for labour shifts to D'. In this case, the combination of the higher wage and the greater demand for labour may result in the competitive level of employment.

Another possible explanation for the absence of a union employment effect is union campaigns to increase the demand for the goods produced by their members. We sometimes see labels on products that proclaim them to be "union made" or "made with union labour." Unions also spend considerably on magazine and television advertising stressing the value of union labour. Some unions also lobby the government to restrict the import of foreign-made products in an attempt to increase Canadian consumers' demand for the domestic products made with union labour. To the extent that these campaigns convince consumers to buy more union-made products than they otherwise would, the result will be an increase in demand for union labour.

Figure 14-8 shows how the combination of the union wage premium and the increases in demand for union labour (either through featherbedding or advertising) can explain the *absence* of an observed union employment effect.

Unanswered Questions

Labour unions have played a significant role in the economies of Canada, the United States, and Europe for many years. It is therefore surprising how little economists actually know about the details of how unions influence economic outcomes. One important unanswered question is how unions affect long-run productivity.

Unions may reduce long-run productivity through a process known as the *hold-up* of capital. Much physical capital, once it is installed, is very difficult to move or resell. For this reason, *installed* capital has a very inelastic supply and, following the discussion from Chapter 13, a large part of its factor payment takes the form of economic rent. The union may be able to extract these rents from the firm in the form of higher wages. That is, once the firm has already installed its capital equipment the union may be able to *hold up* the firm by forcing it to pay higher wages; the firm is stuck with its installed capital and thus pays the higher wages and, in turn, receives lower profits. If firms are forward-looking, however, they can anticipate this sort of behaviour from unions *before* making such investments in physical capital. The possibility of being held up by union wage demands reduces the expected profitability of investment and may result in a reduction in investment. This decision to make fewer investments in physical capital would likely have negative implications for productivity growth in the industry.

There is some empirical evidence that the presence of a union does reduce investment by firms. It is not yet clear, however, whether such reduced investment has long-term effects on productivity. This issue is currently unresolved.

14.3 INCOME INEQUALITY

"By some estimates, income and wealth inequality are near their highest levels in the past hundred years, much higher than the average during that time span and probably higher than for much of American history before then." Janet Yellen, Chair of the Board of Governors of the Federal Reserve in the United States, made this statement in a speech in October 2014. The issue of rising income inequality has become one of great concern, not only to economists and politicians, but to many "ordinary" members of society. While there is little doubt that inequality is rising, there is much debate about its causes, the extent to which it matters, and what governments can do about it. So far in this chapter we have studied how wages and employment are determined in labour markets. Now we ask how a nation's total income is distributed among different segments of the population, and what kinds of things lead to changes in this distribution. To begin, we must first understand how the distribution of income is measured.

Measuring Income Inequality

The founders of Classical economics, Adam Smith (1723–1790) and David Ricardo (1772–1823), were concerned with the distribution of income among what were then the three great social classes: workers, capitalists, and landowners. They defined three factors of production as labour, capital, and land. The payment to each factor was treated as the income of the respective social class.

Smith and Ricardo were interested in what determined the share of total income that each class received. Their theories predicted that as society progressed, landlords would become relatively better off and capitalists would become relatively worse off. Karl Marx (1818–1883) had a different theory, which predicted that as growth occurred, capitalists would become relatively better off and workers would become relatively worse off—until the whole capitalist system collapsed.

These nineteenth-century debates focused on the **functional distribution of income**, defined as the distribution of national income among the major factors of production. Modern economists, however, emphasize the **size distribution of income**. This refers to the distribution of income among different individuals without reference to the source of the income or the "social class" of the individual. If we want to measure and understand the income inequality between individuals, the size distribution of income is the better indicator of the two because in modern society income classes no longer coincide closely with "social" classes. Many capitalists, such as the owners of small retail stores, have relatively low incomes. Conversely, many wage earners, such as professional athletes and corporate executives, have very high incomes.

functional distribution of income The distribution of national income among the major factors of production: labour, capital, and land.

size distribution of income The distribution of income among individuals, without regard to source of income.

Canadian Data Figure 14-9 shows the fraction of Canadian families with pre-tax incomes inside specific intervals in 2012. For example, 18.2 percent of families had annual incomes less than $40 000 whereas 38.4 percent had annual incomes above $100 000. Median family income in 2012 was $81 980.

Another way to show the size distribution of income is found in Figure 14-10. The curves in the figure are **Lorenz curves**, showing how much of total income goes to different proportions of the nations' families. If every family had the same income, 20 percent of total income would go to 20 percent of families, 40 percent of total income would go to 40 percent of families, and so on. In this case, the Lorenz curve would lie exactly along the diagonal and income would be completely equal. The farther the curve bends away from the diagonal, the less equal the distribution of income.

Lorenz curve A graph showing the extent of inequality of income distribution.

FIGURE 14-9 **Distribution of Family income, 2012**

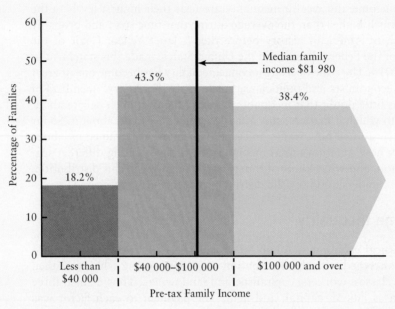

There is considerable inequality in the distribution of income across Canadian families. This figure shows the percentage of Canadian families (couples with or without children and lone-parent families) in each broad income group. Just over 18 percent of families had pre-tax income less than $40 000; almost 44 percent had total income between $40 000 and $100 000; and just over 38 percent of families had total income above $100 000. The median family pre-tax income for 2012 was $81 980.

(*Source*: Author's calculations based on data from CANSIM Table 111-0012.)

The lower Lorenz curve in Figure 14-10 shows that in 2011, the bottom 20 percent of all Canadian families received 1.0 percent of all pre-tax income, whereas the top 20 percent of families received 52.3 percent of all pre-tax income. Canada's tax-and-transfer system, however, had a marked effect on the income distribution. The upper Lorenz curve shows the distribution of *after-tax* family income—that is, income after all taxes have been paid and transfers have been received. The bottom 20 percent of families receive 4.8 percent of after-tax income while the top 20 percent of families receive 44.2 percent. The difference between the two Lorenz curves shows the extent to which Canada's tax-and-transfer system reduces income inequality.

International Data   Income inequality exists in all countries, but there are important differences across countries in the degree of inequality. As a general rule, developed economies tend to have less income inequality than do developing countries, partly because the developed countries have better functioning political and economic institutions that result in greater sharing of economic and political power. However, even the richest developed economies have considerable income inequality.

Figure 14-11 shows one measure of income inequality for 2012 for selected members of the Organisation for Economic Co-operation and Development (OECD). The measure for each country is the ratio of the 90th percentile income to the 10th percentile income, and it applies to households' after-tax incomes. The 90th percentile

FIGURE 14-10   The Lorenz Curve for Canadian Family Income, 2011

Percentage of Families	Pre-tax Income		After-tax Income	
	Percentage	Cumulative Percentage	Percentage	Cumulative Percentage
Lowest 20	1.0	1.0	4.8	4.8
Second-lowest 20	7.2	8.2	10.6	15.4
Middle 20	14.6	22.8	16.3	31.7
Second-highest 20	24.9	47.7	24.1	55.8
Highest 20	52.3	100.0	44.2	100.0

The size of the area between the Lorenz curve and the diagonal is a measure of the inequality of income distribution. If there were complete income equality, the bottom 20 percent of income receivers would receive 20 percent of total income, and so forth, and the Lorenz curve would coincide with the diagonal line. The lower Lorenz curve shows the distribution of pre-tax income. The upper Lorenz curve shows the distribution of after-tax income—income after taxes have been paid and transfers have been received. Since the after-tax income Lorenz curve is closer to the diagonal than the pre-tax income Lorenze curve, Canada's tax-and-transfer system reduces the inequality of income.

(*Source:* Adapted from Statistics Canada, CANSIM Table 202-0701.)

FIGURE 14-11   Income Inequality in OECD Countries, 2012

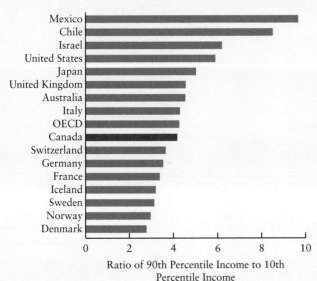

Income inequality is very different across countries. This figure shows the ratio of the after-tax income of the 90th percentile earner to the after-tax income of the 10th percentile earner, for selected OECD countries. For example, in Canada, the income of the 90th percentile earner is just over four times the income of the 10th percentile earner. By this measure, Mexico and Chile have much more unequal incomes than do the Scandinavian countries. Canada's measure lies roughly in the middle.

(*Source:* Based on *Economic Policy Reforms 2012: Going for Growth,* OECD, 2012.)

income is the level of income such that 90 percent of households have incomes below that level, while the 10th percentile income is such that only 10 percent of households have income below it. In Mexico and Chile, for example, the 90th percentile income is roughly 9 times greater than the 10th percentile income. In Canada and Italy the ratio is 4.2, whereas in the Scandinavian countries the ratios are around 3. Though it is not shown in the figure, this measure of income inequality has been increasing for most of the OECD countries over the past 25 years.

Rising Inequality   Growing attention is being paid to *rising* income inequality in Canada and other countries, especially the United States and the United Kingdom. While real *average* per capita income has been growing gradually over many years, the vast majority of the economy's total income growth in recent years has accrued to the very highest income earners, while average incomes among the lowest-income individuals have been approximately stagnant.

Figure 14-12 shows the time-series paths for two different income shares in Canada since 1941. The top solid line shows the share of total pre-tax income (excluding capital gains) received by the top 10 percent of all earners; the top dashed line shows a new measure that replaced the old one in 2000. In 1941, 45 percent of all pre-tax income went to the richest 10 percent, but the fraction fell quickly and remained between 30 and 40 percent until the late 1980s. Since then, however, the fraction has clearly been rising.

The bottom solid line in Figure 14-12 shows the share of total pre-tax income (excluding capital gains) accruing to the richest 1 percent of earners; the bottom dashed line is again a replacement measure beginning in 2000. The richest 1 percent's share of total pre-tax income has also been increasing since the late 1980s, after several decades of relative stability.

FIGURE 14-12   Canadian Income Shares for the Top 1% and Top 10% of Earners

The fraction of Canadian income accruing to the top 10 percent and top 1 percent of earners has been rising in recent years. These fractions fell noticeably in the early part of the 20th century and then remained relatively constant until the mid-1980s, when they both started to rise gradually.

(*Source:* Based on A. Yalnizyan, "The Rise of Canada's Richest 1%," Canadian Centre for Policy Alternatives, December 2010. Updated with data from CANSIM Table 204-0001.)

Causes of Rising Income Inequality

The causes of growing income inequality are actively debated among economists, as are the appropriate policy responses by governments. In this section we provide a brief outline of some of the possible underlying causes identified by researchers. Undoubtedly, some combination of these various forces, and interaction among them, is driving the current trend in income inequality. In the next section we address why inequality matters and how governments might be able to address the issue.

Skill-Biased Technological Change The pace and nature of recent technological change has changed the pattern of the demand for different types of labour. Especially important is the development of computer and robotics equipment that requires high-skilled workers for their operation and, at the same time, automates jobs that previously required middle-skilled "blue collar" workers. The increasing use of these technologies implies an increase in demand for highly skilled, highly educated workers, who benefit with higher wages. The middle-skilled workers, however, find themselves displaced from their once-secure jobs. Some are able to acquire the skills and education needed to join the high-skilled group, but many are not so lucky and find themselves competing for the economy's lowest-skilled jobs.

A further part of the argument that skill-biased technological change is contributing to rising income inequality is that the same technologies that automate the middle-skilled jobs *cannot* do so for many of the economy's lowest-skilled jobs. The work done by janitors, hotel maids, and restaurant servers, for example, cannot be automated by even the most sophisticated robots. As a result, the displaced workers from the "middle" of the income distribution are now increasingly competing with the lowest-skilled workers for scarce jobs at the bottom of the income distribution.

The overall result is what is now called a *hollowing out* of the labour market—growing employment and rising wages among high-skilled workers, falling employment and wages among the middle-skilled workers, and rising employment but falling wages among low-skilled workers. These changes tend to increase income at the top of the distribution and reduce it at the bottom—thus increasing the degree of income inequality.

Globalization The ongoing forces of globalization tend to reinforce these labour-market changes. Especially in manufacturing industries, reductions in communications and transportation costs, combined with increases in competition from foreign firms, is increasingly leading domestic firms to locate their production facilities in countries where costs are low. This "outsourcing" of jobs by firms who close their North American facilities and open lower-cost facilities in Bangladesh or Sri Lanka or Vietnam are likely contributing to growing income inequality in Canada or the United States. (At the same time, however, these same decisions are likely *reducing* income inequality on a global level since they are raising incomes in the low-wage countries in which these firms now operate.)

Other Contributing Causes Other changes in the nature of work and pay have occurred in recent decades, and these are likely contributing to rising income inequality.

Decline of Labour Unions. Union membership has declined gradually since the mid-1970s and today represents about 25 percent of the Canadian labour force. As we saw earlier in the chapter, unions are generally able to secure a wage premium for their members, currently between 10 and 15 percent above the wages earned by non-union members with similar skills. As labour unions have declined in importance in the overall economy, which has been especially marked in the United States and the United Kingdom, a smaller fraction of the labour force will receive these wage and other union-negotiated benefits. Since unions are most important in representing workers whose income places them roughly in the "middle" of the income distribution, this gradual weakening of union influence offers a partial explanation for rising income inequality.

Contract Work.   North American firms are increasingly reducing their costs by changing the nature of the relationship they have with their workers. Rather than hiring full-time employees for specific positions, many firms are instead hiring *contract workers*—individuals who engage in short-term professional contracts with the firms. The skills of the contract workers may be identical to those of the full-time employees. The important difference is that the firm avoids making a long-term commitment to the individual and also avoids having to provide costly benefits such as pension or health benefits. For the individual workers involved, there is usually less employment security and lower (or no) non-wage benefits.

Executive Compensation.   Average compensation to CEOs of large Canadian corporations was recently estimated to be over 200 times the compensation of the average Canadian worker. In the United States this ratio is above 350, the highest such ratio in the world. In contrast, these compensation ratios were approximately 40 during the 1980s. Other data show that, while the average wage in Canada increased by 6 percent between 1998 and 2012, the average compensation to Canada's 100 highest-paid CEOs rose by 73 percent (both figures adjusted for inflation). Some economists argue that these increases in income for top managers and executives have come at the expense of lower wages and benefits for middle and lower-skilled workers.

Superstar Theory.   In a famous paper called "The Economics of Superstars," U.S. economist Sherwin Rosen argues that advances in communications technology allow talented individuals in entertainment and sports to earn far greater incomes than was true in an earlier era with less sophisticated communications. A century ago the world's best singer could physically perform for only one paying audience at a time, perhaps a few hundred people at most. Today that same quality of singer can have his or her talents transmitted instantly to a global paying audience of millions of people by means of Internet, TV, and radio. The demand for any given superstar performer is thus far greater today than a century ago, and the result is the kind of superstar earnings that we all hear about on the news, with individuals earning hundreds of millions of dollars per year.

The Piketty Argument.   Professor Thomas Piketty at the Paris School of Economics argues in his best-selling 2013 book *Capital in the 21st Century* that the economy contains forces that naturally lead to growing income and wealth inequality. His argument begins with the observation that high-income individuals generally have more accumulated wealth than do low-income individuals. Over time, this accumulated stock of wealth generates new income at a rate given by the *return to capital*. At the same time, for most people in low- or middle-income groups, whose income overwhelmingly comes from their labour efforts rather than from their accumulated assets, income grows on average at the economy's per capita growth rate. Piketty then argues that if the return to capital exceeds the economy's growth rate, there will naturally be *growing* income and wealth inequality. Piketty's argument thus provides an explanation for why a given amount of income inequality may naturally rise over time, especially if the economy's overall growth rate is low.

Policy Implications

There is little debate that income inequality is rising in many countries, including Canada. There is more debate about the relative importance of the possible causes, such as those briefly discussed above. There is even more debate about whether inequality really matters and, if it does, what can be done to reduce it.

Does It Matter?   Some argue that *poverty* is obviously important, but *inequality* is not. Economists who make this argument stress the fact that economies will always have income inequality and that what really matters is that people have enough income to live satisfactorily and that they have the ability to increase their incomes through appropriate efforts. A clear exposition of this view is found in a recent book by McGill University's William Watson, *The Inequality Trap*.

Others argue that, aside from poverty, the *inequality of income* is itself important. Recent research emphasizes the negative impact on *social cohesion* that comes from having large income gaps between society's richest and poorest, and the lack of trust between members of society that develops when rich and poor see themselves as members of different communities. This research also notes the strong connection between income inequality and many social problems, including crime, children's educational performance, obesity, and mental illness. A recent book, *The Spirit Level*, by Richard Wilkinson and Kate Pickett, has received considerable attention for showing these relationships across time for a large group of countries.

It is also argued that growing income inequality is harmful to democracy because individuals with more income and wealth are often able to exert undue influence on elected government officials, thus affecting policy and economic outcomes in their favour. To the extent that democracy is weakened in this manner, key economic and political institutions may evolve to the point where they perpetuate and even worsen existing income inequality.

Rising income inequality is also associated with reductions in *social mobility*. It is one thing to have a highly unequal distribution of income when it is relatively easy for low-income people to advance through their efforts to achieve higher incomes. It is quite another, however, if such mobility is very difficult. Current evidence suggests that in countries with rising income inequality, *intergenerational* social mobility is declining. As a result, the chances of a child growing up to be in a different income group than his or her parents are falling. Children of poor parents tend to grow up to be poor whereas children of richer parents tend to grow up to be richer. When social mobility is affected in this way, the inequality of income tends to be self-perpetuating.

What Can Governments Do?   What can governments do to slow or reverse the trend of rising income inequality? Some economists argue that increasing taxes on high-income individuals would be an effective way to reduce the inequality of after-tax income. This is undoubtedly true. Other economists, however, argue that such measures do little to address the underlying *causes* of the pre-tax inequality, and thus do not really solve the problem.

Some argue that policies designed to restrict firms' ability to outsource labour to foreign countries, or to prevent consumers from having such ready access to low-price foreign products, would help reduce income inequality. This is unclear. While the effects on the labour market may work in the desired direction, it is also true that these kinds of trade restrictions reduce consumers' overall well-being by raising the prices paid for products. The overall effect on the income distribution is difficult to predict.

Many economists also agree about the importance of education and the acquisition of skills in determining an individual's earnings. As we saw earlier in this chapter, greater educational attainment is strongly correlated with higher earnings. Such greater skills or training may also help workers adjust to the inevitable forces generated by technological change and globalization, and help them avoid having to compete for the economy's lowest-skilled jobs. But policies aimed at improving education and skills only pay off over the longer term, and do little to change the *current* degree of income inequality.

Few economists would suggest that the process of globalization or the use of information technology are themselves undesirable, even though they may be partly responsible for changing market outcomes in ways that generate more income inequality. The policy challenge is to continue reaping their considerable benefits while designing policies that encourage individuals to acquire valuable skills and also ease their transition between regions and sectors in response to the adjustments that are an inevitable part of a dynamic market economy. We will encounter some of these policies in Chapter 18 when we examine the Canadian taxation and expenditure system.

SUMMARY

14.1 WAGE DIFFERENTIALS

- In a competitive labour market, wages are set by the forces of supply and demand. Differences in wages will arise because some skills are more valued than others, because some jobs are more onerous than others, because of varying amounts of human capital, and because of discrimination based on such factors as gender and race.
- A union entering a competitive market can act as a monopolist and can raise wages but at a predicted cost of reducing employment.

- A profit-maximizing monopsonistic employer entering a competitive labour market will reduce both the wage and the level of employment.
- Governments set some wages above their competitive levels by passing minimum-wage laws. In competitive labour markets, a minimum wage is predicted to reduce employment and create some unemployment. In monopsonistic labour markets, a legislated minimum wage (as long as it is not too high) can raise both wages and employment.

14.2 LABOUR UNIONS

- Labour unions seek many goals when they bargain with management. They may push for higher wages, higher benefits, more stable employment, or less onerous working conditions. Whatever their specific goals, they must recognize the inherent conflict between the level of wages and the size of the union itself.

- There is clear evidence in Canada of a union wage premium: Unionized workers with a particular set of skills in particular types of jobs get paid 10 to 15 percent more than otherwise identical workers who are not union members.

14.3 INCOME INEQUALITY

- The functional distribution of income refers to the shares of total national income going to each of the major factors of production—land, labour, and capital. The size distribution of income refers to the shares of total national income going to various groups of households.
- Canada has considerable inequality in the distribution of pre-tax income. The poorest fifth of families currently receives 1 percent of total income; the richest

fifth receives over 52 percent. Canada's tax-and-transfer system reduces this inequality only modestly.
- Income inequality has been rising in Canada and many other countries over the past few decades.
- Several possible explanations for rising inequality have been examined, including skill-biased technological change, globalization, the declining power of labour unions, and rising executive compensation.

KEY CONCEPTS

Wage differentials in competitive labour markets

Effects of discrimination on wages and employment

Labour unions as monopolists

Single employer as monopsonist

Effects of legislated minimum wages

Collective bargaining

Union goals: wages versus employment

Union wage premium

Functional and size distribution of income

Rising income inequality

Skill-biased technological change

STUDY EXERCISES

MyEconLab

Make the grade with MyEconLab: Study Exercises marked in ⊕ can be found on MyEconLab. You can practise them as often as you want, and most feature step-by-step guided instructions to help you find the right answer.

❶ Fill in the blanks to make the following statements correct.

a. If all workers were identical, all jobs had identical working conditions, and labour markets were perfectly competitive, then all wages would be _____.

b. In reality there is wide variation in wages. Four reasons for wage differentials are _____, _____, _____, and _____.

c. A country that invests in its public education and public health systems is improving the ____ of its population.

d. If there are two groups of workers in a competitive labour market, and one group becomes discriminated against, the labour supply curve for jobs that remain available for that group will shift to the _____ and the wages for these jobs will _____.

❷ Suppose there are only two industries in the economy. All workers have the same skills and the same preferences. But the jobs in the two industries are different. In the Pleasant industry, working conditions are desirable (quiet, safe, and clean). In the Grimy industry, working conditions are awful (noisy, unsafe, and dirty).

a. Draw supply-and-demand diagrams for the labour market in each industry.

b. In which industry are wages higher? Why?

c. Now suppose the Grimy industry made its working conditions just as pleasant as in the Pleasant industry. Explain what happens in *both* labour markets.

❸ Suppose there are two types of restaurant workers—high-skill chefs and low-skill servers. There are 1000 males and 1000 females in the labour force, and each group has an identical distribution between high-skill and low-skill workers. The two diagrams below show an initial outcome in each labour market. Assume there is no discrimination based on gender.

(a) Chefs

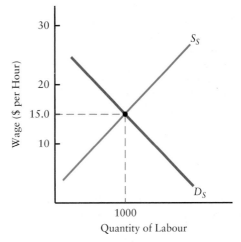

(b) Servers

a. As shown in the figures, the wage paid to chefs is higher than the wage paid to servers. What explains this wage differential?

b. Do men earn more or less, on average, than women? Explain.

c. Now suppose that employers begin to discriminate against female workers and hire only males as chefs. Show in the diagram what happens in each labour market.

d. In the situation in part (c), what happens to the wage differential between chefs and servers? What happens to the wage differential between males and females?

e. In the absence of any government intervention, explain the forces that we expect might eliminate this discrimination over time.

4 Fill in the blanks to make the following statements correct.

a. If workers in a competitive labour market join together to form a union, the effect will be a(n) _____ wage and _____ quantity of labour demanded.

b. If firms in a competitive labour market form an employers' association and become a monopsonist, employment will be _____ and wages will be _____ than in the competitive outcome.

c. A legislated and binding minimum wage in a competitive labour market will lead to a(n) _____ in the quantity of labour demanded and a(n) _____ in the quantity of labour supplied. The actual number of workers employed will _____.

d. A legislated and binding minimum wage in a market where the employer has monopsony power and the wage is initially below the competitive level will lead to a(n) _____ in the number of workers employed.

5 The table below shows how many workers are prepared to work at various hourly wages in the forestry industry. It also shows the workers' marginal revenue product (*MRP*).

Number of Workers	Wage ($)	Marginal Cost of Labour ($)	*MRP* ($)
50	10	14	40
100	12	18	30
150	14	—	24
200	16	—	22
250	18	—	20
300	20	—	18
350	22		

a. On a diagram, draw the supply of labour curve and the demand for labour curve.

b. What is the equilibrium wage and level of employment if the labour market is competitive?

c. Now suppose there is only a single buyer for labour—a *monopsonist*. Compute the marginal cost of labour for each level of employment and fill in the table. (Recall that the *MC* of labour is the change in labour cost divided by the change in employment. The first two rows have been completed for you.)

d. What wage and level of employment would the monopsonist choose? Explain.

6 The following diagram shows the market for labour in a particular industry. It shows both the supply of labour (the average cost of labour) and the marginal cost of labour.

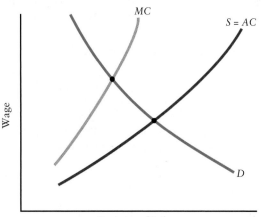

Quantity of Labour

a. Suppose the labour market is competitive. Indicate on the diagram the equilibrium wage and level of employment (call them w^* and L^*).

b. Now suppose the government imposes a minimum wage equal to $w^{\min} > w^*$. Show what happens to wages and employment.

c. In the absence of a minimum wage, show the outcome if there is a monopsony buyer of labour services. Call this wage w^p.

d. Beginning with the monopsony outcome, show what happens if the government imposes a minimum wage above w^p but lower than w^*.

e. Do minimum wages always reduce employment? Explain.

7 For each of the cases below, identify whether the observed wage differential is likely to be an *equilibrium* or a *temporary* differential, and explain why.

a. Pilots in one non-unionized airline earn 20 percent more than pilots in a second non-unionized airline.

b. Construction workers employed near Alberta's oil sands earn 30 percent more than similar workers in Manitoba.

c. Dental surgeons earn far more than dental hygienists.

d. Pilots in a non-unionized airline earn more than flight attendants in the same airline.

e. Economists employed by universities earn significantly less than economists of similar skills employed by commercial banks.

8 Fruitland has a competitive labour market for fruit pickers. Equations for the labour demand and labour supply curves are as follows, and the wage is given as dollars per week.

$$Q_D = 7000 - 5(w)$$

$$Q_S = 625 + 10(w)$$

a. What is the equilibrium level of employment?

b. Suppose all workers join a union and they successfully obtain a wage increase to $500 per week. (The demand curve is not affected.) What is the number of workers employed after unionization?

c. Given the increase in the wage in part (b), how many workers wish to work at this new wage? How many workers are unemployed?

9 The diagram below shows a supply and demand diagram for the services of bike couriers in the downtown core of a large city. Assume all deliveries are identical and the wage is the fee per delivery.

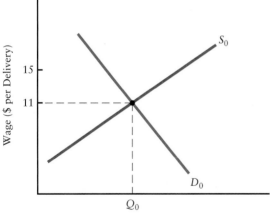

Number of Deliveries

a. Suppose that all of the bike couriers form a union and set a requirement that all members have a minimum height of 6'2". Draw the new supply curve and show the effect on the wage and number of deliveries.

b. Starting from the initial equilibrium, suppose the bike couriers form a union and impose a minimum acceptable wage of $15 per delivery. Draw the new supply curve and show the effect on the wage and number of deliveries.

c. Starting from the initial equilibrium, suppose the local government imposes a legislated minimum wage of $13 per delivery. Draw the new supply curve and show the effect on the wage and number of deliveries.

10 The following diagram shows the market for labour in a particular industry. It shows both the supply of labour (the average cost of labour) and the marginal cost of labour. If the labour market were competitive, the outcome would be w^* and L^*.

a. Suppose the workers in this industry form a union that is able to raise the wage above w^*. Show the expected outcome in the figure.

b. Now suppose there is no union, but there is a monopsony buyer of labour. Show the expected outcome in this market.

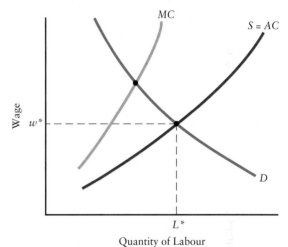

Quantity of Labour

11 In trying to measure the extent to which labour unions are responsible for increasing wages, economists use sophisticated statistical methods to compare the wages of unionized workers with those of non-unionized workers. Explain why it is not legitimate simply to compare the average wage across the two groups and attribute the difference to the effects of unionization.

12 "One can judge the presence or absence of discrimination by looking at the proportion of the population in different occupations." Does such information help? Does it suffice? Consider each of the following examples. Relative to their numbers in the total population, there are

a. Too many blacks and too few Jews among professional athletes

b. Too few male secretaries

c. Too few female judges

d. Too few female prison guards

e. Too few male schoolteachers

f. Too few female graduate students in engineering

13 The table below shows the size distribution of income for Fantasyland.

Household Income Rank	Percentage of Aggregate Income	Cumulative Total
Lowest fifth	6.8	—
Second fifth	14.1	—
Third fifth	21.5	—
Fourth fifth	26.2	—
Highest fifth	31.4	—

a. Compute the cumulative percentage of total income. Fill in the table.

b. On a scale diagram, with the percentage of households on the horizontal axis and the percentage of aggregate income on the vertical axis, plot the Lorenz curve for Fantasyland.

c. How does the diagram show the extent of income inequality in Fantasyland?

d. Now suppose Fantasyland introduces a system that redistributes income from higher-income households to lower-income households. How would this affect the Lorenz curve?

14 Other things being equal, how would you expect each of the following events to affect the size distribution of after-tax income?

a. An increase in unemployment

b. Rapid population growth in an already crowded city

c. An increase in food prices relative to other prices

d. An increase in employment-insurance benefits and premiums

e. Elimination of the personal income-tax exemption for interest earned within an RRSP or TFSA

15

Interest Rates and the Capital Market

CHAPTER OUTLINE	LEARNING OBJECTIVES (LO)
	After studying this chapter you will be able to
15.1 A BRIEF OVERVIEW OF THE CAPITAL MARKET	1 describe how the capital market brings together the borrowing decisions of firms with the lending decisions of households.
15.2 PRESENT VALUE	2 compute the present value of an asset that delivers a stream of future benefits.
15.3 THE DEMAND FOR CAPITAL	3 explain why the demand for investment is negatively related to the interest rate.
15.4 THE SUPPLY OF CAPITAL	4 explain why the supply of saving is positively related to the interest rate.
15.5 EQUILIBRIUM IN THE CAPITAL MARKET	5 understand how the equilibrium interest rate is determined and why it changes over time.

ECONOMISTS use the word *capital* in three different ways. *Human capital*, which we discussed in Chapter 14, is the set of skills that workers acquire through education and on-the-job training. *Physical capital* is a produced factor of production, such as a machine, a factory, or a bridge. *Financial capital* refers to financial assets in the form of loans, bonds, or stocks. In this chapter, we focus on what economists call the "capital market," which involves both physical and financial capital. We also examine the crucial role played in this market by the interest rate.

15.1 A BRIEF OVERVIEW OF THE CAPITAL MARKET

Firms require physical capital to produce their goods and services. Their purchase of new capital equipment is called *investment* in physical capital. They also require working capital—the funds necessary to purchase material inputs and pay workers while the goods are being made and even while the firm is waiting to be paid for its sales.

We saw in Chapter 7 that firms finance their activities in one of four ways. First, they use profits that are not remitted to shareholders—these are called *retained earnings*. Second, they borrow from commercial banks or other financial intermediaries, such as credit unions and trust companies. Third, they issue *bonds* (an IOU) and thereby borrow directly from lenders. Fourth, they issue and sell *stock* (a share of the company) directly to shareholders. However firms choose to finance their activities, their demand for financial capital comes from their demands for physical capital and working capital.

The supply of financial capital comes mostly from households' saving decisions. Every year, millions of households decide how much of their after-tax income to save. These funds are often deposited into various types of accounts at commercial banks, each of which is a loan from a household to the bank. Sometimes the funds are used to buy bonds so that households are lending directly to non-bank borrowers. Households may also decide to purchase stocks, thereby acquiring shares of firms. Finally, some household saving is not done directly by households at all, but rather by employers and the government in the form of employer-sponsored and public pension plans (such as the Canada Pension Plan). Whatever the form, households' saving determines their total supply of financial capital.

Figure 15-1 illustrates the interaction of firms and households in the market for financial capital. Note that some funds flow directly between firms and households (bond and stock purchases) whereas other funds flow through financial intermediaries (bank deposits and loans). Financial intermediaries play an important role in the economy for two reasons. First, they are specialists in assessing the *riskiness* of potential borrowers and thus are better suited than most households to making loans to firms. Second, they have the ability to *pool* the savings from a large number of households and thereby make large loans to firms. Despite the importance of financial intermediaries to the economy, in this chapter we will focus our attention on households and firms, thus focusing on the fundamental determinants of the demand for and supply of financial capital.

During normal times, the process of financial intermediation—the flow of funds between households and firms through institutions, such as commercial banks—works so well that we barely notice its presence. In the financial crisis that began in 2008, however, this process was disrupted by the failure of several

FIGURE 15-1 **The Interaction of Firms and Households in the Capital Market**

The capital market connects households' saving decisions with firms' borrowing decisions. Households save some part of their income. They can lend (make a deposit) to a commercial bank or other financial intermediary. They can lend directly to a firm by buying a bond. Or they can purchase stock and thereby become a part owner in a firm. Firms finance their investments (purchases of new capital equipment) by using their retained earnings, borrowing from a bank, issuing a bond and borrowing directly from a lender, or issuing and selling stock.

large financial institutions in the United States and Europe. With globally integrated financial markets, the result in Canada and elsewhere was an increase in the perceived risks associated with borrowing and lending, and thus a dramatic decline in the flows depicted in Figure 15-1. By 2010, however, these financial flows had returned approximately to normal, partly in response to significant policy actions taken by governments and central banks in many countries.

In this chapter, we look first at firms' demand for physical capital, which leads us to understand their demand for financial capital. As we will see, the interest rate plays an important role in determining how much capital is demanded by firms. We then examine households' saving decisions and thus their supply of financial capital. The interest rate also plays an important role in determining how much financial capital households want to supply. Once we understand the demand and supply for financial capital, we will be ready to put the two sides of the capital market together to determine the equilibrium "price" of financial capital—the interest rate. Finally, we will look at how economic events or policies can affect the equilibrium levels of investment, saving, and the interest rate.

Before beginning our analysis of the demand for capital, it is necessary to clarify one important difference between labour and physical capital as factors of production. When economists speak of the demand and supply for labour, they are referring to the *flow* of labour services. For example, a firm considers hiring the services of a worker for a month, after which the firm and the worker go their separate ways. In contrast, when a firm considers its demand for physical capital, it is considering purchasing a new piece of equipment and thereby adding to its *stock* of capital. This piece of capital equipment will usually deliver services to the firm over many years before it is eventually discarded because it has worn out or become obsolete. The durability of physical capital means that we must distinguish between the *stock* of capital and the *flow* of services that it delivers. We need a way to evaluate the flow of services that a piece of capital equipment delivers for many years into the future. Only then can we determine how much a firm would be willing to pay for the piece of capital equipment. This takes us to the concept of *present value*.

15.2 PRESENT VALUE

Suppose a firm buys a piece of capital equipment and thereby obtains the use of that equipment until it wears out. The capital equipment delivers a flow of benefits over its lifetime—that is, it delivers some benefit every year for many years. The financial benefit to the firm in any given year is the marginal revenue product (*MRP*) of that unit of capital (recall from Chapter 13 that the *MRP* is the extra revenue generated by that unit). A given piece of capital may deliver different *MRP*s in different years—the *MRP* may change because of changes in market conditions or simply because the capital wears out slowly over time. In reality, the stream of future *MRP*s is uncertain. No firm can know with certainty how its market will evolve, how consumers will respond to the product, or even how long the capital equipment will last.

How much would a firm be willing to pay today to purchase a piece of capital equipment that will deliver a stream of benefits into the future? To answer this question we introduce the concept of *present value*. The **present value** of a future amount is the most that someone would be prepared to pay today to get that amount in the future. The concept of present value is used extensively in financial analysis as well as in the analysis of economic policies, where costs and benefits occur at different points in time.

In what follows, we simplify our discussion by assuming that the future benefits from a piece of capital equipment are known with certainty. This allows us to develop

present value The value today of a future stream of payments discounted using the market interest rate.

the central insights about present value and the interest rate without dealing with complications arising from uncertainty.

The Present Value of a Single Future Payment

To begin our analysis, consider a very simple setting in which the piece of capital equipment produces an *MRP* only in one future period. Since most physical capital is durable and thus generates a *stream* of benefits, this assumption is quite unrealistic, but it is only our starting point. In our first example, the *MRP* occurs one period from now. In the second, the *MRP* occurs several periods from now.

One Period in the Future   How much would a firm be prepared to pay now to purchase a capital good that produces an *MRP* of $100 in one year's time, after which time the capital good will be useless? One way to answer this question is to ask a somewhat *opposite* question: How much would the firm have to *lend* now in order to be repaid $100 a year from now? Suppose for the moment that the interest rate is 5 percent per year. If we use *PV* to stand for this unknown amount, we can write $PV \times (1.05) = \$100$. Thus, $PV = \$100/1.05 = \$95.24$. This tells us that the present value of $100 receivable in one year's time is $95.24 when the interest rate is 5 percent. Anyone who lends out $95.24 for one year at 5 percent interest will receive $95.24 back plus $4.76 in interest, or $100 in total. When we calculate this present value, the interest rate is used to *discount* (reduce to its present value) the $100 to be received in one year's time.

The actual present value that we have calculated depended on our assumption that the interest rate was 5 percent. What if the interest rate is 7 percent? At that interest rate, the present value of the $100 receivable in one year's time would be $100/1.07 = \$93.46$.

These examples are easy to generalize. In both cases, we have found the present value by dividing the sum that is receivable in the future by 1 plus the rate of interest. In general, if the interest rate is *i* per year, then the present value of the *MRP* (in dollars) received one year hence is

$$PV = \frac{MRP}{(1 + i)}$$

Table 15-1 computes the present value of an *MRP* of $500, received one year from now, under alternative assumptions of the interest rate. There is a negative relationship between present value and the interest rate.

Several Periods in the Future   Now we know how to calculate the present value of a single sum that is receivable one year in the future. The next step is to ask what would happen if the sum were receivable at a later date. For example, what is the present value of $100 to be received *two* years hence when the interest rate is 5 percent? The answer is $100/[(1.05) (1.05)] = \$90.70$. We can check this by seeing what would happen if $90.70 were lent out for two years. In the first year, the loan would

TABLE 15-1   The Present Value of a Single Sum One Year in the Future

	MRP	Interest Rate per Year	Present Value
1.	$500	4% = 0.04	$500/(1.04) = $480.77
2.	$500	5% = 0.05	$500/(1.05) = $476.19
3.	$500	6% = 0.06	$500/(1.06) = $471.70
4.	$500	7% = 0.07	$500/(1.07) = $467.29
5.	$500	8% = 0.08	$500/(1.08) = $462.96

For any given sum at a given point in the future, the present value of the sum is negatively related to the interest rate. The firm earns an *MRP* of $500 in one year's time. Using the formula developed in the text, it is clear that present value is lower when the interest rate is higher.

earn interest of $(0.05)($90.70) = 4.54, and hence after one year, the outstanding loan would be worth $95.24. If we assume that interest is compounded annually, then in the second year the interest earned would equal $(0.05)($95.24) = 4.76. Hence, after two years the firm would be repaid $100.

In general, the present value of *MRP* dollars received *t* years in the future when the interest rate is *i* per year is

$$PV = \frac{MRP}{(1 + i)^t}$$

This formula simply discounts the *MRP* by the interest rate, repeatedly, once for each of the *t* periods that must pass until the *MRP* becomes available. If we look at the formula, we see that the higher is *i* or *t*, the higher is the whole term $(1 + i)^t$. This term, however, appears in the denominator, so *PV* is *negatively* related to both *i* and *t*.

Table 15-2 computes the present value of an *MRP* of $500 received several years in the future. The table has two parts. In Part A, we keep the date of the *MRP* fixed and vary the interest rate. In Part B, we keep the interest rate fixed and vary the date of the *MRP*. This allows us to see the separate effects of varying *i* and *t*, and leads to the following conclusion.

> **Other things being equal, the present value of a given sum payable in the future will be smaller the more distant the payment date, and it will be smaller the higher the rate of interest.**

TABLE 15-2 The Present Value of a Single Sum Several Years in the Future

Part A: Date Fixed; Interest Rate Variable

	MRP	Date	Interest Rate per Year	Present Value
1.	$500	3 years	4% = 0.04	$500/(1.04)^3 = 444.50
2.	$500	3 years	5% = 0.05	$500/(1.05)^3 = 431.92
3.	$500	3 years	6% = 0.06	$500/(1.06)^3 = 419.81
4.	$500	3 years	7% = 0.07	$500/(1.07)^3 = 408.15

Part B: Date Variable; Interest Rate Fixed

	MRP	Date	Interest Rate per Year	Present Value
1.	$500	2 years	6% = 0.06	$500/(1.06)^2 = 445.00
2.	$500	3 years	6% = 0.06	$500/(1.06)^3 = 419.81
3.	$500	4 years	6% = 0.06	$500/(1.06)^4 = 396.05
4.	$500	5 years	6% = 0.06	$500/(1.06)^5 = 373.63

The present value of a future sum is negatively related to the interest rate and negatively related to the length of time before the sum occurs. In all the rows in Part A, the firm receives an *MRP* of $500 in three years' time, but the interest rate varies. Using the formula from the text, we see that the higher is the interest rate, the lower is the present value of the future *MRP*. In all the rows in Part B, the interest rate is 6 percent per year, but the future date of the *MRP* varies. The computations show that the more distant in time is the *MRP*, the lower is the present value.

The Present Value of a Stream of Future Payments

Now consider the present value of a stream of payments that continues for *many* periods into the future. As we said earlier, the future benefits that a firm receives from a piece of capital equipment may not be constant. Changes in market conditions, technology, or the quality of the capital itself may result in different MRPs in different periods. For example, one new lathe may generate a marginal revenue product equal to $200 one year from now, $180 two years from now, and $210 in the third year—before it wears out and ceases to generate any further benefits.

How do we compute the present value of such an uneven stream of MRPs? The answer is surprisingly simple. We just treat each future MRP as a single MRP that occurs at some point in the future. We then apply our earlier formula to each MRP and add them up. For example, suppose the interest rate is 6 percent per year and the capital generates MRPs equal to $200 in one year, $180 in two years, $210 in three years, and nothing thereafter. The present value of this stream of MRPs is

$$PV = \frac{\$200}{1.06} + \frac{\$180}{(1.06)^2} + \frac{\$210}{(1.06)^3}$$

$$= \$188.68 + \$160.20 + \$176.32$$

$$= \$525.20$$

In general, if MRP_t is the MRP that occurs t years from now, if i is the interest rate, and if the stream of MRPs lasts for N years, the present value of the stream of MRPs is

$$PV = \frac{MRP_1}{1 + i} + \frac{MRP_2}{(1 + i)^2} + \cdots + \frac{MRP_N}{(1 + i)^N}$$

Table 15-3 computes the present value of several streams of MRPs. It confirms the relationships we observed earlier. First, other things being equal, a higher interest rate leads to a lower present value. Second, for a given interest rate, a larger MRP leads to a larger present value. But now that we have a stream of MRPs that lasts for several periods, rather than just a single period, we can add a third general result: The longer a stream of MRPs lasts into the future, the greater is the present value.

Summary

The concept of present value can be confusing at first, but you should now see the straightforward way to evaluate a stream of benefits into the distant future. Let's summarize our findings.

1. A piece of capital is valuable because it generates a *stream* of financial benefits into the future. These benefits in each period are the capital's marginal revenue product (MRP). The value to the firm of owning this capital now is what we have called its *present value*.

2. The larger is each future MRP, or the longer the stream of MRPs lasts, the greater is the present value of the capital.

TABLE 15-3 The Present Value of a Stream of Future Payments

Part A: Alternative Interest Rates

	MRP_1	MRP_2	MRP_3	Interest Rate per Year	Present Value
1.	$500	$400	$300	8% = 0.08	$\dfrac{500}{1.08} + \dfrac{400}{(1.08)^2} + \dfrac{300}{(1.08)^3} = \$1044.05$
2.	$500	$400	$300	5% = 0.05	$\dfrac{500}{1.05} + \dfrac{400}{(1.05)^2} + \dfrac{300}{(1.05)^3} = \$1098.15$

Part B: Alternative MRPs

	MRP_1	MRP_2	MRP_3	Interest Rate per Year	Present Value
3.	$300	$300	$300	5% = 0.05	$\dfrac{300}{1.05} + \dfrac{300}{(1.05)^2} + \dfrac{300}{(1.05)^3} = \$816.97$
4.	$400	$400	$400	5% = 0.05	$\dfrac{400}{1.05} + \dfrac{400}{(1.05)^2} + \dfrac{400}{(1.05)^3} = \$1089.30$

Part C: Alternative Lengths of Stream

	MRP_1	MRP_2	MRP_3	Interest Rate per Year	Present Value
5.	$500	$500	$0	5% = 0.05	$\dfrac{500}{1.05} + \dfrac{500}{(1.05)^2} + 0 = \$929.70$
6.	$500	$500	$500	5% = 0.05	$\dfrac{500}{1.05} + \dfrac{500}{(1.05)^2} + \dfrac{500}{(1.05)^3} = \$1361.62$

The present value of a future stream of sums is negatively related to the interest rate, positively related to the size of each payment, and positively related to the length of time the stream continues. Part A presents a given stream of *MRP*s over three years but considers two different interest rates. The *PV* of the stream of *MRP*s is higher when the interest rate is lower.

Part B uses only a single interest rate of 5 percent but considers two different streams of *MRP*s. One is a stream of $300 that lasts for three years; the other is a higher stream of $400 that also lasts for three years. The stream with the higher *MRP*s has the higher present value.

Part C uses an interest rate of 5 percent and a constant stream of *MRP*s of $500 per year. One stream lasts for two years, whereas the other lasts for three years. The longer-lasting stream of *MRP*s has the higher present value.

3. For a given stream of future *MRP*s, the present value of the capital is negatively related to the interest rate. That is, when interest rates are higher, a given piece of capital is valued less. When interest rates are lower, the capital is valued more highly.

4. Capital that delivers its *MRP*s in the more distant future has a lower present value than capital that delivers the same stream of *MRP*s sooner.

We now go on to examine an individual firm's demand for capital goods. We will then consider the economy's overall demand for capital. Present value and the interest rate play a central role in our analysis.

15.3 THE DEMAND FOR CAPITAL

As we said earlier, a firm's demand for financial capital comes from its demand for physical capital. Economists assume that the amount of physical capital the firm chooses to use comes from its objective of maximizing profit. We now examine this decision in detail.

The Firm's Demand for Capital

An individual firm faces a given interest rate and a given purchase price of capital goods. The firm can vary the quantity of capital that it employs and, as a result, the marginal revenue product of its capital varies. The hypothesis of diminishing marginal returns (see Chapter 7) predicts that the more capital the firm uses, the lower its *MRP*.

The Decision to Purchase a Unit of Capital   Consider a profit-maximizing firm that is deciding whether or not to add to its capital stock and is facing an interest rate of i at which it can borrow or lend money. The first thing the firm has to do is to estimate the expected stream of *MRP*s from the new piece of capital over its lifetime. Then it discounts this stream at the interest rate of i per year to find the present value of the stream of benefits the machine will generate. Having computed the *PV* of the stream of *MRP*s, the firm can then compare this *PV* with the purchase price of the capital good. The decision rule for a profit-maximizing firm is simple: If the *PV* is greater than or equal to the purchase price, the firm should buy the capital good; if the *PV* is less than the purchase price, the firm should not buy it.

Consider the following simple example. Suppose a computer appropriate for high-quality graphic design has an *MRP* of $1000 each year—that is, by buying this computer a graphic-design firm can produce more output and thereby increase its revenues by $1000 each year. Suppose further that the computer delivers benefits this year (now) and for two more years—after that, the computer is completely obsolete and worth nothing. Finally, suppose the interest rate is 6 percent per year. The *PV* of this stream of *MRP*s is then equal to

$$PV = \$1000 + \frac{\$1000}{(1.06)} + \frac{\$1000}{(1.06)^2}$$

$$= \$2833.40$$

The present value tells us how much this flow of future receipts is worth now. If the price of the computer is less than $2833.40, the firm should buy it; if the price is higher, the firm should not buy it.

If a firm wants to maximize its profits, it is worthwhile to buy another unit of capital whenever the present value of the stream of future *MRP*s generated by that unit equals or exceeds its purchase price.

The Firm's Optimal Capital Stock   Because of the law of diminishing marginal returns, the *MRP* of each unit of capital generally declines as the firm buys more capital. The profit-maximizing firm will go on adding to its stock of capital until the present value of the stream of *MRP*s generated by the *last unit* added is equal to the purchase price of that unit.

Figure 15-2 continues our earlier example of a graphic-design firm considering the purchase of a specialized computer. In this case, however, the firm is determining *how many* computers it wants to own and so must compare the purchase price and the present value of the stream of *MRP*s produced by each successive computer. Because the *MRP* of each computer declines as the firm uses more of them, Figure 15-2 shows a negative relationship between the purchase price of the computer and the quantity the firm chooses to own.

What economic events, other than a change in the price of capital, might lead the firm to change its optimal capital stock? In terms of the example shown in Figure 15-2, anything that increases the *PV* of the future *MRP*s of computers will increase the height of the bars in the figure and, for a given purchase price of computers, lead the firm to purchase more computers. More generally, anything that increases the *PV* of the future *MRP*s of capital will lead firms to increase their desired capital stock. This can occur in two general ways.

FIGURE 15-2   The Firm's Optimal Capital Stock

	Annual *MRP*	Present Value	
1st computer	$1000	$1000 + \dfrac{1000}{1.06} + \dfrac{1000}{(1.06)^2}$ = \$2833.40	
2nd computer	$900	$900 + \dfrac{900}{1.06} + \dfrac{900}{(1.06)^2}$ = \$2550.06	
3rd computer	$800	$800 + \dfrac{800}{1.06} + \dfrac{800}{(1.06)^2}$ = \$2266.72	
4th computer	$700	$700 + \dfrac{700}{1.06} + \dfrac{700}{(1.06)^2}$ = \$1983.38	
5th computer	$600	$600 + \dfrac{600}{1.06} + \dfrac{600}{(1.06)^2}$ = \$1700.04	

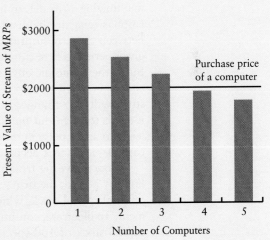

The firm's optimal capital stock is chosen so that the present value of the future *MRP*s on the last unit of capital is its purchase price. In this example, each computer delivers a stream of *MRP*s that begins now and lasts for two years, and the interest rate is 6 percent per year. The second column in the table shows the diminishing marginal revenue product of capital—the annual *MRP* generated by each computer is less than for the previous one. The third column computes the *PV* of the stream of *MRP*s for each computer, and these are plotted in the accompanying figure. If the purchase price of a computer is $2000, the firm will choose to own only three computers; any additional computer delivers a *PV* of *MRP*s that is less than the purchase price and thus is not profitable to the firm. An increase in the purchase price of a computer to $2400 would lead the firm to reduce its desired stock of computers to two.

Increase in Future MRPs. If capital becomes more productive so that the stream of future *MRP*s increases, firms will choose to own more capital, even if the purchase price of capital is unchanged. For example, in Figure 15-2, if a technological improvement increases the annual *MRP* for each computer by 20 percent, each computer's *PV* will also increase by 20 percent. The bars in the figure will increase in height and, for any given purchase price, the firm will increase its desired stock of computers.

The future *MRP*s can also increase if the market price for the firm's product increases (or if demand for its product increases and it operates in an imperfectly competitive market). Even without any technological change, an increase in the firm's product price leads to an increase in the *MRP*s and thus to an increase in the height of the bars in Figure 15-2; the firm would buy more capital at any given purchase price.

Reduction in the Interest Rate. The *PV* of the stream of *MRP*s will also increase if the interest rate falls. A lower interest rate means that future *MRP*s get discounted at a lower rate—and therefore have greater present value. Thus, as the interest rate declines, the firm's optimal capital stock increases. In Figure 15-2, imagine that the interest rate is 3 percent per year instead of 6 percent. In this case, the *PV* of each computer's stream of future *MRP*s will rise, and each bar in the figure will increase in height. For a given purchase price of computers, the firm will therefore increase its desired stock of computers.

> **Anything that causes the present value of future *MRP*s of capital to increase—technological improvement, an increase in the product's price, or a reduction in the interest rate—leads firms to increase their desired capital stock.**

From Capital Stock to Investment Demand We have just examined how a profit-maximizing firm determines its optimal stock of physical capital. It is important to emphasize again the distinction between *stocks* and *flows*—in this case the distinction between the firm's optimal *stock* of capital and its optimal *flow* of investment. In any given period, a firm can determine its optimal stock of capital as shown in Figure 15-2. But if the economic environment changes either because of a change in technology, a change in the firm's market price, or a change in interest rates, the firm's optimal capital stock will also change. In order for the firm to adjust its capital stock appropriately, it needs to carry out *investment*. A positive flow of investment—buying new capital—leads to an increase in the capital stock; a negative flow of investment—selling existing capital—leads to a decline in the capital stock.[1]

How do we get from the firm's optimal capital stock to its demand for investment? For any period, the firm's investment demand is determined by the *change* in the firm's optimal capital stock, which in turn is determined by changes in the economic environment. To illustrate, continue with our example of a graphic-design firm with an optimal capital stock of 100 specialized computers at the beginning of 2016. During the year 2016, suppose interest rates decline, thereby increasing the firm's optimal capital stock to 110 computers. For the year 2016, the firm would therefore have a demand for investment equal to the *change* in this optimal stock—in this case, 10 computers. After the firm carries out this investment (after it buys 10 new computers), it would again possess its optimal capital stock.

---

[1] Positive investment may not add to the firm's capital stock if it is just enough to replace obsolete capital. In this discussion, however, we make the simplifying assumption that all investment is *net* investment and thus increases the firm's capital stock.

> **In any given period, the profit-maximizing firm's investment demand is given by the *change* in the firm's optimal capital stock.**

Emphasis on the Interest Rate In Figure 15-2, there is a negative relationship between the purchase price of a computer and the stock of computers the firm wants to own. Firms use many types of physical capital, however, including buildings, factories, furniture, computer equipment, and various types of tools and machines. Each different type of physical capital has a different price and therefore it is impossible to think of any individual firm's desired capital stock in terms of any single price. For this reason, economists instead focus on the negative relationship between the firm's desired capital stock and the interest rate. Indeed, since firms use financial capital to purchase their physical capital, it is natural to think of the interest rate as the "price" of financial capital.

We just saw that when the interest rate falls, the *PV* of the future stream of *MRP*s will rise. This increase in the present value of capital will lead firms to increase their desired capital stock, and thus the quantity of investment demanded. The opposite happens when the interest rate rises. We thus get a general prediction about firms' investment behaviour:

> **Other things being equal, firms' desired demand for investment (additions to physical capital) is negatively related to the interest rate.**

This negative relationship between the interest rate and the firm's desired investment demand can be given another interpretation. Instead of purchasing physical capital that will generate future benefits, the firm could instead decide to purchase a bond that pays interest in the future. The interest rate on such a bond is the *opportunity cost* the firm faces if it chooses to invest in physical capital. A higher interest rate makes the bond purchase relatively more attractive and the investment in physical capital relatively less attractive, and thus it leads the firm to reduce its desired investment demand.

This negative relationship is shown in Figure 15-3. The negative relationship between the interest rate and the quantity of investment demanded can be thought of as the firm's demand curve for additional physical capital where the relevant "price" is the interest rate.

What would cause a firm's investment demand curve to shift? First, suppose the firm's expectations about future demand for its product improve. This optimism leads the firm to expect an increase in the future stream of *MRP*s produced by capital. With higher expected *MRP*s, the firm is prepared to purchase more units of capital (at any interest rate). The firm's investment demand curve thus

FIGURE 15-3 The Interest Rate and the Firm's Investment Demand

Anything that increases the future stream of MRPs will increase investment demand

The lower the rate of interest, the larger is the firm's demand for investment. The lower the interest rate, the higher is the present value of any given stream of *MRP*s and hence the more capital that the firm will wish to use.

Anything that increases the future stream of *MRP*s produced by the capital leads the firm to demand more units of capital at any interest rate—the investment demand curve shifts to *I'*.

shifts to the right. Second, suppose an improvement in technology increases the future stream of *MRP*s. Again, the higher future *MRP*s lead the firm to purchase more units of capital at any interest rate—a rightward shift in the firm's investment demand curve.

> **Any event that increases the expected future stream of *MRP*s leads to an increase in the firm's investment demand.**

The Economy's Demand for Investment

The economy's overall demand for investment is determined from the demands of individual firms. Thus, there is a negative relationship between the interest rate and the desired *aggregate* investment for the same reasons that the negative relationship exists for any individual firm. The economy's demand for investment can therefore be represented by a downward-sloping curve like the one in Figure 15-3.

The economy's investment demand curve shifts for the same reasons that individual firms' demand curves shift. Anything that increases the future stream of *MRP*s of capital leads to a rightward shift in the investment demand curve. Technological improvements are a key reason for such increases in the demand for investment. (We will say more about this later.)

15.4 THE SUPPLY OF CAPITAL

The supply of financial capital is determined by households' saving decisions. Saving is the difference between income and current spending. At any given time, households have a stock of *assets* that represents the accumulation of their past saving. During any given year, households modify their accumulated stock of assets by either saving or borrowing. (Saving leads to an increase in the accumulated stock of assets; borrowing leads to a reduction in the accumulated stock of assets.) Thus, the annual *flow* of saving by households leads to a change in the total *stock* of assets.

Households' Supply of Saving

Households save because it allows them to spend in the future some of the income they earned today. They do this for several reasons. First, most people work for only part of their lives and, during their retirement, must live off their accumulated assets (plus whatever income they receive from employer or public pensions). Saving in the current year is a way of building up this retirement "nest egg." A second reason people save is that the future is uncertain. Next year they might become unemployed and thus lose their source of income, or they may have to provide for a relative who has lost a job or become incapacitated. In any case, uncertainty about the future provides a good reason to save. Finally, many households save in anticipation of specific large future expenditures. Young couples, for example, save in order to accumulate enough funds for a down payment on a house. Couples with young children save to help finance their children's university education.

Despite the many and varied reasons why any individual household chooses to save a lot or a little, to understand the economy's overall supply of financial capital, economists focus on three key determinants of household saving—current income, expected future income, and the interest rate.

Saving and Current Income   Most people try to *smooth* their spending across time. Instead of spending a lot when income is high and spending only a little when income is low, most people prefer to spend a relatively stable amount from year to year. The result is that in high-income years people tend to save a lot, and in low-income years people tend to save only a little. (In years when income is very low, people may save a negative amount, meaning that they spend partially out of their accumulated assets or go into debt by borrowing to finance their expenditures.) When economists examine statistics across many households in the economy, they find that the positive relationship between total income and total saving is relatively stable.

> Household saving is positively related to current income. An increase in current income increases the supply of financial capital.

Saving and Expected Future Income   For any given level of current income, households tend to save less when their expected *future* income is higher. If people anticipate that their income will be higher in the near future, their desire to smooth their spending (between now and the future) means that they will want to spend some of that higher future income now, thus reducing their *current* saving.

The best example of this behaviour is shown by many of you who are reading this book. Students are busy acquiring human capital and are usually earning little or no income. As we discussed in Chapter 14, people with university degrees earn more on average than people with only a high-school diploma. Thus, students are examples of people whose expected future income is considerably higher than their current income. The result is that many students are spending at levels that would be unaffordable (and quite imprudent!) if they were to earn their current incomes permanently. These students are spending at relatively high levels precisely because they expect to have much higher incomes in the near future. They are borrowing now (from parents or through student loans) because their future income will be high enough to pay back these debts.

> An increase in expected future income leads to a decline in current saving, and thus to a reduction in the supply of financial capital.

Saving and the Interest Rate   How does an increase in the interest rate affect households' desire to save? The interest rate is the "price" of financial capital. Like any price, the interest rate represents an opportunity cost—it is the opportunity cost of spending now rather than in the future. For example, suppose the interest rate is 5 percent per year. Your decision to spend $100 now "costs" you $105 in forgone spending one year from now. An increase in the interest rate increases the "price"—or opportunity

FIGURE 15-4 **The Economy's Supply of Saving**

There is a positive relationship between the interest rate and the flow of saving supplied by households. An increase in the interest rate increases the opportunity cost of current spending and leads households to increase their desired saving.

cost—of current spending. Households respond to an increase in the interest rate by substituting away from (relatively expensive) current spending and toward (relatively inexpensive) future spending.

> **An increase in the interest rate causes households to reduce their spending and increase their saving, thus increasing the quantity of financial capital supplied.[2]**

The Economy's Supply of Saving

The economy's supply of saving is shown in Figure 15-4, which shows a positive relationship between the interest rate and the quantity of financial capital supplied by the economy's households. An increase in the interest rate leads households to increase their total desired saving. This is a movement upward along the supply curve.

An increase in current income leads to an increase in households' desired saving *at any given interest rate* and thus causes the supply curve to shift to the right. An increase in expected future income (holding current income constant) leads to a decrease in households' desired saving *at any given interest rate* and thus causes the supply curve to shift to the left.

15.5 EQUILIBRIUM IN THE CAPITAL MARKET

We have discussed how the economy's demand for capital is related to the interest rate; a rise in the interest rate leads firms to reduce their desired capital stock and thus reduce their need for financial capital. We have also discussed how the economy's supply of capital is related to the interest rate; a rise in the interest rate leads households to increase their desired saving and thus provide more financial capital. We are now ready to put these two sides of the capital market together to examine market equilibrium.

The Equilibrium Interest Rate

There is an important difference between the analysis of individual firms and households on the one hand, and the analysis of the overall capital market on the other.

---

[2] This is the substitution effect of an increase in the interest rate and it works in the same direction for all individuals. There is also an income effect, which operates in one direction for households with negative net assets (debtors) and in the opposite direction for households with positive net assets (creditors). Economists often assume that, when summed across all households in the economy, some of which are debtors and others creditors, the overall effect of a change in the interest rate is dominated by the substitution effect.

Individual firms and households take the interest rate as given because they are so small relative to the entire economy that their own actions have no effect on the interest rate. For firms and households, the interest rate is *exogenous*. In the overall capital market, however, the interest rate is determined by the interaction of demand and supply—that is, the interest rate is *endogenous*. This important distinction is analogous to the one that exists in any competitive market; firms face a given market price for the product they sell, but that price is determined in equilibrium through the interaction of demand and supply.

One thing should be mentioned before we go on. In this chapter we have spent much time discussing the role of the interest rate in determining how firms and households behave. But we have ignored an important distinction between the *nominal* interest rate and the *real* interest rate. The *nominal* interest rate is the rate stated in the loan agreement. The *real* interest rate adjusts the nominal interest rate for the effects of inflation, and better represents the true cost of borrowing. The real interest rate is approximately equal to the nominal interest rate minus the rate of inflation. *Applying Economic Concepts 15-1* examines this distinction in more detail. In the discussion that follows, we restrict our attention to the real interest rate.

FIGURE 15-5 The Capital Market

At the equilibrium interest rate, the quantity of investment demanded equals the quantity of saving supplied. The equilibrium interest rate is i^* where the quantity of investment demanded by firms equals the quantity of saving supplied by households (point E).

Figure 15-5 shows how the interest rate is determined in the capital market. The intersection of the investment demand curve and the saving supply curve determines the equilibrium interest rate, i^*. If the interest rate were above i^*, there would be an excess supply of capital; households' desired saving would exceed firms' desired borrowing. This excess supply of capital would cause the interest rate—the price of financial capital—to fall. Conversely, if the interest rate were below i^*, there would be an excess demand for capital; firms' desired borrowing would exceed households' desired saving. This excess demand for capital would cause the interest rate to rise. Only at i^* is the market in equilibrium—the quantity of investment demanded by firms is just equal to the quantity of saving supplied by households.

Changes in the Market Equilibrium

We are now ready to examine some of the changes that occur in the capital market and how these changes affect the equilibrium interest rate and levels of investment and saving.

Increases in the Supply of Saving Anything that increases the flow of households' desired saving *at the given interest rate* will shift the supply curve for saving to the right. At the initial interest rate, this increase in desired saving will lead to an excess supply of financial capital and thus to a decline in the equilibrium interest rate. As the equilibrium interest rate falls, firms will find it profitable to expand their capital stock and will therefore increase their quantity of investment demanded. The rightward shift in

APPLYING ECONOMIC CONCEPTS 15-1

Inflation and Interest Rates

Inflation means the prices of all goods in the economy are rising. More correctly, it means that the prices of goods are rising on *average*—some prices may be rising and others may be falling, but if there is inflation then the average price is rising. Economists refer to the average price of all goods as the *price level*. When the price level is rising, inflation is positive; if prices are rising at a rate of 5 percent per year, the rate of inflation is 5 percent. When the price level is falling, inflation is negative. If prices are falling at a rate of 2 percent per year, the rate of inflation is –2 percent.

Real and Nominal Interest Rates

In the presence of inflation, we need to distinguish between the *real interest rate* and the *nominal interest rate*. The nominal interest rate is measured simply in dollars paid. If you pay me $7 interest for a $100 loan for one year, the nominal interest rate is 7 percent.

Consider further my one-year loan to you of $100 at the nominal rate of 7 percent. The *real* rate that I earn depends on what happens to the price level during the course of the year. If the price level remains constant over the year, then the real rate that I earn is also 7 percent—because I can buy 7 percent more goods and services with the $107 that you repay me than with the $100 that I lent you. However, if the price level were to rise by 7 percent during the year, the real rate would be zero because the $107 you repay me will buy exactly the same quantity of goods as did the $100 I gave up. If I were unlucky enough to have lent money at a nominal rate of 7 percent in a year in which prices rose by 10 percent, the real rate would be –3 percent. The real rate of interest concerns the ratio of the purchasing power of the money repaid to the purchasing power of the money initially borrowed, and it will be different from the nominal rate whenever inflation is not zero. *The real interest rate is the difference between the nominal interest rate and the rate of inflation.*

If lenders and borrowers are concerned with the real costs measured in terms of purchasing power, the nominal interest rate will be set at the real rate they require plus an amount to cover any expected rate of inflation. Consider a one-year loan that is meant to earn a real return to the lender of 3 percent. If the expected rate of inflation is zero, the nominal interest rate for the loan will also be 3 percent. If, however, a 10 percent inflation is expected, the nominal interest rate will have to be set at 13 percent in order for the real return to be 3 percent.

This point is often overlooked, and as a result people are surprised at the high nominal interest rates that exist during periods of high inflation. But it is the *real* interest rate that matters more to borrowers and lenders. For example, as the accompanying figure shows, in 1981 the nominal interest rate on three-month Treasury bills was almost 18 percent, but the high inflation rate at the time meant that the real interest rate was just over 5 percent. In contrast, a decade later in 1990, nominal rates had fallen to just below 13 percent but inflation had fallen further so that the real interest rate had actually *increased* to almost 8 percent. Thus, the period of lower nominal interest rates was actually a period of higher real interest rates.

Back to Capital

In this chapter we have examined investment demand by firms and the supply of saving by households. In both cases, the interest rate plays an important role. For firms, the interest rate reflects the cost of financial capital required to purchase physical capital. For households, the interest rate reflects the benefit of delaying their spending until the future and thus increasing their current saving. In both cases, though we did not say it, we were referring to the *real* interest rate.

When you go on to study *macroeconomics*, you will learn more about what causes inflation, and thus what forces us to make the distinction between real and nominal interest rates. For now, however, we assume in this chapter that there is no inflation; thus, real and nominal interest rates are the same.

(*Source*: Based on Nominal interest rate: three-month Treasury bill rate, Statistics Canada CANSIM Series V122541. Real interest rate is based on author's calculations of CPI inflation, Series PCPISA from www.bankofcanada.ca.)

the saving supply curve will therefore lead to a movement downward along the investment demand curve. The effect of an increase in the supply of saving is illustrated in part (i) of Figure 15-6. Three possible causes of such an increase in the supply of saving are provided.

1. Income Growth.   As income increases, households desire to consume more, both now and in the future. The greater income leads to an increase in households' desired saving and thus to an increase in the supply of financial capital. Gradual but ongoing income growth over a period of many years is an important reason that the economy's supply of saving continues to increase.

2. Population Growth.   An increase in the population—either through higher birth rates or greater immigration—leads to an increase in the supply of financial capital. The simple reason is that most households save, and so an increase in the number of households leads to an increase in the total amount of desired saving.

3. Policies to Increase Desired Saving.   Some Canadian government policies may increase households' desired saving. Registered Retirement Savings Plans (RRSPs) and Tax-Free Savings Accounts (TFSAs), for example, offer tax benefits to households who contribute to special "registered" savings accounts.

FIGURE 15-6   Changes in the Capital Market

(i) An increase in the supply of saving

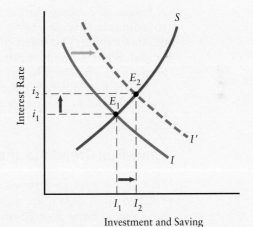

(ii) An increase in investment demand

Changes in the demand for or the supply of financial capital lead to changes in the equilibrium interest rate and levels of investment and saving. Part (i) illustrates an increase in the supply of saving. As households decide to increase the amount of their saving (at any given interest rate), the excess supply of capital leads to a reduction in the interest rate, from i_1 to i_2. As the interest rate falls, firms increase their quantity of investment demanded. The equilibrium level of investment (and saving) increases from I_1 to I_2.

Part (ii) illustrates an increase in investment demand. As firms decide to increase their desired investment, they require more financial capital (at any given interest rate). This leads to an excess demand for capital and to an increase in the interest rate, from i_1 to i_2. As the interest rate rises, households decide to increase their desired saving. The equilibrium level of investment (and saving) increases from I_1 to I_2.

Increases in Investment Demand   Anything that increases firms' desired investment *at the given interest rate* will shift the investment demand curve to the right. At the initial interest rate, this increase in the need for financial capital will lead to an excess demand for capital and thus to a rise in the equilibrium interest rate. As the equilibrium interest rate increases, households will find it desirable to reduce their current spending and increase their saving. The rightward shift in the investment demand curve will therefore lead to a movement upward along the saving supply curve. This case is illustrated in part (ii) of Figure 15-6. There are three possible causes of an increase in the demand for financial capital.

1. Population and Income Growth.   As the economy's total income grows, either through growth in population or in per capita income, the demand for goods and services increases. This increase in the demand for firms' products leads to an increase in the marginal revenue product (*MRP*) of capital. As we saw earlier in the chapter, an increase in capital's *MRP* leads to an increase in the economy's investment demand. The gradual but ongoing growth in the economy's total income is an important explanation for the gradual increase in the economy's investment demand.

2. Technological Improvement.   Over time, there are technological improvements in the quality of factors of production. This is especially true for physical capital. Many of these improvements occur when obsolete or worn-out capital is replaced by new and better capital. For example, the dramatic improvements in computer and information technology over the past two decades have led to large increases in the marginal product of some types of capital and thus an increase in the economy's investment demand.

3. Policies to Encourage Investment.   Over the years, Canadian federal and provincial governments have designed policies to encourage firms to increase their investment in physical capital. One effect of such policies is to increase firms' demand for financial capital. Reductions in corporate income-tax rates, special investment tax credits, support for specific kinds of research and development, and loans guaranteed by governments are four different policies that increase the profitability of investment to firms and likely lead to an increase in their demand for financial capital.

Long-Run Trends in the Capital Market

Part (i) of Figure 15-7 shows the annual flow of net non-residential investment from 1965 to 2013. It is quite volatile over time, though always positive. Part (ii) shows how this volatile flow of investment has led to an ever-increasing non-residential capital stock; it grew at an average annual rate of 2.6 percent over the period shown. Even in years when the flow of investment is relatively large, the growth rate of the overall capital stock rises only slightly, reflecting the small size of the investment *flow* relative to the large accumulated capital *stock*. For similar reasons, large declines in the flow of investment—like the one that occurred during the major recession of 2009—led to only a slight slowdown in the growth of the capital stock. Part (iii) of the figure shows the path of the real interest rate, which is quite volatile and displays no clear trend over the 45-year period. How can we use our model of the capital market to understand these data?

Over long periods of time, technological change and population growth can explain both a rising capital stock and an interest rate with no clear long-run trend.

FIGURE 15-7   Investment, the Capital Stock, and the Real Interest Rate in Canada, 1965–2013

(i) Annual flow of non-residential investment

(ii) Non-residential capital stock

(iii) Real interest rate

The annual flow of investment is quite volatile, although the accumulated capital stock grows more steadily; the real interest rate is quite volatile and has no clear trend. Canada's non-residential capital stock has increased by more than three times since 1965, an average annual growth rate of 2.6 percent. The real interest rate (here measured as the nominal interest rate on three-month Treasury bills minus the annual rate of inflation) is much more volatile.

(*Source:* Author's calculations based on data from statistics Canada's CANSIM data set: Table 031-0002.)

We have already stated that population growth leads to an increase in both the demand for and the supply of financial capital. A larger population implies more demand for goods and services, and thus greater investment demand by firms. A larger population, even with an unchanged level of income per person, leads to more income and greater saving by households. With both the demand and the supply curves for financial capital shifting to the right because of population growth, there will be ongoing growth in the flow of investment and an ever-rising capital stock; the effect on the interest rate will depend on the relative size of the demand and supply shifts.

Technological change also affects both sides of the capital market. Improvements in technology that increase capital's *MRP* lead firms to increase their investment demand. As we have said several times already in this book, technological change also lies at the heart of increasing productivity and growing per capita income. As income grows, so too does the supply of saving. Thus, through its effect on income, technological improvements that stimulate investment demand also lead to an increase in the supply of financial capital. With both the demand

and the supply curves shifting to the right because of technological improvements, there will be growth in the flow of investment and an ever-rising capital stock; the effect on the interest rate will again depend on the relative size of the demand and supply shifts.

> **Ongoing technological improvement and population growth, by increasing both the demand for and the supply of financial capital, explain a rising capital stock with no clear trend in the interest rate.**

SUMMARY

15.1 A BRIEF OVERVIEW OF THE CAPITAL MARKET   LO 1

- The demand for financial capital comes from firms' need to finance their investment in new physical capital. The supply of financial capital comes from households' saving decisions.
- The capital market connects households' saving decisions with firms' financing requirements.

- Financial intermediaries—such as commercial banks—play an important role in bringing the two sides of the capital market together.

15.2 PRESENT VALUE   LO 2

- Since physical capital is durable, it delivers benefits to its owners over many years. As a result, firms need to evaluate the stream of future benefits produced by capital.
- *Present value* is the value today of any stream of future sums; it is computed by discounting the future sums

using the rate of interest. The present value of X receivable in *t* years' time when the interest rate is *i* per year is

$$PV = \frac{X}{(1 + i)^t}$$

15.3 THE DEMAND FOR CAPITAL   LO 3

- Profit-maximizing firms will purchase capital up to the point at which the present value of the future stream of *MRP*s generated by the last unit of capital equals its purchase price.
- Economists focus on the relationship between the interest rate and firms' desired capital stock; an increase in the interest rate reduces the present value of any given stream of future *MRP*s and thus reduces firms' desired capital stock.
- Since firms require financial capital to finance their investment in additional capital equipment, the

economy's demand for financial capital comes from the many individual firms' demand for investment. An increase in the interest rate leads to a decline in firms' quantity of investment demanded.
- An increase in the marginal product of capital increases firms' desired capital stock at any given interest rate and therefore leads to an increase in the economy's demand for financial capital. This is represented by a rightward shift in the economy's investment demand curve.

15.4 THE SUPPLY OF CAPITAL LO 4

- The economy's supply of capital comes from households' flow of desired saving.
- An increase in the interest rate increases the opportunity cost of current spending and thus leads households to increase their desired saving. This is a movement upward along the economy's supply of saving curve.

- An increase in aggregate income—either through population growth or growth in per capita income—leads to an increase in total household saving at any given interest rate. The result is a rightward shift in the economy's supply of saving curve.

15.5 EQUILIBRIUM IN THE CAPITAL MARKET LO 5

- Equilibrium in the capital market is determined where the quantity of capital supplied by households equals the quantity of capital demanded by firms.
- Changes in the demand for capital or the supply of capital lead to changes in the equilibrium interest rate and equilibrium levels of investment and saving.

- Technological improvement and population growth lead to increases in both the demand for and the supply of capital. Continual technological improvement and population growth can therefore explain the ongoing growth in the capital stock with little or no trend in the real interest rate.

KEY CONCEPTS

Physical capital and financial capital
Present value and the interest rate
A firm's optimal capital stock

The economy's demand for investment
Households' saving decisions
The economy's supply of saving

Equilibrium interest rate
Technological change and a rising
  capital stock

STUDY EXERCISES

MyEconLab   Make the grade with MyEconLab: Study Exercises marked in ⊕ can be found on MyEconLab. You can practise them as often as you want, and most feature step-by-step guided instructions to help you find the right answer.

❶ Fill in the blanks to make the following statements correct.

  a. A firm's demand for financial capital is derived from its demand for _____.
  b. A firm that decides to invest in additional machinery will _____ its requirement for financial capital.
  c. An increase in the marginal product of capital will lead firms to _____ their desired capital stock and therefore _____ their demand for financial capital.
  d. An increase in the interest rate will _____ the present value of capital's *MRP* and therefore _____ firms' desired capital stock. The result will

be a _____ in the quantity of financial capital demanded by firms.
  e. An increase in capital's *MRP* results in a _____ in the economy's investment demand curve, whereas an increase in the interest rate results in a _____ the economy's investment demand curve.

❷ Fill in the blanks to make the following statements correct.

  a. An increase in the interest rate leads households to _____ their current spending and _____ their current saving. The result is a(n) _____ in the quantity of financial capital supplied.

b. An increase in current income leads to a(n) _____ in household saving at any given interest rate. This results in a _____ in the economy's supply curve for capital.

c. An increase in expected future income leads to a(n) _____ in current household spending. The result is a(n) _____ in household saving and therefore a(n) _____ in the quantity of capital supplied at any given interest rate. This is represented by a _____ in the economy's supply curve for financial capital.

3 Fill in the blanks to make the following statements correct.

a. The economy's equilibrium interest rate is determined where _____. At an interest rate above the equilibrium interest rate, the quantity of capital supplied _____ the quantity of capital demanded, and the result is a(n) _____ in the interest rate.

b. At an interest rate below the equilibrium interest rate, the quantity of capital demanded _____ the quantity of capital supplied, and the result is a(n) _____ in the interest rate.

c. Beginning in equilibrium in the capital market, an increase in the supply of financial capital leads to a(n) _____ in the equilibrium interest rate, a(n) _____ in borrowing by firms, and a(n) _____ in the equilibrium level of investment and saving.

d. Beginning in equilibrium in the capital market, an increase in the demand for financial capital leads to a(n) _____ in the equilibrium interest rate, a(n) _____ in desired saving by households, and a(n) _____ in the equilibrium level of investment and saving.

e. Technological improvements lead to a(n) _____ in both the demand for and the supply of financial capital. As a result, technological improvements can explain a(n) _____ capital stock and _____ in the interest rate.

4 The following table shows the stream of income produced by several different assets. In each case, P_1, P_2, and P_3 are the payments made by the asset at the end of years 1, 2, and 3.

Asset	i	P_1	P_2	P_3	Present Value
A	8%	$1000	$0	$0	—
B	7%	0	0	5000	—
C	9%	200	0	200	—
D	10%	50	40	60	—

a. For each asset, compute the asset's present value. (Note that the market interest rate, i, is not the same in each situation.)

b. In each case, what is the most a firm would be prepared to pay to acquire the asset?

c. Suppose the listed purchase price for an asset were less than its present value. What would you expect to observe?

5 How would you go about evaluating the present value of each of the following?

a. The existing reserves of a relatively small oil company

b. The total world reserves of an exhaustible natural resource with a known completely fixed supply

c. A long-term bond, issued by a very unstable third-world government, that promises to pay the bearer $1000 per year forever

d. A lottery ticket that your neighbour bought for $10, which was one of 1 million tickets sold for a drawing that will be held in one year's time paying $2 million to the single winner

6 The following table shows how the present value of the future $MRPs$ produced by each unit of capital changes as the firm's total capital stock increases.

Units of Capital	PV of Future $MRPs$
100	$10 000
101	9 000
102	8 000
103	7 000
104	6 000
105	5 000
106	4 000
107	3 000

a. Notice that the present value of the MRP declines as more capital is used. What economic principle accounts for this?

b. If a unit of capital can be purchased for $5000, how many will the firm purchase? Explain.

c. Suppose the market interest rate falls. Explain what happens to the PV of the stream of future $MRPs$. What happens to the firm's profit-maximizing level of capital?

7 Wintertown Snow Removal Co. purchases snowplows for its residential snow clearing business. The purchase price of an additional snowplow is currently $50 000 and it is expected to produce a stream of MRPs for 12 years. The interest rate is 4 percent and the present value of the stream of MRPs is $50 000.

a. With this information, should the company purchase the additional snowplow?

b. Suppose instead the interest rate were 6 percent. How will this affect the future stream of MRPs and the purchase decision?

c. Suppose instead the interest rate were 2 percent. How will this affect the future stream of MRPs and the purchase decision?

d. Suppose again that the interest rate is 4 percent. The company now learns of a new technology that is expected to reduce the price of home snowblowers by 50 percent. How will this affect the future stream of MRPs and the purchase decision?

e. Suppose the interest rate is 4 percent and that new projections are announced for Wintertown that show a booming economy for the next 5–7 years. How will this affect the future stream of MRPs and the purchase decision?

8 CopyCentral provides commercial photocopying services. This profit-maximizing firm purchases copy machines that each have a lifespan of three years, after which they have no value. A machine generates MRPs of $9000 per year for each of those three years. At each of the following annual interest rates, determine the maximum price this firm should be willing to pay for a copy machine.

a. 2 percent
b. 3 percent
c. 6 percent
d. 10 percent

9 The diagram below shows an individual firm's investment demand curve. The market interest rate is i_0.

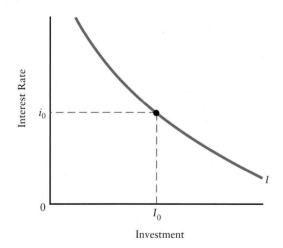

a. Explain why the firm's investment demand curve is downward sloping.

b. Suppose the firm now expects the market for its product to be especially good in the future. Explain what happens to its investment demand curve.

c. Now suppose some technical problem leads to a reduction in the future stream of *MRP*s produced by capital. How does this affect the firm's investment demand curve?

10 For each interest rate below, compute the opportunity cost (in terms of forgone spending next year) to a household of spending $1000 this year:

a. The interest rate is 5 percent per year.
b. The interest rate is 7 percent per year.
c. The interest rate is 9 percent per year.
d. Explain why, other things being equal, households save more when the interest rate is higher.

11 Since the interest rate is the price of financial capital, a change in the interest rate generates both an income effect and a substitution effect.

a. Explain how the substitution effect of an increase in the interest rate influences households' desired saving.

b. Explain how the income effect of an increase in the interest rate influences households' desired saving. Why does the direction of the income effect depend on whether the household is a net debtor or a net creditor?

c. Explain why, for the economy as a whole, the substitution effect is likely to dominate the income effect.

d. What is the importance of the result in part (c) for the economy's supply of financial capital?

12 The accompanying figure shows the economy's capital market, with the initial equilibrium at point E, with an interest rate of i^* and investment (and saving) equal to I^*.

a. Suppose the government introduces a program of tax credits to firms that increase their desired investment in new physical capital. What is the effect on the equilibrium interest rate, investment, and saving of this policy? Show the effect of this policy in the diagram.

b. In part (a), the policy has led to a higher interest rate *and* higher investment by firms. Does this contradict our discussion in this chapter about how firms' desired investment is negatively related to the interest rate? Explain.

c. Now suppose the government introduces a program of tax credits to households who save. What is the effect on the equilibrium interest rate, investment, and saving of this policy? Show the effect of this policy in the diagram.

Investment and Saving

d. In part (c), the policy has led to a lower interest rate and higher saving by households. Does this contradict our discussion in this chapter about how households' desired saving is positively related to the interest rate? Explain.

13 "Profit-maximizing firms will reduce their desired investment when the interest rate rises, other things being equal. As a result, empirical economists should always expect to see a negative correlation between actual investment and the interest rate." Comment.

16 Market Failures and Government Intervention

CHAPTER OUTLINE	LEARNING OBJECTIVES (LO) After studying this chapter you will be able to
16.1 BASIC FUNCTIONS OF GOVERNMENT	**1** discuss the importance of the government's "monopoly of violence."
16.2 THE CASE FOR FREE MARKETS	**2** describe the "informal" defence of free markets.
16.3 MARKET FAILURES	**3** explain why externalities lead to allocative inefficiency. **4** explain why public goods are underprovided by private markets.
16.4 BROADER SOCIAL GOALS	**5** understand why free markets may not achieve some desirable social goals.
16.5 GOVERNMENT INTERVENTION	**6** identify the direct and indirect costs of government intervention, and some of the important causes of government failure.

MANY aspects of Canadian economic life are determined in free markets. Most of the goods and services that you buy are produced by privately owned profit-making firms, and the prices of those goods and services are determined in free markets. The incomes of most Canadian workers are also determined by free-market forces.

At the same time, municipal, provincial, and federal governments provide services to Canadians that are among the most important—public education, healthcare, clean water, and national defence. Government involvement in our market economy is pervasive and takes many forms, including the operation of police forces, national parks, sanitation systems, and the Coast Guard. Crown corporations such as Canada Post, Export Development Canada, and Hydro Quebec sell goods and services to firms and households. Governments also regulate many of our activities through the use of building codes, zoning laws, minimum wages, food inspection, and environmental regulation. In order to finance these various activities, governments in Canada take a significant portion of our incomes in the form of taxes.

Which elements of the economy are best left to free markets and which elements require government intervention? Governments are clearly necessary to provide law and order and to define and enforce property rights. But beyond these basic functions—ones that we all too often take for granted—what is the case for government intervention in otherwise free markets?

The general case for some reliance on free markets is that allowing decentralized decision making is more desirable than having all economic decisions made by a centralized planning body. The general case for *some* government intervention is that almost no one wants to let markets decide *everything* about our economic affairs. Most people believe that there are areas in which markets do not function well and in which government intervention can improve the general social good.

> The operative choice is not between an unhampered free-market economy and a fully centralized command economy. It is rather the choice of which mix of markets and government intervention best suits people's hopes and needs.

In this chapter, we discuss the role of the government in market-based economies, identifying why markets sometimes fail and why government policies sometimes fail. We begin by examining the basic functions of government.

16.1 BASIC FUNCTIONS OF GOVERNMENT

Governments are very old institutions. They arose shortly after the Neolithic Agricultural Revolution turned people from hunter–gatherers into settled farmers about 10 000 years ago. Over the intervening 100 centuries, the functions undertaken by governments have varied enormously. But through all that time, the function that has not changed is to provide what is called a *monopoly of violence*. Violent acts can be conducted by the military and the civilian police arms of government, and through its judicial system the government can deprive people of their liberty by incarcerating them or, in extreme cases, by executing them. This is a dangerous monopoly that is easily abused. For this reason, stable and well-functioning societies have systems of checks and balances designed to keep the government's monopoly directed to the general good rather than to the good of a narrow government circle.

The importance of having a monopoly of violence can be seen in those countries whose governments do not have it. Somalia and Nigeria in recent years and China in the 1920s provide examples of countries in which individual warlords commanded armies that could not vanquish each other. Mexico and Russia provide examples of organized crime having substantial power to commit violence that the government cannot control. In extreme cases where many groups have almost equal ability to exert military violence, power struggles can create havoc with normal economic and social life. Life then becomes "nasty, brutish, and short"—to use the words of the seventeenth-century English political philosopher Thomas Hobbes (1588–1679).

The importance of having checks on the government's arbitrary use of its monopoly is seen in the disasters that ensue in the many dictatorships that misuse their power. The USSR under Stalin, Uganda under Idi Amin, Nigeria under Sanni Abacha, Cambodia under Pol Pot, Iraq under Saddam Hussein, Zimbabwe under Robert Mugabe, and Libya under Muammar Gadaffi are a few of many examples from the past 75 years.

When the government's monopoly of violence is secure and functions with effective restrictions against its arbitrary use, citizens can safely carry out their ordinary economic and social activities.

As the founder of British Classical economics, Adam Smith, wrote over two centuries ago:

The first duty of the sovereign [is] that of protecting the society from the violence and invasion of other independent societies ... The second duty of the sovereign [is] that of protecting, as far as possible, every member of the society from the injustice or oppression of every other member of it.[1]

The provision of national defence is a basic function of government, which helps to allow citizens to carry out their ordinary economic and social activities.

A related government activity is to provide security of property. Governments define and enforce property rights that give people a secure claim to the fruits of their own labour. These property rights include clear definition and enforcement of the rights and obligations of institutions, such as corporations, religious organizations, and non-profit enterprises.

In a modern complex economy, providing these "minimal" government services is no simple task. Countries whose governments are not good at doing these things have seldom prospered economically.

The importance of these basic functions of government should not be under-estimated. In recent years, economists and policymakers in rich, developed countries have come to a greater understanding of the challenges in developing countries that stem from their ineffective political structures. Local corruption, powerful warlords, and a lack of basic political infrastructure combine to make official development aid less effective than it would be in countries with more stable and representative political structures. As a result, a growing share of official assistance to developing countries is taking the form of *political* rather than *economic* assistance—a process often referred to as *institution building*. A 2012 best-selling book *Why Nations Fail* by professors Daron Acemoglu and James Robinson argues the importance of institutions in explaining the economic success or failure of countries.

16.2 THE CASE FOR FREE MARKETS

Within a secure framework of law and order, and well-defined and enforced property rights, a modern economy can function at least moderately well without further government intervention in markets. In this section we review the case for free markets. In subsequent sections we study government functions that arise when free markets fail to produce acceptable results.

Free markets are impressive institutions. Consumers' preferences and producers' costs generate price signals. These signals coordinate separate decisions taken by

---

[1] Adam Smith, *The Wealth of Nations* (1776; New York: Random House, 1937 ed., pp. 653, 669).

millions of independent agents, all pursuing their own self-interest. In doing so, they allocate the nation's resources without conscious central direction. Markets also determine the distribution of income by establishing prices of factors of production, which provide incomes for their owners. Furthermore, modern market economies, where firms compete to get ahead of each other by producing better goods more cheaply, generate the technological changes that have raised average living standards fairly steadily over the past two centuries.

In presenting the case for free markets, economists have used two quite different approaches. The first of these may be characterized as the "formal defence," and is based on the concept of allocative efficiency, discussed in Chapters 5 and 12. The essence of the formal defence of free markets is that if all markets were perfectly competitive, and if governments allowed all prices to be determined by demand and supply, then price would equal marginal cost for all products and the economy would be allocatively efficient. Allocative efficiency means that resources are used in such a way that total surplus to society—consumer surplus plus producer surplus—is maximized. Since we discussed allocative efficiency extensively in earlier chapters, we will say no more about it at this point.

The other defence of free markets—what might be called the "informal defence"—is at least as old as Adam Smith and applies to market economies whether or not they are perfectly competitive. The informal defence is not laid out in a formal model of an economy, but it does follow from some hard reasoning, and over the years it has been subjected to much intellectual probing. The informal defence of free markets is based on three central arguments:

1. Free markets provide automatic coordination of the actions of decentralized decision makers.

2. The pursuit of profits in free markets provides a stimulus to innovation and rising material living standards.

3. Free markets permit a decentralization of economic power.

Automatic Coordination

Defenders of free markets argue that compared with the alternatives, the decentralized market system is more flexible and adjusts more quickly to changes.

Suppose, for example, that the world price of oil rises, which then increases the prices of heating oil, gasoline, and electricity. One household might prefer to respond by maintaining a high temperature in its house and economizing on its driving; another household might do the reverse. A third household might give up air-conditioning instead. This flexibility can be contrasted with centralized control, which would force the same pattern on everyone, say, by rationing heating oil and gasoline, by regulating permitted temperatures, and by limiting air-conditioning to days when the temperature exceeded 27°C.

Furthermore, as conditions continue to change, prices in a market economy will also change, and decentralized decision makers can react continually. In contrast, government quotas, allocations, and rationing schemes are much more difficult to adjust. As a result, there are likely to be shortages and surpluses before adjustments are made. A free market provides automatic signals *as a situation develops* so that not all of the consequences of an economic change have to be anticipated and allowed for by a group of central planners. Millions of responses to millions of changes in thousands of markets are required every year, and it would be a Herculean task to anticipate and plan for them all.

A market system allows for coordination *without anyone needing to understand how the whole system works.* Professor Thomas Schelling, who was awarded the Nobel Prize in economics in 2005, illustrated this idea:

> *The dairy farmer doesn't need to know how many people eat butter and how far away they are, how many other people raise cows, how many babies drink milk, or whether more money is spent on beer or milk. What he needs to know is the prices of different feeds, the characteristics of different cows, the different prices . . . for milk . . ., the relative cost of hired labor and electrical machinery, and what his net earnings might be if he sold his cows and raised pigs instead.*[2]

Producers in market economies have the incentive to provide the goods and services that customers value, and the result is that line-ups rarely exist in these economies. In the former Soviet Union, however, the central planning system was very slow to respond, and line-ups like this were very common.

It is, of course, an enormous advantage that all the producers and consumers of a country collectively can make the system operate—yet not one of them, much less all of them, has to understand the details of *how* that system works.

Innovation and Growth

Technology, preferences, and resource availability are changing all the time, in all economies. Forty years ago there was no such thing as a hand-held GPS or a digital camera. Hybrid cars did not exist. Manuscripts existed only as hardcopy, not as electronic files in an ultralight, wireless, laptop computer. The Internet did not exist—nor did smartphones, tablets, electronic airline tickets, cost-effective solar panels and wind turbines, income-tax software packages, computer-assisted design (CAD) programs, regional jets, standardized containers for transoceanic shipping, and a whole host of other goods and services that we now take for granted.

Digital cameras, tablet computers, social-networking sites, hybrid cars, and regional jets are all products that were invented or developed by individuals or firms in pursuit of profits. An entrepreneur who correctly "reads" the market and perceives that a demand for some product may exist or be created has a profit incentive to develop it.

In a market economy, individuals risk their time and money in the hope of earning profits. Though many fail, some succeed. New products and processes appear and disappear. Some are fads or have little impact; others become items of major significance. The market system works by trial and error to sort them out and allocates resources to what prove to be successful innovations.

In contrast, planners in more centralized systems have to guess which innovations will be productive and which goods will be strongly demanded. Central planning may achieve wonders by permitting a massive effort in a chosen direction, but central planners also may guess incorrectly about the direction and put too many eggs in the

---

[2] T.C. Schelling, 1978. *Micro Motives and Macro Behavior*. New York: Norton.

wrong basket or reject as unpromising something that will turn out to be vital. Perhaps the biggest failure of centrally planned economies was their inability to encourage the experimentation and innovation that have proven to be the driving forces behind long-run growth in advanced market economies. It is striking that since the early 1990s most centrally planned economies abandoned their system in favour of a price system in one fell swoop while the only remaining large planned economy, China, is quickly increasing the role of markets in most aspects of its economy.

Decentralization of Power

Another important part of the case for a free-market economy is that it tends to decentralize power and thus requires less coercion of individuals than any other type of economy. Though the market power of large corporations is sometimes considerable, it tends to be constrained both by the competition of other large entities and by the emergence of new products and firms. This is the process of creative destruction that was described by Joseph Schumpeter and that we examined in Chapter 10. In any case, say defenders of the free market, even such concentrations of private power are far less substantial than government power.

Governments must coerce if markets are not allowed to allocate people to jobs and goods to consumers. Not only will such coercion be regarded as arbitrary (especially by those who do not like the results), but the power also creates major opportunities for bribery, corruption, and allocation according to the preferences of the central administrators. If, at the going prices and wages, there are not enough apartments or coveted jobs to go around, the bureaucrats can allocate some to those who pay the largest bribe, some to those with religious beliefs or political views that they like, and only the rest to those whose names come up on the waiting list.

Of course, even though markets tend to diffuse power, they do not do so completely; large firms and large labour unions clearly have and exercise substantial economic power. In recent years, especially in the United States, many economists have expressed concern about the concentration of economic power within large financial institutions and, in particular, their ability to influence legislation through lobbying and contributions to political parties and candidates.[3]

16.3 MARKET FAILURES

market failure Failure of the unregulated market system to achieve allocative efficiency.

The term **market failure** describes the failure of the market economy to achieve an efficient allocation of resources. As we saw in Chapter 12, efficiency in the allocation of resources requires that price equal marginal cost. If this equality exists in all industries simultaneously, we say that the economy as a whole is *allocatively efficient*.

> Market failure describes a situation in which the free market, in the absence of government intervention, fails to achieve allocative efficiency.

It is useful at this point to recall the distinction between normative and positive statements that we first encountered in Chapter 2. The statement that the economy is

---

[3] For an excellent current discussion of these concerns, see Simon Johnson and James Kwak, *13 Bankers: The Wall Street Takeover and the Next Financial Meltdown*. Pantheon, 2010.

allocatively efficient (or not) is a *positive* statement. We can say that the economy has or has not achieved allocative efficiency without making any value judgement—the statement uses only an observation about the economy and the definition of allocative efficiency. Note, however, that the allocatively efficient outcome may not be the most desirable outcome in a normative sense. For example, an economy may be allocatively efficient even though the distribution of income is judged by some to be undesirable. As we see later in the chapter, such concerns provide another motivation for government intervention.

We now examine four situations in which the free market fails to achieve allocative efficiency—*market power, externalities, non-rivalrous* and *non-excludable goods,* and *asymmetric information.* Many of these market failures provide a justification for government intervention in markets. We then discuss other reasons for government intervention that are not based on market failure—chief among these is intervention to achieve a more equitable distribution of income.

Market Power

Market power is inevitable in any market economy for three reasons. First, in many industries economies of scale are such that there is room for only a few firms to operate at low costs, each having some ability to influence market conditions. Second, in many industries, firms sell differentiated products and thus have some ability to set their prices. Third, firms that innovate with new products or new production processes gain a temporary monopoly until other firms learn what the innovator knows. As we saw in Chapters 10, 11, and 12, firms that have market power will maximize their profit at a level of output at which price exceeds marginal cost. The result is allocatively inefficient, even though it is the inevitable outcome of the kinds of innovation that raise living standards over the long term.

This last reason sets up a conflict between achieving allocative efficiency at any given point in time and encouraging economic growth over time. Government policymakers clearly take the dynamic view of competition. They do not try to turn imperfectly competitive industries into perfectly competitive ones. Nor do they try to induce such firms to produce where marginal cost is equal to price. Not only would this be impossible, given the pervasiveness of oligopoly and monopolistic competition, but it would also be undesirable since much innovation and productivity growth comes from firms with market power. Instead, as we saw in Chapter 12, governments use competition policy to prevent monopolistic practices that permit firms to avoid behaving competitively with respect to one another. The challenge of economic policy is then to accept monopolistic and oligopolistic "imperfect" competition for the range of choices and scale advantages they provide, while keeping firms in active competition with one another so as to gain the economic growth that results from their innovative practices.

Externalities

Recall from Chapter 12 that in order for the economy to be allocatively efficient, marginal benefit must equal marginal cost for all products. But whose benefits and costs are relevant? Firms that are maximizing their *own* profits are interested only in their own costs of production—they may not care about any benefits or costs their actions might create for others. Similarly, insofar as individual consumers are interested in the benefits *they* receive from any given product, they ignore any costs or benefits that

externality An effect on parties not directly involved in the production or use of a commodity. Also called *third-party effects*.

may accrue to others. An **externality** occurs whenever actions taken by firms or consumers directly impose costs or confer benefits on others. If you smoke a cigarette in a restaurant, you impose costs on others present; when you renovate your home, you confer benefits on your neighbours by improving the general look of the neighbourhood. Externalities are also called *third-party effects* because parties other than the two primary participants in the transaction (the buyer and the seller) are affected.

The foregoing discussion suggests the importance of the distinction between *private cost* and *social cost*. **Private cost** measures the cost faced by the private decision maker, including production costs, advertising costs, and so on. **Social cost** includes the private cost (since the decision maker is a member of society) but also includes any other costs imposed on third parties. There is a similar distinction between *private benefit* and *social benefit*. To simplify things, however, we will discuss all externalities in terms of the distinction between private and social cost. But this does not limit our discussion in any way. If we want to consider a situation in which your listening to good music confers benefits to your nearby friends, we can think of your action as increasing their benefits or, equivalently, as decreasing their costs. Similarly, your smoking of cigarettes can be viewed as reducing their benefits or, equivalently, as increasing their costs. By expressing everything in terms of costs (rather than benefits), we merely simplify the discussion.

private cost The value of the best alternative use of resources used in production as valued by the producer.

social cost The value of the best alternative use of resources used in production as valued by society.

> Discrepancies between private cost and social cost occur when there are externalities. The presence of externalities, even when all markets are perfectly competitive, leads to allocatively inefficient outcomes.

Externalities arise in many different ways, and they may be harmful or beneficial to the third parties. When they are harmful, they are called *negative externalities*; when they are beneficial, they are called *positive externalities*. Figure 16-1 shows why an externality leads to allocative inefficiency, even though the market is assumed to be perfectly competitive. Here are two examples.

Consider the case of a firm whose production process for steel generates harmful smoke as a byproduct. Individuals who live and work near the firm bear real costs as they cope with breathing (or trying to avoid breathing) the harmful smoke. When the profit-maximizing firm makes its decision concerning how much steel to produce, it ignores the costs that it imposes on other people. This is a negative externality. In this case, because the firm ignores those parts of social cost that are not its own private cost, the firm will produce too much steel relative to what is allocatively efficient.

A second example involves an individual who renovates her home and thus improves its external appearance. Such improvements enhance the neighbours' view and the value of their property. Yet the individual renovator ignores the benefits that her actions have on the neighbours. This is a positive externality. In this case, because the renovator ignores those parts of social benefits that are not her own private benefits, there will be too little home renovation done relative to what is allocatively efficient.

The airborne emissions from coal-fired power plants are one important example of a negative externality. The social costs associated with these emissions exceed the private costs.

Smileus/Shutterstock

FIGURE 16-1   Externalities Lead to Allocative Inefficiency

(i) A negative externality   (ii) A positive externality

When there is an externality, either too much or too little of the good is produced. If the market for this good is perfectly competitive and there is no government intervention, the equilibrium is shown by p^C and Q^C in both parts of the figure. If there is no externality, social and private marginal cost are the same and so the outcome is allocatively efficient.

Part (i) shows a situation where the production or the consumption of the good imposes costs on third parties. This is a negative externality—social marginal costs are MC_S, above MC_P. The vertical distance between MC_P and MC_S reflects the per-unit external cost. The allocatively efficient quantity is now Q^*, where MB equals MC_S. But the free market will produce Q^C, too much of the good.

Part (ii) shows a situation where the production or consumption of the good instead confers benefits on third parties. This is a positive externality—social marginal costs are MC_S, below MC_P. The vertical distance between MC_P and MC_S reflects the per-unit external benefit. The allocatively efficient quantity is again Q^* where MB equals MC_S. But the free market will produce Q^C, too little of the good.

> **With a positive externality, a competitive free market will produce too little of the good. With a negative externality, a competitive free market will produce too much of the good.**

The allocative inefficiency caused by an externality provides a justification for government intervention. In the case of a negative externality, the government may levy a tax on the firms or consumers responsible, as is often done in the case of pollution; we explore specific policies to address pollution externalities in Chapter 17. In the case of positive externalities, the government may provide a subsidy (a negative tax) to the firms or consumers responsible, as is done in the case of publicly provided education; we examine education and other social policies in Chapter 18.

Non-Rivalrous and Non-Excludable Goods

Economists classify goods and services into four broad categories depending on the *rivalry* for the good and the *excludability* of the good. Table 16-1 shows these four types of goods.

TABLE 16-1 Four Types of Products

	Excludable	Non-Excludable
Rivalrous	*Private Goods* Food A seat on an airplane An hour of legal advice	*Common-Property Resources* Fisheries Rivers and streams Wildlife Clean air
Non-Rivalrous (up to capacity)	*Club Goods* Art galleries Roads Bridges Cable or satellite TV signal	*Public Goods* National defence Public information Public protection Radio signal

Free markets cope best with rivalrous and excludable goods—what we here call "private" goods. The table gives examples of goods in each of four categories, depending on whether consumption of the good or service is rivalrous and whether one can be excluded from consuming it.

A good or service is said to be **rivalrous** if one person's consumption of one unit of the good means that no one else can also consume that same unit. For example, a chocolate bar is rivalrous because if you eat the entire bar, it cannot also be eaten by your friend. In contrast, a radio signal is not rivalrous. You and your friend can sit in your separate living rooms and both receive the same signal, neither of you diminishing the amount available to the other.

A good is said to be **excludable** if people can be prevented from consuming it. A chocolate bar is excludable because you cannot eat it unless you buy it first. A radio signal is not excludable; the signal is there for anyone to access.

Private Goods Most goods and services that you consume are both rivalrous and excludable. Your consumption of food, clothing, a rental apartment, a car, gasoline, CDs, airline tickets, and textbooks are only possible because you pay the seller for the right to own those goods or services. Furthermore, your consumption of those goods reduces the amount available for others. In Table 16-1, we simply refer to these goods as **private goods**.

rivalrous A good or service is rivalrous if one person's consumption of it reduces the amount available for others.

excludable A good or service is excludable if its owner can prevent others from consuming it.

private goods Goods or services that are both rivalrous and excludable.

common-property resource A product that is rivalrous but not excludable.

> **Goods that are both rivalrous and excludable—private goods—pose no particular problem for public policy.**

Common-Property Resources Goods that are rivalrous but non-excludable pose an interesting challenge for public policy. In Table 16-1, the examples of these goods include such things as fisheries, wildlife, rivers and streams, and so on. These are called **common-property resources**.

Because no one person or firm "owns" these resources, there is no incentive for any one user to prevent its overuse or depletion—a situation now referred to as the "tragedy of the commons." *Tragedy of the Commons* was the title of a 1968 article in the journal *Science* by Garrett Hardin in which the author described the dilemma facing villagers in pre-industrial England. The sheep and cows owned by the villagers were allowed to graze on common land surrounding the village. Each additional sheep or cow permitted to graze on that land benefited the owner of that animal, but also contributed to overgrazing of the land, to the detriment of all the villagers.

In terms of marginal costs and benefits, since there is no practical way to exclude me from adding a sheep to the common land, there is no practical way to make me pay for my use of the scarce resource. The result is that there is a zero price. The zero price leads to the obvious result that in the absence of government intervention, private users will tend to *overuse* common-property resources, driving their marginal benefit to zero. At the same time, however, there will be some positive marginal cost to society of using the resource.

Since the marginal cost will exceed the marginal benefit, society would be better off if *less* of the resource was used.

Common-property resources tend to be overused by private firms and consumers.

The overuse of common-property resources is especially noticeable in such cases as the Atlantic cod and Pacific salmon fisheries, where individual fishers have a natural incentive to overfish. After all, if they don't catch a particular fish, they will merely be leaving it to be caught by the next fisher who comes along. It is this natural inclination to overuse the fisheries that has led the Canadian government over the years to develop a system of licences and quotas that restrict access to the common-property resource. *Applying Economic Concepts 16-1* examines the depletion of the world's fisheries.

Excludable but Non-Rivalrous Goods   Goods that are excludable but not rivalrous are sometimes called *club goods*. Many of the obvious examples of these—such as art galleries, roads, and bridges—are typically provided by government. The non-rivalry for these goods means that the marginal cost of providing the good to one extra person is zero. As an example, ask yourself what it costs for an extra person to walk through the Canadian Museum of History in Gatineau, given that it is already open but not many people are there. Or what is the cost of having one more person drive on an uncrowded road? The answer in both cases is zero. But if the marginal cost to society of providing one more unit of the good is zero, then allocative efficiency requires that the price also be zero. Any positive price would prevent some people from using it, but this would be inefficient. As long as their marginal benefit exceeds the social marginal cost of providing the good (zero in this case), it is efficient for these people to use the good.

For this reason, art galleries, museums, libraries, roads, bridges, and national parks are often provided by various levels of government. In some cases, like libraries and roads, the price to consumers is usually zero. In others, like national parks and art galleries, governments are often led to charge a price to help cover some of the operating costs (even though the marginal cost of use is very close to zero).

To avoid inefficient exclusion, the government often provides goods that are non-rivalrous but excludable.

The positive price in some of these cases can be explained by another feature of club goods. What happens in the Canadian Museum of History on a summer Saturday morning? What happens on Highway 401 outside Toronto at rush hour? The answer is *congestion*. When congestion occurs on roads and bridges, or in art galleries and museums, it is no longer true that the marginal cost of providing a club good to one more user is zero.

By increasing the amount of congestion, providing the good to one more person imposes costs on those already using the good. If I enter an already-busy highway, I slow down all the existing traffic. If you visit an already-crowded museum, you make it less pleasant for everybody else. In these cases, a good that is non-rivalrous when uncongested becomes rivalrous when congested. At this point it becomes (in economic terms) a private good, and a positive price is efficient.

Governments that provide such goods often charge a price to help ration the good when rivalry becomes significant. An excellent example of this occurs in several U.S. states where special toll highways, with the aid of powerful cameras and computers,

APPLYING ECONOMIC CONCEPTS 16-1

The World's Endangered Fish

Fish in the ocean are a common-property resource, and theory predicts that such a resource will be overexploited if there is a high enough demand for the product and suppliers are able to meet that demand. In the distant past there were neither enough people eating fish nor efficient enough fishing technologies to endanger stocks. Over the last 50 years, however, the population explosion has added to the demand for fish and advances in technology have vastly increased the ability to catch fish. Large boats, radar detection, and huge bottom-trawling nets allow humans to scoop up more and more fish. As a result, the overfishing prediction of common property theory has been amply borne out. Today, fish are a common-property resource; tomorrow, they could become no one's resource.

Since 1950 the world's annual capture of fish has increased by more than four times, from 20 million tonnes in 1950 to more than 80 million tonnes today (not including the "catch" from farmed fish, which raises the current annual haul to more than 130 million tonnes). The increase was sustained only by substituting smaller, less desirable fish for the diminishing stocks of the more desirable fish and by penetrating ever farther into remote oceans. Today, all available stocks are being exploited, and now even the total tonnage of captured fish is beginning to fall. The UN estimates that the total value of the world's catch could be increased by nearly $30 billion if fish stocks were properly managed by governments interested in the total catch, rather than exploited by individuals interested in their own catch.

The developed countries have so overfished their own stocks that Iceland and the European Union could cut their fleets by 40 percent and catch as much fish as they do today. This is because more fish would survive to spawn, allowing each boat in a smaller fleet to catch about 40 percent more than does each boat in today's large fishing fleet.

The problem became so acute in 1992 that Canada shut down its entire Atlantic cod fishing industry. Tens of thousands of Newfoundland and Labrador residents lost their livelihoods in an industry that had flourished for five centuries (although some of the fishers have since turned to catching lobsters and different species of fish and harvesting farmed mussels).

Some developing countries are taking action to conserve their fish stocks, but in many the need for current prosperity is outweighing the desire to conserve for long-term future benefits. As a result, many developing countries are encouraging rapid expansion of their own fishing fleets with the all-too-predictable results that their domestic waters will soon be seriously overfished.

Worldwide action saved most species of whales. It remains to be seen how many types of fish will be caught to extinction and how many will recover as individual nations slowly learn the lesson of economic theory. Common-property resources need central management if they are not to be overexploited to an extent that risks extinction.

Trends in the State of the World's Marine Fish Stocks

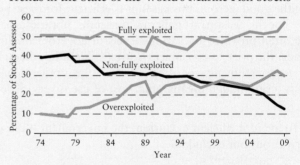

(*Source*: Food and Agriculture Organization of the United Nations. 2014. The State of World Fisheries and Aquaculture. Rome, Italy. http://www.fao.org/3/a-i3720e.pdf. Reproduced with permission.)

charge motorists a different amount per kilometre driven depending on the congestion of the highway. As the traffic slows down because of congestion, the price per kilometre increases to reflect the higher marginal cost. This higher price is indicated on electronic highway signs posted regularly along the highway. Drivers can then choose either to remain on the highway and pay the higher price, or exit the highway and take another (less expensive) route to their destination.

This same principle also applies to city roads in London, England. A daily fee of £10 (roughly $15) is charged to each vehicle entering the city centre. After this road-pricing scheme was first introduced in 2003, there was a 30 percent drop in the volume of downtown traffic and thus a decline in road congestion.

Public Goods   Finally, some goods are neither excludable nor rivalrous. These are called **public goods** or sometimes *collective consumption goods*. The classic case of a public good is national defence. All residents of Canada are equally protected and defended by the Canadian Armed Forces. It is not possible to provide national defence to some residents and not to others.

Information is also often a public good. Suppose a certain food additive causes cancer. The cost of discovering this fact needs to be borne only once. The information is then of value to everyone, and the cost of making the information available to one more consumer is approximately zero. Furthermore, once the information about the newly discovered carcinogen is available, it is impossible to prevent people from using that information. Other public goods include street lighting, weather forecasts (a type of information), and some forms of environmental protection.

All these examples raise what is called the *free-rider problem*. Since public goods are (by definition) not excludable, it is impossible to prevent anyone from using them once they are provided. If the provider charged a price, non-payers would take a *free ride* at the expense of those individuals with a social conscience who do pay. But the existence of free riders, in turn, implies that the private market will generally not produce public goods because producers would not be able to collect the payments required to cover their costs. The obvious remedy in these cases is for the government to provide the good, financed from its general tax revenues.

> Because of the free-rider problem, private markets will usually not provide public goods. In such situations, public goods must be provided by government.

How much of a public good should the government provide? It should provide the public good up to the point at which the *sum* of everyone's individual marginal benefit from the good is just equal to the marginal cost of providing the good. We add everyone's individual marginal benefit to get the total marginal benefit because a public good—unlike an ordinary private good—can be used simultaneously by everyone. It therefore generates value to more than one person at a time. Figure 16-2 shows the optimal provision of a public good in the simple case of only two individuals.

> The optimal quantity of a public good is such that the marginal cost of the good equals the *sum* of all users' marginal benefit of the good.

public goods Goods or services that can simultaneously provide benefits to a large group of people. Also called *collective consumption goods.*

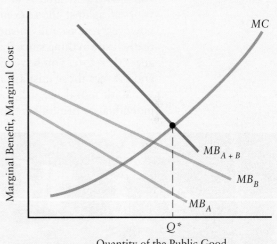

FIGURE 16-2   The Optimal Provision of a Public Good

Determining the optimal provision of a public good requires adding together the marginal benefits for each individual. The figure shows marginal benefit curves for a public good for two individuals, Andrew and Brenda. Since both can consume the good simultaneously, society's marginal benefit of the good is the sum of their own marginal benefits. By adding MB_A and MB_B *vertically*, we derive society's marginal benefit curve, MB_{A+B}. The marginal cost of providing the public good is shown by MC. The allocatively efficient level of the public good is Q^*, where the marginal cost to society is just equal to the marginal benefit to society.

Asymmetric Information

Information is, of course, a valuable commodity, and markets for information and expertise are well developed, as every student is aware. Markets for expertise are conceptually identical to markets for any other valuable service. They can pose special problems, however. One of these we have already discussed: Information is often a public good and, when it is, it tends to be underproduced by a free market.

Even when information is not a public good, markets for expertise are prone to market failure. The reason is that one party to a transaction can often take advantage of special knowledge in ways that change the nature of the transaction itself. Situations in which one party to a transaction has special knowledge are called situations of **asymmetric information**.

asymmetric information A situation in which one party to a transaction has more or better information about the transaction than the other party.

The importance of asymmetric information to the operation of the economy has received considerable attention in recent years. In 2001, Professors George Akerlof, Michael Spence, and Joseph Stiglitz shared the Nobel Prize in economics for their insights about how asymmetric information can lead to market failures. The two important sources of market failure that arise from situations of asymmetric information are *moral hazard* and *adverse selection*.

moral hazard A situation in which an individual or a firm takes advantage of special knowledge while engaging in socially inefficient behaviour.

Moral Hazard In general, **moral hazard** exists when one party to a transaction has both the *incentive* and the *ability* to behave in a way that shifts costs onto the other party. Moral hazard problems often arise from insurance contracts. For example, if you have not insured your home against fire and theft, you have an incentive to protect yourself against those events by installing fire extinguishers and burglar alarms. If, however, you are fully insured against those events, in the event of mishap you do not really lose anything since the costs will be borne by the insurance company. With insurance, therefore, you have less incentive to install fire extinguishers and burglar alarms and prevent those mishaps in the first place.

With moral hazard, the market failure arises because the action by the insured individual or firm raises total costs for society. In our example, the decision not to take action to prevent fire and theft reduces costs for the individual but, in the event of a mishap, increases by much more the costs to the insurance company.

Insurance is not the only context in which moral hazard problems arise. Another example is professional services. Suppose you ask a dentist whether your teeth are healthy or a lawyer whether you need legal assistance. The dentist and the lawyer both face moral hazard in that they both have a financial interest in giving you answers that will encourage you to buy their services, and it is difficult for you to find out if their advice is good. In both cases, one party to the transaction has special knowledge that he or she could use to change the nature of the transaction in his or her favour. Codes of professional ethics and licensing and certification practices, both governmental and private, are reactions to concerns about this kind of moral hazard.

Moral hazard can also be created by government policies, especially those applying to financial

Helen King/Comet/Corbis

Your auto mechanic probably knows far more about cars than you do and is therefore able to benefit by convincing you to make unnecessary expenditures. This is an example of moral hazard caused by asymmetric information. One partial solution to this problem is to get a second (or third!) estimate before you spend any money.

institutions. One argument against deposit insurance, for example, is that the government's guarantee of individuals' bank deposits (as provided by the Canada Deposit Insurance Corporation) may lead commercial banks to undertake more risky lending practices than they otherwise would. And in the 2008 financial crisis, when the U.S. government used more than U.S.$700 billion of taxpayers' funds to inject liquidity into several large commercial banks that were on the edge of bankruptcy, many economists argued that the expectation of similar future policies would lead the banks to continue their excessively risky behaviour. The problem of moral hazard in financial markets is an important topic in macroeconomics; we will say more about it in Chapter 26.

Adverse Selection   **Adverse selection** refers to the tendency for people who are more at risk than the average to purchase insurance and for those who are less at risk than the average to reject insurance. A person who has a heart condition may seek to increase his life insurance coverage by purchasing as much additional coverage as is available without a medical examination. People who buy insurance almost always know more about themselves as individual insurance risks than do their insurance companies. The company can try to limit the variation in risk by requiring physical examinations (for life or health insurance) and by setting up broad categories based on variables, such as age and occupation, over which actuarial risk is known to vary. The rate charged is then different across categories and is based on the average risk in each category, but there will always be much variability of risk *within* any one category.

People who know they are well above the average risk for their category are offered a bargain and will be led to take out more car, health, life, or fire insurance than they otherwise would. Their insurance premiums will also not cover the full expected cost of the risk against which they are insuring. Once again, their private cost (their insurance premium) is less than the total cost (the expected insurance payout by the insurance company). On the other side, someone who knows that she is at low risk and pays a higher price than the amount warranted by her risk is motivated to take out less insurance than she otherwise would. In this case, her private cost (her insurance premium) is more than the total cost (the expected insurance payout). In both cases, resources are allocated inefficiently because the marginal private benefit of purchasing insurance is not equal to the marginal cost of providing it.

An excellent and familiar example of market failure caused by asymmetric information and adverse selection is the apparent overdiscounting of the prices of used cars because of the buyer's risk of acquiring a "lemon." See the discussion of this problem in *Applying Economic Concepts 16-2*.

adverse selection Self-selection, within a single risk category, of persons of above-average risk.

Summary

To summarize, the following four situations result in market failures and, at least in principle, provide a rationale for government intervention:

1. Firms with market power will generally charge a price greater than marginal cost. The level of output in these cases is less than the allocatively efficient level.

2. When there are externalities, social and private marginal costs are not equal. If there is a negative externality, output will be greater than the allocatively efficient level. If there is a positive externality, output will be less than the allocatively efficient level.

APPLYING ECONOMIC CONCEPTS 16-2

Used Cars and the Market for "Lemons"

It is common for people to regard the large loss of value of a new car in the first year of its life as a sign that consumers are overly style conscious and will always pay a big premium for the latest in anything. Professor George Akerlof of the University of California at Berkeley suggests a different explanation. His theory, contained in his now-famous paper "The Market for Lemons," is based on the proposition that the flow of services expected from a one-year-old car that is *purchased on the used-car market* will be lower than that expected from an *average* one-year-old car on the road. Consider his theory.

Any particular model year of car will include a certain proportion of "lemons"—cars that have one or more serious defects. Purchasers of new cars of a certain year and model take a chance on their car turning out to be a lemon. Those who are unlucky and get a lemon are more likely to resell their car than those who are lucky and get a high-quality car. Hence, in the used-car market, there will be a disproportionately large number of lemons for sale. For example, maybe only 1 percent of all 2016 Toyota Corollas have a significant defect and are thus lemons. But in the market for *used* 2016 Toyota Corollas, 20 percent of them may be lemons.

Buyers of used cars are therefore right to be on the lookout for lemons, while salespeople are quick to invent reasons for the high quality of the cars they are selling. Because it is difficult to identify a lemon or a badly treated used car before buying it, the purchaser is prepared to buy a used car only at a price that is low enough to offset the increased probability that it is a lemon.

The market failure in this situation arises because of the asymmetric information between the buyers and the sellers. If there were perfect information, prices would better reflect the quality of the used car. Good used cars would command higher prices than used cars known to be lemons. Buyers and sellers would then conduct more transactions, for two reasons. First, owners wanting to sell good used cars would be more likely to sell them since they know they will get a good price. In contrast, when information is poor, owners of good used cars are less inclined to sell their cars because the prices of used cars reflect the average quality, which of course is diminished by the presence of the lemons. Second, when information is good, consumers know precisely what it is they are buying. Consumers who want to spend more on a good used car can do so; other consumers who want the bargain price on a car known to be a lemon can also be satisfied. A larger number of successful transactions between buyers and sellers means more surplus on both sides of the market—that is, a more efficient outcome.

The now-standard five-year bumper-to-bumper warranties on new cars helps to improve the efficiency of the used-car market. With such warranties, buyers are prepared to pay a higher price for a used car as long as there is still some time remaining on the warranty. Yet even when repairs are covered under warranty, the significant time and inconvenience costs associated with getting a car serviced mean that the unavoidable asymmetric information in the used-car market still leads to inefficient outcomes.

Owners have an incentive to keep good-quality used cars because it is difficult to convince buyers that a used car is not a "lemon." As a result, lemons represent a larger proportion of used-car sales than of the total car proportion.

3. Common-property resources will be overused by private firms and consumers. Public goods will be underprovided by private markets.

4. Situations in which there is asymmetric information—both moral hazard and adverse selection—can lead to allocative inefficiency.

These situations of market failure justify a role for government in a market economy. We now explore some reasons for government intervention that are *not* based on market failures.

16.4 BROADER SOCIAL GOALS

Even if the free-market system were to generate an allocatively efficient outcome, there are broader social goals the market system is unlikely to achieve. For example, the desire for an "equitable" distribution of income is unlikely to ever be achieved by a free market. While this goal is basically an economic one, there are other important social goals that are not economic, such as developing a society in which all people share common values like social responsibility and a belief in basic human rights. Whether society's broader social goals are economic or not, markets are often not an effective means of achieving them, precisely because the "goods" in question are not exchanged in decentralized market transactions.

> **Even in the absence of market failures, the government may choose to intervene in markets to achieve broader social goals.**

Income Distribution

As we saw in Chapter 14, an important characteristic of a market economy is the *distribution of income* that it determines. People whose services are in heavy demand relative to supply, such as good television news anchors, wise corporate CEOs, and outstanding hockey players, earn large incomes, whereas people whose services are not in heavy demand relative to supply, such as high-school graduates without work experience, earn much less.

Such differentials in income, as we discussed in Chapter 14, can be either temporary or equilibrium phenomena. The temporary differentials, caused by changes in demand or supply in specific industries or regions, will eventually be eliminated by the mobility of workers. Equilibrium differentials will persist, whether they are created by differences in non-monetary aspects of the job or by differences in human capital or acquired or inherited skills.

Equilibrium differences in income seem unfair to many people. A free-market system rewards certain groups and penalizes others. Because the workings of the market may be stern, even cruel, society often chooses to intervene. Should heads of households be forced to bear the full burden of their misfortune if, through no fault of their own, they lose their jobs? Even if they lose their jobs through their own fault, should they and their families have to bear the whole burden, which may include starvation? Should the ill and the aged be thrown on the mercy of their families? What if they have no families? Both private charities and a great many government policies are concerned with modifying the distribution of income that results from such things as where one starts, how able one is, how lucky one is, and how one fares in the labour market. We discuss many government policies of this kind in Chapter 18.

We might all agree that it is desirable to have a more equal distribution of income than the one generated by the free market. We might also agree that the pursuit of allocative efficiency is a good thing. It is important to understand, however, that the goal of a more equitable distribution of income often conflicts with the goal of allocative efficiency. To understand why this is so, see *Extensions in Theory 16-1*, which discusses Arthur Okun's famous analogy of the "leaky bucket."

EXTENSIONS IN THEORY 16-1

Arthur Okun's "Leaky Bucket"

Economists recognize that government actions can affect both the allocation of resources and the distribution of income. Resource allocation is easier to talk about simply because economists have developed precise definitions of *efficient* and *inefficient* allocations. Distribution is more difficult because we cannot talk about *better* or *worse* distributions of income without introducing value judgements.

When government policy aims to redistribute income, allocative efficiency will often be reduced. Arthur Okun (1928–1980), who was a noted economist at Yale University, developed the image of a "leaky bucket" to illustrate this problem. Suppose we have a well-supplied reservoir of water and we want to get some water to a household that is not able to come to the reservoir. The only vessel available for transporting the water is a leaky bucket; it works, in that water is deliverable to the intended location, but it works at a cost, in that some of the water is lost on the trip. Thus, to get a litre of water to its destination, more than a litre of water has to be removed from the reservoir. It may be possible to design better or worse buckets, but all of them will leak somewhat.

The analogy to an economy is this: The act of redistribution (carrying the water) reduces the total value of goods and services available to the economy (by the amount of water that leaks on the trip). Getting a dollar to the poor reduces the resources available to everyone else by more than a dollar. Thus, pursuing social goals—like the redistribution of income—conflicts with the goal of allocative efficiency.

Why is the bucket always leaky? Because there is no way to redistribute income without changing the incentives that private households and firms face. For example, a tax-and-transfer system that takes from the rich and gives to the poor will reduce the incentives of both the rich and the poor to produce income. This redistribution of income will often lead to less total income being generated. As another example, a policy of subsidizing goods that are deemed to be important, such as post-secondary education or daycare services, will cause the market prices of those goods to be lower than marginal costs, a result implying that resources used to produce those goods could be used to produce goods of higher value elsewhere in the economy.

Measuring the efficiency costs of redistribution is an important area of economic research. One result from this research is that some methods of redistribution are more efficient than others. For example, most economists agree that programs that directly redistribute income are more efficient (per dollar of resources made available to a given income group) than programs that subsidize the prices of specific goods. One reason for this is that price subsidies apply even when high-income households purchase the goods in question. These high-income households therefore benefit from the subsidy— an unintended (and perhaps undesirable) consequence of the program.

Though redistribution often reduces overall efficiency, this does *not* imply that such programs should not be undertaken. (That buckets leak surely does not imply that they should not be used to transport water, given that we want to transport water and that the buckets we have are the best available tools.) Whatever the social policy regarding redistribution of income, economics has an important role to play in measuring the efficiency costs and distributional consequences of different programs of redistribution. Put another way, it has useful things to say about the design and deployment of buckets.

Preferences for Public Provision

Police protection and justice could, in principle, be provided by private markets. Security guards, private detectives, and bodyguards all provide police-like protection. Privately hired arbitrators, "hired guns," and vigilantes of the Old West represent private ways of obtaining "justice." Yet the members of society may believe that a public police force is *preferable* to a private one and that public justice is preferable to justice for hire.

The question of the boundary between public and private provision is fairly straightforward with regard to justice, but can be more controversial in other arenas. For example, healthcare in Canada is publicly financed, but there is ongoing debate about the extent to which a greater role should be played by the private sector. A few decades ago in Canada, the United States, and Western Europe, many government-owned firms that had provided goods and services for many years were "privatized." For example, various governments decided there was little rationale for public provision of services such as air and rail travel and goods such as retail gasoline.

Governments of mixed economies around the world make different decisions about the extent of public provision, based partly on efficiency arguments and also on other less tangible social factors. Many northern European countries, for example, choose public provision of daycare services, while in the United States these services are almost always private.

A judicial system could be provided privately, with the judges levying charges to plaintiffs and defendants in order to hear their cases. But most people believe that for reasons of fairness and objectivity, it is better for the government to provide the judicial system, financed by money raised through general taxation.

Protecting Individuals from Others

People can use and even abuse other people for economic gain in ways that members of society find offensive. Child labour laws, minimum standards of working conditions, and laws against physical abuse and sexual harassment are responses to such actions. Yet direct abuse is not the only example of this kind of undesirable outcome. In an unhindered free market, the adults in a household would usually decide how much education to buy for their children. Selfish parents might buy no education, while egalitarian parents might buy the same education for all their children, regardless of their abilities. The rest of society may want to interfere in these choices, both to protect the child of the selfish parent and to ensure that some of the scarce educational resources are distributed according to the ability and the willingness to use them rather than according to a family's wealth. The government requires all households to provide a minimum of education for their children, and a number of inducements are offered— through public universities, scholarships, and other means—for talented children to consume more education than they or their parents might choose if they had to pay the entire cost themselves.

Paternalism

Members of society, acting through government, often seek to protect adult (and presumably responsible) individuals, not from others, but from themselves. Laws prohibiting the use of addictive drugs and laws requiring the use of seat belts are intended primarily to protect individuals from their own ignorance or short-sightedness. These kinds of interference in the free choices of individuals are examples of **paternalism**. Whether such actions reflect the wishes of the majority in the society or whether they reflect the actions of overbearing governments, there is no doubt that the market will not provide this kind of protection. Buyers do not buy things they do not want, even if these things are "good for them," and sellers have no motive to provide them.

paternalism Intervention in the free choices of individuals by others (including governments) to protect them against what is presumed to be their own ignorance or folly.

Social Responsibility

In a free-market system, if you can pay another person to do things for you, you may do so. If you persuade someone else to clean your house in return for $75, presumably both parties to the transaction are better off (otherwise neither of you would have voluntarily conducted the transaction). Normally, society does not interfere with people's ability to negotiate mutually advantageous contracts.

Most people do not feel this way, however, about activities that are regarded as social responsibilities. For example, in countries where military service is compulsory, contracts similar to the one between you and a housekeeper could also be negotiated. Some persons faced with the obligation to do military service could no doubt pay enough to persuade others to do their military service for them. Indeed, during the U.S. Civil War, it was common practice for a man to avoid the draft by hiring a substitute to serve in his place. Yet such contracts are usually prohibited by law. They are prohibited because there are values to be considered other than those that can be expressed in a market. In times when it is necessary, military service is usually held to be a duty that is independent of an individual's preferences, wealth, influence, or social position. It is felt that everyone *ought* to do this service, and exchanges between willing traders are prohibited.

Military service is not the only example of a social responsibility. Citizens cannot buy their way out of jury duty or legally sell their voting rights to others, even though in many cases they could find willing trading partners.

A General Principle

We have discussed how the free market may fail to achieve social goals that members of society deem to be desirable. This discussion suggests the following general principle:

> **Even if free markets generated allocatively efficient outcomes, they would be unlikely to generate outcomes consistent with most people's social goals. Furthermore, there is often a tradeoff between achieving these social goals and increasing allocative efficiency.**

16.5 GOVERNMENT INTERVENTION

Since markets sometimes *do* fail, and since even efficient markets produce some undesirable outcomes, there is scope for governments to intervene in beneficial ways. Whether government intervention is warranted in any particular case depends both on the magnitude of the benefits that the intervention is designed to produce and on the costs of the government action itself. For many types of government activity, *cost–benefit analysis* can be helpful in considering the general question of when and to what extent governments can successfully intervene.

cost-benefit analysis An approach for evaluating the desirability of a given policy, based on comparing total (opportunity) costs with total benefits.

The idea behind **cost-benefit analysis** is simple: Add up the total costs associated with a given policy, then add up the benefits, and implement the policy only if the benefits outweigh the costs. In practice, however, cost-benefit analysis is usually quite difficult for three reasons. First, it may be difficult to ascertain what will happen when an action is undertaken. Second, many government actions involve costs and benefits that will occur only in the distant future; thus, they will be more complicated to assess. Third, some benefits and costs are difficult to quantify; for example, the benefits of intervention to protect an endangered animal species. Indeed, some people argue that they cannot be and should not be quantified, as they involve values that are not commensurate with money. The practice then is to use cost–benefit analysis to measure the things that can be measured and to be sure that the things that cannot be measured are not ignored when collective decisions are made. By narrowing the range of things that must be determined by informal judgement, cost-benefit analysis can still play a useful role.

In this chapter, we have been working toward a cost–benefit analysis of government intervention. We have made a general case *against* government intervention, stressing that free markets are great economizers on information and coordination costs. We have also made a general case *for* government intervention, emphasizing that free markets fail to produce allocative efficiency when there are firms with market power, public goods, externalities, or information asymmetries, and may also fail to achieve broader social goals. We now turn to the more specific issues of how governments intervene, the costs of government intervention, and why government intervention sometimes fails to improve on imperfect market outcomes.

The Tools of Government Intervention

The legal power of Canadian governments to intervene in the workings of the economy is limited by the Charter of Rights (as interpreted by the courts), the willingness of Parliament and provincial legislatures to pass laws, and the willingness and ability of the police and courts to enforce them. There are numerous ways in which one or another level of government can alter the workings of the unrestricted market economy.

1. Public Provision   National defence, the criminal justice system, public schools, universities, the highway system, and national parks are all examples of goods or services that are provided by governments in Canada. Public provision is the most obvious remedy for market failure to provide public goods, but it is also often used in the interest of redistribution and other social goals (e.g., public education and healthcare services, neither of which are public goods as defined earlier in the chapter). We will consider public spending in detail in Chapter 18.

2. Redistribution Programs   Taxes and government spending are often used to alter the distribution of income generated by the free market. Government *transfer* programs affect the distribution of income in this way. We examine the distributive effects of the Canadian tax-and-transfer system in Chapter 18.

3. Regulation   Government regulations are public rules that apply to private behaviour. In Chapter 12, we saw that governments regulate private markets to limit the use of monopoly power. In Chapter 17, we will focus on regulations designed to deal with environmental degradation. Among other things, government regulations prohibit minors from consuming alcohol, require that children attend school, penalize racial discrimination in housing and labour markets, and require that all cars have seat belts. Government regulation is used to deal with all of the sources of market failure that we have discussed in this chapter; it applies at some level to virtually all spheres of modern economic life.

The Costs of Government Intervention

Consider the following argument: The market system produces some particular outcome that is deemed to be undesirable; government has the legal means to improve the situation; therefore, the public interest will be served by government intervention.

At first glance this argument is appealing. However, three important considerations must be taken into account. First, the government intervention itself is costly; second, government intervention is generally imperfect and often fails; and third, the decision process regarding what action to take is costly and imperfect. In the remainder of this section we examine the costs of government intervention. We then turn to government failures and government's decision process.

In an effort to better evaluate the costs of government intervention, economists distinguish between *direct costs* and *indirect costs*.

Direct Costs Government intervention uses scarce resources. Civil servants must be paid and computer systems need to be purchased. Paper, photocopying, the steel in the navy's ships, the fuel for the army's tanks, and the pilot of the prime minister's jet—all come at a cost. The same is true of the accountants who administer the Canada Pension Plan, the economists who are employed by the Competition Bureau, and the educators who retrain displaced workers.

Similarly, when government inspectors visit plants to monitor compliance with federally imposed standards of health, industrial safety, or environmental protection, they are imposing costs on the public in the form of their salaries and expenses. When regulatory bodies develop rules, hold hearings, write opinions, or have their staff prepare research reports, they are incurring costs. The costs of the judges, clerks, and court reporters who hear, transcribe, and review the evidence are also imposed by government regulation. None of these activities are possible except by incurring considerable costs.

> **All forms of government intervention use real resources and hence impose direct costs.**

The direct costs of government intervention are fairly easy to identify, as they almost always involve well-documented expenditures. In 2014, the total expenditures by all levels of government in Canada were $778 billion, just under 40 percent of total national income.

Indirect Costs Most government interventions in the economy impose costs on firms and households over and above the direct financial costs of the policy. Here are three examples.

1. Changes in Costs of Production. Government safety and emissions standards for cars raise the costs of both producing and operating cars. Environmental policies that require firms to treat their waste products and emissions increase the overall costs of those firms. In both cases, these costs are much greater than the direct financial costs of administering the regulations.

2. Costs of Compliance. Government regulation and supervision generate a flood of reporting and related activities that are often referred to collectively as *red tape*. The number of hours of business time devoted to understanding, reporting, and contesting

regulatory provisions is enormous. Regulations dealing with occupational safety and environmental control have all increased the size of non-production payrolls. The legal costs alone of a major corporation sometimes can run into tens or hundreds of millions of dollars per year.

Households also bear compliance costs directly. The annual exercise of completing income-tax returns requires every taxpayer to spend considerable time or money making sure that the forms are correctly filled out and submitted on time. In addition to costs of compliance, there are costs borne as firms and households try to avoid regulation. There is a substantial incentive to find loopholes in regulations. Resources that could be used elsewhere are devoted to the search for such loopholes and then, in turn, by regulators to counteract such behaviour.

Farmers in Canada often request government assistance to offset the effects of low crop prices or bad weather. This is one example of rent seeking.

3. Rent Seeking.   Private firms, households, and business groups can use political influence to seek *economic rents* from the government in ways that impose costs on society as a whole—a phenomenon known as **rent seeking**. These economic rents can come in the form of legislated quotas or price controls, favourable regulations or direct subsidies, or even lucrative contracts that do not use public funds in a prudent manner. In all cases the individual or firm involved will be better off and will likely argue that their private interests are aligned with the public interest. Unless there is a market failure to be corrected, however, it is more likely that the government is simply pandering to a vocal and well-organized interest group by redistributing resources in their direction. And these resources do not come for free; they must be provided in some way by the taxpayers who finance government activities.

Rent seeking is endemic to mixed economies. Because of the many things that governments are called on to do, they have the power to act in ways that transfer resources among private entities. Because they are democratic, they are responsive to public pressures of various kinds. If a government's behaviour can be influenced, whether by voting, campaign contributions, lobbying, or bribes, real resources will be used in trying to do so.

> **rent seeking** Behaviour whereby private firms and individuals try to use the powers of the government to enhance their own economic well-being in ways that are not in the social interest.

> **In the aggregate, indirect costs of government intervention are substantial but difficult to measure and are usually dispersed across a large number of firms and households.**

Government Failure

Even in the cases in which the benefits and costs of government intervention can be easily identified and measured, governments, like private markets, are imperfect. Often they will fail, in the same sense that markets do, to achieve their potential.

The reason for government failure is not that public-sector employees are less able, honest, or virtuous than people who work in the private sector. Rather, the causes of

Public choice theory seeks to explain how public officials make their decisions. They are assumed to act not in the best interests of their constituents but according to their own agendas, which often conflict with the public interest.

government failure are inherent in government institutions, just as the causes of market failure stem from the nature of markets. Importantly, some government failure is an inescapable cost of democratic decision making.

Decision Makers' Objectives By far the most important cause of government failure arises from the nature of the government's own objectives. Traditionally, economists did not concern themselves greatly with the motivation of government. The theory of economic policy implicitly assumed that governments had no objective other than to protect the public interest. As a result, economists needed only to identify places where the market functioned well on its own, and places where government intervention could improve the market's functioning. Governments would then stay out of the former markets and intervene as necessary in the latter.

This model of government behaviour never fitted reality, and economists were gradually forced to think more deeply about the motivation of governments. Today economists no longer assume that governments are only guided by the public interest. Instead they are modelled just as are producers and consumers—as units with their own objectives, which they seek to maximize.

Governments undoubtedly do care about the social good to some extent, but public officials have their own careers, self-interest, and prejudices as well. As a result, public officials' own needs are seldom wholly absent from their consideration of the actions they will take. Similarly, their definition of the public interest is likely to be influenced heavily by their personal views of what policies are best. It is therefore often the case that the policies supported by the public are different from the policies advocated by policymakers.

Modelling governments as maximizers of their own welfare, and then incorporating them into theoretical models of the working of the economy, was a major intellectual breakthrough. One of the pioneers of this development was the American economist James Buchanan, who was awarded the 1986 Nobel Prize in economics for his work in this field. The theory that he helped to develop is called *public choice theory*.

Public Choice Theory Full-blown public choice theory deals with three maximizing groups. Elected officials seek to maximize their votes. Civil servants seek to maximize their salaries and their influence. Voters seek to maximize their own utility. To this end, voters look to the government to provide them with goods and services and income transfers that raise their personal utility. No one cares about the general interest!

On the one hand, this surely is not a completely accurate characterization of motives. Some elected officials have acted in what they perceive to be the public interest, hoping to be vindicated by history even if they know they risk losing the next election. Some civil servants expose inside corruption—so-called whistleblowers—even though it can cost them their jobs. Some high-income individuals vote for the political party that advocates the most, not the least, income redistribution, and some poorer taxpayers vote for a party that advocates lower taxes on the rich and lower transfers to the poor.

On the other hand, the characterization is close to the mark in many cases. Most of us have read of politicians whose only principle appears to be "What will get me the most votes?" And many voters ask only "What is in it for me?" This is why the theory can take us a long way in understanding what we see, even though real behaviour is more complex.

Here is one example relevant to Canada and many other developed economies. Why, in spite of strong advice from economists, have governments persisted in assisting agriculture for decades, until many governments now have major farm crises on their hands? Public choice theory considers the winners and the losers among the voters.

The winners from agricultural supports are farmers. They are a politically powerful group and are aware of what they will lose if farm supports are reduced. They would show their disapproval of such action by voting against any government that even suggests it. The losers are the entire group of consumers or taxpayers. Although they are more numerous than farmers, and although their total loss is large, each individual suffers only a small loss. Citizens have more important things to worry about, and so they do not vote against the government just because it supports farmers. As long as the average voters are unconcerned about, and often unaware of, the losses they suffer, the vote-maximizing government will ignore the interests of the many and support the interests of the few. The vote-maximizing government will consider changing the agricultural policy only when the cost of agricultural support becomes so large that ordinary taxpayers begin to be concerned by the cost. What is required for a policy change, according to this theory, is that those who lose become sufficiently aware of their losses for this awareness to affect their voting behaviour.

Governments as Monopolists Governments face the same problems of cost minimization that private firms do but often operate in an environment in which they are monopoly producers without shareholders. Large governments (provinces, big cities, the federal government) face all of the organizational problems faced by large corporations. They tend to use relatively rigid rules and hence respond slowly to change. Building codes are an example of this type of problem. Most local governments have detailed requirements regarding the materials that must go into a new house, factory, or office building. When technology changes, the codes often lag behind. For example, plastic pipe, which is cheaper and easier to use than copper pipe, was prohibited by building codes for decades after its use became efficient. Changes in technology may make a regulation inefficient, but the regulation may stay in place for a long time.

In the private sector, market forces often push firms into revising their view of the problem at hand, whereas there is ordinarily no market mechanism to force governments to adopt relatively efficient regulations. Put another way, government failure often arises precisely because governments do not have competitors and are not constrained by the "bottom line."

How Much Should Government Intervene?

Do governments intervene too little, or too much, in response to market failure? This question reflects one aspect of the continuing debate over the role of government in the economy. Although many economists might agree on the principles that should guide government intervention in selected cases, there is more disagreement about the broader role of government in the economy. Unfortunately, the issue is often framed ideologically. Those on the "right wing" tend to compare heavy-handed government with a hypothetical and perfectly operating competitive market. In contrast, those on the "left wing" tend to compare hypothetical and ideal government intervention with a laissez-faire economy rife with market failures. Both perspectives are in danger of missing the more relevant debate.

> **Evaluating the costs and benefits of government intervention requires a comparison of the private economic system as it actually works (not as it might work ideally) with the pattern of government intervention as it actually performs (not as it might perform ideally).**

Over the last three decades in most of the advanced industrial countries, the mix of free-market determination and government ownership and regulation has been shifting toward more market determination. No reasonable person believes that government intervention can, or should, be reduced to zero. Do we still have a long way to go in reversing the tide of intrusive government that flowed through most of the twentieth century? Or have we gone too far by giving some things to the market that governments could do better? These questions lie at the heart of one of the great social debates of our time.

In general, the cases we have made for the costs and benefits of government intervention are both valid, depending on time, place, and the values that are brought to bear. At this point, we turn to the issue of what government actually does, something that will perhaps illuminate the question of what it could do better. In Chapter 12, we discussed government action that is designed to affect monopoly and competition. In the next two chapters, we discuss in some detail three other important types of intervention in the Canadian economy today: environmental regulation, taxation, and public spending.

SUMMARY

16.1 BASIC FUNCTIONS OF GOVERNMENT — LO 1

- The government's monopoly of violence gives it the ability to enforce laws and protect its citizens. But restrictions on the government's power are required to ensure that individuals' rights are not unnecessarily violated.

16.2 THE CASE FOR FREE MARKETS — LO 2

- The case for free markets can be made in two different ways. The "formal defence" is based on the concept of allocative efficiency, as seen in Chapter 12.
- The "informal defence" of free markets is not specifically based on the idea of allocative efficiency and thus applies to market structures other than just perfect competition. The informal defence of free markets is based on three central arguments:

1. Free markets provide automatic coordination of the actions of decentralized decision makers.
2. The pursuit of profits, which is central to free markets, provides a stimulus to innovation and economic growth.
3. Free markets permit a decentralization of economic power.

16.3 **MARKET FAILURES**

- Market failure refers to situations in which the free market does not achieve allocative efficiency. Four main sources of market failure are
  1. market power
  2. externalities
  3. public goods
  4. information asymmetries
- Pollution is an example of an externality. A producer who pollutes the air or water does not pay the social cost of the pollution and is therefore not motivated to avoid the costs. Private producers will therefore produce too much pollution relative to what is allocatively efficient.
- National defence is an example of a public good. Markets fail to produce public goods because the benefits of such goods are available to people whether they pay for them or not.
- Information asymmetries cause market failure when one party to a transaction is able to use personal expertise to manipulate the transaction in his or her own favour. Moral hazard and adverse selection are consequences of information asymmetries.

16.4 **BROADER SOCIAL GOALS**

- Changing the distribution of income is one of the roles for government intervention that members of a society may desire. Others include values that are placed on public provision for its own sake, on protection of individuals from themselves or from others, and on recognition of social responsibilities.

16.5 **GOVERNMENT INTERVENTION**

- Major tools of microeconomic policy include (a) public provision, (b) redistribution, and (c) regulation.
- The costs and benefits of government intervention must be considered in deciding whether, when, and how much intervention is appropriate. Among the costs are the direct costs that are incurred by the government, the costs that are imposed on the parties who are regulated, and the costs that are imposed on third parties. These costs are seldom negligible and are often large.
- The possibility of government failure, as well as the costs of successful intervention, must be balanced against the potential benefits of removing market failure. It is neither possible nor efficient to correct all market failure; neither is it always efficient to do nothing.

KEY CONCEPTS

Market failure	Private goods	Cost-benefit analysis
Externalities	Common-property resources	Costs of government intervention
Private and social cost	Public goods	Rent seeking
Excludable and non-excludable goods	Information asymmetries	Government failure
Rivalrous and non-rivalrous goods	Moral hazard and adverse selection	Public choice theory

STUDY EXERCISES

MyEconLab Make the grade with MyEconLab: Study Exercises marked in ● can be found on MyEconLab. You can practise them as often as you want, and most feature step-by-step guided instructions to help you find the right answer.

1 Fill in the blanks to make the following statements correct.

a. The "formal defence" of free markets is that, if all markets were perfectly competitive, then prices would equal _____ for all products and the economy would be _____.

b. The "informal defence" of free markets is based on the following three central arguments:

- _____
- _____
- _____

c. A situation in which the free market, in the absence of government intervention, fails to achieve allocative efficiency is called _____.

d. There are four major market failures that, in principle, justify government intervention in markets. They are:

- _____
- _____
- _____
- _____

2 Fill in the blanks to make the following statements correct.

a. The marginal cost faced by the private decision maker is known as _____. The marginal cost faced by the private decision maker *plus* any other costs imposed on third parties is known as _____. If there is a divergence between these two marginal costs, then we can say that _____ are present.

b. An economic outcome is allocatively efficient when marginal social cost and marginal social benefit are _____.

c. Suppose a potato chip plant is operating beside a residential neighbourhood and produces noise and an unpleasant odour. We can say that there is a _____ externality because the marginal social cost of producing potato chips is _____ the marginal private cost of producing potato chips. As a result, the free market is producing too _____ potato chips.

d. Suppose an apple orchard is operating beside a residential neighbourhood and provides beautiful blossoms and a pleasant fragrance. We can say that there is a _____ externality because the marginal social cost of apples is _____ the marginal private cost of apples. As a result, the free market is producing too _____ apples.

3 Fill in the blanks to make the following statements correct.

a. A good or service that is rivalrous and excludable (e.g., a restaurant meal or a sofa) is known as a _____ good and is most efficiently provided by the _____.

b. A good that is rivalrous and non-excludable (e.g., fish in the ocean, or common grazing land) is known as a _____ and tends to be overused by _____.

c. Goods that are non-rivalrous and excludable (e.g., roads, museums, and parks) are often provided by government because the marginal cost of provision to society is _____ and so the allocatively efficient price is _____.

d. Goods and services that are non-rivalrous and non-excludable (e.g., national defence, a lighthouse) are known as _____. Private markets will not provide these goods or services because of the _____ problem.

e. If an auto mechanic tells you that your car needs a new transmission, there is the possibility of market failure in the form of _____.

f. If you take up cliff diving as a new hobby and increase your life insurance, just in case, there is a possible market failure in the form of _____.

4 In each case, identify any divergence between social and private costs.

a. Cigarette smoking
b. Getting a university education
c. Private ownership of guns
d. Drilling for offshore oil

5 For each of the situations in the table below, indicate whether there is a positive or a negative externality. Indicate in each case whether social marginal cost (MC_S) is greater than or less than private marginal cost (MC_P).

	Positive or negative externality?	MC_S greater than or less than MC_P?
You smoke a cigarette and blow the smoke into others' faces.		
You cut your lawn early on a Sunday morning.		
A firm conducts R&D and generates useful "basic" knowledge that is freely available.		
A firm produces aluminum, but also produces toxic waste as a by-product.		

6 Consider the following diagram showing the monthly market demand for electricity, where the electricity is generated by burning coal. The mining, processing, and burning of coal have considerable environmental and health costs associated that are not reflected in the market price for the final product—electricity. The diagram below shows the market demand for electricity and private marginal costs of production.

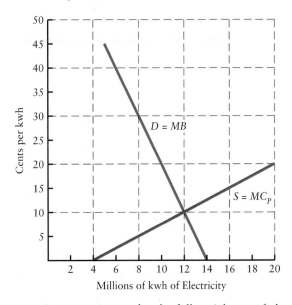

Millions of kwh of Electricity

a. Current estimates for the full social cost of electricity generated by burning coal vary greatly but suggest that it could be many times higher than current market prices in Canada and the United States. Supposing the external cost associated with producing one kilowatt hour (kwh) of electricity is $0.25, draw the marginal social cost curve for this market.

b. What quantity of electricity will be produced and consumed in the absence of government intervention in this market? What will be the price?

c. What is the socially optimal price per kwh and quantity consumed of electricity? Explain.

d. Explain how a special tax might be used to get electricity-producing firms to produce the allocatively efficient level of output.

7 Suppose health care is provided privately in a free market and families are responsible for paying for polio vaccinations for their children. The following supply and demand diagram shows the private marginal costs and private marginal benefits in this market.

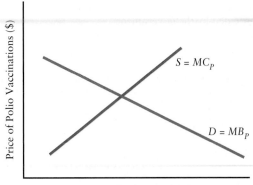

Quantity of Polio Vaccinations

a. Show on the diagram the quantity of polio vaccinations that would be undertaken in the absence of government intervention.

b. Describe the externality associated with having a polio vaccination.

c. Draw a curve showing the *social* marginal cost of vaccinations. Show the socially optimal quantity of vaccinations. Explain.

d. Explain why the government might choose to subsidize vaccinations (or perhaps even provide them for free). Are there both efficiency and equity motivations for government involvement in this market?

8 What market failures does public support of higher education seek to remedy? How would you go about evaluating whether the benefits of this support outweigh the costs?

9 For each of the listed goods, indicate whether they are rivalrous or non-rivalrous, and whether the use of them is excludable or non-excludable.

	Rivalrous?	Excludable?
Laptop computer		
Clothing		
Library		
Lighthouse		
Medical services		
Published product safety information		
Pacific salmon		

a. Which of the goods in the table are public goods? Explain.

b. Which are common-property resources? Explain.

10 Art galleries, museums, roads, and bridges are usually provided by the government.

   a. Explain why uncrowded goods of this sort should have a price of zero if allocative efficiency is to be achieved.

   b. Would allocative efficiency be achieved if private firms provided these goods? Explain.

   c. What happens when access to these goods becomes congested? Does efficiency still require a zero price? Explain.

11 In this chapter we discussed common-property resources such as common grazing land. Suppose the social marginal benefits and social marginal costs of using the grazing land are as shown below.

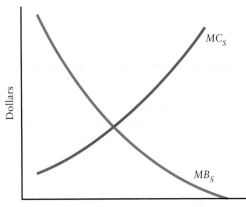

Number of Animals Grazing
on Fixed Quantity of Land

   a. If residents are permitted unlimited access to the use of the grazing land at a zero price, what is the *private* marginal cost of grazing? Draw the MC_P curve in the diagram.

   b. Given your answer to part (a), what level of grazing will occur if there is unrestricted access to the land?

   c. Is the outcome from part (b) efficient? Why or why not?

   d. What is the efficient level of grazing, and how is this shown in the diagram? Explain.

   e. Explain why charging residents a fee per unit of access would improve allocative efficiency. How would this be shown in the diagram?

   f. Explain why selling individual parcels of the grazing land to the town's residents is also likely to improve efficiency.

12 Consider a small town deciding whether to build a public park. The town council conducts a survey of its 100 residents and asks them how much they would each value the park. The survey results are as follows:

Number of people	Value of park per person	Total
10	$1000	$10 000
30	500	15 000
30	200	6 000
20	50	1 000
10	0	0
100		$32 000

   a. Suppose it costs $35 000 to build the park. Should the town do it?

   b. Suppose the park costs only $20 000 to build. Should the town build the park?

   c. Suppose the town builds the park but charges people $50 for an annual pass. Does this present a problem for efficiency? Explain.

13 In the text we discussed how rent seeking is one of the costs of government intervention. Consider a group of pig farmers who are lobbying the federal government for some form of financial assistance (as they have done in the past when the world price of pork declined steeply).

   a. Explain why economists call such lobbying "rent seeking."

   b. Suppose the farmers spend $500 000 in their lobbying efforts but have no effect on government policy. What is the cost to society of the rent seeking? Explain.

   c. Suppose the $500 000 of lobbying *does* lead to a change in government policy. Now what is the social cost of the rent seeking?

17

The Economics of Environmental Protection

CHAPTER OUTLINE	LEARNING OBJECTIVES (LO) After studying this chapter you will be able to
17.1 THE ECONOMIC RATIONALE FOR REGULATING POLLUTION	1 explain how an externality can be internalized, and how this can lead to allocative efficiency.
17.2 POLLUTION-CONTROL POLICIES	2 understand why direct pollution controls are often inefficient. 3 describe how market-based policies, such as emissions taxes and tradable pollution permits, can improve economic efficiency.
17.3 THE ECONOMIC CHALLENGE OF GLOBAL CLIMATE CHANGE	4 discuss some basic facts about global climate change and the associated economic challenges.

IN almost everything we do, we are subject to some form of government regulation. The system of criminal law regulates our interactions with people and property. Local zoning laws regulate the ways we use land. Regulatory commissions set rates for electricity, natural gas, local telephone service, and a host of other goods and services. Seat belts, brake lights, turn signals, air bags, internal door panels, bumpers, and catalytic converters are compulsory and regulated in quality—all in a single industry. The list goes on and on. A good case can be made that various governments in Canada have more effect on the economy through regulation than through taxing and spending.

The focus in this chapter is on a specific type of government regulation, one that has become increasingly important in recent years. In particular, we examine the negative externalities that lead to

environmental degradation and the various government policies designed to address them. As we will see, policies intended to protect the environment do not always do so in an efficient manner. One of the central themes in this chapter is that the information available to the regulatory agencies, especially regarding firms' technologies for reducing pollution, is generally incomplete. This lack of good information leads to the result that *market-based* environmental regulations are usually more successful than methods based on the government's *direct control*.

The chapter concludes with a discussion of a crucial policy issue. We examine how greenhouse gas emissions are contributing to global climate change, the technical challenges associated with reducing these emissions, and policies designed to address this enormous challenge.

17.1 THE ECONOMIC RATIONALE FOR REGULATING POLLUTION

As a consequence of producing or consuming goods and services, "bads" are produced as well. Steel plants produce smoke in addition to steel. Farms produce chemical runoff as well as food. Logging leads to soil erosion that contaminates fish breeding grounds. Cars, trucks, and factories, by burning carbon-rich fossil fuels, such as coal, oil, and natural gas, produce carbon dioxide and other greenhouse gases that contribute to global climate change. Households produce human waste and garbage as they consume goods and services.

In all of these cases, the acts of production and consumption automatically generate pollution, which is a *negative externality*. As we saw in Chapter 16, externalities are an important type of market failure and lead to an inefficient allocation of resources. This inefficiency provides the rationale for government policy to improve the market outcome.

FIGURE 17-1 A Pollution Externality in a Competitive Market

A negative externality implies that a competitive free market will produce more output than the allocatively efficient level; if the externality can be internalized, allocative efficiency can be achieved. A competitive free market will produce where the demand and supply curves intersect—that is, at Q^c and p^c. If each unit of output of this good also generates an external cost of MEC, then social marginal cost is greater than private marginal cost by this amount. The allocatively efficient level of output is where social marginal benefit equals social marginal cost—that is, at Q^*. The competitive free market therefore produces too much output.

If firms in this industry are now required to pay a tax of $\$MEC$ per unit of output, the private marginal cost curve, MC_P, shifts up to MC_S. The externality will be internalized because firms will be forced to pay the social marginal cost of their production. The new competitive equilibrium will be p^*, Q^*, and allocative efficiency will be achieved.

Pollution as an Externality

Polluting firms that are profit maximizers do not regard a clean environment as a scarce resource and therefore fail to consider the full costs of using this resource when producing their product. When a paper mill produces newsprint, the production affects more than just the firm's suppliers, employees, and customers. Its water-discharged effluent damages natural ecosystems and imposes costs on all those who use the nearby water for drinking or swimming. The emissions from its smokestacks affect the cleanliness of the air and impose costs on people who rely on its purity. The profit-maximizing paper mill neglects these external effects of its actions because its profits are not directly affected by them.

As shown in Figure 17-1, allocative efficiency requires that the price (the value consumers place on the marginal unit of output) be just equal to the marginal social cost (the value of resources society gives up to produce the marginal unit of output). When there are negative externalities, *social* marginal cost exceeds *private* marginal cost because the act of production generates costs for society that are not faced by the producer.

By producing where price equals private marginal cost and thereby ignoring the externality, the firms are maximizing profits but producing too much output. The price that consumers pay just covers the private marginal cost but does not pay for the external damage. The *social benefit* of the last unit of output (the market price) is less than the social cost (private marginal cost plus the extra cost to society from the externality). Reducing output would increase allocative efficiency and make society as a whole better off.

Making polluting firms bear the entire social cost of their production is called **internalizing the externality**. This leads them to produce a lower level of output, as shown in Figure 17-1. Indeed, at the optimal level of output, where the externality is completely internalized, consumer prices would just cover the *social* marginal cost of production. We would have the familiar condition for allocative efficiency that marginal benefits to consumers are just equal to the social marginal cost of producing these benefits.

Internalizing the externality
A process that results in a producer or consumer taking account of a previously external effect.

> The socially optimal level of output is such that the social marginal cost equals the social marginal benefit.

In order to internalize the externality successfully, it is necessary to measure its size accurately. Looking at Figure 17-1, we must be able to measure the magnitude of the marginal external cost, *MEC*. In practice, however, external costs are quite difficult to measure. This measurement is especially difficult in the case of air pollution, where the damage is often spread over hundreds of thousands of square kilometres and can affect millions of people.

The Optimal Amount of Pollution Abatement

Notice from Figure 17-1 that the allocatively efficient outcome still has some pollution being generated. This is because the production of each unit of output in Figure 17-1 generates some pollution. It is simply impossible to produce goods and services without generating *some* environmental damage. The economic problem is then to determine how much environmental damage to allow or, equivalently, how much pollution abatement (reduction) to implement. In general, it is not optimal to eliminate all pollution.

> Eliminating all pollution is generally not allocatively efficient.

The economics of determining how much pollution to reduce, and therefore how much to allow, is summarized in Figure 17-2, which depicts the social marginal benefits and social marginal costs of pollution abatement. The analysis might be thought of as applying, for example, to water pollution in a specific watershed. It is drawn from the perspective of a public authority whose mandate is to maximize social welfare.

Note that the figure is drawn in terms of the amount of pollution that is reduced (or abated) rather than the total amount of pollution. We do this because pollution abatement (rather than pollution itself) is a "good" of economic value, and we are more familiar with applying the concepts of supply and demand for goods with positive values. If no pollution is abated, the watershed will be subjected to the amount of pollution that would occur in an unregulated market. The greater the amount of pollution abated, the smaller the amount of pollution that remains. Thus, as we move to the right along the horizontal axis, there is more pollution abatement and therefore less remaining pollution. On the vertical axis, measured in dollars per unit, we show the marginal benefit and marginal cost of pollution abatement.

FIGURE 17-2 **The Optimal Amount of Pollution Abatement**

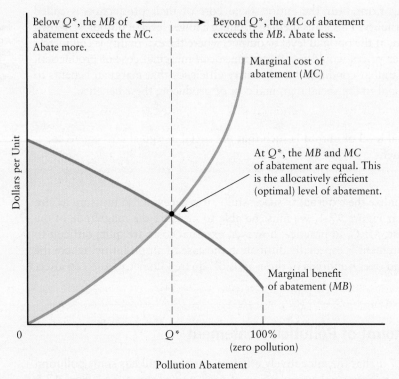

The optimal amount of pollution abatement occurs where the marginal cost of reducing pollution is just equal to the marginal benefits from doing so. *MB* represents the social marginal benefit of reducing pollution by one unit. *MC* represents the social marginal cost of reducing pollution by one unit. The optimal level of pollution abatement is *Q**, where *MB* = *MC*. Notice that not all pollution is eliminated. For each unit up to *Q**, the marginal benefit derived from pollution abatement exceeds the marginal cost. The total net benefit from the optimal amount of pollution abatement is given by the shaded area. Any further efforts to reduce pollution beyond *Q** would add more to social costs than to social benefits.

Marginal Cost of Abatement   The marginal cost of abating pollution is often small at low levels of abatement but rises steeply after some point. This is the upward-sloping line shown in Figure 17-2. There are two reasons for believing that this shape is accurate. First is the familiar logic behind increasing marginal costs. Because some antipollution measures can be taken fairly easily, the first units of pollution abatement will be cheap relative to later units. In addition, it is likely that pollution reduction of any degree will be easier for some firms than for others. New facilities are likely to run more cleanly than old ones, for example. Pollution abatement in a factory that was designed in the era of environmental concern may be much easier than obtaining similar abatement in an older factory. After some point, however, the easy fixes are exhausted, and the marginal cost of further pollution abatement rises steeply.

Marginal Benefit of Abatement   The downward-sloping curve in Figure 17-2 is the "demand" for pollution abatement and reflects the marginal benefit of pollution reduction. The curve slopes downward for much the same reason that a typical demand curve slopes downward. Starting at any level of pollution, people will derive some benefit from reducing the level of pollution, but the marginal benefit from a given amount of abatement will be lower, the lower the level of remaining pollution (or the higher the level of abatement). Put another way, in a very dirty environment, a little cleanliness will be much prized, but in a very clean environment, a little more cleanliness will be of only small additional value.

Optimal Abatement   The optimal amount of pollution abatement occurs where the marginal benefit is equal to the marginal cost—where "supply" and "demand" in Figure 17-2 intersect. Since the optimal amount of abatement is usually not 100 percent, some pollution will exist at the optimal outcome. As we said earlier, zero pollution is generally not allocatively efficient.

In trying to reach this optimum, the government faces three serious problems. First, although Figure 17-2 looks like a supply–demand diagram, we have already seen that the private sector will not by itself create a market in pollution control. Hence, the government must intervene in private-sector markets if the outcome shown in Figure 17-2 is to be attained.

The second problem is that the optimal level of pollution abatement is not easily known because the marginal benefit and the marginal cost curves shown in Figure 17-2 are not usually observable. In practice, the government can only estimate these curves, and accurate estimates are often difficult to obtain, especially when the technology of pollution abatement is changing and the health consequences and other costs associated with various pollutants are not easily measured. An important example of our ignorance regarding the marginal costs and benefits of pollution abatement is related to the effects of greenhouse-gas emissions on global climate change. Though there is now an overwhelming consensus among scientists that humankind's emissions of greenhouse gases are contributing to global climate change, the estimates of the *magnitude* of the effects of Earth's climate change, as well as the resulting costs, vary considerably.

The third problem is that the available techniques for reducing pollution are themselves imperfect. Even if the optimal level of pollution abatement were known with precision, there are both technical and legal impediments to achieving that level through regulation.

This brings us to a discussion of the various policies governments can use to reduce pollution. As we will see, some policies are more effective than others.

17.2 POLLUTION-CONTROL POLICIES

We examine three different types of policies designed to bring about the optimal amount of pollution abatement. These are *direct controls, emissions taxes*, and *tradable pollution permits*.

Direct Controls

Direct control is the form of environmental regulation that is used most often in Canada and the United States, although it is often invisible to consumers. (Policies of direct control are sometimes referred to as *command-and-control* policies.) Automobile emissions standards are one example. The standards must be met by all new cars that are sold in Canada. They require that emissions per kilometre of a number of smog-producing pollutants be less than certain specified amounts, and the standards are the same no matter where the car is driven.

Another form of direct control is the simple prohibition of certain polluting behaviours. For example, many cities and towns prohibit the private burning of leaves and other trash because of the air pollution problem (as well as the fire dangers) that the burning would cause. A number of communities have banned the use of wood-burning stoves for the same reason. Some provinces outlaw the use of weed-control products because of the contamination they cause in the ground water. Similarly, the Canadian federal government gradually reduced the amount of lead allowed in gasoline and then eliminated leaded gasoline altogether.

When the policy objective is to *eliminate* a specific type of pollution, direct pollution controls are probably the most practical policy instrument. In the case of weed-control products, for example, the costs imposed on homeowners by prohibiting their use of certain products are almost certainly smaller than the benefits from removing the contamination from the groundwater. In the case of leaded gasoline, the gradual reduction in the permissible lead content allowed producers and consumers to substitute toward unleaded gasoline at relatively low cost, while society gained the considerable benefits of the cleaner automobile emissions.

In other situations, however, when the policy objective is to *reduce*, rather than eliminate a particular type of pollution, and when it may not be so clear to governments *how* the pollution can most effectively be reduced, direct pollution controls are far less effective. For example, if the goal is to reduce the emissions of sulphur dioxide from hundreds of factory smokestacks, we need to recognize that some firms may be able to reduce their emissions much more cheaply than others. In this situation, direct controls would generally not be the *least-cost* method of reducing harmful emissions.

Problems with Direct Controls In the terminology of Chapter 12, direct pollution controls are often not *productively efficient* because the total cost of achieving a given amount of pollution abatement is not minimized.

> **Pollution is being reduced at the lowest possible cost when the marginal cost of pollution abatement is the same for all firms.**

When firms are required to abide by the same direct pollution controls, however, the marginal cost of pollution abatement is usually *not* equated across firms. To see this, consider two firms that have different technologies and thus face different marginal costs of pollution abatement, as shown in Figure 17-3. These firms may be in the same industry, producing similar products, or they may be in different industries altogether. In either case, they are assumed to have different abilities to abate pollution. Suppose that, for any level of pollution abatement, Firm A's marginal costs of abatement are lower than those for Firm B.

In this situation, consider a system of direct pollution controls that requires Firm A and Firm B each to reduce pollution by a given amount, say Q_R. As shown in Figure 17-3, Firm A's marginal cost at Q_R (C_A) is less than Firm B's marginal cost (C_B). As long as C_A is less than C_B, it is possible to reduce the *total* cost of this total amount of pollution abatement by reallocating it between the two firms. For example, suppose C_A is

$10 and C_B is $18. If Firm A abated one more unit of pollution, its total costs would rise by $10; if Firm B abated one *less* unit of pollution, its total costs would fall by $18. By reallocating one unit of pollution abatement from Firm B to Firm A, total pollution abatement would be unaffected, but the total cost of the abatement would be reduced by $8. As long as the two firms' marginal costs of abatement are not equal, it is possible to reduce total costs by further redistributing the abatement between the firms. Only when marginal costs are equal across the two firms is the given level of pollution abatement being achieved at the lowest possible cost.

Direct pollution controls are usually inefficient because they do not minimize the total cost of a given amount of pollution abatement.

Direct controls are also expensive to monitor and to enforce. The regulatory agency has to check—factory by factory, farm by farm—how many pollutants of what kinds are being emitted. It then also needs a mechanism for penalizing offenders. Accurate monitoring of all potential sources of pollution requires a considerable level of resources. Moreover, the system of fines and penalties needs to be harsh enough to induce potential polluters to obey the law. A potential polluter, required to limit emissions of a pollutant to so many kilograms or litres per day, will take into account the cost of meeting the standard, the probability of being caught, and the severity of the penalty before deciding how to behave. If the chances of being caught and the penalties are small, the direct controls may have little effect. As we will see, however, the considerable costs of monitoring and enforcement apply in a similar way to all kinds of pollution policies.

FIGURE 17-3 The Inefficiency of Direct Pollution Controls

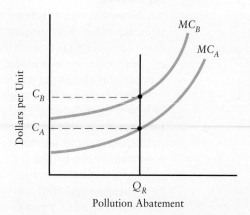

Requiring equal amounts of pollution abatement from different polluters is inefficient when the different polluters have different technologies of pollution abatement. Firm A is able to abate pollution according to the marginal cost curve MC_A. Firm B has a different abatement technology and has a higher marginal cost of abatement, MC_B. Suppose a regulatory authority requires that the two firms reduce pollution by the same amount, Q_R. Firm A will have a marginal cost of pollution abatement of C_A, whereas Firm B's marginal cost will be C_B, which is larger than C_A.

To see that this outcome is inefficient, consider what happens if Firm A increases its pollution abatement by one unit while Firm B decreases its abatement by one unit. Total pollution remains the same, but total costs fall.

Emissions Taxes

An alternative method of pollution control is to levy a tax on emissions at the source. The advantage of imposing a tax on each unit of pollution emitted is that each individual polluting firm is forced to *internalize* the negative externality associated with the pollution it is producing. This can lead to *efficient* pollution abatement.

Again, suppose Firm A can reduce emissions cheaply, while it is more expensive for Firm B to reduce emissions. And further suppose that all firms are required to pay a tax equal to t per unit of pollution emitted. For example, assume that the tax is $10 per unit of pollution. Since firms must pay $10 for every unit of pollution they produce, they will save $10 for every unit of pollution they *do not produce*. It follows that the emissions tax of $10 is each firm's marginal benefit of pollution abatement. The goal of profit maximization will then lead firms to reduce emissions to the point where the marginal cost of further reduction is just equal to $10. Such a situation is illustrated in Figure 17-4.

Note that when all firms facing an emissions tax are maximizing their profits, they will each abate pollution until their own marginal cost is equal to the tax. It follows that their marginal costs will be equated and thus the condition will be satisfied for *efficient* pollution abatement. This efficiency is the central appeal of emissions taxes, especially as compared to direct pollution controls.

The above analysis applies to any level of an emissions tax. But what is the level at which an emissions tax should be set to achieve allocative efficiency? If the regulatory agency is able to obtain a good estimate of the marginal cost generated by the pollution, it could set the tax rate just equal to that amount. In such a case, polluters would be forced by the tax to internalize the full pollution externality and allocative efficiency would be achieved. In terms of Figure 17-1, each firm's private marginal cost curve would shift up by the full amount of the tax (set to equal the marginal external cost, *MEC*) and thus the allocatively efficient level of output (and pollution) would be produced.

A second advantage of using emissions taxes is that regulators are not required to specify anything about *how* polluters should abate pollution and thus are not required to have expertise about the firms' technologies. Rather, polluters themselves can be left to find the most efficient abatement techniques. The profit motive will lead them to do so because they will want to avoid paying the tax.

> Emissions taxes lead profit-maximizing firms to abate pollution in a cost-minimizing manner. If the tax is set equal to the marginal external cost of the pollution, the externality will be fully internalized and the allocatively efficient amount of pollution abatement (and output) will be produced.

A third advantage of an emissions tax is the incentive it creates for innovation. With direct controls, firms are required to reduce pollution only to the point where the regulation is satisfied; there is no economic incentive to reduce further. In contrast, an emissions tax attaches a price to any amount of pollution and so firms have an ongoing financial incentive to innovate so as to reduce emissions. As long as the tax is in place, firms will continually be trying to reduce their emissions.

Problems with Emissions Taxes Emissions taxes can only be applied if it is possible for the government regulator to measure emissions with reasonable accuracy. For some kinds of pollution-creating activities, this does not pose much of a problem, but for many other types of pollution, good measuring devices that can be installed at reasonable cost do not exist. In these cases, emissions

FIGURE 17-4 The Efficiency of Emissions Taxes

Emission taxes can lead to efficient pollution abatement. As in Figure 17-3, Firm A faces a lower marginal cost of pollution abatement than does Firm B. Suppose the regulatory authority imposes a tax of t dollars per unit of pollution emitted. Since each firm would then save t dollars for each unit of pollution it does not produce, t can be viewed as each firm's marginal benefit of pollution abatement.

Firm A chooses to reduce its pollution by Q_A. Up to this point, the tax saved (marginal benefit) from reducing pollution exceeds the marginal cost of reducing pollution. Firm B chooses to abate only a small amount of pollution, Q_B. Since the marginal cost of abatement is equated across firms, the total amount of pollution abatement ($Q_A + Q_B$) is achieved at minimum cost. This is efficient pollution abatement.

taxes cannot work, and direct controls are the only feasible approach (although appropriate enforcement may still be a problem).

Another problem with emissions taxes involves setting the tax rate. Ideally, the regulatory agency would obtain an estimate of the marginal external cost of each pollutant and set the tax equal to this amount. This ideal tax rate would perfectly internalize the pollution externality. However, the information that is needed to determine the marginal external cost (MEC) shown in Figure 17-1 is often difficult to obtain. If the regulatory agency sets the tax rate too high, too many resources will be devoted to pollution control. If the tax is set too low, there will be too little pollution abatement and thus too much pollution.

Tradable Pollution Permits: "Cap and Trade"

The third general policy approach to pollution reduction is often referred to as a system of "cap and trade." This system comprises two fundamental parts. First, the government mandates a limit (or "cap") on the total amount of pollution of some specific type. Second, the government distributes permits to firms (either by granting or auctioning) allowing the firms to emit a specified amount of pollution. These permits can be traded among them at prices determined in a free market. For example, the government might issue permits for a total of 10 000 megatonnes of annual sulphur dioxide emissions and distribute to each of 20 firms a permit for 500 megatonnes. In any given year, a firm is restricted to emitting an amount of sulphur dioxide no greater than the amount allowed by the permits it holds. Firms can then trade the permits freely among themselves and a market-determined price will be established. For obvious reasons, a cap-and-trade system is also referred to as a system of **tradable pollution permits**.

Like emissions taxes, tradable pollution permits can minimize the cost of a given amount of pollution abatement. To see this, consider starting from a situation similar to that with direct pollution controls. In Figure 17-5, both firms are abating pollution by Q^* units. (The inefficiency of this initial situation is reflected by the differential in marginal

tradable pollution permits Rights to emit specific amounts of specified pollutants that private firms may buy and sell among themselves. The total quantity of permits is set by government policy.

FIGURE 17-5   The Efficiency of Tradable Pollution Permits ("Cap and Trade")

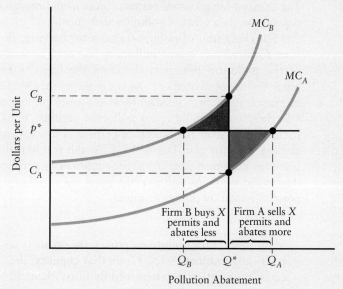

Firm B buys X permits and abates less | Firm A sells X permits and abates more

A cap-and-trade system is an efficient way to achieve a given amount of pollution abatement. As in Figure 17-3 and Figure 17-4, Firm A has lower marginal costs of pollution abatement than does Firm B. If each firm abates pollution by Q^* units, the firms' marginal costs are not equated and the pollution abatement is inefficient.

All firms can be better off if they are issued tradable pollution permits even though total pollution abatement remains unchanged. The price of the permits reflects firms' marginal benefit of pollution abatement. If the price is p^*, Firm A would sell X permits to Firm B. Firm B would reduce its abatement to Q_B and reduce its costs by the red area, while Firm A would increase its abatement to Q_A and increase its net earnings by the blue area. Since the marginal costs of abatement are then equated across firms, this is efficient pollution abatement.

costs of the two firms.) Now suppose the government issues permits for a total amount of emissions consistent with the same total amount of pollution abatement (= $2 \times Q^*$ in the figure). What should each of the firms do? Should they abate more pollution, or less?

Note that at Q^* units of pollution abatement, the marginal costs for Firm B exceed the marginal costs for Firm A—pollution abatement is more difficult for Firm B than for Firm A. Suppose the two firms could agree on a price p^* at which to buy and sell permits. Who would buy, and who would sell? Firm B, the high-abatement-cost firm, would rather buy permits at p^* and avoid having to reduce pollution at high marginal costs. By buying X pollution permits from Firm A, Firm B ends up abating Q_B units of pollution and reduces its costs by the red-shaded area. Firm A, the low-abatement-cost firm, would rather sell its permits at p^* and abate more pollution at low marginal cost. By selling X permits to Firm B, Firm A ends up abating Q_A units of pollution and increases its profits by the blue-shaded area.

Therefore, with low-abatement-cost firms selling pollution permits to high-abatement-cost firms, both types of firms are better off than when they are subject to direct pollution controls even though the total amount of pollution abatement is unchanged. Since the marginal cost of abatement is now equal across firms, we know from our earlier discussion that the given amount of pollution abatement is being achieved at the lowest possible cost.

> With tradable pollution permits, profit-maximizing firms will reduce pollution until their marginal abatement costs equal the price of pollution permits. The costs of a given amount of pollution abatement will be minimized.

FIGURE 17-6   The Market for Tradable Pollution Permits

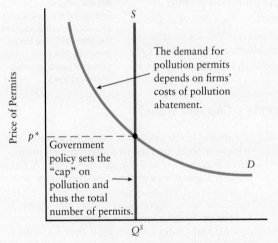

The demand for pollution permits depends on firms' costs of pollution abatement.

Government policy sets the "cap" on pollution and thus the total number of permits.

Number of Pollution Permits

The equilibrium price in the market for pollution permits is determined by government policy and by firms' technology of pollution abatement. The government sets the total quantity of pollution permits at Q^S. This is the vertical supply curve. At a lower price for permits (the marginal benefit of abatement) firms decide to abate less pollution and they therefore require more pollution permits. The demand curve for permits is therefore downward sloping. At the equilibrium price, the quantity of permits demanded by firms is equal to the number issued by the government.

What determines the equilibrium market price for pollution permits? The total supply of pollution permits is determined by the government policy—the government-mandated "cap" on pollution. Let this amount be Q^S—it is represented by a vertical supply curve in Figure 17-6. The demand for pollution permits comes from firms and depends on their costs of pollution abatement.

For every unit of pollution that a firm abates, the firm requires one fewer pollution permit. The price of the pollution permit is therefore the firms' marginal benefit of abatement. As the price of the permit increases, each firm decides to abate more pollution and therefore demand fewer pollution permits. Thus, the demand curve for pollution permits is downward sloping, as shown in Figure 17-6. At the equilibrium price for pollution permits, p^*, the number of permits demanded by firms will exactly equal the number of permits issued by the government.

> In the market for pollution permits, the quantity is set by government policy. Given that quantity, the equilibrium price is determined by firms' demand for pollution permits.

Technological Improvement   One problem with direct pollution controls is that they tend, like much government regulation, to respond only slowly to changes in technology or market conditions. In contrast, tradable pollution permits, because they are a market-based method of pollution control, maintain their efficiency even in the midst of frequent and substantial changes in technology. As technological advances occur that reduce the marginal costs of pollution abatement, profit-maximizing firms will choose to abate more pollution at any given price for the pollution permits (see Figure 17-5). But this decision will imply a reduced overall demand for pollution permits and thus the equilibrium price for the permits will fall (see Figure 17-6). Whatever the market price for permits, profit-maximizing firms will equate the price to their marginal abatement costs, thus minimizing the total cost of a given amount of pollution abatement.

> **Improvements in abatement technology will lead to a reduction in the demand for emissions permits and thus a reduction in their equilibrium price. The total cost of a given amount of pollution abatement will still be minimized.**

Problems with Tradable Pollution Permits   Tradable permits pose some problems of implementation. There are technical difficulties in measuring pollution and in designing mechanisms to ensure that firms and households comply with regulations (the same problems that exist for direct controls and emissions taxes). Furthermore, the potential efficiency gains arising from tradable permits cannot be realized if regulatory agencies are prone to change the rules under which trades may take place. Such changes have been a problem in the past, but they are a problem that can be corrected.

One problem with tradable permits is more political than economic, but it is certainly important in explaining why such policies are relatively rare. Opponents of tradable permits often argue that by providing permits, rather than simply outlawing pollution above some amount, the government is condoning the "crime" of polluting the environment. Direct controls, according to this argument, have much greater normative force because they suggest that violating the standards is simply wrong. In contrast, emissions taxes and markets for pollution permits make violating the standards just one more element of cost for the firm to consider as it pursues its private goals.

Most economists find arguments of this kind unpersuasive. An absolute ban on pollution is impossible because any production of goods and services generates at least some pollution. In choosing how much pollution to allow, society must recognize the tradeoff between devoting resources toward pollution abatement and other valuable things. Economic analysis has a good deal to say about how a society might minimize the cost of *any* degree of pollution abatement. By taking the moral attitude that pollution is wrong and pollution permits should not be allowed, the result is that *less* pollution is abated for any given amount of society's scarce resources that are allocated toward this goal.

Pricing Pollution

The economic advantage of using emissions taxes or tradable emissions permits as opposed to direct controls is that these policies "attach a price" to pollution and then rely on firms' natural inclination to maximize profits. In the pursuit of high profits (and low costs), firms seek out the lowest cost way to reduce their polluting activities. It is this behaviour that explains the efficiency of market-based pollution-reduction policies.

The general principle behind pricing pollution can be applied to many different settings. Whenever there are multiple sources of a given type of pollution, and the

APPLYING ECONOMIC CONCEPTS 17-1

Using Prices to Reduce Pollution and Conserve Resources

Policies that attach a price to pollution are increasingly being used to achieve effective and low-cost pollution reduction. By requiring households and firms to pay a tax or fee every time they pollute, powerful incentives are created to reduce pollution. At the same time, polluters are led to adopt or develop innovative and non-polluting ways of conducting their activities. Moreover, as long as there is a price attached to pollution, there is always an incentive to reduce further and save additional money. The same principle applies to the use of scarce resources such as water and land; by attaching a price to the use of the resource, people are led to economize on their use. Here are three examples to illustrate how pricing is being used effectively to reduce pollution and conserve resources.

Solid Waste in the United Kingdom

Disposal of solid waste in landfills occupies scarce land and leads to emissions of greenhouse gases, common air pollutants, and the contamination of local groundwater. In the late 1990s, the United Kingdom introduced landfill taxes for organic waste from all sources—commercial, industrial, and residential. The current tax rate is £80 per tonne of solid waste. Over a five-year period following the introduction of the tax, the volume of solid waste sent to landfills fell by between 30 and 40 percent.

Water Conservation in Singapore

Singapore's domestic supply of fresh water is severely limited, so it relies on costly imports of water by pipeline from neighbouring Malaysia. With scarce domestic supply and growing demand driven by population growth, conservation is an important objective of Singapore's water policy. In the late 1990s, Singapore introduced a water tariff system in which price closely reflects the full economic and ecological costs of shipping and treatment. Some of the revenues collected by the water tariff are returned to lower-income households to prevent an undue decline in their overall purchasing power. Over a ten-year period after the water tariff was implemented, Singapore's per capita water consumption fell by 10 percent. It is expected to decline further in response to households' growing efficiency in water use.

Road Congestion in London, England

Highly congested roads lead to economic costs from wasted time and traffic accidents, as well as contributing to greater air pollution and greenhouse gas emissions. In 2003, the City of London introduced a daily fee (currently £11.50) for any vehicle travelling inside a "congestion charge zone," along with stiff penalties for any owners of vehicles not paying the fee. Most of the revenues raised by the fee are used to finance improvements in public transit, thereby improving alternatives for those who choose not to travel by car. Over the first 10 years of the program, the volume of traffic in the congestion zone fell by about 30 percent.

For more on the case for pricing pollution and "recycling" the revenues to generate economic benefits, see *Smart, Practical, Possible*, Canada's Ecofiscal Commission, 2014, www.ecofiscal.ca.

different polluters have different marginal costs of abatement, a market-based policy stands to be significantly more efficient than a policy based on direct controls. See *Applying Economic Concepts 17-1* for a discussion of how this principle has been effectively used to reduce landfill waste, conserve water, and reduce traffic congestion.

17.3 THE ECONOMIC CHALLENGE OF GLOBAL CLIMATE CHANGE

So far in this chapter we have discussed the general case of environmental externalities and the types of policies that can be used to address them. We now go on to examine the particular case of global climate change, undoubtedly the most complex environmental externality the world has ever seen. Recall that a negative externality is an example of a market failure, where the private market fails to take account of the external cost associated with the production or use of a commodity. There is now an overwhelming consensus in the scientific community that the burning of fossil fuels and the resulting emission of green-house gases is directly affecting the global climate and raising Earth's average temperature. Correcting this market failure will require coordinated actions by all countries. It is no surprise that global climate change has been described as the "mother of all externalities."

In this section we review the basic facts about the emission of greenhouse gases, their accumulation in the atmosphere, and the effects on Earth's climate. In addition, we examine the case for global collective action to reduce these emissions. Finally, we discuss the considerable technical challenges that must be overcome if emissions are to be reduced on a scale sufficient to stabilize Earth's climate. As will become clear, the issue of global climate change presents a complex combination of economic, political, and scientific challenges.

Greenhouse-Gas Emissions

Greenhouse gases include carbon dioxide, methane, and nitrous oxide, all of which are emitted through various industrial processes, especially the burning of fossil fuels, the production of cement, and the use of nitrogen-rich fertilizers in agriculture. As these greenhouse gases (GHGs) accumulate in the atmosphere, the rising atmospheric concentration increases Earth's average temperature. It is common to measure greenhouse gases in terms of their equivalent amount of carbon dioxide, referred to as CO_2e.

Flows Versus Stocks The world's total emissions of greenhouse gases is currently approximately 50 billion tonnes of CO_2e, two-thirds of which are related to the production or consumption of energy—residential and commercial heating, transportation, electricity generation, and industrial processes. These emissions are a *flow* that occur annually and have been on a significant upward trend over the past century. Through the natural respiration of forests and absorption by the oceans, Earth can absorb only about 5 billion tonnes of GHGs every year. For each year that the total flow of GHG emissions exceed this natural absorptive level, the atmospheric concentration of greenhouse gases increases.

In the mid-1800s, before the Industrial Revolution began, current estimates suggest that the concentration of greenhouse gases in the atmosphere was roughly 280 parts per million (ppm) of CO_2e. But as the Industrial Revolution progressed, the burning of coal to operate steam engines and generate electricity became widespread, and later the burning of petroleum-based fuels was developed to fuel automobiles, diesel locomotives, ships, and airplanes. As the world's emissions of GHGs rose above Earth's absorptive capacity, the gases began to accumulate in the atmosphere. Today, a century and a half later, the atmospheric concentration of greenhouse gases has increased by over 50 percent to 435 ppm of CO_2e.

The Effect on Global Climate Why is the growing atmospheric concentration of greenhouse gases a problem? The accumulation of GHGs in the atmosphere acts like the walls and roof of a greenhouse to hold in the infrared radiation from Earth, thus raising Earth's average temperature. If the atmospheric concentration increases to a level of 550 ppm of CO_2e, Earth's average temperature is predicted to rise above its pre-industrial level by 1.5 to 4.5°C. Even such an apparently modest increase in temperature is predicted to have potentially devastating effects, including:

- melting of the world's glaciers, resulting in a loss of fresh-water supplies, especially in South Asia, China, and South America;

- melting of the Greenland and Antarctic ice caps, resulting in rising sea levels and the likely displacement of tens of millions of people from their current homes (especially in the low island states of the developing world);
- a reduction of animal habitat and the extinction of some species, leading to a reduction in biodiversity;
- reduced crop yields (especially in Africa and parts of Asia), resulting in reduced food supplies in regions already facing hunger problems; and
- rising intensity of storms and increasing volatility of weather patterns.

The costs associated with these changes are easy to imagine but difficult to quantify precisely. Current estimates of the effects of climate change, expressed in terms of a permanent reduction in world GDP, range from 3 percent to 20 percent. The width of this range indicates just how much uncertainty and debate continues to exist about the effects of global climate change, but even the lower bound of this range—an annual global cost of U.S.$1.2 trillion forever—represents an enormous sum. Even worse, these costs will probably be unevenly distributed across the world's population; the developing world is likely to bear the lion's share of the burden of global climate change.

In summary, the atmospheric concentration of greenhouse gases is already 50 percent above its pre-industrial levels and some climate change is already occurring. But if the global climate is to be stabilized in the long run (albeit at a higher average temperature than today's), the atmospheric concentration of greenhouse gases must also be stabilized, at least eventually. Such stabilization will eventually require an enormous cut in the annual flow of GHG emissions from its current level of 50 billion tonnes of CO_2e to about 5 billion tonnes per year, the amount Earth can naturally absorb annually. Such a reduction in the annual flow of global GHG emissions is an enormous task and will take many years to accomplish.

The Case for Global Collective Action

The emission of greenhouse gases is a *negative externality*. Many production and consumption activities of individual firms and households emit greenhouse gases, and thereby impose costs on others. But because they are not required to incorporate these external costs into their own calculations, most firms and individuals act as if these external costs do not exist. As a result, they carry out too many of these polluting activities relative to what is socially optimal; the market outcome is allocatively inefficient.

When such negative externalities occur within a community, bylaws can be enacted by local government to alter individuals' behaviour. We thus have bylaws in some cities preventing the use of wood-burning stoves. When negative externalities occur within larger regions, governments often step in to correct the market failure, and so we get provincial governments enforcing such laws as banning the dumping of toxic waste in waterways.

In the case of greenhouse-gas emissions, however, the negative externality is truly global. The GHG emissions that come from a coal-burning

One of the predicted effects of ongoing climate change is the increasing frequency and severity of extreme weather events, such as the massive flood in Calgary in 2013.

Jonathan Hayward/The Canadian Press

electricity plant in Canada or China rise into the atmosphere and disperse around the globe. They add to the atmospheric stock of existing GHGs and therefore contribute to the ongoing process of climate change. In both cases, the costs are imposed on people all over the world. As Professor Nicolas Stern says in his 2006 report written for the U.K. Treasury, "Climate change is the greatest market failure the world has ever seen"—its solution will require collective action on a global scale.

The Kyoto Protocol   The global scale of the problem motivated the United Nations to sponsor a set of conferences, aimed at developing a coordinated solution to climate change. In 1997, this process was brought to the world's attention with a conference held in Kyoto, Japan, at which many countries signed an international agreement aimed at reducing GHG emissions. This agreement came to be called the *Kyoto Protocol*, and within a decade had been ratified by the parliaments of 166 signatory countries.

The countries participating in the Kyoto Protocol agreed to an aggregate emissions-reduction target of 5 percent below the 1990 level of emissions by 2012. Each country also agreed to its own emissions-reduction target over the same period. But the countries who signed the Protocol were responsible for only about one-third of global GHG emissions. Notably absent from the agreement were the developed countries of the United States and Australia, and the large developing countries of China, India, and Indonesia.

Performance   Figure 17-7 shows the change in annual GHG emissions for selected countries between 1995 and 2011. Some countries, including Canada, have experienced significant *increases* in their annual emissions, despite their stated commitments to achieve modest reductions. On the other hand, many countries have been able to reduce their annual GHG emissions significantly since 1995. In some cases, such as France, Sweden, and the United Kingdom, the emissions reductions were achieved despite continued growth in annual income (GDP) over the 25-year period. In other cases, however, notably the Russian Federation (and to a lesser extent Germany), a large part of the emissions reductions were associated with the steep economic declines that occurred as the former Eastern Bloc countries made the difficult transition from centrally planned to market economies.

FIGURE 17-7   Changes in Annual GHG Emissions, 1995-2011

There is considerable variation across countries in terms of the change in annual emissions of greenhouse gases since 1995. The data show the percentage change in annual GHG emissions between 1995 and 2011.

(*Source:* Adapted from World Resources Institute. Data are GHG emissions including those due to land use, land-use change, and forestry (LULUCF); www.wri.org.)

One important lesson from Figure 17-7 is that the mere act of signing an international treaty and committing to a specific outcome does not guarantee the achievement of that outcome. Without effective policies being put in place, emissions reductions are unlikely to occur. We say more about specific policies below.

Beyond Kyoto   Some countries achieved their Kyoto targets while many did not. By the time the Kyoto Protocol expired in 2012, however, it was increasingly clear to most countries that subsequent phases of international actions to reduce greenhouse-gas emissions needed to include participation by the world's largest emitters, including the United States, China, India, and Indonesia.

In Durban, South Africa, in 2011, a U.N.-sponsored conference achieved a notable success. All countries agreed to negotiate a legally binding emission-reduction agreement by 2015, to be implemented by 2020. Many observers hailed this as a major breakthrough because for the first time *all* countries would be taking part in emissions reductions, even though the details were yet to be determined. Critics pointed out that the "details" were crucial and that, in any event, delaying implementation until 2020 might prove to be too late to prevent an excessive increase in Earth's temperature. The Durban-inspired agreement was scheduled to be negotiated at another U.N.-sponsored conference in December 2015 in Paris. As this book went to press late that year, the outcome of the Paris conference was unknown.

There is no doubt that getting agreement on emissions reductions from a large number of countries is a complex and difficult task. But even apart from the politics and the diplomacy, there are enormous *technological* challenges involved in reducing greenhouse-gas emissions. We now turn to examine these challenges.

Energy Use, GDP, and Greenhouse-Gas Emissions

The data in Figure 17-7 suggest that it is not easy for a country to achieve significant reductions in greenhouse-gas emissions. If it were straightforward to achieve sizable reductions, then presumably emissions would not have *grown* in several large countries that claimed to be committed to achieving their stated emissions-reduction targets. Why are such reductions so difficult to achieve?

To organize our thoughts, it is useful to think about the following identity, which expresses GHG emissions in terms of three essential components.

$$\text{GHG} = \frac{\text{GHG}}{\text{Energy}} \times \frac{\text{Energy}}{\text{GDP}} \times \text{GDP} \tag{17-1}$$

where "GHG" is the world's annual emissions of greenhouse gases, "Energy" is the amount of energy consumed globally per year, and "GDP" is the world's annual gross domestic product. It is obvious that Equation 17-1 is identically true since one could easily cancel out the "GDP" and "Energy" terms to get GHG = GHG.

The value of this identity is that it shows us three essential components of the world's annual emissions of greenhouse gases. Each time the annual rate of GHG emissions increases, at least one of the three components must have increased. There has been either an increase in GDP, an increase in the energy intensity of GDP (Energy/GDP), or an increase in the GHG intensity of energy (GHG/Energy). Conversely, if we are to reduce the world's annual GHG emissions, then at least one of these three components must fall. Let's consider these three components in turn and determine which specific route to reducing global GHG emissions appears to be most promising.

Reducing Global GDP   It should not be surprising that, *ceteris paribus*, GHG emissions rise when GDP rises. The production of most goods and services requires the use of energy, which in turn tends to be associated with the release of greenhouse gases.

For two reasons, it is unrealistic to consider a reduction in the world's GDP as a fruitful approach to reducing global GHG emissions. First, based on current trends, the world's population will rise from its current 7 billion people to approximately 10 billion over the next century. These 3 billion extra people will require more GDP just to be fed, clothed, and housed, not to mention to receive the various "extras" that most of us take for granted.

Second, even if we ignore the challenge of global population growth, it is likely that per capita GDP will continue to rise over time. It is probably inherent to human nature that individuals—in rich and poor countries alike—strive to do better and improve their quality of life. And this desire to increase per capita income will inevitably lead to increases in world GDP.

As a result, world GDP can be expected to *rise* over time, not fall. For the world as a whole, the average GDP growth rate is usually between 4 and 5 percent per year. It follows that with unchanged "intensities" in Equation 17-1, the typical growth in world GDP will lead to growth in GHG emissions of between 4 and 5 percent per year.

Reducing the Energy Intensity of GDP   Now consider the second component in Equation 17-1, the energy intensity of GDP—the amount of energy that is used to produce one dollar's worth of real GDP. Taken by itself, a reduction in the energy intensity of GDP will reduce the annual emissions of greenhouse gases.

Improvements in technology, driven in part by firms' efforts to economize on inputs that are becoming increasingly scarce and expensive, are one driver for reductions in the energy intensity of GDP. Another is that as the structure of the economy continues its gradual adjustment away from energy-intensive manufacturing and toward the less-energy-intensive service sector, less energy is used even if the same level of aggregate output is produced. In countries like Canada and the United States, the energy used per dollar of real GDP has fallen by about one percent annually over the past 40 years. Similar declines have been observed in other developed economies.

Can we rely on reductions in energy intensity to achieve the necessary reductions in the world's greenhouse-gas emissions? The answer, again, is probably not. Reductions in energy intensity are ongoing, but are probably insufficient for the task at hand. With world GDP growing at 4 or 5 percent per year on average, even a 1.5 percent annual improvement in energy intensity means that the second two terms in Equation 17-1 are still likely to grow at a combined rate of about 3 percent per year.

Reducing the GHG Intensity of Energy   We are thus left with only one remaining way to achieve sizable reductions in the annual flow of global GHG emissions: We must significantly cut the GHG intensity of our energy. In other words, we need to produce and consume energy in ways that release far fewer GHG emissions into the atmosphere.

Two general approaches are available. The first is to switch, on a large scale, away from fossil fuel–based energy toward alternative forms of energy. Call this the *substitution* approach. The second is to continue using fossil fuels to generate energy, but to prevent the resulting greenhouse gases from being released into the atmosphere. Call this the *emissions-prevention* approach. Let's examine these two approaches in turn.

The Substitution Approach: Alternative Energy.   The burning of fossil fuels is an extremely efficient and economical method of producing energy. The sun's heat and the weight

Ken Gillespie/Newscom

This facility in Estevan, Saskatchewan is designed to capture and store carbon dioxide. If it proves to be sufficiently effective and inexpensive, this procedure could be used to significantly reduce Canada's GHG emissions.

of Earth's crust have combined over hundreds of millions of years to concentrate a tremendous amount of energy into every barrel of oil, bucket of coal, or cubic metre of natural gas. As a result, the burning of these fossil fuels is a very efficient way to produce energy. In addition, the costs (not including the negative externalities) of extracting and refining these fossil fuels are relatively low. The combination of these two factors results in a large economic advantage for fossil-fuel-based energy (sometimes called carbon-based energy) relative to non-carbon alternatives. It is therefore no wonder that roughly 80 percent of the world's energy is produced by burning fossil fuels.

The substitution approach to reducing GHG emissions is difficult because it requires making a substitution *away from* a low-cost and efficient energy source on an immense scale. In order to reduce the world's annual GHG emissions by 90 percent (even if we assumed that total energy consumption was held constant), it would be necessary to expand *by many times* the amount of energy currently being produced by hydroelectric dams, nuclear reactors, and renewable power sources such as solar and wind. These alternative sources of energy have their own limitations, however, and in most cases it is unlikely that large-scale expansion can be readily achieved.

The large-scale expansion of hydro power, for example, relies on being able to find enough new locations appropriate to the damming of large rivers, but such sites are already becoming quite scarce. Expansion of nuclear power is politically difficult for the simple reason that this method of power generation carries its own considerable environmental challenges—the safe storage of nuclear waste and the ongoing risk of nuclear accidents. Wind power and solar power, though currently growing in use, both require large amounts of land, and this land often has a considerable opportunity cost. In addition, the capital costs for both types of renewable power are considerable, and without government subsidies, operators are currently unable to cover their costs if they must compete with cheaper, conventional carbon-based power. Another disadvantage of wind and solar power is their inherent intermittence; as the wind dies down or the sun moves behind the clouds, power generation naturally falls off. A major challenge for wind and solar power is therefore the development of efficient, large-capacity storage batteries.

In summary, the large-scale substitution away from carbon-based energy and toward alternative, cleaner energy is not feasible in the short term. The various alternative energy sources have their own limitations, which probably explain why they are currently so rarely used as compared with carbon-based energy. Such a large-scale substitution, however, is possible over a much longer time frame. In the next section we will discuss several policies that may encourage a substitution toward alternative fuels.

The Emissions-Prevention Approach: Carbon Capture and Storage. The second approach to reducing the GHG intensity of energy—the emissions-prevention approach—is to continue reaping the enormous economic benefits that come from carbon-based energy production, but to minimize the associated environmental costs. In other words, we continue to burn fossil fuels to produce energy but prevent the harmful GHG emissions from escaping into the atmosphere. Instead, the GHGs could be "captured" and stored safely, either in secure manufactured storage containers or, perhaps more realistically, in the sedimentary layers from which the oil and natural gas were originally extracted.

In principle, this is a promising possibility, as the depleted oil and gas reservoirs at thousands of locations around the world could accommodate the pressurized greenhouse gases that the world will continue to produce.

The technology for *carbon capture and storage* (CCS) currently exists, and some small projects are currently operating in Saskatchewan and in the United States. But the process is quite expensive, and there remains considerable doubt regarding the extent to which the process can be scaled up to the degree necessary for CCS to play a large role in the reduction of global GHG emissions.

Significant Policy Challenges

If climate change is the greatest market failure the world has ever seen, then it may also represent the largest scope for government intervention that has ever existed. It is one thing to suggest a role for government policy but quite another to design a set of policies that achieves the objectives in an effective manner. Our brief discussion of climate-change policy examines separately the complexity of international negotiations, the outlines of coherent policy, and the current state of policy in Canada.

International Negotiations   As we said earlier, meeting through the UN-sponsored process, all countries have now agreed to design a legally binding emissions-reduction agreement by 2015, to be implemented by 2020. The details of this agreement are not yet determined, however, and importantly, it is not clear *who* will be responsible for *how much* emissions reduction. There is a powerful tension here between the developed and the developing nations.

The developed countries argue that in order for their domestic voters to accept stringent emissions-reductions policies, the developing countries must be seen to be equally committed to slowing and eventually reducing their own GHG emissions. The rich-country voters do not want the developing countries to be "free riding" on their costly actions.

The developing countries respond by pointing out that the vast majority of the greenhouse gases emitted over the past century have come from the developed countries and that it is unfair to expect developing countries to now slow their rate of economic advance. They argue that they should be allowed to continue their process of economic development while the rich countries take on the primary responsibility of reducing global GHG emissions. They also suggest that if the richer countries feel so strongly about reducing GHG emissions in the developing world, then the rich countries should be prepared to pay for it—by making large financial contributions to the developing countries to help finance the adoption of non-emitting technologies.

The developed countries respond in two ways. First, they point out that the structure of the world economy is changing dramatically, and that over the next 50 years, the lion's share of GHG emissions will come from the developing world, not the developed world. This is partly due to the higher rates of economic growth in the developing world and partly due to the greater reliance on energy-intensive production in those economies. Second, and not surprisingly, the developed economies respond by suggesting that they have only limited public funds that can be transferred to the developing countries.

In short, the international climate-change negotiations contain a fascinating but complex set of challenges, including many details that have not been discussed here. But most economists agree that the global nature of the climate-change problem requires a global policy solution. It is therefore important that these negotiations continue and culminate in an effective international agreement.

Mark Garten/United Nations Photo Library

Climate change is a global challenge. Complex negotiations between a large number of developed and developing countries are required to reach binding agreements regarding the reduction of global greenhouse-gas emissions.

Coherent Climate Policy   Any coherent and effective policy directed at reducing greenhouse-gas emissions is likely to incorporate two central elements: a policy that, first, places a price on GHG emissions and that, second, provides strong public support for technological development. Both elements can work to reduce the GHG intensity of our energy.

A Price on GHG Emissions.   As we saw earlier in this chapter, two policies would place a price on GHG emissions: an emissions tax and a cap-and-trade system. A tax on GHG emissions would directly increase the cost to polluters; a cap-and-trade system would force polluters to purchase costly permits in order to emit greenhouse gases.

Putting a price on GHG emissions would have two main advantages. First, by raising the price of carbon-based energy, users would be led to economize. Large cars would eventually be replaced by smaller vehicles, and carpooling and public transportation would become more attractive. The higher price of energy would also show up on electricity bills very quickly, thus providing people with a clear incentive to examine how best to reduce energy use within the home.

The second advantage of having a price on GHG emissions is that it would raise the relative price of carbon-based energy and thus make alternative, cleaner energy sources more competitive. For example, the current price of electricity in Alberta is roughly 8 cents per kilowatt hour, and much of Alberta's power is produced in coal-burning electricity plants. At this price, operators of wind turbines and solar panels cannot fully cover their costs, and thus very little of this alternative power is available. But suppose a tax on emissions raises the price of electricity to 10 cents per kilowatt hour. At this higher price, wind and solar power may be able to cover their costs, even though there has been no change in their basic technology. By forcing the owners of carbon-based energy to sell their product at a price that includes the price on GHG emissions, thereby better reflecting the relevant external costs, the producers of cleaner energy would be able to enter the market and compete.

Public Support for Technology.   The second element of an effective climate-change policy is public support for the development of non-emitting technologies. We just argued that placing a price on GHG emissions would produce incentives for firms and consumers to switch from carbon-based energy systems to cleaner, non-emitting systems. But the *amount* of adoption of non-emitting technologies will depend crucially on the relevant elasticities of supply. Especially in the short run, however, these supplies are likely to be quite inelastic (unresponsive to price increases), and so even a substantial price on emissions may have only a modest effect on the adoption and development of non-emitting technologies.

A direct boost to the adoption of these cleaner technologies can be provided with carefully designed government policies to fund research. The government could even go so far as to sponsor a "technology race," not unlike the "space race" that the United States government entered in the late 1950s. In this case, the race would be to develop technologies that could increase the scale of alternative energy sources and overcome some of their existing technical challenges, and develop cost-effective methods of capturing and safely storing greenhouse gases.

Canadian Climate-Change Policy   On several occasions in recent years, the Canadian federal government has started and then halted the development of a climate-change policy. As of early 2015, when it was clear that the country was not on track to achieve the federal government's emissions-reduction targets for 2020, no new policy had been proposed for implementation.

Each of the Canadian provinces has also established emissions-reductions targets for 2020 and, as of mid-2015, most provinces were projected to miss those targets with the policies then in place. New and more stringent policies will be required if the provinces are to achieve these targets. Even more stringent policies will be required in the longer term if Canada's GHG emissions are to fall by anything like 80 percent from current levels by 2050.

Three Canadian provinces have carbon-pricing policies in place. British Columbia implemented a carbon tax in 2008 that has been effective at reducing per capita GHG emissions. The tax rate is currently $30 per tonne of CO_2e and the policy is designed to be revenue neutral; the revenues generated by the carbon tax are used to reduce personal and business income taxes by the same amount.

Quebec has recently put in place a cap-and-trade system that applies to a large share of provincial emissions of CO_2e and is linked (for permit trading) to a similar system in California. The policy is designed to become more stringent over time as the aggregate level of the emissions cap declines gradually, thus pushing up the equilibrium price of permits. The policy is too new to determine its effectiveness in reducing GHG emissions.

Alberta has a regulatory approach that is more complex than the systems in B.C. and Quebec, though it still has elements of carbon pricing. Large industrial emitters that cannot reduce their emissions *intensity* (emissions per unit of output) below a specific threshold are required to pay a fee of $30 per tonne into a Technology Fund. The money in the fund is then used to finance the development of low-carbon technologies in the business sector. The specific design of Alberta's system has resulted in only a small share of the province's GHG emissions being priced and thus has generated only weak incentives for overall emissions reductions.

As this book went to press in the fall of 2015, Ontario was designing a province-wide cap-and-trade system for carbon pricing, one that will eventually be linked to the systems in Quebec and California. At the same time, Alberta was re-designing its system to improve its simplicity and strengthen its incentives to reduce GHG emissions.

Summary

It is essential that we recognize the likely impact of the ongoing process of climate change. It is just as important to realize that stabilizing Earth's climate, albeit at a temperature a few degrees above the current average, will require tremendous economic changes. Significant reductions in global greenhouse-gas emissions will not be achieved through a large number of small actions that are barely noticeable in our daily lives. Instead, bold but carefully designed government policies are needed to alter some of the prices that we face to better reflect the full social costs of our activities—both as consumers and as producers. Considerable resources will also have to be devoted to the development of new technologies. None of this will be simple, and real sacrifices will be involved. But these sacrifices today and in the near future may be far less than the long-term costs we will face if we do not take up the challenge now.

SUMMARY

17.1 THE ECONOMIC RATIONALE FOR REGULATING POLLUTION   LO 1

- Pollution is a negative externality. Polluting firms and households going about their daily business do harm to the environment and fail to take account of the costs they impose on others.
- In a market that produces pollution as a by-product, the external cost of the pollution implies that too much of the good is produced compared with what is allocatively efficient.

- The allocatively efficient level of pollution is generally not zero; it is the level at which the marginal cost of further pollution reduction is just equal to the marginal benefit of pollution reduction.
- If a firm or a household faces incentives that cause it to internalize fully the costs that pollution imposes, it will choose the allocatively efficient level of pollution.

17.2 POLLUTION-CONTROL POLICIES   LO 2, 3

- Pollution can be regulated either directly or indirectly. Direct controls are used most often. They are often inefficient because they require that all polluters meet the same standard regardless of the benefits and costs of doing so.
- Efficient pollution abatement requires that the marginal cost of abatement is equated across firms. This can be achieved with market-based policies, such as emissions taxes or tradable pollution permits.
- Emission taxes work by requiring polluters to pay a tax per unit of pollution produced. The tax becomes the

marginal benefit of pollution abatement to the firms. Since all firms face the same tax per unit of pollution, their profit-maximizing behaviour will bring about efficiency in pollution abatement.
- Tradable pollution permits work by the government issuing permits to firms and then allowing those permits to be freely traded. The market price of the permit then represents firms' marginal benefit of pollution abatement. Efficiency in pollution abatement is achieved because firms' profit-maximizing behaviour leads their marginal abatement costs to be equated.

17.3 THE ECONOMIC CHALLENGE OF GLOBAL CLIMATE CHANGE   LO 4

- There is a clear scientific consensus that the burning of fossil fuels is adding to the atmospheric concentration of greenhouse gases (GHGs) and leading to increases in average global temperatures.
- Global emissions of GHGs can be reduced by reducing global GDP, by reducing the energy intensity of GDP, or by reducing the GHG intensity of the world's energy.

- Significant reductions in world GHG emissions will likely require dramatic reductions in the GHG intensity of energy.
- Most economists agree that an effective policy for reducing GHG emissions must involve placing a price on GHG emissions. Either an emissions tax or a cap-and-trade system could be effective.

KEY CONCEPTS

Negative pollution externalities
Marginal external cost
Costs and benefits of pollution abatement

The efficient level of pollution
Direct pollution controls
Emissions taxes

Tradable pollution permits (cap and trade)
Global climate change
Greenhouse-gas emissions

STUDY EXERCISES

MyEconLab   Make the grade with MyEconLab: Study Exercises marked in ⊕ can be found on MyEconLab. You can practise them as often as you want, and most feature step-by-step guided instructions to help you find the right answer.

❶ Consider the following costs and benefits associated with cleaning up a polluted city lake.

Cleanliness of Water (%)	Marginal Cost ($)	Marginal Benefit ($)
0	50 000	550 000
20	100 000	400 000
40	160 000	300 000
60	230 000	230 000
80	350 000	180 000
100	infinite	150 000

a. Explain why the marginal cost of pollution reduction increases as the cleanliness of the water increases. Plot the *MC* curve in a diagram.
b. Explain why the marginal benefit of pollution reduction falls as the cleanliness of the water increases. Plot the *MB* curve in the same diagram.
c. What is the optimal level of water cleanliness?
d. Explain why the efficient level of pollution is greater than zero.

❷ Fill in the blanks to make the following statements correct.

a. When there are pollution externalities associated with the production of steel, _____ marginal costs of steel production exceed _____ marginal costs of steel production.
b. By imposing a _____ on the production of steel, the externality can be _____.
c. If the tax is chosen to be exactly equal to the _____, the externality can be completely internalized. The result will be that private firms produce the _____ level of steel (and pollution).

❸ Fill in the blanks to make the following statements correct.

a. Suppose the Canadian government announced that all homeowners must insulate their homes with R-40 insulation. As a pollution-control policy, this is an example of _____.
b. Suppose the Canadian government announced a tax of $2.50 per litre of home heating oil consumed. As a pollution-control policy, this is an example of _____.
c. Suppose the Canadian government distributed coupons to all homeowners allowing them to burn specified amounts of fossil fuels for home heating, and allowed homeowners to buy and sell these coupons. As a pollution-control policy, this is an example of _____. A _____ would develop for these coupons.

❹ Consider the market for lumber, which we assume here to be perfectly competitive.

a. Suppose that for each unit of lumber produced, the firms also generate $10 of damage to the environment. Draw the social marginal cost curve in the diagram.
b. What is the allocatively efficient level of lumber output? Explain.
c. Describe and show the new market outcome if lumber producers are required to pay a tax of $10 per unit of lumber produced. Explain.
d. In part (c), does the equilibrium price of lumber rise by the full $10 of the tax? Explain.

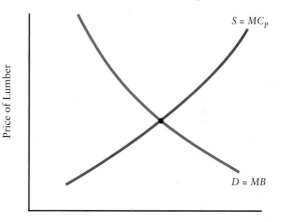

❺ A large urban hospital produces solid waste. The table below shows the hospital's marginal cost of reducing waste and the marginal benefit to society of doing so.

Tonnes of waste abated	MC($)	MB($)
1st	1000	4000
2nd	1500	3800
3rd	2000	3500
4th	3000	3000
5th	4500	2000
6th	7000	200

a. Draw a scale diagram of the marginal costs and benefits of reducing solid waste.
b. What is the socially optimal amount of waste to abate?
c. What is the net benefit to society of abating the socially optimal amount of waste?
d. What is the net benefit to society of abating the final tonne of waste if the hospital abates 6 tonnes?

6 The following diagram shows society's marginal benefit and marginal cost for abating a particular type of pollution—say greenhouse-gas emissions.

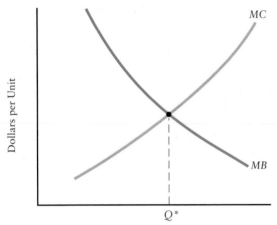

Amount of Pollution Abatement

a. Explain why the marginal cost curve is upward sloping.
b. Explain why the marginal benefit curve is downward sloping.
c. At Q^*, are all greenhouse-gas emissions eliminated? Explain.
d. Is there an "optimal" level of greenhouse-gas emissions? Explain.

7 The runoff from agricultural fertilizers contains compounds that damage local watersheds. Suppose the private marginal costs of production and the demand (marginal benefit) in the market are as follows:

$$MC_P = 20 + 0.5Q$$

$$MB = 50 - 0.25Q$$

The social marginal cost of production is:

$$MC_S = 30 + 0.75Q$$

a. What level of output will be produced in a competitive free market?
b. What is the allocatively efficient level of output?
c. What is the marginal external cost at the competitive free-market equilibrium?
d. What is the marginal external cost at the allocatively efficient level of output?
e. What level of emissions tax ($ per unit produced) would lead to the allocatively efficient level of output?

8 Suppose there are only two firms—Softies Inc. and Cuddlies Inc.—producing disposable diapers. Both firms are releasing dioxins into the same river. To reduce the pollution, the regulatory agency must choose between using direct controls and emissions

Abatement by Softies Inc.

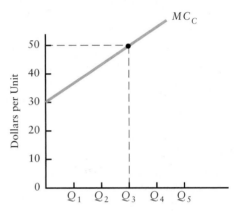

Abatement by Cuddlies Inc.

taxes. The following diagrams show each firm's marginal cost of pollution abatement.

a. Suppose the regulatory agency requires that the two firms each abate Q_3 units of pollution. What is each firm's marginal abatement cost at Q_3?
b. Could the total cost of this amount of pollution abatement be reduced? Explain how.
c. Now suppose the regulatory agency instead imposes an emissions tax of $40 per unit of emissions. Explain why this tax can be thought of as each firm's "marginal benefit of abatement."
d. In part (c), how much pollution will each firm choose to abate?
e. Is it possible to reduce the total cost of the amount of abatement being done in part (d)?

9 Suppose the government issues a fixed quantity, Q^*, of tradable pollution permits, each one permitting the emission of one tonne of sulphur dioxide. Use the accompanying figure to help answer the following questions.

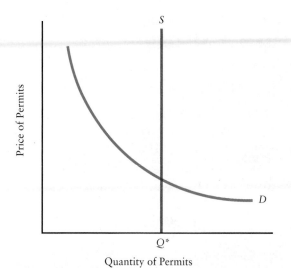

Quantity of Permits

a. Explain what determines firms' demand for permits.
b. If there is a competitive market for pollution permits, explain why the equilibrium price of the permit will equal firms' marginal abatement cost.
c. Explain why the equilibrium price of permits will fall if polluting firms experience a technological improvement that reduces their marginal abatement costs.
d. One advantage of tradable pollution permits is that they allow the public to express their preferences for pollution reduction through the market. What happens if Greenpeace decides to buy a large number of pollution permits and "retire" them?

10 Fill in the blanks to make the following statements correct.
a. The emission of greenhouse gases is a good example of a(n) _____ externality. Firms and individuals have not internalized the _____.
b. Geographically, the _____ externalities associated with greenhouse gas emissions are a(n) _____ problem, which was the motivation behind the _____ of 1997.
c. It is estimated that, in order to stabilize Earth's climate, the annual flow of global GHG emissions must fall by approximately _____ percent from its current level.
d. Most economists believe that it is necessary to impose a(n) _____ on GHG emissions, which would force polluters to _____ the externality. Two market-based policy options to achieve this outcome are a(n) _____ and a(n) _____ system.

11 The following identity shows the three essential components of the world's annual emissions of greenhouse gases:

$$GHG = \frac{GHG}{Energy} \times \frac{Energy}{GDP} \times GDP$$

a. Explain the meaning of the first component, GHG/Energy.
b. Explain the meaning of the second component, Energy/GDP.
c. Explain why world GDP is likely to continue growing over time. How is this related to world population growth?
d. Explain why the second term is likely to fall over time but by less than the growth in world GDP.
e. Given your answers to parts (c) and (d), what is the implication for the path of GHG/Energy if overall GHG emissions are to be reduced significantly?

12 The European Union has a system for tradable permits for the emission of greenhouse gases. The authorities initially set the cap on emissions at a level that was expected to generate a permit price of about 20€ per tonne of emissions, and during the early 2000s the equilibrium price was close to 20€.
a. During the global recession of 2008–2009, many European firms reduced their output of goods and services. Why would this also reduce their demand for emission permits?
b. Could this explain why the market price for permits fell to as low as 7€ per tonne during this period? Explain.
c. Some commentators have argued that the observed price volatility within the European trading system shows that a cap-and-trade system does not work in practice, even though it has theoretical appeal. Does a properly functioning cap-and-trade system display constant permit prices? Why or why not?
d. Is there a particular problem associated with volatile permit prices in a cap-and-trade system? (Hint: Consider firms' incentives to make investments in either using or developing non-emitting technologies.)

13 The federal government has imposed many regulations aimed at reducing the pollution that is generated by driving. The more familiar regulations are direct—mandatory catalytic converters, fuel-efficiency standards, and the like.
a. Given the discussion in the chapter, why do you think the government opted for such direct controls?
b. Can you think of any indirect controls currently in use to reduce automobile pollution?
c. The federal government is also considering using direct controls to regulate the emission of greenhouse gases. Can you think of a *political* reason why the government might prefer direct controls over either emissions taxes or tradable emission permits?

18 Taxation and Public Expenditure

CHAPTER OUTLINE	LEARNING OBJECTIVES (LO)
	After studying this chapter you will be able to
18.1 TAXATION IN CANADA	1 describe the main taxes in use in Canada.
18.2 EVALUATING THE TAX SYSTEM	2 explain why a tax can lead to allocative inefficiency.
18.3 PUBLIC EXPENDITURE IN CANADA	3 discuss the concept of fiscal federalism in Canada.
	4 describe Canada's major social programs.
18.4 EVALUATING THE ROLE OF GOVERNMENT	5 consider the costs and benefits of government intervention in the economy.

IN Chapter 16, we saw some of the reasons the scope of government is so extensive. Taxation is needed to finance government expenditures, and also plays a policy role in its own right. Both taxes and government expenditure affect the distribution of income—some people are taxed more than others and some people benefit more from government programs than others. Moreover, taxation and public expenditure influence the allocation of resources. In some cases, government policy is carefully designed with such effects in mind; in other cases, the effects are unintended byproducts of policies pursued for other purposes.

In this chapter, we examine the various sources of government tax revenues and the various types of government expenditures. We examine how to evaluate a tax system, emphasizing the distinction between equity and efficiency. The types of public expenditures in Canada are examined along with the important concept of fiscal federalism. Finally, we briefly discuss Canada's main social programs, which account for approximately 65 percent of the total spending of governments in this country.

18.1 TAXATION IN CANADA

Governments at all levels in Canada—federal, provincial, and municipal—use a complex array of taxes to collect revenue. Some are highly visible, like the GST or income tax, while others are levied directly on producers and we may not even be aware of them. We pay tax on what we earn, what we own, and on what we spend. The resulting tax revenues for all levels of government combined are almost $750 billion each year. Table 18-1 shows the revenue raised by the different types of taxes in 2014.

At almost 38 percent of GDP, Canada lies roughly in the middle of other developed countries in terms of total government revenues as a share of GDP. Among the major industrialized countries, Denmark and Norway collect over 55 percent of GDP in taxes and non-tax revenues. The lowest-tax industrialized countries are Japan and the United States, which each collect about 34 percent of GDP in government revenues.

Progressive Taxes

Before discussing details about the Canadian tax system, we examine the concept of *progressivity* of taxes.

When the government taxes one income group in society more heavily than it taxes another, it influences the distribution of income. The effect of taxes on the distribution of income can be summarized in terms of *progressivity*. A **progressive tax** takes a larger percentage of income from high-income people than it does from low-income people. A **proportional tax** takes amounts of money from people in direct proportion to their

progressive tax A tax that takes a larger percentage of income at higher levels of income.

proportional tax A tax that takes a constant percentage of income at all levels of income.

TABLE 18-1 Total Revenues of Canadian Governments, 2014

	Billions of Dollars	Percent of GDP
Taxes on income, profits, and capital gains	$292.5	14.8
Consumption taxes (GST, provincial sales taxes, and excise taxes)	144.2	7.3
Property and related taxes	61.8	3.1
Other taxes	4.4	0.2
Health and social insurance premiums	104.5	5.3
Total tax revenues	$607.4	30.7
Non-tax revenues (sales of goods and services, investment income)	137.9	7.0
Total government revenues	$745.3	37.7

Canadian governments (at all levels) collect over $745 billion from various sources, almost 38 percent of GDP. These data show total tax revenues for all levels of government combined. Notice that Canadian governments have considerable revenue, almost $140 billion in 2014, from non-tax sources.

(*Source:* Adapted from Statistics Canada, Table 385-0032.)

regressive tax A tax that takes a greater percentage of income at lower levels of income.

incomes—for example, every individual might pay 10 percent of his or her income in taxes. A **regressive tax** takes a larger percentage of income from low-income people than it does from high-income people.

Note that the progressivity or regressivity of a tax is expressed in terms of *shares* of income rather than absolute dollar amounts. Thus, a tax that collects $1000 from each individual clearly collects the same dollar amount from everybody, though it collects a higher share of income from low-income people than from higher-income people. A tax of this type is therefore a regressive tax. It is often called a *lump-sum tax*, one that is the same at all levels of income.

average tax rate The ratio of total taxes paid to total income earned.

marginal tax rate The fraction of an additional dollar of income that is paid in taxes.

The progressivity of a tax involves an important distinction between the average tax rate and the marginal tax rate. The **average tax rate** is the percentage of income that the individual pays in taxes. The **marginal tax rate** is the percentage *of the next dollar* earned that the individual pays in taxes. Progressivity of a tax requires an *average* tax rate that rises with income; we will see in this chapter that such progressivity can be achieved with either rising or constant marginal tax rates.

Progressive taxes play an important role in an overall tax and expenditure system designed to redistribute some income toward lower-income individuals. Since a progressive tax collects more from high-income individuals than it does from those with low incomes, a progressive tax system can achieve more redistribution than can proportional or regressive ones. Let's now go on to examine the various elements of the Canadian tax system.

The Canadian Tax System

Taxes are collected by the federal government, by each of the provinces, and by thousands of cities and towns. Here is a brief guide to the most important taxes in Canada.

tax bracket A range of taxable income for which there is a constant marginal tax rate.

Personal Income Taxes   Personal income taxes are paid directly to the government by individuals. The amount of tax any individual pays is the result of a fairly complicated set of calculations. All types of income are included in what is called total income, although certain types of income qualify for total or partial exemption. Then a number of allowable deductions are subtracted from total income to determine taxable income. The most important deduction is called the "basic personal amount" and in 2015 was equal to $11 138. Once taxable income is calculated, the amount of tax payable is then computed by applying different tax rates to different levels of income. There are four federal personal income tax rates, each applying within what is called a tax bracket. In 2015, the four **tax brackets** and marginal tax rates within each bracket were as follows:

- $0–$44 701: marginal tax rate = 15 percent
- $44 702–$89 401: marginal tax rate = 22 percent
- $89 402–$138 586: marginal tax rate = 26 percent
- $138 587 and over: marginal tax rate = 29 percent

To see how to compute the amount of taxes payable with this system of tax brackets, we consider Christine, who has a taxable income of $100 000. To the federal government she pays at a rate of 15 percent on the first $44 701 of taxable income ($6705), at a rate of 22 percent on her next $44 700 ($9834), and at a rate of 26 percent on her last $10 599 (=$100 000 - $89 401) of income ($2756). Since her taxable income is less than $138 587, she never enters the highest tax bracket and therefore does not face the 29 percent tax rate. Christine's total federal tax payable is therefore $19 295. Recalling the definition of average and marginal tax rates, Christine's *average* tax rate is 19 295/100 000 or 19.3 percent. Her *marginal tax rate*—the rate on an additional dollar of income—is 26 percent.

The four federal personal income-tax rates do not represent the complete taxation of personal income in Canada because the provincial and territorial governments also tax personal income. Quebec operates its own income-tax system, whereas the other nine provinces simply use the federal tax base (and federally distributed tax forms) to calculate provincial income taxes according to their own legislated income-tax rates. In all provinces other than Quebec, taxpayers pay a single amount to the Canada Revenue Agency (CRA), which then distributes the total between the federal government and each province according to the amount collected from residents of that province.

The Canada Revenue Agency, with headquarters in the Connaught Building in Ottawa, is the government department that collects all federal tax revenues in Canada.

The provincial taxation of income implies that Canada's highest marginal income-tax rate is not the highest *federal* rate, 29 percent. As of 2015, the highest combined (provincial plus federal) marginal tax rates varied from a low of 39 percent in Alberta to 55 percent in Quebec.

Corporate Income Taxes   The federal corporate income tax is a flat-rate (proportional) tax on profits as defined by the taxing authorities. As of 2015, the federal corporate income-tax rate for large businesses was 15 percent; provincial rates vary somewhat but the average is about 12 percent. Small businesses—those with business income below $500 000 per year—are taxed at lower rates by both the federal and (most) provincial governments.

Some corporate after-tax profits get distributed as dividends to shareholders. These dividends represent the shareholder's share of after-tax profits and would ordinarily be taxed along with his or her other income. To avoid double taxation on this income, however, individual shareholders get a personal income-tax credit for their share of the corporate tax already paid by the firm. In this way, the corporate and personal income-tax systems are said to be *integrated*.

When governments in Canada consider changes to income-tax rates, a debate usually occurs regarding which taxes should be changed: personal income taxes or corporate income taxes. Some people argue that corporate income-tax rates are already too low and that firms are not paying their "fair share" of the tax burden. Others argue that corporate taxes end up being paid partly by firms' customers and employees, and partly by the individuals who own shares in firms, which now include most individuals through some form of employer-sponsored or self-administered pension plan. In addition, they argue that corporate taxes, by reducing the rate of return on investment, impede the economy's long-run growth.

EXTENSIONS IN THEORY 18-1

Who Really Pays the Corporate Income Tax?

As we saw in Chapter 7, there are two different measures of a firm's profit—*accounting* profit and *economic* profit. Accounting profit is the difference between the firm's revenues and its explicit costs, such as labour, materials, overhead, and depreciation. The same firm's economic profit would also take into account the opportunity costs of the owner's time and financial capital. Since there are additional costs included, economic profits are less than accounting profits. As it turns out, the burden of the corporate income tax depends crucially on which measure of profit is used as the basis for the tax.

Let's examine two alternative taxes: one that applies to economic profits and another that applies to accounting profits. To illustrate the two taxes, we consider an imaginary firm that produces hockey equipment—Canada Hockey Inc. (CHI), located in Brampton, Ontario. Suppose in 2016 CHI earns accounting profits of $1.5 million. Also suppose the opportunity cost of the owner's capital and time is $1.1 million. Once these opportunity costs are considered, CHI's economic profits are equal to $400 000.

A Tax on Economic Profits

Recall that *economic* profits are the return to the owner's capital over and above what could be earned elsewhere. Specifically, CHI's $400 000 of economic profits represents the firm's return to its capital in excess of what that capital could earn in the (equally risky) next-best alternative investment. If CHI faces a 30 percent corporate tax

that applies to its economic profits of $400 000, it will pay $120 000 in corporate taxes, and it will still have after-tax economic profits equal to $280 000. Since CHI is still earning positive economic profits—that is, it is still earning more than it could earn elsewhere—it has no incentive to leave this industry.

In fact, the firm has no incentive to do anything differently than it was doing previously—the tax on the firm's economic profit has *no effect* on the firm's output, prices, employment, or long-run investment choices. Before the tax, CHI was making output, employment, price, and investment decisions to maximize its (economic) profits. With the tax, some fraction of these economic profits must be paid to the government, but CHI still chooses to maximize its profits by doing whatever it was doing before the tax.

The implication is that if the corporate income tax applies to *economic* profits, firms and their owners bear the entire burden of the tax. But the tax will have no effect on the allocation of resources, and in this sense the tax would be efficient.

A Tax on Accounting Profits

Now consider the alternative case in which the corporate income tax applies not to economic profit but to *accounting* profit. CHI's *accounting* profits are $1.5 million, which are greater than (and include) its economic profits. If CHI faces a 30 percent corporate tax on accounting profits of $1.5 million, it will pay

---

Extensions in Theory 18-1 discusses taxes on corporate income and highlights the important difference between taxing *accounting* profits and *economic* profits—a distinction we first saw in Chapter 7.

Taxes on Expenditure   As we first saw in Chapter 4, an *excise tax* is a tax levied on a particular commodity. In many countries, such goods as tobacco, alcohol, and gasoline are singled out for high rates of excise taxation. Because these goods usually account for a much greater proportion of the expenditure of lower-income than higher-income groups, the excise taxes on them are regressive. A *sales tax* applies to the sale of all or most goods and services. All provinces except Alberta impose a retail sales tax. Such a tax is mildly regressive, because poorer families tend to spend a larger proportion of their incomes than richer families. Both excise and sales taxes are often referred to as

$450 000 in corporate taxes. CHI's after-tax accounting profits will now be $1.05 million. But the presence of the corporate tax does not change the opportunity cost of the owner's capital and time; when including these costs ($1.1 million), CHI's economic profits are −$50 000. Negative economic profits indicate that the owner's capital is now earning less than what is available in the (equally risky) next-best alternative investment. In this situation, CHI may soon leave this industry.

Negative economic profits and the exit from the industry will obviously have implications for its output and employment decisions. In particular, as CHI scales down its operations, its workers will be laid off or have their wages reduced. And as supply in this industry falls, product prices will rise until the remaining firms earn enough profits to keep them in the industry.

The bottom line is that if the corporate income tax applies to accounting profits (and results in negative economic profits), some of the burden of the tax falls on consumers and workers. Only part of the burden of the tax falls on firms and their owners. Because the tax leads to changes in the allocation of resources, it also generates some inefficiency. We will see this idea in more detail later in this chapter when we discuss what economists call the "excess burden" of taxation.

A large body of economic research suggests that the biggest burden of the corporate income tax in this case is on the economy's long-run growth. By taxing accounting profits rather than economic profits, investment in physical capital is made less attractive. The result will be lower investment in new machinery and equipment, and thus less adoption of many of the newest technologies embodied in such physical capital. The overall result for the economy is lower productivity growth and, eventually, slower growth in average living standards.

Which Tax Do We Use?

In Canada and other countries, corporations are taxed on the basis of their *accounting* profits, not their economic profits, despite the greater efficiency of the latter. Why do we use such a tax, given its inefficiency? The explanation comes down to simplicity: Accounting profits are easy to measure, whereas economic profits require an identification and measurement of the opportunity cost of the owner's time and capital. The precise identification of such opportunity costs, for each and every firm and group of owners, would be technically impossible for the tax authorities.

The end result is that the burden of the corporate tax in Canada is not borne only by firms and their owners—consumers and workers share the burden through higher product prices and lower wages. These effects are subtle but nonetheless important. Equally subtle, and probably more important, are the longer-term effects on the growth rate of the economy and Canadians' average standard of living.

"indirect" taxes to contrast them with income taxes, which are levied directly on the income of individuals or firms.

Canada has a nationwide expenditure tax, the Goods and Services Tax (GST), which applies to the sale of almost all goods and services, currently set at a rate of 5 percent. The GST has now been harmonized with the sales taxes in several provinces, in which case it is referred to as the Harmonized Sales Tax (HST), with a rate equal to 5 percent plus the rate of the province-specific component.

With the notable exception of the United States, most developed economies levy a tax similar to our GST, referred to in Europe as a *value-added tax* and in some countries as a *consumption tax*. The main advantage of the GST (and other value added taxes) is that it taxes expenditure rather than income, and for this reason it generates no disincentive to save. In contrast, since income taxes

FIGURE 18-1 **The Operation of a GST of 5%**

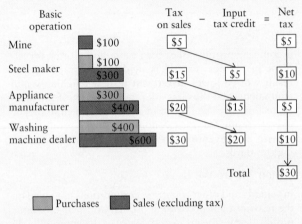

A tax on value added is the same as a tax on the value of final goods with a credit allowed for the tax paid for purchased inputs. The example is for the stages involved as iron ore is mined and then sold to a steel maker, the steel then sold to an appliance manufacturer, and the washing machine sold to a retailer and then to a consumer. The example makes the simplifying assumption that no produced inputs are used in the mining operation (so that the value of the iron ore is all value added); at all further stages, however, the use of produced inputs makes the firm's value added less than the value of final output at that stage. The steel maker's value added is $200, and its tax is thus $10; $15 on the total value of its output less the $5 credit on the taxes already paid to the mine on the value of the iron ore. Total taxes paid equal $30, which is 5 percent of the $600 value of the final product; each firm pays 5 percent of its share in creating that $600 value.

apply to all sources of income, including interest income, they tend to discourage saving.

In practice, the GST works by taxing a firm on the gross value of its output and then allowing a tax credit equal to the taxes paid on the inputs that were produced by other firms. Thus, the GST taxes each firm's contribution to the value of final output—its value added. Figure 18-1 shows how the GST is calculated at each stage from the mining of iron ore to the final retail sale of a washing machine.

Since the GST applies to expenditure rather than to income, it is mildly regressive, because the proportion of income saved, and hence not taxed, rises with income. This regressivity is reduced, however, by exempting food and, more importantly, by giving low- and middle-income households a refundable tax credit. For the lowest-income households, the GST is a progressive tax because the refundable tax credit exceeds the value of GST that they would pay even if they spent all of their incomes on taxable commodities.

Property Taxes The property tax is the most important source of revenue for Canadian municipalities, but it is quite different than the taxes we have discussed so far. Personal and corporate income taxes and expenditure taxes are all related to an actual transaction (earning income or making a purchase) whereas a property tax applies to the value of owned property.

Taxing the value of existing property creates two problems. First, someone has to assess the current market value of the property that may not have changed hands in many years. Because the assessment is only an estimate, it is always subject to challenge. Second, sometimes owners of valuable real estate property have low *incomes* and thus have difficulty paying the tax from their available funds.

The progressivity of the property tax has been studied extensively. The rich typically live in more expensive houses than the poor and thus typically pay more in property taxes. This does not mean, however, that the rich pay more property taxes *as a fraction of their total income* than the poor. Thus, it is not readily apparent that property taxes are progressive. Indeed, most studies have shown that the property tax is mildly regressive.

18.2 EVALUATING THE TAX SYSTEM

We have described several individual taxes in Canada, and in each case noted the tax's possible effects on behaviour as well as its progressivity. The overall tax *system*, however, is a complex combination of these various taxes. More important than evaluating each individual tax is evaluating the system as a whole. Economists focus on two key aspects of a tax system—efficiency and equity. Efficiency matters because governments strive to raise tax revenues in a manner that imposes the least overall cost on society. Equity matters because, as we saw in Chapter 16, governments often strive to redistribute resources toward low-income people. A natural challenge when designing an overall tax system is to raise the revenue required to finance necessary public expenditures while at the same time improving equity and achieving as efficient a system as possible. We begin by exploring how taxation can affect equity.

Taxation and Equity

Debates about income distribution and tax policy usually involve the important but hard-to-define concept of *equity*. *Equity* (or *fairness*) is a normative concept; what one group thinks is fair may seem outrageous to another. Two principles can be helpful in assessing equity in taxation: equity according to *ability to pay*, and equity according to *benefits received*.

The Ability-To-Pay Principle   Most people view an equitable tax system as being based on people's ability to pay taxes. In considering equity that is based on ability to pay, two concepts need to be distinguished.

Vertical equity concerns equity *across* income groups. Vertical equity refers to the idea that those people with a greater ability to pay tax should pay more than those with less ability to do so. The higher is your income, the more you have available after the necessities of life have been met, and thus the more you are able to pay. Thus, an ability-to-pay standard of equity requires progressive taxation.

Horizontal equity concerns equity *within* income groups. Individuals and families with the same income may have very different abilities to pay depending on their circumstances, such as the number of children to support, aging or disabled family members to care for, or extra expenses necessary for earning income. It is difficult for a tax system to account for all such factors, but some effort is made by allowing taxpayers to deduct some of these expenses from their taxable income. However, corrections like these are rough at best.

The Benefit Principle   According to the benefit principle, taxes should be paid in proportion to the benefits that taxpayers derive from public expenditure. From this perspective, the ideal taxes are *user charges*, such as those that would be charged if private firms provided the government services.

The benefit principle is the basis for the excise tax on gasoline, since gasoline usage is closely related to the services obtained from using public roads. The benefit principle may also explain high taxes on cigarettes, since smokers tend to require more health-care services that, in Canada, are mostly provided by government. Although there are other examples, especially at the local level, the benefit principle has historically played only a minor role in the design of the Canadian tax system. But its use is growing in Canada and elsewhere as governments seek new ways to finance many of their expenditures. For example, two decades ago Statistics Canada supplied data for free to anybody who wanted it. Now, Statistics Canada charges on a "cost recovery basis" for any data other than the most general data, which it makes available on its website. So instead of covering the cost of producing the data from the general taxpayer, some costs are recovered from those who use it. The benefit principle can be easily applied to some government-provided goods and services. But it is difficult to see how the benefit principle could be applied to many of the most important categories of government spending. Who gets how much benefit from national defence, interest on the public debt, the judicial system, or environmental protection?

How Progressive Is the Canadian Tax System?   Assessing how the entire tax system affects the distribution of income is complicated by two factors. First, the progressivity of the system depends on the mix of the different taxes. Federal taxes tend to be somewhat progressive; the progressivity of the income-tax system and the use of a low-income GST tax credit more than offset the regressivity of the federal GST. Provincial and municipal governments rely heavily on sales and property taxes and thus have tax systems that are probably slightly regressive.

Second, income from different sources is taxed at different rates. For example, in the federal personal income tax, income from royalties on oil wells is taxed less than income from royalties on books, and profits from sales of assets (capital gains) are taxed less than wages and salaries. To evaluate progressivity, therefore, one needs to know how different *levels* of income are related to different *sources* of income.

> **Many economists have concluded that the overall Canadian tax system is roughly proportional for middle-income classes and mildly progressive for low- and high-income persons.**

Taxation and Efficiency

The tax system influences the allocation of resources by altering such things as the relative prices of various goods and factors and the relative profitability of various industries. Individual taxes shift consumption and production toward goods and services that are taxed relatively lightly and away from those that are taxed more heavily. This alteration of free-market outcomes often affects allocative efficiency.

Of course, in a world with no taxes, it would be impossible to pay for the government programs and public goods that we desire as a society. In practice, then, the relevant objective for tax policy is to design a tax system that minimizes inefficiency, *holding constant the amount of revenue to be raised*. In designing such a tax system, a natural place to start would be with taxes that both raise revenue and enhance efficiency. An example of such a tax is the pollution emissions tax that we discussed in Chapter 17. Unfortunately, such taxes cannot raise nearly enough revenue to finance all of government expenditure.

In the following discussion we examine how taxes affect the economy's allocation of resources. We focus on the effects of expenditure taxes and income taxes since these are the main taxes used by Canadian governments to raise revenues.

The Two Burdens of Taxation   A tax normally does two things. It takes money from the taxpayers, and it changes their behaviour. The money taken away from taxpayers is used to finance government activity. So, while the money taken from taxpayers, called the **direct burden** of the tax, is clearly a cost to taxpayers, it is *not* a cost to society overall; it is merely a transfer of resources within the economy.

direct burden For an individual tax, the amount of money that is collected from taxpayers.

When a tax changes behaviour, however, there are costs to taxpayers as well as to society overall. The cost that results from the induced changes in behaviour is called the **excess burden** and reflects the allocative inefficiency or *deadweight loss* of the tax.[1]

excess burden The allocative inefficiency or deadweight loss generated by a tax.

> The direct burden of a tax is the amount paid by taxpayers. The excess burden reflects the allocative inefficiency of the tax.

Figure 18-2 shows an example that illustrates this important distinction. Suppose your provincial government imposes a $2 excise tax on the purchase of compact discs. Suppose further that you are a serious music lover and that this tax does not change your quantity demanded of CDs—that is, your demand for them is perfectly inelastic and hence you continue to buy your usual five CDs per month. In this case, you pay $10 in excise taxes per month, and you therefore have to reduce your consumption of other goods (or your saving) by $10 per month.

The direct burden to you of this excise tax is $10 because that is what you pay to the government in taxes. There is no excess burden to you because the tax does not cause you to reduce your purchases of CDs. The absence of any excess burden from this tax is just another way of saying that there is no allocative inefficiency; the cost of raising $10 a month for the provincial government is just the $10 a month that you pay in taxes. In this case, the tax is *purely* a redistribution of resources from you to the government.

FIGURE 18-2   Direct and Excess Burdens of an Excise Tax

The allocative inefficiency of a tax is measured by its excess burden. The excess burden is greater the more elastic is demand. Part (i) shows your demand for CDs. It is perfectly inelastic at five CDs per month. When the government imposes an excise tax of $2 per CD, the price rises from $15 to $17. Your quantity demanded is unchanged, so you pay $10 per month in taxes ($2 tax per CD × 5 CDs). The direct burden of the tax is $10; but because your quantity of CDs demanded is unchanged, there is no excess burden.

Part (ii) shows your friend's demand. Her quantity demanded falls from two CDs per month to zero as a result of the tax. Since she pays no tax (because she buys no CDs), she bears no direct burden of the tax. But because she has lost consumer surplus, she bears an excess burden from the tax.

Part (iii) shows the entire market demand. There is both a direct burden, the red shaded area, and an excess burden, the purple shaded area. The more elastic is the demand curve, the larger is the excess burden of the tax.

---

[1] Note that some taxes change behaviour and correct a market failure, as in the environmental taxes discussed in Chapter 17. In these cases, the tax *improves* allocative efficiency. Our discussion of excess burden applies to situations where a tax is imposed in an otherwise efficient market.

FIGURE 18-3   Direct and Excess Burdens of an Income Tax

An income tax generates both a direct and an excess burden. Without an income tax, the labour-market equilibrium has employment of L_0 and a wage of w_0. An income tax shifts the supply of labour curve upward. The result is an increase in the pre-tax wage to w_1 and a reduction in the level of employment to L_1. The tax revenue generated is the red area; this is the direct burden of the income tax. The tax also generates a deadweight loss, as shown by the purple area; this is the excess burden of the income tax.

Now suppose a friend of yours is also a music lover but is not quite as dedicated—she has a downward-sloping demand curve for CDs. The tax leads her to cut back on her consumption of CDs from two per month to none. In this case, your friend pays no taxes and therefore experiences no reduction in her overall purchasing power. The direct burden of the tax is therefore zero. However, your friend is still worse off as a result of this tax. She is worse off by the amount of consumer surplus that she would have received had she made her usual purchases of two CDs per month. In this case, the direct burden is zero (because no tax is paid) but there *is* an excess burden equal to her loss in consumer surplus from the two CDs per month that she no longer enjoys.

When an excise tax is imposed, some people behave like the music buff and do not change their consumption of the taxed good at all, others cease consuming the taxed good altogether, and most simply reduce their consumption. There will be an excess burden for those in the latter two groups. Thus, the revenue collected will *understate* the total cost to taxpayers of generating that revenue.

The same basic analysis applies to income taxes. Figure 18-3 shows the effect of levying a tax on workers' incomes. The income tax shifts the labour supply upward because workers will be prepared to supply any given amount of labour services only if the pre-tax wage is increased to offset the effect of the tax.

The income tax generates both a direct burden and an excess burden. The tax raises revenue by collecting some percentage of workers' wages. This is a cost borne by both workers and firms. By reducing the equilibrium level of employment and creating a deadweight loss, the income tax also creates an excess burden. As with the case of excise taxes, the revenue collected by the tax understates the total cost of the tax.

> **Excise taxes and income taxes impose costs in two ways. By taking resources from market participants (consumers, firms, workers), they impose a direct burden. By reducing the volume of specific market transactions, they also generate a deadweight loss—this is the excess burden of the tax.**

Efficient and Equitable Taxation   An efficient tax is one that raises a given amount of revenue (the direct burden) while minimizing the size of the excess burden. As can be inferred from Figures 18-2 and 18-3, the efficiency of either an excise tax or an income tax is related to the relevant demand and supply elasticities.

For example, as Figure 18-2 shows, the excess burden of an excise tax is smaller when the demand for the product is less elastic. In the extreme case of a perfectly inelastic demand, the excess burden of an excise tax is zero; the tax raises revenue but leads to no reduction in consumption of the specific product. Unfortunately, because the demand for many of life's necessities (such as food) is very inelastic, a tax system that was based only on imposing excise taxes on goods with inelastic demands would prove to be very regressive.

Many economists argue that taxing income is more efficient *and* more equitable than imposing large numbers of excise taxes on products. The greater efficiency of the income tax comes from the fact that the supply of labour is relatively inelastic with respect to the real wage. Figure 18-3 shows that an income tax does generate an excess burden. But if the labour supply curve is very steep—as most empirical evidence suggests—the excess burden is small, and the income tax is therefore relatively efficient. The greater equity of the income tax comes from the fact that it can be designed to be either proportional or progressive, thus permitting some redistribution from high-income households to low-income households.

Disincentive Effects of Income Taxes   Our discussion of income taxes, and the illustration in Figure 18-3, shows how an income tax affects workers' incentives. If an increase in the income-tax rate leads to a reduction in the amount of work effort, it is possible that total tax revenue might actually *fall* as a result.

FIGURE 18-4   A Laffer Curve

Increases in income-tax rates beyond some level will decrease rather than increase tax revenues. The curve relates the government's tax revenue to the tax rate. As drawn, revenue reaches a maximum level of R_0 at the tax rate t_0. If the tax rate were t_1, then reducing it to t_0 would increase the government's tax revenue.

This possibility is illustrated in Figure 18-4, which shows what economists call a *Laffer curve*, named after well-known U.S. economist Arthur Laffer.

The reasoning behind the general shape of the Laffer curve is as follows. At a zero tax rate, no revenue would be collected. As rates are raised above zero, some revenue will be gained. But as rates continue to rise, revenue will eventually fall because the very high tax rates will lead people to work less and less. At a tax rate of 100 percent, they will not bother to work at all (because all of their income would go to the government) and so tax revenue will again be zero. It follows that there must be *some* tax rate, greater than zero and less than 100 percent, at which tax revenue reaches a maximum.

Figure 18-4 is drawn under the assumption that there is a steady increase in tax revenue as tax rates rise to t_0, and a steady decrease in tax revenues as tax rates continue to rise toward 100 percent. This particular shape—with a single peak in tax revenues—is not necessary. But the precise shape is beside the point. The key point is that there is *some* tax rate like t_0 that maximizes total tax revenue. And therefore tax rates above or below t_0 will generate less tax revenue than the amount raised at t_0.

In Canada and the United States, it is not uncommon to hear heated debates regarding the appropriate level of income-tax rates. In such debates, one side will often cite the logic of the Laffer curve, arguing that a reduction in tax rates will lead to such an increase in economic activity that total tax revenues will rise. This outcome is possible, but by no means guaranteed. Revenue will only increase if current tax rates are so high as to be above t_0 in Figure 18-4. The problem is that we do not know for sure where t_0 is, although some recent research in the United States suggests that t_0 may be as high as 80 percent, far above current tax rates.

18.3 PUBLIC EXPENDITURE IN CANADA

Spending by the consolidated public sector—which includes federal, provincial, and municipal governments—is currently about 40 percent of Canadian GDP. Table 18-2 gives the distribution of consolidated government spending across a number of major *functions*

TABLE 18-2 **Expenditures by Canadian Governments, 2009**

Category of Spending	Billions of Dollars	Percent of GDP
General government services	22.8	1.5
Protection of persons and property	50.8	3.2
Transportation and communication	32.2	2.1
Health	121.6	7.8
Social services	190.3	12.2
Education	95.7	6.1
Resource conservation, environment, and industrial development	36.9	2.4
Recreation and culture	16.3	1.0
Housing	6.1	0.4
Labour, employment, and immigration	2.4	0.2
Foreign affairs and international aid	6.5	0.4
Debt charges	43.6	2.8
Other expenditures	6.0	0.4
Total spending	631.3	40.3

Expenditures on health, social services, and education together make up almost 65 percent of total government expenditure. These data show the various categories of spending by all levels of government combined.

(*Source:* Adapted from Statistics Canada, "Consolidated Government Revenue and Expenditures," www.statcan.gc.ca.)

for 2009. These data are now over six years old, but unfortunately Statistics Canada no longer collects data on the functional spending categories of Canadian governments. Fortunately, however, while the total dollar spending in each category generally rises over time as the economy grows, the spending in each category as a share of GDP tends to be roughly constant, at least over periods of just a few years. So the second column in the table still gives us a very good indication of how Canadian governments are spending their resources.

As can be seen in Table 18-2, health care, education, and social services are very large items; collectively, they make up roughly 65 percent of total government spending. Interest on the public debt makes up about 7 percent of total spending. The remaining 28 percent covers everything else, from police protection and sanitation to general administration of government, environmental protection, and foreign aid.

Table 18-2 does not show which of the three levels of government actually do the spending. For example, of the $95.7 billion spent on education in 2009, the vast majority was spent by provincial and municipal governments. In contrast, expenditures on national defence and foreign aid are made exclusively by the federal government. Expenditures on social services are about equally divided between the federal and provincial governments, with only a small role played by the municipalities. Another thing that Table 18-2 does not show is the important distinction between the purchase of goods and services by government, and *transfers* that are made to individuals or firms.

Government Purchases and Transfers

The government *purchases* goods and services and provides them to the public, as when the government pays for physicians' services, highway repair, primary and secondary education, and so on. Included in this category of expenditures are the salaries that the government pays to its employees. Also included is the interest that governments pay on their outstanding stock of debt. A government's stock of debt is equal to the accumulation of its past budget deficits, where the deficit is the excess of spending over revenues.

transfer payment A payment to an individual, a firm, or an organization that is not made in exchange for a good or service.

The government also makes **transfer payments**. These are payments to individuals, firms, organizations, or other levels of government that are *not* made in exchange for a good or a service. For example, when the federal government pays employment insurance benefits to an unemployed individual, the government is not getting any good or service in return. Similarly, when provincial governments give money to universities to finance part of their operating costs, it is getting nothing in return. Table 18-3 shows total government transfers to *individuals*, which totalled $205 billion in 2014, about 26 percent of total government spending and roughly 10 percent of national income.

Canadian "Fiscal Federalism"

Canada is a federal state with governing powers divided between the central authority and the ten provinces and three territories. Municipalities provide a third level of government, whose powers are determined by the provincial legislatures. Understanding the fiscal interaction of the various levels of government is central to understanding the nature of government expenditure in Canada. In this section, we examine the concept of *fiscal federalism*; in the next section we examine how fiscal federalism affects the operation of Canada's social programs.

The Logic of Fiscal Federalism   The essence of Canadian fiscal federalism is the recognition that Canada is a country with many different fiscal authorities (federal, provincial, and municipal governments) that need a certain amount of coordination to be responsive to the needs and desires of the citizens—who are free to move from one area to another. Four main considerations are important in understanding Canada's system of fiscal federalism.

1. Differences in Tax Bases.   Canadian provinces vary considerably in terms of their average levels of prosperity. Alberta and Saskatchewan are currently well above the national average (as measured by per capita GDP) whereas Prince Edward Island and Nova Scotia are below the average. Ontario is slightly below the national average of about $52 000 per person.

In order to provide services as varied as medical care, highways, and judicial systems, the provincial governments must levy various types of provincial taxes. Provinces that are more prosperous, and thus have larger tax bases, are able to provide a given amount of services while having relatively low tax rates. In contrast, less affluent provinces with smaller tax bases would only be able to provide the same amount of services if they had higher tax rates, but excessive tax rates create their own problems, as we saw earlier.

One of the guiding principles in Canada's system of fiscal federalism is that individuals, no matter where they live, should have approximately the same access to what is regarded as a reasonable level and quality of public services and should face approximately the same tax rates to finance those services. Since revenue sources do not always match revenue needs at each level of government, some transfers *between* governments are necessary. We examine these transfers shortly.

2. Geographic Scope of Services.   Because the government of a province or a municipality is unlikely to be responsive to the needs of citizens outside its

TABLE 18-3   Government Transfer Payments to Individuals, 2014

	Billions of Dollars
Federal Government	96.9
Child Tax Benefit	10.3
War pensions and veterans' allowances	2.5
Employment Insurance benefits	15.8
Old Age Security payments	44.0
Grants to Aboriginal persons	7.1
GST tax credit	4.7
Other transfers	12.5
Provincial Governments	53.1
Current transfers to households	39.9
Grants to non-profit institutions	12.0
Other transfers	1.2
Local Governments	5.5
Canada/Quebec Pension Plan	49.4
Total Transfers	204.9

(*Source:* Adapted from Statistics Canada, "Government Transfer Payments to Persons," www.statcan.gc.ca.)

jurisdiction, some public services may not be provided adequately unless responsibility for them is delegated to the level of government appropriate to the scope of the service provided. For example, national defence is normally delegated to the central government because it provides benefits to all residents of the country. At the other extreme is fire protection. If fire protection is to be effective, it is necessary to have fire stations serving small geographic areas. Accordingly, responsibility for fire stations lies with municipal governments.

3. Regional Differences in Preferences.   The delegation of some functions to lower levels of government may provide a political process that is more responsive to regional differences in preferences for public versus private goods. Some people may prefer to live in communities with higher-quality schools and police protection, and they may be prepared to pay the high taxes required. Others may prefer lower taxes and lower levels of services. The differences in provincial tax rates that we noted earlier partially reflect each provincial government's own view of the appropriate level of taxation.

4. Administrative Efficiency.   Administrative efficiency requires that duplication of the services provided at different levels of government be minimized and that related programs be coordinated. For this reason, in all provinces except Quebec, income taxes are reported on a single form and paid to the federal government, which then remits the appropriate share of those taxes to the relevant provincial government. This coordination avoids the administrative burden that would exist if each province had its own tax-collection system.

Intergovernmental Transfers   Canada's system of fiscal federalism requires transfers between various levels of government. Some of these transfers are purely administrative, such as when the federal government collects provincial income taxes on behalf of the provinces (except Quebec) and then remits the funds back to the provinces. Other transfers, however, are federal funds given to the provinces to help them finance particular programs in their jurisdictions, such as health care and education. Still other transfers of federal funds are made to provinces that are less prosperous than the average, and these funds are unrestricted in their use.

Canada Health and Social Transfers.   The federal government makes two block grants to each provincial and territorial government every year—one for expenditures on health care and the other for expenditures on post-secondary education, social assistance, and early learning and childcare. Though the Canada Health Transfer (CHT) and the Canada Social Transfer (CST) are each described as being directed at these specific categories of expenditure, there is no practical way to prevent provincial governments from spending this money on whatever they deem to be appropriate. These block grants are financial support with "no strings attached."

The CHT and CST are allocated to provinces on an equal per capita basis. The total CST payment is scheduled to grow annually at the rate of 3 percent, and in 2015–2016 the total amount to all provinces was $13 billion. The total CHT payment is scheduled to grow more quickly to accommodate the rapidly growing demands on Canada's public health-care system. In 2015–2016, the total CHT payment was $34 billion, and it was scheduled to grow at a 6 percent annual rate until 2017. After 2017, the CHT will grow at the rate of national income which is expected to be about 4.5 percent annually.

Equalization Payments.   The Constitution of Canada, which was formally amended and repatriated from the United Kingdom in 1982, explicitly includes a provision for less prosperous provinces to receive **equalization payments** from the federal government. The Constitution states that "Parliament and the government of Canada are committed to the principle of making equalization payments to ensure that provincial governments have sufficient revenues to provide reasonably comparable levels of public

equalization payments Transfers of funds from the federal government to the low-income provinces.

services at reasonably comparable levels of taxation." Since the federal government collects revenues from economic activity generated in *all* provinces, and uses this revenue to support the lower-income ones, the equalization program is effectively a redistribution program from high-income to low-income provinces. Equalization payments are calculated by a complicated formula that involves five different revenue sources: personal income taxes, corporate income taxes, GST, property taxes, and natural resource taxes. From their inception in 1957, equalization payments have increased significantly. In the 2015–2016 fiscal year, total equalization payments were forecast to be $17.3 billion.

Canadian Social Programs

Table 18-2 shows that government spending on health, education, and other social services represents roughly two-thirds of total government spending in Canada. Given their obvious fiscal importance, it is worth briefly reviewing Canada's major social programs.

Some social programs are universal, in the sense that they pay benefits to anyone meeting only such minimal requirements as age or residence. These are referred to as **demogrants**. Other programs are selective, in the sense that they pay benefits only to people who qualify by meeting specific conditions, such as having young children, having very low income, or being unemployed. When these conditions are related to the individual's income, the term **income-tested benefits** is used.

In this section we examine the five pillars of Canadian social policy: education, health care, income support, employment insurance, and retirement benefits.

demogrants Social benefits paid to anyone meeting only minimal requirements such as age or residence; in particular, not income-tested.

Income-tested benefits Social benefits paid to recipients who qualify because their income is less than some critical level.

Education   Public education, one of the earliest types of social expenditure in Canada, remains one of the most important. It has been supplemented over the years by numerous other public programs aimed at developing human capital. All levels of education are the responsibility of provincial governments, although the federal government makes the CST transfers to the provinces to finance part of the costs.

Primary and Secondary Education.   Basic education is publicly financed for both efficiency and equity reasons. In terms of efficiency, a literate and numerate population is necessary for an informed electorate that can participate in democratic society. Therefore, society as a whole is better off when all its citizens have at least a basic level of education. The equity argument is based on the fact that basic skills acquired in primary and secondary schools are usually necessary in order for individuals to secure careers that can provide reasonable incomes. If basic education were not financed by the government, many low-income households could not afford to send their children to school. The result in many cases would be a vicious circle of poverty in which children from low-income families would lack basic education and thus secure only poor jobs and earn only low incomes themselves.

Post-Secondary Education.   In Canada, universities are public institutions, and university education is heavily subsidized by government. In 2013, total revenues for universities and colleges were $33.6 billion, with 51 percent coming from various levels of government. Only 24 percent came from student tuition fees and the remaining 25 percent came from various other sources.

There is both an efficiency argument and an equity argument for subsidizing higher education. The efficiency argument is based on the claim that there are positive externalities from higher education—that is, that the country as a whole benefits when a student receives higher education. In many cases these externalities cannot be internalized by the students receiving the education, so, left to their own maximizing decisions, students who had to pay the full cost of their education would choose less than the socially

Brian Sytnyk/Masterfile

Roughly half of the operating revenues of Canadian universities comes from provincial governments. Only a quarter of revenues comes from students' tuition fees. There is an active debate in Canada about how much students should be paying toward the full costs of their post-secondary education.

optimal amount. The equity argument is that if students were forced to pay anything like the full cost of the services they receive, a university education would become prohibitively expensive to low- and even middle-income families. Government subsidies help provide education according to ability rather than according to income.

Proponents of charging higher tuition fees to finance a larger fraction of the costs of running universities start with the observation that the value of many kinds of post-secondary education is internalized and recaptured in higher incomes earned by the recipients later in their life. This is particularly true of professional training in such fields as law, medicine, dentistry, management, and computer science (although students in these fields typically pay a smaller proportion of their real education costs than students in the arts do, where the argument for externalities is greatest). Further, subsidized education does represent a significant income transfer from taxpayers to students, even though the average taxpayer may have a lower income than the average post-secondary student can expect to earn in the future.

Health Care   In Canada, basic health care is financed mainly by the provincial governments, with significant transfers from the federal government under the CHT. In most provinces, residents pay nothing to receive medical attention—health care is free to users and is financed out of the government's general tax revenues. Though health care is publicly financed, physicians and private hospitals working on a "fee for service" basis form the core of Canada's health-care delivery system. Thus, the Canadian health-care system is based on public *financing* but private *delivery*.

Health care is financed by government for reasons of both efficiency and equity. The efficiency argument is much the same as for basic education—a healthy population is as important to the smooth functioning of a democratic country as is an educated one. The equity argument is even more powerful: Most people believe that basic health care is so important that denying it to people who cannot afford it would be unacceptable. But even when this equity argument is generally accepted, there is still a decision as to what and how much to provide for free.

Cost Containment.   Taking federal and provincial payments into account, Canada's public health-care system is the country's single most expensive social program. In 2014, government expenditure on health care was just over $150 billion, over 19 percent of total government expenditure and 7.8 percent of GDP. Private spending on health care brought total spending up to over 11 percent of GDP. In other words, more than one out of every nine dollars in income produced in the Canadian economy is spent on health care. This ratio is expected to rise as the baby-boom generation continues to age, and increases the average age and health-care needs in the Canadian population.

"Cost containment" in the health-care sector has become a priority for most provincial governments and the debate currently rages over what reforms would be effective and acceptable. Most observers agree that some type of expenditure-controlling reform is urgently needed. Unfortunately, agreement stops there.

The Role of the Private Sector.   Much of the debate over the reform of Canada's health-care system rests on the appropriate role of the private sector in what is a publicly financed system. Some provincial governments, notably Quebec and Alberta, have suggested that allowing a greater role for private, for-profit hospitals and clinics can reduce waiting lists and therefore improve the overall quality of health care that citizens receive.

The main concern with allowing a greater role for private clinics and hospitals is that private hospitals may begin "extra billing" their patients. In this case a "two-tiered" health-care system would develop in which individuals with higher incomes would have faster access to health care than would individuals with lower incomes. If extra billing becomes a feature of private hospitals and clinics, then only those individuals who can afford to pay the extra fees will be able to use them. Furthermore, it is argued that many nurses and doctors who are currently within the financially strapped public health-care system may move to the private facilities if salaries or working conditions are better there. The overall concern, therefore, is that the

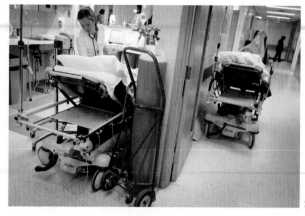

Dramatically rising costs in Canada's publicly financed health-care sector represent a serious challenge for Canadian governments.

introduction of private hospitals and clinics into the existing public health-care system, while reducing waiting lists and providing more health-care services overall, may result in a high-quality system for the wealthy and a low-quality system for lower-income people. People who take this view argue that such a two-tiered health-care system would destroy the equity that the public system was initially designed to promote.

Advocates of allowing a greater role for private hospitals and clinics argue that, to a significant extent, Canada already has a two-tiered system. For example, for such services as laser eye surgery and diagnosis with MRIs, private clinics have existed for several years; people have a choice between waiting in line for service in the public hospitals, sometimes for many months, or going to a private clinic immediately and paying for the service. They also argue that two-tier systems do not seem to lead to major health-care inequalities in the countries of the European Union, most of which operate some form of two-tier system.

Income-Support Programs   Canada has various programs that provide assistance for people in dire financial need—these programs constitute what is often called the "social safety net." The overriding objectives of this safety net are to reduce poverty and increase individuals' sense of economic security. Though no longer as prevalent as it was in Canada's past and still is in many other countries, poverty remains a matter of real concern to Canadian policymakers.

Statistics Canada defines the **poverty line** or *low-income cutoff* as the level of income below which the typical household spends more than 63 percent of its income on the three necessities of food, shelter, and clothing. (The average Canadian household spends only 43 percent of its income on these three necessities.) Not surprisingly, this poverty line varies depending on the size of the family and where it lives. In 2012, Statistics Canada's estimated poverty line for a family of four living in a major urban centre was $43 942. A family of four with pre-tax income less than this amount would be defined to be living in poverty. In 2012, 9.7 percent of families had incomes below Statistics Canada's estimated poverty line. This percentage includes some of the working poor, whether stuck in low-paying jobs or doing their first job; some who were not working at all; and some whose incomes were only temporarily below the poverty line, such as students or trainees.

There is considerable debate, however, about the methods used to estimate poverty. Central to this debate is whether poverty is best viewed as an *absolute* or a *relative* concept. If poverty is viewed as an absolute concept, then anybody without enough income

poverty line An estimate of the annual family income that is required to maintain a minimum adequate standard of living.

to purchase a certain amount of food, shelter, and clothing is said to be in poverty. With such an absolute definition of poverty, sufficient growth in the economy could, at least in principle, eliminate poverty entirely as low-income households eventually see their income rise above the threshold level.

With a *relative* definition of poverty, however, there will *always* be some families defined to be poor. For example, suppose households are defined to be poor whenever their income is less than 50 percent of the economy's average household income. Since any realistic distribution of income will contain *some* households whose income is less than 50 percent of the average, there will always be some poverty when it is defined this way. Advocates of a relative measure of poverty argue that poverty is more than just the absence of enough food and clothing—it is also the social exclusion from mainstream society that typically comes from having much lower income than most households. (Recall our discussion of income inequality in Chapter 14.)

Whatever the precise definition, all experts agree that many Canadians live in poverty. Canada has several income-support programs designed to address this important problem. First, we will discuss welfare and child benefits, both designed to assist individuals and families whose incomes are deemed to be too low to provide an adequate standard of living. Next, we will look at employment insurance, which is designed to assist those in need because of temporary job loss. Finally, we examine retirement benefits designed to provide income assistance to the elderly.

Welfare.   Social assistance for individuals below retirement age, usually called *welfare*, is mainly a provincial responsibility in Canada. The details of the programs vary considerably across the provinces even though they are partly financed by transfers received from the federal government under the CST.

One important problem with welfare occurs with what are called *poverty traps*. **Poverty traps** occur whenever the tax-and-transfer system results in individuals having very little incentive to increase their pre-tax income because such an increase would make them ineligible for some financial benefits and might even make them worse off overall. Current research on the Canadian tax system shows that some Canadian families with incomes of approximately $20 000 are in this situation. The presence of such poverty traps reflects a tax-and-transfer system that has been modified in many small steps over many years, the result of which is a plethora of programs often working at cross-purposes. The elimination of poverty traps requires that the tax-and-transfer system be examined in its entirety rather than on a piecemeal basis. *Applying Economic Concepts 18-1* discusses one possible reform of the tax-and-transfer system that maintains progressivity of the system while eliminating poverty traps. This is the idea of the "negative income tax."

poverty trap Occurs whenever individuals have little incentive to increase their pre-tax income because the resulting loss of benefits makes them worse off.

Child Benefits.   The Canada Child Tax Benefit is a federal non-taxable payment to parents of children under 18 and varies according to the number of children in the family and family income. For families with net income of $40 000, the benefit pays about $170 per month per child under the age of 18. There is an extra payment for third and additional children. The benefit declines as the family's net income rises, and disappears altogether for net incomes above $160,000. For families with very low incomes (below $24 000 per year) there are additional child-support payments.

In addition to these income-tested programs, there is also a taxable federal Universal Child Care Benefit which pays parents $160 per month for each child under the age of six plus $60 per month for each child aged 6 through 17. The payments are taxed in the hands of the lower-earning parent. Some provinces also have child benefits that are separate from and in addition to these federal programs.

APPLYING ECONOMIC CONCEPTS 18-1

Poverty Traps and the Negative Income Tax

The underlying principle of the negative income tax (NIT) is that a family of a given size should be *guaranteed* a minimum annual income. The tax system must be designed, however, to guarantee this income without eliminating the household's incentive to be self-supporting.

As an example, consider a system in which each household is guaranteed a minimum annual income of $10 000 and the marginal tax rate on all earned income is 40 percent. Money can be thought of as flowing in two directions; the government gives every household $10 000, and then every household remits 40 percent of any *earned income* back to the government. The *break-even* level of earned income in this example is $25 000. All households earning less than $25 000 pay negative taxes overall; they receive more money from the government than they remit in taxes. Households earning exactly $25 000 pay no net taxes—their $10 000 from the government exactly equals the taxes they remit to the government on their earned income. All households earning more than $25 000 pay more than $10 000 in taxes so they are paying *positive* taxes overall.

The figure shows the operation of this scheme by relating earned income on the horizontal axis to after-tax income on the vertical axis. The red 45° line shows what after-tax income would be if there were no taxes.

The blue line shows after-tax income with an NIT. It starts at the guaranteed annual income of $10 000, rises by 60 cents for every one dollar increase in earned income, and crosses the 45° line at the break-even level of income, $25 000. The vertical distance between the two lines shows the net transfers between the household and the government.

Note that the NIT is a progressive tax, despite the *constant* marginal income-tax rate. To see this, note that a household's *average* tax rate is equal to the total taxes paid divided by total earned income. If I_E is earned income, then

$$\text{Average tax rate} = \frac{(0.40) \times I_E - 10\,000}{I_E}$$

$$= (0.40) - \frac{10\,000}{I_E}$$

The average tax rate for the household rises as earned income rises, but the average tax rate is *always less* than the marginal tax rate (40 percent). That the average tax rate rises with earned income means that higher-income households pay a larger fraction of their income in taxes than is paid by lower-income households—that is, the NIT is progressive.

Supporters of the NIT believe that it would be an effective tool for reducing poverty. The NIT provides a minimum level of income as a matter of right, not of charity, and it does so without removing the work incentives for people who are eligible for payments; every dollar earned adds to the after-tax income of the family. Poverty traps are avoided.

A step toward the NIT was taken in 2007 with the introduction of the Working Income Tax Benefit (WITB). The WITB is aimed at low-income working Canadians and is designed to reduce the marginal income-tax rate and thereby provide greater incentives for low-income people to increase their labour-force participation. The WITB works by offering a *refundable tax credit* for every dollar earned within a specific range. A *refundable* tax credit means that even if the individual pays no income tax, the credit would result in money being paid to (refunded to) the individual. The WITB is a small but important step toward the reduction of poverty traps in Canada.

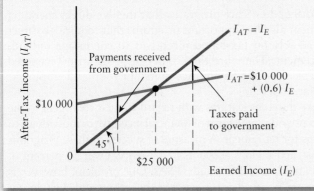

Employment Insurance   Employment insurance (EI) is a federal program designed to provide temporary income support to workers who lose their jobs. Employers and employees remit EI premiums to the government equal to a small percentage of wages and salaries. These premiums then finance the EI payments to unemployed workers who qualify for the benefits. In boom times, when there is little unemployment, the total amount of EI premiums collected exceeds the total amount dispersed as EI benefits; in times of high unemployment, the benefits exceed the premiums. As a result, the EI program is approximately self-financing over the duration of the average six-to seven-year business cycle.

In its current form, the EI system provides workers with incentives to remain in seasonal jobs and in areas with poor employment prospects for longer than would otherwise be the case. In some extreme cases, the individuals are accused of taking EI-financed "holidays". That the EI system encourages behaviour that increases unemployment and reduces regional mobility does not mean that the unemployed themselves are responsible for the abuses of the system that sometimes occur. The responsibility lies with those who designed the incentives and those who strive to preserve them. They can alter the system to make it deliver the intended benefits with fewer incentives for undesired behaviour.

Retirement Benefits   There are three components of the system of retirement benefits. These are the Canada Pension Plan (CPP), retirement income-support programs such as Old Age Security (OAS) and Guaranteed Income Supplement (GIS), and tax-assisted saving plans.

The Canada Pension Plan (CPP).   The CPP provides a basic level of retirement income for all Canadians who have contributed to it over their working lives. A separate but similar scheme exists in Quebec—the Quebec Pension Plan or QPP. Unlike some private programs, the pension provided by the CPP is *portable*—changing jobs does not cause any loss of eligibility.

Retirement Income-Support Programs.   Two programs provide benefits to the elderly in Canada. First, the Old Age Security (OAS) benefit is a monthly payment of $564 that goes to all Canadians over age 65 with an annual income of less than $116 103, a cut-off that provides some element of income testing. The OAS benefit is further income tested because it begins to be recaptured by a tax "clawback" for individuals with incomes above $71 592. Second, the Guaranteed Income Supplement (GIS) is a more explicitly income-tested benefit specifically targeted to low-income elderly Canadians. The GIS provides for most of the progressivity in the elderly benefits system. Over the past few decades, these two programs have together played a central role in significantly reducing poverty among Canada's elderly.

Tax-Assisted Saving Plans.   The OAS and GIS are programs that involve direct spending by the government. The government also has important programs that require no direct government spending but instead rely on tax-based incentives to encourage individuals to save more for their retirement. There are three types of programs: Registered Retirement Savings Plans (RRSPs), Tax-Free Saving Accounts (TFSAs), and employer-sponsored Registered Pension Plans (RPPs).

While the three programs have different features with regard to their treatment in the tax system, they are all designed to provide some form of financial incentive to individuals to increase their own personal savings for retirement. A measure of success of these programs is the high number of these tax-assisted savings accounts in existence. Over 50 percent of Canadian taxpayers contribute regularly to RRSPs and TFSAs. One problem, however, is that Canadians with low-incomes are not well-represented in this group and thus do not receive the considerable benefits that accrue to middle and higher-income Canadians.

18.4 EVALUATING THE ROLE OF GOVERNMENT

Earlier we stated that it is more informative to assess the progressivity of the overall tax system than any individual tax. It is even more informative to assess the progressivity of the combination of taxes and expenditures—that is, the entire tax-expenditure system. For example, a tax-expenditure system could be highly progressive even if all taxes were proportional, as long as government expenditures and transfers accounted for a higher portion of real incomes of the poor than of the rich. The evidence is that the overall Canadian tax-expenditure system is progressive and succeeds in successfully narrowing the inequalities of income generated by the market.

Even if there is widespread agreement that the Canadian tax-expenditure system helps to produce a more desirable distribution of income, there is nonetheless considerable disagreement regarding the appropriate scale of government activity in the economy.

Public Versus Private Sector

When the government raises money by taxation and spends it on an activity, it increases the spending of the public sector and decreases that of the private sector. Since the public sector and the private sector spend on different things, the government is changing the allocation of resources. Is this change good or bad? Should there be more schools and fewer houses or more houses and fewer schools? More generally, should we have more private consumption and fewer public goods, or less private consumption and more public goods?

John Kenneth Galbraith's 1958 book, *The Affluent Society*, proclaimed that a correct assignment of marginal utilities would show them to be higher for an extra dollar's worth of public parks, clean water, and education than for an extra dollar's worth of TVs, shampoo, or cars. In Galbraith's view, the political process often fails to translate preferences for public goods into effective action; thus more resources are devoted to the private sector and fewer to the public sector than would be the case if the political mechanism were as effective as the market. He lamented the resulting "private opulence and public squalor." Many economists would argue that Galbraith's observations are even truer today, almost 60 years after he first published them.

An alternative view has many supporters who agree with Nobel Laureate James Buchanan that society has reached a point where the value of the *marginal* dollar spent by government is less than the value of that dollar left in the hands of households or firms. Advocates of this view argue that because bureaucrats are spending other people's money, they care very little about a few million or billion dollars here or there. They have only a weak sense of the opportunity cost of public expenditure and, thus, tend to spend beyond the point at which social marginal benefits equal social marginal costs.

Scope of Government Activity

One of the most difficult problems for the student of the Canadian economic system is to maintain the appropriate perspective about the scope of government activity in the market economy. On the one hand, one can look at the thousands of laws, regulations, and policies that affect firms and households and decide that a general reduction in the role of government would be desirable. On the other hand, private decision makers still have an enormous amount of discretion about what they do and how they do it.

One danger is to become so concerned with the many ways in which government activity impinges on the individual that one

In his classic book The Affluent Society, *the late John Kenneth Galbraith argued that Western democracies often undervalue public goods and place too much value on private consumption. He lamented the resulting contrast between "private opulence" and "public squalor."*

fails to see that these various government activities nonetheless leave individuals free to make the vast majority of their own decisions in a market system. It is in the private sector that most individuals choose their occupations, earn their living, spend their incomes, and live their lives. In this sector, too, firms are formed, choose products, live, grow, and sometimes die.

The opposite danger is to fail to see that a significant share of the taxes paid by the private sector is used to buy goods and services that add to the welfare of individuals. By and large, the public sector complements the private sector, doing things the private sector would leave undone or would do differently. For example, Canadians pay taxes that are used to finance expenditures on health and education. But certainly Canadians would continue to use hospitals and attend schools even if the various levels of government did not provide these goods and instead left more money in people's pockets. Thus, in many cases, the government is levying taxes to raise money to finance goods that people would have purchased anyway. To recognize that we often benefit directly from government spending, however, in no way denies that it is often wasteful, and sometimes worse.

Evolution of Policy

Public policies in operation at any time are not the result of a single master plan that specifies precisely where and how the public sector will seek to complement or interfere with the workings of the market mechanism. Rather, as individual problems arise, governments attempt to meet them by passing appropriate legislation to deal with the problem. These laws stay on the books, and some become obsolete and unenforceable. This pattern is generally true of systems of law.

Many anomalies exist in our economic policies; for example, laws designed to support the incomes of small farmers have created some agricultural millionaires, and commissions created to ensure competition between firms often end up creating and protecting monopolies. Neither individual policies nor whole programs are above criticism.

In a society that elects its policymakers at regular intervals, however, the majority view on the amount of government intervention that is desirable will have some considerable influence on the amount of intervention that actually occurs. Fundamentally, a free-market system is retained because it is valued for its lack of coercion and its ability to do much of the allocating of society's resources better than any known alternative. But we are not mesmerized by it; we feel free to intervene in pursuit of a better world in which to live. We also recognize, however, that sometimes government intervention has proved ineffective or even counterproductive.

SUMMARY

18.1 TAXATION IN CANADA

LO 1

- Although the main purpose of the tax system is to raise revenue, tax policy is potentially a powerful device for income redistribution because the progressivity of different kinds of taxes varies greatly.
- The most important taxes in Canada are the personal income tax, the corporate income tax, excise and sales taxes (including the nationwide GST), and property taxes.

- The progressivity of a tax is determined by how the average tax rate (taxes paid divided by income) changes as income changes. If the average tax rate rises as income rises, the tax is progressive. If the average tax rate falls as income rises, the tax is regressive.

18.2 EVALUATING THE TAX SYSTEM

- Evaluating the tax system involves evaluating the efficiency and progressivity of the entire system, rather than of individual taxes within the system.
- The total Canadian tax structure is roughly proportional, except for very low-income and very high-income groups (where it is mildly progressive).
- Taxes often generate allocative inefficiency. The allocative inefficiency of a tax is measured by the excess burden.

Because of the excess burden, a tax is more costly than just the amount paid by the taxpayers (the direct burden).

- There are potentially important disincentive effects of taxation, as represented by a Laffer curve. After some point, increases in the tax rate reduce the incentive to produce taxable income, and thus reduce tax revenue.

18.3 PUBLIC EXPENDITURE IN CANADA

- A large part of public expenditure is for the provision of goods and services. Other types of expenditures, including subsidies, transfer payments to individuals, and intergovernmental transfers, are also important.
- Fiscal federalism is the idea that the various fiscal authorities should be coordinated in their spending plans and should have a mechanism for transfers between the various levels of government.

- The five pillars of Canadian social policy are

  1. Education
  2. Health care
  3. Income support programs (welfare and child benefits)
  4. Employment insurance
  5. Retirement benefits (CPP, GIS, OAS, and tax-assisted saving plans)

18.4 EVALUATING THE ROLE OF GOVERNMENT

- Government taxation and expenditure have a major effect on the allocation of resources. The government determines how much of society's total output is devoted to education, health care, highways, the armed forces, and so on.
- When evaluating the overall role of government in the economy, we should keep three basic issues in mind:
  1. What is the appropriate mix between public goods and private goods?

  2. Much government activity is directed to providing goods and services that add directly to the welfare of the private sector.
  3. We should continually re-evaluate existing programs; some that were needed in the past may no longer be needed; others may have unintended and undesirable side effects.

KEY CONCEPTS

Progressive, proportional, and regressive taxes
The benefit principle and the ability-to-pay principle

Vertical and horizontal equity
Direct and excess burdens of a tax
Disincentive effects of taxation
Transfer payments to individuals

Fiscal federalism
Intergovernmental transfers
Canadian social programs

STUDY EXERCISES

MyEconLab Make the grade with MyEconLab: Study Exercises marked in ⊕ can be found on MyEconLab. You can practise them as often as you want, and most feature step-by-step guided instructions to help you find the right answer.

⊕ 1 Fill in the blanks to make the following statements correct.

a. Suppose you earn an annual income of $22 500 and you paid a total of $3600 in taxes. Your average tax rate is _____.

b. Suppose you earn an annual income of $22 500 and each dollar earned is taxed at the same rate. Your marginal tax rate is the same as _____.

c. Suppose the marginal tax rate on the first $25 000 of income is 20 percent, and on any income above that, the rate rises to 30 percent. If your annual income is $42 000, you will pay total income tax of _____.

d. Lower-income groups typically spend a higher proportion of their income than do higher-income groups. For this reason, excise and sales taxes are considered to be somewhat _____.

e. The most important source of revenue for municipalities is the _____ tax. Rather than being a tax on income or expenditure, it is a tax on _____.

❷ Fill in the blanks to make the following statements correct.

a. Evaluating a tax system requires consideration of the following two aspects of taxation: _____ and _____.

b. Taxation usually causes allocative inefficiency because it distorts the equality between marginal _____ and marginal _____ of a given activity.

c. Economists refer to the revenue collected as a result of a tax as the _____ burden of taxation. Economists refer to other costs imposed on society because of the tax as the _____ burden of taxation.

d. An efficient tax system is one that collects a given amount of revenue while minimizing the amount of _____.

e. The Laffer curve suggests that above some tax rate, further increases in the tax rate will _____ tax revenue.

❸ Consider an income-tax system that has four tax brackets. The following table shows the marginal tax rate that applies to the income in each tax bracket.

Earned Income	Tax Rate in Bracket
Up to $20 000	0%
$20 001–$40 000	15%
$40 001–$80 000	30%
$80 001 and higher	35%

a. Compute the average income-tax rate at income levels $10 000, $20 000, and each increment of $10 000 up to $120 000.

b. What is the marginal income-tax rate for each level of income in part (a)?

c. On a graph with the tax rates on the vertical axis and income on the horizontal axis, plot the average and marginal tax rates for each level of income.

d. Is this tax system progressive? Explain.

❹ The table below provides information about two individuals, Michael and Lindsay. Assume the following:

- income tax brackets are the same as in Study Exercise 3.
- all after-tax income is either saved or spent.
- there is a sales tax of 7 percent on all goods and services.

	Michael	Lindsay
Annual pre-tax taxable income	$35 000	$400 000
Percentage of after-tax income saved	10%	40%
Income tax paid ($)		
After-tax income		
Sales tax paid ($)		
Percentage of pre-tax income paid in income tax		
Percentage of pre-tax income paid in sales tax		
Overall average tax rate		

a. Calculate the income tax and sales taxes that each individual will pay annually and complete the remainder of the table.

b. Is the income tax progressive or regressive? How do you know?

c. Is the sales tax progressive or regressive? How do you know?

d. What effect does the sales tax have on the progressivity of this tax system overall? What government policy could address this effect?

❺ The diagrams below show the market for gasoline in two countries, Midas and Neptune. In Midas, demand is perfectly inelastic; in Neptune, demand is relatively elastic. In both countries, supply is identical and upward sloping. The government in each country imposes an excise tax of $t per litre on the producers of gasoline. This tax shifts the supply curve up by $t.

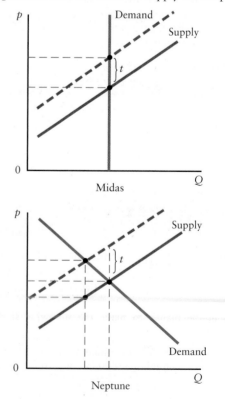

a. In each case, shade the area that is the direct burden of the tax.

b. In each case, shade the area that is the excess burden of the tax.

c. In which country does the tax cause the greater allocative inefficiency? Explain.

6 The diagram below shows the market for gasoline in two island economies, Island Flatland and Island Steephills, which have similar populations but have different elasticities of demand for the product. On each island a tax of $0.20 per litre of gasoline is imposed.

Island Flatland

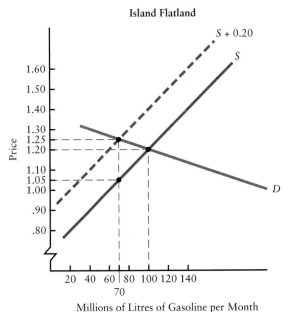

Millions of Litres of Gasoline per Month

Island Steephills

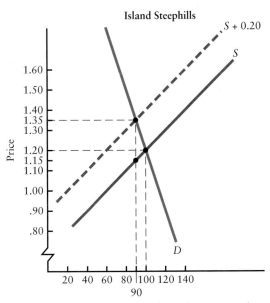

Millions of Litres of Gasoline per Month

a. What is the producers' net revenue *before* imposition of the tax on each island (in dollars)? What is their net revenue *after* imposition of the tax?

b. What is the direct burden of this tax on each island?

c. What is the excess burden of the tax on each island?

d. Is the tax more allocatively efficient on one island than another? How do you explain this?

7 In Canada, capital gains—which occur when assets are sold at prices greater than their earlier purchase price—are taxed at half the rates applicable to other income.

a. Who are the likely beneficiaries of this policy?

b. What are the likely effects on the distribution of income and the allocation of resources?

8 "Taxes on tobacco and alcohol are nearly perfect taxes. They raise lots of revenue and discourage smoking and drinking."

a. To what extent are the two effects inconsistent? (Hint: think about elasticity.)

b. How is the burden of an excise tax related to the extent to which it discourages use of the product?

9 Rank the following taxes according to which has the highest excess burden relative to the direct burden. Start with the highest. Recall that the direct burden of the tax is equal to the revenue that the tax raises.

a. An excise tax on one brand of breakfast cereal

b. An excise tax on all breakfast cereals

c. An excise tax on all food

d. An excise tax on everything

10 Classify each of the following government expenditures as either a transfer payment or a purchase of goods and services. Which ones clearly tend to decrease the inequality of income distribution?

a. Payments of wages and family living allowances to Canadian soldiers overseas

b. Employment insurance payments to unemployed workers

c. Payments to provinces for support of highway construction

d. Pensions of retired Supreme Court justices

e. Salaries paid to government workers

11 Governments in Canada, at all levels, make considerable transfer payments to individuals and to businesses. This question will show you how significant these transfer payments are. Go to Statistics Canada's website (www.statcan.gc.ca), and answer the following questions.

a. For the years 2013–2015, what were the federal transfers for employment insurance benefits?
b. Were total government transfers to individuals growing faster or slower than GDP over these years?
c. For the years 2013–2015, what were total revenues for Canada's universities and colleges?
d. In part (c), how much of these revenues came as transfers from the federal and provincial governments?

⑫ The negative income tax has been proposed as a means of increasing both the efficiency and the equity of Canada's tax system (see *Applying Economic Concepts 18-1*). The most basic NIT can be described by two variables: the guaranteed annual income and the marginal tax rate. Suppose the guaranteed annual income is $8000 and the marginal tax rate on *every dollar earned* is 35 percent. With this NIT, after-tax income is given by

After-tax income =
$$8000 + (1 - 0.35) \times \text{(Earned income)}$$

a. On a scale diagram with after-tax income on the vertical axis and earned income on the horizontal axis, draw the NIT relationship between earned income and after-tax income.
b. What is the level of income at which taxes paid on earned income exactly equal the guaranteed annual income?
c. The average tax rate is equal to total *net* taxes paid divided by earned income. Provide an algebraic expression for the average tax rate.
d. On a scale diagram with earned income on the horizontal axis and tax rates on the vertical axis, plot the average and marginal tax rates for the NIT. Is the NIT progressive?

⑬ Fill in the blanks to make the following statements correct.

a. Canada has different fiscal authorities, in the form of federal, provincial, territorial, and municipal governments. The coordination of the taxing and spending powers of these governments gives rise to our system of _____. One of the guiding principles of this system is that individuals, no matter where they live in Canada, should have access to a comparable level and quality of _____ and should face approximately the same _____.
b. The two major programs by which cash is transferred from Canada's federal government to provincial governments are _____ and _____.
c. What are the five pillars of Canada's social policy?

_____

_____

_____

_____

_____

d. Education and health care are primarily ___ responsibilities even though the _____ government makes large _____ to the provincial governments to help finance these programs.
e. Employment insurance is operated by the _____. It is designed to be approximately _____ over the course of the typical business cycle.
f. The government encourages households to save for their retirement by offering special tax treatment in _____ and _____.

⑭ It is common to read articles in the newspapers by people who think Canadians pay too much in taxes. One popular concept is "tax freedom day," the day in the year beyond which you get to keep your income rather than pay it to the government as taxes. For example, if the government collects 33 percent of GDP in taxes, then "tax freedom day" is the 122nd day of the year, May 2.

a. Does everyone in the economy have the same tax freedom day, no matter what his or her income?
b. How sensible is the concept of "tax freedom day" in a country where the government provides some goods and services to the people that they would otherwise purchase on their own, such as primary education and health-care services?

32 The Gains from International Trade

CHAPTER OUTLINE	LEARNING OBJECTIVES (LO) After studying this chapter you will be able to
32.1 THE GAINS FROM TRADE	**1** explain why the gains from trade depend on the pattern of comparative advantage. **2** understand how factor endowments and climate can influence a country's comparative advantage.
32.2 THE DETERMINATION OF TRADE PATTERNS	**3** describe the law of one price. **4** explain why countries export some goods and import others.

TRADE between peoples and nations has been going on throughout human history, and humans have gone to great lengths and endured severe hardship in order to reap the benefits of trade. Centuries ago, for example, the inhabitants of remote islands in Southeast Polynesia travelled the open ocean in canoes for days at a time to trade oyster shells, volcanic glass, basalt, and food items with inhabitants of other, distant islands.

Today, the logistics for trade may be less demanding, but the transactions themselves are no less important. Canadian consumers buy cars from Germany, Germans take holidays in Italy, Italians buy spices from Africa, Africans import oil from Kuwait, Kuwaitis buy Japanese cameras, and the Japanese buy Canadian lumber. *International trade* refers to the exchange of goods and services that takes place across international boundaries.

The founders of modern economics were concerned with the costs and benefits of foreign trade. The eighteenth-century British philosopher and economist David Hume (1711–1776), one of the first to work out the theory of the price system, developed his concepts mainly in terms of prices in foreign trade. Adam Smith (1723–1790), in *The Wealth of Nations*, attacked government restriction of international trade. David Ricardo (1772–1823) developed the basic theory of the gains from trade that we study in this chapter. The 1846 repeal of the Corn Laws—tariffs on the importation of corn and other grains into the United Kingdom—and the transformation of that country during the nineteenth century from a country of high tariffs to one of complete free trade were to some extent the result of arguments by economists whose theories of the gains from international trade led them to condemn tariffs.

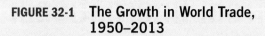

FIGURE 32-1 **The Growth in World Trade, 1950–2013**

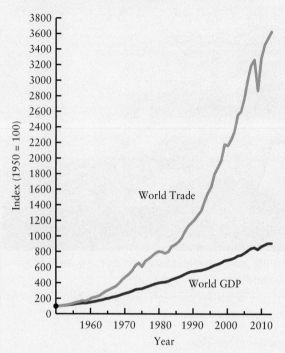

The volume of world trade has grown much faster than world GDP over the past six decades. The figure shows the growth of real GDP and the volume of trade since 1950. Both are expressed as index numbers, set equal to 100 in 1950. Real world GDP has increased more than eight times since 1950; world trade volume has increased by over 35 times. The major global recession in 2009 is clearly evident with the sharp decline in the flow of trade in that year.

(*Source:* Adapted from World Trade Organization, *International Trade Statistics 2014*, Table A1. www. wto.org.)

International trade is becoming increasingly important, not just for Canada but for the world as a whole. As Figure 32-1 shows, the volume of world trade has grown much faster than world real GDP over the past six decades. Since 1950, the world's real GDP has increased by more than eight times, an average annual growth rate of 3.6 percent. Over the same period, however, the volume of world trade has increased by more than 35 times, an average annual growth rate of 5.9 percent.

Figure 32-2 shows some data for Canadian trade in 2014. The bar chart shows the value of Canadian exports and imports of goods in several broad industry groupings. There are three important points to note from the figure. First, international trade is very important for Canada. In 2014, Canada exported $529 billion and imported $524 billion in goods—if we added trade in services, each of these values would be higher by about $100 billion; each flow (exports and imports) amounts to about 32 percent of GDP. Second, exports and imports are roughly the same size, so that the *volume* of trade is much larger than the *balance* of trade—the value of exports minus the value of imports. Third, in most of the industry groupings there are significant amounts of both imports and exports. Such *intra-industry trade* will be discussed later in the chapter. Canada does not just export resource products and import manufactured goods; it also imports many resource products and exports many manufactured goods.

In this chapter, we examine the increases in average living standards that result from international trade. We find that the source of the gains from trade lies in differing cost conditions among geographical regions. World income would be vastly lower if countries did not specialize in the products in which they have the lowest opportunity costs of production. These costs are partly determined by natural endowments (geographical and climatic conditions), partly by public policy, and partly by historical accident.

32.1 THE GAINS FROM TRADE

open economy An economy that engages in international trade.

closed economy An economy that has no foreign trade.

An economy that engages in international trade is called an **open economy**; one that does not is called a **closed economy**. A situation in which a country does no foreign trade is called one of *autarky*.

Although politicians often regard foreign trade differently from domestic trade, economists from Adam Smith on have argued that the causes and consequences of international trade are simply an extension of the principles governing trade between domestic firms and individuals. What are the benefits of trade among individuals, among groups, among regions, or among countries?

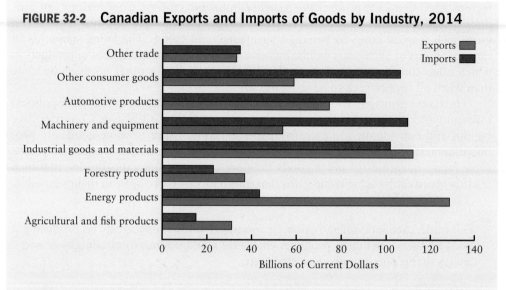

FIGURE 32-2   Canadian Exports and Imports of Goods by Industry, 2014

Canada exports and imports large volumes of goods in most industries. The data show the value of goods exported and imported by industry in 2014 (trade in services is not shown). The total value of goods exported was $529 billion; the total value of goods imported was $524 billion.

(*Source:* These data are available on Statistics Canada's website: www.statcan.gc.ca.)

Interpersonal, Interregional, and International Trade

To begin, consider trade among individuals. Without trade, each person would have to be self-sufficient: Each would have to produce all the food, clothing, shelter, medical services, entertainment, and luxuries that he or she consumed. Because no individual could effectively produce such a large range of products, a world of individual self-sufficiency would be a world with extremely low living standards: individuals would work very hard but not be able to produce or consume very much.

Trade among individuals allows people to specialize in activities they can do well and to buy from others the goods and services they cannot easily produce. A good doctor who is a bad carpenter can provide medical services not only for her own family but also for a good carpenter without the training or the ability to practise medicine. Trade and specialization are intimately connected.

Without trade, everyone must be self-sufficient; with trade, people can specialize in what they do well and satisfy other needs by trading.

The same principle applies to regions. Without interregional trade, each region would be forced to be self-sufficient. With trade, each region can specialize in producing products for which it has some natural or acquired advantage. Prairie regions can specialize in growing grain, mountain regions in mining and forest products, and regions with abundant power can specialize in manufacturing. Cool regions can produce wheat and other crops that thrive in temperate climates, and hot regions can grow such tropical crops as bananas, sugarcane, and coffee. The living standards of the inhabitants of all regions will be higher when each region specializes in products in which it has some natural or acquired advantage and obtains other products by trade than when all regions seek to be self-sufficient.

This same principle also applies to countries. A national boundary is a political invention and rarely delimits an area that is naturally self-sufficient. Countries, like regions and individuals, can gain from specialization. More of some goods are produced domestically than residents want to consume, while residents would like to consume larger quantities of other goods than are produced domestically. International trade is necessary to achieve the gains that international specialization makes possible.

> **With trade, each individual, region, or country is able to concentrate on producing goods and services that it produces efficiently while trading to obtain goods and services that it does not produce efficiently.**

Specialization and trade go hand in hand because there is no incentive to achieve the gains from specialization without being able to trade the goods produced for goods desired. Economists use the term **gains from trade** to embrace the results of both.

gains from trade The increased output attributable to the specialization that is made possible by trade.

Illustrating the Gains from Trade

Our discussion so far has emphasized the *differences* that exist between individuals, regions, and countries, and how these differences lie behind the benefits derived from trade. In order to show these benefits more precisely, we will focus on trade between two countries. We make the important assumption that within each country the average cost of production of any good is independent of *how much* of that good is produced.

absolute advantage When one country can produce some commodity at lower absolute cost than another country.

That is, we are making the assumption of *constant costs.* (We relax this assumption later.) Our example involves two countries and two products, but the general principles apply to the case of many countries and many products.

Absolute Advantage   One region is said to have an **absolute advantage** over another in the production of good *X* when an equal quantity of resources can produce more *X* in the first region than in the second. Or, to put it differently, if it takes fewer resources to produce one unit of good *X* there than in another country. Table 32-1 shows an example. The two "countries" are Canada and the European Union (EU), and the two goods are wheat and cloth. The table shows the *absolute cost* of producing one unit of wheat and one unit of cloth in each country. The absolute cost is the dollar cost of the labour, capital, and other resources required to produce the goods. Thus, the country that can produce a specific good with fewer resources can produce it at a lower absolute cost.

TABLE 32-1   Absolute Costs and Absolute Advantage

	Wheat (kilograms)	Cloth (metres)
Canada	$1 per kilogram	$5 per metre
EU	$3 per kilogram	$6 per metre

Absolute advantage reflects the differences in absolute costs of producing goods between countries. The numbers show the dollar cost of the total amount of resources necessary for producing wheat and cloth in Canada and the EU. Note that Canada is a lower-cost producer than the EU for both wheat and cloth. Canada is therefore said to have an absolute advantage in the production of both goods.

In Table 32-1, the absolute cost for both wheat and cloth is less in Canada than in the EU. Canada is therefore said to have an *absolute advantage* over the EU in the production of both wheat and cloth because it is a more efficient producer—it takes less labour and other resources to produce the goods in Canada than in the EU.

The situation in Table 32-1 is hypothetical, but it is encountered often in the real world. Some countries, because they have access to cheap natural resources or low-cost labour or more sophisticated capital equipment, are low-cost producers for a wide range of products. Does this mean that high-cost countries stand no chance of being successful producers in a globalized world of international trade? Will the low-cost countries produce everything, leaving nothing to be done by high-cost countries? The answer is no. As we will see immediately, the gains from international trade do *not* depend on the pattern of absolute advantage.

Comparative Advantage   The great English economist David Ricardo (1772–1823) was the first to provide an explanation of the pattern of international trade in a world in which countries had different costs. His theory of *comparative advantage* is still accepted by economists as a valid statement of one of the major sources of the gains from international trade. A country is said to have a **comparative advantage** in the production of good X if the cost of producing X *in terms of forgone output of other goods* is lower in that country than in another. Thus, the pattern of comparative advantage is based on *opportunity costs* rather than absolute costs. Table 32-2 illustrates the pattern of comparative advantage in the Canada–EU example. The opportunity cost in Canada for one kilogram of wheat is computed by determining how much cloth must be given up in Canada in order to produce an additional kilogram of wheat. From Table 32-1, the absolute costs of wheat and cloth were $1 per kilogram and $5 per metre, respectively. Thus, in order to produce one extra kilogram of wheat, Canada must use resources that could have produced one-fifth of a metre of cloth. So the opportunity cost of one kilogram of wheat is 0.2 metres of cloth. By exactly the same reasoning, the opportunity cost of one metre of cloth in Canada is 5.0 kilograms of wheat. These opportunity costs are shown in Table 32-2.

> **comparative advantage** When a country can produce a good with less forgone output of other goods than can another country.

Even though a country may have an absolute advantage in all goods (as Canada does in Table 32-1), it *cannot* have a comparative advantage in all goods. Similarly, even though a country may be inefficient in absolute terms and thus have an absolute disadvantage in all goods (as is the case for the EU in Table 32-1) it *cannot* have a comparative disadvantage in all goods. In Table 32-2, Canada has a comparative advantage in the production of wheat because Canada must give up less cloth to produce one kilogram of wheat than must be given up in the EU. Similarly, the EU has a comparative advantage in the production of cloth because the EU must give up less wheat in order to produce one metre of cloth than must be given up in Canada.

TABLE 32.2	**Opportunity Costs and Comparative Advantage**
Canada:	opportunity cost of 1 kg of wheat = 0.2 m cloth
EU:	opportunity cost of 1 kg of wheat = 0.5 m cloth
Canada:	opportunity cost of 1 m of cloth = 5 kg wheat
EU:	opportunity cost of 1 m of cloth = 2 kg wheat

Comparative advantages reflect opportunity costs that differ between countries. The opportunity costs are computed using the data provided in Table 32-1. For example, for Canada to produce one additional kilogram of wheat, it must use resources that could have been used to produce 0.2 metres of cloth; the opportunity cost of 1 kg of wheat in Canada is therefore 0.2 metres of cloth. The comparative advantages for each country are shown by the shaded rows. Canada has a comparative advantage in wheat production because it has a lower opportunity cost for wheat than does the EU. The EU has a comparative advantage in cloth because its opportunity cost for cloth is lower than that in Canada.

TABLE 32-3   **The Gains from Specialization**

Changes from each country producing more units of the product in which it has the lower opportunity cost		
	Wheat (kilograms)	Cloth (metres)
Canada	+5.0	−1.0
EU	−4.0	+2.0
Total	+1.0	+1.0

Whenever opportunity costs differ between countries, specialization can increase the world's production of both products. These calculations show that there are gains from specialization given the opportunity costs of Table 32-2. To produce five more kilograms of wheat, Canada must sacrifice 1.0 m of cloth. To produce two more metres of cloth, the EU must sacrifice 4.0 kg of wheat. This combination of changes increases world production of both wheat and cloth.

The gains from specialization and trade depend on the pattern of comparative, not absolute, advantage.

In our example, total world wheat production can be increased if Canada devotes more resources to the production of wheat and fewer resources to the production of cloth. Similarly, total world cloth production can be increased if the EU devotes more resources to the production of cloth and fewer to wheat. In the extreme case, Canada could *specialize* by producing *only* wheat and the EU could specialize by producing only cloth. Such reallocations of resources increase total world output because each country is producing more of the good in which it has the lowest opportunity cost. The gains from specialization along the lines of comparative advantage are shown in Table 32-3.

World output increases if countries specialize in the production of the goods in which they have a comparative advantage.

Not *every possible* pattern of specialization, however, is beneficial for the world. In our example, if Canada were to specialize in cloth and the EU in wheat, total world output would *fall*. To see this, note that in order to produce one extra metre of cloth in Canada, five kilograms of wheat must be sacrificed (see Table 32-2). Similarly, in order to produce four extra kilograms of wheat in the EU, two metres of cloth must be sacrificed. Thus, if each country produced these additional units of the "wrong" good, total world output of wheat would fall by one kilogram and total output of cloth would fall by one metre.

Specialization of production *against* the pattern of comparative advantage leads to a decline in total world output.

Production Possibilities Boundaries   We have discussed comparative advantage in terms of opportunity costs. We can also illustrate it by considering the two countries' production possibilities boundaries. Recall from Chapter 1 the connection between a country's production possibilities boundary and the opportunity costs of production. The slope of the production possibilities boundary indicates the opportunity costs. The existence of different opportunity costs across countries implies comparative advantages that can lead to gains from trade. Figure 32-3 illustrates how two countries can both gain from trade when they have different opportunity costs, which are independent of the level of production. An alternative diagrammatic illustration of the gains from trade appears in *Extensions in Theory 32-1*, where the production possibilities boundary is concave (which means that the opportunity cost for each good is higher when more of that good is being produced).

FIGURE 32-3 The Gains from Trade with Constant Opportunity Costs

International trade leads to specialization in production and increased consumption possibilities. The bottom, purple lines in parts (i) and (ii) represent the production possibilities boundaries for Canada and the EU, respectively. In the absence of any international trade, these also represent each country's consumption possibilities.

The difference in the slopes of the production possibilities boundaries reflects differences in comparative advantage, as shown in Table 32-2. In each part the opportunity cost of increasing production of wheat by the same amount (measured by the distance *ba*) is the amount by which the production of cloth must be reduced (measured by the distance *bc*). The relatively steep production possibilities boundary for Canada thus indicates that the opportunity cost of producing wheat in Canada is less than that in the EU.

If trade is possible at some relative prices between the two countries' opportunity costs of production, each country will specialize in the production of the good in which it has a comparative advantage. In each part of the figure, the slope of the upper, green line shows the relative prices at which trade takes place. Production occurs in each country at point *S* (for specialization); Canada produces only wheat, and the EU produces only cloth.

Consumption possibilities for each country are now given by the upper, green line that passes through point *S*. Consumption possibilities are increased in both countries; consumption may occur at some point, such as *d*, that involves a combination of wheat and cloth that was not attainable in the absence of trade.

The conclusions about the gains from trade arising from international differences in opportunity costs are summarized below.

1. The opportunity cost of producing *X* is the output of other products that must be sacrificed in order to increase the output of *X* by one unit.

2. Country A has a comparative advantage over Country B in producing a product when its opportunity cost of production is lower. This implies, however, that Country A has a comparative *dis*advantage in some other product(s).

3. When opportunity costs for all products are the same in all countries, there is no comparative advantage and there is no possibility of gains from specialization and trade.

4. When opportunity costs differ in any two countries and both countries are producing both products, it is always possible to increase production of both products by a suitable reallocation of resources within each country.

Though the concepts of comparative advantage and specialization are relatively straightforward, it is helpful to work through numerical examples to solidify your

EXTENSIONS IN THEORY 32-1

The Gains from Trade More Generally

Examining the gains from trade is relatively easy in the case where each country's production possibilities boundary is a straight line. What happens in the more realistic case where the production possibilities boundary is concave? As this box shows, the same basic principles of the gains from trade apply to this more complex case.

International trade leads to an expansion of the set of goods that can be consumed in the economy in two ways:

1. By allowing the bundle of goods consumed to differ from the bundle produced

2. By permitting a profitable change in the pattern of production

Without international trade, the bundle of goods produced must be the same as the bundle consumed. With international trade, the consumption and production bundles can be altered independently to reflect the relative values placed on goods by international markets.

Fixed Production

In each part of the figure, the purple curve is the economy's production possibilities boundary. In the absence of international trade, the economy must consume the same bundle of goods that it produces. Thus, the production possibilities boundary is also the consumption possibilities boundary. Suppose the economy produces and consumes at point a, with x_1 of good X and y_1 of good Y, as in part (i) of the figure.

Next suppose that production remains at point a but we now allow good Y to be traded for good X internationally. The consumption possibilities are now shown by the line tt drawn through point a. The slope of tt indicates the quantity of Y that exchanges for a unit of X on the international market—that is, the relative price of X in terms of Y.

Although production is fixed at point a, consumption can now be anywhere on the line tt. For example, the consumption point could be at b. This could be achieved

understanding. *Applying Economic Concepts 32-1* provides two examples and works through the computations of absolute and comparative advantage.

The Gains from Trade with Variable Costs

So far, we have assumed that opportunity costs are the same whatever the scale of output, and we have seen that there are gains from specialization and trade as long as there are differences in opportunity costs across countries. If costs vary with the level of output, or as experience is acquired via specialization, *additional* gains are possible.

Economies of Scale   In many industries, production costs fall as the scale of output increases. The larger the scale of operations, the more efficiently large-scale machinery can be used and the more a detailed division of tasks among workers is possible. Small by exporting y_2y_1 units of Y and importing x_1x_2 units of X. Because point b (and all others on line tt to the right of a) lies outside the production possibilities boundary, there are potential gains from trade. Consumers are no longer limited by their own country's production possibilities. Let us suppose that they prefer point b to point a. They have achieved a gain from trade by being allowed to exchange some of their production of good Y for some quantity of good X and thus to consume more of good X than is produced at home.

Variable Production

In general, however, openness to trade with other countries will change the pattern of domestic production, and this will create *further* gains from trade. The country can now produce the bundle of goods that is most valuable in world markets. That is represented by the bundle d in part (ii). The consumption possibilities boundary is shifted to the line $t't'$ by changing production from a to d and thereby increasing the country's degree of specialization in good Y. For every point on the original consumption possibilities boundary tt, there are points on the new boundary $t't'$ that allow more consumption of both goods—for example, compare points b and f. Notice also that, except at the zero-trade point d, the new consumption possibilities boundary lies *everywhere above the production possibilities boundary*.

The benefits of moving from a no-trade position, such as point a, to a trading position, such as points b or f, are the *gains from trade* to the country. When the production of good Y is increased and the production of good X decreased, the country is able to move to a point, such as f, by producing more of good Y, in which the country has a comparative advantage, and trading the additional production for good X.

countries (such as Switzerland, Belgium, and Israel) whose domestic markets are not large enough to exploit economies of scale would find it prohibitively expensive to become self-sufficient by producing a little bit of everything at very high cost.

One of the important lessons learned from patterns of world trade since the Second World War has concerned scale economies and product differentiation. Virtually all of today's manufactured consumer goods are produced in a vast array of differentiated product lines. In most industries, any one firm produces only one or a few of the different versions of the product. It does this because it is producing for a larger foreign market, and by focusing on only a few versions of the product, it can achieve the benefits of the associated scale economies. The result is that different countries specialize in different *versions* of similar products, and then trade with one another. Such trade is referred to as *intra-industry trade* and reflects the prevalence of scale economies and product differentiation in many industries.

This aspect of trade was first dramatically illustrated when the European Common Market (now known as the European Union) was established in the late 1950s.

APPLYING ECONOMIC CONCEPTS 32-1

Two Examples of Absolute and Comparative Advantage

Example #1

Argentina and Brazil can both produce fish and leather. The table shows the total resource cost, in dollars, of producing one kilogram of each good in both countries.

	Fish (kg)	Leather (kg)
Argentina	$2	$5
Brazil	$3	$4

Absolute Advantage Argentina is the more efficient producer of fish since its total resource cost ($2) is less than Brazil's ($3), and so it has the absolute advantage in producing fish. Brazil has the absolute advantage in producing leather.

Comparative Advantage To know the pattern of comparative advantage, we must compute the *opportunity costs of production*. In Argentina, producing one more kilogram of leather requires using $5 of resources—the amount that could have been used to produce 2.5 kg of fish. Thus, producing 1 kg of leather involves giving up 2.5 kg of fish. In Brazil, however, one extra kilogram of leather only requires a sacrifice of 1.33 kg of fish. Since Brazil has the lower opportunity cost for leather (it gives up the least fish), it has the comparative advantage in leather production.

The opportunity cost for fish production *must* be the inverse of that for leather. In Argentina, one extra kilogram of fish "costs" 0.4 kg of leather. In Brazil, one extra kilogram of fish "costs" 0.75 kg of leather. Since Argentina has the lower opportunity cost of fish, it has the comparative advantage in fish production.

Specialization If Argentina and Brazil were to trade with each other, total production would be increased if each country specialized in the production of the good in which it has the comparative advantage. Argentina should produce fish and buy its leather from Brazil; Brazil should produce leather and buy its fish from Argentina.

Example #2

Switzerland and Austria can both produce glass and chocolate. Each country has 1000 units of identical resources, which we will call "labour." The table shows the maximum amount of each good that each country could produce if it devoted all of its labour to the production of that good.

	Glass (tonnes)	Chocolate (kg)
Austria	5 000	400 000
Switzerland	4 000	200 000

Absolute Advantage Each unit of labour in Austria can produce 5 tonnes of glass or 400 kg of chocolate. The identical unit of labour in Switzerland can produce only 4 tonnes of glass or 200 kg of chocolate. Switzerland is less efficient than Austria in the production of both goods; Austria therefore has the absolute advantage in *both* goods.

Comparative Advantage Once again, we need to know the opportunity costs of production. In Austria, producing one extra tonne of glass requires giving up 80 kg (= 400 000/5000) of chocolate. In Switzerland, producing one extra tonne of glass "costs" 50 kg (= 200 000/4000) of chocolate. Switzerland has the lower opportunity cost for glass and thus has the comparative advantage in glass production. It follows that Austria *must* have the comparative advantage in the production of chocolate. Austria's opportunity cost of 1 kg of chocolate is 1/80 tonne of glass, whereas Switzerland's opportunity cost of 1 kg of chocolate is 1/50 tonne of glass.

Specialization If the two countries engaged in international trade, total output would be maximized if Austria specialized in the production of chocolate and Switzerland specialized in the production of glass.

Economists had expected that specialization would occur according to the theory of comparative advantage, with one country specializing in cars, another in refrigerators, another in fashion and clothing, another in shoes, and so on. This is not the way it worked out. Instead, much of the vast growth of trade was in intra-industry trade—that is, trade of goods or services within the same broad industry. Today, one can buy French, English, Italian, and German fashion goods, cars, shoes, appliances, and a host of other products in Paris, London, Rome, and Berlin. Ships loaded with Swedish furniture bound for London pass ships loaded with English furniture bound for Stockholm, and so on.

learning by doing The reduction in unit costs that often results as workers learn through repeatedly performing the same tasks. It causes a downward shift in the average cost curve.

But the firms involved in this production are more likely to reap the benefits of the economies of scale than they could if they were producing only for their own domestic markets.

The same increase in intra-industry trade driven by scale economies happened with Canada–U.S. trade over successive rounds of tariff cuts that were negotiated after the Second World War, the most recent being those associated with the 1989 Canada–U.S. Free Trade Agreement, and its 1994 expansion into the North American Free Trade Agreement (NAFTA), which included Mexico. In several broad industrial groups, including automotive products, machinery, textiles, and forestry products, both imports and exports increased in each country. What free trade in Europe and North America did was to allow a proliferation of differentiated products, with different countries each specializing in different sub-product lines and reaping the benefits of the scale economies in production. Consumers have shown by their expenditures that they value this enormous increase in the range of choice among differentiated products, and producers have gained economies by being able to operate at a larger scale.

> In industries with significant scale economies, small countries that do not trade will have low levels of output and therefore high costs. With international trade, however, small countries can produce for the large global market and thus produce at lower costs. International trade therefore allows small countries to reap the benefits of scale economies.

Learning by Doing The discussion so far has assumed that costs vary with the *level* of output. But they may also vary with the *accumulated experience* in producing a product over time.

Early economists placed great importance on a concept that is now called **learning by doing**. They believed that as countries gained experience in particular tasks, workers and managers would become more efficient in performing them. As people acquire expertise, costs tend to fall. There is substantial evidence that such learning by doing does occur. It is particularly important in many of today's knowledge-intensive high-tech industries. The distinction between this phenomenon and economies of scale is illustrated in Figure 32-4. It is one more example of the difference between a movement along a curve and a shift of the curve.

Wine is a good example of an industry in which there is much intra-industry trade. Canada, for example, imports wine from many countries but also exports Canadian-made wine to the same countries.

FIGURE 32-4 Economies of Scale Versus Learning by Doing

Specialization may lead to gains from trade through scale economies, learning by doing, or both. Consider a country that wants to consume the quantity Q_0. Suppose it can produce that quantity at an average cost per unit of c_0. Suppose further that the country has a comparative advantage in producing this product and can export the quantity Q_0Q_1 if it produces Q_1. This may lead to cost savings in two ways.

First, the increased level of production of Q_1 compared with Q_0 permits it to move along its long-run cost curve from a to b, thereby reducing costs per unit to c_1. This is an economy of scale.

Second, as workers and management become more experienced, they may be able to produce at lower costs. This is learning by doing and it shifts the cost curve from $LRAC$ to $LRAC'$. At output Q_1, costs per unit fall to c_2. The movement from a to b' incorporates both economies of scale and learning by doing.

The opportunity for learning by doing has an important implication: Policymakers need not accept current comparative advantages as given. Through such means as education and tax incentives, they can seek to develop new comparative advantages. Moreover, countries cannot complacently assume that their existing comparative advantages will persist. Misguided education policies, the wrong tax incentives, or policies that discourage risk taking can lead to the rapid erosion of a country's comparative advantage in particular products and industries.

Sources of Comparative Advantage

David Ricardo's analysis teaches us that the gains from trade arise from the pattern of comparative advantage. However, his analysis does not explain the *sources* of a country's comparative advantage. Why do comparative advantages exist? Since a country's comparative advantage depends on its opportunity costs, we could also ask: Why do different countries have different opportunity costs?

Different Factor Endowments   One answer to this question was offered early in the twentieth century by two Swedish economists, Eli Heckscher and Bertil Ohlin. Ohlin was subsequently awarded the Nobel Prize in economics for his work in the theory of international trade. According to their theory, the international cost differences that form the basis for comparative advantage arise because factor endowments differ across countries. This is often called the *factor endowment theory of comparative advantage.*

To see how this theory works, consider the prices for various types of goods in countries *in the absence of trade*. A country that is well endowed with fertile land but has a small population will find that land is cheap but labour is expensive. It will therefore produce land-intensive agricultural goods cheaply and labour-intensive goods, such as machine tools, only at high cost. The reverse will be true for a second country that is small in size but possesses abundant and efficient labour. As a result, the first country will have a comparative advantage in agricultural production and the second in goods that use much labour and little land.

> According to the Heckscher-Ohlin theory, countries have comparative advantages in the production of goods that use intensively the factors of production with which they are abundantly endowed.

For example, Canada is abundantly endowed with forests relative to most other countries. According to the Heckscher-Ohlin theory, Canada has a comparative advantage in goods that use forest products intensively, such as paper, framing materials, raw lumber, and wooden furniture. In contrast, relative to most other countries, Canada is sparsely endowed with labour. Thus, Canada has a comparative disadvantage in goods that use labour intensively, such as cotton or many other textile products.

Different Climates   The factor endowment theory provides only part of the entire explanation for the sources of comparative advantage. Another important influence comes from all those natural factors that can be called *climate* in the broadest sense. If you combine land, labour, and capital in the same way in Costa Rica and in Iceland, you will not get the same output of most agricultural goods. Sunshine, rainfall, and average temperature also matter. You can, of course, artificially create any climate you want in a greenhouse, but it costs money to create what is freely provided elsewhere.

A country's comparative advantage is influenced by various aspects of its climate.

Of course, if we consider "warm weather" a factor of production, then we could simply say that countries like Costa Rica are better endowed with that factor than countries like Iceland. In this sense, explanations of comparative advantage based on different climates are really just a special case of explanations based on factor endowments.

Canada is extremely well endowed with forests. It is no surprise, therefore, that it has a comparative advantage in a whole range of forestry products.

Human Capital   Acquired skills, what economists call *human capital*, matter greatly in determining comparative advantage. Beginning in the late nineteenth century, Germany had an excellent set of trade schools that were attended by virtually every male who did not go on to higher academic education. As a result, Germany developed, and still maintains, a strong comparative advantage in many consumer goods that require significant engineering skills to produce, such as home appliances, power tools, and small machines. The people of Persia (now Iran) produced carpets of high quality over the centuries, and from childhood their workers developed skills in carpet making that few others could match. So they had a comparative advantage in high-quality carpets and some related commodities. Early on, Americans developed the skills necessary to mass-produce goods of reasonable quality made from standardized parts. So the United States developed a comparative advantage in many consumer goods made with mass-production techniques.

Acquired Comparative Advantage   The example of human capital makes it clear that many comparative advantages are *acquired*. Further, they can change. Thus, comparative advantage should be viewed as being *dynamic* rather than static. Many of today's industries depend more on human capital than on fixed physical capital or natural resources. The skills of a computer designer or a video game programmer are acquired by education and on-the-job training. Natural endowments of energy and raw materials cannot account for Silicon Valley's leadership in computer technology, for Canada's prominence in auto-parts manufacturing, for Taiwan's excellence in electronics, or for Switzerland's prominence in private banking.

If comparative advantage can be acquired, it can also be *lost*. If firms within one country fail to innovate and adopt the latest technologies available in their industry, but competing firms in other countries are aggressively innovating and reducing their production costs, the first country will eventually lose whatever comparative advantage it once had in that industry. In recent years, for example, pulp and paper mills in Canada have been closing, driven out of the industry by Scandinavian firms that more aggressively pursue improvements in productivity.

With today's growing international competition and rapidly changing technologies, no country's comparative advantages are secure unless its firms innovate and keep up with their foreign competitors and its education system produces workers, managers, and innovators with the requisite skills.

Contrasting Views? The view that a country's comparative advantages change over time and can be influenced by education, innovation, and government policy is a relatively modern one. It contrasts sharply with the traditional view that a country's natural endowments of land, labour, and natural resources are the prime determinants of its comparative advantage. The traditional view suggested that a government interested in maximizing its citizens' material standard of living should encourage specialization of production in goods for which it *currently* had a comparative advantage. If all countries followed this advice, each would have been specialized in a relatively narrow range of distinct products. Germans would have produced engineering products, Canadians would have produced resource-based primary products, Americans would have been farmers and factory workers, Central Americans would have been banana and coffee growers, the Chinese would have produced rice and cheap toys, and so on.

There are surely elements of truth in both views. It would be unwise to neglect the importance of resource endowments, climate, culture, social patterns, and institutional arrangements. But it would also be unwise to assume that all advantages are innate and immutable.

32.2 THE DETERMINATION OF TRADE PATTERNS

Comparative advantage has been the central concept in our discussion about the gains from trade. If Canada has a comparative advantage in lumber and Italy has a comparative advantage in shoes, then the total output of lumber and shoes can be increased if Canada specializes in the production of lumber and Italy specializes in the production of shoes. With such patterns of specialization, Canada will naturally export lumber to Italy and Italy will export shoes to Canada.

It is one thing to discuss the *potential* gains from trade if countries specialized in the production of particular goods and exported these to other countries. But do *actual* trade patterns occur along the lines of comparative advantage? In this section of the chapter we use a simple demand-and-supply model to examine why Canada exports some products and imports others. We will see that comparative advantage, whether natural or acquired, plays a central role in determining actual trade patterns.

There are some products, such as coffee and mangoes, that Canada does not produce (and will probably never produce). Any domestic consumption of these products must therefore be satisfied by imports from other countries. At the other extreme, there are some products, such as nickel and potash, for which Canada is one of the world's major suppliers, and demand in the rest of the world must be satisfied partly by exports from Canada. Finally, there are some products, such as houses and crushed stone, that are so expensive to transport that every country produces approximately what it consumes.

Our interest in this section is with the vast number of intermediate cases in which Canada is only one of many producers of an internationally traded product, as with beef, oil, copper, wheat, lumber, and newsprint. Will Canada be an exporter or an importer of such products? And what is the role played by comparative advantage?

The Law of One Price

Whether Canada imports or exports a product for which it is only one of many producers depends to a great extent on the product's price. This brings us to what economists call the *law of one price*.

The law of one price states that when a product is traded throughout the entire world, the prices in various countries (net of any specific taxes or tariffs) will differ by no more than the cost of transporting the product between countries. Aside from differences caused by these transport costs, there is a single world price.

Many basic products—such as copper wire, steel pipe, iron ore, and computer RAM chips—fall within this category. The world price for each good is the price that equates the quantity demanded worldwide with the quantity supplied worldwide. The world price of an internationally traded product may be influenced greatly, or only slightly, by the demand and supply coming from any one country. The extent of one country's influence will depend on how important its quantities demanded and supplied are in relation to the worldwide totals.

The simplest case for us to study arises when the country, which we will take to be Canada, accounts for only a small part of the total worldwide demand and supply. In this case, Canada does not itself produce enough to influence the world price significantly. Similarly, Canadian purchases are too small a proportion of worldwide demand to affect the world price in any significant way. Producers and consumers in Canada thus face a world price that they cannot influence by their own actions.

In this case, the price that rules in the Canadian market must be the world price (adjusted for the exchange rate between the Canadian dollar and the foreign currency). The law of one price says this must be so. What would happen if the Canadian domestic price diverged from the world price? If the Canadian price were below the world price, no supplier would sell in the Canadian market because higher profits could be made by selling abroad. The absence of supply to the Canadian market would thus drive up the Canadian price. Conversely, if the Canadian domestic price were above the worldwide price, no buyer would buy from a Canadian seller because lower prices are available by buying abroad. The absence of demand on the Canadian market would thus drive down the Canadian price.

The Pattern of Foreign Trade

Let us now see what determines the pattern of international trade in such circumstances.

An Exported Product To determine the pattern of Canadian trade, we first show the Canadian domestic demand and supply curves for some product, say, lumber. This is done in Figure 32-5. The intersection of these two curves tells us what the price and quantity would be in Canada *if there were no foreign trade*. Now compare this no-trade price with the world price of that product.[1] If the world price is higher, the actual price in Canada will exceed the no-trade price. In this situation there will be an

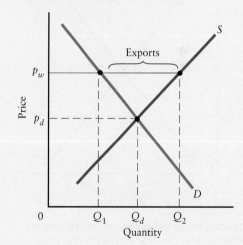

FIGURE 32-5   An Exported Good

Exports occur whenever there is excess supply domestically at the world price. The domestic demand and supply curves are D and S, respectively. The domestic price in the absence of foreign trade is p_d, with Q_d produced and consumed domestically. The world price of p_w is higher than p_d. At p_w, Q_1 is demanded while Q_2 is supplied domestically. The excess of the domestic supply over the domestic demand is exported.

---

[1] If the world price is stated in terms of some foreign currency (as it often is), the price must be converted into Canadian dollars by using the current exchange rate between the foreign currency and Canadian dollars.

excess of Canadian supply over Canadian demand. Domestic producers want to sell Q_2 units of lumber but domestic consumers want to buy only Q_1 units. If Canada were a closed economy, such excess supply would drive the price down to p_d. But in an open economy with a world price of p_w, this excess supply is exported to Canada's trading partners.

What is the role of comparative advantage in this analysis? We have said that Canada will export lumber if the world price exceeds Canada's no-trade price. Note that in a competitive market the price of the product reflects the product's marginal cost, which in turn reflects the opportunity cost of producing the product. That Canada's no-trade price for lumber is lower than the world price reflects the fact that the opportunity cost of producing lumber in Canada is less than the opportunity cost of producing it in the rest of the world. Thus, by exporting goods that have a low no-trade price, Canada is exporting the goods for which it has a comparative advantage.

> Countries export the goods for which they are low-cost producers. That is, they export goods for which they have a comparative advantage.

An Imported Product   Now consider some other product—for example, computer RAM chips. Once again, look first at the domestic demand and supply curves, shown this time in Figure 32-6. The intersection of these curves determines the price that would exist in Canada if there were no foreign trade. The world price of RAM chips is below the Canadian no-trade price so that, at the price ruling in Canada, domestic demand is larger and domestic supply is smaller than if the no-trade price had ruled. The excess of domestic demand over domestic supply is met by imports.

Again, this analysis can be restated in terms of comparative advantage. The high Canadian no-trade price of RAM chips reflects the fact that the production of RAM chips has a higher opportunity cost in Canada than elsewhere in the world. This high cost means that Canada has a comparative disadvantage in RAM chips. So Canada imports goods for which it has a comparative disadvantage.

FIGURE 32-6   An Imported Good

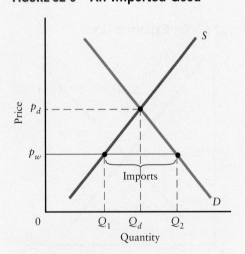

Imports occur whenever there is excess demand domestically at the world price. The domestic demand and supply curves are D and S, respectively. The domestic price in the absence of foreign trade is p_d, with Q_d produced and consumed domestically. The world price of p_w is less than p_d. At the world price Q_2 is demanded, whereas Q_1 is supplied domestically. The excess of domestic demand over domestic supply is satisfied through imports.

> Countries import the goods for which they are high-cost producers. That is, they import goods for which they have a comparative disadvantage.

Is Comparative Advantage Obsolete?

It is sometimes said that the theory of comparative advantage is nearly 200 years old, and things have changed so much since then that the theory must surely be obsolete.

Contrary to such assertions, comparative advantage remains an important and valid economic concept. At any one time—because comparative advantage is reflected in international relative prices, and these relative prices determine what goods a country will import and what it will export—the operation of the price system will result in trade that follows the current pattern of comparative advantage. For example, if Canadian costs of producing steel are particularly low relative to other Canadian costs, Canada will export steel at international prices (which it does). If Canada's costs of producing textiles are particularly high relative to other Canadian costs, Canada will import textiles at international prices (which it does). Thus, there is no reason to change the view that David Ricardo long ago expounded: *Current comparative advantage is a major determinant of trade under free-market conditions.*

What has changed, however, is economists' views about the *determinants* of comparative advantage. It is now clear that current comparative advantage is more open to change by private entrepreneurial activities and by government policy than was previously thought. Thus, what is obsolete is the belief that a country's current pattern of comparative advantage, and hence its current pattern of imports and exports, must be accepted as given and unchangeable.

The theory that comparative advantage is a major influence on trade flows is not obsolete, but the theory that comparative advantage is completely determined by forces beyond the reach of decisions made by private firms and by public policy has been discredited.

One caveat should be noted. It is one thing to observe that it is *possible* for governments to influence a country's pattern of comparative advantage. It is quite another to conclude that it is *advisable* for them to try. The case in support of a specific government intervention requires that (1) there is scope for governments to improve on the results achieved by the free market, (2) the costs of the intervention be less than the value of the improvement to be achieved, and (3) governments will actually be able to carry out the required interventionist policies (without, for example, being sidetracked by considerations of electoral advantage).

In many cases, governments have succeeded in creating important comparative advantages. For example, the Taiwanese government virtually created that nation's electronics industry and then passed it over to private hands in which it became a world leader. The government of Singapore created a computer-parts industry that became a major world supplier. However, there are also many examples in which governments failed in their attempts to create comparative advantage. The government of the United Kingdom tried to create a comparative advantage in computers and failed miserably, wasting much public money in the process. The government of Ireland tried to create a comparative advantage in automobile production and failed to create more than a modest, unprofitable industry that eventually disappeared. The world is strewn not only with spectacular successes, which show that it can be done, but also with abject failures, which show that the attempt to do so is fraught with many dangers.

One other comment needs to be made regarding the relevance of the concept of comparative advantage. For understanding international trade in copper wire, lumber, oil, bananas, coffee, textiles, and many other relatively simple products, the concept of comparative advantage is very useful. In some manufacturing industries, however, where products have dozens or perhaps hundreds of components, the determinants of trade flows are more complex than the theory of comparative advantage suggests. For example, it is difficult to see why Canada might have a comparative advantage in the production of automobile transmissions but not in automobile brake systems or air-conditioning systems. Yet, the automobile sector is perhaps the best example of an industry in which a firm's "supply chain" includes products made by several other firms in several countries. *Applying Economic Concepts 32-2* discusses how economies of scale and the forces of globalization have led to the development of complex global supply chains.

The Terms of Trade

We have seen that world production can be increased when countries specialize in the production of the goods for which they have a comparative advantage and then trade with one another. We now ask: How will these gains from specialization and trade be shared among countries? The division of the gain depends on what is called the **terms of trade**, which relate to the quantity of imported goods that can be obtained per unit of goods exported. The terms of trade are measured by the ratio of the price of exports to the price of imports.

terms of trade The ratio of the average price of a country's exports to the average price of its imports.

A rise in the price of imported goods, with the price of exports unchanged, indicates a *fall in the terms of trade*; it will now take more exports to buy the same quantity of imports. Similarly, a rise in the price of exported goods, with the price of imports unchanged, indicates a *rise in the terms of trade*; it will now take fewer exports to buy the same quantity of imports. Thus, the ratio of these prices measures the amount of imports that can be obtained per unit of goods exported.

The terms of trade can be illustrated with a country's production possibilities boundary, as shown in Figure 32-7. The figure shows the hypothetical case in which Canada can produce only wheat and cloth. As we saw earlier, the slope of Canada's production possibilities boundary shows the relative opportunity costs of producing the two goods in Canada. A steep production possibilities boundary indicates that only a small amount of cloth must be given up to get more wheat; thus cloth is relatively costly and wheat is relatively cheap. A flatter production possibilities boundary indicates that a larger amount of cloth must be given up to get more wheat; thus cloth is relatively cheap and wheat is relatively expensive. Thus, the slope of the production possibilities boundary in Figure 32-7 shows the relative price of cloth (in terms of wheat) that Canada faces in the absence of international trade.

If, through international trade, Canada has access to different relative prices, Canada will be led to specialize in the production of one good or the other. In Figure 32-7, we show a case in which the world relative price of cloth is lower than the relative price Canada would have if it did not trade. (This lower *world* relative price of cloth reflects the fact that other countries can produce cloth more cheaply than Canada.) Faced with a lower relative price of cloth, Canada ends up specializing in the production of the relatively high-priced product (wheat), and importing the relatively low-priced product (cloth). This point of specialization is point S in Figure 32-7.

FIGURE 32-7   An Improvement in the Terms of Trade

A rise in the relative price of exports is a terms-of-trade improvement and expands consumption possibilities

Changes in the terms of trade lead to changes in a country's consumption possibilities. The hypothetical production possibilities boundary is shown for Canada. With international trade at relative prices T_0, Canada specializes in the production of wheat, producing at point S, but is able to consume at a point like A. It pays for its imports of cloth with its exports of wheat.

If the price of wheat rises relative to the price of cloth, production remains at S but the line T_1 shows Canada's new consumption possibilities. Consumption can now take place at a point like B where consumption of both wheat and cloth has increased. The increase in the terms of trade makes Canada better off because of the increase in consumption possibilities.

APPLYING ECONOMIC CONCEPTS 32-2

Comparative Advantage and Global Supply Chains

The discussion of comparative advantage developed in this chapter applies easily to many products with one or even a few components. One can sensibly speak of national comparative advantages for whole products, such as Costa Rica for bananas, Canada for sawn logs, Chile for copper, Korea for steel, and Saudi Arabia for oil.

For many manufactured products, however, and even for some resource-based products and service industries, production is carried out in complex and integrated "global supply chains," with a product's several different components being produced in different countries and often by different firms. In this world of "integrative trade," it is no longer clear where some products are "made," even though one could easily determine where each of the product's many components is produced and where they are all assembled into a final product.

This method of decentralized production has several causes. First, the existence of scale economies provides an incentive for individual firms to reduce their costs by concentrating the production of each individual component in a different specialized large factory. Second, differences in national wage rates for various types of labour provide an incentive for these production facilities to be located in different countries. Third, the current very low costs of communication and transportation make it possible to coordinate supply chains globally and ship parts and final products anywhere at low cost. (If fuel becomes expensive enough to make transport costs a significant part of total costs, it will become economic to do much more production closer to final markets than it has been over the last several decades.)

Consider three examples. The iPhone sold by Apple clearly says "Made in China" on the box, but most of the value from its design occurs in the United States, many electronic components come from Korea and Japan, and only the iPhone's final assembly occurs in China. Apple chooses to locate assembly in China, using components manufactured elsewhere, because by doing so it can maximize its product quality and minimize costs.

Bombardier jet aircraft designed and assembled in Canada also involve global supply chains. Fuselage parts come from Japan, the wings are produced in Northern Ireland, engines are imported from the United States, and the avionics are engineered in the United States but sourced from Asian suppliers. Bombardier adopts this business model because costs can be reduced and quality maximized by using specialty suppliers at each link in the global supply chain.

Such global supply chains even exist for some products that appear to have few "components," such as fish. For example, a Canadian firm may hire a Chilean trawler to fish in the Indian Ocean, land its catch in Malaysia where it is frozen, and then send it to China for further processing before it is finally sold to Japanese wholesalers.

There are three implications for how we think about international trade in the presence of integrated global supply chains. First, we should not view countries as having comparative advantages in entire products but rather in the specific productive activities that take place along the global supply chain. China may not have a comparative advantage in "producing" consumer electronics but may have one in assembling them. Canada may not have a comparative advantage in "producing" jet aircraft but may have one in designing them.

Second, these comparative advantages may not be long-lasting because they are sensitive to changes in the economic environment and in technology. For example, significant changes in national corporate tax rates, exchange rates, and wages for factory workers will generally change the optimal location for the production of a product's various components. Also, newly developed technologies for producing existing products and creating new ones can alter the patterns of comparative advantage significantly and quickly.

Third, traditional data on international trade does not capture the extent of integration in global supply chains. The iPhone assembled in China and exported to the United States appears simply as a Chinese export; but the significant value generated by the U.S.-based design team may appear in no trade statistics whatsoever. It follows that the measured flow of a country's exports of some products does not necessarily correspond closely with the level of local economic activity (production and employment) actually generated by those products. Even in Canada's resource sector, the domestic content of exports is not 100 percent, although it is typically more than 75 percent, meaning that up to one-quarter of the value of the final exported product comes from imported inputs. In most manufacturing industries, however, the domestic content of exports is 50 percent or lower, and in the automobile industry it is only 35 percent.

The presence of such highly integrated global supply chains indicates the importance of two-way trade in the Canadian economy: Access to low-price and high-quality imports is as crucial to the Canadian economy as is our access to world markets where we can sell our intermediate and final products.

The upper two *green* lines in the figure show alternative values of the world relative prices—that is, alternative values for Canada's terms of trade. A rise in the terms of trade indicates a fall in the relative price of cloth (or a rise in the relative price of wheat). This increase in the terms of trade is shown as an upward rotation of the green line from T_0 to T_1. A reduction in the terms of trade is shown as a downward rotation in the green line, from T_1 to T_0.

It should be clear from Figure 32-7 why changes in the terms of trade are important. Suppose the international relative prices are initially given by T_0. Canada specializes in the production of wheat (point S) but consumes at some point like A, where it finances its imports of cloth with exports of wheat. Now suppose there is a shift in world demand toward wheat and away from cloth, and this leads to an increase in the relative price of wheat. The terms of trade increase to T_1 and, with unchanged production at point S, Canada can now afford to consume at a point like B where consumption of both wheat and cloth has increased.

A rise in a country's terms of trade is beneficial because it expands the country's consumption possibilities.

Conversely, a reduction in the price of a country's exports (relative to the price of its imports) is harmful for a country. In Figure 32-7, this is shown as a change of the

FIGURE 32-8 **Canada's Terms of Trade, 1961–2014**

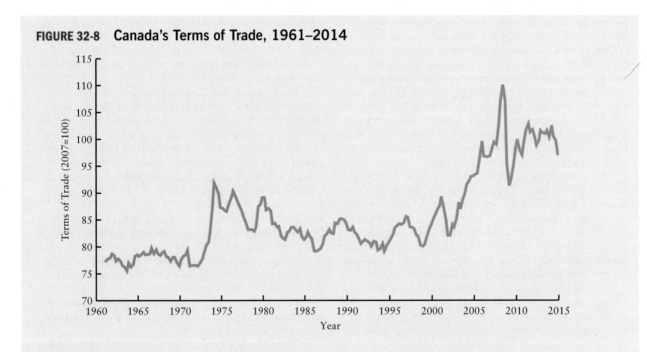

Canada's terms of trade have been quite variable over the past 50 years. The data shown are Canada's terms of trade—the ratio of an index of Canadian export prices to an index of Canadian import prices. As the relative prices of lumber, oil, wheat, electronic equipment, textiles, fruit, and other products change, the terms of trade naturally change.

(*Source:* Author's calculations using data from Statistics Canada, CANSIM database, Table 380-0066.)

terms of trade from T_1 to T_0. Even though production may remain unchanged, the range of goods available to be consumed falls, and this reduction in consumption possibilities leads to an overall loss of welfare.

How do we measure the terms of trade in real economies? Because international trade involves many countries and many products, we cannot use the simple ratio of the prices of two goods as in Figure 32-7. The basic principle, however, is the same. A country's terms of trade are computed as an index number:

$$\text{Terms of trade} = \frac{\text{Index of export prices}}{\text{Index of import prices}} \times 100$$

A rise in the index is referred to as a *favourable* change in a country's terms of trade (sometimes called a terms of trade *improvement*). A decrease in the index of the terms of trade is called an *unfavourable* change (or a terms of trade *deterioration*). For example, oil-exporting countries experienced significant terms-of-trade improvements when the world price of oil increased sharply in the mid-1990s and again in the mid-2000s. When world oil prices fell sharply in 2014–2015, the same countries experienced a large deterioration in their terms of trade. The opposite was true for oil-importing economies like the United States and the European Union.

Canada's terms of trade since 1961 are shown in Figure 32-8. As is clear, the terms of trade are quite variable, reflecting frequent changes in the relative prices of different products. Note the dramatic increase (improvement) in Canada's terms of trade in the early 1970s, reflecting the large increase in oil prices caused by OPEC's output restrictions. Since Canada is a net exporter of oil, its terms of trade improve when the price of oil increases. An even larger increase occurred in the 2002–2008 period, when the world prices of most commodities, especially energy-related commodities, increased sharply.

SUMMARY

32.1 THE GAINS FROM TRADE
LO 1, 2

- Country A has an *absolute* advantage over Country B in the production of a specific product when the absolute cost of the product is less in Country A than in Country B.
- Country A has a *comparative* advantage over Country B in the production of a specific good if the forgone output of other goods is less in Country A than in Country B.
- Comparative advantage occurs whenever countries have different opportunity costs of producing particular goods. World production of all products can be increased if each country transfers resources into the production of the products for which it has a comparative advantage.
- International trade allows all countries to obtain the goods for which they do not have a comparative

advantage at a lower opportunity cost than if they were to produce all products for themselves; specialization and trade therefore allow all countries to have more of all products than if they tried to be self-sufficient.
- A nation that engages in trade and specialization may also realize the benefits of economies of large-scale production and of learning by doing.
- Traditional theories regarded comparative advantage as largely determined by natural resource endowments that are difficult to change. Economists now know that some comparative advantages can be acquired and consequently can be changed. A country may, in this view, influence its role in world production and trade.

32.2 THE DETERMINATION OF TRADE PATTERNS LO 3, 4

- The law of one price says that the national prices of tradable goods (net of taxes and tariffs) must differ by no more than the costs of transporting these goods between countries. After accounting for these transport costs, there is a single world price.
- Countries will export a good when the world price exceeds the price that would exist in the country if there were no trade. The low no-trade price reflects a low opportunity cost and thus a comparative advantage in that good. Thus, countries export goods for which they have a comparative advantage.
- Countries will import a good when the world price is less than the price that would exist in the country if

there were no trade. The high no-trade price reflects a high opportunity cost and thus a comparative disadvantage in that good. Thus, countries import goods for which they have a comparative disadvantage.

- The terms of trade refer to the ratio of the prices of goods exported to the prices of those imported. The terms of trade determine the quantity of imports that can be obtained per unit of exports.
- A favourable change in the terms of trade—a rise in export prices relative to import prices—is beneficial for a country because it expands its consumption possibilities.

KEY CONCEPTS

Interpersonal, interregional, and international specialization
Absolute advantage and comparative advantage
Opportunity cost and comparative advantage

The gains from trade: specialization, scale economies, and learning by doing
The sources of comparative advantage
Factor endowments

Acquired comparative advantage
The law of one price
The terms of trade

STUDY EXERCISES

MyEconLab Make the grade with MyEconLab: Study Exercises marked in ● can be found on MyEconLab. You can practise them as often as you want, and most feature step-by-step guided instructions to help you find the right answer.

❶ Fill in the blanks to make the following statements correct.

a. The "gains from trade" refers to the increased _____ caused by specialization and trade.

b. Suppose Argentina can produce one kilogram of beef for $2.50 and Brazil can produce one kilogram of beef for $2.90. Argentina is said to have a(n) _____ in beef production over Brazil. The gains from trade do *not* depend on _____.

c. Comparative advantage is based on _____ rather than absolute costs.

d. It is possible for a country to have a comparative advantage in some good and a(n) _____ in none.

e. If all countries specialize in the production of goods for which they have a comparative advantage, then world output will _____.

f. If opportunity costs are the same in all countries, there is no _____ and no possibility of _____.

❷ Fill in the blanks to make the following statements correct.

a. Such a product as coffee beans is cheaply transported and is traded around the world. The law of _____ tells us that it will tend to have _____ worldwide price.

b. If the domestic price of copper wire in Canada (in the absence of trade) is $20 per unit and the world price is $24 per unit, then Canada will have an excess _____, which it will then _____. The opportunity cost of producing copper wire in Canada is _____ than the opportunity cost of producing it in the rest of the world.

c. Canada will import goods for which it has an excess _____ at the world price. In the absence of trade, the _____ price of these goods would be less than the _____ price.

d. A rise in Canada's terms of trade means that the average price of Canada's _____ has risen compared with the average price of Canada's _____. This change is referred to as a terms of trade _____.

e. The terms of trade determine the quantity of _____ that can be obtained per unit of _____.

❸ The following diagram shows the production possibilities boundary for Arcticland, a country that produces only two goods, ice and fish. Labour is the only factor of production. Recall that a linear production possibilities boundary reflects *constant* opportunity costs for both products.

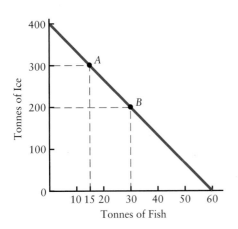

a. Beginning at any point on Arcticland's production possibilities boundary, what is the opportunity cost of producing 100 more tonnes of ice?

b. Beginning at any point on Arcticland's production possibilities boundary, what is the opportunity cost of producing 10 more tonnes of fish?

❹ The following table shows the production of wheat and corn in Brazil and Mexico. Assume that both countries have one million acres of arable land.

	Brazil	Mexico
Wheat	90 bushels per acre	50 bushels per acre
Corn	30 bushels per acre	20 bushels per acre

a. Which country has the absolute advantage in wheat? In corn? Explain.

b. What is the opportunity cost of producing an extra bushel of wheat in Brazil? In Mexico? Which country has the comparative advantage in wheat production? Explain.

c. Which country has the comparative advantage in corn production? Explain.

d. Explain why one country can have an absolute advantage in both goods but cannot have a comparative advantage in both goods.

e. On a scale diagram with wheat on the horizontal axis and corn on the vertical axis, draw each country's production possibilities boundary.

f. What is shown by the slope of each country's production possibilities boundary? Be as precise as possible.

❺ The following table shows how many tonnes of dairy products and beef products can be produced in New Zealand and Australia with one unit of equivalent resources.

	Dairy Products (tonnes)	Beef Products (tonnes)
New Zealand	12	4
Australia	12	16

a. Which country has an absolute advantage in dairy products? In beef products? Explain.

b. What is the opportunity cost of producing an extra tonne of dairy products in New Zealand? In Australia? What is the opportunity cost of producing an extra tonne of beef products in New Zealand? In Australia?

c. What is the pattern of comparative advantage between these two countries?

d. Assume that both countries have 100 units of equivalent resources. On a scale diagram with beef products on the horizontal axis and dairy products on the vertical axis, draw each country's production possibilities boundary.

e. What is the interpretation of the slope of the production possibilities boundary?

❻ The following diagrams show the production possibilities boundaries for Canada and France, both of which produce only two goods, wine and lumber.

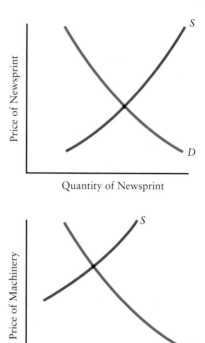

a. Which country has the comparative advantage in lumber? Explain.

b. Which country has the comparative advantage in wine? Explain.

c. Suppose Canada and France are initially not trading with each other and are producing at points C_1 and F_1, respectively. Suppose when trade is introduced, the free-trade relative prices are shown by the slope of the dashed line. Show in the diagrams which combination of goods each country will now produce.

d. In this case, what will be the pattern of trade for each country?

7 The following diagrams show the Canadian markets for newsprint and machinery, which we assume to be competitive.

a. Suppose there is no international trade. Show on the diagram the equilibrium price and quantity in the Canadian newsprint and machinery markets.

b. Now suppose Canada is open to trade with the rest of the world and the world price of newsprint is higher than the price of newsprint from part (a). Show in the diagram the quantities of domestic consumption and production and the quantity of newsprint that is either exported or imported.

c. Similarly, suppose the world price of machinery is lower than the price of machinery from part (a). Show in the diagram the quantity of domestic consumption and production and the quantity of machinery that is either exported or imported.

8 The table below shows indexes for the prices of imports and exports over several years for a hypothetical country.

Year	Import Prices	Export Prices	Terms of Trade
2011	90	110	—
2012	95	87	—
2013	98	83	—
2014	100	100	—
2015	102	105	—
2016	100	112	—
2017	103	118	—

a. Compute the terms of trade in each year for this country and fill in the table.

b. In which years do the terms of trade improve?

c. In which years do the terms of trade deteriorate?

d. Explain why a terms of trade "improvement" is good for the country.

9 For each of the following events, explain the likely effect on Canada's terms of trade. Your existing knowledge of Canada's imports and exports should be adequate to answer this question.

a. A hurricane damages much of Brazil's coffee crop.

b. OPEC countries succeed in significantly restricting the world supply of oil.

c. Several new large copper mines come into production in Chile.

d. A major recession in Southeast Asia reduces the world demand for pork.

e. Russia, a large producer of wheat, experiences a massive drought that reduces its wheat crop by more than 30 percent.

f. Three major potash-producing firms form a cartel and restrict the world's output of potash.

10 When the North American Free Trade Agreement (NAFTA) was being negotiated in the early 1990s, there was a great deal of debate. One critic argued that "it can't be in our interest to sign this deal; Mexico gains too much from it." What does the theory of the gains from trade have to say about that criticism?

11 Adam Smith saw a close connection between a nation's wealth and its ability and willingness "freely to engage" in trade with other countries.

a. Based on what you have learned in this chapter, what is the connection?

b. Explain why trading with countries that are "most different" from our own is likely to generate the most benefits. Which differences are of central importance?

c. Under what circumstances are there *no* benefits from a country specializing and trading with other countries?

d. Illustrate the argument from part (c) in a simple diagram of a country's production possibilities boundary.

12 Predict what each of the following events would do to the terms of trade of the importing country and the exporting country, other things being equal.

a. A blight destroys a large part of the coffee beans produced in the world.

b. Korean producers cut the price of the steel they sell to Canada.

c. General inflation of 4 percent occurs around the world.

d. Violation of OPEC output quotas leads to a sharp fall in the price of oil.

33 Trade Policy

CHAPTER OUTLINE	LEARNING OBJECTIVES (LO)
	After studying this chapter you will be able to
33.1 FREE TRADE OR PROTECTION?	**1** describe the various situations in which a country may rationally choose to protect some industries.
	2 discuss the most common invalid arguments in favour of protection.
33.2 METHODS OF PROTECTION	**3** explain the effects of tariffs and quotas on imported goods.
	4 understand why trade-remedy laws are sometimes just thinly disguised protection.
33.3 CURRENT TRADE POLICY	**5** distinguish between trade creation and trade diversion.
	6 discuss the main features of the North American Free Trade Agreement.

CONDUCTING business in a foreign country is not always easy. Differences in language, in local laws and customs, and in currency often complicate transactions. Our concern in this chapter, however, is not with these complications but with government policy toward international trade, which is called *trade policy*. At one extreme is a policy of free trade—that is, an absence of any form of government interference with the free flow of international trade. Any departure from free trade designed to protect domestic industries from foreign competition is called *protectionism*.

We begin by briefly restating the case for free trade and then go on to examine various valid and invalid arguments that are commonly advanced for some degree of protection. We then explore some of the methods commonly used to restrict trade, such as tariffs and quotas. Finally, we examine the many modern institutions designed to foster freer trade on either a global or a regional basis. In particular, we discuss the North American Free Trade Agreement (NAFTA) and the World Trade Organization (WTO).

33.1 FREE TRADE OR PROTECTION?

Today, most governments accept the proposition that a relatively free flow of international trade is desirable for the health of their individual economies. But heated debates still occur over trade policy. Should a country permit the *completely* free flow of international trade, or should it use policies to restrict the flow of trade and thereby protect its local producers from foreign competition? If some protection is desired, should it be achieved by tariffs or by non-tariff barriers? **Tariffs** are taxes designed to raise the domestic price of imported goods. **Non-tariff barriers (NTBs)** are policies other than tariffs designed to reduce the flow of imports; examples are import quotas and customs procedures that are deliberately more cumbersome than necessary.

tariff A tax applied on imports of goods or services.

non-tariff barriers (NTBs) Restrictions other than tariffs designed to reduce imports.

The Case for Free Trade

The gains from trade were presented in Chapter 32. Comparative advantages arise whenever countries have different opportunity costs. Free trade encourages all countries to specialize in producing products in which they have a comparative advantage. This pattern of specialization maximizes world production and hence maximizes average world living standards (as measured by the world's per capita GDP).

However, free trade does not necessarily make *everyone* better off than they would be in its absence. For example, reducing an existing tariff often results in individual groups receiving a smaller share of a larger world output so that they lose even though the average person gains. If we ask whether it is *possible* for free trade to improve everyone's living standards, the answer is yes because the larger total value of output that free trade generates could, at least in principle, be divided up in such a way that every individual is better off. If we ask whether free trade always does so in practice, however, the answer is, not necessarily.

Free trade makes the country as a whole better off, even though it may not make every individual in the country better off.

In today's world, a country's products must stand up to international competition if they are to survive. Over even as short a period as a few years, firms that do not develop new products and new production methods fall seriously behind their foreign competitors. If one country protects its domestic firms by imposing a tariff, those firms are likely to become complacent about the need to adopt new technologies, and over time they will become less competitive in international markets. As the technology gap between domestic and foreign firms widens, the tariff wall will provide less and less protection. Eventually, the domestic firms will succumb to foreign competition. Meanwhile, domestic living standards will fall relative to foreign ones.

Given that any country can be better off by specializing in those goods in which it has a comparative advantage, one might wonder why most countries of the world continue in some way to restrict the flow of trade. Why do tariffs and other barriers to trade continue to exist two centuries after Adam Smith and David Ricardo argued the case for free trade? Is there a valid case for some protection?

Countries whose economies are based on the production of only a few goods face risks from fluctuations in world prices. For this reason, protection to promote diversification may be viewed as desirable.

The Case for Protection

A country engages in trade **protection** whenever it uses policies that restrict the flow of trade in a way that favours domestic firms over their foreign competitors. There are several valid arguments for protection, including

- promoting diversification
- protecting specific groups
- improving the terms of trade
- protecting infant industries
- earning economic profits in foreign markets

We will discuss each of these arguments briefly. Note that the first two arguments generally involve achieving some worthy objective at the cost of a *reduction* in national income. The last three arguments are reasons for protection as a means of *increasing* a country's national income.

protection Any government policy that interferes with free trade in order to protect domestic firms and workers from foreign competition.

Promoting Diversification For a very small country, specializing in the production of only a few products—though dictated by comparative advantage—might involve risks that the country does not want to take. One such risk is that technological advances may render its basic product obsolete. Another risk, especially for countries specialized in producing a small range of agricultural products, is that swings in world prices lead to large swings in national income. By using protectionist policies, the government can encourage the creation of some domestic industries that may otherwise not exist. The cost is the loss of national income associated with devoting resources to production in industries in which there is no domestic comparative advantage. The benefit is that overall national income and employment become less volatile.

Protecting Specific Groups Although specialization according to comparative advantage will maximize *average* per capita GDP, some specific groups may have higher incomes under protection than under free trade. Of particular interest in Canada and the United States has been the effect that greater international trade has on the incomes of unskilled workers.

Consider the ratio of skilled workers to unskilled workers. There are plenty of both types throughout the world. Compared with much of the rest of the world, however, Canada has more skilled and fewer unskilled people. When trade is expanded because of a reduction in tariffs, Canada will tend to export goods made by its abundant skilled workers and import goods made by unskilled workers. (This is the basic prediction of the *factor endowment theory* of comparative advantage that we discussed in Chapter 32.) Because Canada is now exporting more goods made by skilled labour, the domestic demand for such labour rises. Because Canada is now importing more goods made by unskilled labour, the domestic demand for such labour falls. This specialization according to comparative advantage raises average Canadian living standards, but it will also tend to raise the wages and employment prospects of skilled Canadian workers relative to the wages of unskilled Canadian workers.

If increasing trade has these effects, then reducing trade by erecting protectionist trade barriers can have the opposite effects. Protectionist policies may raise the incomes of unskilled Canadian workers, giving them a larger share of a smaller total GDP.

The conclusion is that trade restrictions can improve the earnings of one group whenever the restrictions increase the demand for that group's services. This is done, however, at the expense of a reduction in *overall* national income and hence the country's average living standards.

> **Social and distributional concerns may lead to the rational adoption of protectionist policies. But the cost of such protection is a reduction in the country's *average* living standards.**

Improving the Terms of Trade   Tariffs can be used to change the terms of trade in favour of a country that makes up a large fraction of the world demand for some product that it imports. By restricting its demand for that product through a tariff, it can force down the price that foreign exporters receive for that product. The price paid by domestic consumers will probably rise but as long as the increase is less than the tariff, foreign suppliers will receive less per unit. For example, a 20 percent U.S. tariff on the import of Canadian softwood lumber might raise the price paid by U.S. consumers by 12 percent and lower the price received by Canadian suppliers by 8 percent (the difference between the two prices being received by the U.S. Treasury). This reduction in the price received by the Canadian suppliers of a U.S. import is a terms-of-trade improvement for the United States (and a terms-of-trade deterioration for Canada).

Note that not all countries can improve their terms of trade by levying tariffs on imported goods. A *necessary* condition is that the importing country has *market power*—in other words, that its imports represent a large proportion of total world demand for the good in question, so that its restrictive trade policies lead to a decline in the world price of its imports. Small countries, like Canada, are not large enough importers of any good to have a significant effect on world prices. For small countries, therefore, tariffs cannot improve their terms of trade.

> **Large countries can sometimes improve their terms of trade (and thus increase their national income) by levying tariffs on some imported goods; small countries cannot.**

Protecting Infant Industries   The oldest valid arguments for protection as a means of raising living standards concern economies of scale or learning by doing. It is usually called the **infant industry argument**. An infant industry is nothing more than a new, small industry. If such an industry has large economies of scale or the scope for learning by doing, costs will be high when the industry is small but will fall as the industry grows. In such industries, the country that first enters the field has a tremendous advantage. A developing country may find that in the early stages of development, its industries are unable to compete with established foreign rivals. A trade restriction may protect these industries from foreign competition while they "grow up." When they are large enough, they will be able to produce as cheaply as their larger foreign rivals and thus be able to compete without protection.

Most of the now industrialized countries developed their industries initially under quite heavy tariff protection. (In Canada's case, the National Policy of 1876 established a high tariff wall behind which many Canadian industries developed and thrived for many years.) Once the industrial sector was well developed, these countries reduced

infant industry argument The argument that new domestic industries with potential for economies of scale or learning by doing need to be protected from competition from established, low-cost foreign producers so that they can grow large enough to achieve costs as low as those of foreign producers.

their levels of protection, thus moving a long way toward free trade. Electronics in Taiwan, automobiles in Japan, commercial aircraft in Europe (specifically the consortium of European governments that created Airbus), and shipbuilding in South Korea are all examples in which protection of infant industries was successful. In each case, the national industry, protected by its home government, developed into a major player in the global marketplace.

One practical problem with this argument for protection is that some infants "never grow up." Once the young firm gets used to operating in a protected environment, it may resist having that protection disappear, even though all economies of scale may have been achieved. This is as much a political problem as an economic one. Political leaders must therefore be careful before offering protection to infant industries because they must recognize the political difficulties involved in removing that protection in the future. The countries that were most successful in having their protected industries eventually grow up and succeed in fierce international competition were those, such as Taiwan and South Korea, that ruthlessly withdrew support from unsuccessful infants within a specified time period.

Earning Economic Profits in Foreign Markets

Another argument for protectionist policies is to help create an advantage in producing or marketing some product that is expected to generate economic profits through its sales to foreign consumers. If protection of the domestic market, which might include subsidizing domestic firms, can increase the chance that one of the domestic firms will become established and thus earn high profits, the protection may pay off. The economic profits earned in foreign markets may exceed the cost to domestic taxpayers of the protection. This is the general idea of *strategic trade policy*.

Opponents of strategic trade policy argue that it is nothing more than a modern version of age-old and faulty justifications for tariff protection. Once all countries try to be strategic, they will all waste vast sums trying to break into industries in which there is no room for most of them. Domestic consumers would benefit most, they say, if their governments let other countries engage in this game. Consumers could then buy the cheap, subsidized foreign products and export traditional non-subsidized products in return. The opponents of strategic trade policy also argue that democratic governments that enter the game of picking and backing winners are likely to make more bad choices than good ones. One bad choice, with all of its massive development costs written off, would require that many good choices also be made in order to make the equivalent in profits that would allow taxpayers to break even overall.

An ongoing dispute between Canada and Brazil illustrates how strategic trade policy is often difficult to distinguish from pure protection. The world's two major producers of regional jets are Bombardier, based in Montreal, and Embraer SA, based in Brazil. For several years, each company has accused its competitor's government of using illegal subsidies to help the domestic company sell jets in world markets. Brazil's Pro-Ex program provides Embraer's customers with low-interest loans with which to purchase Embraer's jets. Export Development Canada (EDC) provides similar loans to Bombardier's customers.

PAULO WHITAKER/Reuters/Landov

For many years, Canada and Brazil have been in a trade dispute centred on each country's alleged support of aerospace manufacturers. Canada's Bombardier and Brazil's Embraer both receive considerable financial assistance from their respective governments.

There have been several complaints brought to the World Trade Organization (WTO) by both the Canadian and Brazilian governments. In various rulings the WTO determined that both governments were using illegal subsidy programs to support their aerospace firms. Both countries, however, naturally view their respective programs as necessary responses to the other country's subsidization. Many economists believe that an agreement to eliminate both programs would leave a "level playing field," while saving Brazilian and Canadian taxpayers a considerable amount of money. As of 2015, however, governments in both countries continue to support their respective aerospace firms and both sets of taxpayers continue to foot the bill.

A country can potentially increase its national income by protecting infant industries and by subsidizing "strategic" firms. Unless carefully applied, however, such policies can end up being redistributions from consumers and taxpayers to domestic firms, without any benefit to overall living standards.

Invalid Arguments for Protection

We have seen that free trade is generally beneficial for a country overall even though it does not necessarily make every person better off. We have also seen that there are some situations in which there are valid arguments for restricting trade. For every valid argument, however, there are many invalid arguments. Here we review a few arguments that are frequently heard in political debates concerning international trade.

Keep the Money at Home   This argument says that if I buy a foreign good, I have the good and the foreigner has the money, whereas if I buy the same good locally, I have the good and our country has the money, too. This argument is based on a common misconception. It assumes that domestic money actually goes abroad physically when imports are purchased and that trade flows only in one direction. But when Canadian importers purchase Japanese goods, they do not send dollars abroad. They (or their financial agents) buy Japanese yen and use them to pay the Japanese manufacturers. They purchase the yen on the foreign-exchange market by giving up dollars to someone who wants to use them for expenditure in Canada. Even if the money did go abroad physically—that is, if a Japanese firm accepted a bunch of Canadian $100 bills—it would be because that firm (or someone to whom it could sell the dollars) wanted them to spend in the only country where they are legal tender—Canada.

Canadian currency ultimately does no one any good except as purchasing power in Canada. Actually, it would be miraculous if Canadian money could be exported to other countries in return for real goods. After all, the Bank of Canada has the power to create as much new Canadian money as it wants (at almost zero direct cost). It is only because Canadian money can buy Canadian products and Canadian assets that others want it.

Protect Against Low-Wage Foreign Labour   This argument says that the products of low-wage countries will drive Canadian products from the market, and the high Canadian standard of living will be dragged down to that of its poorer trading partners. For example, if Canada imports cotton shirts from Bangladesh, higher-cost Canadian textile firms may go out of business and Canadian workers may be laid off. This argument says that Canada is worse off *overall* by trading with Bangladesh. Is this really true?

As a prelude to considering this argument, think what the argument would imply if taken out of the context of countries and applied instead to individuals, where the same principles govern the gains from trade. Is it impossible for a rich person to gain by trading with a poor person? Would Bill Gates and Warren Buffett really be better off if they did all their own gardening, cooking and cleaning? No one believes that a rich person gains nothing by trading with those who are less rich.

Why, then, must a rich group of people lose when they trade with a poor group? "Well," some may say, "the poor group will price its goods too cheaply." Consumers gain, however, when they can buy the same goods at a lower price. If Vietnamese, Mexican, or Indian workers earn low wages and the goods they produce are sold at low prices, Canadians will gain by obtaining imports at a low cost in terms of the goods that must be exported in return. The cheaper our imports are, the better off we are in terms of the goods and services available for domestic consumption.

As we said earlier in this chapter, *some* Canadians may be better off if Canada places high tariffs on the import of goods from Mexico or India or other developing nations. In particular, if the goods produced in these countries compete with goods made by unskilled Canadian workers, then those unskilled workers will be better off if a Canadian tariff protects their firms and thus their jobs. But Canadian income overall—that is, average per capita real income—will be higher when there is free trade.

Exports Are Good; Imports Are Bad Exports create domestic income; imports create income for foreigners. Surely, then, it is desirable to encourage exports by subsidizing them and to discourage imports by taxing them. This is an appealing argument, but it is incorrect.

Exports raise GDP by adding to the value of domestic output and income, but they do not add to the value of domestic consumption. The standard of living in a country depends on the level of consumption, not on the level of income. In other words, income is not of much use except that it provides the means for consumption.

If exports really were "good" and imports really were "bad," then a fully employed economy that managed to increase exports without a corresponding increase in imports ought to be better off. Such a change, however, would result in a reduction in current standards of living because when more goods are sent abroad but no more are brought in from abroad, the total goods available for domestic consumption must fall.

The living standards of a country depend on the goods and services consumed in that country. The importance of exports is that they provide the resources required to purchase imports, either now or in the future.

Create Domestic Jobs It is sometimes said that an economy with substantial unemployment, such as Canada during and immediately after the 2009 recession, provides an exception to the case for freer trade. Suppose tariffs or import quotas reduce the imports of Japanese cars, Indian textiles, German kitchen equipment, and Polish sausages. Surely, the argument goes, these polices will create more employment in Canadian industries producing similar products. This may be true but it will also *reduce* employment in other industries.

The Japanese, Indians, Germans, and Poles can buy products from Canada only if they earn Canadian dollars by selling their domestically produced goods and services to Canada (or by borrowing dollars from Canada).[1] The decline in their sales of cars, textiles, kitchen equipment, and sausages will decrease their purchases of Canadian lumber, software, banking services, and holidays. Jobs will be lost in Canadian export industries and gained in industries that formerly faced competition from imports. The major long-term effect is that the same amount of total employment in Canada will merely be redistributed among industries. In the process, average living standards will be reduced because employment expands in inefficient import-competing industries and contracts in efficient exporting industries.

A country that imposes tariffs in an attempt to create domestic jobs risks starting a "tariff war" with its trading partners. Such a trade war can easily leave every country worse off, as world output (and thus income) falls significantly. An income-reducing trade war followed the onset of the Great Depression in 1929 as many countries increased tariffs to protect their domestic industries in an attempt to stimulate domestic production and employment. Most economists agree that this trade war made the Great Depression worse than it otherwise would have been. *Lessons from History 33-1* discusses this relationship between tariffs and recession and how it resurfaced during the major recession that followed the 2008 global financial crisis.

33.2 METHODS OF PROTECTION

We now go on to explore the effects of two specific protectionist policies. Both cause the price of the imported good to rise and the quantity demanded by domestic consumers to fall. They differ, however, in how they achieve these results.

Tariffs

A tariff, also called an *import duty*, is a tax on imported goods. For example, consider a Canadian firm that wants to import cotton T-shirts from India at $5 per shirt. If the Canadian government levies a 20 percent tariff on imported cotton shirts, the Canadian firm pays $5 to the Indian exporter *plus* $1 (20 percent of $5) in import duties to the Canada Revenue Agency. The immediate effect of a tariff is therefore to increase the domestic firm's cost to $6 per T-shirt. This tariff has important implications for domestic consumers as well as domestic producers. The effect of a tariff is shown in Figure 33-1.

The initial effect of the tariff is to raise the domestic price of the imported product above its world price

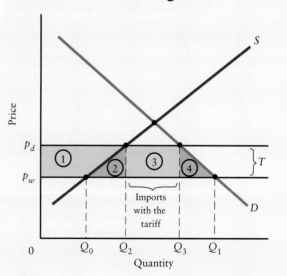

FIGURE 33-1 The Deadweight Loss of a Tariff

A tariff imposes a deadweight loss for the importing country. Before the tariff, the price in the domestic economy is the world price, p_w. Imports are Q_0Q_1. With a tariff of T per unit, the domestic price rises to p_d. Domestic consumption falls to Q_3, and consumer surplus falls by areas ① + ② + ③ + ④. Domestic production rises to Q_2 and producer surplus increases by area ①. Imports fall to Q_2Q_3, and the government collects tariff revenue equal to area ③. The sum of areas ② and ④ represents the deadweight loss of the tariff.

---

[1] They can also get dollars by selling to other countries and then using their currencies to buy Canadian dollars. But this intermediate step only complicates the transaction; it does not change its fundamental nature. Other countries must have earned the dollars by selling goods to Canada or borrowing from Canada.

LESSONS FROM HISTORY 33-1

Trade Protection and Recession

In 1929, at the start of the Great Depression, governments in many countries responded to internal political pressures to protect domestic jobs. In the United States, Congress passed the Smoot-Hawley Tariff Act in June 1930, legislation that raised tariffs on hundreds of different imported products. At the time, a petition against the legislation was signed by 1028 economists who argued that such tariffs would be costly for America and would initiate a "tariff war" between the United States and its trading partners, thereby worsening the economic situation.

In retrospect, the economists were clearly correct. Dozens of countries protested the increase in U.S. tariffs but then retaliated by increasing their own tariffs. Here in Canada, Liberal Prime Minister Mackenzie King raised tariffs on imported U.S. products and lowered them on imports from the rest of the British Empire. Confident that he would earn the public's support for his aggressive actions, he promptly called a federal election. But the Conservatives under R.B. Bennett argued that the Liberal actions were far too timid, and the voters apparently agreed. The Liberals were soundly defeated, Bennett became prime minister, and Canadian tariffs on U.S. products were raised even further.

Economists today agree that the widespread increase in tariffs in the 1930s contributed significantly to a reduction in global trade and made the economic situation worse. In January of 1929, before the onset of the Depression, the annual volume of world trade was $5.3 billion. Four years later, at the depth of the Depression, world trade had collapsed to $1.8 billion, a reduction of 66 percent. The net effect, instead of increasing employment in any country, was to shift jobs from efficient export industries to inefficient domestic industries, supplying local markets in place of imports.

When the most recent worldwide recession began in the wake of the 2008 global financial crisis, world leaders were mindful of this important lesson from the Great Depression. When meeting in Washington, D.C., to coordinate their policy responses, the leaders of the world's largest developed and developing countries (the G20 group of countries) publicly committed to not raising any tariffs for at least one year.

Despite this commitment, however, protectionist measures soon emerged. In the United States, the fiscal stimulus package passed by Congress included a "buy American" clause prohibiting any funds from the

by the amount of the tariff. Imports fall. The price received on domestically produced units rises, as does the quantity produced domestically. On both counts, domestic producers earn more. However, the cost of producing the extra production at home exceeds the price at which it could be purchased on the world market. Thus, the benefit to domestic producers comes at the expense of domestic consumers. Indeed, domestic consumers lose on two counts: First, they consume less of the product because its price rises, and second, they pay a higher price for the amount that they do consume. This extra spending ends up in two places: The extra that is paid on all units produced at home goes to domestic producers, and the extra that is paid on units still imported goes to the government as tariff revenue.

The overall loss to the domestic economy from levying a tariff is best seen in terms of the changes in consumer and producer surplus. Before the tariff, consumer surplus was equal to the entire area below the demand curve and above the price line at p_w.

After the tariff, the price increase leads to less consumption and less consumer surplus. The loss of consumer surplus is the sum of the areas ①, ②, ③, and ④ in Figure 33-1. As domestic producers respond to the higher domestic price by increasing their production and sales, they earn more producer surplus, equal to area ①. Finally, the taxpayers gain the tariff revenue equal to area ③. This is simply a redistribution of surplus away from consumers toward taxpayers. In summary:

package being spent on imported construction materials. Similar kinds of protection were built in to the fiscal stimulus packages in China and some European countries. Canada and other major trading nations were understandably concerned by these actions and soon began threatening their own retaliatory measures. The Canadian government went to great lengths to argue that U.S. trade protection would not only hurt Canada but would also hurt the United States by raising prices for American consumers, thus making economic recovery more difficult.

While the lessons from history were being forgotten by some political leaders, a few prominent voices were arguing the dangers of increased trade protection. The World Bank issued a report in March 2009 indicating that in the previous four months world leaders had proposed or implemented 78 different protectionist measures. The president of the World Bank urged leaders to rethink these policies: "Leaders must not heed the siren-song of protectionist fixes, whether for trade, stimulus packages or bailouts. . . . Economic isolationism can lead to a negative spiral of events such as those we saw in the 1930s, which made a bad situation much, much worse."

Canadian Prime Ministers Bennett (left) and Mackenzie King (right) both learned in the 1930s that protectionist policies often make better politics than economics.

Loss of consumer surplus	= ① + ② + ③ + ④
Gain of producer surplus	= ①
Gain of tariff revenue	= ③
Net loss in surplus	= ② + ④

The overall effect of the tariff is therefore to create a deadweight loss to the domestic economy equal to areas ② plus ④. Domestic consumers are worse off, while domestic firms and taxpayers are better off. But the net effect is a loss of surplus for the economy as a whole. This is the overall cost of levying a tariff.

A tariff imposes costs on domestic consumers, generates benefits for domestic producers, and generates revenue for the government. But the overall net effect is negative; a tariff generates a deadweight loss for the economy.

FIGURE 33-2 **The Deadweight Loss of an Import Quota**

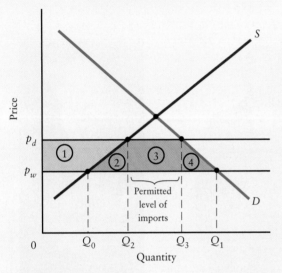

An import quota drives up the domestic price and imposes a deadweight loss on the importing country. With free trade, the domestic price is the world price, p_w. Imports are Q_0Q_1. If imports are restricted to only Q_2Q_3 (through either quotas or VERs), the domestic price must rise to the point where the restricted level of imports just satisfies the domestic excess demand—this occurs only at P_d. The rise in price and reduction in consumption reduces consumer surplus by areas ① + ② + ③ + ④. Domestic producers increase their output as the domestic price rises, and producer surplus increases by area ①. Area ③ does not accrue to the domestic economy; instead this area represents extra producer surplus for the foreign firms that export their product to this country. The net effect of the quota or VER is a deadweight loss for the importing country of areas ② + ③ + ④. Import quotas are therefore worse than tariffs for the importing country.

import quota A limit set on the quantity of a foreign product that may be imported in a given time period.

voluntary export restriction (VER) An agreement by an exporting country to limit the amount of a good exported to another country.

Quotas and Voluntary Export Restrictions (VERs)

The second type of protectionist policy directly restricts the quantity of imports of a specific product. A common example is the **import quota**, by which the importing country sets a maximum quantity of some product that may be imported each year. Another measure is the **voluntary export restriction (VER)**, an agreement by an exporting country to limit the amount of a product that it sells to the importing country.

Figure 33-2 shows that a quantity restriction and a tariff have similar effects on domestic consumers and producers—they both raise domestic prices, increase domestic production, and reduce domestic consumption. But a direct quantity restriction is actually *worse* than a tariff for the importing country because the effect of the quantity restriction is to raise the price received by the foreign suppliers of the good. In contrast, a tariff leaves the foreign suppliers' price unchanged and instead generates tariff revenue for the government of the importing country.

> **Import quotas and voluntary export restrictions (VERs) impose larger deadweight losses on the importing country than do tariffs that lead to the same level of imports.**

Canada, the United States, and the European Union have used VERs extensively, and the EU makes frequent use of import quotas. Japan has been pressured into negotiating several VERs with Canada, the United States, and the EU in order to limit sales of some of the Japanese goods that have had the most success in international competition. For example, in 1983, the United States and Canada negotiated VERs whereby the Japanese government agreed to restrict total sales of Japanese cars to these two countries for three years. When the agreements ran out in 1986, the Japanese continued to restrict their automobile sales by unilateral voluntary action. Japan's readiness to restrict its exports to North America reflects the high profits that Japanese automobile producers were making under the system of VERs, as explained in Figure 33-2. In recent years, such VERs have become less important because Japan's major automobile producers have established manufacturing plants in Canada.

Tariffs Versus Quotas: An Application

The dispute that raged for several years between Canada and the United States over the exports of Canadian softwood lumber (spruce, pine, fir, cedar) illustrates an important distinction between tariffs and quotas. The United States protected its softwood lumber industry in two ways:

- by imposing tariffs on U.S. imports of Canadian softwood lumber
- by pressuring Canadian governments to place quotas on Canadian exports to the United States

Analysis of Figure 33-1 and 33-2 reveals that the choice between tariffs and quotas matters greatly for Canadian producers.

In the case of a U.S. tariff on imported Canadian softwood lumber, Figure 33-1 illustrates the U.S. market. An import tariff raises the domestic price for U.S. lumber users and also increases the profits of U.S. lumber producers. Canadian lumber producers are harmed because there is less demand for their product at the unchanged world price. Area ③ in the figure represents U.S. tariff revenue collected on the imports of Canadian lumber—revenue that accrues to the United States government.

Figure 33-2 illustrates the U.S. market for softwood lumber when a quota is placed on the level of Canadian exports (U.S. imports). As with the tariff, the restricted supply of Canadian lumber to the U.S. market drives up the price to U.S. users and also raises profits for U.S. producers. But with a quota there is an important difference: The higher price in the U.S. market is received by the Canadian lumber producers, as shown by area ③ in the figure.

While a tariff and quota may lead to the same reduced volume of exports, the tariff permits some surplus to be captured by the importing country, whereas the quota allows some surplus to be captured by the exporting country (area ③ in both cases). In the U.S.–Canadian softwood lumber dispute, both tariffs and quotas were used. And while both systems were to be preferred *overall* by a system of free trade, Canada had an interest in imposing quotas on Canadian lumber exporters rather than having the same export reduction accomplished by a U.S. tariff.

Trade-Remedy Laws and Non-Tariff Barriers

As tariffs in many countries were lowered over the years since the Second World War, countries that wanted to protect domestic industries began using, and often abusing, a series of trade restrictions that came to be known as *non-tariff barriers* (NTBs). The original purpose of some of these barriers was to remedy certain legitimate problems that arise in international trade and, for this reason, they are often called *trade-remedy laws*. All too often, however, such laws are misused and over time become powerful means of simple protection.

Dumping   Selling a product in a foreign country at a lower price than in the domestic market is known as **dumping**. For example, if U.S.-made cars were sold for less in Canada than in the United States, the U.S. automobile firms would be said to be *dumping*. Dumping is a form of price discrimination studied in the theory of firms with price-setting power (see Chapter 10). Most governments have antidumping duties designed to protect their own industries against what is viewed as unfair foreign pricing practices.

dumping The practice of selling a commodity at a lower price in the export market than in the domestic market for reasons unrelated to differences in costs of servicing the two markets.

> Dumping, if it lasts indefinitely, can be a gift to the receiving country. Its consumers get goods from abroad at lower prices than they otherwise would.

Dumping is more often a temporary measure, designed to get rid of unwanted surpluses, or a predatory attempt to drive competitors out of business. In either case, domestic producers complain about unfair foreign competition. In both cases, it is accepted international practice to levy *antidumping duties* on foreign imports. These duties are designed to eliminate the discriminatory elements in their prices.

Unfortunately, antidumping laws have been evolving over the past three decades in ways that allow antidumping duties to become barriers to trade and competition rather than to provide redress for genuinely unfair trading practices.

Several features of the antidumping system that is now in place in many countries make it highly protectionist. First, any price discrimination between national markets is classified as dumping and is subject to penalties. Thus, prices in the producer's domestic market become, in effect, minimum prices below which no sales can be made in foreign markets, whatever the nature of demand in the domestic and foreign markets. Second, many countries' laws calculate the "margin of dumping" as the difference between the price that is charged in that country's market and the foreign producer's average cost. Thus, when there is a global slump in some industry so that the profit-maximizing price for all producers is below average cost, foreign producers can be convicted of dumping. This gives domestic producers enormous protection whenever the market price falls temporarily below average cost. Third, law in the United States (but not in all other countries) places the onus of proof on the accused. Facing a charge of dumping, a foreign producer must prove that the charge is unfounded. Fourth, U.S. antidumping duties are imposed with no time limit, so they often persist long after foreign firms have altered the prices that gave rise to them.

Antidumping laws were first designed to permit countries to respond to predatory pricing by foreign firms. More recently, they have been used to protect domestic firms against any foreign competition.

---

countervailing duty A tariff imposed by one country designed to offset the effects of specific subsidies provided by foreign governments.

Countervailing Duties   A **countervailing duty** is a tariff imposed by one country designed to offset the effects of specific subsidies provided by foreign governments to their exporting firms. For example, if the German government provided subsidies to its firms that produce and export machine tools, the Canadian government might respond by imposing a countervailing duty—a tariff—on the imports of German machine tools designed to "level the playing field" between German and Canadian firms in that industry. Countervailing duties, which are commonly used by the U.S. government but much less so elsewhere, provide another case in which a trade-remedy law can become a covert method of protection.

There is no doubt that countervailing duties have sometimes been used to counteract the effects of foreign subsidies. Many governments complain, however, that countervailing duties are often used as thinly disguised protection. At the early stages of the development of countervailing duties, only subsidies whose prime effect was to distort trade were possible objects of countervailing duties. Even then, however, the existence of equivalent domestic subsidies was not taken into account when decisions were made to put countervailing duties on subsidized imports. Thus, the United States levies some countervailing duties against foreign goods even though the foreign subsidy is less than the domestic (U.S.) subsidy in the same industry. This does not create a level playing field.

Over time, the type of subsidy that is subject to countervailing duties has evolved until almost any government program that affects industry now risks becoming the object of a countervailing duty. Because all governments, including most U.S. state governments, have programs that provide direct or indirect assistance to industry, the potential for the use of countervailing duties as thinly disguised trade barriers is enormous.

> **Countervailing duties can be used to offset the effects of foreign export subsidies, but often they are nothing more than thinly disguised protection.**

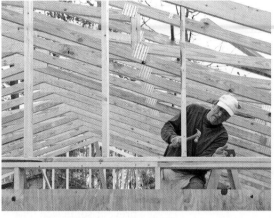

Softwood lumber (spruce, pine, and fir) is used extensively in North America for the framing of houses and small buildings. For many years, the United States levied countervailing duties on Canadian softwood lumber exports, alleging that Canadian provinces unfairly subsidized production. In 2006, the Canadian and U.S. governments reached an agreement to end the dispute.

The best-known example in Canada of a U.S. countervailing duty is the 27 percent duty imposed on U.S. imports of Canadian softwood lumber in the early 2000s. The U.S. government's claim was that Canadian provincial governments provided a subsidy to domestic lumber producers by charging artificially low *stumpage fees*—the fees paid by the companies to cut trees on Crown land. In 2006, the U.S. government agreed to eliminate the countervailing duty but only if restrictions were placed on Canadian lumber exports. Thus, a tariff was replaced by a combination of an export quota and an export tax.

33.3 CURRENT TRADE POLICY

In the remainder of the chapter, we discuss trade policy in practice. We start with the many international agreements that govern current trade policies and then look in a little more detail at the NAFTA.

Before 1947, in the absence of any international agreement, any country was free to impose tariffs on its imports. However, when one country increased its tariffs, the action often triggered retaliatory actions by its trading partners. During the Great Depression in the 1930s, widespread increases in protection occurred as many countries sought to raise their employment and output by raising its tariffs. The end result was lowered efficiency, less trade, and a deeper economic decline. Since the end of the Second World War, much effort has been devoted to reducing tariff barriers, both on a multilateral and on a regional basis.

The GATT and the WTO

One of the most notable achievements of the post–Second World War era was the creation in 1947 of the General Agreement on Tariffs and Trade (GATT). The principle of the GATT was that each member country agreed not to make unilateral tariff increases. This prevented the outbreak of "tariff wars" in which countries raised tariffs to protect particular domestic industries and to retaliate against other countries' tariff increases. The GATT has since been replaced by the World Trade Organization (WTO), which continues the work of the GATT.

Through various "rounds" of negotiations under the auspices of the GATT and the WTO, the average level of tariffs has declined considerably since 1947. In addition to the tariff reductions, an important success of the WTO negotiations has been the creation of a formal dispute-settlement mechanism. This mechanism allows countries to take cases of alleged trade violations—such as illegal subsidies or tariffs—to the WTO for a formal ruling, and obliges member countries to follow the ruling. A notable failure of the WTO process has been the inability to significantly liberalize trade in agricultural products, an industry that still receives massive subsidies and other government support in many developed and developing countries.

Despite the WTO's successes in recent years, the organization has many critics. One common criticism is that the WTO's process of negotiating trade agreements pays insufficient attention to environmental and labour standards, especially as they exist in the developing countries. Another criticism is that the presence of the WTO does not prevent some rich and powerful countries from ruthlessly pursuing their own interests, often to the detriment of economic conditions in weaker countries. *Applying Economic Concepts 33-1* addresses some of the often-heard criticisms of the WTO and argues that, as imperfect as the institution may be, it holds out much promise for continued progress in trade liberalization.

Regional Trade Agreements

Regional agreements seek to liberalize trade over a much smaller group of countries than the WTO membership. Three standard forms of regional trade-liberalizing agreements are *free trade areas, customs unions*, and *common markets.*

free trade area (FTA) An agreement among two or more countries to abolish tariffs on trade among themselves while each remains free to set its own tariffs against other countries.

A **free trade area** (**FTA**) is the least comprehensive of the three. It allows for tariff-free trade among the member countries, but it leaves each member free to establish its own trade policy with respect to other countries. As a result, members are required to maintain customs points at their common borders to make sure that imports into the free trade area do not all enter through the member that is levying the lowest tariff on each item. They must also agree on *rules of origin* to establish when a good is made in a member country and hence is able to pass tariff-free across their borders, and when it is imported from outside the FTA and hence is subject to tariffs when it crosses borders within the FTA. The three countries in North America formed a free-trade area when they created the NAFTA in 1994.

In recent years, Canada has signed bilateral free-trade agreements with Israel, Chile, Costa Rica, Peru, Colombia, and Jordan and is currently negotiating with Japan. In 2014, Canada completed negotiations with the European Union of a Comprehensive Economic and Trade Agreement (CETA). The agreement currently awaits ratification by the Canadian Parliament. In 2012, Canada gained admission to the Trans-Pacific Partnership (TPP), a new proposed free-trade agreement between several Pacific-rim countries, including Australia, New Zealand, the United States, Chile, Singapore, Vietnam, and others. The details of the agreement are currently being negotiated.

customs union A group of countries that agree to have free trade among themselves and a common set of barriers against imports from the rest of the world.

A **customs union** is a free trade area in which the member countries agree to establish a common trade policy with the rest of the world. Because they have a common trade policy, the members need neither customs controls on products moving among themselves nor rules of origin. Once a product has entered any member country it has met the common rules and regulations and paid the common tariff and so it may henceforth be treated the same as one that is produced within the union. An example of a customs union is Mercosur, an agreement linking Argentina, Brazil, Paraguay,

APPLYING ECONOMIC CONCEPTS 33-1

Does the WTO Do More Harm Than Good?

There are many critics of the World Trade Organization. Extremists argue that all institutions supporting globalization should be abolished. Other critics admit that globalization is inevitable but say that the WTO is so faulty in providing a rules-based system that it does more harm than good.

Supporters of the WTO argue that it is the best hope for poor countries that would be most oppressed in a lawless world in which rich countries, particularly the United States and members of the European Union, could behave as they wanted. Rather than allowing the poorer countries to flounder in a lawless world, the WTO provides a rules-based regime and has a dispute-settlement function that has heard more than 300 cases. Even if the rich countries do exert undue power over the negotiations, at least the WTO meetings provide a forum for poor nations to speak out and broker alliances. The alternative—no voice in a no-rules system—would be much worse.

Critics often respond that while the existence of the dispute-settlement mechanism may be beneficial, the enforcement of those settlements is undermined by disparities in economic power. Nations with large economies can use trade sanctions against small nations, but the small nation that attempts the same often inflicts the most harm on its own economy. Supporters of the WTO agree that this *is* a major defect, but the dispute-settlement mechanism has accomplished much, and to discard it because of imperfect enforcement would be a great loss. What is needed is *reform*—with larger economies agreeing to graduated enforcement mechanisms, including stiffer penalties for themselves.

Critics also claim that the WTO is a failure because it does not permit the imposition of trade sanctions against countries that pollute their own environments or exploit their own workers. But the poorest countries, many of whom are strong WTO supporters, fear that advanced countries would use environmental and labour standards written into the body of trade agreements as disguised non-tariff barriers. To the poorer countries it would be "policy imperialism" to argue that they should be forced to accept the standards of environmental and labour protection that the rich countries can only now afford. Nonetheless, environmental and labour protections are being written into some new trade agreements, and it remains to be seen if they will work beneficially or harmfully—or not at all.

Critics also complain that the WTO is undemocratic. In response, supporters point out that it is representatives of sovereign nations, usually elected ones, who conduct the negotiations, and that any agreements must be ratified by respective national parliaments before they come into effect. It is unlikely that any organization able to achieve agreement among 161 member-country governments could be any more democratic while still being effective.

Finally, some critics claim that the WTO is simply a tool for those who advocate a doctrinaire form of laissez-faire capitalism. It is true that some WTO supporters believe that unfettered free markets can meet all social requirements. A far larger number of supporters, however, believe that the market system needs government involvement if it is to meet societal needs for social justice and growth. The vast majority of supporters agree that most, if not all, trade restrictions are harmful and that the WTO, with its mission of continued trade liberalization, can create significant benefits to rich and poor countries alike.

and Uruguay. A **common market** is a customs union that also has free movement of labour and capital among its members. The European Union is by far the largest example of a common market.

> **common market** A customs union with the added provision that labour and capital can move freely among the members.

Trade Creation and Trade Diversion

A major effect of regional trade liberalization is to alter the pattern of production and trade as countries reallocate their resources toward the production of goods in which they have a comparative advantage. Economists divide the effects on trade into two categories: *trade creation* and *trade diversion*. These concepts were first developed by

Jacob Viner, a Canadian-born economist who taught at the University of Chicago and Princeton University in the first half of the twentieth century.

trade creation A consequence of reduced trade barriers among a set of countries whereby trade within the group is increased and trade with the rest of the world remains roughly constant.

Trade creation occurs when producers in one member country find that they can export products to another member country that previously were produced there because of tariff protection. For example, when the North American Free Trade Agreement (NAFTA) eliminated most cross-border tariffs among Mexico, Canada, and the United States, some U.S. firms found that they could undersell their Canadian competitors in some product lines, and some Canadian firms found that they could undersell their U.S. competitors in other product lines. As a result, specialization occurred, and new international trade developed among the three countries.

Trade creation represents efficient specialization according to comparative advantage.

trade diversion A consequence of reduced trade barriers among a set of countries whereby trade within the group replaces trade that used to take place with countries outside the group.

Trade diversion occurs when exporters in one member country *replace* more efficient foreign exporters as suppliers to another member country. For example, trade diversion occurs when U.S. firms find that they can undersell competitors from the rest of the world in the Canadian market, not because they are the cheapest source of supply, but because their tariff-free prices under NAFTA are lower than the tariff-burdened prices of imports from other countries. This effect is a gain to U.S. firms and Canadian consumers of the product. U.S. firms get new business and therefore they clearly gain. Canadian consumers buy the product at a lower, tariff-free price from the U.S. producer than they used to pay to the third-country producer (with a tariff), and so they are also better off. But Canada as a whole is worse off as a result of the trade diversion. Canada is now buying the product from a U.S. producer at a higher price with no tariff. Before the agreement, it was buying from a third-country producer at a lower price (and collecting tariff revenue).

From the global perspective, trade diversion represents an inefficient use of resources.

The main argument *against* regional trade agreements is that the costs of trade diversion may outweigh the benefits of trade creation. While recognizing this possibility, many economists believe that regional agreements, especially among only a few countries, are much easier to negotiate than multilateral agreements through the WTO. In addition, regional agreements may represent effective *incremental* progress in what is a very lengthy process of achieving global free trade.

The North American Free Trade Agreement

The NAFTA dates from 1994 and is an extension of the 1989 Canada–U.S. Free Trade Agreement (FTA). It established a free trade area, as opposed to a customs union; each member country retains its own external trade policy, and rules of origin are needed to determine when a good is made within North America and thus allowed to move freely among the members.

National Treatment   The fundamental principle that guides the NAFTA is that of *national treatment*. The principle of national treatment is that individual countries are free to establish any laws they want, with the sole proviso that these laws must not discriminate on the basis of nationality. For example, Canada can choose to have stringent laws against releasing pollutants in waterways or against the emission of noxious gases into the atmosphere. The principle of national treatment requires that the Canadian government enforce these laws equally on all firms located in Canada, independent of their ownership or nationality. It is against the NAFTA conditions to apply more stringent laws to foreign-owned firms than to domestic firms, or vice versa. Canada can also choose to impose strict product standards related to the chemical content of paint or the nutritional content of foods, but again the NAFTA condition requires that such laws be applied to products independent of where they are produced. For example, it would be against the NAFTA rules to require a specific level of fuel efficiency on imported cars but not on those cars produced and sold in Canada.

The principle of national treatment allows each member country a maximum of policy independence while preventing national policies from being used as trade barriers. In the absence of national treatment, Canada could impose stringent environmental or product standards on the products of *foreign* firms only and thereby offer effective protection to its domestic firms who need only satisfy less stringent standards.

Other Major Provisions   There are several other major provisions in the NAFTA.

1. All tariffs on trade between Canada, the United States, and Mexico were eliminated as of 2010.

2. The principle of national treatment (described above) applies to foreign investment once it enters a country, but each country can screen foreign investment before it enters.

3. Some restrictions on trade and investment are not eliminated by the agreement. In Canada's case, the main examples are supply-managed agricultural products and cultural industries such as magazine and book publishing.

4. Trade in most non-agricultural service industries is liberalized and subject to the principle of national treatment.

5. A significant amount of government procurement is open to cross-border bidding, though a large part is still exempt from NAFTA.

Dispute Settlement   From Canada's point of view, by far the biggest setback in the negotiations for the Canada–U.S. FTA was the failure to obtain agreement on a common regime for countervailing and antidumping duties. In view of that failure, no significant attempt was made to deal with this issue in the subsequent NAFTA negotiations. The U.S. Congress was unwilling to abandon the unilateral use of these powerful weapons.

In the absence of such a multilateral regime, a NAFTA dispute-settlement mechanism was created. Under it, the justifications required for the levying of antidumping and countervailing duties are subject to review by a panel of Canadians, Americans, and Mexicans. This international review replaces appeal through the domestic courts.

The panel has the power to suspend any duties until it is satisfied that the domestic laws have been correctly and fairly applied.

The establishment of the dispute-settlement mechanism in NAFTA was path breaking: for the first time in its history, the United States agreed to submit the administration of its domestic laws to *binding* scrutiny by an international panel that often contains a majority of foreigners.

Results   The Canada–U.S. FTA aroused a great debate in Canada. Indeed, the Canadian federal election of 1988 was fought almost entirely on the issue of free trade. Supporters looked for major increases in the security of existing trade from U.S. protectionist attacks and for a growth of new trade. Detractors predicted a flight of firms to the United States, the loss of many Canadian jobs, and even the demise of Canada's political independence.

By and large, however, both the Canada–U.S. FTA and the NAFTA agreements worked out just about as expected by their supporters. Industry restructured in the direction of greater export orientation in all three countries, and trade creation occurred. The flow of trade among the three countries increased markedly, but especially so between Canada and the United States. As the theory of trade predicts, specialization occurred in many areas, resulting in more U.S. imports of some product lines from Canada and more U.S. exports of other goods to Canada. In 1988, before the Canada–U.S. FTA took effect, Canada exported $85 billion in goods to the United States and imported $74 billion from the United States. By 2014, the value of Canada–U.S. trade had more than quadrupled—Canadian exports of goods to the United States had increased to $400 billion and imports from the United States had increased to $351 billion. (Note that these figures exclude trade in services; with services included, the increase in Canada–U.S. trade between 1988 and 2014 would be larger by about $100 billion in each direction.)[2]

It is hard to say how much trade diversion there has been and will be in the future. The greatest potential for trade diversion is with Mexico, which competes in the Canadian and U.S. markets with a large number of products produced in other low-wage countries. Southeast Asian exporters to the United States and Canada have been worried that Mexico would capture some of their markets by virtue of having tariff-free access denied to their goods. Most estimates predict, however, that trade creation will dominate over trade diversion.

Most transitional difficulties were initially felt in each country's import-competing industries, just as theory predicts. Such an agreement as the NAFTA brings its advantages by encouraging a movement of resources out of protected but inefficient import-competing industries, which decline, and into efficient export industries, which expand because they have better access to the markets of other member countries. Southern Ontario and parts of Quebec had difficulties as some traditional exports fell and labour and capital were shifting to sectors where trade was expanding. By the late 1990s, however, Southern Ontario was booming again and its most profitable sectors were those that exported to the United States.

[2] These data are in nominal dollars, which naturally grow over time along with real GDP and the price level. As a share of GDP, however, Canadian trade with the United States has also grown substantially. In 1988, exports and imports of goods (excluding services) with the United States were each roughly 13 percent of Canadian GDP; by 2014, they were each about 18 percent of Canadian GDP.

APPLYING ECONOMIC CONCEPTS 33-2

Canadian Wine: A Free-Trade Success Story

Before the Canada–U.S. FTA was signed in 1989, great fears were expressed over the fate of the Canadian wine industry, located mainly in Ontario and British Columbia. It was heavily tariff protected and, with a few notable exceptions, produced mainly cheap, low-quality products. Contrary to most people's expectations, rather than being decimated, the industry now produces a wide variety of high-quality products, some of which win international competitions.

The nature of the pre-FTA protection largely explains the dramatic turnaround of the Canadian wine industry once the FTA took effect. First, Canadian wine producers had been protected by high tariffs on imported wine but were at the same time required by law to produce wine by using only domestically grown grapes. The domestic grape growers, however, produced varieties of grapes not conducive to the production of high-quality wines, and with a captive domestic market, they had little incentive to change their behaviour. Thus, Canadian wine producers concentrated their efforts on "hiding" the attributes of poor-quality grapes rather than enhancing the attributes of high-quality grapes. The result was low-quality wine.

The second important aspect of the protection was that the high Canadian tariff was levied on a per unit rather than on an *ad valorem* basis. For example, the tariff was expressed as so many dollars per litre rather than as a specific percentage of the price. Charging a tariff by the litre gave most protection to the low-quality wines with low value per litre. The higher the per-litre value of the wine, the lower the percentage tariff protection. For example, a $5-per-litre tariff would have the following

effects. A low-quality imported wine valued at $5 per litre would have its price raised to $10, a 100 percent increase in price, whereas a higher-quality imported wine valued at $25 per litre would have its price increased to $30, only a 20 percent increase in price.

Responding to these incentives, the Canadian industry concentrated on producing low-quality wines. The market for these wines was protected by the nearly prohibitive tariffs on competing low-quality imports and by the high prices charged for high-quality imports. In addition, protection was provided by many hidden charges that the various provincial governments' liquor monopolies levied in order to protect local producers.

When the tariff was removed under the FTA, the incentives were to move up-market, producing much more value per hectare of land. Fortunately, much of the Canadian wine-growing land in the Okanagan Valley in B.C. and the Niagara Peninsula in Ontario is well suited for growing the grapes required for good wines. Within a very few years, and with some government assistance to grape growers to make the transition from low-quality to high-quality grapes, Canadian wines were competing effectively with imported products in the medium-quality range. More recently, Canadian wineries have also started producing wines of higher quality.

The success of the wine industry is a good example of how tariffs can distort incentives and push an industry into a structure that makes it dependent on the tariff. Looking at the pre-FTA industry, very few people suspected that it would be able to survive, let alone become a world-class industry.

There were also some pleasant surprises resulting from free trade. Two Canadian industries that many economists expected to suffer from the FTA and the NAFTA were winemaking and textiles. Yet both of these industries prospered as Canadian firms improved quality, productivity, and benefited from increased access to the huge U.S. market. *Applying Economic Concepts 33-2* discusses the success of the Canadian wine industry after the tariffs on wine were eliminated.

Finally, the dispute-settlement mechanism seems to have worked well. A large number of disputes have arisen and have been referred to panels. Panel members have usually reacted as professionals rather than as nationals. Most cases have been decided on their merits; allegations that decisions were reached on national rather than professional grounds have been rare.

SUMMARY

33.1 FREE TRADE OR PROTECTION?   LO 1, 2

- The case for free trade is that world output of all products can be higher under free trade than when protectionism restricts regional specialization.
- Trade protection may be advocated to promote economic diversification or to provide protection for specific groups. The cost of such protection is lower average living standards.
- Protection can also be urged on the grounds that it may lead to higher living standards for the protectionist country than would a policy of free trade. Such a result might come about by using market power to influence the terms of trade or by developing a dynamic comparative advantage by allowing inexperienced or uneconomically small industries to become efficient enough to compete with foreign industries.
- Some invalid protectionist arguments are that (a) buying abroad sends our money abroad, while buying at home keeps our money at home; (b) our high-paid workers must be protected against the competition from low-paid foreign workers; and (c) imports are to be discouraged because they reduce national income and cause unemployment.

33.2 METHODS OF PROTECTION   LO 3, 4

- A tariff raises the domestic price of the imported product and leads to a reduction in the level of imports. Domestic consumers lose and domestic producers gain. The overall effect of a tariff is a deadweight loss for the importing country.
- A quota (or voluntary export restriction) restricts the amount of imports and thus drives up the domestic price of the good. Domestic consumers lose and domestic producers gain. The overall effect is a *larger* deadweight loss than with a tariff because, rather than the importing country collecting tariff revenue, foreign producers benefit from a higher price.
- Antidumping and countervailing duties, although providing legitimate restraints on unfair trading practices, are often used as serious barriers to trade.

33.3 CURRENT TRADE POLICY   LO 5, 6

- The General Agreement on Tariffs and Trade (GATT), under which countries agreed to reduce trade barriers through multilateral negotiations and not to raise them unilaterally, has greatly reduced world tariffs since its inception in 1947.
- The World Trade Organization (WTO) was created in 1995 as the successor to GATT. It has 161 member countries and contains a formal dispute-settlement mechanism.
- Regional trade-liberalizing agreements, such as free trade areas and common markets, bring efficiency gains through trade creation and efficiency losses through trade diversion.
- The North American Free Trade Agreement (NAFTA) is the world's largest and most successful free trade area, and the European Union is the world's largest and most successful common market.
- NAFTA is based on the principle of "national treatment." This allows Canada, the United States, and Mexico to implement whatever social, economic, or environmental policies they choose providing that such policies treat foreign and domestic firms (and their products) equally.

KEY CONCEPTS

Free trade and protection
Tariffs and import quotas
Voluntary export restrictions (VERs)
Countervailing and antidumping
  duties

The General Agreement on Tariffs and
  Trade (GATT)
The World Trade Organization (WTO)
Common markets, customs unions,
  and free-trade areas

Trade creation and trade diversion
Non-tariff barriers
The North American Free Trade
  Agreement (NAFTA)

STUDY EXERCISES

MyEconLab Make the grade with MyEconLab: Study Exercises marked in ⊕ can be found on MyEconLab. You can practise them as often as you want, and most feature step-by-step guided instructions to help you find the right answer.

❶ Fill in the blanks to make the following statements correct.

a. The _____ argument provided the rationale for Canada's National Policy of 1876. A high tariff wall allowed many Canadian industries to develop where they may not have been able to compete otherwise.

b. Advertisements that encourage us to "buy Canadian" are promoting a(n) _____ argument for protection. The reason is that money spent on imported goods must ultimately be spent on _____ goods and services anyway.

c. Invalid arguments for protection usually come from a misunderstanding of the gains from _____ or from the misbelief that protection can increase total _____.

❷ Fill in the blanks to make the following statements correct.

a. A tariff imposed on the import of leather shoes will cause a(n) _____ in the domestic price. Total quantity of leather shoes sold in Canada will _____. Domestic (Canadian) production of leather shoes will _____ and the quantity of shoes imported will _____.

b. The beneficiaries of the tariff described above are _____ because they receive a higher price for the same good and _____ because they receive tariff revenue. The parties that are clearly worse off are _____ because they now pay a higher price for the same good, and _____ because they sell less in the Canadian market.

c. The overall effect of a tariff on the importing country is a(n) _____ in welfare. The tariff creates a(n) _____ loss for the economy.

d. Suppose an import quota restricted the import of leather shoes into Canada to 20 000 pairs per year when the free trade imported amount was 40 000 pairs. The domestic price will _____, total quantity sold in Canada will _____, and domestic production will _____.

e. The beneficiaries of the quota described above are _____ and _____ because they both receive a higher price in the Canadian market. The party that is clearly worse off is _____ because they are now paying a higher price.

f. The overall effect of an import quota on the importing country is a(n) _____ in welfare. The quota imposes a(n) _____ loss for the economy.

❸ Fill in the blanks to make the following statements correct.

a. A regional trade agreement, such as the NAFTA, or a common market, such as the European Union, allows for _____, whereby trade within the group of member countries is increased.

b. A regional trade agreement, such as the NAFTA, or a common market, such as the European Union, also results in _____, whereby trade within the group of member countries replaces trade previously done with other _____.

c. The fundamental principle that guides the NAFTA is the principle of _____, which means that any member country can implement the policies of its choosing, as long as _____ and _____ firms are treated equally.

❹ Canada produces steel domestically and also imports it from abroad. Assume that the world market for steel is competitive and that Canada is a small producer, unable to affect the world price. Since Canada imports steel, we know that in the absence of trade, the Canadian equilibrium price would exceed the world price.

a. Draw a diagram showing the Canadian market for steel, with imports at the world price.

b. Explain why the imposition of a tariff on imported steel will increase the price of steel in Canada.

c. Who benefits and who is harmed by such a tariff? Show these effects in your diagram.

❺ The diagram below shows the Canadian market for leather shoes, which we assume to be competitive. The world price is p_w. If the Canadian government imposes a tariff of t dollars per unit, the domestic price then rises to $p_w + t$

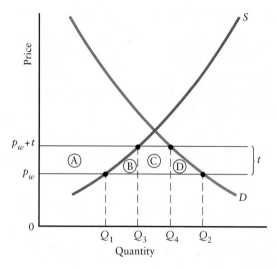

a. What quantity of leather shoes is imported before the tariff is imposed? After the tariff?

b. What is the effect of the tariff on the Canadian production of shoes? Which areas in the diagram show the increase in domestic producer surplus?

c. Which areas in the diagram show the reduction in domestic consumer surplus as a result of the higher Canadian price?

d. The Canadian government earns tariff revenue on the imported shoes. Which area in the diagram shows this tariff revenue?

e. What is the overall effect of this tariff on the economy? Which area in the diagram shows the deadweight loss?

6 Use the diagram from Question 5 to analyze the effects of imposing an import quota instead of a tariff to protect domestic shoe producers. Draw the diagram as in Question 5 and answer the following questions.

a. Explain why an import quota of $Q_3 Q_4$ raises the domestic price to $p_w + t$.

b. With import quotas, the Canadian government earns no tariff revenue. Who gets this money now?

c. Is the import quota better or worse than the tariff for Canada as a whole? Explain.

7 Under pressure from the Canadian and U.S. governments in the early 1980s, Japanese automobile producers agreed to restrict their exports to the North American market. After the formal agreement ended, the Japanese producers decided unilaterally to continue restricting their exports. Carefully review Figure 33-2 and then answer the following questions.

a. Explain why the Japanese producers would voluntarily continue these restrictions.

b. Explain why an agreement to export only 100 000 cars to North America is better for the Japanese

producers than a North American tariff that results in the same volume of Japanese exports.

c. Who is paying for these benefits to the Japanese producers?

8 Go to Statistics Canada's website: www.statcan.gc.ca. Search for "exports and imports," and answer the following questions related to imports and exports of *goods* (trade data for *services* are generally harder to obtain).

a. For the most recent year shown, what was the value of Canada's exports to the United States? To the European Union?

b. For the same year, what was the value of Canada's imports from the United States? From the European Union?

c. Compute what economists call the "volume of trade" (the sum of exports and imports) between Canada and the United States. How has the volume of trade grown over the past five years? Has trade grown faster than national income?

9 The table below shows the prices *in Canada* of cotton towels produced in the United States, Canada, and Bangladesh. Assume that all cotton towels are identical.

Producing Country	Canadian Price ($) Without Tariff	Canadian Price ($) With 20% Tariff
Canada	4.75	4.75
United States	4.50	5.40
Bangladesh	4.00	4.80

a. Suppose Canada imposes a 20 percent tariff on imported towels from any country. Assuming that Canadians purchase only the lowest-price towels, from which country will Canada buy its towels?

b. Now suppose Canada eliminates tariffs on towels from all countries. Which towels will Canada now buy?

c. Canada and the United States now negotiate a free-trade agreement that eliminates all tariffs between the two countries, but Canada maintains the 20 percent tariff on other countries. Which towels now get imported into Canada?

d. Which of the situations described above is called trade creation and which is called trade diversion?

10 In the past few years, trade between Canada and China has been growing quickly (though from a very low level). Many observers are concerned that Canadian firms are not able to compete with Chinese ones and that Canada may therefore be harmed by trading more with China. Comment on the following points in relation to the above worries:

a. "Chinese are the most expensive cheap labour I have ever encountered." Statement by the owner of a Canadian firm that is moving back to Canada from China.

b. The theory of the gains from trade says that a high-productivity, high-wage country can gain from trading with a low-wage, low-productivity country.

c. Technological change is rapidly reducing labour costs as a proportion of total costs in many products; in many industries that use high-tech production methods this proportion is already well below 20 percent.

⑪ Consider a mythical country called Forestland, which exports a large amount of lumber to a nearby country called Houseland. The lumber industry in Houseland has convinced its federal government that it is being harmed by the low prices being charged by the lumber producers in Forestland. You are an advisor to the government in Forestland. Explain who gains and who loses from each of the following policies.

a. Houseland imposes a tariff on lumber imports from Forestland.

b. Forestland imposes a tax on each unit of lumber exported to Houseland.

c. Forestland agrees to restrict its exports of lumber to Houseland.

d. Which policy is likely to garner the most political support in Houseland? In Forestland?

⑫ Canada has recently imposed antidumping duties of up to 43 percent on hot-rolled steel imports from France, Russia, Slovakia, and Romania. The allegation is that these countries were dumping steel into the Canadian market.

a. Who benefits from such alleged dumping? Who is harmed?

b. Who benefits from the imposition of the antidumping duties? Who is harmed?

c. Is Canada as a whole made better off by the imposition of the duties? Explain.

Mathematical Notes

1. Because one cannot divide by zero, the ratio $\Delta Y / \Delta X$ cannot be evaluated when $\Delta X = 0$. However, as ΔX *approaches* zero, the ratio $\Delta Y / \Delta X$ increases without limit:

$$\lim_{\Delta X \to 0} \frac{\Delta Y}{\Delta X} = \infty$$

Therefore, we say that the slope of a vertical line (when $\Delta X = 0$ for any ΔY) is equal to infinity.

2. Many variables affect the quantity demanded. Using functional notation, the argument of the next several pages of the text can be anticipated. Let Q^D represent the quantity of a commodity demanded and

$$T, \overline{Y}, N, \hat{Y}, p, p_j$$

represent, respectively, tastes, average household income, population, income distribution, the commodity's own price, and the price of the jth other commodity.

The demand function is

$$Q^D = D(T, \overline{Y}, N, \hat{Y}, p, p_j), \qquad j = 1, 2, \ldots, n$$

The demand schedule or curve is given by

$$Q^D = d(p) \bigg|_{T, \overline{Y}, N, \hat{Y}, p_j}$$

where the notation means that the variables to the right of the vertical line are held constant.

This function is correctly described as the demand function with respect to price, all other variables being held constant. This function, often written concisely as $Q^D = d(p)$, shifts in response to changes in other variables. Consider average income: if, as is usually hypothesized, $\partial Q^D / \partial \overline{Y} > 0$, then increases in average income shift $Q^D = d(p)$ rightward and decreases in average income shift $Q^D = d(p)$ leftward. Changes in other variables likewise shift this function in the direction implied by the relationship of that variable to the quantity demanded.

3. Quantity demanded is a simple and straightforward but frequently misunderstood concept in everyday use, but it has a clear mathematical meaning. It refers to the dependent variable in the demand function from note 2:

$$Q^D = D(T, \overline{Y}, N, \hat{Y}, p, p_j)$$

It takes on a specific value whenever a specific value is assigned to each of the independent variables. The value of Q^D changes whenever the value of any independent variable is changed. Q^D could change, for example, as a result of a change in any one price, in average income, in the distribution of income, in tastes, or in population. It could also change as a result of the net effect of changes in all of the independent variables occurring at once.

Some textbooks reserve the term *change in quantity demanded* for a movement along a demand curve, that is, a change in Q^D as a result *only* of a change in p. They then use other words for a change in Q^D caused by a change in the other variables in the demand function. This usage is potentially confusing because it gives the single variable Q^D more than one name.

Our usage, which corresponds to that in more advanced treatments, avoids this confusion. We call Q^D *quantity demanded* and refer to any change in Q^D as a *change in quantity demanded*. In this usage it is correct to say that a movement along a demand curve is a change in quantity demanded, but it is incorrect to say that a change in quantity demanded can occur *only because of* a movement along a demand curve (because Q^D can change for other reasons, for example, a *ceteris paribus* change in average household income).

4. Similar to the way we treated quantity demanded in note 2, let Q^S represent the quantity of a commodity supplied and

$$C, X, p, w_i$$

represent, respectively, producers' goals, technology, the product's price, and the price of the ith input.

The supply function is

$$Q^S = S(C, X, p, w_i), \qquad i = 1, 2, \ldots, m$$

The supply schedule or curve is given by

$$Q^S = s(p) \Big|_{C, X, w_i}$$

This is the supply function with respect to price, all other variables being held constant. This function, often written concisely as $Q^S = s(p)$, shifts in response to changes in other variables.

5. Equilibrium occurs where $Q^D = Q^S$. For *specified values of all other variables*, this requires that

$$d(p) = s(p) \qquad [5.1]$$

Equation 5.1 defines an equilibrium value of p; although p is an *independent* or *exogenous* variable in each of the supply and demand functions, it is an *endogenous* variable in the economic model that imposes the equilibrium condition expressed in Equation 5.1. Price is endogenous because it is assumed to adjust to bring about equality between quantity demanded and quantity supplied. Equilibrium quantity, also an endogenous variable, is determined by substituting the equilibrium price into either $d(p)$ or $s(p)$.

Graphically, Equation 5.1 is satisfied only at the point where the demand and supply curves intersect. Thus, supply and demand curves are said to determine the equilibrium values of the endogenous variables, price and quantity. A shift in any of the independent variables held constant in the d and s functions will shift the demand or supply curves and lead to different equilibrium values for price and quantity.

6. The axis reversal arose in the following way. Alfred Marshall (1842–1924) theorized in terms of "demand price" and "supply price," which were the prices that would lead to a given quantity being demanded or supplied. Thus,

$$p^D = d(Q) \qquad [6.1]$$

$$p^S = s(Q) \qquad [6.2]$$

and the condition of equilibrium is

$$d(Q) = s(Q)$$

When graphing the behavioural relationships expressed in Equations 6.1 and 6.2, Marshall naturally put the independent variable, Q, on the horizontal axis.

Leon Walras (1834–1910), whose formulation of the working of a competitive market has become the accepted one, focused on quantity demanded and quantity supplied *at a given price*. Thus,

$$Q^D = d(p)$$

$$Q^S = s(p)$$

and the condition of equilibrium is

$$d(p) = s(p)$$

Walras did not use graphical representation. Had he done so, he would surely have placed p (his independent variable) on the horizontal axis.

Marshall's work influenced later generations of economists, in particular because he was the great popularizer of graphical analysis in economics. Today, we use his graphs, even for Walras's analysis. The axis reversal is thus one of those historical accidents that seem odd to people who did not live through the "perfectly natural" sequence of steps that produced it.

7. The definition in the text uses finite changes and is called *arc elasticity* because it is being computed across an *arc* of the demand curve. The parallel definition using derivatives is

$$\eta = \frac{dQ}{dp} \cdot \frac{p}{Q}$$

and is called *point elasticity*.

8. The propositions in the text are proved as follows. Letting *TE* stand for total expenditure, we can write

$$TE = p \cdot Q$$

It follows that the change in total expenditure is

$$dTE = Q \cdot dp + p \cdot dQ \qquad [8.1]$$

Multiplying and dividing both terms on the right-hand side of Equation 8.1 by $p \cdot Q$ yields

$$dTE = \left[\frac{dp}{p} + \frac{dQ}{Q} \right] \cdot (p \cdot Q)$$

Because dp and dQ are opposite in sign as we move along the demand curve, dTE will have the same sign as the term in brackets on the right-hand side that dominates—that is, on which percentage change is largest.

A second way of arranging Equation 8.1 is to divide both sides by dp to get

$$\frac{dTE}{dp} = Q + p \cdot \frac{dQ}{dp} \qquad [8.2]$$

From the definition of point elasticity in note 7, however,

$$Q \cdot \eta = p \cdot \frac{dQ}{dp} \qquad [8.3]$$

which we can substitute into Equation 8.1 to obtain

$$\frac{dTE}{dp} = Q + Q \cdot \eta = Q \cdot (1 + \eta) \qquad [8.4]$$

Because η is a negative number, the sign of the right-hand side of Equation 8.4 is negative if the absolute value of η exceeds unity (elastic demand) and positive if it is less than unity (inelastic demand).

Total expenditure is maximized when dTE/dp is equal to zero. As can be seen from Equation 8.4, this occurs when elasticity is equal to –1.

9. The distinction between an incremental change and a marginal change is the distinction for the function $Y = Y(X)$ between $\Delta Y/\Delta X$ and the derivative dY/dX. The latter is the limit of the former as ΔX approaches zero. We shall meet this distinction repeatedly—in this chapter in reference to marginal and incremental *utility* and in later chapters with respect to such concepts as marginal and incremental *product, cost,* and *revenue.* Where Y is a function of more than one variable—for example, $Y = f(X,Z)$—the marginal relationship between Y and X is the partial derivative $\partial Y/\partial X$ rather than the total derivative dY/dX.

10. The hypothesis of diminishing marginal utility requires that we can measure utility of consumption by a function

$$U = U(X_1, X_2, \dots, X_n)$$

where $X_1, \dots, X_n$ are quantities of the n products consumed. It really embodies two utility hypotheses: first,

$$\partial U/\partial X_i > 0$$

which says that the consumer can get more utility by increasing consumption of the product; second,

$$\partial^2 U/\partial X_i^2 < 0$$

which says that the utility of *additional* consumption of some product declines as the amount of that product consumed increases.

11. Because the slope of the indifference curve is negative, it is the absolute value of the slope that declines as one moves downward to the right along the curve. The algebraic value, of course, increases. The phrase *diminishing marginal rate of substitution* thus refers to the absolute, not the algebraic, value of the slope.

12. The relationship between the slope of the budget line and relative prices can be seen as follows. In the two-good example with prices held constant, a change in expenditure (ΔE) is given by the equation

$$\Delta E = p_C \cdot \Delta C + p_F \cdot \Delta F \qquad [12.1]$$

Expenditure is constant for all combinations of F and C that lie on the same budget line. Thus, along such a line we have $\Delta E = 0$. This implies

$$p_C \cdot \Delta C + p_F \cdot \Delta F = 0 \qquad [12.2]$$

and thus

$$\Delta C/\Delta F = - p_F/p_C \qquad [12.3]$$

The ratio $\Delta C/\Delta F$ is the slope of the budget line. It is negative because, with a fixed budget, one must consume less C in order to consume more F. In other words, Equation 12.3 says that the negative of the slope of the budget line is the ratio of the absolute prices (i.e., the relative price). Although prices do not show directly in Figure 6A-3, they are implicit in the budget line: Its slope depends solely on the relative price, while its position, given a fixed money income, depends on the absolute prices of the two goods.

13. *Marginal product,* as defined in the text, is really *incremental* product. More advanced treatments distinguish between this notion and marginal product as the limit of the ratio as ΔL approaches zero.

Marginal product thus measures the rate at which total product is changing as one factor is varied and is the partial derivative of the total product with respect to the variable factor. In symbols,

$$MP = \frac{\partial TP}{\partial L}$$

14. We have referred specifically both to diminishing *marginal* product and to diminishing *average* product. In most cases, eventually diminishing marginal product implies eventually diminishing average product. This is not true in *all* cases, however, as the accompanying figure shows.

In the figure below, marginal product diminishes after v units of the variable factor are employed. Because marginal product falls toward, but never quite reaches, a value of m, average product rises continually toward, but never quite reaches, the same value.

15. Let Q be the quantity of output and L the quantity of the variable factor. In the short run,

$$TP = Q = f(L) \qquad [15.1]$$

We now define

$$AP = \frac{Q}{L} = \frac{f(L)}{L} \qquad [15.2]$$

$$MP = \frac{dQ}{dL} \qquad [15.3]$$

We are concerned with the relationship between AP and MP. Where average product is rising, at a maximum, or falling is determined by its derivative with respect to L:

$$\frac{d(Q/L)}{dL} = \frac{L \cdot (dQ/dL) - Q}{L^2} \qquad [15.4]$$

The right-hand side may be rewritten

$$\frac{1}{L} \cdot \left[\frac{dQ}{dL} - \frac{Q}{L} \right] = \frac{1}{L} \cdot (MP - AP) \qquad [15.5]$$

Clearly, when MP is greater than AP, the expression in Equation 15.5 is positive and thus AP is rising. When MP is less than AP, AP is falling. When they are equal, AP is neither rising nor falling.

16. The text defines *incremental cost*. Strictly, marginal cost is the rate of change of total cost with respect to output, Q. Thus,

$$MC = \frac{dTC}{dQ}$$

From the definitions, $TC = TFC + TVC$. Fixed costs are not a function of output. Thus, we may write $TC = Z + f(Q)$, where $f(Q)$ is total variable costs and Z is a constant. From this we see that $MC = df(Q)/dQ$. MC is thus independent of the size of the fixed costs.

17. This point is easily seen if a little algebra is used:

$$AVC = \frac{TVC}{Q}$$

but note that $TVC = L \cdot w$ and $Q = AP \cdot L$, where L is the quantity of the variable factor used and w is its cost per unit. Therefore,

$$AVC = \frac{L \cdot w}{AP \cdot L} = \frac{w}{AP}$$

Because w is a constant, it follows that AVC and AP vary inversely with each other, and when AP is at its maximum value, AVC must be at its minimum value.

18. A little elementary calculus will prove the point:

$$MC = \frac{dTC}{dQ} = \frac{dTVC}{dQ} = \frac{d(L \cdot w)}{dQ}$$

If w does not vary with output,

$$MC = \frac{dL}{dQ} \cdot w$$

However, referring to note 15 (Equation 15.3), we see that

$$\frac{dL}{dQ} = \frac{1}{MP}$$

Thus,

$$MC = \frac{w}{MP}$$

Because w is fixed, MC varies negatively with MP. When MP is at a maximum, MC is at a minimum.

19. Strictly speaking, the marginal rate of substitution refers to the slope of the tangent to the isoquant at a particular point, whereas the calculations in Table 8A-1 refer to the average rate of substitution between two distinct points on the isoquant. Assume a production function

$$Q = Q(K,L) \qquad [19.1]$$

Isoquants are given by the function

$$K = I(L, \overline{Q}) \qquad [19.2]$$

derived from Equation 19.1 by expressing K as an explicit function of L and Q. A single isoquant relates to a particular level of output, $\overline{Q}$. Define Q_K and Q_L as an alternative, more compact notation for $\partial Q/\partial K$ and $\partial Q/\partial L$, the marginal products of capital and labour. Also, let Q_{KK} and Q_{LL} stand for $\partial^2 Q/\partial K^2$ and $\partial^2 Q/\partial L^2$, respectively. To obtain the slope of the isoquant, totally differentiate Equation 19.1 to obtain

$$dQ = Q_K . dK + Q_L \cdot dL$$

Then, because we are moving along a single isoquant, set $dQ = 0$ to obtain

$$\frac{dK}{dL} = -\frac{Q_L}{Q_K} = MRS$$

Diminishing marginal productivity implies $Q_{LL} < 0$ and $Q_{KK} < 0$, and hence, as we move down the isoquant of Figure 8A-1, Q_K is rising and Q_L is falling, so the absolute value of MRS is diminishing. This is called the *hypothesis of a diminishing marginal rate of substitution*.

20. Formally, the problem is to choose K and L in order to maximize

$$Q = Q(K, L)$$

subject to the constraint

$$p_K \cdot K + p_L \cdot L = C$$

To do this, form the Lagrangean,

$$\pounds = Q(K,L) - \lambda(p_K \cdot K + p_L \cdot L - C)$$

where λ is called the Lagrange multiplier.

The first-order conditions for this maximization problem are

$$Q_K = \lambda \cdot p_K \qquad [20.1]$$
$$Q_L = \lambda \cdot p_L \qquad [20.2]$$
$$p_K \cdot K + p_L \cdot L = C \qquad [20.3]$$

Dividing Equation 20.1 by Equation 20.2 yields

$$\frac{Q_K}{Q_L} = \frac{p_K}{p_L}$$

That is, the ratio of the marginal products, which is −1 times the MRS, is equal to the ratio of the factor prices, which is −1 times the slope of the isocost line.

21. Marginal revenue is mathematically the derivative of total revenue with respect to output, dTR/dQ. Incremental revenue is $\Delta TR/\Delta Q$. However, the term *marginal revenue* is used loosely to refer to both concepts.

22. For notes 22 through 24, it is helpful first to define some terms. Let

$$\pi_n = TR_n - TC_n$$

where π_n is the profit when Q_n units are sold.

If the firm is maximizing its profits by producing Q_n units, its profits must be at least as large as the profits at output zero. That is,

$$\pi_n \geq \pi_0 \qquad [22.1]$$

This condition says that profits from producing must be greater than profits from not producing. Condition 22.1 can be rewritten as

$$\begin{aligned} TR_n - TVC_n - TFC_n \\ \geq TR_0 - TVC_0 - TFC_0 \end{aligned} \qquad [22.2]$$

However, note that by definition

$$TR_0 = 0 \qquad [22.3]$$
$$TVC_0 = 0 \qquad [22.4]$$
$$TFC_n = TFC_0 = Z \qquad [22.5]$$

where Z is a constant. By substituting Equations 22.3, 22.4, and 22.5 into Condition 22.2, we get

$$TR_n - TVC_n \geq 0$$

from which we obtain

$$TR_n \geq TVC_n$$

This proves Rule 1.

On a per-unit basis, it becomes

$$\frac{TR_n}{Q_n} \geq \frac{TVC_n}{Q_n} \qquad [22.6]$$

where Q_n is the number of units produced.

Because $TR_n = Q_n \times p_n$, where p_n is the price when n units are sold, Condition 22.6 may be rewritten as

$$p_n \geq AVC_n$$

23. Using elementary calculus, we may prove Rule 2.

$$\pi_n = TR_n - TC_n$$

each of which is a function of output Q. To maximize π, it is necessary that

$$\frac{d\pi}{dQ} = 0 \qquad [23.1]$$

From the definitions,

$$\frac{d\pi}{dQ} = \frac{dTR}{dQ} - \frac{dTC}{dQ} = MR - MC \qquad [23.2]$$

From Equations 23.1 and 23.2, a necessary condition for attaining maximum π is $MR - MC = 0$, or $MR = MC$, as is required by Rule 2.

24. To prove that for a negatively sloped demand curve, marginal revenue is less than price, let $p = p(Q)$. Then

$$TR = p \cdot Q = p(Q) \cdot Q$$

$$MR = \frac{dTR}{dQ} = Q \cdot \frac{dp}{dQ} + p$$

For a negatively sloped demand curve, dp/dQ is negative, and thus MR is less than price for positive values of Q.

25. The equation for a downward-sloping straight-line demand curve with price on the vertical axis is

$$p = a - b \cdot Q$$

where a is the vertical intercept (when $Q = 0$) and $-b$ is the slope of the demand curve. Total revenue is price times quantity:

$$TR = p \cdot Q = a \cdot Q - b \cdot Q^2$$

Marginal revenue is

$$MR = \frac{dTR}{dQ} = a - 2 \cdot b \cdot Q$$

Thus, the MR curve and the demand curve are both straight lines, they have the same vertical intercept (a), and the (absolute value of the) slope of the MR curve ($2b$) is twice that of the demand curve (b).

26. The marginal revenue produced by the factor involves two elements: first, the additional output that an extra unit of the factor produces and, second, the change in price of the product that the extra output causes. Let Q be output, R revenue, and L the number of units of the variable factor hired. The contribution to revenue of additional labour is $\partial R/\partial L$. This, in turn, depends on the contribution of the extra labour to output $\partial Q/\partial L$ (the marginal product of the factor) and the contribution of the extra output to revenue $\partial R/\partial Q$ (the firm's marginal revenue). Thus,

$$\frac{\partial R}{\partial L} = \frac{\partial Q}{\partial L} \cdot \frac{\partial R}{\partial Q}$$

We define the left-hand side as marginal revenue product, MRP. Thus,

$$MRP = MP \cdot MR$$

27. The proposition that the marginal labour cost is above the average labour cost when the average is rising is essentially the same mathematical proposition proved in note 15. Nevertheless, let us do it again, using elementary calculus.

The quantity of labour supplied depends on the wage rate: $L^s = f(w)$. Total labour cost along the supply curve is $w \cdot L^s$. The average cost of labour is $(w \cdot L^s)/L^s = w$. The marginal cost of labour is

$$\frac{d(w \cdot L^s)}{dL^s} = w + L^s \cdot \frac{dw}{dL^s}$$

Rewrite this as

$$MC = AC + L^s \cdot \frac{dw}{dL^s}$$

As long as the supply curve slopes upward, $dw/dL^s > 0$; therefore, $MC > AC$.

28. In the text, we define MPC as an incremental ratio. For mathematical treatment, it is sometimes convenient to define all marginal concepts as derivatives: $MPC = dC/dY_D$, $MPS = dS/dY_D$, and so on.

29. The basic relationship is

$$Y_D = C + S$$

Dividing through by Y_D yields

$$\frac{Y_D}{Y_D} = \frac{C}{Y_D} + \frac{S}{Y_D}$$

and thus

$$1 = APC + APS$$

Next, take the first difference of the basic relationship to get

$$\Delta Y_D = \Delta C + \Delta S$$

Dividing through by ΔY_D gives

$$\frac{\Delta Y_D}{\Delta Y_D} = \frac{\Delta C}{\Delta Y_D} + \frac{\Delta S}{\Delta Y_D}$$

and thus

$$1 = MPC + MPS$$

30. The total expenditure over all rounds is the sum of an infinite series. If we let A stand for autonomous expenditure and z for the marginal propensity to spend, the change in autonomous expenditure is ΔA in the first round, $z \cdot \Delta A$ in the second, $z^2 \cdot \Delta A$ in the third, and so on. This can be written as

$$\Delta A \cdot (1 + z + z^2 + \ldots + z^n)$$

If z is less than 1, the series in parentheses converges to $1/(1 - z)$ as n approaches infinity. The total change in expenditure is thus $\Delta A/(1 - z)$. In the example in the box, $z = 0.80$; therefore, the change in total expenditure is

$$\frac{\Delta A}{1 - z} = \frac{\Delta A}{0.2} = 5 \cdot \Delta A$$

31. The "rule of 72" says that any sum growing at the rate of X percent per year will double in approximately $72/X$ years. For two sums growing at the rates of X percent and Y percent per year, the *difference* between the two sums will double in approximately $72/(X - Y)$ years. The rule of 72 is only an approximation, but at low annual rates of growth it is extremely accurate.

32. A simple example of a production function is $GDP = z(LK)^{1/2}$. This equation says that to find the amount of GDP produced, multiply the amount of labour by the amount of capital, take the square root, and multiply the result by the constant z which is a technology parameter. This production function has positive but diminishing marginal returns to either factor. This can be seen by evaluating the first and second partial derivatives and showing the first derivatives to be positive and the second derivatives to be negative.

For example,

$$\frac{\partial GDP}{\partial K} = \frac{z \cdot L^{1/2}}{2 \cdot K^{1/2}} > 0$$

and

$$\frac{\partial^2 GDP}{\partial K^2} = -\frac{z \cdot L^{1/2}}{4 \cdot K^{3/2}} < 0$$

33. The production function $GDP = z(LK)^{1/2}$ displays constant returns to scale. To see this, multiply both L and K by the same constant, θ, and see that this multiplies the whole value of GDP by θ:

$$z(\theta L \cdot \theta K)^{1/2} = z(\theta^2 \cdot LK)^{1/2} = \theta z(LK)^{1/2} = \theta \cdot GDP$$

34. This is easily proved. The banking system wants sufficient deposits (D) to establish the target ratio (v) of deposits to reserves (R). This gives $R/D = v$. Any change in D of size ΔD has to be accompanied by a change in R of ΔR of sufficient size to restore v. Thus, $\Delta R/\Delta D = v$, so $\Delta D = \Delta R/v$ and

$\Delta D/\Delta R = 1/v$. This can be shown also in terms of the deposits created by the sequence in Table 26-7. Let v be the reserve ratio and $e = 1 - v$ be the excess reserves per dollar of new deposits. If X dollars are initially deposited in the system, the successive rounds of new deposits will be X, eX, e^2X, e^3X, ... The series

$$X + eX + e^2X + e^3X + \ldots$$

$$= X \cdot [\, 1 + e + e^2 + e^3 + \ldots \,]$$

has a limit of $X \cdot \dfrac{1}{1 - e}$

$$= X \cdot \frac{1}{1 - (1 - v)} = \frac{X}{v}$$

This is the total new deposits created by an injection of \$X of new reserves into the banking system. For example, when $v = 0.20$, an injection of \$100 into the system will lead to an overall increase in deposits of \$500.

35. Suppose the public wants to hold a fraction, c, of deposits in cash, C. Now suppose that X dollars are injected into the system. Ultimately, this money will be held either as reserves by the banking system or as cash by the public. Thus, we have

$$\Delta C + \Delta R = X$$

From the banking system's reserve behaviour, we have $\Delta R = v \cdot \Delta D$, and from the public's cash behaviour, we have $\Delta C = c \cdot \Delta D$. Substituting into the above equation, we get the result that

$$\Delta D = \frac{X}{v + c}$$

From this we can also relate the change in reserves and the change in cash holdings to the initial injection:

$$\Delta R = \frac{v}{v + c} \cdot X$$

$$\Delta C = \frac{c}{v + c} \cdot X$$

For example, when $v = 0.20$ and $c = 0.05$, an injection of \$100 will lead to an increase in reserves of \$80, an increase in cash in the hands of the public of \$20, and an increase in deposits of \$400.

36. Let d be the government's debt-to-GDP ratio and let Δd be the annual change in d. The percentage change in d over the year is therefore $\Delta d/d$, which for small percentage changes is very closely approximated by

$$\Delta d/d = \Delta D/D - \Delta \text{GDP}/\text{GDP}$$

where ΔD is the budget deficit and is equal to $G - T + iD$. The second term is the percentage change in *nominal* GDP, which is approximately equal to $g + \pi$, where g is the growth rate of real GDP and π is the rate of inflation. We therefore rewrite the expression as

$$\Delta d/d = (G - T + iD)/D - (g + \pi)$$

Now, multiply both sides by d to get:

$$\Delta d = (G - T + iD)/\text{GDP} - (g + \pi)d$$

We can now let x be the primary budget deficit $(G - T)$ as a share of GDP. The equation then becomes

$$\Delta d = x + (i - \pi - g)d$$

Finally, note that the real interest rate on government bonds is $r = i - \pi$, and so our final equation becomes

$$\Delta d = x + (r - g)d$$

Timeline of Great Economists

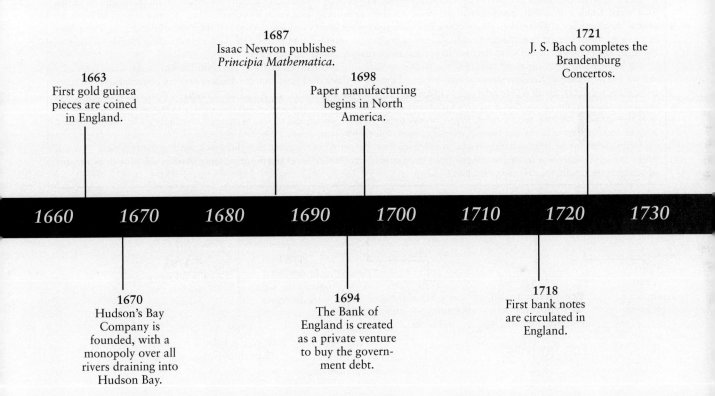

1663
First gold guinea pieces are coined in England.

1687
Isaac Newton publishes *Principia Mathematica*.

1698
Paper manufacturing begins in North America.

1721
J. S. Bach completes the Brandenburg Concertos.

| 1660 | 1670 | 1680 | 1690 | 1700 | 1710 | 1720 | 1730 |

1670
Hudson's Bay Company is founded, with a monopoly over all rivers draining into Hudson Bay.

1694
The Bank of England is created as a private venture to buy the government debt.

1718
First bank notes are circulated in England.

ADAM SMITH *(1723–1790)*

Adam Smith was born in 1723 in the small Scottish town of Kirkcaldy. He is perhaps the single most influential figure in the development of modern economics, and even those who have never studied economics know of his most famous work, *The Wealth of Nations,* and are familiar with the terms *laissez-faire* and the *invisible hand,* both attributable to Smith. He described the workings of the capitalist market economy, the division of labour in production, the role of money, free trade, and the nature of economic growth. Even today, the breadth of his scholarship is considered astounding.

Smith was raised by his mother, as his father had died before his birth. His intellectual promise was discovered early, and at age 14 Smith was sent to study at Glasgow and then at Oxford. He returned to an appointment as professor of moral philosophy at University of Glasgow, where he became one of the leading philosophers of his day. He lectured on natural theology, ethics, jurisprudence, and political economy to students who travelled from as far away as Russia to hear his lectures.

In 1759, Smith published *The Theory of Moral Sentiments,* in which he attempted to identify the origins of moral judgment. In this early work, Smith writes of the motivation of self-interest and of the morality that keeps it in check. After its publication, Smith left his post at the University of Glasgow to embark on a European tour as the tutor to a young aristocrat, the Duke of Buccleuch, with whom he travelled for two years. In exchange for this assignment Smith was provided with a salary for the remainder of his life. He returned to the small town of his birth and spent the next 10 years alone, writing his most famous work.

An Inquiry into the Nature and Causes of the Wealth of Nations was published in 1776. His contributions in this book (generally known as *The Wealth of Nations*) were revolutionary, and the text became the foundation for much of modern economics. It continues to be reprinted today. Smith rejected the notion that a country's supply of gold and silver was the measure of its wealth—rather, it was the real incomes of the people that determined national wealth. Growth in the real incomes of the country's citizens—that is, economic growth—would result from specialization in production, the division of labour, and the use of money to facilitate trade. Smith provided a framework for analyzing the questions of income growth, value, and distribution.

Smith's work marked the beginning of what is called the Classical period in economic thought, which continued for the next 75 years. This school of thought was centred on the principles of natural liberty (laissez-faire) and the importance of economic growth as a means of bettering the conditions of human existence.

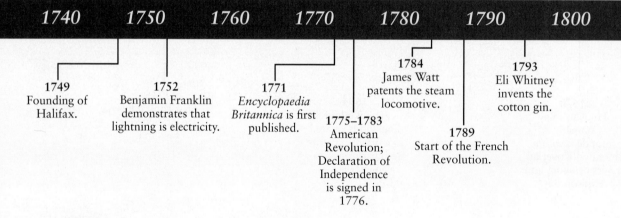

1740   1750   1760   1770   1780   1790   1800

1749
Founding of Halifax.

1752
Benjamin Franklin demonstrates that lightning is electricity.

1771
Encyclopaedia Britannica is first published.

1775–1783
American Revolution; Declaration of Independence is signed in 1776.

1784
James Watt patents the steam locomotive.

1789
Start of the French Revolution.

1793
Eli Whitney invents the cotton gin.

THOMAS MALTHUS *(1766–1834)*

Thomas Malthus was born into a reasonably well-to-do English family. He was educated at Cambridge, and from 1805 until his death he held the first British professorship of political economy in the East India Company's college at Haileybury. In 1798 he published *An Essay on the Principle of Population as It Affects the Future Improvement of Society,* which was revised many times in subsequent years until finally he published *A Summary View of the Principle of Population* in 1830.

It is these essays on population for which Malthus is best known. His first proposition was that population, when unchecked, would increase in a geometric progression such that the population would double every 25 years. His second proposition was that the means of subsistence (i.e., the food supply) cannot possibly increase faster than in arithmetic progression (increasing by a given number of units every year). The result would be population growth eventually outstripping food production, and thus abject poverty and suffering for the majority of people in every society.

Malthus's population theory had tremendous intellectual influence at the time and became an integral part of the Classical theory of income distribution. However, it is no longer taken as a good description of current or past trends.

DAVID RICARDO (1772–1823)

David Ricardo was born in London to parents who had emigrated from the Netherlands. Ricardo's father was very successful in money markets, and Ricardo himself was very wealthy before he was 30 by earning money on the stock exchange. He had little formal education, but after reading Adam Smith's *The Wealth of Nations* in 1799, he chose to divide his time between studying and writing about political economy and increasing his own personal wealth.

Ricardo's place in the history of economics was assured by his achievement in constructing an abstract model of how capitalism worked. He built an analytic "system" using deductive reasoning that characterizes economic theorizing to the present day. The three critical principles in Ricardo's system were (1) the theory of rent, (2) Thomas Malthus's population principle, and (3) the wages-fund doctrine. Ricardo published *The Principles of Political Economy and Taxation* in 1817, and the work dominated Classical economics for the following half-century.

Ricardo also contributed the concept of comparative advantage to the study of international trade. Ricardo's theories regarding the gains from trade had some influence on the repeal of the British Corn Laws in 1846—tariffs on the importation of grains into Great Britain—and the subsequent transformation of that country during the nineteenth century from a country of high tariffs to one of completely free trade.

1837
Victoria becomes
Queen of England
(until 1901).
Rebellions in
Upper and Lower
Canada.

1831
The first horse-
drawn buses
appear in
New York.

1814
British forces burn
Washington, D.C., in the
War of 1812.

1800   **1810**   **1820**   **1830**

1805
Admiral Horatio
Nelson's victory
(and death)
at Trafalgar.

1815
Napoleon
defeated at Waterloo
and exiled to
St. Helena;
Corn Laws passed
in Britain.

1822
First textile
mills are built
in Lowell,
Massachusetts.

JOHN STUART MILL (1806–1873)

John Stuart Mill, born in London, was the son of James Mill, a prominent British historian, economist, and philosopher. By age 12 he was acquainted with the major economics works of the day, and at 13 he was correcting the proofs of his father's book, *Elements of Political Economy*. J. S. Mill spent most of his life working at the East India Company—his extraordinarily prolific writing career was conducted entirely as an aside. In 1848 he published his *Principles of Political Economy*, which updated the principles found in Adam Smith's *The Wealth of Nations* and which remained the basic textbook for students of economics until the end of the nineteenth century. In *Principles*, Mill made an important contribution to the economics discipline by distinguishing between the economics of production and of distribution. He pointed out that economic laws had nothing to do with the distribution of wealth, which was a societal matter, but had everything to do with production.

Previous to Mill's *Principles* was his *System of Logic* (1843), which was the century's most influential text on logic and the theory of knowledge. His essays on ethics, contemporary culture, and freedom of speech, such as *Utilitarianism* and *On Liberty*, are still widely studied today.

KARL MARX *(1818–1883)*

Karl Marx was born in Trier, Germany (then part of Prussia), and studied law, history, and philosophy at the universities of Bonn, Berlin, and Jena. Marx travelled between Prussia, Paris, and Brussels, working at various jobs until finally settling in London in 1849, where he lived the remainder of his life. Most of his time was spent in the mainly unpaid pursuits of writing and studying economics in the library of the British Museum. Marx's contributions to economics are intricately bound to his views of history and society. *The Communist Manifesto* was published with Friedrich Engels in 1848, his *Critique of Political Economy* was published in 1859, and in 1867 the first volume of *Das Kapital* was completed. (The remaining volumes, edited by Engels, were published after Marx's death.)

For Marx, capitalism was a stage in an evolutionary process from a primitive agricultural economy toward an inevitable elimination of private property and the class structure. Marx's "labour theory of value," whereby the quantity of labour used in the manufacture of a product determined its value, held the central place in his economic thought. He believed that the worker provided "surplus value" to the capitalist. The capitalist would then use the profit arising from this surplus value to reinvest in plant and machinery. Through time, more would be spent for plant and machinery than for wages, which would lead to lower profits (since profits arose only from the surplus value from labour) and a resulting squeeze in the real income of workers. Marx believed that in the capitalists' effort to maintain profits in this unstable system, there would emerge a "reserve army of the unemployed." The resulting class conflict would become increasingly acute until revolution by the workers would overthrow capitalism.

1846
Britain repeals
the Corn Laws.

1859
Charles
Darwin
publishes
*On the Origin
of Species.*

1867
British North America Act
establishes the Dominion of
Canada. Alfred Nobel
invents dynamite.

1840   **1850**   **1860**   **1870**

1844
Electric
telegraph
opens between
Washington
and Baltimore.

1861–1865
The U.S. Civil War;
Abraham Lincoln is
assassinated in
1865.

1869
Opening of the
Suez Canal.

1840
Act of Union
unites Upper
and Lower
Canada.

LEON WALRAS *(1834–1910)*

Leon Walras was born in France, the son of an economist. After being trained inauspiciously in engineering and performing poorly in mathematics, Walras spent some time pursuing other endeavours, such as novel writing and working for the railway. Eventually he promised his father he would study economics, and by 1870 he was given a professorship in economics in the Faculty of Law at the University of Lausanne in Switzerland. Once there, Walras began the feverish activity that eventually led to his important contributions to economic theory.

In the 1870s, Walras was one of three economists to put forward the marginal utility theory of value (simultaneously with William Stanley Jevons of England and Carl Menger of Austria). Further, he constructed a mathematical model of general equilibrium using a system of simultaneous equations that he used to argue that equilibrium prices and quantities are uniquely determined. Central to general equilibrium analysis is the notion that the prices and quantities of all commodities are determined simultaneously because the whole system is interdependent. Walras's most important work was *Elements of Pure Economics,* published in 1874. In addition to all of Walras's other accomplishments in economics (and despite his early poor performance in mathematics!), we today regard him as the founder of mathematical economics.

Leon Walras and Alfred Marshall are regarded by many economists as the two most important economic theorists who ever lived. Much of the framework of economic theory studied today is either Walrasian or Marshallian in character.

CARL MENGER   *(1840–1921)*

Carl Menger was born in Galicia (then part of Austria), and he came from a family of Austrian civil servants and army officers. After studying law in Prague and Vienna, he turned to economics and in 1871 published *Grundsatze der Volkswirtschaftslehre* (translated as *Principles of Economics*), for which he became famous. He held a professorship at the University of Vienna until 1903. Menger was the founder of a school of thought known as the "Austrian School," which effectively displaced the German historical method on the continent and which survives today as an alternative to mainstream Neoclassical economics.

Menger was one of three economists in the 1870s who independently put forward a theory of value based on marginal utility. Prior to what economists now call the "marginal revolution," value was thought to be derived solely from the inputs of labour and capital. Menger developed the marginal utility theory of value, in which the value of any good is determined by individuals' subjective evaluations of that good. According to Menger, a good has some value if it has the ability to satisfy some human want or desire, and *utility* is the capacity of the good to do so. Menger went on to develop the idea that the individual will maximize total utility at the point where the last unit of each good consumed provides equal utility—that is, where marginal utilities are equal.

Menger's emphasis on the marginal utility theory of value led him to focus on consumption rather than production as the determinant of price. Menger focused only on the demand for goods and largely ignored the supply. It would remain for Alfred Marshall and Leon Walras to combine demand and supply for a more complete picture of price determination.

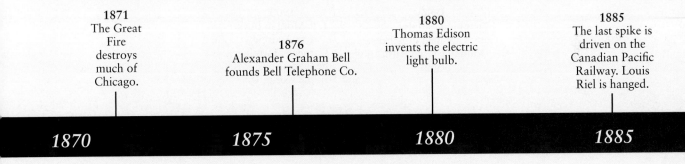

| 1871 The Great Fire destroys much of Chicago. | 1876 Alexander Graham Bell founds Bell Telephone Co. | 1880 Thomas Edison invents the electric light bulb. | 1885 The last spike is driven on the Canadian Pacific Railway. Louis Riel is hanged. |

1870   *1875*   *1880*   *1885*

ALFRED MARSHALL   *(1842–1924)*

Alfred Marshall was born in Clapham, England, the son of a bank cashier, and was descended from a long line of clerics. Marshall's father, despite intense effort, was unable to steer the young Marshall into the church. Instead, Marshall followed his passion for mathematics at Cambridge and chose economics as a field of study after reading J. S. Mill's *Principles of Political Economy*. His career was then spent mainly at Cambridge, where he taught economics to John Maynard Keynes, Arthur Pigou, Joan Robinson, and countless other British theorists in the "Cambridge tradition." His *Principles of Economics*, published in 1890, replaced Mill's *Principles* as the dominant economics textbook of English-speaking universities.

Marshall institutionalized modern marginal analysis, the basic concepts of supply and demand, and perhaps most importantly the notion of economic equilibrium resulting from the interaction of supply and demand. He also pioneered partial equilibrium analysis—examining the forces of supply and demand in a particular market provided that all other influences can be excluded, *ceteris paribus*.

Although many of the ideas had been put forward by earlier writers, Marshall was able to synthesize the previous analyses of utility and cost and present a thorough and complete statement of the laws of demand and supply. Marshall refined and developed microeconomic theory to such a degree that much of what he wrote would be familiar to students of this textbook today.

It is also interesting to note that although Alfred Marshall and Leon Walras were simultaneously expanding the frontiers of economic theory, there was almost no communication between the two men. Though Marshall chose partial equilibrium analysis as the appropriate method for dealing with selected markets in a complex world, he did acknowledge the correctness of Walras's general equilibrium system. Walras, on the other hand, was adamant (and sometimes rude) in his opposition to the methods that Marshall was putting forward. History has shown that both the partial and the general equilibrium approaches to economic analysis are required for understanding the functioning of the economy.

THORSTEIN VEBLEN   *(1857–1929)*

Thorstein Veblen was born on a farm in Wisconsin to Norwegian parents. He received his Ph.D. in philosophy from Yale University, after which he returned to his father's farm because he was unable to secure an academic position. For seven years he remained there, reading voraciously on economics and other social sciences. Eventually, he took academic positions at the University of Chicago, Stanford University, the University of Missouri, and the New School for Social Research (in New York). Veblen was the founder of "institutional economics," the only uniquely North American school of economic thought.

In 1899, Veblen published *The Theory of the Leisure Class*, in which he sought to apply Charles Darwin's evolutionism to the study of modern economic life. He examined problems in the social institutions of the day, and savagely criticized Classical and Neoclassical economic analysis. Although Veblen failed to shift the path of mainstream economic analysis, he did contribute the idea of the importance of long-run institutional studies as a useful complement to short-run price theory analysis. He also reminded the profession that economics is a *social* science, and not merely a branch of mathematics.

Veblen remains most famous today for his idea of "conspicuous consumption." He observed that some commodities were consumed not for their intrinsic qualities but because they carried snob appeal. He suggested that the more expensive such a commodity became, the greater might be its ability to confer status on its purchaser.

1896
First modern Olympic Games are held in Athens. Klondike Gold Rush begins.

1900
J. P. Morgan buys out Andrew Carnegie, forming the biggest business in the world, U.S. Steel.

1890   *1895*   *1900*   *1905*

1889
Gustave Eiffel designs the Eiffel Tower for the Paris World Exposition.

1898
Spanish-American War.

1903
The Wright Brothers' first successful flight.

VILFREDO PARETO   *(1848–1923)*

Vilfredo Pareto was an Italian, born in Paris, and was trained to be an engineer. Though he actually practised as an engineer, he would later succeed Leon Walras to the Chair of Economics in the Faculty of Law at the University of Lausanne.

Pareto built on the system of general equilibrium that Walras had developed. In his *Cours d'économie politique* (1897) and his *Manuel d'économie politique* (1906), Pareto set forth the foundations of modern welfare economics. He showed that theories of consumer behaviour and exchange could be constructed on assumptions of ordinal utility, rather than cardinal utility, eliminating the need to compare one person's utility with another's. Using the indifference curve analysis developed by F. Y. Edgeworth, Pareto was able to demonstrate that total welfare could be increased by an exchange if one person could be made better off without anyone else becoming worse off. Pareto applied this analysis to consumption and exchange as well as to production. Pareto's contributions in this area are remembered in economists' references to *Pareto optimality* and *Pareto efficiency*.

JOSEPH SCHUMPETER   *(1883–1950)*

Joseph Schumpeter was born in Triesch, Moravia (now in the Czech Republic). He was a university professor and later a minister of finance in Austria. In 1932, he emigrated to the United States to avoid the rise to power of Adolf Hitler. He spent his remaining years at Harvard University.

Schumpeter, a pioneering theorist of innovation, emphasized the role of the entrepreneur in economic development. The existence of the entrepreneur meant continuous innovation and waves of adaptation to changing technology. He is best known for his theory of "creative destruction," where the prospect of monopoly profits provides owners the incentive to finance inventions and innovations. One monopoly can replace another with superior technology or a superior product, thereby circumventing the entry barriers of a monopolized industry. He criticized mainstream economists for emphasizing the static (allocative) efficiency of perfect competition—a market structure that would, if it could ever be achieved, retard technological change and economic growth.

Schumpeter's best known works are *The Theory of Economic Development* (1911), *Business Cycles* (1939), and *Capitalism, Socialism and Democracy* (1943).

1912
Titanic sinks on her maiden voyage, killing 1513 people.

1914
Opening of the Panama Canal. First World War begins.

1918
Treaty of Versailles ends First World War.

1908
Henry Ford introduces the Model T.

1917
Bolshevik Revolution in Russia brings V. I. Lenin to power.

1905   1910   1915   1920

JOHN MAYNARD KEYNES   *(1883–1946)*

John Maynard Keynes was born in Cambridge, England. His parents were both intellectuals, and his father, John Neville Keynes, was a famous logician and writer on economic methodology. The young Keynes was educated at Eton and then at Kings College, Cambridge, where he was a student of Alfred Marshall and Arthur Pigou. His career included appointments to the Treasury in Britain during both world wars, a leading role in the establishment of the International Monetary Fund (through discussions at Bretton Woods, New Hampshire, in 1944), and editorship of the *Economic Journal* from 1911 to 1945, all in addition to his academic position at Kings College.

Keynes published extensively during his life, but his most influential work, *The General Theory of Employment, Interest, and Money,* appeared in 1936. This book was published in the midst of the Great Depression when the output of goods and services had fallen drastically, unemployment was intolerably high, and it had become clear to many that the market would not self-adjust to achieve potential output within an acceptable period of time. Fluctuations in economic activity were familiar at this point, but the failure of the economy to recover rapidly from this depression was unprecedented. Neoclassical economists held that during a downturn both wages and the interest rate would fall low enough to induce investment and employment and bring about a recovery. They believed that the persistent unemployment during the 1930s was caused by inflexible wages and they recommended that workers be convinced to accept wage cuts.

Keynes believed that this policy, though perhaps correct for a single industry, was not correct for the entire economy. Widespread wage cuts would reduce the consumption portion of aggregate demand, which would offset any increase in employment. Keynes argued that unemployment could be cured only by manipulating aggregate demand, whereby increased demand (through government expenditure) would increase the price level, reduce real wages, and thereby stimulate employment.

Keynes's views found acceptance after the publication of his *General Theory* and had a profound effect on government policy around the world, particularly in the 1940s, 1950s, and 1960s. As we know from this textbook, Keynes's name is associated with much of macroeconomics, from its basic theory to the Keynesian short-run aggregate supply curve and the Keynesian consumption function. His contributions to economics go well beyond what can be mentioned in a few paragraphs—in effect, he laid the foundations for modern macroeconomics.

EDWARD CHAMBERLIN *(1899–1967)*

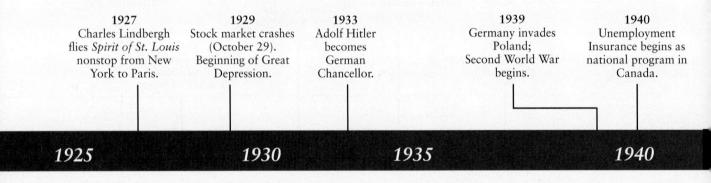

Edward Chamberlin was born in La Conner, Washington, and received his Ph.D. from Harvard University in 1927. He became a full professor at Harvard in 1937 and stayed there until his retirement in 1966. He published *The Theory of Monopolistic Competition* in 1933.

Before Chamberlin's book (which appeared more or less simultaneously with Joan Robinson's *The Economics of Imperfect Competition*), the models of perfect competition and monopoly had been fairly well worked out. Though economists were aware of a middle ground between these two market structures and some analysis of duopoly (two sellers) had been presented, it was Chamberlin and Robinson who closely examined this problem of imperfect markets.

Chamberlin's main contribution was explaining the importance of product differentiation for firms in market structures between perfect competition and monopoly. Chamberlin saw that though there may be a large number of firms in the market (the competitive element), each firm created for itself a unique product or advantage that gave it some control over price (the monopoly element). Specifically, he identified items such as copyrights, trademarks, brand names, and location as monopoly elements behind a product. Though Alfred Marshall regarded price as the only variable in question, Chamberlin saw both price and the product itself as variables under control of the firm in monopolistically competitive markets.

1927
Charles Lindbergh flies *Spirit of St. Louis* nonstop from New York to Paris.

1929
Stock market crashes (October 29). Beginning of Great Depression.

1933
Adolf Hitler becomes German Chancellor.

1939
Germany invades Poland; Second World War begins.

1940
Unemployment Insurance begins as national program in Canada.

1925   1930   1935   1940

1922
The Soviet Union is formed; Joseph Stalin named Secretary General of the Communist Party.

FRIEDRICH AUGUST VON HAYEK *(1899–1992)*

Friedrich von Hayek was born in Vienna and studied at the University of Vienna, where he was trained in the Austrian tradition of economics (a school of thought originating with Carl Menger). He held academic positions at the London School of Economics and the University of Chicago. He returned to Europe in 1962 to the University of Freiburg in what was then West Germany and the University of Salzburg in Austria. He was awarded the Nobel Prize in Economics in 1974.

Hayek contributed new ideas and theories in many different areas of economics, but he is perhaps best known for his general conception of economics as a "coordination problem." His observation of market economies suggested that the relative prices determined in free markets provided the signals that allowed the actions of all decision makers to mesh—even though there was no formal planning taking place to coordinate these actions. He emphasized this "spontaneous order" at work in the economy as the subject matter for economics. The role of knowledge and information in the market process became central to Hayek, an idea that has grown in importance to the economics profession over the years.

Hayek's theory of business cycles provided an example of the breakdown of this coordination. A monetary disturbance (e.g., an increase in the money supply) would distort the signals (relative prices) by artificially raising the return to certain types of economic activity. When the disturbance disappeared, the boom caused by these distorted signals would be followed by a slump. Although Hayek's business-cycle theory was eclipsed by the Keynesian revolution, his emphasis on economics as a coordination problem has had a major influence on contemporary economic thought.

Hayek was also prominent in advocating the virtues of free markets as contributing to human freedom in the broad sense as well as to economic efficiency in the narrow sense. His *The Road to Serfdom* (1944) sounded an alarm about the political and economic implications of the then-growing belief in the virtues of central planning. His *Constitution of Liberty* (1960) is a much deeper philosophical analysis of the forces, economic and otherwise, that contribute to the liberty of the individual.

MILTON FRIEDMAN   *(1912–2006)*

Milton Friedman completed graduate studies in economics at the University of Chicago and at Columbia University, where he received his Ph.D. in 1946. Most of Friedman's academic career was spent as a professor at the University of Chicago, and after retiring in 1977 he was a senior research fellow at the Hoover Institution at Stanford University. Friedman is best known as one of the leading proponents of Monetarism and for his belief in the power of free markets. His work greatly influenced modern macroeconomics.

Friedman made his first significant mark on the profession with the publication of *The Theory of the Consumption Function* in 1957. There he developed the permanent income hypothesis and argued that consumption depends on long-run average income rather than current disposable income, as it does in Keynesian analysis. This was an early example of a macroeconomic theory that emphasized the importance of forward-looking consumers. In 1963, he co-authored with Anna Schwartz his most influential book, *A Monetary History of the United States, 1867–1960*, where they presented evidence in support of the Monetarist view that changes in the supply of money can cause dramatic fluctuations in the level of economic activity. Although this view was seriously challenged by subsequent research, Friedman helped the profession to understand the power of and the limitations of monetary policy.

Capitalism and Freedom (1962) and *Free to Choose* (1980), the latter co-written with his wife, Rose Friedman, are part of Friedman's attempts to communicate his ideas about economics and, in particular, the power of the free market, to a mass audience of non-economists. Both books became international bestsellers, and these books, in addition to his writing for newspapers and magazines, made Milton Friedman one of the most famous modern economists. He was awarded the Nobel Prize in Economics in 1976.

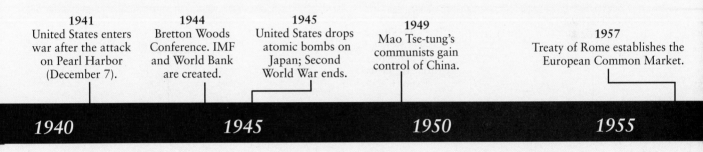

1941
United States enters war after the attack on Pearl Harbor (December 7).

1944
Bretton Woods Conference. IMF and World Bank are created.

1945
United States drops atomic bombs on Japan; Second World War ends.

1949
Mao Tse-tung's communists gain control of China.

1957
Treaty of Rome establishes the European Common Market.

1940   *1945*   *1950*   *1955*

JOHN KENNETH GALBRAITH   *(1908–2006)*

John Kenneth Galbraith was born on a farm in southeastern Ontario, to a family of Scottish-Canadian farmers. He began his undergraduate education at the Ontario Agricultural College in Guelph in 1926, where he studied agricultural economics and animal husbandry. He moved to California to study at the University of California at Berkeley and completed a Ph.D. in agricultural economics in 1934. Galbraith was hired by Harvard University in 1934 and, aside from his government and diplomatic postings, remained on staff there until his death.

Galbraith was heavily influenced by the ideas of John Maynard Keynes, Thorstein Veblen, and the "institutional" school of economics. He rejected the technical and mathematical approach of Neoclassical economics. Instead he emphasized the interplay of economics, politics, culture, and tradition, a combination that does not lend itself well to mathematical modelling. He was much more of a "political economist" in the style of the nineteenth century than a theoretical economist of the late twentieth century.

His most famous book was *The Affluent Society* (1958), where he argued that the United States had become obsessed with overproducing consumer goods and instead should be making large public investments in highways, education, and other public services. His expression "private opulence and public squalor" became well known, and many would agree is even more relevant today than it was when he wrote the words more than 50 years ago. In a later book, *The New Industrial State* (1967), Galbraith argued that very few U.S. industries fit economists' model of perfect competition, and that the economy was dominated by large, powerful firms. In general, Galbraith continued to write about topics that he believed the economics profession had neglected—topics such as advertising, the separation of corporate ownership and management, oligopoly, and government and military spending.

Because of Galbraith's desire to focus on the interplay of economics, politics, and society, he was often criticized (or ignored) by mainstream economists. But he was undeterred. And while many economists disagreed with his approach and some of his political views, he was widely recognized as a gifted and insightful writer and speaker.

KENNETH ARROW *(b. 1921)*

Kenneth Arrow was born and educated in New York City. He began graduate work at Columbia University and received an M.A. in mathematics in 1941. Over the following 10 years, after Arrow had completed his Ph.D. course work, he served in the U.S. Army Air Corps during World War II and held various research jobs while searching for a dissertation topic. His dissertation, which earned him his Ph.D. from Columbia in 1951, subsequently became a classic in economics, *Social Choice and Individual Values* (1951). Kenneth Arrow is currently professor emeritus at Stanford University.

In his 1951 book, Arrow presented his "Impossibility Theorem," in which he shows that it is not possible to construct a set of voting rules for making public choices that is simultaneously democratic and efficient. This theorem led to decades of work by economists, philosophers, and political scientists in the field of social choice theory.

Arrow also made significant contributions in other areas of economics. In 1954 (with Gerard Debreu) he constructed a mathematical model of an economy with many individual, interrelated markets and proved the existence of a theoretical general market-clearing equilibrium. Arrow's work in the economics of uncertainty was also a major contribution. In *Essays in the Theory of Risk-Bearing* (1971), he introduced the concepts of moral hazard and adverse selection (among other ideas about risk), which we encounter in Chapter 16 of this book. Arrow was one of the first economists to develop the idea of "learning by doing," which has played an important role in modern theories of economic growth.

Arrow was awarded the Nobel Prize in 1972 (jointly with British economist John Hicks) and in 2004 was awarded the National Medal of Science, the United States' highest scientific honour.

1962 Cuban Missile Crisis (October).

1967 Canada celebrates its Centennial; Montreal hosts Expo '67.

1973 First OPEC oil shock.

1960   **1965**   **1970**   **1975**

1959 St. Lawrence Seaway officially opens.

1963 U.S. President John F. Kennedy assassinated.

1969 Neil Armstrong is first person to walk on the moon.

1975 Bill Gates and Paul Allen found Microsoft Corporation.

PAUL SAMUELSON *(1915–2009)*

Paul Samuelson was born in Gary, Indiana, the son of a drugstore owner. He received his PhD in economics in 1941 from Harvard University and spent his academic career at the Massachusetts Institute of Technology (MIT).

Samuelson is generally regarded as one of the greatest economic theorists of the twentieth century. While still a graduate student at Harvard, Samuelson wrote most of *Foundations of Economic Analysis* (1947), which was path-breaking at the time and used mathematical analysis and constrained optimization techniques to shed insight into economic behaviour. He systematized economic theory into a more rigorous mathematical discipline, which has had enormous effects on the way economics is studied today.

Though Samuelson made major contributions to many branches of economics, three are particularly notable. First, he showed how the central predictions of demand theory could be tested using the "revealed preferences" of consumers from observed market behaviour. Second, in international trade theory, he made important contributions in the analysis of the gains from trade and the effects of tariff protection on the distribution of income. Third, most familiar to readers of this book, he is credited with introducing the 45°-line model of short-run national income determination. This diagram, encountered throughout Chapters 21 and 22 of this book, has become the standard tool for teaching the Keynesian theory of national-income determination in the short run. Samuelson's work also provided valuable insights in other areas of economics, including government taxation and expenditure, capital theory, and theories of economic growth.

Samuelson was also well known for his famous introductory economics textbook, *Economics,* first published in 1948, which provided a systematic treatment of both micro- and macroeconomics in a way that had not been presented before. In general, he is credited with raising the level of scientific and mathematical analysis in economics. Samuelson was awarded the Nobel Prize in Economics in 1970, and was the first American scholar to receive this honour.

Index

Common Abbreviations Used in the Text

Greek Letters	η	(eta)	Elasticity
	Δ	(delta)	Change in

Abbreviations

Microeconomics

ATC	Average Total Cost
AVC	Average Variable Cost
D	Demand
i	Interest Rate
LRAC	Long-Run Average Cost
MC	Marginal Cost
MP	Marginal Product
MR	Marginal Revenue
MRP	Marginal Revenue Product
S	Supply
TC	Total Cost
TR	Total Revenue

Macroeconomics

AD	Aggregate Demand
AS	Aggregate Supply
AE	(Desired) Aggregate Expenditure
C	Aggregate Consumption Expenditure
CPI	Consumer Price Index
G	Government Purchases
GDP	Gross Domestic Product
GNP	Gross National Product
I	Aggregate Investment Expenditure
i	Nominal Interest Rate
IM	Imports of Goods and Services
M_S, M_D	Money Supply/Money Demand
M1, M2, M2+	Measures of Money Supply
P	Price Level
r	Real Interest Rate
S	Private Saving
T	Government Tax Revenue (Net of Transfers)
U	Unemployment Rate
U^*	Natural Rate of Unemployment (NAIRU)
X	Exports of Goods and Services
X-IM *or* NX	Net Exports of Goods and Services
Y	Real GDP
Y^*	Potential GDP
Y_D	Disposable Income

Education and Employment Income, 2007

The Growth in World Trade, 1950–2010

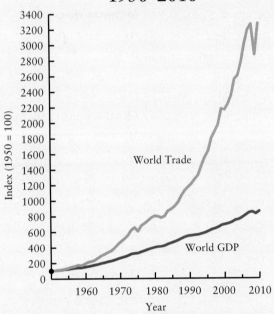

Inflation and Money Growth Across Many Countries, 1978–2010

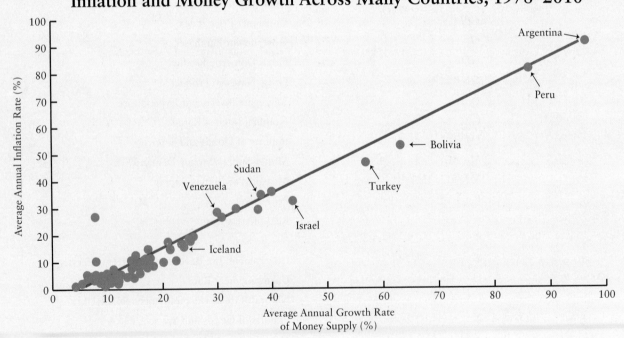